PSYCHOLOGY
for AS Level

PSYCHOLOGY
for AS Level

THIRD EDITION

Michael W. Eysenck

Psychology Press
Taylor & Francis Group

HOVE AND NEW YORK

First edition published 2000

Second edition published 2003

Third edition published 2005 by Psychology Press Ltd
27 Church Road, Hove, East Sussex, BN3 2FA

www.psypress.co.uk
www.a-levelpsychology.co.uk

Simultaneously published in the USA and Canada
by Psychology Press Inc
270 Madison Avenue, New York, NY 10016

Psychology Press is part of the Taylor & Francis Group

© 2000, 2003, 2005 by Psychology Press Ltd

Some exam questions quoted in this book, where referenced,
appear with kind permission from the Assessment and
Qualifications Alliance (AQA)

British Library Cataloguing in Publication Data
A catalogue record for this book is available from the British Library

ISBN 1–84169–378–2

Cover created by Richard Massing, based on a design by
Hurlock Design, Lewes, East Sussex
Typeset in India by Newgen Imaging Systems (P) Ltd
Printed and bound in Slovenia

To Maria, with love

CONTENTS

ABOUT THE AUTHOR

Michael W. Eysenck is one of the best-known British psychologists. He is Professor of Psychology and head of the psychology department at Royal Holloway University of London, which is one of the leading departments in the United Kingdom. His academic interests lie mainly in cognitive psychology, with much of his research focusing on the role of cognitive factors in anxiety in normal and clinical populations.

He is an author of many titles, and his previous textbooks published by Psychology Press include *Psychology for A2 Level* (2001), *Key Topics in A2 Psychology* (2003), *Psychology: An International Perspective* (2004), *Psychology: A Student's Handbook* (2000), *Simply Psychology, Second Edition* (2002), *Cognitive Psychology: A Student's Handbook, Fifth Edition* (2005, with Mark Keane), *Perspectives on Psychology* (1994), *Individual Differences: Normal and Abnormal* (1994), and *Principles of Cognitive Psychology, Second Edition* (2001). He has also written the research monographs *Anxiety and Cognition: A Unified Theory* (1997), and *Anxiety: The Cognitive Perspective* (1992), along with the popular title *Happiness: Facts and Myths* (1990). He is also a keen supporter of Crystal Palace football club.

The study skills you need to be successful in the AS exam are based on psychological principles involving learning and memory. So psychology students should already be well placed to gain maximum advantage in the exam room! This chapter is divided into two sections that address your own study skills and the ways in which the exam will be assessed and marked.

SECTION 1
How can I study effectively? p.3
How to develop your study skills, including increasing your motivation and improving reading skills using the SQ3R approach. Managing your time to get the best results from your work.

SECTION 2
How can I do well in the examination? p.6
Discover your own personal learning style, and how your performance in the exam will benefit from this knowledge. What the examiners will be looking for, and how they award marks. Hints from the Chief Examiner on how to stay calm and be effective once you are in the exam room.

PREPARING FOR THE AS EXAM
By Roz Brody

From the start of your course in AS-level psychology you should be aware of how you will be examined. Study skills are also important—all too often students realise, too late, that they haven't been studying effectively. This chapter will give you some helpful hints on how to go about studying throughout the year so that you will be well prepared for the exam. We also provide guidance on how you will be examined so you can apply these study skills during the exam for maximum effect. You are likely to refer back to this chapter as you go through the book—you can start being a serious student of psychology by reading the evidence now!

SECTION 1
HOW CAN I STUDY EFFECTIVELY?

Students of psychology should find it easy to develop good study skills because they are based on psychological principles. For example, study skills are designed to promote effective learning and remembering, and learning and memory are key areas within psychology. Study skills are also concerned with motivation and developing good work habits, and these also fall very much within psychology, although they are not part of your AS-level course. Most of what is involved in study skills is fairly obvious, so we will focus on detailed pieces of advice rather than on vague generalities (e.g. "Work hard", "Get focused").

Motivation

Most people find it hard to maintain a high level of motivation over long periods of time. We all know what happens. You start out with high ideals and work hard for the first few weeks. Then you have a bad week and/or lose your drive, and everything slips. What can you do to make yourself as motivated as possible? One psychological theory of motivation (Locke, 1968) suggested the following seven ways to set appropriate goals and maintain motivation:

1. You must set yourself a goal that is hard but achievable.
2. You need to commit yourself as fully as possible to attaining the goal, perhaps by telling other people about your goal.
3. You should focus on goals that can be achieved within a reasonable period of time (e.g. no more than a few weeks). A long-term goal (e.g. obtaining a grade A in your AS-level exam) needs to be broken down into a series of short-term goals (e.g. obtaining an excellent mark on your next essay).
4. You should set yourself clear goals, and avoid vague goals such as "doing well".

Set a realistic goal.   Commit to achieving the goal.   Enjoy your achievement!

5. You should do your best to obtain feedback on how well you are moving towards your goal (e.g. checking your progress with a teacher or friend).

6. You should feel pleased whenever you achieve a goal, and then move on to set slightly harder goals in future.

7. You should try to learn from any failure encountered by being very honest about the reasons why you failed: was it really "just bad luck"?

Your attempts to motivate yourself are only likely to be successful if you make use of all seven points. If you set yourself a very clear, medium-term goal, and obtain feedback, but the goal is impossible to achieve, then you are more likely to *reduce* rather than *increase* your level of motivation.

Reading Skills

You will probably spend a fair amount of time reading psychology books (or at least reading this book), and it is obviously important to read in as effective a way as possible. Morris (1979) described the **SQ3R** approach—Survey, Question, Read, Recite, Review, representing the five stages in effective reading—which has proved to be very useful. We will consider these five stages with respect to the task of reading a chapter.

Survey

The Survey stage involves getting an overall view of the way in which the information in the chapter is organised. If there is a chapter summary, this will probably be the easiest way to achieve that goal. Otherwise, you could look through the chapter to find out what topics are discussed and how they are linked to each other.

Question

The Question stage should be applied to fairly short parts of the chapter of no more than six pages. The essence of this stage is that you should think of relevant questions to which you expect this part to provide answers.

? Have you got any questions? Always question everything you read by saying, for example, "Does this explain my own knowledge of the world?" or "Do I understand all the words?"

Read

The Read stage involves reading through each part identified at the Question stage. There are two main goals at this stage: (1) you should try to answer the questions that you thought of during the previous stage; (2) you should try to integrate the information provided in that part of the chapter with your pre-existing knowledge of the topic.

Recite

The Recite stage involves you trying to remember all the key ideas that were contained in the part of the chapter you have been reading. If you cannot remember some of them, then you should go back to the Read stage.

Review

The Review stage occurs when you have read the entire chapter. If all has gone well, you should remember the key ideas from the chapter, and you should be able to combine information from different parts into a coherent structure. If you cannot do these things, then go back to earlier stages in the reading process.

The most important reason why the SQ3R approach works so well is because it ensures that you do not simply read in a passive and mindless way. Instead, it encourages you to engage with the reading material in an *active* and *proactive* way. Remember that if you read a book chapter in a passive way you may convince yourself that all is well when the material in it seems familiar, but that doesn't mean you'll be able to produce it during a stressful examination.

> **EXAM HINT**
>
> In order to succeed in examinations, you must be able to recall the information you need. The Recite and Review stages of the SQ3R approach are designed to achieve precisely that.

Time Management

What do you do with the 100 or so hours a week during which you are awake? Probably the honest answer is that you only have a vague idea where most of the time goes. As time is such a valuable commodity, it is a good idea to make the most efficient use of it as you will probably be surprised at how much time you tend to waste. Here are some suggestions on how to manage your time:

- Create a timetable of the times that are available and unavailable over a week. Now indicate which subjects you can study on different days, and how much time within each day you are going to spend on any subject.
- Decide what is, for you, a reasonable span of attention (possibly 30–40 minutes). Set aside a number of periods of time during the week for study. Make a commitment to yourself to use these periods for study.
- Note that the more of a habit studying becomes, the less effortful it will be, and the less resistant you will be to making a start.
- No-one has limitless concentration. After initially high levels of concentration, the level decreases until the end is in sight. So make sure that the time you commit to studying is realistic. You can probably improve your level of

One motivational strategy is to reward yourself at regular intervals. For example, after you have read 10 pages, or worked for an hour have a cup of tea, go for a brief walk, or phone or text a friend. Make sure your rewards are for easily achievable goals— but not too easy!

concentration by including short (10-minute) rest periods. Remember to avoid distractions like the television in your study area (don't kid yourself that you can watch TV *and* study—reward yourself later with an hour slumped in front of the TV).

- During these study times, there will be a tendency to find other things to do (e.g. phoning a friend). This is where the hard part begins. You must try to be firm and say to yourself that this is time you have committed to studying, and that is what you are going to do. However, you will have time available later for other things. It is hard to do to start with, but it gets easier.

Planning fallacy

? Why do many people fail to achieve work targets, despite the fact that they really should know better?

We are almost all familiar with the **planning fallacy**, even though we may never have heard it called that. Kahneman and Tversky (1979) defined the planning fallacy as "a tendency to hold a confident belief that one's own project will proceed as planned, even while knowing that the vast majority of similar projects have run late". In other words, we all kid ourselves that it will be easy despite knowing that, on previous occasions, we and other people have not managed to fulfil our planned intentions.

As we are psychologists, we might be interested to know if there is evidence to support this planning fallacy, and indeed there is. Buehler, Griffin, and Ross (1994) found that, on average, students submitted a major piece of work 22 days later than they had predicted, even when they were specifically told that the purpose of the study was to examine the accuracy of people's predictions. Buehler et al. found that students were much better at predicting completion times for other students than for themselves. The reason for this is that they were more likely to use what is called "distributional" information (which comes from knowledge about similar tasks completed in the past) when making predictions about other students, whereas with themselves they tended to use "singular" information (related to the current task).

SECTION 2
HOW CAN I DO WELL IN THE EXAMINATION?

We don't want to lessen your enjoyment of psychology by reducing it to a set of examination techniques—but ultimately your pleasure will be increased by being able to use what you know to achieve a good mark.

Three key factors will help you do well in the examination:

- Knowing how you learn.
- Knowing how you will be assessed.
- Knowing what you will be examined on.

If you know what to expect in the exam it removes the stress and allows you to:

- organise your information;
- plan how you will learn the information;
- understand how you can use the information to answer questions in the examination.

Coping with stress in examinations

In chapter 5 you will be studying stress and how to manage it. Here is some advice from that chapter:

- THINK POSITIVELY: This will increase your sense of control: "I can only do my best."
- AVOID DEFENCE MECHANISMS SUCH AS DENIAL: Recognise the feeling of stress and intellectualise your problem.
- RELAX: At intervals during the examination have a break and think positive thoughts unrelated to the exam.
- SOCIAL SUPPORT: Think about comforting people or things.
- PHYSICAL EXERCISE AND EMOTIONAL DISCHARGE: Go for a run before the exam, stretch your legs, find some means of discharging tension during the exam (that doesn't disturb anyone else).

Knowing How You Learn

Think about the strategies that work for you. Some students like summarising their notes onto cards. Others devise posters or put "post-its" around their room. Others find it much easier to learn information by discussing their ideas with a friend.

Try the quiz below to help you think about how you learn.

Look at the following questions and answer yes or no	YES	NO
1. I often see my notes in my head when I sit an exam.		
2. I can never seem to start my work.		
3. When I explain my ideas to someone else, they often become clearer to me.		
4. I find it easy to remember conversations word for word.		
5. If a friend phones me I'll stop working and chat for hours.		
6. I often say what I am writing down to myself.		
7. I find it easier to remember my notes when I highlight key points.		
8. I can remember my notes by repeating them over and over again to myself.		
9. I often look at my book, but nothing ever goes in.		
10. I like it when people ask me questions about psychology and I can explain things to them.		
11. I like using different coloured pens when making revision notes.		
12. I find it hard to work on my own.		
13. I can always find something else to do when I am meant to be studying.		
14. I can remember where things are on a page.		
15. I enjoy talking about psychology to my friends.		
16. I often hear my teacher's voice when I read through my notes.		

Throughout the book the red boxes, like this one, give cross-references to *Revise Psychology for AS Level* by Roz Brody and Diana Dwyer (the revision guide).

See p.2 of the revision guide for a summary of revision techniques.

- If you answered yes to questions 1, 7, 11, and 14, you enjoy learning using a visual approach. Making posters, using "post-its" and coloured pens and highlighters will help you for the exam.
- If you answered yes to questions 2, 5, 9, and 13, you are easily distracted and find it hard to start work. You need to remove all distractions (e.g. mobile phone) and realise that it might take you 5–10 minutes to settle into doing the work. Focus on the task you have set yourself for a certain amount of time (e.g. 30 minutes) and then take a break.
- If you answered yes to 3, 10, 12, and 15, you enjoy learning in a social way. Working with a friend as you revise and discussing ideas will help you for the exam.
- If you answered yes to questions 4, 6, 8, and 16, you enjoy learning information using sound. Some students make tape recordings of the key points they need to remember, and then listen to them before they go to sleep.
- If you answered yes to a range of questions, you don't have a preferred method of learning information and may use a range of strategies to help you.

Knowing How You Will Be Assessed

There are three main skills that are examined in the AS examination: AO1, AO2, and AO3. AO means assessment objective.

- AO1 is concerned with your *knowledge and understanding* of:
  - Psychological theories
  - Psychological terminology and concepts
  - Psychological studies
  - Psychological methods
- AO2 is concerned with *analysing and evaluating*:
  - Psychological theories
  - Psychological terminology and concepts
  - Psychological studies
  - Psychological methods
- AO3 is only assessed in the research methods question and is concerned with designing, conducting, and reporting psychological investigations.

Because they are assessing different skills, the AO1 questions differ from the AO1/AO2 questions. You will never meet pure AO2 questions in the exam. Those that assess AO2 skills combine this assessment with testing AO1 skills.

Typical AO1 questions include:

- *Describe/outline* **one** *explanation of forgetting in short-term memory.*
- *Describe the [two out of aims/procedures/findings/conclusion and criticisms] of a given study.*
- *Outline the findings of research into the role of control in stress.*
- *Describe* **one** *study that demonstrates the long-term effects of privation.*
- *Give* **two** *criticisms of this study.*
- *Describe how personality can play a role in how people respond to stress.*

EXAM HINT

AO1 questions can be:
- Key terms
- Key studies (APFCCs); findings and conclusions
- Theories and explanations
- Compare/contrast

- *Outline **two** attempts to define psychological abnormality.*
- *What is meant by minority influence?*

Typical part (c) questions (AO1/AO2) include:

- *Outline and evaluate any **two** explanations for conformity.*
- *To what extent have attempts to explain attachment taken account of cultural variation?*
- *Critically consider the effectiveness of stress management techniques.*

Each question in the exam (except those on research methods) consists of three parts:

- Part (a) is out of 6 marks and examines AO1.
- Part (b) is out of 6 marks and examines AO1.
- Part (c) is out of 18 marks: 6 marks for AO1 and 12 marks for AO2.

EXAM HINT

In comparison questions (e.g. give two differences between . . .) make sure you draw the comparison, rather than describing each separately and expecting the examiner to identify the comparison, as this would receive no marks! So make sure you've used WHEREAS or IN COMPARISON.

Key Studies

The questions on studies test your knowledge and understanding (AO1) and so are worth 6 marks. Throughout the book we provide examples of relevant studies in APFCC format (describing the Aims, Procedure, Findings, Conclusions, Criticisms). For an example see the Peterson and Peterson (1959) Key Study on page 46.

These key studies are examined using the following type of question:

- *"Describe the [two out of aims/procedure/ findings/conclusions/criticisms] of a given study."* (6 marks)

You may be asked to give any two components from an appropriate study, for instance the "aims and procedure", the "procedure and findings" or the "procedure and conclusions", and so on. In your answer you should try to write 3 marks-worth on each component. However, do bear in mind that this guideline is just an approximation. In some cases the two components do not have to be exactly equal, as the aims are often shorter than the procedure or findings.

If you are describing a criticism, remember, you can evaluate the study in terms of application, methodology, ethics, culture, and gender. All studies have methodological criticisms so you can refer to Chapter 8 on Research Methods and transfer your knowledge from this topic. Remember that criticism means evaluation in this context and so the criticism can be positive as well as negative!

■ **Activity:** To see if you have got the idea of the differences, see if you can identify whether the following questions are measuring AO1 or AO1/AO2 skills.

(a) Outline research into the effects of privation.
(b) Outline and evaluate two or more attempts to define abnormality.
(c) To what extent does psychological research support the view that eyewitness testimony will always be unreliable?
(d) Outline the aims and findings of any one study on obedience.
(e) Describe the characteristics of anorexia nervosa and bulimia nervosa.
(f) How effective have psychologists been in dealing with the ethical issues raised by social influence research?

See overleaf for the answers.

EXAM HINT

Avoid "common-sense" answers: you must convince the examiner that your answer is drawn from what you have learned, not from everyday knowledge.

Key studies can also be used to answer the following types of question:

- *"Outline the findings of research into . . ."* (6 marks)

This means you will need to describe research findings. For maximum marks you should outline findings from two or three studies that relate to the topic. Remember to focus on findings and not the other components of your studies.

- *"Outline the conclusions of research into . . ."* (6 marks)

This question is similar to the one above, however this time it asks you to describe the conclusions of a given study, and supportive studies on the same topic.

Key Studies

The key studies that feature in this book relate to the 16 key study topic areas specified by the syllabus:

Cognitive psychology topics
1. A study into the nature of short-term memory
2. A study into the nature of long-term memory
3. A study of reconstructive memory
4. A study into the role of leading questions in eyewitness testimony

Developmental psychology topics
5. A study of individual differences in attachments
6. A study of cross-cultural differences in attachments
7. A study into the effects of privation

Physiological psychology topics
8. A study into the relationship between stress and cardiovascular disorders
9. A study into the relationship between stress and the immune system
10. A study into life changes as a source of stress
11. A study into workplace stressors

Individual differences topics
12. A study into biological explanations of eating disorders
13. A study into psychological explanations of eating disorders

Social psychology topics
14. A study into conformity
15. A study into minority influence
16. A study into obedience to authority

The studies we have presented as examples are not compulsory, and you may choose to learn different studies on these topics. However, remember you will not be asked to describe studies in the exam that do not relate to these key topic areas.

■ Activity answers

(a) AO1
(b) AO1/AO2
(c) AO1/AO2
(d) AO1
(e) AO1
(f) AO1/AO2

How the Examinations are Marked

Examiners are given mark schemes to enable them to work out how many marks to award to an answer. Some mark schemes are based on skill cluster AO1 and others are based on skill cluster AO2, as can be seen in the box below.

Mark scheme for AQA specification AS-level examinations

Assessment objective 1 (AO1)

6–5 marks   The description is *accurate* and *detailed*.

4–3 marks   The description is *limited*. It is generally *accurate* but *less detailed*.

2–1 marks   The description is *basic*, *lacking detail*, and may be *muddled* and/or *flawed*.

0 marks   The description is *inappropriate* or the description is *incorrect*.

Where an answer is marked out of 3, then the marks are changed accordingly.

Assessment objective 2 (AO2)

12–11 marks   There is an *informed commentary* and *reasonably thorough analysis* of the relevant psychological research. Material has been used in an *effective* manner, within the time constraints of answering this part of the question.

10–9 marks   There is a *reasonable commentary* and *slightly limited analysis* of the relevant psychological studies/methods. Material has been used in an *effective* manner.

8–7 marks   There is a *reasonable commentary* but *limited analysis* of the relevant psychological studies/methods. Material has been used in a *reasonably effective* manner.

6–5 marks   There is a *basic commentary* with *limited analysis* of the relevant psychological studies/methods. Material has been used in a *reasonably effective* manner.

4–3 marks   There is *superficial commentary* and *rudimentary analysis* of the relevant psychological studies/methods. There is *minimal interpretation* of the material used.

2–1 marks   Commentary is *just discernible* (for example, through appropriate selection of the material). Analysis is *weak* and *muddled*. The answer may be *mainly irrelevant* to the problem it addresses.

0 marks   Commentary is *wholly irrelevant* to the problem it addresses.

Some idea of how examiners use this mark scheme can be shown by looking at the following questions:

Question: *Describe the procedures and findings of* **one** *study of duration of short-term memory. (6 marks)*

Candidate's answer: Peterson and Peterson did a study on the capacity of short-term memory. Participants were shown three-letter consonants, such as RTG. Then they were asked to recall them either after 3, 12, 15, or 18 seconds. The longer the interval, the worse their recall was.

Examiner's comment: The candidate has included some information, such as who did the study and what they did, but there is minimal detail. The findings have been treated rather briefly and certain other details were omitted (such as what the participants did while they were waiting to recall the digits). Therefore this answer would be described as "limited", close to "basic", and would get 3 out of 6 marks.

Remember that your answer needs to be *accurate and detailed* to gain full marks.

EXAM HINT

Remember: There are no right answers, only answers that are well-informed, well-constructed, well-argued, and in which the material used is well-selected.

Question: "People who witness a crime want to be able to provide useful information to the police to help them catch the criminal." With reference to psychological research, consider the extent to which it is possible for eyewitnesses to provide useful information. (18 marks)

Candidate's answer: Psychological research has investigated many areas of memory that are relevant to eyewitness testimony.

The first area I will consider is Loftus' research on the way the language used in questioning the eyewitness will affect recall. In her experiment it was found that, if people were asked "About how fast were the cars going when they smashed into each other?", they estimated the cars' speed as being faster than if the word "hit" was used in the question. This shows that the accuracy of their recall is very much influenced by the way they are asked questions.

Another line of evidence has looked at flashbulb memories. It has been suggested that certain events are printed in our memories because they occur at times of high emotion, such as when the World Trade Centre was attacked, and you remember exactly what you were doing at the time. The same thing might be true of a crime scene so that you can see a picture of what actually happened. However, research into flashbulb memories suggests that they are not as accurate as people think. McCloskey et al. interviewed people shortly after the explosion of the space shuttle *Challenger* and then re-interviewed the same people nine months later. McCloskey et al. found that the participants did forget elements. We should also consider evidence which showing that high emotion may lead to poorer recall. Freud suggested that people repress memories that create anxiety and there is evidence to support this.

This research on flashbulb memories and emotion suggests that eyewitness recall may be less accurate than people like to think it is.

Another kind of evidence is that people often don't remember things until they have their memory jogged. Psychologists have shown that a lot of forgetting can be explained in terms of not having the right cues (Tulving & Psotka, 1971). This is why it is good for police to stage reconstructions of a crime scene to help witnesses recall what happened.

Finally we should consider face recognition. It is very hard to recognise an unfamiliar face and one that is still rather than moving.

Examiner's comment: The candidate has presented a well-structured answer to the question. It is all relevant and there has been good use of evidence—the candidate has not just presented evidence but has also explained what it demonstrates ("effective use of material"). Some of the points have not been backed up by specific references but they continue to demonstrate that the candidate is reasonably "informed". The AO1 material (description of psychological research) is detailed but limited (3 out of 6 marks). The AO2 material (commentary on the research) is reasonable but perhaps slightly limited (10 out of 12 marks). This gives a total of 14 marks, which would be equivalent to a Grade A.

See pp.11–12 of the revision guide for a summary of the exam format.

EXAM HINT

AO1 questions are either 2 + 2 + 2 marks or 3 + 3 marks. Be careful not to write too much or too little. Your answers may be correct but just lacking in detail. Use research evidence and examples to increase the content.

Strategies You Can Use to Improve Your AO2 Marks

One way to think about how you can improve your marks for AO2 questions is to think about how you can evaluate the research and theories you have studied. Focus on:

- *Application*. Can the research or theories be applied to everyday life? Does the research benefit humanity?

- *Methodology.* How was the research done?
  What sampling technique was used, and can we generalise from this sample?
  Did the participants simply do what they thought the researcher wanted them to do?
  Could the researcher have been biased?
- *Ethics.* Did the research cause physical or psychological harm?
  Do you consider the research treated the participants with respect?
  How have psychologists used the information they have gained?
- *Culture/gender.* How universal are the findings?
  Do the findings have any relevance for non-Western societies and are the findings gender specific?
- *Commentary/constructing a coherent answer.* Use evidence to support your answer.
  Consider the strengths and weaknesses of the evidence.
  Explore how psychologists have challenged different theories.
  Discuss how effective these challenges have been.

Don't expect the examiner to read your mind. Unless it is written down, they cannot know what you intended to say. Spell out the points to the examiners. Use phrases like:

- "This research on eyewitness testimony clearly has applications to everyday life where mistaken identity has led to the wrong person being imprisoned . . ."
- "One major problem with this research was that the sample was male and hence it is unclear whether these findings can be generalised to females . . ."
- "Although it is clear that Milgram's research caused his participants stress, there has been some debate as to whether the means justified the ends . . ."
- "It is important to recognise the limitations of this definition in that what may be seen as normal in one culture (e.g. having three wives) might be seen as abnormal in other cultures."

Constructing coherent arguments takes practice. One way to construct your argument is by thinking about your conclusion, and then working backwards. For example if you were given the question:

To what extent does day care affect the social development of the child?

You might want your conclusion to make the following point:

- Day care can have a beneficial effect on social development.

Working backwards your answer would need to include:

- The evidence that might support your view.
- The strengths and weaknesses of this evidence.
- Other factors that need to be taken into consideration such as:
  - The type of day care being offered.
  - Individual differences.
  - The alternative care provided at home.

Some examiners suggest that answers to 18-mark questions can be broken down into three paragraphs. Using the knowledge that you can only get 6 marks for AO1

EXAM HINT
When in doubt, try writing a sentence that starts "This suggests that . . ." or "Therefore, one can conclude . . .".

See p.10 of the revision guide for guidance on what not to say in the exam!

EXAM HINT
A common mistake in essay answers is writing too much AO1 and too little AO2. You must aim to write twice as much AO2 as AO1 if you are to access the 12 AO2 marks. Achieving these marks rather than missing them can make a difference between a C/D or B/A grade.

and that 12 marks are given for AO2, the first paragraph can be predominantly an AO1 response while the second two paragraphs would be AO2. For example if you were given the question:

To what extent have studies of obedience been shown to lack validity?

- *Paragraph 1* might describe the concerns that psychologists have about internal and external validity in the context of research into obedience.
- *Paragraph 2* might weigh up the evidence for and against the view that studies on obedience lack internal validity.
- *Paragraph 3* might weigh up the evidence for and against the view that studies on obedience lack external validity.

See pp.5–9 of the revision guide for more detail on how you will be assessed and how to evaluate psychological studies.

Knowing What You Will Be Examined On

The AS psychology exam is divided into three units:

- UNIT 1: Cognitive Psychology and Developmental Psychology
- UNIT 2: Physiological Psychology and Individual Differences
- UNIT 3: Social Psychology and Research Methods

Each topic in each unit is broken down into three subsections. Use the unit map opposite to make sure you are clear about what topics are covered in each section.
   To help you prepare for the exam:

- Make a glossary of the key terms or concepts for each topic.
- Make sure you can describe each of the key studies you need to know in terms of:
   - THE AIMS
   - THE PROCEDURE
   - THE FINDINGS
   - THE CONCLUSIONS
   - THE CRITICISMS
- Make sure you can evaluate the studies and theories both positively and negatively in terms of:
   - APPLICATION
   - METHODOLOGY
   - ETHICS
   - CULTURE

So now you know what each unit is about, and how you will be assessed. The last aspect of doing well in exams is to focus on examination technique.

EXAM HINT

Answer the part (c) essay questions before you tackle the (a) and (b) AO1 questions. This strategy can help you move up a grade because often students run out of time for the essays and lose the chance to access these marks. The key to this strategy is timing—do NOT get caught up in the essays. Spend about 15 minutes on each essay and then move on to parts (a) and (b).

Preparing For the Exam

- Revise the topics you know you will be tested on.
- Make sure you know how you will be assessed.
- Make sure you know the difference between AO1 and AO2.
- Make sure you know how many marks are assigned to each question.

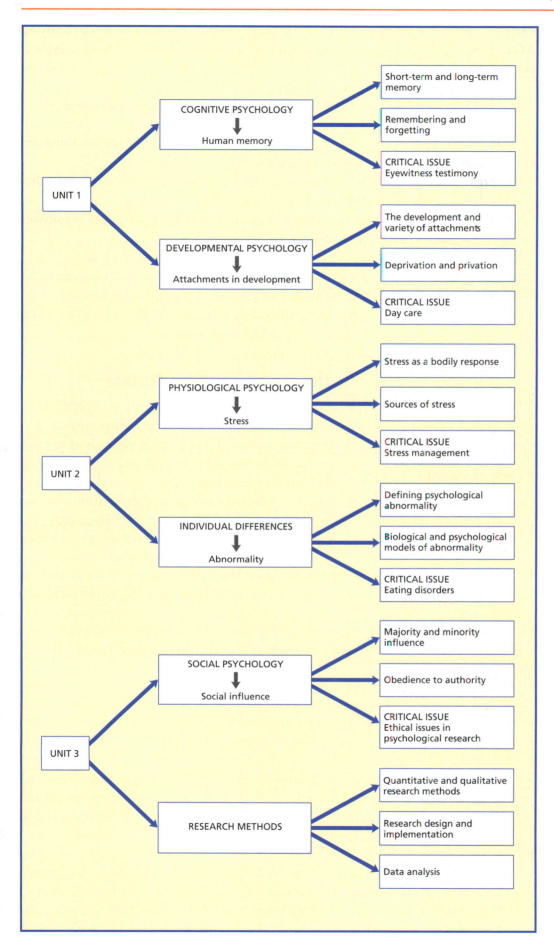

COGNITIVE PSYCHOLOGY
↓
Human memory
- Short-term and long-term memory
- Remembering and forgetting
- CRITICAL ISSUE Eyewitness testimony

DEVELOPMENTAL PSYCHOLOGY
↓
Attachments in development
- The development and variety of attachments
- Deprivation and privation
- CRITICAL ISSUE Day care

UNIT 1

PHYSIOLOGICAL PSYCHOLOGY
↓
Stress
- Stress as a bodily response
- Sources of stress
- CRITICAL ISSUE Stress management

INDIVIDUAL DIFFERENCES
↓
Abnormality
- Defining psychological abnormality
- Biological and psychological models of abnormality
- CRITICAL ISSUE Eating disorders

UNIT 2

SOCIAL PSYCHOLOGY
↓
Social influence
- Majority and minority influence
- Obedience to authority
- CRITICAL ISSUE Ethical issues in psychological research

RESEARCH METHODS
- Quantitative and qualitative research methods
- Research design and implementation
- Data analysis

UNIT 3

EXAM HINT

Read the specification—this will help you reduce the amount you need to revise! Check where the important phrase **E.G.** has been used, as in these cases you can choose between various studies, explanations, or techniques to decide which to revise in depth. Two is the magic number—for instance, most questions will ask for two explanations from a given selection.

- Have a look at past exam papers so that the layout of the examination paper is familiar to you (these are often obtainable from your teachers or the AQA).
- Have a look at the chief examiner's reports on previous exams (obtainable from the AQA), so you know what mistakes other students have made.
- Practise writing answers in timed conditions.
- Make up questions that you think might come up in the exam. Write your ideal paper and your worst case scenario.
- Get a good night's sleep before the exam.
- Think positively about the exam. You want to let the examiner know what you have learned.
- Remember that you can still get an A even if you don't give a perfect answer.

EXAM HINT

The list of AO1 and essay questions may seem long but is not infinite. Prepare model AO1 and essay answers as you work your way through a topic so you will have a complete set of all questions to revise from. Practising writing perfect answers in timed conditions can be much more effective as revision than just reading or writing notes. You can then compare your answers with the sample answers in the textbook and revision guide and on the website.

In the Examination Room

- Read all the questions carefully BEFORE YOU START WRITING. Students often realise too late that although they can give a good answer to question (a), their knowledge for answering (b) and (c) is lacking.
- Underline the key words in the question, so that if you are asked to describe the <u>procedures</u> and <u>findings</u> of a study, you don't waste time on describing the aims and conclusions.
- Before you start writing, quickly jot down the key points you want to include in your answer, so you don't forget your points as you start answering the question.
- Keep focused on the question set so that you don't fall into the trap of:
  - writing down everything you know about the topic, whether it is relevant or not;
  - repeating the same point over and over again;
  - drifting away from the question.
- Make sure each paragraph relates back to the question.
- Don't make the mistake of trying to answer both questions when you only have to answer one.
- Use the marks by the side of the question to help you plan your time. You have 30 minutes to answer each question, which is about a mark a minute. If the question is worth 18 marks you need to spend three times as long answering this question as a 6-mark question.
- Be careful about how you express yourself:
  - Avoid making sweeping, inaccurate, ill-informed, or judgemental statements.
  - Avoid expressing personal opinions such as "I really don't like this study." Instead use phrases like "This study has been criticised for causing the participants stress."

EXAM HINT

Remember that quantity doesn't equal quality. Stick to the point and organise your answer clearly so that the examiner can follow your argument.

- ○ Always back up your views with evidence.
- ○ Avoid one-word criticisms like "this study was unethical". Instead expand on your answer by stating why the study was unethical.
- And above all else, DON'T PANIC. Even if the examination questions aren't the ones you wanted, if you have prepared for the exam and understand how you can gain marks, you will be able to write an answer.

See pp.13–16 of the revision guide for more advice on exam technique before, during, and after the exams.

Examiner's Viewpoint

And finally, a word to sum up from the current Chief Examiner:

This chapter has provided many hints on ways to approach your own learning and in particular how to *use* what you know in answering the demands of the AS examinations. It is sad but true that many candidates do badly in the exams. For some it is simply that they know too little, but for others it is worse; they know a fair amount, but fail to use it effectively and/or make some basic errors. It is frustrating for the examiner to see a good candidate throw away marks, as believe it or not they actually want you to do well! Most of these issues have been covered in this chapter, but the following mistakes are ones seen *repeatedly* in these exams, so focus on them.

Time management

- Despite the pressure on you, take two minutes to read the questions carefully. In general, go for the question where you can score good AO2 marks on section (c).
- Do you know how much you can write in three minutes? Six minutes? If not, find out. That is what you should do for the section (a) and (b) questions depending on whether they are 6 marks or 3 + 3 marks. Not less, not more.

Proper preparation for the exam, and an understanding of how to gain marks, will increase your chances of getting a good grade.

One good paragraph may earn you 6 marks, and extending it to a page doesn't add any more marks.

- One sentence is unlikely to earn good marks. A general rule for sections (a) and (b) is to make a point, elaborate it a little, then use an example or research finding to illustrate it.
- Section (c) questions should be roughly 15–18 minutes' writing time, i.e. three times as long as (a) and (b). That is what the examiner expects. 6 marks for AO1 and 12 for AO2, so make your AO1 similar in amount to sections (a) and (b), i.e. about 5–6 minutes on AO1 and 10–12 minutes on AO2.

Answer the question

- You now know that sections (a) and (b) are AO1, knowledge and understanding, so avoid evaluation and commentary—they will not earn marks however impressive.
- *One* strength, or *one* weakness, or *one* criticism, means exactly that. For good marks you must name and elaborate on *one*, not give a *list* of different strengths, weaknesses etc. If you do, only one will be marked and it is unlikely to do well.
- Similarly, if you are asked for *two* of anything, just provide two; balance your coverage roughly equally between them, but don't give more than two as they will not earn marks.
- For the APFCC questions try to focus on the two aspects asked for. Again, irrelevant material will not earn marks. In these questions the two aspects do not have to be perfectly balanced for full marks.
- In research methods questions watch for the phrase "*in this study*" or similar. It means that your answer *must* refer to the study described in the question to earn full marks.

AO2

This is the area that candidates find most difficult. You need to be able to provide several points of evaluation, but don't forget that examiners realise you have limited time so we do not expect long essays. Just a few points *made well* can score good marks.

Check the sections in this chapter on strategies for improving your AO2 marks. In general these can be at three levels (but make sure you are answering the question!):

- Evaluate studies: Validity, generalisability, ethics etc. *but* remember, don't simply list points—relate them to the specific study. Two or three points made effectively will earn more marks than five or six simply listed.
- Evaluate the theory/approach: Is the theory/approach still relevant (e.g. Milgram's obedience work; Selye's GAS; the multistore model of memory)? Has it stimulated further work? Is it completely outdated and now replaced by later work? You can use *alternative* theories/approaches as AO2, but only by comparing them with the target theory/approach. Don't just describe them, but point out how they are better/worse and why. This is *effective* use of material and earns AO2 credit.

- General commentary/conclusions: Are eating disorders likely to have a *single* explanation? Is day care definitely good/bad/neutral? Has work on conformity contributed to our understanding of human behaviour? Ending your section (c) in this way makes it look organised and structured.
- Use of research findings to support your comments is impressive. Don't worry if you can't remember names/dates or much detail. The phrase "Research has shown that . . ." is very useful! Examiners know studies and will give you credit however you refer to them.

Finally, don't panic! Examiners understand the pressures on you. Marking is positive, so they ignore anything wrong or irrelevant—if in doubt, *put it down*.

Throughout the book we provide hints and tips on exam technique. We also provide references to the revision guide (*Revise Psychology for AS Level* by Roz Brody and Diana Dwyer) where the content is summarised to make exam preparation easier. This will help you if you choose to read the revision guide in conjunction with the textbook from the start of the course. Alternatively, you may prefer to read the revision guide when the exams are around the corner. Further exam advice as well as structured guidance on studying the course can be found in our *Psychology for AS Level Workbook* by Clare Charles.

REVISION QUESTIONS

At the end of each chapter you will find sample exam questions. These will give you an idea of the type of questions you will be asked in the exam. You could also use them to practise writing answers under timed conditions and can then check your work against the sample answers we provide. These give two levels of answer, one at grade C and one at grade A, with examiner comments on how to raise your grade. One sample answer for each chapter is given in Chapter 8 of *Revise Psychology for AS Level* by Roz Brody and Diana Dwyer. The other can be found on our website "AS Level On-Line: Teacher Resources" (see http://www.a-levelpsychology.co.uk/asp3).

Some questions, where referenced, appear with kind permission from the Assessment and Qualifications Alliance (AQA).

It is very important to read this chapter of the book because it sets the scene for all that follows. You might be asking some of the following questions:

"What is psychology?"

"Is psychology just common sense?"

"What is research?"

"What do psychologists do?"

"How do psychologists explain behaviour?"

This chapter of the book is divided into two sections to look at these questions.

SECTION 3
Introducing psychology p.21

A brief look at what psychology is, and how it is more than just common sense. In addition, there is an explanation of what psychological research involves. We also take a look at what psychologists do, considering the core areas of psychology.

SECTION 4
Psychological explanations p.25

A look at the psychologists' "toolkit" containing a set of explanations and theoretical approaches (tools) they use to explain behaviour.

The content of this chapter is not included in the exam syllabus so there will be no direct exam questions on it, but we hope it will help foster an interest in psychology and explain the later concepts.

STARTING PSYCHOLOGY

Welcome to psychology. Presumably you are reading this book because you have elected to study AS-level psychology, and what a good choice! The AS-level course should give you some fundamental and lasting insights into human behaviour to help you to cope better with your own life and with the people around you. Besides learning about human behaviour, you should also learn how to express yourself coherently, how to challenge information, how to be confident about yourself, and to be a better friend, employee, and member of society! The previous chapter, "Preparing for the AS Exam", has been written to provide guidance on exam strategy and help you gain the maximum marks, but this chapter is designed to introduce you to the general issues that make psychology so fascinating.

SECTION 3
INTRODUCING PSYCHOLOGY

What is Psychology?

Psychology is the science of mind, behaviour, and experience.

The term "science" refers to the objective study of something. Psychologists study *behaviour*—what people (and other animals) *do*. "Behaviour" includes being aggressive or kind, thinking and seeing, breathing and walking, growing up and getting old, being a friend or a parent, and so on. These are all examples of "behaviour".

Psychologists are also interested in "experience". If we want to understand behaviour we also need to consider what the experience is like for the individual doing the behaving. For example, if we want to study aggression, it matters what the person who is behaving aggressively *feels like*.

Psychology is concerned with the study of all human and non-human animals. In this book, however, we will focus on the study of human behaviour.

Is Psychology Just Common Sense?

Many people say "Well, psychology is only common sense!" Everyone is an "armchair psychologist". We all have views about why people behave as they do and, in a sense, these are "theories of psychology". For example, your friend might say "Those football fans act like that because they're hooligans". By saying "They're hooligans" your friend is presumably offering an explanation for the fans' behaviour, such as "They have no care for the feelings of others". But how do we *know* this explanation is correct? That's the starting point for psychological

Common sense can be contradictory: "Look before you leap" vs. "He who hesitates is lost".

research. Psychologists observe behaviour, put forward an explanation or theory to account for the behaviour, and then conduct a test to see if their theory is correct. Consider the following example:

Several years ago, a young woman was stabbed to death in the middle of a street in a residential section of New York City. Although such murders are not entirely routine, the incident received little public attention until several weeks later when the New York Times disclosed another side to the case: at least 38 witnesses had observed the attack—and none had even attempted to intervene. Although the attacker took more than half an hour to kill Kitty Genovese, not one of the 38 people who watched from the safety of their own apartments came out to assist her. Not one even lifted the telephone to call the police. (From A.M. Rosenthal, 1964, Thirty-eight witnesses. New York: McGraw-Hill.)

? Have you ever been in a situation where someone was in trouble and you did nothing? Can you explain why you did not help?

Two psychologists John Darley and Bibb Latané (1968) read this report. It made them wonder, "Why *do* bystanders in an emergency fail to offer assistance?" The *common-sense* answer, given by the *New York Times*, was that city dwellers were a callous and uncaring lot of people. Darley and Latané thought that perhaps the reason was related to the number of bystanders—in this case there were 38 "silent witnesses". Could it be that each individual witness assumed someone else was taking action to end the emergency situation and therefore they personally didn't need to do anything?

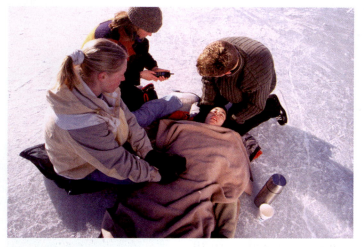

We expect bystanders to help in emergency situations, but sometimes they don't. Why is this? Psychological research has tried to find clear answers to this so-called "bystander behaviour".

Up to this point you might say that Darley and Latané's thinking was not necessarily more than common sense (although it *was* an unusual explanation). But what they did next is what distinguishes psychology from common sense. They set up an experiment to test their opinions—they arranged for students to discuss personal problems with each other over an intercom. Except that there was only one actual student involved: the other participants were confederates of the experimenter pretending to be participants. During the conversation, one of the "students" appeared to have an epileptic fit. If the real student was under the impression that five people were listening to the conversation it took them three times longer before they offered help than if they thought there were only two people.

This study appears to demonstrate that it is the number of people present that affects how likely one is to offer help in an emergency situation. This is psychology—the attempt to explain why people behave in the way they do, and to support these explanations with objective evidence.

Hindsight bias

You still might think "I knew it all along", but this is called **hindsight bias**—the tendency to be wise after the event. Two psychologists, Fischhoff and Beyth, conducted a study to demonstrate hindsight bias in action. Fischhoff and Beyth (1975) asked American students to estimate the probability of various possible outcomes on the eve of President Nixon's trips to China and Russia. After the trips were over, the students were asked to do the same task, but without taking into account their knowledge of what had actually happened. In spite of these instructions, participants did use the benefit of hindsight and couldn't remember how uncertain things had looked before the trips, thus demonstrating hindsight bias.

Hindsight bias seems to be very strong, and is hard to eliminate. In another study, Fischhoff (1977) told the participants about hindsight bias, and encouraged them to avoid it. However, this had little or no effect on the size of the hindsight bias. Hindsight bias poses a problem for teachers of psychology, because it produces students who are unimpressed by almost everything in psychology!

What is Research?

Darley and Latané's bystander study, described earlier, is an example of one kind of psychological research. It is an **experiment**. Psychologists use other methods of research besides the experiment, and we will look at them in Chapter 8 of this book. Some of the methods are rather less "artificial" and more like real life. For example, in another study of bystander behaviour, that took place in 1969, Piliavin, Rodin, and Piliavin (or Piliavin et al., 1969) arranged for someone to "collapse" on an underground train, in one instance appearing sober but carrying a black cane and in the other appearing to be drunk, and timed how long it took for people on the train to offer help.

If research is like "real life" we say it has greater **external validity**—therefore perhaps it will tell us more about "real" behaviour. The problem is that the more the research is like real life, the less easy it is to control other factors that might influence the particular behaviour we want to study (called the "target behaviour")—in our example the extent of helping behaviour. The case of Kitty Genovese was in fact real life, but just observing what happened did *not* allow us to know for sure why the witnesses didn't respond. We have to narrow down the possibilities to determine if the number of people was the cause. There may be other explanations as well, and to find them out we would need to conduct other research. In each research study, we have to control irrelevant factors to demonstrate the effect of the one we think is important. We will consider external validity again, later in the book.

What Do Psychologists Do?

If you don't quite understand what psychology is, then maybe another way to approach it is to ask, "What do psychologists do?" Some psychologists conduct research into different branches of psychology, such as the core areas of cognitive, developmental, physiological, individual differences, and social psychology. Other psychologists apply this research in areas such as health, business, crime, and education, and many work as clinical psychologists helping people with mental disorders.

Terms in black bold are explained in the glossary at the back of the book. Key terms are in blue bold.

? Can you think of any ways in which we could try to eliminate hindsight bias?

When there are more than two authors of a research paper we use "et al.", which means "and others", to refer to all the other researchers.

KEY TERM
External validity: the validity of an experiment outside the research situation itself; the extent to which the findings of a research study are applicable to other situations, especially "everyday" situations.

Cognitive psychology

Cognitive psychologists look at topics such as memory, perception, thought, language, attention, and so on. In other words they are interested in mental processes and seek to explain behaviour in terms of these mental processes.

There are many applications of cognitive psychology, ranging from suggestions about how to improve your memory (useful for examination candidates!) to how to improve performance in situations requiring close attention (such as air traffic control).

The experiences we have during childhood have a great impact on our adult lives.

Developmental psychology

Developmental psychologists study the changes occurring over a person's lifetime, starting from conception and infancy through adolescence, adulthood, and finally old age. This approach has also been called lifespan psychology. Developmental psychologists focus on how particular behaviours change as individuals grow older, for instance, they look at the changes in the way children think. They also look at how children acquire language; at moral, social, and gender development; and at changes such as coping with retirement or with memory loss.

Physiological psychology

Physiological psychologists are interested in how to explain behaviour in terms of bodily processes. They look at topics such as how the nerves function, how hormones affect behaviour, and how the different areas of the brain are specialised and related to different behaviours.

> **Physiological and psychological explanations**
>
> Neurology and biochemistry underlie all behaviour. What happens when a person sees a sunset? The physiological explanation would be that light reflected from the landscape forms an image on the retina, which is converted into a neural signal and transmitted to the brain, and so on. No-one disputes that this is true, and the process is absolutely essential, but does it give a full and adequate explanation of what is going on? A psychological explanation would probably include the personal and social relevance of the experience, which many would argue are of equal value.

Individual differences

The study of "individual differences" is literally the study of the ways that individuals differ in terms of their *psychological* characteristics, for example, intelligence, aggressiveness, willingness to conform, masculinity and femininity, and just about every behaviour you can think of.

An important individual difference can be found in the degree to which a person is mentally healthy. This is specifically referred to as the study of abnormal behaviour and forms the basis of **abnormal** or **atypical psychology**, which studies childhood and adult disorders such as dyslexia, autism, schizophrenia, and depression, seeking to find explanations and valid methods of treatment.

Social psychology

Social psychologists are interested in the way people affect each other. They look at, for example, interpersonal relationships, group behaviour, leadership, majority and minority influence, obedience to those in authority, and the influence of the media. Social psychology differs from sociology in placing greater emphasis on the individual as a separate entity; sociologists are interested in the structure and functioning of groups, whereas social psychologists look at how these processes influence the individual members of a social group.

Other branches of psychology

The five core areas just described form the basis of this book, but there are other areas of psychology as well. For example, **comparative psychology** is the study of non-human animals—comparisons are made between animals of different species to find out more about human behaviour. The study of **animal behaviour** is a field of study in its own right and straddles psychology and biology.

Comparative psychologists study non-human animals and make comparisons between them and humans.

SECTION SUMMARY

- ❖ Psychology is the science of behaviour and experience.
- ❖ It is more than common sense because psychologists conduct and apply research and use research-based evidence to support their theories.
- ❖ This research aims to achieve a balance between external validity and a good control of irrelevant factors.

What is psychology?

- ❖ The core areas of psychology include:
  - Cognitive psychology: examines mental processes.
  - Developmental psychology: explores the physical and psychological changes that occur in relation to age.
  - Physiological psychology: looks at bodily processes.
  - Individual differences: looks at how we differ from each other, for example in terms of differing degrees of mental health.
  - Social psychology: considers the way in which individuals of the same species affect each other.

What are the core areas of psychology?

SECTION 4
PSYCHOLOGICAL EXPLANATIONS

How Do Psychologists Explain Behaviour?

In discussing the issue of what psychologists do, we have touched on the question of *how* they explain behaviour. For example, physiological psychologists clearly explain behaviour in terms of bodily processes, and social psychologists explain behaviour in terms of the interactions between people. The ways that psychologists explain behaviour are explored in later sections of the book.

Some kinds of explanation are more general to all areas of psychology, such as learning theory, social learning theory, psychodynamic theory, cognitive or information-processing theory, and evolutionary theory. We will now consider all these more general kinds of explanation.

Learning Theory

One way to explain behaviour is in terms of **learning**. This form of explanation is called **learning theory** and is based on the principles of **conditioning**.

Classical conditioning

The origins of behaviourism lie in Ivan Pavlov's (1849–1936) work as a physiologist. He was conducting research into the digestive system and accidentally discovered a new form of learning by association. This is how it happened. When his experimental dogs were offered food, saliva production increased. But he also noticed something particularly interesting—salivation started to increase as soon as a researcher opened the door to bring them the food. The dogs had learned that "opening door" signalled "food coming soon". It was in their nature to salivate when they smelled food—a reflex response—but the dogs had now *learned* a link between "door" and their reflex response (salivation). What Pavlov had demonstrated is **classical conditioning**, which is learning by association.

Just to make the basic idea clear, here is another example of classical conditioning. Imagine you have to go to the dentist. As you lie down on the reclining chair, you may feel frightened. Why are you frightened *before* the dentist has caused you any pain? The sights and sounds of the dentist's surgery lead you to expect or predict that you are shortly going to be in

Ivan Pavlov (1849–1936), a Russian physiologist.

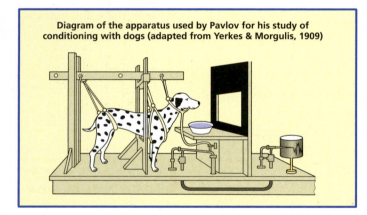

Diagram of the apparatus used by Pavlov for his study of conditioning with dogs (adapted from Yerkes & Morgulis, 1909)

Have you ever noticed how a cat comes running as soon as it hears the cupboard door opening? Classical conditioning can explain this.

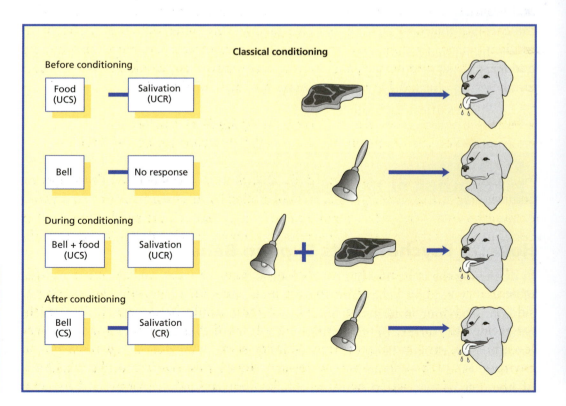

Classical conditioning

Before conditioning

| Food (UCS) | — | Salivation (UCR) |

| Bell | — | No response |

During conditioning

| Bell + food (UCS) | — | Salivation (UCR) |

After conditioning

| Bell (CS) | — | Salivation (CR) |

pain. Thus, you have formed an *association* between the neutral stimuli of the surgery and the painful stimuli involved in drilling.

Drilling is an unconditioned stimulus (US) and fear is an unconditioned response (UR). No learning is required for this stimulus–response (S–R) link, which is why both stimulus and response are described as "unconditioned".

The sights and sounds of the dentist's surgery form a neutral stimulus (NS). There is no inborn reflex response to being in the surgery.

If an NS and a US occur together repeatedly they become associated, until eventually the NS also causes the UR. Now the NS is called a conditioned stimulus (CS) and the UR becomes a conditioned response (CR) to this—the CS will produce the CR. A new **S–R link** has been learned, and you start to experience fear before the dentist has set to work on you.

Operant conditioning

Classical conditioning may be important, but it doesn't explain *all* learning. Another important form of learning was studied by Edward Thorndike (1874–1949). He suggested that learning could take place through *trial and error*, rather than just by association as in classical conditioning. He demonstrated this by placing a hungry cat in a "puzzle box" with a fish hanging nearby. The cat scratched and clawed and miaowed to try to get out of the box, and eventually, by accident, tripped the catch and could jump out. The next time the cat was placed in the box, it went through the same sequence of somewhat random behaviours but took less time to escape. After a few more trials the cat had learned what to do and, each time it was imprisoned, would release the catch immediately. This led Thorndike to state his "Law of Effect":

- Positive effects (rewards) lead to the *stamping in* of a behaviour.
- Negative effects (punishments) lead to the *stamping out* of a behaviour.

This theory was further developed by B.F. Skinner (1904–1990) into **operant conditioning**, which is learning that is controlled by its consequences (i.e. rewards or punishments). Thorndike's and Skinner's approaches were similar in that they concentrated on the *effects* of behaviour, in contrast with Pavlov's focus on the behaviours themselves.

The essence of operant conditioning can be seen in Skinner's (1938) experiments with rats. A rat was placed in a cage with a lever sticking out on one side. If the lever was pressed, a pellet of food would be delivered. At first the rat accidentally pressed the lever but soon learned that there was a link between lever pressing and food appearing. Skinner stated that the rat *operated* on the environment. When there was a reward (food) this **reinforced** the likelihood of the behaviour occurring again. When an animal performs a behaviour

■ **Activity:** Consider the following situations and, for each, try to identify the US, UR, NS, CS, CR:

A puff of air is directed at your eye. Your reflex response is to blink. At the same time as the air is blown, a bell is sounded. In time, the bell produces a blink response.

As you walk into the examination room you are filled with a sense of dread. There is a smell of roses from outside the window. A few weeks later you smell the same perfume of roses and are filled, inexplicably, with a sense of fear.

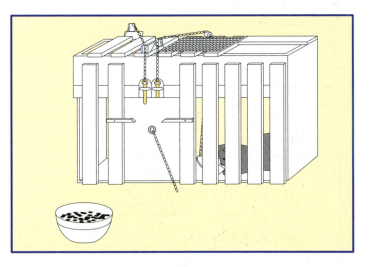

The concepts of classical and operant conditioning are important elements in the psychologist's toolkit. It is important that you try to learn the terminology that is used.

B.F. Skinner, 1904–1990.

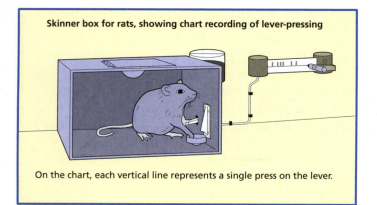

Skinner box for rats, showing chart recording of lever-pressing

On the chart, each vertical line represents a single press on the lever.

(or operates on the environment) there are four possible consequences:

- *Positive reinforcement* is pleasurable (e.g. receiving food) and therefore increases the likelihood of a behaviour occurring again.
- *Negative reinforcement* refers to the avoidance of an unpleasant stimulus, but the result is that it is also pleasurable (like positive reinforcement) and thus increases the likelihood of a behaviour. For example, if the floor of the cage was electrified and pressing the lever stopped this, then the rat would be more likely to press the lever.

> Note that reinforcement always makes behaviour more likely.

- *Positive punishment* such as receiving an electric shock decreases the likelihood of a behaviour, e.g. if the rat received a shock every time it pressed the lever it would stop doing it.
- *Negative punishment* such as removing a pleasant stimulus decreases the likelihood of a behaviour, e.g. a teenager being grounded for staying out late. The removal of a desirable option (going out) reduces the likelihood of staying out late.

John Watson and behaviourism

John Watson was very impressed with the principles of conditioning and felt they offered psychology a way to become a more objective science. This led him to found behaviourism, based on the principles of learning outlined by Pavlov and Thorndike. The behaviourists argued that a scientific approach to psychology involves focusing on things that can be *observed* and *measured*, especially behaviour. It is easy to measure the amount of salivation produced by a dog, the time taken by a cat escape from a puzzle box, or the number of lever presses of a rat in 5 minutes.

"Well, I simply trained them to give me fish by pressing this over and over again."

? How do classical and operant conditioning differ?

We can perhaps see the appeal of behaviourism when we think of what came before it. Up until the end of the 19th century, psychology was still quite close to philosophy and most research relied on **introspection**, studying human behaviour by asking well-trained participants to report what was going on in their mind. Watson argued that this approach was vague and subjective. He and other behaviourists felt there was no need to explain what went on in the mind, or as they called it, the "**black box**"; it was sufficient to talk in terms of a stimulus and a response.

Evaluation of learning theory

The greatest strength of the behaviourist approach was that it was a systematic attempt to turn psychology into a proper science via the careful observation and measurement of behaviour. All psychologists accept that the learning theory put forward by the behaviourists explains *some* aspects of behaviour, and so it is

---

Assumptions of the behaviourist approach

- Behaviourists think that behaviour is all that matters: the stimulus and the response.
- It doesn't matter what goes on inside the "black box".
- All behaviour is learned.
- The same laws apply to all animal behaviour, including humans. Attempts have been made to justify this in terms of the **theory of evolution**, which shows that we have evolved from non-human animals. However, we are quite different from other species in having language.

---

an important part of our toolkit. The evidence of Pavlov, Thorndike, Skinner, and others shows clearly that classical conditioning and operant conditioning both exist. However, no psychologists today claim that we can explain *all* behaviour in terms of learning theory. As you may have noticed, learning theory was originally developed through work with non-human animals such as dogs, cats, and rats. Many experts argue that learning theory is more relevant to the learning shown by these species than it is to human learning. We are more complex than other species, and possess language, and much of our learning seems to go beyond classical and operant conditioning.

What is "evaluation"?

- At the start of this chapter, you found out that psychology would help you to learn how to challenge information. The skill of "evaluation" is the key to this. To evaluate means to determine the value of something.
- Is it good? Positive criticism considers what is right with a theory. We might consider to what extent a theory has been useful. Or to what extent it has been supported by research studies.
- As an example of positive criticism, there is the point that behaviourism changed psychology by making it more scientific and objective through its emphasis on observable behaviour.
- Another example of positive criticism is the point that there is much research support for both classical and operant conditioning.
- Is it bad? Negative criticism considers what is wrong with a theory. It might not be supported by all studies. It might apply only in some situations. It might lead to undesirable applications.
- As an example of negative criticism, there is the point that the behaviourist approach is more relevant to non-human species than to the human species.
- Another example of negative criticism is that the behaviourist approach raises some ethical issues concerning attempts to control human behaviour.

There are ethical concerns about behaviourist explanations. A central aim of the behaviourists is the prediction and control of behaviour. Both Watson and Skinner wanted to use their principles of learning to produce a better society. Behaviourist approaches have been used in this way. For example, people in some prisons, schools, and psychiatric institutions are trained to behave in "desirable" ways. Some people regard this as a good thing, but many others feel it may be unethical. The issue of ethics will be considered later in this book.

Social Learning Theory

Albert Bandura was one of the first psychologists to propose an alternative to learning theory that incorporated mental processes. In **social learning theory,**

A theory is basically an organised collection of related statements that seem to explain observed phenomena.

Bandura suggested that behaviour is learned *but* not always through direct conditioning. We often learn by watching what other people do. If they appear to be rewarded for their actions then we are likely to imitate them. This is called **vicarious reinforcement**.

A key difference between *social* learning theory and learning theory is the introduction of mental states. In order to imitate someone's behaviour there must be an intervening cognitive state (i.e. we perceive and interpret their behaviour). Whereas behaviourists rejected the concept of mind, saying there was no need for it, social learning theorists introduced a role for cognition (internal mental processes) as well as the influence of social factors.

The social learning of aggression

A classic study used to support Bandura's theory deals with the social learning of aggression in children. According to Bandura's theory, **observational learning** or **modelling** is of great importance in producing aggressive behaviour. Observational learning is a form of learning in which the behaviour of others is copied. Bandura, Ross, and Ross (1961) carried out a study in which young children watched as an adult (the model) behaved aggressively towards a Bobo doll, punching the doll and hitting it with a hammer. After 10 minutes the children were moved to another room where there were some toys, including a hammer and a Bobo doll. They were watched through a one-way mirror and rated for their aggression. The children who had watched the model behaving aggressively were more violent and imitated exactly some of the behaviours they had observed, as compared with children who had either seen no model or watched a model behaving in a non-aggressive manner.

Bandura (1965) carried out another study on aggressive behaviour towards the Bobo doll. One group of children simply saw a film of an adult model kicking and punching the Bobo doll. A second group saw the same aggressive behaviour performed, but this time the model was rewarded by another adult for his aggressive behaviour by being given sweets and a drink. A third group saw the

Children watched adults behaving aggressively with a "Bobo" doll. Afterwards they were filmed imitating this behaviour.

same aggressive behaviour, but the model was punished by another adult, who warned him not to be aggressive in future.

Those children who had seen the model rewarded, and those who had seen the model neither rewarded nor punished, behaved much more aggressively towards the Bobo doll than did those who had seen the model punished. The children in all these groups showed comparable levels of memory for the aggressive behaviour they had seen, and thus had the same amount of observational learning. However, those who had seen the model punished were least likely to apply this learning to their own behaviour.

There are reasons for arguing that Bandura exaggerated the meaning of his findings, as it is unlikely that those children would so readily imitate aggressive behaviour towards another child. Bandura consistently failed to distinguish between real aggression and playfighting, and it is likely that much of the behaviour observed by Bandura was playfighting (Durkin, 1995). Also, as a novelty item, the Bobo doll provided interest to young children. Cumberbatch (1990) reported that children unfamiliar with the doll were *five* times more likely to imitate aggressive behaviour against it than those children who had played with it before. Finally, it could be argued that the whole set-up of the experiment indicated to the children that they should behave aggressively towards the Bobo doll. In other words, the Bobo doll experiment provided cues that "invited" the children to behave in certain predictable ways.

Evaluation of social learning theory

The social learning explanation is found throughout psychology and is an important one. It is a neo-behaviourist account because it still emphasises the role of learning as a way of explaining why people behave as they do, but with the additional involvement of cognitive (mental) and social factors. Children learn many of their behaviours by observing others and modelling their own behaviour on what they have seen. Likely role models include parents, friends, TV characters, pop stars, footballers, and fashion models.

A limitation is that behaviour doesn't depend only on observational learning; people's internal emotional state, their interpretation of the current situation, and their personality are other important factors that need to be taken into account.

Psychodynamic Theory

In the 19th century another form of psychological explanation grew out of Sigmund Freud's (1856–1939) theory of personality development. Freud practised as a psychiatrist in Vienna and collected a lot of information from his patients about their feelings and experiences, especially those related to early childhood. He developed his ideas into a theory (**psychodynamic theory**) and a form of therapy (**psychoanalysis**).

Psychodynamic theory tries to explain human development in terms of an interaction between **innate** drives (such as the desire for pleasure) and early experience (the extent to which early desires were gratified). The idea is that individual personality differences can be traced back to early conflicts between desire and experience. For example, a child may want to behave badly (e.g. steal sweets) but be in conflict because of the guilt experienced afterwards. Some of

? Does this study have external validity? In other words, to what extent can we generalise the findings obtained in this study to real life?

? What are some of the limitations of Bandura's research?

? How important do you think observational learning is with respect to producing aggressive behaviour?

Sigmund Freud, 1856–1939.

A "Freudian slip" is a mistake that betrays the concerns of the unconscious mind. Think of a time when you might have called someone by the wrong name. In what way might this have been a Freudian slip?

these conflicts remain with the adult and are likely to influence his/her behaviour. In order to understand this we need to look briefly at Freud's description of development.

The structure of the personality

You probably imagine that most (or even all) of the mind exists at the conscious level. The fact that you are generally consciously aware of why you have the emotions you do, and why you behave as you do, suggests that our conscious mind has full access to all relevant information about ourselves. However, Freud's views were very different. He argued that the conscious mind was like the tip of an iceberg, with most of the mind (like most of the iceberg) out of sight. More specifically, Freud assumed there were *three* levels of the mind:

- The conscious—those thoughts that are currently the focus of attention; in other words, what we are thinking about at any moment.
- The preconscious—information and ideas that can be retrieved easily from memory and brought into consciousness.
- The unconscious—this is the largest part of the mind, containing information that is almost impossible to bring into conscious awareness. Much of the information in the unconscious mind relates to very emotional experiences from our past (e.g. being bullied at school; being rejected by someone of great importance in our lives).

We have just seen that Freud assumed that the mind exists at three different levels. He also assumed that the mind is divided into *three* parts. In broad terms, Freud argued that the mind contains basic motivational forces (the id), the cognitive system used to perceive the world and for thinking and problem solving (the ego), and a conscience based on the values of family and of society generally (the superego). Let's now consider each of these parts of the mind in more detail.

Note that the term "sexual" is roughly equivalent to "physical pleasure".

1. *Id.* This contains basic motivational forces, especially innate sexual and aggressive instincts. The id follows the **pleasure principle**, with the emphasis being on *immediate* satisfaction. It is located in the unconscious mind. The sexual instinct is known as libido.
2. *Ego.* This is the conscious, rational mind, and it develops during the first two years of life. It works on the **reality principle**, taking account of what is going on in the environment.
3. *Superego.* This develops at about the age of 5 and embodies the child's conscience and sense of right and wrong. It is formed when the child adopts many of the values of the same-sexed parent (the process of identification).

Defence mechanisms

An important part of Freud's theory was the notion that there are frequent *conflicts* among the id, ego, and superego, which cause the individual to experience anxiety. More specifically, what generally happens is that there are conflicts between the id (which wants immediate satisfaction) and the superego (which wants the person to behave in line with society's rules). These conflicts force the ego to devote much time to trying to resolve them. The ego protects itself

by using a number of **defence mechanisms** (strategies designed to reduce anxiety), some of which are as follows:

1. *Repression*. Keeping threatening thoughts out of consciousness, e.g. not remembering a potentially painful dental appointment.
2. *Displacement*. Unconsciously moving impulses away from a threatening object and towards a less threatening object, e.g. someone who has been made angry by their teacher may shout at their brother.
3. *Projection*. An individual may attribute their undesirable characteristics to others, e.g. someone who is unfriendly may accuse other people of being unfriendly.
4. *Denial*. Refusing to accept the existence or reality of a threatening event, e.g. patients suffering from life-threatening diseases often deny that their lives are affected.
5. *Intellectualisation*. Thinking about threatening events in ways that remove the emotion from them, e.g. responding to a car ferry disaster by thinking about ways of improving the design of ferries.

Psychosexual development

One of Freud's key assumptions was that adult personality depends very much on childhood experiences. In his theory of **psychosexual development**, Freud assumed that all children go through *five* stages:

1. *Oral stage* (occurs during the first 18 months of life). During this stage, the infant obtains satisfaction from eating, sucking, and other activities using the mouth.
2. *Anal stage* (between about 18 and 36 months of age). Toilet training takes place during this stage, which helps to explain why the anal region becomes so important.
3. *Phallic stage* (between 3 and 6 years of age). The genitals become a key source of satisfaction during this stage. At about the age of 5, boys acquire the **Oedipus complex**, in which they have sexual desires for their mother and therefore want to get rid of their father, who is a rival. They then also fear their father, who might realise what they are thinking. This complex is resolved by identification with their father, involving adopting many of their father's attitudes and developing a superego. So far as girls are concerned, Freud argued that girls come to recognise that they don't have a penis and blame their mother for this. The girl's father now becomes her love-object and she substitutes her "penis envy" with a wish to have a child. This leads to a kind of resolution and ultimate identification with her same-sex parent. If you think Freud's ideas of what goes on in the phallic stage are very fanciful, you're absolutely right!
4. *Latency stage* (from 6 years of age until the onset of puberty). During this stage, boys and girls spend very little time together.
5. *Genital stage* (from the onset of puberty and throughout adult life). During this stage, the main source of sexual pleasure is in the genitals.

Personality theory

Freud coupled the theory of psychosexual development with a theory of personality. If a child experiences severe problems or excessive pleasure at any

Useful mnemonic

To help you remember Freud's stages of psychosexual development, the following mnemonic is made from the initial letter of each stage: Old Age Pensioners Love Greens!

Freud suggested that adult personality types could be linked with fixations during each stage of development.

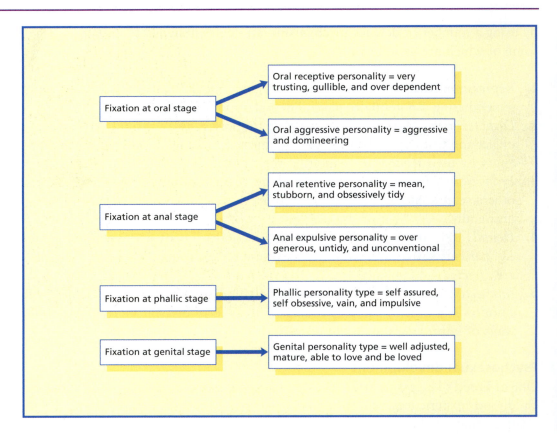

stage of development, this leads to **fixation**, in which basic energy or libido becomes attached to that stage for many years. Later in life, adults who experience very stressful conditions are likely to show **regression**, in which their behaviour becomes less mature, and more like that displayed during a psychosexual stage at which they fixated as children. According to Freud, these processes of fixation and regression play important roles in determining adult personality. Some personality types are shown in the box above, along with descriptions and a link to the stage of psychosexual development at which fixation may have occurred.

Evaluation of psychodynamic theory
- Freud and his psychodynamic theory have had an enormous impact on psychology. Indeed, he is the most influential psychologist of all time.
- As Freud argued, adult personality depends in part on the experiences of early childhood.
- There is increasing evidence that our conscious minds are less powerful than we like to think, and that Freud was right to emphasise the importance of the unconscious mind.
- It is to Freud's credit that he put forward what was probably the first systematic theory of personality.
- Freud's method of investigation was to focus on the individual, observing particular "cases" in fine detail. Many people see this approach as a drawback, mainly because Freud's observations were largely based on a rather narrow sample of people: white, middle-class Victorian Viennese women.

Freud developed his Oedipus complex at a time when lone-parent families were very rare. What bearing do you think this had on his theorising?

Freud's work was largely with middle-class women in Vienna in the 1890s and 1900s. How relevant do you think his ideas are to other cultures, particularly given the social changes during the 20th century?

? Considering that Freud was working in a strict Victorian society, why was sexual behaviour so strongly emphasised in his theory of development?

- Freud over-emphasised sex, because he developed his theory at a time of great sexual repression, which may have caused sex to be something that was repressed in many minds (Banyard & Hayes, 1994).
- Freud's stage-based theory suggests that personality development occurs in a neater and tidier way than is actually the case.
- It is very hard to prove that early childhood experiences have actually determined adult personality many years later, and so the theory is hard to test properly.

> **Assumptions of the psychoanalytic approach**
> - Development is the result of an interaction between innate drives and early experience.
> - Childhood experiences are of fundamental importance.
> - Early conflicts result in unconscious forces that drive many aspects of adult behaviour.

Cognitive or Information-processing Theory

Cognitive psychology developed in the 1950s because of a growing dissatisfaction with the behaviourist approach. It is very hard to understand cognitive abilities, such as language or problem solving, from the behaviourist perspective, with its emphasis on observable behaviour. For example, what someone is thinking is generally not obvious from their behaviour. What is also needed is a focus on internal processes, and this is what cognitive psychologists tried to do.

The arrival of the computer revolution provided an ideal analogy and a good basis for understanding human cognition, with cognitive psychologists explaining human cognition in terms of an information-processing system. There is input in the form of data or information to the brain and to the computer. This is followed by various kinds of information processing in the brain and the computer. Finally, there is some kind of output. Suppose you are given an input in the form of a problem in

> **Assumptions of the cognitive approach**
> - Whereas the behaviourists reduced psychology to stimulus and response (S–R), cognitive psychologists have added another dimension.
> - Cognitive psychologists focus on a central, internal stage (stimulus–information processing–response).
> - The internal cognitive processes and the issue of how the stimulus provokes the response are not dismissed.

mathematics (e.g. 13 × 12 = ?). You engage in information processing, and then finally you output the answer by saying (hopefully!) 156. In similar fashion, computers can be programmed to work out the answer when given the same problem, printing it out or displaying it on the screen.

Evaluation of the cognitive theory

Cognitive explanations tend to be as machine-like as behaviourist ones, often ignoring the role of emotion or the influence of other people—not surprising when they are based on the behaviour of a machine. Also, the research on which they are based is often rather artificial, lacking external validity, because most experiments are carried out under highly controlled laboratory conditions.

Evolutionary Theory

Charles Darwin, 1809–1882.

Charles Darwin presented the most influential theory of evolution. Darwin composed a theory to account for the fact that animal species have evolved and continue to evolve (i.e. change their characteristics). The essential principles of this theory are:

- Environments are always changing, or animals move to new environments.
- Living things are constantly changing, partly because of sexual reproduction where two parents create a new individual by combining their **genes**, and also through chance **mutations** of the genes. In both cases new **traits** are produced.
- Those individuals who possess traits best adapted to the environment are more likely to survive to reproduce (it is reproduction rather than survival that matters); or, to put it another way, those individuals who best "fit" their environment survive (survival of the fittest); or, to put it still another way, the *genes* of the individuals with these traits are naturally selected.

All dogs have the same distant ancestors, but selective breeding (artificial selection) has resulted in major variations.

In order to understand the concept of **natural selection** consider this example. A farmer chooses which males and females have the best characteristics for milk production or for increased reproduction (giving birth to lots of twins), and mates these individuals. This is selective breeding or artificial selection. In nature, no-one does the selecting, it is natural pressures that do it—it is called "natural selection".

The end result is that the genes carrying physical characteristics and behaviours that are **adaptive**, i.e. help the individual to better fit its environment, are the ones that survive to the next generation. Those traits that are non-adaptive tend to disappear. However, it should be emphasised it is not the individual but his/her genes that disappear.

The adaptive role of genes

A classic example of the adaptive role of the genes can be seen in the tendency for parents to risk their lives to save their offspring. This is described as **altruism**. Darwin could not explain this behaviour because, according to his theory, it is only the *individuals* who survive that count. If a parent dies saving their offspring this would appear to be a non-adaptive behaviour. However, altruism is adaptive at the level of the genes. A parent who dies in order to save his or her offspring is ensuring that their **genetic** line survives. Therefore altruism can be seen to be adaptive behaviour.

Evaluation of evolutionary theory

The theory of natural selection offers a good account of the facts. However, we can only point to fossil records and the evidence from a few species who have changed before our eyes, seemingly in response to environmental demands. A good example of this is the peppered moth, which is described in the **Case Study** given below.

One criticism is that the theory of evolution offers mainly *post-facto* (after the fact) evidence. It is hard to know whether a behaviour is actually beneficial, and that's why it remained, or whether it was simply neutral, and was never selected against.

> **Assumptions of the evolutionary approach**
>
> - Animal species have evolved and continue to evolve.
> - Physical characteristics and behaviours that are adaptive are kept, whilst the genes for non-adaptive characteristics and behaviours disappear.
> - It is the genes, not the individuals, that are either selected or disappear with natural selection.

CASE STUDY: THE PEPPERED MOTH

What has often been regarded as fairly direct support for some of the assumptions of Darwin's theory was obtained by Kettlewell (1955). He studied two variants of the peppered moth, one of which was darker than the other. The difference in colour is inherited, with the offspring of the darker type being on average darker than those of the lighter type. Both types of peppered moth are eaten by birds such as robins and redstarts that rely on sight to detect them. Kettlewell observed the moths when they were on relatively light lichen-covered trees and when they were on dark, lichen-less trees in industrially polluted areas. The lighter-coloured moths survived better on the lighter trees and the darker-coloured moths survived better on the darker trees.

According to Darwin's theory, the number of darker moths should increase if there is an increase in the proportion of dark trees. Precisely this happened in England due to the industrial revolution, when pollution killed the lichen and coated the trees with sooty deposits. The proportion of peppered moths that were dark apparently went from almost nil to over half the resident population in a period of about 50 years. However, the baseline evidence that there were few dark peppered moths before the industrial revolution comes from moth collections. As Hailman (1992, p.126) pointed out, "Those collections were not scientific samples but were made by amateurs . . . Perhaps they did not like ugly black moths." ■

Approaches in Psychology

All of these different kinds of explanation can also be called "approaches" or "perspectives". They are ways to approach the problem of explaining behaviour. Different psychologists prefer different approaches. However, some might favour one kind of approach when explaining, say, aggression, but another approach when offering an account of why some individuals develop mental disorders.

No single explanation is "right" and no explanation is right for every behaviour. Each is appropriate in different contexts and many can be used together. They form part of the psychologist's "toolkit". You must choose the psychological explanations that make best sense to you in the context of different behaviour.

Two colours of peppered moth on the bark of a tree. These two forms, light (upper left) and dark (lower right), are a famous example of natural selection.

> ■ **Activity:** Divide the class into five groups and give each group one of the approaches covered: behaviourist, psychoanalytic, cognitive, social learning, evolutionary. They should draw up a list of the advantages and disadvantages of their approach. Each group should give a brief presentation of their approach and, at the end of the lesson, let everyone decide which approach gets their vote for being the most valuable.

SECTION SUMMARY

The range of
explanations

❖ Psychologists use a range of different explanations, or "tools" to explain behaviour. For instance:
- Physiological explanations explore our behaviour in terms of our bodily processes.
- Social psychological explanations look at our behaviour in terms of our interactions with each other.

❖ There are general explanations that are used more or less throughout psychology, which are each described below.

Learning theory

❖ One key explanation of behaviour is learning theory. This theory suggests that all our behaviour is learned, and was largely developed from studies on animal behaviour.

❖ Learning theory is based on two types of conditioning:
- Classical conditioning: occurs when a neutral stimulus is paired with an unconditioned stimulus, eventually producing a conditioned stimulus and response.
- Operant conditioning: the result of reinforcement or punishment, which either increases or decreases the likelihood of a behaviour being repeated.

❖ Learning theory has been criticised:
- first, for being based on animal research;
- second, in its application to humans, where the emphasis on controlling behaviour has led to ethical concerns.

Social learning theory

❖ Social learning theory adds to the learning theory explanations by explaining learning in terms of conditioning *and* observation.

❖ This theory suggests that we also learn via vicarious reinforcement and identification or modelling.

❖ Some of the findings apparently supporting social learning are open to other interpretations.

Psychodynamic theory

❖ Another important psychological theory is psychodynamic theory. This theory is both an account of personality development and a therapy.

❖ This theory focuses on the unconscious mind, and suggests that our early experiences may result in unconscious conflicts that motivate adult behaviour.

❖ Freud described the mind in terms of three levels (conscious, preconscious, and unconscious) and three structures:
- The ID: is made up of our innate sexual and aggressive instincts and follows the pleasure principle.
- The EGO: describes our conscious rational mind and follows the reality principle.
- The SUPEREGO: embodies the child's conscience.

❖ These structures are likely to come into conflict because they are motivated by different principles.

❖ Conflicts create anxieties that are dealt with by defence mechanisms.

❖ These defence mechanisms include:
- repression,
- displacement,

- – projection,
- – denial,
- – intellectualisation.
❖ Freud also suggested that there were five stages in development:
 1. oral,
 2. anal,
 3. phallic,
 4. latency,
 5. genital.
❖ Children may fixate at any one of these stages, and this fixation can be linked to their adult personality.
❖ Freudian theory has been criticised in terms of bias, but there is no doubt that his theories have had an enormous influence on 20th-century thought.

❖ Cognitive explanations of behaviour focus on mental processes and use the analogy of information-processing systems.
❖ This comparison of human thought and behaviour to computer systems has resulted in the accusation of offering mechanistic explanations of behaviour.

Cognitive explanations

❖ Evolutionary explanations of behaviour describe behaviour in terms of adaptiveness.
❖ They suggest that any characteristic that enhances reproduction is more likely to be perpetuated than those that do not. Natural selection chooses those genes that are desirable. Altruism is a good example.
❖ One major problem with evolutionary explanations centres on the evidence used to support the theory.

Evolutionary explanations

❖ It is important to stress that no one explanation or approach is right.
❖ They are all used as part of the psychologist's "toolkit" for studying behaviour.

Which explanation is right?

FURTHER READING

Two useful books on perspectives are C. Tavris and C. Wade (1997) *Psychology in perspective* (New York: Longman), and W.E. Glassman (1995) *Approaches to psychology* (Milton Keynes, UK: Open University Press). Books written more specifically for AS and A-level include M.W. Eysenck (1994) *Perspectives on psychology* (Hove, UK: Psychology Press), and A.E. Wadeley, A. Birch, and A. Malim (1997) *Perspectives in psychology (2nd Edn.)* (Basingstoke, UK: Macmillan). For a general introduction to psychology you could try J.C. Berryman, D.J. Hargreaves, C.R. Hollin, and K. Howells (1987) *Psychology and you* (Leicester, UK: BPS Books), or M.W. Eysenck (2002) *Simply Psychology (2nd Edn.)* (Hove, UK: Psychology Press). There is also an amusing series of introductory books written by Nigel Benson (1998), including *Introducing psychology*, *Introducing Freud*, and *Introducing evolutionary psychology* (Duxford, UK: Icon Books).

Cognitive psychology is an approach or perspective in psychology. Cognitive psychologists are interested in internal mental (cognitive) processes such as those of perceiving, thinking, talking, and attention. Behaviour and experience are explained in terms of these internal processes rather than in terms of external influences. The emphasis is on how we perceive and interpret a stimulus rather than the stimulus itself. Here is an example to clarify the point. Consider the stimulus, "I would like to go to the cinema with you." That stimulus would probably have a very different effect on someone who understands English than on someone who knows no English at all. Thus, what is important is how a stimulus is interpreted. Essentially, cognitive psychology is the study of how the mind works and how it influences our behaviour and experience.

SECTION 5
Short-term memory and long-term memory p.41

Short-term memory (STM) is the part of the memory system where information is initially stored. Information that we remember is held in long-term memory (LTM). What causes memories to be moved from STM to LTM? The answer is offered by various models of memory.

Specification content: Research into the nature of short-term memory (STM) and long-term memory (LTM) (e.g. encoding, capacity, and duration). The multi-store model of memory (Atkinson & Shiffrin) and at least one alternative to this (e.g. working memory: Baddeley & Hitch; levels of processing: Craik & Lockhart).

SECTION 6
Remembering and forgetting p.63

Why do we forget? Why do we fail to retrieve some memories? What factors influence our ability to remember and forget information?

Specification content: Explanations of forgetting in short-term memory (e.g. decay and displacement). Explanations of forgetting in long-term memory (e.g. retrieval failure and interference). The role of emotional factors in memory, including flashbulb memories and repression (e.g. Freud).

SECTION 7—CRITICAL ISSUE
Eyewitness testimony p.74

This section looks at a practical application of memory research. Eyewitness reports involve identifying suspects or describing what happened when a crime was committed. How reliable are eyewitnesses when they try to recall what happened or when they describe a person's face?

Specification content: Research into reconstructive memory (e.g. Bartlett). Memory research into eyewitness testimony (e.g. Loftus), including the role of leading questions.

COGNITIVE PSYCHOLOGY:
Human Memory

You may think that in an ideal world we would remember every detail of things that happen, especially when they are important. However, if we did remember everything, our memories would be very full, and we would find it hard to think because of the enormous wealth of detail we would always be remembering. In fact, of course, we actually forget lots of things, many of them things we didn't want to forget. What makes some things memorable, and others forgettable?

This chapter explores one topic in cognitive psychology—human memory. How important is memory? Imagine if we were without it. We would not recognise anyone or anything as familiar. We would not be able to talk, read, or write, because we would remember nothing about language. We would be like newborn babies.

We use memory for numerous purposes—to keep track of conversations, to remember telephone numbers while we dial them, to write essays in examinations, to make sense of what we read, and to recognise people's faces. There are many different *kinds* of memory, which suggests that we have a number of memory systems. This chapter explores in detail some of the sub-divisions of human memory, as well as the reverse side of the coin—forgetting.

SECTION 5
SHORT-TERM MEMORY AND LONG-TERM MEMORY

What is Memory?

Memory is the process of retaining information after the original thing is no longer present. There are close links between **learning** and **memory**. Something that is learned is lodged in memory, and we can only remember things learned in the past.

Memory and learning can most clearly be demonstrated by good performance on a memory test, such as giving someone a list of words for a specified period of time, removing the list, and later asking them to recall the list. When learning and memorising the words in the list, there are three stages:

1. **Encoding.** When the person is given the list they encode the words. They place the words in

> **KEY TERM**
>
> **Memory**: the mental processes used to encode, store, and retrieve information. Encoding takes many forms; visual, auditory, semantic, taste, and smell. Storage refers to the amount of information that can be held in memory. Retrieval refers to the processes by which information is "dug out" of memory, and includes recognition, recall, and reconstruction. It is useful to distinguish between two types of memory: short-term or immediate memory and long-term or more permanent memory.

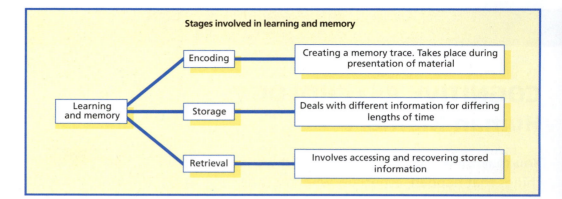

Stages involved in learning and memory

Learning and memory

Encoding — Creating a memory trace. Takes place during presentation of material

Storage — Deals with different information for differing lengths of time

Retrieval — Involves accessing and recovering stored information

? **Are learning and memory different? If so, what is the difference?**

memory. "Encoding" means to put something into a code, in this case the code used to store it in memory—some kind of chemical **memory trace**. For example, if you hear the word "Chair", you might encode it in terms of your favourite chair that you normally sit in at home. In other words, your encoding of the word "Chair" involves converting or changing the word you hear into a meaningful form.

2. **Storage**. As a result of encoding, the information is stored within the memory system. As we will see, some information remains stored in memory for decades or even an entire lifetime.

3. **Retrieval**. Recovering stored information from the memory system. This is known as "recall" or "remembering".

Psychologists who are interested in learning focus on encoding and storage, whereas those interested in memory concentrate on retrieval. However, all these processes depend on each other.

Short-term and long-term memory
Most psychologists agree that there is a distinction between two kinds of memory: short-term and long-term memory. One lasts for only a short time, while the other lasts theoretically forever or at least for a long time.

Trying to remember a telephone number for a few seconds is an everyday example of the use of the **short-term memory**, illustrating two of its key features: a very limited **capacity** and a very limited **duration**. Long-term memory, on the other hand, has unlimited capacity and lasts (potentially) forever. As an example, you might think of your childhood memories.

The multi-store model of memory
The model of memory put forward by Atkinson and Shiffrin (1968) is the most important theoretical approach based on the notion that there are separate

---

Testing memory

Psychologists use various methods to test recall or learning.

- Free recall. Give participants some words to learn and then ask them to recall the words in any order.
- Cued recall. After presenting the material to be learned, provide cues to help recall. For example, saying that some of the items are minerals.
- Recognition. Giving a list of words which includes some of those in the initial presentation. Participants are asked to identify those in the original list.
- Paired-associate learning. Participants are given word pairs to learn and then tested by presenting one of the words and asking them to recall the other word.
- Nonsense syllables. Participants are asked to memorise meaningless sets of letters. These may be trigrams (three letters).

KEY TERMS

Short-term memory: a temporary place for storing information during which it receives limited processing (e.g. verbal rehearsal). Short-term memory has a very limited capacity and short duration, unless the information in it is maintained through rehearsal.
Long-term memory: a relatively permanent store, which has unlimited capacity and duration. Different kinds of long-term memory have been identified, including episodic (memory for personal events), semantic (memory for facts and information), and procedural (memory for actions and skills).

short-term and long-term memory stores. In fact, they argued that there are *three* kinds of memory stores, which explains why their approach is known as the **multi-store model** of memory. Here are the crucial assumptions built into this model:

1. Human memory consists of three kinds of memory stores.
2. Information from the environment is initially received by the sensory stores. There is one sensory store for each sense modality, so there is one for what we see, one for what we hear, and so on. Information lasts for a very short period of time (fractions of a second, or a second or two) in these sensory stores.
3. Some of the information in the sensory stores is attended to (and processed further) by the short-term store. The main feature of the short-term store is that it has limited capacity—we cannot keep more than about *seven* items in this store at any one time.
4. Some of the information processed in the short-term store is transferred to the long-term store. How does information get into the long-term store? We need to rehearse or repeat verbally information in the short-term store to put it into the long-term store. The more something is rehearsed, the stronger the memory trace in long-term memory.
5. The key feature of the long-term store is that information in it can often last for a long time. Indeed, in some cases, information in the long-term store remains there for our entire lifetime.

We all know that certain kinds of information disappear from memory in a few seconds whereas others last for years and years. Accordingly, you may think it is obvious that there are separate short-term and long-term memory stores. However, if we are going to prove the point (or get as close to proof as we can), then we need to start by listing *all* the likely differences between the short-term and long-term memory stores. When we have done that, we can have a look at the relevant research evidence. Then, finally, we will evaluate the evidence, and decide how accurately the multi-store model actually accounts for human

You may be familiar with the following experience: Your mother says "Are you listening to me?" You weren't listening, but remarkably you are able to repeat the last few things she said. This is because that information is in a sensory memory store, where it is held for a few seconds before entering short-term memory.

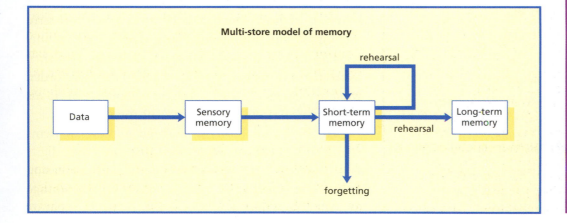

Multi-store model of memory

memory. Here is a list of possible differences between the short-term and long-term memory stores:

1. *Encoding*: Remember that encoding involves changing the information presented into a different form. Since words or other items in the short-term store are rehearsed or repeated in the short-term store, we might assume they are encoded in terms of their sound (this is known as acoustic coding). In contrast, the information we have stored in long-term memory nearly always seems to be stored in terms of its meaning (this is known as semantic coding).

2. *Capacity*: The short-term store has very limited capacity. As mentioned already, its capacity is about seven items. In contrast, the capacity of the long-term memory is assumed to be so large that we are in no danger of filling it. We probably have millions of pieces of information stored in long-term memory already, but that doesn't stop us from adding a lot of new information every day.

3. *Duration*: It is pretty obvious from the names short-term memory store and long-term memory store that information has greater duration (i.e. it lasts longer) in the long-term store than in the short-term store! As we will see, there is evidence that information in the short-term store, if not rehearsed, will disappear within about 18–20 seconds. In contrast, we will see that elderly people can recognise the names of fellow students from 48 years previously (Bahrick et al., 1975; see page 50). Thus, we have proof that long-term memory can last virtually 50 years at least.

Now we will have a look at the evidence relating to these various assumptions about the short-term and long-term memory stores. That will take us some time, and after that, we will evaluate the multi-store model, trying to identify its main strengths and weaknesses.

■ **Activity:** Read quickly through the following list of digits once. Cover the list and try to write the digits down in the correct order.

7 3 5 1 5 6 9 8 2 7 4

How many did you remember in the correct order? This is one way of measuring your memory span. Now try the following digits:

1 9 3 9 1 0 6 6 1 8 0 5 1 2 1 5

More digits, but if you recognised the "chunks" you should have remembered them all:

1939 Start of Second World War
1066 Battle of Hastings
1805 Battle of Trafalgar
1215 Signing of the Magna Carta

Did you find any primary or recency effects when you tried to recall the list of digits? Try the test again (with different data) with this in mind.

Short-term Memory

Capacity of short-term memory

It's not as easy as you might think to estimate the capacity of short-term memory. Psychologists have devised two main strategies: span measures, and the recency effect in free recall.

Span measures

In 1887, Joseph Jacobs used memory span as a measure of how much can be stored in short-term memory at any time. Jacobs presented his participants with a random sequence of digits or letters, and then asked them to repeat the items back in the same order. **Memory span** was the longest sequence of items recalled accurately at least 50% of the time.

Jacobs found that the average number of items recalled was between five and nine, and that digits were recalled better (9.3 items) than letters (7.3 items), with both spans increasing with age. These findings suggested that short-term memory has a limited storage capacity of between about five and nine items.

Why is Jacobs' study important? First, he provided the first proper assessment of the capacity of short-term memory. Second, his conclusion that the capacity of short-term memory is about seven items has been confirmed.

Jacobs' approach was limited. First, his research lacked **mundane realism** because his span tasks were not representative of everyday memory demands. Second, if we could only remember a few letters, we would be unable to remember the following sequence of ten letters: P S Y C H O L O G Y! In fact, we can remember that sequence because it's easy to organise the information in memory. Miller (1956) took account of that point, and argued that the span of immediate memory is "seven, plus or minus two", whether the units are numbers, letters, or words. He claimed we should focus on **chunks** (integrated pieces or units of information). About seven chunks of information can be held in short-term memory at any time. The question of what constitutes a "chunk" depends on your personal experience. For example, "IBM" could be one chunk or three chunks (the letters stand for International Business Machines).

Herb Simon (1974) carried out a thorough study to test Miller's ideas about the importance of **chunking**. Simon argued that the size of a chunk corresponds to the highest-level integration of the stimulus material available to the participant. In his research, he studied memory span for words, two-word phrases, and eight-word phrases. When he focused on the number of words in the span, he found this increased from seven words to nine with two-word phrases and 22 with eight-word phrases. At the level of chunks, Simon argued that an entire phrase should be regarded as a single chunk. When he did this, the number of chunks fell from six or seven with unrelated words to four with two-word phrases and three with eight-word phrases.

Simon confirmed that it makes sense to measure memory span in terms of chunks. However, the number of chunks in the memory span varied across different types of material more than expected on Miller's hypothesis. Such research has useful applications—for example, if you chunk phone numbers, they are easier to remember. This skill is becoming less useful now that most people store numerous phone numbers in their mobile phones! As with Jacobs' earlier research, this study by Simon (1974) lacks mundane realism in that the demands on the participants were very different from those of our everyday lives.

The recency effect

A familiar example of the **recency effect** is the observation that a pop group is only as good as their last hit song. People generally remember most-recent things well. In relation to short-term memory, the recency effect can be measured using free recall; participants are shown a list of words or syllables, and immediately asked to recall them in any order. The recency effect is demonstrated by the fact that the last few items in a list are usually much better remembered than items from the middle of the list.

Glanzer and Cunitz (1966) found that introducing an **interference** task involving counting backwards for only 10 seconds between the end of list presentation and the start of recall eliminated the recency effect, but otherwise had no effect on recall of the rest of the list. The two or three words at the end of the list were in a fragile state (not well encoded) in short-term memory, and so were easily wiped out by the task of counting backwards. In contrast, the other list items were in the long-term store, and so were unaffected.

[?] To what extent can we apply the findings of Jacobs to everyday life?

[?] Are there any problems with using letter or digit span as a measure of the capacity of short-term memory?

[?] If you were shown these ten words: cat, butter, car, house, carpet, tomato, beer, river, pool, tennis; and then asked to recall them immediately in any order, what words are likely to be best remembered?

The recency effect suggests that the capacity of the short-term store is about two or three items. However, span measures indicate a capacity of about seven items. Why do these two techniques produce different results? One reason relates to different patterns of **rehearsal**. Participants carrying out a span task rehearse as many items as possible, whereas those asked to learn a list for free recall rehearse only a few items at a time. Both measures indicate that the capacity of short-term memory is strictly limited. In contrast, no effective limits on the capacity of long-term memory have been discovered.

Duration in short-term memory

We have seen that the capacity of short-term memory is very limited. However, this leaves open another important issue: how long does information last in short-term memory? This is a crucial question. If information is lost rapidly from short-term memory, this must limit our ability to think about several things at once.

The classic study to work out the duration of short-term memory was carried out by Peterson and Peterson (1959, see Key Study below), using what became known as the Brown–Peterson technique. In essence, the participants were shown a trigram (three consonants such as BVM), and then recalled it after a few seconds. This task would have been very easy, but for the fact that the participants were given an interference task between the initial presentation of the trigram and its subsequent recall. The interference task was to count backwards in threes from a three-digit number. (Try it and you'll find it stops you thinking of anything else!) The reason for using an interference task was to prevent the participants from rehearsing the trigram. If they had been allowed to rehearse the trigram, their performance would have been perfect, and we would have learned nothing about *forgetting* from short-term memory!

Key Study: Duration in short-term memory

Peterson and Peterson's (1959) study of the duration of short-term memory.

Aims: In a laboratory experiment, Peterson and Peterson aimed to study how long information remains in short-term memory (STM), using simple stimuli and not allowing the participants to rehearse the material presented to them. They aimed to test the hypothesis that information not rehearsed is lost rapidly from short-term memory.

Procedure: Peterson and Peterson used what is known as the Brown–Peterson technique. On each trial, participants were presented with a trigram consisting of three consonants (e.g. BVM, CTG), which they knew they would be asked to recall in the correct order. Recall was required after a delay of 3, 6, 9, 12, 15, or 18 seconds. The participants counted backwards in threes from a random 3-digit number (e.g. 866, 863, 860, and so on) between the initial presentation of the trigram and the time when they were asked to recall it. This was done to prevent rehearsal of the trigram, because rehearsal would have improved performance by keeping information in STM. Recall had to be 100% accurate and in the correct order (serial recall) in order to count. The participants were tested repeatedly with the various time delays. The experimenters varied the time delay, and the effect of time delay on memory was assessed in terms of the number of trigrams recalled.

Findings: There was a rapid increase in forgetting from STM as the time delay increased. After 3 seconds 80% of the trigrams were recalled, after 6 seconds 50% were recalled, and after 18 seconds fewer than 10% of the trigrams were recalled. Thus, there was a rapid rate of forgetting, and very little information remained in STM for more than 18 seconds or so.

Conclusions: The findings from this study suggest strongly that information held in STM is lost rapidly when there is little or no opportunity to rehearse it. Thus, information in STM is fragile and easily forgotten. We can also conclude that STM is distinct from LTM in that forgetting is enormously faster from STM than from LTM.

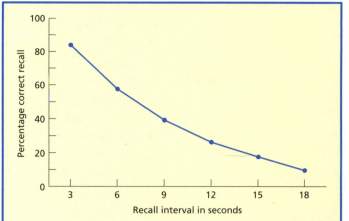

The graph shows a steady decline in short-term memory recall after longer retention intervals (from Peterson & Peterson, 1959).

Criticisms

- Peterson and Peterson made use of very artificial stimuli (i.e. trigrams), which are essentially lacking in meaning. Thus, the study lacks mundane realism and external validity. For example, STM is likely to be better for the meaningful stimuli encountered in everyday life than for the stimuli used in this study.
- The findings of Peterson and Peterson depended in part on the fact that the participants were given many trials with different trigrams and may have become confused. Keppel and Underwood (1962) used the same task as Peterson and Peterson (1959), but observed *no* forgetting over time on the very first trial. Why was this? Forgetting is caused in part by proactive interference (disruption of current learning and memory by previous learning), and only the first trigram presented is free from proactive interference.
- Peterson and Peterson only considered STM duration for one type of stimulus. Their study did not provide information about the duration of STM for other kinds of stimuli (e.g. pictures; melodies; smells).

Note: If the question asks for findings or conclusions only, you could include research by Glanzer and Cunitz (1966, see p.45).

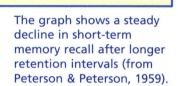 **Why was information in short-term memory forgotten so quickly?**

Was the approach taken by Peterson and Peterson (1959) too artificial to tell us much about short-term forgetting in everyday life?

The research of Peterson and Peterson (1959) is important, because it provided the first detailed analysis of the rate of forgetting from short-term memory. It confirmed what most of us would have guessed, namely, that information in short-term memory is lost rapidly, especially if it is not rehearsed. Peterson and Peterson (1959) didn't provide a full account of *why* information is lost from short-term memory, but this issue has been considered by other researchers (see page 64).

Encoding in short-term memory vs long-term memory

When psychologists talk about **encoding** they are referring to the way the information is stored in memory. One of the ways to compare encoding is in terms of acoustic (sound) or semantic (meaning) coding. The words "cap" and "can" are acoustically similar; "cap" and "hat" are semantically similar. One can remember words by the way they sound or by their meaning.

It seems that short-term and long-term memory differ in the way information is coded. If you have to remember something for a short time, such as a phone number, you probably repeat it to yourself (rehearsal). People do this whether they heard the number or saw it, suggesting that short-term memory may encode information acoustically. Conrad (1964) investigated this by comparing performance with acoustically and visually presented information. Participants, presented with six letters each displayed for 0.75 seconds, had to recall the letters in the same order. When the letters *sounded* alike (even though they were presented *visually*), errors were made in terms of sound confusions, for example S was recalled instead of X.

Conrad's (1964) study was important because it increased our understanding of short-term memory. However, it failed to address one key issue. During the 1960s, there was much interest in trying to find major differences between short-term and long-term memory. Conrad had focused *only* on short-term memory, and so his study could not identify such differences. This was an important omission, because there was some controversy at the time as to whether or not short-term and long-term memory were really separate from each other. If they really are separate forms of memory, then there should be some major differences between them.

This was the context in which Baddeley (1966) carried out an important study on coding in short-term and long-term memory. He confirmed Conrad's (1964) finding that short-term memory depends mainly on **acoustic coding**: if participants recalled words from short-term memory they didn't confuse words having the same meaning (e.g. "big" and "large") but they often confused words that sounded similar (e.g. remembering "cat" instead of "cap"). The *opposite* was true for long-term memory. This suggests that short-term memory largely uses an acoustic code, and that long-term memory depends mostly on **semantic coding** based on the meaning of words. These findings convinced many psychologists that the distinction between short-term and long-term memory is both genuine and important.

Baddeley's (1966) approach was limited in that he didn't consider the possibility of *visual* codes existing in short-term memory. Posner (1969) found evidence that visual codes *are* used. For example, when "A" was followed by "A", people were faster to decide it was the same letter than when "A" was followed by "a". The visual code for the second letter differed from that of the first letter when "A" was followed by "a", and that slowed people down.

In fact, information in long-term memory can be encoded acoustically, visually, or by taste or smell. This suggests that the coding distinction between short-term and long-term memory is not as clear-cut as Baddeley's study suggested. It would not make

■ **Activity:** You could test the effects of semantic and acoustic recall by using Baddeley's word lists and asking for immediate or delayed recall.

Construct four word lists: acoustically similar, acoustically dissimilar, semantically similar, and semantically dissimilar.

Divide participants into two groups—immediate recall (short-term memory) and longer-term recall. Participants should be randomly allocated to conditions to ensure that both groups of participants are equivalent.

For each group, which lists are they best at recalling and which lists do they perform least well on?

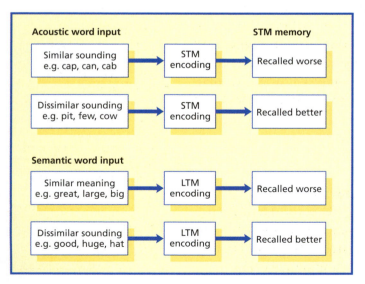

sense to suggest that all information in long-term memory is in semantic form. If you consider the example of processing a word that is presented visually in a short-term memory task, you only know how to pronounce that word because information about word sounds is stored in your long-term memory!

Evidence about short-term memory from studies of brain damage

The strongest evidence for a distinction between short-term and long-term memory comes from the study of brain-damaged patients. In **amnesia,** a person loses much of their long-term memory, often due to an accident that has caused brain damage. Such patients usually have almost normal short-term memories. In contrast, there are other patients with brain damage who have no problem with their long-term memories, but their short-term memory is very poor. Shallice and Warrington (1970) studied KF, who suffered brain damage as a result of a motorcycle accident. KF had no problem with long-term memory, but his digit span was only two items (i.e. he could only remember two digits at a time instead of the average seven digits). These findings suggest that different parts of the brain are involved in short-term and long-term memory.

In addition, Warrington and Shallice (1972) found that KF's short-term forgetting of auditory letters and digits (things that were heard) was much greater than his forgetting of visual stimuli. They also found that KF's short-term memory deficit was limited to verbal materials (e.g. letters, words), and didn't extend to meaningful sounds (e.g. cats miaowing). This suggests that there is not just *one* short-term memory but a number of different stores, each represented in different parts of the brain. These distinctions within short-term memory are important and we will return to them later.

Evaluation of studies of brain-damaged patients

When we consider the effects of brain damage, it is important to remember that it is a complex matter to relate such findings to the functioning and behaviour of intact individuals.

External validity of short-term memory research

Before we move on to long-term memory, it is worth noting that all the research considered so far has been *experimental* and conducted in *laboratories*. However, your emotional state and social circumstances influence your memory considerably, and therefore it may be that we are studying one particular *kind* of memory and not all kinds of memory. This is especially true of studies of long-term memory. The conclusion must be that generalisation from these studies to all situations may not be reasonable.

Long-term Memory

Long-term memory covers all those things that we remember for a long time. Regarding encoding in long-term memory, see text above. The long-term storage space in your brain is essentially unlimited in capacity and the duration of these memories is also thought to be potentially unlimited. The main differences between short-term and long-term memory are summarised in the box on page 53.

> **EXAM HINT**
> You may be asked to distinguish between STM and LTM. The easiest way to do this is to compare encoding, capacity, and duration. Note then that the research on encoding, capacity, and duration supports the concept that STM and LTM are different stores. You could also consider the differences in forgetting.

CASE STUDY: THE MAN WHO NEVER GOT OLDER

In the 1950s a man known as "HM" sought medical help for his epileptic seizures. He had been forced to give up his job because the seizures had became so frequent and severe, and it was not possible to control them with drugs. In desperation the doctors decided to remove a structure called the hippocampus from both hemispheres of his brain because this was the seat of his seizures. No-one quite knew what the outcome would be. The operation did reduce his epilepsy but it also had a dramatic effect on his memory.

His personality and intellect remained the same, but his memory was severely affected. Some aspects of his memory were fairly intact: he could still talk and recall the skills he knew previously (semantic memory), he continued to be able to form short-term memories, but was unable to form any new long-term ones. For example, given the task of memorising a number he could recall it 15 minutes later but, after being distracted, he had no recollection. He could read the same magazine over and over again without realising that he had read it before.

HM moved house after his operation and had great difficulty learning his new route home. After 6 years he was finally able to at least find his way around the house. This shows that he did have some memory capacity and, intellectually, he was quite "intact" so he did have some awareness of his predicament.

For many years he reported that the year was 1953 and he was 27 years old. As time went on he clearly realised this could not be true and he started to guess a more appropriate answer. In other words he tried to reconstruct his memories, although not very successfully. ■

Some memories never fade. Can you remember the names of your primary-school classmates?

Capacity of long-term memory

The capacity of the human brain for storing information is enormous and compares well with many computers (Solso, 1991). Believe it or not, you can remember a vast amount of information. Information stored in memory includes the route you take to get home, what your primary school looked like, the names of all the people you know and other things about those people, how to eat and what food you like, the letters of the alphabet and the rules of arithmetic, what you learned in psychology class today . . . the list is endless. There must be some physical limit in terms of the actual brain cells available, but unlike the limited-capacity store of short-term memory, in long-term memory we never reach this upper limit. Indeed, some experts believe that we only use a surprisingly small fraction of our brain's capacity and power.

Impressive evidence of the capacity of long-term memory was provided by Standing et al. (1970). Participants were presented with 2560 pictures over a number of days. When they were given a subsequent test of long-term memory, about 90% of the pictures were recognised!

Duration in long-term memory

How can one assess how long a memory lasts? Even if you can't remember something at this moment, it might be there somewhere, but you simply cannot bring it into your conscious mind. If you can remember something, it may be an inaccurate memory and one you have "confabulated" (made-up details) from relevant cues.

If we are to assess how long information can remain in long-term memory, we need to carry out research into "very-long-term memory" (VLTM). It is said that the elderly never lose their childhood memories and many skills (e.g. riding a bicycle) are never forgotten. It is not easy to study very-long-term memory. We generally don't know exactly what happened many years ago, and so the accuracy of our participants' memory for the distant past is hard to assess.

Bahrick, Bahrick, and Wittinger (1975, see Key Study) carried out a clever study of very-long-term memory using photographs from high-school yearbooks (an annual publication in American High Schools in which everyone's picture is shown with their name and other details). What they found was that even after 34 years, ex-students could still name 90% of the photographs of their classmates, which is a truly impressive achievement.

Why is this study by Bahrick et al. so important? First, it provided a good method of assessing the accuracy of very-long-term memories. Second, it showed more clearly than previous research that people can retain accurate memories going back several decades. Our very-long-term memory (at least for faces) seems to be better than many people had feared was the case!

Key Study: Duration in long-term memory

Bahrick et al.'s (1975) study of memory for classmates.

Aims: Bahrick et al. aimed to investigate the duration of very-long-term memory (VLTM) to see if memories could last over several decades, and thus support the assumption that the duration of memory can be a lifetime. They aimed to test VLTM in a way that showed external validity by testing memory for real-life information.

Procedure: An opportunity sample of 392 American ex-high-school students aged from 17–74 years was formed. They were tested in a number of ways:

1. Free recall of the names of as many of their former classmates as possible.
2. A photo recognition test where they were asked to identify former classmates in a set of 50 photos, only some of which were of their classmates.
3. A name recognition test.
4. A name and photo matching test.

These tests assessed VLTM, because the time since leaving high school was up to 48 years. Participants' accuracy (and thus duration of memory) was assessed by comparing their responses with high-school yearbooks containing pictures and names of all the students in that year.

Findings: Bahrick et al. found 90% accuracy in face and name recognition, even with those participants who had left high school 34 years previously. After 48 years this declined to 80% for name recognition and 40% for face recognition. Free recall was considerably less accurate: 60% accurate after 15 years and only 30% accurate after 48 years.

Conclusions: The findings show that classmates are rarely forgotten once recognition cues have been given. Thus, Bahrick et al.'s aim to demonstrate that people have very-long-term memories was supported. The findings also support the claim that recognition is better than recall. The research demonstrates VLTM for a particular type of information. It cannot be concluded that VLTM exists for all types of information. It can be concluded that memory may not be as unreliable and subject to confabulation (inaccuracy) as is often claimed. However, the finding that free recall was only 30% after 48 years indicates that many of the memories were fairly weak.

? Why do you think that people have such good long-term memories of their classmates from school?

? Why was name recognition much better than face recognition after 48 years?

Criticisms

- Before this research by Bahrick et al. it had often been assumed that information could remain in LTM for very long periods of time. However, there had been practically no direct experimental tests of this assumption.
- Classmates' faces and names are a very particular type of information. They might have emotional significance, and there will have been opportunity for a great deal of rehearsal, given the daily contact classmates will have experienced. The same is *not* true of other types of information and so the findings on VLTM cannot be generalised to other types of information.
- Compared to the vast majority of memory research, which takes place in the laboratory, Bahrick et al.'s research has high mundane realism. Asking participants to recall their classmates tests real-life memory. Thus, the research is more representative of natural behaviour and so has high external validity. Thus, it may be possible to generalise the findings to other settings.

Is there *one* long-term memory store?

According to Atkinson and Shiffrin's (1968) multi-store model, there is only *one* long-term memory store. As soon as you start thinking about it, that seems unlikely. An enormous wealth of information is stored in long-term memory, including such different things as the knowledge that Nicole Kidman is a film star, how to ride a bicycle, that we had fish and chips for lunch yesterday, and the meaning of the word "bling". It seems improbable that *all* this knowledge is stored within a *single* long-term memory store, so different kinds of memory could have greater duration or might be affected by forgetting in different ways. Some of the main suggestions for *multiple* long-term stores are considered briefly next.

Episodic and semantic memory

Tulving (1972) argued for a distinction between two types of long-term memory: episodic memory and semantic memory. **Episodic memory** has an autobiographical flavour. It contains the memories of specific events or episodes occurring in a particular place at a particular time, e.g. what you did yesterday or what you had for lunch last Sunday. In contrast, **semantic memory** contains information about our knowledge of the world, e.g. the rules and the words of our language, how to calculate percentages, how to set the video, the capital of France, and the stars of *Lord of the Rings*.

Vargha-Khadem et al. (1997) studied two children, Beth and Jon, both of whom had suffered brain damage at a very early age. Beth and Jon had very poor episodic memory for the day's activities and television programmes. However, their semantic memory was fine, as shown by the fact that they attended ordinary schools and had normal language development and factual knowledge. This suggests that episodic memory and semantic memory are different forms of long-term memory.

Research such as that on Beth and Jon indicates that episodic memory and semantic memory are separate from each other. Nevertheless, they depend

I remember that hot day when my ice-cream melted faster than I could eat it. EPISODIC MEMORY

Ice-cream melts unless it is kept cold. SEMANTIC MEMORY

heavily on each other. For example, remembering what you had for lunch last Sunday basically involves episodic memory. However, semantic memory is also involved, as your knowledge of the world is needed to identify the different foods you ate.

Declarative and procedural knowledge

Cohen and Squire (1980) argued that long-term memory is divided into two memory systems: **declarative knowledge** and **procedural knowledge**. Ryle (1949) uses corresponding terms "knowing that" and "knowing how", e.g. we know *that* we had roast pork for Sunday lunch (declarative knowledge), and we know *how* to ride a bicycle (procedural knowledge). Much of our procedural knowledge

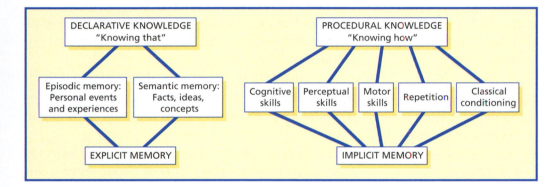

is in the form of motor skills such as how to play various sports, play the piano, and so on.

Evidence for the distinction comes from brain-damaged patients with amnesia (severe problems with long-term memory). Spiers et al. (2001) reviewed 147 cases of amnesia. Every one of them had poor declarative knowledge, but *none* of them had any problems with procedural knowledge. The procedural skills the amnesic patients had acquired included learning to play the piano and mirror tracing (tracing a figure reflected in a mirror). That is convincing evidence that declarative knowledge and procedural knowledge are separate forms of long-term memory.

■ **Activity:** State whether the following involve procedural or declarative knowledge.

- Your name
- Driving a car
- The capital city of Japan
- The value of m^2 when $m = 6$
- Balancing on one leg

Think of some other examples of procedural and declarative knowledge.

? Which type of memory (procedural or declarative) is likely to be tested in a memory experiment?

Summary

There is good evidence that there are several kinds of long-term memory. First, there is an important distinction between episodic memory and semantic memory.

Comparing STM and LTM	Short-term memory	Long-term memory
Duration (how long it lasts)	Short (seconds)	Long, potentially forever
Capacity (how much it holds)	Limited by duration	Unlimited
Encoding differences	Acoustic	Semantic
Serial position effect	Recency effect (last material is better remembered because of interference)	Primacy effect (earlier material is better remembered because it is better rehearsed)
Brain damage	Some patients only lose short-term memory whereas others only lose long-term memory.	

Second, there is another significant distinction between declarative knowledge and procedural knowledge. The existence of all these types of long-term memory is inconsistent with the multi-store model.

Evaluation of the multi-store model

We have considered much evidence concerned with short-term and long-term memory, and it is now time to draw up a balance sheet of the strengths and limitations of the multi-store model. We start with the strengths followed by the limitations:

- Strength: Evidence from brain-damaged patients supports the distinction between short-term and long-term memory. Patients with amnesia have problems with long-term memory but not with short-term memory, and some other brain-damaged patients have problems with short-term memory but not with long-term memory (Shallice & Warrington, 1970).
- Strength: There is evidence that encoding is different in short-term and long-term memory. For example, Baddeley (1966) found evidence for acoustic or sound encoding in short-term memory and semantic or meaning encoding in long-term memory.
- Strength: There is convincing evidence that the capacity of the two stores is radically different. The capacity of the short-term store is about seven items (Jacobs, 1887; Simon, 1974). In contrast, there are no known limits to the capacity of the long-term store, and Standing et al. (1970) found that 90% out of 2560 pictures presented once each were remembered in a test of long-term memory.
- Strength: There are huge differences in the duration of information in short-term and long-term memory. Unrehearsed information in short-term memory has vanished within about 20 seconds (Peterson & Peterson, 1959). In contrast, some information in long-term memory is still there 48 years after learning (Bahrick et al., 1975).
- Limitation: The model argues that the transfer of information from short-term to long-term memory is through rehearsal. However, in daily life most people devote very little time to active rehearsal, although they are constantly storing away new information in long-term memory. Rehearsal may describe what happens when psychologists conduct experiments in laboratories but this isn't true to life.
- Limitation: It is assumed that information in the short-term store is encoded in terms of its sound (acoustic coding) whereas information in the long-term store is encoded in terms of its meaning (semantic coding), and there is an arrow leading from one store to the other. I don't want to be frivolous, but it seems like magic for information to change from sound to meaning as it proceeds along an arrow!
- Limitation: The model is oversimplified in its assumption that there is a *single* long-term memory store. As we have seen (e.g. Spiers et al., 2001), it makes sense to identify several long-term memory stores: episodic memory; semantic memory; declarative knowledge; and procedural knowledge. Atkinson and Shiffrin (1968) focused almost exclusively on declarative knowledge and had practically nothing to say about procedural knowledge (e.g. skills learning).

EXAM HINT
If you have a question asking you to outline the main features of the multi-store model, you might find it useful to include a diagram in your answer, IN ADDITION TO the written description.

- Limitation: The model is oversimplified in its assumption that there is a *single* short-term store. There is evidence from brain-damaged patients suggesting that there are a number of different short-term stores (Shallice & Warrington, 1972). Additional convincing evidence that there is more than a single short-term store comes from work on the working memory model, to which we now turn.

The Working Memory Model

Baddeley and Hitch (1974) described a more detailed multi-component model of short-term or "working" memory (that area of memory used while working on things). There were *two* main reasons why they did this. First, they argued that short-term memory is much more useful in everyday life than was assumed by previous researchers. For example, whenever we are working on a complex problem (e.g. in arithmetic) we use short-term memory to keep track of where we have got to in the problem. In other words, we use short-term memory most of the time and *not* just when psychologists give us a short-term memory task or we are trying to remember a phone number. Second, they argued (very reasonably) that we need to include rehearsal as one (but only one) of the possible processes occurring in short-term memory. This led them to put forward a **working memory system** consisting of three components:

- **Central executive**: a modality-free component. It has a limited capacity and is like attention.
- **Phonological loop** (originally called the articulatory loop): the loop is divided into a phonological store, directly concerned with speech *perception*, and an articulatory process, linked to speech *production*.
- **Visuo-spatial sketchpad** (sometimes called a scratch pad): this is specialised for spatial and/or visual coding, a kind of writing pad for visual and spatial data.

Baddeley, Thomson, and Buchanan (1975) studied the phonological loop by asking their participants to recall sets of five words immediately in the correct order. Participants' ability to do this was better with short words than with long ones, i.e. recall was a function of word length. Further investigation of this *word-length effect* showed that the participants could recall as many words as they could read out loud in two seconds. This suggests that the capacity of the phonological or articulatory loop is determined by how long it takes to rehearse verbal information.

In everyday life the phonological or articulatory loop is used in reading difficult material, making it easier for readers to retain information about the

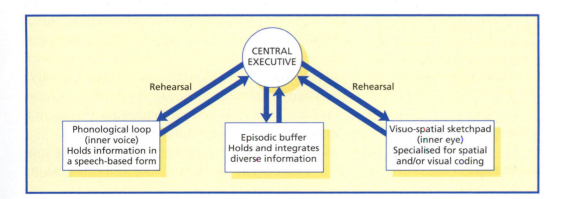

order of words in text. For example, Baddeley and Lewis (1981) gave their participants sentences to read and asked them to say whether the sentences were meaningful. Some were not because two words in a meaningful sentence had been switched round (e.g. "The tree flew up into the birds"). When the participants were prevented from using the phonological or articulatory loop by saying something meaningless repeatedly, their ability to decide whether sentences were meaningful was reduced because they could not re-examine the sentences repeatedly. Gathercole and Baddeley (1990) found that children with reading problems had an impaired memory span and had difficulty in saying whether words rhymed, suggesting they had a phonological loop deficit.

Evaluation of the working memory model

- **Strength:** The **working memory model** is an advance on the account of short-term memory provided by the multi-store model because it is concerned with both active processing and the brief storage of information. As a result, it is relevant to activities such as mental arithmetic, verbal reasoning, and comprehension, as well as to traditional short-term memory tasks. Thus it is much more than just a theory of memory.
- **Strength:** The model can be used to predict whether or not two tasks can be performed successfully at the same time. Every component of the working memory system has limited capacity, and is relatively independent of the other components. Two predictions follow:
  1. If two tasks make use of the same component, they cannot be performed successfully together.
  2. If two tasks make use of different components, it should be possible to perform them as well together as separately.

Hitch and Baddeley (1976) tested these predictions by asking participants to carry out a verbal reasoning task to decide whether each in a set of sentences provided a true or a false description of the letter pair that followed it. This task requires extensive use of the central executive. At the same time, the participants had to do either a task where little thought or attention was involved (only using the phonological or articulatory loop by saying 1 2 3 4 5 6 rapidly), or a task that involved the central executive as well as the phonological or articulatory loop. As predicted, reasoning performance was slowed down by the additional task *only* when it involved using the central executive. So this model accounts for many findings that are hard to explain within the multi-store approach.

- **Strength:** The working memory model views verbal rehearsal as an *optional* process occurring within the articulatory or phonological loop, which doesn't have to be used to remember things. Information in working memory can be processed in the visuo-spatial sketchpad or central executive without involving rehearsal. This view is more realistic than the central importance of verbal rehearsal in the multi-store model.
- **Limitation:** Little is known about the central executive. It has limited capacity, but this capacity

KEY TERM

Working memory model: a model of memory proposed by Baddeley and Hitch as an alternative to the multi-store model. The model consists of a central executive (an attentional system, which has a limited capacity and which is involved in decision-making), together with two slave systems (the articulatory-phonological loop, and visuo-spatial sketch pad). This model is concerned with both active processing and the brief storage of information.

■ **Activity:** Try the dual-task technique used by Hitch and Baddeley for yourself. Read a page in a book you have not read before. You should find that you have understood what was being written about, and could explain what you have read to another person. Now turn to a different page and try to read it while saying "the, the, the" aloud repeatedly. You may find that you have some difficulty understanding the text, and your reading rate may have been reduced. Can you explain what you have read to someone else? If you can, how would you explain this?

has not been measured accurately. It is argued that the central executive is "modality-free" (i.e. it does not rely on any specific way of receiving information, such as sound or vision) and is used in many different processing operations, but the precise details of its functioning are not known.

- Limitation: It's not very clear how the three components of the working memory system interact with each other.
- Limitation: The model is concerned with memory, but tells us very little about long-term memory and the ways in which processing in the working memory system relate to long-term storage of information.

Levels-of-processing Theory

Craik and Lockhart (1972) put forward an alternative to the multi-store model of memory, called the **levels-of-processing** theory. They argued that the concept of rehearsal is *not* sufficient to account for long-term memory—evidence shows that the cognitive processes operating at the time of learning determine what is stored in long-term memory. More specifically, they proposed that it's the *level* of **processing** that determines whether something is stored in long-term memory. If you process information a lot in terms of its meaning, or "deeply", then it will be stored; if you only process something rather superficially then it won't be stored effectively.

Depth of analysis

Craik and Lockhart predicted that the **depth of processing** (involving meaning) of a stimulus has a substantial effect on its memorability, i.e. how well it is remembered, and that deeper levels of analysis produce more elaborate, longer lasting, and stronger memory traces than do shallow levels of analysis. The crucial assumptions are that deep processing involves the processing of meaning and leads to good long-term memory, whereas shallow processing does *not* involve the processing of meaning and leads to poor long-term memory. Rehearsal or repetition is *not* a form of deep processing because it only involves a repeated "number of analyses", and does not lead to an increase in the extent to which meaning is processed.

In a classic piece of research to demonstrate the levels-of-processing theory, Craik and Tulving (1975) used **semantic processing** (processing of meaning) to represent deep processing and the physical analysis of a stimulus to represent more **shallow processing**. As the theory would predict, participants remembered those words that were deeply processed better than those processed more shallowly.

Craik and Tulving's (1975) series of experiments aimed to demonstrate that memory is an automatic by-product of semantic processing. If information has more meaning, then it should be more memorable. In one experiment, participants were shown a list of words (five-letter concrete nouns such as "table") and asked a question for each. For each question the

> **KEY TERM**
>
> **Levels of processing**: the extent to which something (e.g. a list of words) is processed, not in terms of how much processing is done (as in repetition), but in terms of how much meaning is extracted. Shallow processing focuses on the superficial features of the information (e.g. whether a word is in upper or lower case). In contrast, deep processing focuses on the meaning of the information and generally (but not always) leads to better long-term memory.

> ■ **Activity:** Try to construct a list of words that have approximately the same frequency of usage. Now think of questions to ask that will involve deep processing (e.g. Is this the opposite of . . .?) or shallow processing (e.g. Does this word include the letter G?). It will be easier if your questions have yes/no answers. Divide the list in half, give each half to a naive participant, such as a member of your family, and ask the questions. Take the list away and give the participant a blank piece of paper for a free recall test. Your findings should be in line with those of Craik and Lockhart: deep processing should lead to better recall.

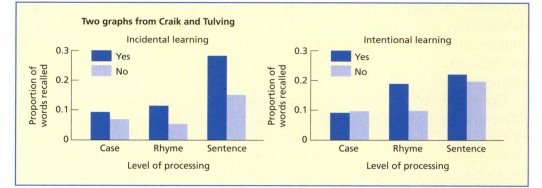

The graphs show recall for all three conditions with incidental and intentional learning. You can see that deeper processing produced better recall in both kinds of learning, and that learning was not greater when participants were pre-warned. The graphs also show the difference between recall when the questions had a "yes" answer (better recall).

answer was "yes" or "no". The questions were of three types:

- Shallow processing (involving case decisions), such as "Is the word in capital letters?"
- **Phonemic processing** (involving rhyme decisions based on the sounds of the words), such as "Does the word rhyme with 'able'?"
- Semantic or deep processing (involving sentence decisions), such as "Would the word fit in the sentence 'They met a _____ in the street'?"

Craik and Tulving found that words processed semantically were recalled best and those processed phonemically were processed second best (see graphs above). You might think that the reason participants did better on the semantic task was because they took longer to process the "semantic" questions in comparison with the "shallow" questions. To test this, Craik and Tulving conducted a further experiment where the shallow questions were more difficult to perform and thus would take longer than a "deeper" semantic task. For example, the participant had to say whether the word shown had the pattern CCVVC (C = consonant and V = vowel). The deeper but shorter sentence task still produced better recall. This further supports the importance of "depth" rather than time/effort.

It is possible that the reason participants had better recall for the words that were semantically processed was because this matched the method by which memory was tested. Morris, Bransford, and Franks (1977), in a study discussed more fully later, found phonemic processing sometimes led to *better* memory than semantic processing. This occurred when the memory test involved being given words and deciding which ones *rhymed* with list words, with none of the actual list words themselves being presented. It makes sense that it would be easier to do this memory test if you had focused on the sounds of list words during learning.

However, it became apparent that the concept of "depth" alone was an oversimplification, and so various other forms of processing were included to extend the concept of "processing".

Elaboration

An important factor in learning is **elaboration of processing**. The basic idea is that if you do a lot of processing of meaning (high elaboration) this will produce better long-term memory than doing only a little processing of meaning (low elaboration). For example, if you try to remember the word "cat" on a list by thinking of your pet cat whose name is Bella and who had black fur, loves fish, and likes sitting in the sun (high elaboration), you are more likely to remember it than if you simply think "four-footed animal" when you see the word "cat".

Craik and Tulving's (1975) classic study (just discussed) also looked at how elaboration of processing can lead to greater recall. Participants were presented on each trial with a word and a sentence containing a blank and asked to decide whether the word fitted into the incomplete sentence. Elaboration was manipulated by varying the complexity of the sentence between the simple (e.g. "She cooked the . . .") and the complex (e.g. "The great bird swooped down and carried off the struggling . . ."). Recall was twice as high for words accompanying complex sentences, suggesting that elaboration benefits long-term memory.

Elaboration of learning, e.g. thinking of details of your pet cat, when trying to remember the word "cat" on a list, helps us to remember things in long-term memory.

We have seen that elaboration of processing is important for good long-term memory, and so is depth of processing. As Craik and Tulving (1975) showed, long-term memory is better when processing involves both depth *and* elaboration than when it involves only one of these factors.

Organisation

Research has shown that organisation creates a lasting memory. No conscious processing needs to take place. Mandler (1967) demonstrated this by giving participants a pack of 52 picture cards, each printed with a word. Participants sorted the cards into piles, using between two and seven categories, according to any system they wished. They repeated the sorting until they had assigned all the words to the same categories on two different attempts at sorting. If anyone was still trying to achieve this after 1¼ hours they were excluded from the experiment! Most participants took about six sorts to gain 95% consistency. At this point they were given an unexpected free recall test. Mandler found that recall was poorest for those who had decided to use only two categories, and best for those who used seven categories. According to Mandler, those participants who used several categories in sorting were imposing more organisation on the list than were those who used only a few, concluding (p.328) that "memory and organisation are not only correlated, but organisation is a necessary condition for memory".

> ■ **Activity:** You can demonstrate that organisation aids memory by constructing two lists of the same words. List 1 will be a categorised word list containing a number of words belonging to several categories (e.g. four-footed animals, sports, flowers, articles of furniture). List 2 will consist of the same words but presented in a random order (e.g. golf, rose, cat, tennis, carnation, and so on). To avoid bias you should allocate participants to conditions (list 1 or list 2) on a random basis. Give them a set time to study the list. After an interval (they could count backwards in threes to prevent rehearsal), give them a test of free recall. You should find that the participants in condition 1 were able to recall more words than those in condition 2 and that the words were recalled category by category. The experiment shows how organisation aids memory.

Distinctiveness

Another factor that needs to be considered is distinctiveness, which refers to how different or unique is an item's processing. Distinctive or unique memory traces are more memorable than those closely resembling others. Michael Eysenck and Christine Eysenck (1980) tested this theory by using nouns having irregular pronunciations (e.g. "comb" with its silent "b"; "pint" which would rhyme with "hint" and "mint" if it had a regular pronunciation). The participants performed the shallow task of saying such words as if they were regular (e.g. pronouncing the "b" in "comb" thus producing "com-ber", pronouncing "pint" to rhyme with

"I'll never forget what's-her-name."

"hint"), resulting in a unique memory trace (the shallow distinctive condition). In another condition, nouns were simply pronounced in their normal fashion. In the semantic conditions, nouns were processed in terms of their meaning.

On an unexpected test of recognition memory, there was a large difference between the two shallow conditions. Words in the shallow distinctive condition (comb/pint) were much better remembered than words that had been pronounced normally. Indeed, they were remembered almost as well as the words in the two semantic conditions. These findings show that distinctiveness is important and can lead to good long-term memory even for words processed only at a shallow level.

Distinctiveness depends in part on the context in which a given stimulus is processed. For example, the name "Smith" if presented in the list "Jones, Robinson, Williams, Baker, Smith, Robertson" would not be distinctive. However, it would stand out in the following list: "Zzitz, Zysblat, Vangeersadaele, Vythelingum, Smith, Uwejeyah" (I am indebted to the telephone directory for these names!).

Bransford (1979) showed how effective distinctiveness is by comparing participants' recall of sentences such as "A mosquito is like a raccoon because they both have hands, legs, and jaws" (elaborative processing) with "A mosquito is like a doctor because they both draw blood" (distinctive processing). Distinctive processing led to better recall than did elaborative processing.

> ■ **Activity:** It would be fairly easy to manipulate distinctiveness in a similar manner to the "Smith" example and to observe its effects on long-term memory, if you wanted to carry out an experiment in this area.

? From what you have learned so far about recall, what advice would you give to doctors about how to improve their patients' recall of medical advice?

Evaluation of levels-of-processing theory

- Strength: Processes occurring at the time of learning have a major impact on long-term memory. Factors such as depth, elaboration, and distinctiveness are all important in determining long-term memory. That sounds obvious, but the view before 1972 was that memory could be explained in terms of structure and rehearsal.
- Strength: The depth of processing theory, developed in line with Craik and Tulving's classic studies reported in 1975, offered a model that could be applied to improving memory. If you find it hard to remember someone's name, don't just repeat it—elaborate on it or make the memory distinctive.
- Limitation: It is often hard to decide whether a particular task involves shallow or deep processing, because of the lack of any independent measure of processing depth. Craik and Tulving (1975) assumed that semantic processing involved greater "depth" than phonemic processing, with no real evidence.
- Limitation: Participants may not stop at the expected level of processing. For example, suppose you were told to decide whether each word in a list was in capital letters. If you knew your memory was going to be tested you would be tempted to process the meaning of the words to improve your performance!
- Limitation: Some evidence doesn't support the theory. Morris, Bransford, and Franks (1977) found that stored information is remembered only if it is *relevant*

to the memory test. Some of their participants were tested with a rhyming recognition test: they were given several words on the test and had to decide which ones rhymed with the words previously presented; unusually, *none* of the list words was presented on the test. Participants remembered words that had been processed in terms of their sound (shallow processing) better than those that had been processed for meaning (deep processing). This disproves the prediction of levels of processing theory that deep processing is *always* better than shallow processing. The reason is that processing the meaning of the list words was of little help when the memory test required the identification of words rhyming with list words. The information acquired from the shallow rhyme task was far more relevant, and so memory performance was higher in this condition.

- Limitation: Craik and Lockhart (1972) failed to provide a detailed account to explain the effectiveness of different kinds of processing. *Why* does deep, elaborative, or distinctive processing lead to better long-term memory than shallow, non-elaborative, or non-distinctive processing?

SECTION SUMMARY

❖ Memory and learning involve the retention of information, but the *study* of memory focuses on cognitive processes and retrieval.

❖ Memory tests assess learning.

❖ Psychologists distinguish between short-term memory and long-term memory in terms of:
  – capacity,
  – duration,
  – encoding.

What is memory?

❖ The short-term memory is described as:
  – having limited capacity of 7 plus or minus 2 chunks;
  – having limited duration;
  – using mainly acoustic coding.

Research into the nature of short-term memory (STM)

❖ Capacity: Span measures indicate an STM capacity of about 7 items but this can be increased by chunking. Capacity for STM can also be seen in recency effects, caused by higher recall for the last few items in a list.

❖ Duration: The Brown–Peterson technique is a means of demonstrating STM duration. If rehearsal is prevented, there is little recall beyond 18 seconds.

❖ Encoding: This differs from long-term memory which is more semantically coded.

❖ Evidence about different kinds of short-term memory comes from the study of brain-damaged individuals, which also supports a distinction between short-term and long-term memory. However, it is difficult to generalise from case studies.

Research into the nature of long-term memory (LTM)

❖ The long-term memory is described as:
- having an unlimited capacity;
- lasting forever;
- using mainly semantic coding.

❖ Capacity: Unlike in STM we never reach the upper limit of the LTM capacity store.

❖ Duration: Its duration has been demonstrated in studies of VLTMs (very-long-term memories).

❖ Encoding: This differs from long-term memory which is more acoustically coded.

❖ In addition the long-term memory has been further divided into:
- Semantic memory: Contains knowledge about the world.
- Episodic memory: Concerned with events and autobiographical experiences.
- Procedural memory: Concerned with "knowing how" rather than "knowing that".

❖ These distinctions are important for criticising the validity of the multi-store model (see below).

The distinction between STM and LTM

❖ This distinction between the long-term memory and short-term memory has been supported by:
- The recency effect.
- Miller's research into the magical number seven.
- Studies from brain-damaged individuals.
- Research into acoustic and semantic coding.

Models of memory

❖ In an attempt to help us understand how we acquire, store, and retrieve information, psychologists have proposed different models of memory.

❖ They offer accounts of how information is transferred from STM to LTM.

❖ The three models described are:
1. The multi-store model (Atkinson & Shiffrin).
2. The working memory model (Baddeley & Hitch).
3. Levels-of-processing theory (Craik & Lockhart).

The multi-store model

❖ The multi-store model of memory supports the distinction between three separate stores and proposes that information is transferred from the short-term memory into the long-term memory by rehearsal.

❖ This model has been criticised in that:
- It is too simple, and ignores the evidence that there is more than one component to short-term memory and more than one long-term memory store.
- Rehearsal does not always lead to storage in the long-term store.
- The model cannot easily explain flashbulb memories (see later).

The working memory model

❖ This model offers a more accurate representation of STM and can account for empirical findings as well as representing more active processing.

❖ It focuses on linking memory with attention and introduces the idea of a central executive and slave systems such as the visuo-spatial sketchpad and phonological loop.

❖ While this model has practical applications in that it can be used to help children read it has been criticised in that:
  – More detail is needed about how the central executive functions.

❖ This approach focuses attention on how information is encoded. It argues that information that is processed at a deep level is more likely to be recalled.

❖ Deep processing includes:
  – semantic processing,
  – elaboration,
  – organisation,
  – distinctiveness.

❖ While this model recognises that encoding is active and has some practical applications it has been criticised in that:
  – The concept of depth is circular.
  – By focusing on acquisition it ignores the importance of retrieval cues.

Levels of processing

See pp.20–24 of the revision guide.

SECTION 6
REMEMBERING AND FORGETTING

When we considered the evidence related to the *capacity* of short-term and long-term memory we overlooked the issue of **forgetting**. The reason a memory is no longer present may *not* be due to the capacity of the store, but because it has been forgotten. We all know the experience of forgetting, but we need to understand forgetting in more detail. A classic study by Hermann Ebbinghaus (1885) produced the first clear experimental evidence of how forgetting generally increases over time.

Ebbinghaus was both the experimenter and the only participant (a dubious approach not to be copied!). He learned a list of meaningless items known as nonsense syllables (e.g. MAZ, TUD) until he could recall all of them. After a short period of time, his recall was good. However, his recall decreased as the retention interval (the time between learning and recall) increased, especially over the first hour after learning, after which forgetting increased more slowly. Ebbinghaus also made another discovery. He re-learned the list and measured his level of remembering in terms of "savings". Each time he re-learned the list he recorded the number of trials required to get back to having full recall. Each time he re-learned the list, fewer trials were required. He called this re-learning "savings". His key finding was that re-learning was slower (and so the savings were less) the longer the interval of time since he originally learned a list. In other words, Ebbinghaus showed increased forgetting over time.

It is important to note that the participant in this case study (Ebbinghaus) was not representative of people generally. He was an extremely intelligent individual who may have had an especially good memory. He was also both experimenter and participant, which could mean that the data he collected were biased. We must question whether his expectations might have influenced his performance.

All memory experiments rely on retrieving information from memory, and assume that, if it can't be retrieved, then it must be forgotten. The concept

KEY TERM

Forgetting: this is the inability to recall or recognise information. Forgetting may occur because the information no longer exists in memory and so is not available for retrieval. Alternatively, it can occur because it cannot be found and so is not accessible (cue-dependent forgetting). Forgetting is more likely with information that needs to be recalled, as recognition is generally easier than recall.

? How might this concept of "savings" be used to explain successful revision techniques?

of "forgetting" suggests that something has disappeared from memory (it is not available, i.e. it has ceased to exist). However, another possibility is that the memory is simply "mislaid" (it is not accessible, i.e. we might find it given time or the right clues).

Forgetting in short-term memory is likely to be due to a failure of availability—because it is a limited-capacity store it is unlikely that we could not find something still stored there. Forgetting in long-term memory may be due to a lack of availability and/or a lack of accessibility. We will consider explanations of forgetting in short-term memory first.

Forgetting in Short-term Memory

Trace decay
In the study by Peterson and Peterson (see page 46) it was found that recall dropped over time. What caused this drop to occur? One possible explanation comes from **trace decay** theory, based on the idea that memories have a physical basis (a "trace") that will decay in time unless it is passed to long-term memory by rehearsal. The trace disappears just like a photographic image that is not fixed with chemicals. Information in short-term memory certainly does disappear but it may not be because of spontaneous decay—it may be the result of interference. One of the problems with trace decay theory is that it is hard to test. For example, there is no obvious way of manipulating the situation to speed up or slow down the rate of decay.

Displacement
Another possibility is that forgetting in short-term memory is due to **displacement**. If we think of the short-term state as resembling a box with limited capacity, then it could be argued that new items can only be put into the box by displacing or removing one or more of the items currently in it. Perhaps the requirement in Peterson and Peterson's study to count backwards by threes displaced the initial information and caused forgetting to occur. This approach assumes we have limited short-term memory capacity because of *structural* limitations (the short-term memory box is too small). In fact, it is much more likely that what is happening is that we can only attend to a limited number of things at once, and the capacity of short-term memory is limited because of this limitation in attention.

After reorganising the contents of, for example, the fridge or a cupboard you may find yourself looking for something in its old location, even weeks after everything has been moved. This is an example of interference—memory for the old location is interfering with memory for the new one.

Interference
Instead of thinking in terms of displacement, we could argue that forgetting occurs because new information interferes with (or disrupts) the information currently in short-term memory. Waugh and Norman (1965) compared the decay and interference explanations in a study in which the participants heard a series of digits followed by a probe digit (this was a final digit to which they had to respond). Their task was to recall the digit that had *previously* followed the probe

digit in the series. The number of intervening digits was varied, and the digits were presented rapidly or slowly.

If interference is what matters, recall should depend on the number of intervening digits. In contrast, if decay is what matters, recall should depend on the speed of presentation—the faster the presentation the less the decay. Recall decreased as the number of intervening digits increased, but was unaffected by the rate of presentation. These findings suggest that interference in the form of the intervening digits caused forgetting. This is known as **retroactive interference**, because the interference occurred in the period of time between being presented with the digit and the memory test. The fact that speed of presenting the digits had no effect suggests that time-based decay was not a factor.

Diversion of attention

Another possibility is that forgetting occurs because attention is diverted away from the to-be-remembered information. Watkins et al. (1973) obtained evidence favouring the diversion of attention theory. Some of their participants had to listen to musical notes, then hum them, and finally identify them, whereas others simply had to listen to the notes. The former showed much forgetting, whereas the latter showed no forgetting. Watkins et al. argued that forgetting occurred because the requirements to hum and identify the notes diverted attention away from the to-be-remembered information.

Conclusion

It has proved difficult to identify *why* information in short-term memory is generally forgotten within a few seconds as shown by Peterson and Peterson (1959). However, much of the observed forgetting is probably due to interference. It is also likely that diversion of attention is important, as is shown by the common experience of forgetting a telephone number you are about to dial when something distracts your attention. There is less evidence that time decay or displacement explains forgetting in short-term memory.

Forgetting can occur when attention is diverted.

> Interference involves displacement of one set of material by another. However, psychologists use the term "displacement" to refer to the loss of information from the short-term memory store because it is replaced by other information, whereas interference involves a loss of availability of information in long-term memory due to other, similar, information being more readily accessible.

Forgetting in Long-term Memory: Availability

Trace decay theory

Forgetting in long-term memory might be due to the gradual physical decay of the memory traces, as was suggested for short-term memory. It has proved hard to study these physical or physiological changes directly, so tests of trace decay theory have been somewhat indirect. The assumption is that if a person does very little during the time of initial learning and subsequent recall (called the retention interval) and they forget the material, then the only explanation can be that the trace has disappeared.

Jenkins and Dallenbach (1924) asked two students to recall **nonsense syllables** (meaningless items) at retention intervals between one and eight hours. The students were either awake or asleep during the retention interval. There was much

> **EXAM HINT**
> Use research evidence to support the two explanations for STM. Peterson and Peterson (1959) for trace decay and Waugh and Norman (1965) for displacement. Be aware of how the latter study supports displacement over decay.

What were you doing when you heard about the terrorist attack on the twin towers in New York? Why do so many people have a vivid memory for this and other extremely emotional and important events?

? What were the independent and dependent variables in the Jenkins and Dallenbach study? Were there any confounding variables?

less forgetting when the students were asleep during the retention interval than when they were awake. If trace decay theory were correct, we would expect the same amount of forgetting whether they were asleep or awake. The fact that they forgot more when awake suggests that interference from other activities (which would be much greater when the participants were awake rather than asleep) was responsible for the increased forgetting. The fact that *some* forgetting took place when the participants were asleep could be explained in terms of interference from dreams, or perhaps there may indeed have been some trace decay.

Evaluation of trace decay theory

Jenkins and Dallenbach's experiment was flawed because there was no control over what was happening when the participants were awake or asleep. Also, in the asleep condition, the students learned the material in the *evening*, whereas their learning usually occurred in the *morning* in the awake condition. Thus, the high level of forgetting in the awake condition could have occurred *either* because the students were awake throughout the retention interval, *or* because learning is worse in the morning. Hockey, Davies, and Gray (1972) tested the effects of morning versus evening learning. They found that the rate of forgetting was rapid during daytime sleeping, suggesting that forgetting depends mostly on the time at which learning occurs.

In sum, there is very little support for trace decay theory. If all memory traces are subject to decay, it is surprising how well we can remember many events that happened several years ago although rarely thought about or rehearsed. For example, most people remembered in detail for some years what they were doing when they heard the news of former Prime Minister Margaret Thatcher's resignation in 1990 (Conway et al., 1994) and the same is true for memories of the 11 September terrorist attack on New York. Accurate and long-lasting memories for very significant events are known as flashbulb memories (discussed later in this section). Trace decay may play some causal role in forgetting, but it is by no means the main explanation.

Interference theory

If you had asked psychologists during the 1930s, 1940s, or 1950s what caused forgetting, you would probably have received the answer, "Interference". It was assumed that learning one thing in some way interferes with learning something else and wipes out the memory. When previous learning interferes with later learning and retention, this is known as **proactive interference**. For example, suppose you have become highly practised at carrying out some operation on the computer. At some point, you update your software, so that now you need to carry out the same operation in a rather different way. You would probably find yourself trying to carry out the operation in the old way before you remembered the new way of doing it.

When later learning disrupts memory for earlier learning, this is known as retroactive interference (which was the kind of interference proposed for short-term memory). For example, suppose as a child you went to the same place for your summer holiday four years running. All the events and experiences you had on the last three holidays will probably interfere with your ability to remember clearly what happened on the first of those holidays.

Interference theory has been tested by means of **paired-associate learning**. Some participants are initially presented with several pairs of words (e.g. cat–tree;

candle–table). The first word in each pair is known as the stimulus term, and the second is the response term. Learning continues until the participants can recall each response term when presented with the stimulus term. The participants then learn a second list of paired associates (e.g. cat–glass; candle–whale).

- *Proactive interference*: Participants' recall is tested for the *second* list of paired associates. Proactive interference should mean that the experimental group (who learned both lists) do less well than the control group (who learned only the second list).
- *Retroactive interference*: Participants' recall is tested on the *first* list of paired associates. Retroactive interference should mean that the experimental group do less well than the control group.

There is strong evidence for both proactive and retroactive interference when the same stimulus terms are used in both lists of paired associates (list A contains cat–tree and list B contains cat–glass, the same stimulus word "cat" appears in both lists). However, little proactive or retroactive interference is found when *different* stimulus terms are used in the two lists (Underwood & Postman, 1960). Read through the activity on the right if you are still feeling confused!

Jacoby, Debner, and Hay (2001) argued that proactive interference might occur for two different reasons: (1) the incorrect response from the first list is very strong; or (2) the correct response from the second list is very weak. What they found was that proactive interference was due mainly to the strength of the incorrect response rather than to the weakness of the correct response.

Lists of paired associates: words that could be used to test proactive and retroactive interference

List A:		List B:	
	cat–tree		cat–glass
	candle–table		candle–whale
	book–tractor		book–revolver
	apple–lake		apple–sadness
	doll–kettle		doll–pedal
	glacier–poster		glacier–cane
	locker–cigar		locker–bullet
	jelly–moss		jelly–time
	hammer–monk		hammer–pencil
	ankle–blister		ankle–head

■ **Activity:** You could try testing interference yourself. Arrange for one group of participants (group 1) to learn list A until they can remember all the response terms when you say the stimulus term.

Then ask them to learn list B in the same way.

Ask another group (group 2) to just learn list B.

Afterwards test both groups on list B. Group 1 should do less well, in terms of number of items correctly recalled, than group 2 because of proactive interference.

Test group 1 on list A. They should do less well, in terms of number of items correctly recalled, than group 2 did for list B. This is retroactive interference.

Try the experiment again using the following list instead of the original list B (and use a new set of participants):

hostage–glass
bandage–whale
pear–revolver
pin–sadness
trumpet–pedal
day–cane
soup–bullet
money–time
mast–pencil
toy–head

Are your findings any different? Why?

Evaluation of interference theory

Interference theory probably has somewhat limited applicability to everyday life even though it has been supported in numerous laboratory studies. It is not common in everyday life for two different responses to be attached to the same stimulus and therefore much of our forgetting is unlikely to be due to interference. However, that situation does happen sometimes in everyday life. Consider, for example, the 19th-century German psychologist Hugo Munsterberg, who moved his pocket-watch from one pocket to another. When asked "What time is it, Hugo?" (this is the recurrent stimulus), Munsterberg would often fumble about in confusion, and put his hand into the wrong pocket (proactive interference because past experience is interfering with current recall). In addition, it has been found (Loftus & Palmer, 1974; see p.79) that the way in which an eyewitness is questioned after observing an event can disrupt memory, with the disruption being due to retroactive interference.

An important criticism of interference theory is that the effects sometimes disappear when **cued recall** (recall assisted by the provision of useful cues) rather than free recall (in which words are recalled in any order without cues) is used. This was clarified in a study by Tulving and Psotka (1971). Participants were given six different word lists, each with 24 words. Each set of words was divided into six different categories of four words (therefore 36 categories in all of the six word lists). The words were presented category by category, so that the organisation and the categories were quite obvious. For example, one list could be: cat, tiger, dog, whale, ruby, diamond, sapphire, emerald, chair, table, sofa, bed, apple, pear, orange, lemon, oak, maple, birch, elm, lake, river, sea, pond.

Some participants learned six lists, with the words being shown one at a time. After each list had been presented, the participants free-recalled as many words as possible (the original learning). After all the lists had been presented, the participants tried to recall the words from all the lists that had been presented (total free recall). Finally, all the category names were presented, and the participants tried again to recall all the words from all the lists (total free cued recall—cued because they were given the category names). There were two main findings:

1. In the test of total free recall, many more words were recalled from the last few lists than from the first few. The apparent reason why recall was so poor from the early lists was because they were subject to retroactive interference— in other words, the presentation of several other word lists to be learned between learning the early lists and total free recall caused massive interference.

2. When the participants were given the total cued recall test, the effects of retroactive interference totally disappeared! About 70% of the words in each list (even the first few) were recalled. Thus, the apparent evidence for retroactive interference in total free recall can be explained better in terms of a lack of adequate cues on the total free recall test. As we will see, there is much evidence for the importance of cues in determining remembering and forgetting (see next section).

There is a final criticism of interference theory. We have good evidence for the existence of proactive and retroactive interference, but interference theory doesn't provide us with a clear account of the *processes* underlying these forms of interference.

There is a danger that "proactive interference" and "retroactive interference" merely describe effects that we observe, but fail to explain them.

Forgetting in Long-term Memory: Retrieval Failure

Cue-dependent forgetting

Cue-dependent forgetting is a classic example of forgetting because of retrieval failure. The information is stored in memory, and so is available, but just cannot be retrieved until an appropriate cue is given. In essence, the more relevant

? What is the difference between cued recall tests and free recall tests?

? Is forgetting always a bad thing? Do we need to remember everything?

information (cues) you have available to you when trying to remember something, the more likely you are to do so. For example, you are at a party and you spot a girl who looks vaguely familiar but you can't remember where you have seen her before or what her name is. A bit later, you see her talking in an animated way with two people from the local college. That cue leads you to remember that she is at the same college, and you then finally remember her name.

Evidence of the importance of cue-dependent forgetting was provided in the study by Tulving and Psotka (1971), described in the previous section. The relatively better performance with cued recall occurred because the participants were better able to *retrieve* their memory. The words they had forgotten on the total free recall test (which was non-cued) were temporarily "forgotten" but available on the total cued recall test.

Some psychologists have argued that virtually all forgetting is cue-dependent forgetting. They claim that we store all (or almost all) information *permanently* somewhere in long-term memory, even if it cannot be retrieved. It is very hard to *prove* or to *disprove* this idea, even though it seems unlikely that all information remains in long-term memory.

Encoding specificity principle

Remembering something hinges on having the right cues. Tulving (1979) used this notion to put forward his **encoding specificity principle**: this is the idea that the more *similar* the retrieval cue is to the information stored in memory, the greater the likelihood that the cue will be successful in retrieving the memory. For example, "Ted" is a good cue for the information stored in memory ("Fred") because they rhyme. "Frank" is also a good cue because it starts with the same sound. Even "Flintstone" might be helpful!

The encoding specificity principle is also hard to test, because we do not usually know how much *similarity* there is between retrieval cue and memory trace. For some people "Ted" might be a good cue for "Fred", but is it better than "Frank"?

In addition, according to the encoding specificity principle, retrieval (or its opposite, forgetting) occurs fairly rapidly and with little thinking involved. However, retrieval often involves problem-solving activities that take time and conscious thought. For example, if asked what you were doing last Friday, you might reply: "Let's see, on Friday I usually play badminton, but last week was half term, and so I went to see a film with a friend."

The role of context

Tulving's studies of cue-dependent forgetting involved *external cues* (e.g. presenting category names). However, cue-dependent forgetting has also been shown with *internal* cues (e.g. mood state), which is called **mood-state-dependent memory**. People tend to remember material better when there is a *match* between their mood at learning and at retrieval, which shows that we tend to store information about our mood states in long-term memory. The effects of mood-state-dependent memory are usually stronger when the participants are in a positive mood than a negative mood (Ucros, 1989).

These internal cues are a form of context. They place the memory in a context and the context serves as the retrieval cue. An experimental study of the effects of external context was conducted by Abernethy (1940). A group of psychology

> Laura: "Do you remember what that boy was called?"
> Holly: "No, but it was something like 'Ted' or 'Frank'."
> Laura: "Oh that's it, it was Fred!"

? Do you have to remember the names of researchers when describing a study? No, but the name may act as a useful cue for recall.

students was given a set of tests before their four-week course began. All students had the same lecturer and all lessons were in the same room. At the end of each week they were all tested. Some were tested in the same room by their usual lecturer, or by a different lecturer. Others were tested in a different room either by their normal lecturer or a different one. Those students tested in their usual room by their usual lecturer did best of all on the tests. Presumably the context (same room, same lecturer) acted as a retrieval cue, assisting recall. Perhaps the students looked around the room when they couldn't think of an answer and something they saw jogged their memory and so acted as a cue. This has obvious applications to your own studies, except that you probably won't be taking your psychology examinations in the same room used for teaching the subject!

Emotional Factors in Forgetting

Repression

A further reason for not being able to retrieve a memory is that emotionally threatening material is repressed, or held from conscious awareness. Freud (1915; see pages 31 to 35 of this book) suggested that anxiety-causing material may be dealt with in a number of ways—repression is one of these methods of **ego defence** (strategies used by the rational mind or ego to protect itself).

The concept of repression can be used to explain forgetting, e.g. someone who dislikes going to the dentist may "forget" their appointment—the anxiety caused by the memory in some way represses it from conscious thought.

It is hard to test Freud's theory, and therefore to prove or disprove the validity of the concept of repressed memories, mainly because of ethical issues. Freud argued that repression is caused by traumatic and other very stressful events, but it is totally unacceptable to create such events in the laboratory.

It is in this context that a study by Levinger and Clark (1961) is important. They managed to find a clever way of testing Freud's ideas about repression in an ethically acceptable way under controlled conditions in the laboratory. In essence, they told their participants to give free associations (say whatever came into their minds) when presented with various neutral (e.g. "tree"; "window") and negative emotionally charged (e.g. "war"; "fear") words. Shortly afterwards, the participants were presented for a second time with the neutral and emotionally charged words, and asked to recall their associations. The key finding was that the participants took longer to recall their associations to the negative emotionally charged words than to the neutral ones. Levinger and Clark also found at recall that the emotional words produced a higher galvanic skin response (GSR, which is a measure of emotional arousal caused by sweating on the palm of the hand). They interpreted these findings by assuming that repression slowed down participants' recall of associations to the emotionally charged words.

Why is the study by Levinger and Clark important? First, they devised a good way of assessing

? What problems can you see in this study by Levinger and Clark (1961)?

KEY TERMS

Repression: this is one of the main defence mechanisms suggested by Freud. What happens is that memories causing great anxiety (e.g. traumatic memories) are kept out of conscious awareness in order to protect the individual. Thus, repression is a good example of motivated forgetting. Information that has been repressed still exists, and can often be recalled during psychoanalysis.

Ethical issues: ethical issues arise in the implementing of research when there is conflict between how the research should be carried out (e.g. with no deception to the participants) and the methodological consequences of observing this (e.g. reduced validity of the findings). Another issue is that of participants versus society. Is it justifiable to infringe upon the rights of participants if the research will be of benefit to society? Such issues are an inevitable consequence of researching people and resolving the issues can be difficult.

repression under controlled conditions. Second, the study focused on unpleasant associations of *relevance* to each individual participant, thus ensuring that negative emotions were created in the participants. Third, there were increasing doubts at the time as to the existence of repression, and the findings of Levinger and Clark provided some evidence that repression is a genuine phenomenon.

The concept of repression is related to the idea of recovered memories. Some adults seem to have repressed memories for childhood sexual abuse. These repressed memories often emerge when the individual concerned is receiving therapy because of their emotional condition. In one study, Williams (1994) interviewed 129 women who had suffered acts of rape and sexual abuse more than 17 years previously. All of them had been 12 or younger at the time, and 38% had no recollection of the sexual abuse they had suffered. However, 16% of the women who recalled being abused said there had been periods of time in the past when they could not remember the abuse.

A difficult issue is that there is often no concrete evidence to confirm the accuracy of recovered memories. Brewin, Andrews, and Gotlib (1993, p.94) discussed the issues involved, and came to the following conclusion: "Provided that individuals are questioned about the occurrence of specific events or facts that they were sufficiently old and well placed to know about, the central features of their accounts are likely to be reasonably accurate." However, the whole issue of recovered memories of abuse is very sensitive and controversial. It raises major ethical and legal issues concerning the therapist's responsibilities, the effects of accusations on other members of the family, and so on.

Even if we accept that repression does exist (and it probably does), that certainly doesn't mean that we can explain most forgetting in terms of repression. As we all know to our cost, we forget many things, but only a small fraction of them are associated with anxiety or trauma.

Flashbulb memories

There are some situations in which powerful negative emotions produce very strong memories. The term **flashbulb memory**, first coined by Brown and Kulik (1977), describes long-lasting and vivid memories of highly important and dramatic events having personal consequences for the individual. Flashbulb memories often contain information about the person supplying the news, the place where the news was heard, and the individual's own emotional state. Many people have vivid memories of what they were doing at the time of learning about the death of Diana, Princess of Wales and the terrorist atrocities of 11 September 2001. It is as if a flash photograph was taken at the very moment of the event with every detail indelibly printed in memory. Flashbulb events don't have to be negative or to concern international events. Happy events can also apparently create a "photographic" image, such as a wedding or the birth of a child. However, in practice nearly all studies of flashbulb memories have focused on dramatic world events. Flashbulb memories for personal events (e.g. being told of the death of a family member) may be remembered in a very different way from flashbulb memories for world events (Di Dwyer, personal communication).

> **?** **How possible is it to study repression under laboratory conditions?**

> **EXAM HINT**
> There are a number of explanations of forgetting in LTM to choose from: trace decay, interference, retrieval failure (cue-dependent forgetting), and repression (motivated forgetting). Cue-dependent and repression tend to be more memorable and provide plenty of content to write about. If you cover these two be familiar with Tulving and Psotka's (1971) study of cue-dependent memory, and Levinger and Clark's (1961) study of repression.

> **KEY TERM**
> **Flashbulb memory**: a long-lasting and vivid memory of a specific event and the context in which it occurred. The event is important and emotionally significant (e.g. a national or personal event). The term "flashbulb" refers to the fact that it is as if a photographic image of the event and setting has been encoded, as the memory is so detailed and accurate. Examples include the atrocities of September 11th 2001, and the deaths of Princess Diana and John F. Kennedy.

Can you remember what you were doing when you heard about the death of Princess Diana? What other flashbulb memories do you have?

Clearly, the emotional nature of such events contributes to the way they remain in memory. Brown and Kulik suggested that flashbulb memories were distinctive because they were both enduring and accurate. The concept of flashbulb memories seems to contradict the notion that thorough processing in the short-term store is needed for good long-term memory, and to support the idea that distinctiveness and emotional factors are important in memory.

What causes a flashbulb memory?

Brown and Kulik suggested that a special neural mechanism might be responsible for flashbulb memories. Other psychologists have suggested that it is because they are rehearsed or thought about so often (e.g. when people discuss the impact these emotionally significant events have had on their lives).

More recently Cahill and McGaugh (1998) suggested that flashbulb memories may have an adaptive function in that, at times of high emotional arousal, **hormones** are produced that have a two-fold effect. In the short-term, emotional hormones create a sense of arousal that helps the animal respond to an emotionally charged situation. In the long-term, future responses to the same emotional (important) situation will be enhanced because the events surrounding the original emotional experience are well remembered. This was shown in an experiment where rats were injected with a stimulant drug (like a hormone) just after they learned something new. The drug successfully enhanced the rats' recall of the task.

Are flashbulb memories accurate?

Are flashbulb memories as accurate and reliable over time as they have been described? Some of the strongest evidence suggesting that they are was reported by Conway et al. (1994), who argued that the resignation of Mrs Thatcher as Prime Minister in 1990 should have produced flashbulb memories. According to them, this was an event that was surprising and consequential to most people in the UK. They tested people within a fortnight of the event and again 11 months later. They found that 86% of their UK participants still had flashbulb memories after 11 months, compared to only 29% in other countries. The UK participants' memories were vivid, detailed, accurate, and consistent over time. A weakness of this study was sample drop-off, with not all of the original participants taking part in the follow-up of 11 months. This may have left a biased sample. Another problem is that Conway et al.'s initial assessment of participants' flashbulb memories typically occurred only several days after Mrs Thatcher's resignation. As a result, they probably obtained an inadequate measure of the original memories, because there is evidence that memories for dramatic events change over the first few days after the event (Winningham, Hyman, & Dinnel, 2000).

Why is the study by Conway et al. important? First, they studied an event apparently fulfilling the necessary criteria for the creation of flashbulb memories. Second, they obtained some of the clearest evidence ever reported for the existence of flashbulb memories. Third, their findings re-awakened interest in flashbulb memories after other researchers had failed to find much evidence of such memories.

? **Why might we have expected to find flashbulb memories for Mrs Thatcher's resignation?**

Different findings were reported by Talarico and Rubin (2003). On 12 September 2001, they assessed students' memories for the events of the previous day and for a very recent everyday event. The students were then tested again between 1 and 32 weeks later. The participants claimed that their flashbulb memories remained very vivid over the entire 32-week period. In fact, however, their flashbulb memories were not very accurate or consistent over time; indeed, they were no more consistent than their everyday memories! Interestingly, even President George W. Bush's flashbulb memories for 11 September are inaccurate. On 5 January 2002 he said, "When we walked into the classroom, I had seen this plane fly into the first building. There was a TV set on" (Greenberg, 2004, p.364). This must be wrong, because footage of the *first* plane crashing into the building was not shown on television that early in the day.

? How do you know that your flashbulb memories are accurate?

SECTION SUMMARY

❖ Forgetting may occur because of:
  – Problems of availability, usually linked to the short-term memory.
  – Problems of accessibility in retrieving information that is still stored in memory.

Reasons for forgetting

❖ Forgetting from the short-term memory may be due to:
  – trace decay;
  – interference;
  – diversion of attention;
  – brain damage.
  The first three causes are all examples of lack of availability.

Explanations of forgetting in STM

❖ Forgetting from the long-term memory may be due to:
  – Proactive or retroactive interference which can account for forgetting when stimulus material is similar. However, this explanation may apply less well in real life than in the laboratory.
  – A lack of retrieval cues.
❖ Retrieval failure can be explained in terms of cue-dependent forgetting and emotional factors.
❖ The encoding specificity principle states that the closer cues are to actual memory the more effective they are.

Explanations of forgetting in LTM

❖ Increased anxiety and emotional factors resulting in repression may explain the forgetting of emotionally unpleasant memories.
❖ However, flashbulb memories suggest that emotional factors may enhance our memories.
❖ Some memories may be more accurate and longer lasting because of hormones produced at times of high emotion, suggesting that such memories have an adaptive function.
❖ However, flashbulb memories are often less accurate and consistent than used to be believed.

The role of emotional factors

See pp.25–31 of the revision guide.

SECTION 7—CRITICAL ISSUE
EYEWITNESS TESTIMONY

In this section, our focus will be on a major practical application of our knowledge of human memory—eyewitness testimony.

Brown (1986, p.258) suggested that there is a paradox to eyewitness testimony: "Judges, defense attorneys and psychologists believe it to be just about the least trustworthy kind of evidence of guilt, whereas jurors have always found it *more* persuasive than any other sort of evidence." Brown's concerns were confirmed in a study by Wells, Liepe, and Ostrom (1979). In the cubicle where participants were told to wait before the study started there was a calculator and, while each participant waited, a **confederate** of the experimenter appeared and popped it into her purse. When the participants were asked to identify the "thief" from a set of six photographs, only 58% were correct. Even more worryingly, when the same participants were asked to "testify" at a mock trial, 80% of them were believed by the jury.

The Devlin report (1976) to the British Home Secretary found that in 1973 there were 850 cases where eyewitness testimony was the only evidence of guilt. In 74% of them, the accused was found guilty by a jury. The Devlin committee considered the evidence about the **reliability** of such testimony and advised that no jury should convict on eyewitness testimony alone. This is supported by evidence from DNA tests, which can establish definitely who was responsible for certain crimes. In the United States, more than 100 convicted people have been shown to be innocent by DNA tests, with 75% of them being found guilty on the basis of mistaken eyewitness identification. The 100th innocent person freed following DNA testing was Larry Mayes of Indiana. He was convicted of raping a cashier at a filling station after she identified him in court, and spent 21 years in prison for a crime he didn't commit (Loftus, 2004).

Unreliable Evidence

Why is eyewitness testimony so unreliable, and what can we do to improve it? There are various explanations for the unreliability of eyewitness testimony. For example, people often don't have total recall for events and they fill in the gaps in their memory on the basis of what they *think* might have happened. This is called reconstructive memory and relies on stereotypes, e.g. you might not expect a crime to be committed by a little old woman wearing a suit so you might "recall" that it was a man rather than a woman. If you have to "reconstruct" your memory, it will be affected by your stereotypes.

A further issue is the effect of language. If you are asked "What was the doctor wearing?" it would lead you to give a different answer from "What was the

? **Wells et al.'s study involved deceiving the participants. Do you feel this is acceptable?**

EXAM HINT

With regard to eyewitness testimony be ready to discuss two issues in essay questions:

- The reliability of eyewitness testimony.
- How research has helped to improve the reliability of eyewitness testimony.

KEY TERMS

Eyewitness testimony: evidence supplied by people who witness a specific event or crime, relying only on their memory. Statements often include descriptions of the criminal (facial appearance and other identifiable characteristics) and subsequent identification, and details of the crime scene (e.g. the sequence of events, time of day, and if others witnessed the event, etc.). There is good evidence that eyewitness testimony can be incorrect, because eyewitness memories of events tend to be fragile and easily distorted (e.g. by leading questions).

Reconstructive memory: it is often assumed that recall from long-term memory involves reconstruction. This is an active process in which information from the to-be-remembered material *and* information from our knowledge and experience of the world are combined. Information based on our knowledge and experience of the world is contained in schemas, which are packets of knowledge. What often happens is that what we recall is *not* an accurate reproduction of the original material, because our recall is distorted by schemas, which have been used to fill in the gaps in our memory.

woman wearing?" The language used when questioning eyewitnesses may lead them to give certain answers.

Eyewitness testimony has been found by psychologists to be extremely unreliable, yet jurors tend to find such testimony highly believable. This is very worrying. What can we do about it?

Reconstructive nature of memory

In this section, we are concerned with reconstructive memory. Suppose you are trying to remember some event. Reconstructive memory would involve combining the scraps of information about the event you can remember with your relevant knowledge and experience to reconstruct what probably happened. The concept of reconstructive memory is related to **schema theory**. During the course of life we develop schemas. A **schema** is an organised package of information containing your knowledge about the world; it helps us to make sense of it all. Schemas are stored in long-term memory. Your schemas tell you that if you were wearing a short-sleeved shirt it was likely to be summer. Bower, Black, and Turner (1979) demonstrated that most people share similar schemas. Several people listed the most important events associated with having a restaurant meal. Most included the following events: sitting down, looking at the menu, ordering, eating, paying the bill, and leaving the restaurant.

In the early 1930s, it was generally assumed that memory simply involves remembering the information presented to us. However, Bartlett argued that memory was often more complex than that, in that prior knowledge in the form of schemas has an impact on our memory. How could he show this? He argued that what was of key importance was to ask participants to memorise a text selected to produce *conflict* between its contents and their knowledge of the world. As a result, the participants would impose their own schemas on the contents, and this would result in distortion of the material. For example, if people read a story taken from a different culture, then this would contain words and concepts that were foreign. It would be likely that the participants' prior knowledge would influence the way this information was remembered, making it more conventional and acceptable from the standpoint of their own cultural background.

In a study by Allport and Postman (1947) participants were shown this picture. Later they were more likely to recall that the black man was holding the razor, presumably because this fitted in with the stereotype at the time.

In one study, Bartlett (1932, see Key Study overleaf) asked English participants to read a North American Indian folk tale, after which they tried to recall the story. Their recall distorted the content and style of the original story, with the distortions increasing over successive recalls. Most of the recall errors were in the direction of making the story read more like an ordinary English story and to make it more coherent.

Key Study: Reconstructive memory

Bartlett's (1932) study of reconstructive memory.

Aims: Bartlett wanted to investigate the effects of schemas (packets of knowledge about the world) on participants' recall. He aimed to test his own schema theory, which states that memory involves an active reconstruction at the time of recall. In more detail, he wanted to find out if what we remember depends on the following two factors: (1) the information presented to us; and (2) distortions created by our reliance on schemas. Such distortions would be most likely to occur when the participants' schemas were of little relevance to the material being learned.

Procedure: Twenty English participants took part in a natural experiment. Participants were presented with a range of stimuli, including different stories and line drawings. A repeated reproduction method was used as participants were asked to reproduce the stimulus they had seen repeatedly at different time intervals. The time interval varied between days, months, and even years. The story called "The War of the Ghosts" is the best-known example of Bartlett's materials. This story was selected because it was from a different culture (North American Indian) and so would conflict with the participants' prior knowledge contained in their schemas. The participants' story reproductions were analysed in order to assess the distortions produced.

The War of the Ghosts

The most well-known of the stimulus materials used by Bartlett was the North American Indian folk tale called "The War of the Ghosts", part of which follows:
One night two young men from Edulac went down the river to hunt seals, and while they were there it became foggy and calm. Then they heard war-cries, and they thought: "Maybe this is a war-party." They escaped to the shore, and hid behind a log. Now canoes came up, and they heard the noise of paddles, and saw one canoe coming up to them. There were five men in the canoe, and they said: "What do you think? We wish to take you along. We are going up the river to make war on the people."

? Do you think that the kinds of errors and distortions observed by Bartlett would be found with other kinds of material?

Findings: Bartlett found considerable distortions in the participants' recollections. The distortions increased over successive recalls and most of these reflected the participants' attempts to make the story more like a story from their own culture. Changes from the original included: rationalisations (these made the story more coherent as the story was shortened and phrases changed to be more similar to their own language); flattening (failure to recall unfamiliar details, e.g. the ghosts); and sharpening (elaboration of certain content and altering of its importance). These changes made the story easier to remember.

Conclusions: Bartlett concluded that the accuracy of memory is low. The changes to the story on recall showed that the participants were actively reconstructing the story to fit their existing schemas, so his schema theory was supported. He believed that schemas affect retrieval rather than encoding or storage. He also concluded that memory was forever being reconstructed because each successive reproduction showed more changes, which contradicted Bartlett's original expectation that the reproductions would eventually become fixed. This research has important implications for the reporting of events requiring great accuracy, such as in eyewitness testimony.

Criticisms

- Bartlett's research is important, because it provided some of the first evidence that what we remember depends in an important way on our prior knowledge in the form of schemas. It also possesses more external validity than most memory research, because schemas play a major role in everyday memory.
- Bartlett assumed that the distortions in recall produced by his participants were due to genuine problems with memory. However, the instructions he used were very vague. It is probable that many of these distortions were simply guesses made by the participants trying to make their recall seem coherent and complete.
- Bartlett assumed that schemas influence what happens at the time of retrieval, but have no effect on what happens at the time of comprehension of a story. Other evidence suggests that schemas influence comprehension (encoding and storage) *and* retrieval.

Note: If the question asks for findings or conclusions only, you could include research by Cohen (1981, see p.78).

> **?** Why do you think that Bartlett's research has been so influential in the study of memory?

Why is Bartlett's research so important? First, he devised a good method for studying the effects of past knowledge on memory by using texts involving a *conflict* between their content and the participants' past knowledge. Second, he provided one of the first clear demonstrations that our long-term memory can be strongly affected by our past knowledge and experience, and this influences memory research even today. Third, Bartlett showed that our long-term memory is prone to various distortions and errors, and his schema theory helped to predict the most common kinds of memory distortions. Fourth, Bartlett's approach has been very influential recently in explaining some of the limitations in eyewitness testimony.

Bartlett's work suggested that the process of remembering things is an *active* reconstruction of the bits that are stored. What is involved here has been compared to using a few dinosaur bones to reconstruct what the dinosaur probably looked like. When you learn something, it is actually only elements of the experience that are stored.

So reconstructions are made by combining the real elements of a memory with your knowledge of the world—these things that are called schemas. Schema theory indicates that prior expectations will influence our perceptions—our prejudices and stereotypes will influence what we think we have seen, and how we subsequently recall the information, as we will see in a moment. Before that, let's briefly consider the nature of stereotypes.

> **■ Activity:** In small groups, write your own schemas for the following:
>
> - Catching a train
> - Buying a newspaper
> - Starting school
>
> How easy was it to agree on a uniform pattern of events? Were any of the themes easier to agree on than the others? Why might this be?

Stereotypes

In Bartlett's classic study he showed how our cultural expectations or **stereotypes** lead to predictable changes in memory. Stereotypes are schemas that summarise

A stereotypical image of an Italian matriarch which gives rise to many expectations of what she is likely to wear, say, do, and so on.

? We all use stereotypes, usually without even thinking about them, e.g. "Essex girl", "trainspotter", "teacher". Think of some other examples in common use. Are stereotypes always necessarily negative or inaccurate?

large amounts of data. Like schemas, stereotypes influence memory. If you are told that a target person is a waitress rather than a librarian, this may influence your recall of that person. Cohen (1981) showed participants a 15-minute video of a man and woman eating a meal, and celebrating a birthday. The woman was either described as a waitress or a librarian. Later participants were asked to describe the woman's behaviour, appearance, and personality. Participants were more likely to recall information that was consistent with the stereotype than information that was inconsistent. (Consistent **traits** were established in a pilot study.)

Furthermore, if the "occupational information" was provided *before* the videotape then later recall was more accurate than if participants were told the woman's occupation *after* watching the video. When the information about whether the woman was a waitress or a librarian was given before watching the video, it served to generate expectations which enhanced recall. Bartlett (1932) argued that schemas affect the retrieval process rather than initial storage, but Cohen's study shows that schemas and stereotypes are important at both stages of memory: initial storage *and* retrieval.

Influence of schemas on eyewitness memory

According to Bartlett (1932), schemas can be useful because they provide a way of organising information and thus enhancing long-term memory. Support for this idea was reported by Tuckey and Brewer (2003a). First of all, they obtained information about people's bank robbery schema, which typically include the following aspects: robbers are male; they wear disguises; they wear dark clothes; they make demands for money; and they have a getaway car with a driver in it. After that, participants were shown a video of a simulated bank robbery and their memory for the events was tested afterwards.

What did Tuckey and Brewer (2003a) find? First, as predicted by Bartlett's reconstructive memory theory, eyewitnesses had better recall for information *relevant* to the bank robbery schema than for information that was *irrelevant* (e.g. the colour of the getaway car). Thus, eyewitnesses used schematic information to assist in their recall of the bank robbery. Second, eyewitnesses were good at recalling information relevant to their bank robbery schema even when the details differed from those contained in the schema (e.g. robbers wearing light clothes; robbers had no guns). According to Bartlett (1932), there should have been a tendency to *misremember* these details as being consistent with the schema (e.g. remembering the robbers wearing dark clothes even though they wore light clothes). Presumably eyewitnesses attended closely to aspects of the crime relevant to their bank robbery schema, and this allowed them to remember them accurately.

In another study, Tuckey and Brewer (2003b), the findings were more directly in line with predictions from Bartlett's approach. Eyewitnesses tried to recall the details of a simulated crime they observed, and what was of interest was how they remembered ambiguous information. As expected, eyewitnesses tended to interpret the ambiguous information as being consistent with their crime schema—this led them to make memory errors based on information in the crime schema but not in the crime they had observed.

Evaluation of the reconstructive approach

- Strength: Schemas influence the way data are stored and can explain how data are actively retrieved. Schemas can enhance memory by making it easier for eyewitnesses to organise the information they possess about a crime (Tuckey & Brewer, 2003a).
- Strength: Studies such as that of Tuckey and Brewer (2003b) show that eyewitness memory can be distorted by schemas. We sometimes "remember" information that is consistent with our schematic knowledge but didn't actually happen.
- Limitation: Many psychologists believe that schema theory goes too far in the direction of claiming that memory is usually inaccurate. We often remember accurately the personal remarks that others make about us, and actors and actresses need to remember their lines perfectly. Such phenomena aren't easily explained by schema theory, with its emphasis on the ways in which schemas change what has been presented in systematic ways.
- Limitation: Schema theory often fails to make clear predictions. We often don't know what schemas someone is using to understand or to recall information, and this limits our ability to predict *what* they will remember and *how* they will remember it.

Leading questions

One obvious reason why eyewitness testimony is so unreliable is because the events they witness are typically unexpected, and so eyewitnesses may not be paying close attention to what is going on. A less obvious reason is that the memories eyewitnesses have of an event are fragile, and can easily be distorted and made inaccurate by the questions asked of an eyewitness. The most celebrated study in the whole history of research on eyewitness testimony was by Elizabeth Loftus and John Palmer (1974), and it was on precisely this issue (see Key Study below).

Key Study: Eyewitness testimony

Loftus and Palmer's (1974) study of the effects of language on recall in eyewitness testimony.

Aims: To test their hypothesis that eyewitness testimony (EWT) is fragile and can easily be distorted. Loftus and Palmer aimed to show that leading questions could distort EWT accounts via the cues provided in the question. To test this hypothesis, Loftus and Palmer used different forms of questions to ask people to estimate the speed of motor vehicles after they had observed a car accident. The estimation of vehicle speed is something people are generally quite poor at and so, therefore, they may be more open to suggestion by leading questions.

Procedure: Forty-five American students formed an opportunity sample. This was a laboratory experiment with five conditions, only one of which was experienced by each participant (an independent measures design). Participants were shown a brief film depicting a car accident involving a

KEY TERM

Leading questions: questions that are relevant to eyewitness testimony. They are questions phrased in such a way as to lead witnesses to a particular answer, such as "Did you see THE broken glass?" instead of "Did you see ANY broken glass?". Another example would be Loftus and Palmer's (1974) study showing that speed estimates varied with the word (contacted, bumped, smashed etc.) used in the question.

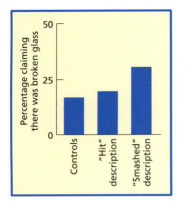

Results from Loftus and Palmer's (1974) study showing how the verb used in the initial description of a car accident affected recall of the incident after one week.

? **What are some of the practical implications of this research?**

? **How confident can we be that such laboratory-based findings resemble what would be found in the real world?**

number of cars. They were then asked to describe what had happened as if they were eyewitnesses. After they had watched the film, the participants were asked specific questions, including the question "About how fast were the cars going when they [hit/smashed/collided/bumped/contacted—the five conditions] each other?" Thus, the independent variable was the wording of the question and the dependent variable was the speed reported by the participants. A week after the participants were shown the film of the car accident they were asked, "Did you see any broken glass?" In fact, no broken glass was shown in the film.

Findings: Loftus and Palmer found that estimated speed was influenced by the verb used. The verb implied information about the speed, which systematically affected the participants' memory of the accident. Those who were asked the question where the verb used was "smashed" thought the cars were going faster than those who were asked the question with "hit" as the verb. The mean estimate when "smashed" was used was 41mph, versus 34mph when "hit" was used. Thus, participants in the "smashed" condition reported the highest speeds, followed by "collided", "bumped", "hit", and "contacted" in descending order. In answering the follow-up question, a higher percentage of participants who heard "smashed" said they had seen broken glass (32%) compared to those who heard "hit" (14%).

Conclusions: The questions asked can be termed "leading" questions because they affected the participants' memory of the event. The answer to a leading question is implicit in the question—that is, the question contains information about what the answer should be. Thus, language can have a distorting effect on EWT, which can lead to confabulated (inaccurate) accounts of the witnessed event. It is possible that the original memory had been reconstructed. However, it is also possible that the original memory may have been replaced or subject to interference. This has important implications for the questions used in police interviews of eyewitnesses.

Criticisms

- The research lacks mundane realism, as what the observers saw in the laboratory would not have had the same emotional impact as witnessing a real-life accident. It also differs from real life, in that the participants knew that something interesting was going to be shown to them, and were paying full attention to it. In real life, eyewitnesses are typically taken by surprise and often fail to pay close attention to the event or incident.
- This research by Loftus and Palmer is important in showing that the memories of eyewitnesses can easily be distorted. However, the main distortion produced in this study was for a relatively unimportant piece of information (i.e. presence vs absence of broken glass). It has proved harder to produce distortions for information of central importance (e.g. the weapon used by a criminal).
- The participants witnessed a brief film, which may have contained much less information than would be available when observing an incident or crime in real life.

Note: If the question asks for findings or conclusions only, you could include follow-up research by Loftus and Zanni (1975, see p.81).

Loftus' contribution

Loftus and Zanni (1975) later obtained similar findings to Loftus and Palmer (1974). They showed their participants a short film of a car accident. Some of the participants were asked, "Did you see *a* broken headlight?", whereas others were asked, "Did you see *the* broken headlight?" There was no broken headlight in the film, but the latter question implies that there was. Only 7% of those asked about a broken headlight said they had seen it, compared to 17% of those asked about the broken headlight.

Evidence showing how difficult it is to stop eyewitnesses being influenced by post-event information was reported by Eakin, Schreiber, and Segent-Marshall (2003). Eyewitnesses watched slides of a maintenance man repairing a chair in an office and stealing some money and a calculator. As predicted, memory was worse when eyewitnesses had been presented with misleading post-event information. More surprisingly, memory was made worse by misleading information even when the eyewitnesses were warned immediately that misleading information had been presented.

Why is the study by Loftus and Palmer (1974) so important? First, it showed that eyewitness memory is fragile, and can easily be distorted by questions asked after the memory has been formed. This is a very good example of retroactive interference (discussed on page 65), which involves information presented between learning and memory test disrupting memory. Second, it provided evidence that juries listening to eyewitness testimony should be careful before accepting the validity of what eyewitnesses have to say. Third, the study was useful for the police, because it showed the need to be very careful when questioning eyewitnesses in order to prevent their memories from being distorted.

Subsequent research

The tendency for eyewitness memory to be influenced by misleading post-event information is very strong. Eakin et al. (2003) found that eyewitness memory was impaired by misleading post-event information. Of key importance, there was often memory impairment even when the eyewitnesses were warned immediately about the presence of misleading information.

Although the majority of studies show that eyewitness memory can be unreliable and can be distorted, there have been studies showing that real-life recall can be very accurate. One such study is by Yuille and Cutshall (1986). Yuille and Cutshall interviewed people who had witnessed a crime where one person was shot dead and another person seriously injured. These interviews (given some months later), along with interviews given to the police immediately after the incident, were analysed. The eyewitness accounts were found to be very accurate, and the accuracy and amount of information recalled did not diminish over time. The eyewitnesses' accounts were also not distorted by leading questions. Yuille and Cutshall

Eyewitness memory can be impaired by misleading post-event information. However, important information, such as the weapon used in a crime, is less likely to be distorted than trivial information.

concluded that laboratory studies such as those outlined above are not generalisable to real life (i.e. Yuille and Cutshall's study has more **external validity**) and that more field research is needed.

There is another limitation with research on the effects of post-event information on eyewitness memory: what has typically been found is that such information can distort memory of relatively minor details (e.g. broken glass). Heath and Erickson (1998) found that there was less memory distortion for central or important details than for trivial ones. This may limit the practical importance of this line of research.

How Can Evidence Be Made More Reliable?

Many innocent people have been put in prison purely on the basis of eyewitness testimony. Mistakes by eyewitnesses may occur because of what happens at the time of the crime or incident, or because of what happens afterwards.

Implications for police procedures

It follows from the research we have discussed that the questions asked during a police interview may distort an eyewitness' memory, and thus reduce its reliability. What happened at one time in the United Kingdom was that an eyewitness' account of what had happened was repeatedly interrupted. The interruptions made it hard for the eyewitness to concentrate fully on the process of retrieval, and thus reduced recall. As a result of psychological research, the Home Office issued guidelines recommending that police interviews should proceed from free recall to general open-ended questions, concluding with more specific questions.

Geiselman et al. (1985) argued that interview techniques should take account of some basic characteristics of human memory:

- Memory traces are complex, and contain various features and/or kinds of information.
- The effectiveness of a retrieval cue depends on the extent to which the information it contains is *similar* to information stored in the memory trace— the encoding specificity principle (see page 69).
- Various retrieval cues may permit access to any given memory trace, for example, reconstructing a crime can provide useful cues to retrieve memories.

Geiselman et al. used these considerations to develop the basic **cognitive interview**. The eyewitness tries to recreate mentally the context that existed at the time of the crime, including environmental and internal (e.g. mood state) information. The eyewitness then simply reports everything he/she can think of relating to the incident, even if the information is fragmented. In addition, the eyewitness reports the details of the incident in various orders, and from various perspectives (e.g. that of another eyewitness).

EXAM HINT

When discussing the reliability of eyewitness testimony make sure you are not too one-sided as research such as Yuille and Cutshall (1986) suggests real-life EWT is much more reliable.

? What empirical evidence demonstrated the value of retrieval cues?

KEY TERM

External validity: the validity of an experiment outside the research situation itself; the extent to which the findings of a research study are applicable to other situations, especially "everyday" situations.

Geiselman et al. compared the effectiveness of the basic cognitive interview with that of the standard police interview. The average number of correct statements produced by eyewitnesses was 41.1 using the basic cognitive interview, compared to only 29.4 using the standard police interview. Fisher et al. (1987) devised the more effective enhanced cognitive interview, which makes use of the following recommendations (Roy, 1991, p.399):

Investigations should minimise distractions, induce the eyewitness to speak slowly, allow a pause between the response and next question, tailor language to suit the individual eyewitness, follow up with interpretive comment, try to reduce eyewitness anxiety, avoid judgmental and personal comments, and always review the eyewitness's description of events or people under investigation.

Evidence that the enhanced cognitive interview is generally very effective was reported by Kohnken et al. (1999) in a meta-analysis combining data from over 50 studies. The enhanced cognitive interview consistently elicited more correct information than standard police interviews. Indeed, the average eyewitness given an enhanced cognitive interview produced more correct items of information than 81% of eyewitnesses given a standard interview. However, there was a small cost in terms of reduced accuracy, with the average eyewitness given an enhanced cognitive interview producing more errors than 61% of those given a standard interview.

Use of hypnosis

The media have reported numerous cases in which hypnosis seems to have been remarkably effective in bringing forgotten memories to light. Indeed, many police forces (but *not* in the UK) use hypnosis to collect relevant evidence from eyewitnesses about matters such as car number plates and the physical features of wanted criminals. The term **hypermnesia** has been used to refer to the enhance memory allegedly created by hypnosis.

What are the facts? Geiselman et al. (1985) compared hypnosis against the cognitive interview and standard police procedures as a way of obtaining more information from eyewitnesses. They found that hypnosis was more effective than standard police procedures, but it was less effective than the cognitive interview. However, the real problem with hypnosis is that it makes people much less cautious in what they claim to remember, and so more liable to make errors in recall. For example, hypnotised individuals will sometimes confidently "recall" events from the future! Putnam (1979) showed people a videotape of an accident involving a car and a bicycle. They were then asked various questions, some of which contained misleading information. Some of

Putnam (1979) used a videotape of scenes like this to test the memory of eyewitnesses. He asked hypnotised and non-hypnotised participants about their memories of the accident and the events leading up to it. He found that the hypnotised individuals made more errors in their answers than those who had not been hypnotised. The hypnotised people were also more suggestible—i.e. giving positive answers to misleading questions.

"Well I know he was wearing tights."

the eyewitnesses were asked these questions while hypnotised, whereas others were not hypnotised. The hypnotised individuals made more errors in their answers than did the non-hypnotised ones, especially with the misleading questions.

Identity parades

The police often make use of identity parades in which the suspect and several other people who look similar to the suspect are placed in a line. The eyewitness is then asked to try to identify the person they saw committing the crime. One of the problems is that the eyewitness may feel under pressure to select someone, even if they are not really sure that the suspect is in the line-up. An obvious approach to take is to warn the eyewitness in advance that the suspect may not be present, and that he/she is not required to select anyone unless they are confident.

Steblay (1997) carried out a meta-analysis based on numerous studies. Steblay found that such warnings reduced mistaken identification rates by 42% when the guilty person was absent. However, there was a small cost to pay, in that accurate identification was reduced by 2% when the guilty person was in fact present, because the warnings made eyewitnesses more cautious.

Expert witnesses

In important criminal cases psychologists are sometimes asked to explain the reliability of eyewitness testimony to the jury. Elizabeth Loftus, mentioned earlier,

? One method used to produce lots of ideas is called "brainstorming", where all ideas are received without criticism. How reliable would such evidence be?

acted as an **expert witness** at the trial of José Garcia, a Mexican-American accused of robbing a liquor store in California and killing one of two clerks in the store. The only evidence of Garcia's guilt was the eyewitness testimony of the surviving clerk, Joseph Melville, who was only asked to identify the attacker two weeks after the incident. Loftus was called in to help the jury decide how much weight to give to Melville's testimony. In answer to questions, she explained that people do forget over time, that situations of high stress can lead to impaired memory, that people have been found to be less good at cross-racial identification, and that memory is influenced by stereotypes (Loftus, 1979).

The jury in this case could not agree on a verdict and José Garcia was acquitted. Presumably the jury were not convinced about the accuracy of the eyewitness testimony. One note of criticism is that the evidence that was presented by Elizabeth Loftus was based on laboratory experiments and may not therefore be valid in real life.

> **EXAM HINT**
>
> If you are asked how research has improved the reliability of eyewitness testimony you need to assess how well research in this area has been applied to improve real-life eyewitness testimony. Use the research evidence from the cognitive interview and insights from research on leading questions, cue-dependent memory, and the role of emotional factors.

SECTION SUMMARY

❖ Schema theory describes memory retrieval as a process of active reconstruction relying on, and being biased by, schemas and stereotypes.

❖ Our use of schemas and stereotypes (schema theory) can influence both the acquisition and retrieval of information.

❖ However, this theory cannot account for occasions when memory is extremely accurate.

The reconstructive nature of memory

❖ There are serious concerns as to whether we can trust eyewitness testimony.

❖ Factors that may contribute to the unreliability of eyewitness testimony include:
  – the reconstructive nature of memory;
  – emotional distress;
  – leading questions.

❖ However we need to be cautious about disregarding all eyewitness testimony, since much of the research has been undertaken in the laboratory. Studies exploring real-life crime have shown that important information about the crime is not easily distorted.

The reliability of eyewitness testimony

❖ When eyewitnesses are questioned after an event, the language used may affect the way information is stored, and thus affect later recall.

Leading questions

❖ There is general evidence that language affects recall, but the research on leading questions is based on laboratory studies.

Attempts to improve the reliability of eyewitness testimony

❖ There are implications from psychological research for improvements in the collection and use of eyewitness testimony. These can include:

❖ Developing the basic and enhanced cognitive interview:
  – Reinstating the context for the witness.
  – Getting witnesses to recall anything whether it seems relevant or not.
  – Getting witnesses to recall the information from a different perspective.

❖ Reducing eyewitness anxiety by:
  – Establishing a rapport with the witness.
  – Stating that the culprit might not be in an identity parade line-up, to avoid pressurising the witness into making an identification. (Warning eyewitnesses that the suspect may not be present in identity parades also makes them less liable to select the wrong person.)
  – Allowing the witness to volunteer information.

❖ Minimising distractions by:
  – Suggesting sequential line-ups.

❖ Hypnosis has also been used, but is liable to increase errors in recall.

❖ Psychologists can be used as expert witnesses in criminal trials to advise jurors on the reliability of eyewitness testimony.

See pp.32–38 of the revision guide.

> You have reached the end of the chapter on cognitive psychology. Cognitive psychology is an approach or perspective in psychology. The material in this chapter has exemplified the way that cognitive psychologists explain behaviour. They look at behaviour in terms of the way that it can be explained by reference to mental (cognitive) processes. This is sometimes regarded as a rather "mechanistic" approach to the study of behaviour because it focuses on machine-like processes and tends to exclude the influence of social or emotional factors.

FURTHER READING

Nearly all the topics discussed in this chapter are dealt with in Chapters 5 and 6 of M.W. Eysenck (2001) *Principles of cognitive psychology (2nd Edn.)* (Hove, UK: Psychology Press). A much fuller account of human memory is contained in M.W. Eysenck and M.T. Keane (2005) *Cognitive psychology: A student's handbook (5th Edn.)* (Hove, UK: Psychology Press). Several key topics in memory are discussed in an accessible way in J.A. Groeger (1997) *Memory and remembering: Everyday memory in context* (Harlow, UK: Addison Wesley Longman). There is an interesting discussion of eyewitness testimony in Chapter 6 of R. Brown (1986) *Social psychology: The second edition* (London: Free Press).

REVISION QUESTIONS

The examination questions aim to sample the material in this whole chapter. For advice on how to answer such questions refer to Chapter 1, Section 2.

Whenever you are asked to describe a study try to include some or all of the following details: research aim(s), participants, research method (e.g. experiment or observation), procedure, findings, and conclusion.

You will always have a choice of two questions in the AQA AS-level exam and 30 minutes in which to answer the question you choose:

Question 1 (AQA, 2004)
a. Describe *one* alternative to the multi-store model of memory. (6 marks)
b. Describe the procedures and findings of *one* study of repression. (6 marks)
c. Outline and evaluate research (theories *and/or* studies) related to eyewitness testimony (EWT). (18 marks)

Question 2
a. Outline *two* explanations of forgetting in long-term memory. (3 marks + 3 marks)
b. Describe the procedures and findings of one study of capacity in short-term memory. (6 marks)
c. Outline and evaluate the working memory model. (18 marks)

Developmental psychology is an approach or perspective in psychology, and it is concerned with the way people change as they get older. Some of these changes are innate, e.g. puberty occurs as a result of a hormonal surge that is biologically driven. However, many of the changes that occur during development are a result of experience, e.g. a girl learns many aspects of feminine behaviour by modelling herself on women around her. Therefore, developmental changes occur as a result of an interaction between innate factors (nature) and experience (nurture). Developmental psychologists aim to describe how children and adults develop and also explain why they develop as they do.

SECTION 8
The development and variety of attachments p.89
When do infants first become attached? What is the sequence of attachment development, and are there individual differences and cultural variations? Are there theories that can account for why children form attachments, and why they become attached to one person rather than another?

Specification content: Stages in the formation of attachments (e.g. Schaffer). Research into individual differences in attachment, including secure and insecure attachments (e.g. Ainsworth) and cross-cultural variations. Explanations of attachment (e.g. learning theory, Bowlby's theory).

SECTION 9
Deprivation and privation p.116
What happens when children are separated from their main caregivers? In the short term infants become anxious. We will examine how this subsequently influences the child's development, and explore the important distinction that has been made between deprivation (separation from caregivers) and privation (a lack of attachment).

Specification content: Bowlby's maternal deprivation hypothesis, including evidence on which it is based. Research into the effects of privation (e.g. studies of extreme privation and institutionalisation), including the extent to which the effects of privation can be reversed.

SECTION 10—CRITICAL ISSUE
Day care p.128
Children in day care experience short-term separations from their main caregivers. Does this affect their development, and if so how?

Specification content: The effects of day care on children's cognitive and social development.

DEVELOPMENTAL PSYCHOLOGY: Attachments in Development

People develop attachments to all sorts of things—footwear, favourite restaurants, friends, lovers, and parents. You form attachments throughout your life but among the most important ones are those that are formed early in development.

Attachment is like a piece of invisible string that binds individuals in a way that allows healthy development. The tie is reciprocal: parents are as attached to their children as the children are to their parents. Attachment is a central topic in developmental psychology. In this chapter we will consider how attachment develops and why it happens at all, as well as other related issues.

SECTION 8
THE DEVELOPMENT AND VARIETY OF ATTACHMENTS

What is Attachment?

According to Shaffer (1993), an attachment is "a close emotional relationship between two persons, characterised by mutual affection and a desire to maintain proximity [closeness]". It is an emotional relationship experienced throughout the lifespan. When you are attached to someone, it makes you feel good to be in that person's company and also makes you feel anxious when they are not there. You may also experience a longing to be reunited. This is the "desire to maintain proximity".

Maccoby (1980) identified four key behaviours of attachment:

- *Seeking proximity to primary caregiver.* The infant tries to stay close to its "attachment figure".
- *Distress on separation.* When caregiver and infant are separated, *both* experience feelings of distress.
- *Pleasure when reunited.* Obvious pleasure is shown when the child is reunited with his/her caregiver.
- *General orientation of behaviour towards primary caregiver.* The infant is aware of his/her caregiver at all times and may frequently make contact for reassurance.

> **KEY TERM**
>
> **Attachment:** this is a strong, reciprocal, emotional bond between an infant and his or her caregiver(s) that is characterised by a desire to maintain proximity. Attachments take different forms, such as secure or insecure. Infants display attachment through the degree of separation distress shown when separated from the caregiver, pleasure at reunion with the caregiver, and stranger anxiety.

There are certain behaviours that characterise attachment: distress on separation, pleasure when reunited, seeking out the attachment figure, and general orientation to each other.

Parenting is one of the most important relationships in adult life. A person's attachment to their own parents will influence their subsequent relationship with their own child.

? Who are you most attached to? How do you think this attachment has affected your development?

The earliest attachment, between an infant and his/her caregivers, has a special role to play in development, as we will see.

It is important to recognise that all attachments are *reciprocal*. Both partners must be involved for the bond to be forged. Maurer and Maurer (1989) wrote, "Attachments are not formed by a congenital [existing at birth] glue held in limited supply: they are welded in the heat of interactions." In other words, attachments depend on interaction rather than two people just being together. Next we look at a number of questions we can ask about the development of attachments.

Why Do Infants Form Attachments?

Attachment serves various purposes, some immediate and others longer-term.

Immediate benefits

Young animals are relatively helpless at birth and need caregivers to provide food and protection in order to ensure their survival. Any young animal with an **innate** behaviour that will ensure closeness between itself and a caregiver will be more likely to survive. Attachment is likely to be an innate behaviour because it increases reproductive success.

Long-term benefits of attachment

In the long term, attachment provides a basis for emotional relationships. The early bond between caregiver and infant is the basis for all later emotional involvements, i.e. the infant is learning how to form an emotional or "love" relationship. According to Eibl-Eibesfeldt (1995) only warm-blooded animals form these bonds. Fish and reptiles may gather in groups but they form no bonds of love. Where animals care for their young, long-lasting affectionate bonds develop.

John Bowlby (1969) suggested that the means by which the early attachment relationship influences emotional development is via an **internal working model** about relationships. This model or schema represents the infant's knowledge about his/her relationship with the primary caregiver, generating expectations about other relationships. The model predicts how other people will behave and react to the child, about whether to trust other people, and so on—in short, it is a template [pattern] for all future relationships. Supporting evidence comes from Hazan and Shaver (1987; see page 110). They found that the type of attachments adults had had with their parents in childhood predicted their current style of love. Of key importance, those adults who reported that they had secure and warm attachments to their parents when they were young were the ones most likely to describe their adult love experiences as happy and trusting.

Grossmann and Grossmann (1991) found that children who were securely attached to their mothers as infants enjoyed close friendships later in childhood, whereas those who were avoidant or anxious reported either having no friends or few friends.

Perhaps even more importantly a relationship has been found between early attachment experiences and later styles of parenting. Quinton, Rutter, and Liddle (1984) studied women who had spent much of their early lives in institutions where they had little opportunity to form any attachments. These institutionalised women interacted poorly with their own children and were less sensitive, less supportive, and less warm than a group of non-institutionalised women.

How important are early attachments?

The research evidence suggests that early attachments form a basis for later relationships because they act as a model for these relationships. However, many other factors determine how successfully children cope with later relationships. For example, children who have formed close early attachments but then experience parental divorce later in childhood may have problems with later relationships. There are also important individual differences. For example, Lewis et al. (1984) looked at behaviour problems in older children and found a greater incidence of maladjustment in *boys* who had been classed as insecure at an earlier age, but not *girls*. Therefore we must be very cautious about the generalisations we make.

Perhaps more fundamentally, Harris (1998) suggested that the concept of *one* internal working model is just wrong. She claimed that the infant is well aware that the model is only of use with a particular person and will not function with, for example, an indifferent babysitter or a playful peer. So you can see that not everyone accepts that attachments are the basis for later relationships. An alternative model would be that each of us has an innate **temperament** (a character we have inherited) which determines how well we form relationships. If you are good at forming relationships because of the temperament you have inherited, this would explain why you had good early attachments and were also good at later relationships, and vice versa.

When Does an Infant Begin to Form an Attachment?

Stages in the development of attachment

The stage approach is a popular way to describe how children develop—to identify the ages at which certain typical changes occur, such as when an infant first crawls and then walks, and talks. Bowlby (1969) described four phases in the development of attachments (see box on page 106).

Schaffer and Emerson's stage theory

Schaffer and Emerson (1964) also developed a stage theory of attachment, arguing that infants go through *three* stages in the early development of attachments to others (see box below).

This was based on findings from their classic large-scale longitudinal study in which they followed 60 infants from a mainly working-class area of Glasgow over a period of two years, keeping a detailed record of their observations. The infants were observed every four weeks until they were 1 year old and then again at

Stages of attachment		
Asocial stage 0–6 weeks	**Indiscriminate attachment** 6 weeks–7 months	**Specific attachments** 7–11 months
Smiling and crying, not directed at any special individuals	Attention sought from different individuals	Strong attachment to one individual. Good attachments to others often follow

18 months. At the start of the investigation the youngest participant was 5 weeks and the oldest was 23 weeks old. Attachment was measured in two ways:

? **In what way might the sample used by Schaffer and Emerson make it difficult to generalise from these data?**

- *Using **separation protest** in seven everyday situations.* The infant was left alone in a room, left with other people, left in his/her pram outside the house, left in his/her pram outside the shops, left in his/her cot at night, put down after being held by an adult, or passed by while sitting in his/her cot or chair.
- *Using **stranger anxiety**.* Every visit started with the researcher approaching the infant and noting at what point the infant started to whimper, thus displaying anxiety.

Separation protest and stranger anxiety are signs that an attachment has formed. Before this stage of specific attachments, infants show neither of these behaviours.

Schaffer and Emerson found that half of the children showed their first specific attachment between 25 and 32 weeks (6–8 months). Fear of strangers occurred about a month later in all the children. Also, the intensity of attachment peaked in the first month after attachment behaviour first appeared, as measured by the strength of separation protest.

However, there were large individual differences. Intensely attached infants had mothers who responded quickly to their demands (high responsiveness) and who offered the child the most interaction, whereas infants who were weakly attached had mothers who failed to interact. In addition, soon after one main attachment was formed, the infants also became attached to other people, and by 18 months very few (13%) were attached to only one person and 31% had five or more attachments, such as the father, grandparent, or older sibling. In 65% of the children the first specific attachment was to the mother, and in a further 30% the mother was the first joint object of attachment. Finally, Schaffer and Emerson found that in 39% of the cases the person who usually fed, bathed, and changed the child was *not* the child's primary attachment object. Thus, many of the mothers (and some of the fathers) were not the person who performed these tasks yet they were the main attachment object.

? **Compare the method of measuring attachment behaviour used here with the methods used in the Strange Situation (see pages 95–96).**

Methodological criticisms can be made of this study, as data were collected *either* by direct observation *or* from the record kept by mothers, and these are both prone to bias and inaccuracy. Mothers were asked to record situations where separation protest was shown, and to whom these protests were directed. It is possible that a busy mother may have had to manufacture these records some days after the events. On the other hand, such data would have been more accurate than the retrospective recollections used in many studies, and would have had more ecological validity than data collected in laboratory observations (e.g. the Strange Situation, which is described shortly).

Evaluation of Schaffer and Emerson's stage theory

This stage theory is generally correct, in as much as infants are easily comforted by anyone. As they get older, they are less willing to be separated from their caregiver, and will show **separation anxiety**. This is the main characteristic of being attached. We know when an infant is attached because he/she recognises the *absence* of an attachment figure and becomes anxious. Prior to this, absence causes little concern.

Infants distrust strangers and cling to familiar people.

In addition, infants also start to show stranger anxiety—when a strange person comes close and tries to interact, the infant may withdraw and show signs of distress. Both of these forms of anxiety show that the infant has now formed schemas for known and unknown people, and has reached an emotional stage of development where the unknown creates a fear response.

However, the asocial stage (in which infants' emotional reactions are not directed at specific individuals) may not be quite as asocial as Schaffer and Emerson presumed. Even very young infants actually do respond to one special person in a unique way. Carpenter (1975) demonstrated that 2-week-old infants can recognise their mother's face and voice. He set up a situation in which infants looked at a face while hearing a voice. Sometimes the face and the voice belonged to the same person, and sometimes they did not. The infants looked at the face for the longest time when it was the mother's face, and when it was accompanied by her voice. More convincing evidence that the infants recognised their mother's face and voice was obtained when they were presented with their mother's face but an unfamiliar voice, or vice versa. Most of the infants found this distressing, and rapidly looked away from the face.

A problem with Carpenter's study is that those rating the behaviour of the infants knew which condition was being used at any time. However, the findings have been supported by other research using improved versions of Carpenter's design. For example, Bushnell, Sai, and Mullin (1989) presented 2-day-old babies with the faces of their mother and a female stranger until they had spent a total of 20 seconds fixating on one of the faces. Almost two-thirds of them showed a preference for their mother over the stranger, indicating that they had some ability to recognise their own mother within a few days of birth.

? Might Carpenter have predicted that infants would become distressed by seeing their mother's face but hearing someone else's voice? If so, to what extent was this study ethical?

? How else could the problems of interpretation of Carpenter's study have been overcome?

Individual Differences in Attachment

Most psychological theories are written in a way which suggests that everyone is the same. However, as I am sure you will agree, each one of us is different. For example, Schaffer and Emerson found that some babies like cuddling whereas others prefer not to be touched. We also saw in this same study that some infants are attached to one person, whereas others have multiple attachments (remember that, at 18 months, only 13% of the children were attached to only one person).

These are **individual differences**. The same can be said about differences both within and between **cultures**. In the next part of this section we will look at cross-cultural differences. First of all we will consider individual differences *within* our culture.

All normal children are attached to a caregiver, even those children who have been neglected or abused (see box on abuse and attachment, page 97). The main individual difference lies in the degree to which a child is attached, known as **secure** and **insecure attachment**.

Secure and insecure attachment

Most child psychologists claim that the nature of the attachment between an infant and its caregiver (e.g. mother) is of great importance to its emotional

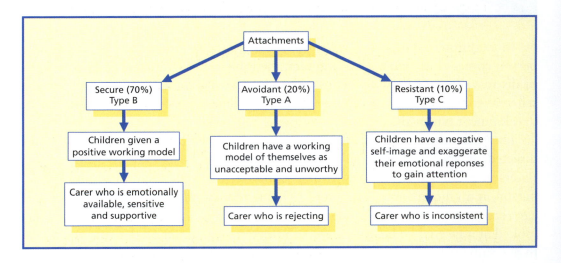

Ainsworth and Bell proposed three attachment types (A, B, and C). Main and Soloman proposed a fourth category, Type D, which they described as "Insecure: Disorganised".

development. However, it is rarely possible for researchers to observe infants and their caregivers over long periods of time in the home setting, and this makes it hard to assess infant–caregiver attachments. When we describe a child as "being attached" this implies a secure attachment. Alas, not all children are as securely attached as others. Mary Ainsworth provided us with the **Strange Situation** as a means to test the quality of an infant's attachment to its caregiver. Studies using this form of assessment have found there are four types of attachment: **secure** (also called type B), **avoidant** (type A), **resistant** (type C), and **disorganised** (type D). All the last three are examples of different kinds of insecure attachment. Secure attachment is most likely to be related to healthy emotional and social development.

Ainsworth and Bell (1970, see Key Study below) devised the most popular way of assessing infant attachment in their Strange Situation procedure, and that helps to make this study of major importance. An infant (normally aged between 12 and 18 months) is observed during a sequence of eight short episodes. For some of the time, the infant is with its caregiver. At other times, it is with its caregiver and a stranger, or just with a stranger, or on its own. Overall, the key observations that are made relate to the child's reactions to the stranger (**stranger anxiety**), to separation from the caregiver (**separation anxiety**), and to being reunited with its caregiver.

Key Study: Secure/insecure attachments

Ainsworth and Bell's (1970) study of individual differences in types of attachments using the Strange Situation.

Aims: Ainsworth and Bell aimed to investigate individual variation in infant attachments; in particular differences between secure and insecure attachments. They hoped that their method of assessing attachments, the Strange Situation test, would prove to be a reliable and valid measure of attachments.

Procedure: The Strange Situation test lasts for just over 20 minutes and was used on American infants aged between 12 and 18 months. It takes place in the laboratory and the method used is controlled observation.
The Strange Situation consists of EIGHT stages or episodes as follows:

Stage	People in the room	Procedure
1 (30 seconds)	Mother or caregiver and infant plus researcher	Researcher brings the others into the room and rapidly leaves
2 (3 minutes)	Mother or caregiver and infant	Mother or caregiver sits; infant is free to explore
3 (3 minutes)	Stranger plus mother or caregiver and infant	Stranger comes in and after a while talks to mother or caregiver and then to the infant. Mother or caregiver leaves the room
4 (3 minutes)	Stranger and infant	Stranger keeps trying to talk and play with the infant
5 (3 minutes)	Mother or caregiver and infant	Stranger leaves as mother or caregiver returns to the infant. At the end of this stage, the mother or caregiver leaves
6 (3 minutes)	Infant	Infant is alone in the room
7 (3 minutes)	Stranger and infant	Stranger returns and tries to interact with the infant
8 (3 minutes)	Mother or caregiver and infant	Mother or caregiver returns and interacts with the infant, and the stranger leaves

? **What are the strengths of the experimental approach used by Ainsworth and Bell?**

EXAM HINT
If you are asked to outline individual differences in attachment, you could use Ainsworth's research and identify:
- Secure attachment: Describe the characteristics of Type B
- Insecure attachments: Describe the characteristics of Type A, (anxious/avoidant), and Type C (anxious/resistant).

Findings: Several important findings were reported by Ainsworth and Bell (1970) and by Ainsworth et al. (1978). There were considerable individual differences in behaviour and emotional response in the Strange Situation.

Most of the infants displayed behaviour categorised as typical of secure attachment (70%), while 10% were resistant, and 20% avoidant. The securely attached infants were distressed when separated from the caregiver, and sought contact and soothing on reunion. Resistant attachment was characterised by ambivalence (conflicting emotions) and inconsistency, as the infants were very distressed at separation but resisted the caregiver on reunion. Avoidant attachment was characterised by detachment as the infants did not seek contact with the caregiver and showed little distress at separation.

Conclusions: The Strange Situation is generally regarded as a good measure of attachment in that it allows us to discriminate between attachment types. It was concluded that secure attachment is the preferred type of attachment. Implications include the linking of secure attachment to healthy emotional and social development and the type of attachment to maternal sensitivity and responsiveness.

Criticisms

- The validity of the classification was questioned and a fourth attachment type suggested by Main and Solomon (1986). They found that a small number of infants displayed disorganised attachment, in which the infants showed no consistent pattern of behaviour, and fitted none of the three main attachment types. However, Main and Solomon accepted the validity of the three attachment types identified by Ainsworth et al. (1978).
- The Strange Situation was created and tested in the USA. As a result, it may be culturally biased (ethnocentric), reflecting the norms and values of American culture. The Strange Situation test assumes that behaviour has the same meaning in ALL cultures, which is unlikely. This probable lack of generalisability means that the Strange Situation's **external validity** (validity outside the original context in which it was used) must be questioned. There is more information on this in the Key Study of Van IJzendoorn and Kroonenberg (1988), which is discussed shortly.
- The Strange Situation is artificial in ways that may well distort behaviour. For example, some mothers or other caregivers are likely to behave differently towards their child when they know they are being observed than they would do at home when they are alone with their child.
- Ainsworth and Bell (1970) put infants into three categories. This is neat and tidy, but oversimplifies matters because infants *within* any given category differ from each other in their attachment behaviour. This issue is discussed further below.

Note: If the question asks for findings or conclusions only, you could include research by Main and Solomon (1986, see above), Main and Weston (1981, see p.98), Kagan (1984, see p.99), and Belsky and Rovine (1987, see p.99).

[?] **What factors determine infants' attachment style?**

The findings from several studies using the Strange Situation were reported by Ainsworth et al. (1978). The infant's reactions to the various episodes allow us to categorise its attachment type (disorganised attachment was discovered later and is discussed shortly):

- *Secure attachment*: the infant is distressed by the caregiver's absence. However, he/she rapidly returns to a state of contentment after the caregiver's return, immediately seeking contact with the caregiver. There is a clear difference in the infant's reaction to the caregiver and to the stranger. Ainsworth et al. reported that 70% of American infants show secure attachment.

- *Resistant attachment*: the infant is insecure in the presence of the caregiver, and becomes very distressed when the caregiver leaves. He/she resists contact with the caregiver upon return, and is wary of the stranger. About 10% of American infants were found to be resistant.
- *Avoidant attachment*: the infant doesn't seek contact with the caregiver, and shows little distress when separated. The infant avoids contact with the caregiver upon return. The infant treats the stranger in a similar way to the caregiver, often avoiding him/her. About 20% of American infants were avoidant.

Why do some infants have a secure attachment with their caregiver, whereas others do not? According to Ainsworth's (1982) caregiving hypothesis, the *sensitivity* of the caregiver is of crucial importance. Most of the caregivers of securely attached infants are very sensitive to their needs, and respond to their infants in an emotionally expressive way. In contrast, the caregivers of resistant infants were interested in them, but often misunderstood their infants' behaviour. Of particular importance, these caregivers tended to vary in the way they treated their infants. As a result, the infant could not rely on the caregiver's emotional support.

Finally, there are the caregivers of avoidant infants. Ainsworth et al. (1978) reported that many of these caregivers were uninterested in their infants, often rejecting them, and tending to be self-centred and rigid in their behaviour. However, some caregivers of avoidant infants behaved rather differently. These caregivers acted in a suffocating way, always interacting with their infants even when the infants didn't want any interaction. What these types of caregivers have in common is that they are not very sensitive to the needs of their infants.

According to Ainsworth (1982), securely attached infants have caregivers that are emotionally sensitive to their needs.

Abuse and attachment

Harris (1998) notes that it is a "sad and paradoxical fact that abuse may actually increase a child's clinginess." A number of studies have investigated the consequences of neglect or abuse on the bonds that form between caregiver and infant. In one of Harlow's studies of rhesus monkeys, the cloth "mother" blasted the infant monkey with a strong current of compressed air (Rosenblum & Harlow, 1963). The findings were that these abused monkeys appeared to be *more* strongly attached to their "mother" than the other monkeys. This is confirmed by a report from a researcher studying imprinting in ducklings. He found that when he accidentally stepped on the foot of one of the ducklings who had already imprinted on him, then the duckling followed him more closely than ever (Harris, 1998).

However, this link between abuse and attachment may not extend to humans. Lynch and Roberts (1982) suggested that abuse leads to bonding failure rather than stronger attachment. One example is seen in mothers described as "primary rejectors" (Jones et al., 1987). These tend to be middle-class women who have had an unwanted child, a difficult pregnancy, and/or experienced early separation from their infant due to problems at the time of birth. The mothers may have good relationships with other children. Rejection starts from the time of birth and the mother–infant relationship never recovers. It is possible that children who experience this "primary rejection" go on to suffer from reactive attachment disorder, which is described on page 103. These children do not appear to be attached to their rejecting caregiver, and in fact are unable to form any attachments. Therefore, this suggests that abuse does not create a stronger bond in humans.

Why is the research reported by Ainsworth and Bell (1970) and by Ainsworth et al. (1978) important? First, Ainsworth devised an effective way of assessing infants' attachment behaviour in a relatively short period of time. Second, the three main types of infant attachment identified by Ainsworth et al. are still regarded as the most important ones even after numerous studies by other researchers and the identification of a small number of infants showing disorganised attachment (Main & Solomon, 1986). Third, as we will see, there is reasonable evidence that the type of attachment shown by infants influences their subsequent emotional development.

Evaluation of the Strange Situation assessment

Studies that have used the Strange Situation have found it is both reliable and valid. The question of **reliability** is determined by seeing if the same child, tested at different times, produces the same result. Main, Kaplan, and Cassidy (1985) assessed infants in the Strange Situation before the age of 18 months with both their mothers and fathers. When the children were retested at the age of 6, the researchers found that 100% of the secure babies were still classified as secure, and 75% of avoidant babies remained in the same classification. When differences occur, these are often associated with changes in the form of care, such as separation of parents (Melhuish, 1993). Bar-Heim, Sutton, Fox, and Marvin (2000) found that only 38% of children stayed in the same attachment category between 14 and 58 months of age. Those whose attachment category changed were much more likely to have mothers who reported several negative life events than were those whose attachment category remained the same. Overall, the Strange Situation often produces reasonably reliable results unless there are major changes or problems within the family.

The issue of **validity** concerns the extent to which the Strange Situation measure is "true" in the sense of measuring what it is supposed to be measuring. In terms of attachment, if the Strange Situation assessment is valid, then we would expect that securely attached infants should be better adjusted socially and emotionally at later ages than an insecurely attached child. Most of the evidence suggests the Strange Situation is reasonably valid within most Western cultures—even though its external validity across cultures may be limited. For example, Stams, Juffer, and van IJzendoorn (2002) assessed child–mother attachment security at the age of 12 months in adopted children. Children who were securely attached at that age had superior social and cognitive development six years later.

It appears that the Strange Situation is both a reliable and a valid form of assessment—although we have raised doubts about its external validity. However, there is one significant flaw to the procedure. The essential concept of the Strange Situation assessment is that one is testing something about the *child*, some aspect of their personality—how securely (or insecurely) attached they are. But this may not be the case. One may be testing the *relationship* between the infant and their caregiver, rather than the resulting attachment type. Main and Weston (1981) found that children behaved differently depending on which parent they were with in the Strange Situation, which suggests that attachment type is *not* a consistent individual difference. But *most* children tend to have the same relationships throughout childhood and so it *appears* that this is their attachment type. This line of argument suggests that the whole basis of the Strange Situation assessment is somewhat flawed.

There is a second important issue. It is neat and tidy to assign all infants to one out of three (or four) attachment categories, but real life is *not* neat and

Studies that look at the association between two variables have the drawback that they appear to demonstrate cause and effect, whereas all they really show is whether a correlation exists.

tidy. For example, two children may both be put into the category of secure attachment, but one child may be significantly more securely attached than the other. Fraley and Spieker (2003) argued that we should do away with categories and instead focus on the extent to which children show certain types of behaviour (e.g. angry and resistant strategies; avoidant/withdrawal strategies). This allows us to identify small differences among children, and is a more sensitive and flexible approach than the one based on a small number of categories.

The temperament hypothesis

An alternative way to explain the correlation between early attachment type and later development is by using the **temperament hypothesis**. Kagan (1984) proposed that an infant's relationships, both attachments with primary caregivers and those later in life, can be explained in terms of the infant's innate temperament (the character that it inherits through its genes). Some people are innately good at forming relationships whereas others aren't.

Kagan further argued that the caregiving sensitivity hypothesis (see page 114) exaggerates the role played by the caregiver in the development of attachment and ignores the part played by the infant's temperament or personality in determining his/her attachment to the mother. Belsky and Rovine (1987) reported that newborns who showed signs of behavioural instability (e.g. tremors or shaking) were less likely to become securely attached to their mother. In other words, it was their innate personality that was the key factor in the formation of an attachment.

Evaluation of the temperament hypothesis

Much of the evidence fails to support Kagan's temperament hypothesis. For example, infants' temperament as assessed by their parents is not usually associated with their attachment type as determined by the Strange Situation assessment (Durkin, 1995).

It is probable that neither relationship (caregiver sensitivity) nor temperament is wholly responsible for the development of attachment, but that there is an *interaction* between them (Belsky & Rovine, 1987), meaning that *both* factors make a contribution in combination. Supporting evidence was reported by Spangler (1990) in a study of German mothers whose responsiveness to their infants was influenced by their perceptions of the infants' temperament.

Cross-cultural Variation in Attachment

If attachment is an innate behaviour then we would expect attachment behaviours to be very similar around the world.

Secure and insecure attachment

Cross-cultural variations in attachment have been studied using the Strange Situation test. Findings for

> **EXAM HINT**
> If you are asked what factors are important in the development of attachments, the two factors that you should mention are:
> - The infant (temperament hypothesis).
> - The caregiver (sensitivity hypothesis).

> **KEY TERM**
> **Cross-cultural variations in attachment:** cross-cultural variations refer to the fact that behaviour, attitudes, norms, and values differ across cultures. This is because cultures socially construct different values and norms, etc. Thus, the relationships between infants and caregivers vary across cultures because of different childrearing styles and beliefs about which qualities should be nurtured. This is evident in the cross-cultural differences that research has suggested between individualistic and collectivist cultures.

? How similar is attachment behaviour in different cultures?

infants in the United States, Israel, Japan, and Germany were reported by Sagi, van IJzendoorn, and Koren-Karie (1991). Their findings for the American infants were similar to those reported by Ainsworth et al. (1978): 71% of them showed secure attachment, 12% showed anxious and resistant attachment, and 17% were anxious and avoidant.

The Israeli infants behaved rather differently. Secure attachment was shown by 62% of the Israeli infants, 33% were anxious and resistant, and only 5% were anxious and avoidant. These infants lived on a Kibbutz, looked after much of the time by adults who were not part of their family. As they had a close relationship with their mothers, they tended not to be anxious and avoidant.

Japanese mothers practically never leave their infants alone with a stranger. In spite of the differences in child-rearing practices in Japan and Israel, the Japanese infants showed similar attachment styles to the Israeli ones. Two-thirds of them (68%) had a secure attachment, 32% were anxious and resistant, and none was anxious and avoidant.

Israeli children are accustomed to being separated from their mother, but rarely encounter complete strangers, so their resistant behaviour was perhaps due to the presence of the stranger. In contrast, Japanese children are practically never separated from their mother, and this would be the main cause of their resistant attachment behaviour.

Finally, the German infants showed a different pattern of attachment from the other three groups of infants. Only 40% of them were securely attached, 49% were anxious and avoidant, and 11% were anxious and resistant. Grossmann et al. (1985) obtained very similar findings, suggesting that German culture requires distance between parents and children: "the ideal is an independent, non-clinging infant who does not make demands on the parents but rather unquestioningly obeys their commands" (p.253).

Evaluation of cross-cultural attachment studies

As we have seen, there is much research using the Strange Situation test suggesting that there are interesting cross-cultural differences in infant attachment. This

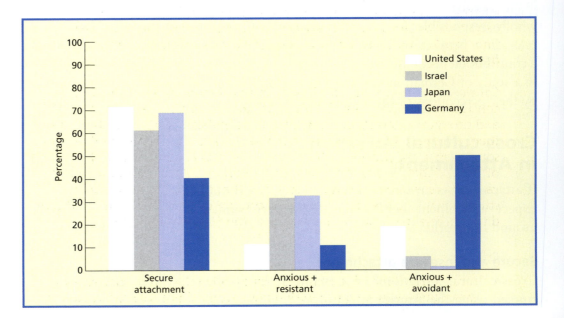

Children from different countries vary in their attachment types. The graph summarises research from Sagi et al. (1991) and Ainsworth and Bell (1970).

research has led to various theories trying to identify what is responsible for the variations in infant attachment from one culture to another.

Van IJzendoorn and Kroonenberg (1988; see Key Study below) added greatly to our understanding of cross-cultural differences in infant attachment. They carried out a meta-analysis (which involves combining data from many studies) to assess attachment based on research in many countries. One of their key findings was that the variation in attachment *within* cultures was 1½ times greater than the variation *between* cultures.

Key Study: Cross-cultural variation

Van IJzendoorn and Kroonenberg's (1988) study of cross-cultural variation in attachment.

Aims: Van IJzendoorn and Kroonenberg aimed to investigate cross-cultural variation in attachment types through a meta-analysis of research (combining data from many studies) in which attachments in other cultures had been considered. They compared ONLY the findings of studies that had used the Strange Situation in order to draw inferences about the external validity of this as a measure of attachment in other populations and other settings.

Procedure: A meta-analysis was conducted which compared the findings of 32 studies that had used the Strange Situation to measure attachment and to classify the attachment relationship between the mother and the infant. Research from eight different nations was compared, including Western cultures (e.g. USA, Great Britain, Germany) and non-Western cultures (e.g. Japan, China, Israel). Van IJzendoorn and Kroonenberg researched various databases for studies on attachment.

Findings: Considerable consistency in the overall distribution of attachment types was found across all cultures. Secure attachment was the most common type of attachment in all eight nations. However, significant differences were found in the distributions of insecure attachments. For example, in Western cultures the dominant insecure type is avoidant, whereas in non-Western cultures it is resistant, with China being the only exception, as avoidant and resistant were distributed equally. A key finding was that there was 1½ times greater variation *within* cultures than *between* cultures.

Conclusions: The overall consistency in attachment types leads to the conclusion that there may be universal characteristics that underpin infant and caregiver interactions. However, the significant variations show that there are greater variations in attachment types among different groups in society than had previously been assumed. Implications include the linking of the variation in attachment to child-rearing practices. Also, the greater variation found *within* cultures suggests that sub-cultural comparison studies may be more valid than cross-cultural comparisons. The significant differences also question the validity of the Strange Situation.

? Are there problems with using the Strange Situation in very different cultures?

Criticisms

- This study is limited in that it doesn't really tell us WHY patterns of attachment vary so much within any given culture. We can speculate that variations in child-rearing practices are important, but the study didn't provide any concrete evidence to support this.

- The greater variation found within than between cultures shows that it is wrong to think of any culture as a whole. This means that cross-cultural comparisons based on the assumption that there is uniformity of behaviour within each culture lack validity. It is oversimplified to view Britain or America as one single culture, as within each country there are many sub-cultures differing in the nature of attachment types. Thus, the findings may not be representative of the culture they are assumed to represent, and will generalise back only to the sub-cultures that were sampled.

- The Strange Situation was created and tested in the USA, which means that it may be culturally biased (ethnocentric). In other words, the Strange Situation reflects the norms and values of American culture (e.g. the belief that attachment is related to anxiety on separation). Those who use the Strange Situation assume that behaviour has the same meaning in all cultures, when in fact social constructions of behaviour differ greatly. For example, in Japan young infants are very rarely parted from their mother. As a result, the Strange Situation poses more of a threat to them than to Western infants, and so their severe distress may not be indicative of insecure attachment. Thus, the Strange Situation lacks external validity, which means the findings and insights may be less meaningful than used to be thought.

- In spite of its limitations, the Strange Situation is the only test of infant attachment that has been used in several different countries. Perhaps findings from the test could be used to understand some of the main sub-cultural differences found within any given country.

Note: If the question asks for findings or conclusions only, you could include research by Sagi et al. (1991, see p.100) and Grossmann et al. (1985, see p.100).

EXAM HINT

If you are asked to outline two cross-cultural variations in attachment, you could use the Van IJzendoorn and Kroonenberg (1988) study to discuss:

- The higher number of avoidant infants in individualistic cultures.
- The higher number of resistant infants in collectivistic cultures.

If you are asked to outline two factors that influence cross-cultural attachment, you could discuss:

- Child-rearing practices.
- The different cultural norms of individualistic vs collectivistic cultures.

If you are asked to outline two effects of cross-cultural variation in attachment, you could discuss:

- The higher incidence of avoidant attachment in individualistic cultures.
- The higher incidence of resistant attachment in collectivistic cultures.

Why are van IJzendoorn and Kroonenberg's findings important? First, they were the first researchers to carry out a thorough meta-analysis to consider *all* cross-cultural findings using the Strange Situation. Second, their findings indicate strongly that it is wrong to think of any given culture as consisting of the same practices. The notion that there is a *single* British or American culture is a gross oversimplification. In fact, there are several sub-cultures within most large countries which probably differ very much in their child-rearing practices. Third, and related to the second point, the findings of van IJzendoorn and Kroonenberg suggest that the idea of making cross-cultural comparisons lacks validity.

Therefore, we can see that the Strange Situation is based on cultural assumptions. This is called an **imposed etic**, the use of a technique developed in one culture to study another culture. This means that the cross-cultural evidence is inherently flawed by the use of an invalid measuring tool. The same conclusion may be true for sub-cultures within America and Britain.

Explanations of Attachment

We will now consider some of the major theories of attachment. They *all* provide explanations for why attachments are formed and maintained.

The psychodynamic approach

Sigmund Freud (1924) put forward a simple account of the infant's attachment to its mother: "The reason why the infant in arms wants to perceive the presence of its mother is only because it already knows by experience that she satisfies all its needs without delay." In other words, babies like being with their mothers because the mother is their source of food, comfort, and warmth. This explanation is sometimes referred to as focusing on "cupboard love"

Freud's views on early attachment stemmed from his theory of development, described on pages 33 to 34. According to this theory, adult personality depends very much on childhood experiences. Childhood can be divided into *five* stages of psychosexual development, stages during which the child is biologically driven to seek pleasure in certain ways. The first stage of psychosexual development is the oral stage when pleasure is derived orally, for example sucking at the mother's breast. The result is an attachment to the mother because she is associated with the satisfaction of pleasure. This first attachment has long-lasting effects. Freud argued that the mother's status was "established unalterably for a whole lifetime as the first and strongest love-object and as the prototype of all later love-relations" (1924, p.188). The mother's role as a prototype means that she serves as a model or example for an infant or young child, influencing his/her choice of partners and experiences of love as an adult.

Evaluation of the psychodynamic approach

Freud's theory suggests that attachment behaviour in babies will be related to feeding but we will see later that this is *not* the case. Harlow's research with young monkeys (see page 112) showed that food alone could not explain attachment. Schaffer and Emerson (1964, see page 91) found with about 40% of human infants that the adult who fed, bathed, and changed the infant was *not* the person to whom the infant was most attached. Thus, there is not the simple link between food and attachment behaviour assumed by Freud. Infants are most likely to become attached to adults who are responsive to them, and who provide them with much stimulation in the form of touching and playing.

? Do you think that there are problems with generalising from the behaviour of one species to another?

Learning theory

The basic principle of **learning theory** is that all behaviour has been learned (it is not innate). Learning theorists (also called "behaviourists") believe that learning is the result of conditioning—either **classical conditioning** or **operant conditioning** (see Chapter 2, Section 4). A reminder of these processes is shown in the box, see overleaf.

An infant is born with reflex responses. The stimulus of food (an unconditioned stimulus) produces a sense of pleasure (an unconditioned response). The person providing the food (usually the mother) becomes associated with this pleasure and therefore becomes a conditioned stimulus which independently will produce the

Classical conditioning

- Unconditioned stimulus (US) e.g. food → causes → reflex response e.g. salivation.
- Neutral stimulus (NS) e.g. bell → causes → no response.
- NS and US are paired in time (they occur).
- NS (e.g. bell) is now a conditioned stimulus (CS) → which produces → a conditioned response (CR) [a new stimulus–response link is learned, the bell causes salivation].

Operant conditioning

- A behaviour that has a positive effect is more likely to be repeated.
- Negative reinforcement (escape from aversive stimulus) is agreeable.
- Punishment is disagreeable.

unconditioned stimulus (pleasure). The food-giver then becomes a source of pleasure independent of whether or not food is supplied. This, according to learning theory, is the basis of the attachment bond.

Dollard and Miller (1950) offered a further learning theory explanation for the development of attachments that focuses on motivation, the explanation of what it is that drives behaviour:

- All humans possess various primary motives or drives, such as the primary drives of hunger and thirst.
- A person will be "driven" to seek food to satisfy hunger.
- Obtaining food results in drive reduction which is rewarding.
- According to the principles of operant conditioning anything that is rewarding is more likely to be repeated and therefore this behaviour is repeated (learned).
- The caregiver provides the food which reduces the drive, thus becoming a **secondary reinforcer**.
- From then on the infant seeks to be with this person because they are now a source of reward in themselves. The infant has thus become attached.

Mothers also learn to be attached to their infants because of reinforcement. For example, mothers may be rewarded when they make their offspring smile or stop crying.

Evaluation of learning theory

In fact, as we have just seen, infants often become attached to adults who are *not* involved in feeding or basic caregiving (Schaffer & Emerson, 1964), so learning theory cannot be the whole explanation. Learning theory is generally criticised for being **reductionist**, "reducing" the complexities of human behaviour to oversimple ideas such as stimulus, response, and reinforcement, then using these ideas as building blocks to explain complex human behaviours such as attachment. It may well be that these ideas are too simple to explain a complex behaviour such as attachment.

Social learning theory

Social learning theory is a more sophisticated version of this type of theory. Learning theory proposes that conditioning takes place *directly*, with no intervening mental process. In other words, direct links are formed between stimuli and responses. For example, the rat sees a lever and presses it to receive food. Social learning theory, on the other hand, suggests that we also learn in a more *indirect* way which is known as vicarious reinforcement. What happens in **vicarious reinforcement** is that we learn a new behaviour by seeing someone else performing that behaviour and being rewarded or reinforced for performing it. According to social learning theorists, the kind of imitation involved in vicarious reinforcement is very important.

Hay and Vespo (1988) used social learning theory to explain attachment. They suggested that attachment occurs because parents "deliberately teach their children to love them and to understand human relationships" (p.82), for example by:

- *Modelling*: Learning based on observing and imitating a model's behaviour.
- *Direct instruction*: Providing reward or reinforcement when the child behaves in the required way.
- *Social facilitation*: Using the presence of others to encourage the child to understand positive relationships between people.

Some psychologists think of attachment behaviour as something that is learned because it is reinforced. Young children may learn about human relationships by imitating the affectionate behaviours of their parents.

Evaluation of social learning theory

The greatest strength of the social learning approach is that it has led to a detailed consideration of the interactional processes occurring between parents and children. Also, at least some of the attachment learning shown by infants does depend on processes such as these. On the negative side, as Durkin (1995) pointed out, the strong emotional intensity of many parent–child attachments is not really *explained* by social learning theorists.

Bowlby's theory of attachment

John Bowlby (1907–1990) was a child psychoanalyst whose main interest was in the relationship between caregiver and child. He realised that Freud's views of the importance of maternal care could be combined with the ethological concept of imprinting to produce a new theory. What does that mean? **Ethologists** study animals in their natural surroundings, and **imprinting** is the tendency for the young of some species of birds to follow the first moving object they see and to continue to follow it after that. The idea was that infants would show imprinting to their own mother, and this would explain the strong attachment most infants have for their mother. This theory has had a profound effect on the way psychologists think about attachment and infant development. This key aspect of Bowlby's approach is discussed in more detail on page 111.

The fundamental principle of Bowlby's theory is that **attachment** is an innate and **adaptive** process, for both infant and parent, and as such it provides an evolutionary perspective. Attachment behaviour has evolved and endured because it promotes survival, as proposed by Darwin's **theory of evolution**. Attachment promotes survival in many ways:

1. *Safety*. Attachment results in a desire to maintain proximity and thus ensure safety. Both infant and caregiver experience feelings of anxiety when separated and this creates a proximity-seeking drive (striving to be close to the other person).
2. *Emotional relationships*. Attachment enables the infant to learn how to form and conduct healthy emotional relationships. Bowlby used the concept of the **internal working model**—a set of conscious and/or unconscious rules and expectations regarding our relationships with others—to explain how this

EXAM HINT
You need to know two explanations of attachment BUT it is best to make sure one of these is BOWLBY's explanation as this provides the most content and so would be the most suitable for the question: "Outline ONE explanation of attachment" for six marks.

happens. This model develops out of the primary attachment relationship and is a model or **schema** used as a template for future relationships.

3. *A secure base for exploration.* Attachment also provides a safe base for exploration, a process that is of fundamental importance for mental development. The child often returns periodically to "touch base" with their attachment figure. An insecurely attached child is less willing to wander. Exploration is very important for cognitive development, as shown in a study by Bus and van IJzendoorn (1988). They assessed the attachment types of children aged 2 years old, using the Strange Situation. Three years later the children were assessed in terms of their reading interests and skills, and their pre-school teachers also

---

Bowlby's proposed phases in the development of attachment

Bowlby proposed that an infant is born with a set of behavioural systems that are ready to be activated, for example crying, sucking, and clinging (all called "social releasers"), and an ability to respond to the "stimuli that commonly emanate from a human being"—sounds, faces, and touch. Shortly thereafter other behaviours appear which are equally innate though not present at birth, such as smiling and crawling. From these small beginnings, sophisticated systems soon develop.

In the table below, four phases in the development of attachments are described, with very approximate ages.

Phase 1 Birth–8 weeks	Orientation and signals towards people without discrimination of one special person	Infants behave in characteristic and friendly ways towards other people but their ability to discriminate between them is very limited, e.g. they may just recognise familiar voices
Phase 2 About 8/10 weeks–6 months	Orientation and signals directed towards one or more special people	Infants continue to be generally friendly but there is beginning to be a marked difference of behaviour towards one mother-figure or primary caregiver
Phase 3 6 months through to 1–2 years old	Maintenance of proximity to a special person by means of locomotion as well as signals to that person	The infant starts to follow his or her mother-figure, greet her (him) when she (he) returns, and use her (him) as a base from which to explore. The infant selects other people as subsidiary attachment figures. At the same time the infant's friendly responses to other people decrease and the infant treats strangers with increasing caution
Phase 4 Starts around the age of 2	Formation of a goal-corrected partnership	The child develops insight into the mother-figure's behaviour and this opens up a whole new relationship where the infant can consciously influence what she (or he) does. This is the beginning of a real partnership

Adapted from J. Bowlby (1969), *Attachment and love, Vol. 1: Attachment,* London: Hogarth.

completed a questionnaire about preparatory reading and intelligence. The securely attached children showed more interest in written material than did the insecurely attached children, regardless of their intelligence and the amount of preparatory reading instruction.

The role of social releasers

According to Bowlby, attachment must be innate, or the infant or parent might not show it. It must also be reciprocal because both infant and caregiver must actively take part. The infant innately elicits caregiving from its mother-figure by means of **social releasers**, behaviours such as smiling or crying which encourage a response—humans are innately programmed to respond to these social releasers.

Most people feel uncomfortable when they hear an infant, or an adult, crying, which helps to ensure that someone will respond. It is a mechanism that has evolved to maximise survival by keeping the caregiver(s) close. These innate behaviours and innate responses are a fundamental part of the process of forming an attachment.

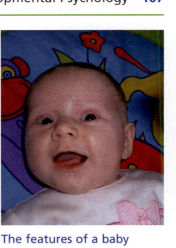

The features of a baby face are very appealing. They act as a "social releaser", a social stimulus that "releases" a desire to offer caregiving.

? **How should you respond when you hear a baby cry?**

A critical period

I mentioned earlier that Bowlby was influenced in his thinking by the work of the ethologists, who study various species in their natural environment. The ethologists emphasise the concept of a **critical period**. In the case of biological characteristics, development has to take place during a set period, otherwise it won't take place at all. As was mentioned earlier, ethologists suggested that this principle of a critical period might apply to attachment. One ethologist, Konrad Lorenz, found that the young of some species of birds tended to follow the first moving object they saw on hatching, and they continued to follow it thereafter. This is imprinting, the chief characteristics of which are:

1. It occurs during a short critical period. If the infant is not exposed to a "mother" within a critical time window, then imprinting will not take place.
2. It is irreversible. Once an imprint is formed it cannot be changed.
3. It has lasting consequences. It results in the formation of a bond between caregiver and its young and so has consequences in the short term for safety and food. It also affects the individual in the long term because it acts as a template or pattern for future reproductive partners. For example, Immelmann (1972) arranged for zebra finches to be raised by Bengalese finches, and vice versa. In later years, when the finches were given a free choice, they preferred to mate with the species on which they had imprinted.

> **Imprinting**
>
> The BBC television series *Supernature* used imprinting as a means of obtaining spectacular close-up film of geese in flight. A member of the production company made sure he was the first thing a group of goslings saw when they hatched, and from then on the birds followed him everywhere, even into the office! When the geese were young adults, their adopted "parent" took to the skies as a passenger in a microlight aircraft. The geese followed and flew alongside, allowing him to film their flight to produce a truly breathtaking sequence for the television series.

Like attachment, this **bonding** process is desirable because it means the offspring are more likely to survive and therefore the parents' genes are passed on.

Lorenz hatched some goslings and arranged it so that he would be the first thing that they saw. From then on they followed him everywhere and showed no recognition of their actual mother. The goslings formed a picture (imprint) of the object they were to follow.

Imprinting as an explanation of attachment. These characteristics of imprinting have been challenged to some extent. For example, Guiton (1966) found he could reverse imprinting in chickens. Guiton's chickens were initially imprinted on some yellow rubber gloves. When the chickens matured, this early imprint acted as a mate template or pattern and the chickens tried to mate with the rubber gloves, which appears to support the claims made for imprinting. However, Guiton found that later, after spending time with their own species, the chickens were able to engage in normal sexual behaviour with their own kind.

The idea of a critical period is too strong and it would be more appropriate to describe it as a **sensitive period**. Thus, even though imprinting is *less* likely to occur outside a particular time window, imprinting does still occur at other times. The notion of a sensitive period is that imprinting takes place most easily at a certain time but still may happen at any time during development.

Applying imprinting to humans. Bowlby (1969) claimed that something like imprinting occurs in infants. He proposed that infants have an innate tendency to orient towards one individual. This attachment is innate, and like all biological mechanisms should have a critical period for its development. Bowlby argued that this critical period ends at some point between 1 and 3 years of age, after which it would no longer be possible to establish a powerful attachment to the caregiver.

Klaus and Kennell (1976) were in general agreement with Bowlby (1958) that early contact between infant and mother is of great importance. In fact they argued that there is a *sensitive period* immediately after birth in which bonding (an initial part of the attachment process) can occur through skin-to-skin contact. Klaus and Kennell compared the progress of two groups of infants. One group had much more contact with their mother during the first three days of life. One month later, more bonding had occurred in the extended-contact group than in the routine contact group. During feeding, the extended-contact mothers cuddled and comforted their babies more, and they also maintained more eye contact with them.

Later research generally failed to repeat the findings of Klaus and Kennell (1976). Durkin (1995) pointed out that most of the mothers in the original study were unmarried teenagers from disadvantaged backgrounds; therefore, it may not be

? Do you think that there are any ethical issues related to studies such as Klaus and Kennell's?

? What is an "atypical sample" and how might this problem be overcome?

CASE STUDY: AMOROUS TURKEYS

Some psychologists were conducting research on the effects of hormones on turkeys. In one room there were 35 full-grown male turkeys. If you walked into the room, the turkeys fled to the furthest corner and if you walked towards them, the turkeys slid along the wall to maintain a maximum distance between you and them. This is fairly normal behaviour for wild turkeys. However, in another room, there was a group of turkeys who behaved in a very different manner. These turkeys greeted you by stopping dead in their tracks, fixing their eyes on you, spreading their tail into a full courtship fan, putting their heads down and ponderously walking towards you, all at the same time. Their intention was clearly one of mating. (Fortunately turkeys in mid-courtship are famously slow so it is easy to avoid their advances.)

What was the difference between these two groups? The first set were raised away from humans, whereas the second group had received an injection of the male hormone, testosterone, when they were younger. The hormone created an artificial sensitive period during which the turkeys imprinted on their companion at the time—a male experimenter. Subsequently, these turkeys showed little interest in female turkeys, however they were aroused whenever they saw a male human—displaying their tail feathers and strutting their stuff.

It has been suggested that the reason this learning was so strong and apparently irreversible was because it took place at a time of high arousal—when hormones were administered. In real life, hormones may be involved as well. Perhaps, for these birds, a moving object creates a sense of pleasure and this pleasure triggers the production of endorphins, opiate-like biochemicals produced by the body, which in turn create a state of arousal that is optimal for learning.

(From Howard S. Hoffman, 1996, *Amorous turkeys and addicted ducklings: A search for the causes of social attachment*. Boston, MA: Author's Cooperative.) ■

reasonable to generalise from this rather atypical sample. The extended-contact mothers may have become more involved with their babies because of the special attention they received, rather than because of the hours of skin-to-skin contact.

Cross-cultural evidence supports these conclusions. Lozoff (1983) reported that mothers were no more affectionate towards their babies in cultures encouraging early bodily contact between mother and baby. However, some support for the skin-to-skin hypothesis. De Chateau and Wiberg (1977) found that mothers who had skin-to-skin contact with their unwashed babies immediately after birth, and also immediately put the baby to their breast to suckle, engaged in significantly more kissing and embracing with their infants, and breastfed on average for 2½ months longer than "traditional contact" mothers.

The general view nowadays is that the relationship between mother and baby develops and changes over time rather than being fixed shortly after birth, although early bonding experiences may be helpful.

Klaus and Kennell suggested that prolonged skin-to-skin contact between baby and mother gave rise to greater bonding. However, recent research, including cross-cultural studies, indicates that other forms of attention also promote bonding.

Monotropy or multiple attachments?

Schaffer and Emerson's research (see page 91) gave us several answers to the question "to whom do infants become attached?" One thing they noted was that infants usually become attached to one person first and this is then followed by attachments to many others. They also considered the amount of time spent with caregivers and found that attachments were not necessarily formed with the person who spent most time with the infant. We will now consider further evidence.

The attachment between a child and his or her caregiver serves many important functions. According to Bowlby, it maintains proximity for safety, the caregiver acts as a secure base for exploration, and the attachment relationship acts as a template for all future relationships.

There has been much debate about whether infants become attached to one person (which is called "monotropy", meaning "leaning towards one thing") or to many people. To some extent the debate stems from the claim made by Bowlby (1953) that infants have a hierarchy of attachments, at the top of which is one central caregiver—he called this the **monotropy hypothesis**. This one person is *often* the mother but not invariably. The terms "maternal" and "mothering" do not have to refer to a woman. Bowlby (1988) said "it is because of this marked tendency to monotropy that we are capable of deep feelings".

The special significance of monotropy is that it alone provides the experience of an intense emotional relationship which forms the basis of the internal working model, the schema a child has for forming future relationships. However, it is generally accepted that Bowlby exaggerated the notion that young children typically have only *one* very close attachment.

Do early attachments affect future relationships?

Bowlby's concept would lead us to expect a correlation or association between early attachment experiences and later relationships. Evidence supporting this expectation comes from Hazan and Shaver (1987), who devised a "love quiz" consisting of a simple adjective checklist of childhood relationships with parents, and parents' relationships with each other, as a measure of attachment style, and a questionnaire that assessed individuals' beliefs about romantic love. The quiz was printed in a local newspaper, and the first 620 replies were analysed. Hazan and Shaver used the answers to classify respondents (1) as secure, ambivalent, or avoidant "types" based on their description of their childhood experiences, and (2) on their adult style of romantic love. They found a consistent relationship between attachment "type" and adult style of love. Secure types described their love experiences as happy, friendly, and trusting, and were able to accept their partners regardless of any faults. Ambivalent types experienced love as involving obsession, desire for reciprocation, intensity, and jealousy, and worry that their partners might abandon them. Avoidant lovers typically feared intimacy, emotional highs and lows, and jealousy and believed that they didn't need to be loved to be happy. These attachment "types" are based on research examined earlier in this section using the Strange Situation (see page 95).

One major problem with this study was that some of the data were collected retrospectively, and an individual's recall of their childhood experiences might not be very reliable. A second problem was that the data were collected through self-report questionnaires, and people don't always give truthful answers. Finally, the sample was biased because the participants were self-selected, as only certain types of people complete and send in questionnaires.

Is it really this simple? Not everyone agrees with Bowlby. The disagreement is about the relative importance of these multiple attachments. Some psychologists feel that healthy psychological development is *not* best served by having one primary attachment. Thomas (1998) suggests it may be better to have a network of close attachments to sustain the needs of a growing infant who has a variety of demands for social and emotional interactions. This is certainly true in some cultures, such as Caribbean countries. Even in European cultures, infants do form several attachments which are all beneficial probably because of the differences among them. For example, fathers' style of play is more often physically stimulating and unpredictable whereas mothers are more likely to hold their infants, soothe them, attend to their needs and read them stories (Parke, 1981).

However, there is **cross-cultural evidence** to support Bowlby's (1969) argument that within these multiple attachments there was always a hierarchy. For example, Tronick, Morelli, and Ivey (1992) studied an African tribe, the Efe, from Zaire who live in extended family groups. The infants were looked after and even breastfed by different women but usually they slept with their own mother at night. By the age of 6 months, the infants still showed a preference for their mothers.

Cross-cultural research

There are several reasons for conducting cross-cultural research; that is, research that looks at the customs and practices of different countries and makes comparisons with our own cultural norms. First of all, such research can tell us about what might be universal in human behaviour. If the same behaviours are observed in many different cultures, all of which have different ways of socialising children, then the behaviour may be due to innate (universal) factors rather than learning. The second reason for conducting cross-cultural research is that it offers us insights into our own behaviour. Insights that we may not otherwise be aware of. Perhaps that is the appeal of watching programmes on the television that show foreign lands and different people.

There are some major weaknesses to cross-cultural research. First of all, any sample of a group of people may well be biased and therefore we may be mistaken in thinking that the observations made of one group of people are representative of that culture. Second, where the observations are made by an outsider, that person's own culture will bias how they interpret the data they observe. Finally, the psychological tools that are used to measure people, such as IQ tests and the Strange Situation, are designed in one particular culture and based on assumptions of that culture. They may not have any meaning in another culture.

Therefore cross-cultural research has the potential to be highly informative about human behaviour but also has many important weaknesses.

Evaluation of Bowlby's theory

Bowlby explained the purpose of attachment in terms of adaptation, and believed that the primary caregiver will be the individual who is most responsive to the infant's social releasers, entering into mutual interactions.

It is important to recognise the enormous influence of Bowlby's theory. It has generated a great deal of research—studies that have tried to prove or disprove it, and theories that have modified it. It has also had important practical applications, as we will see in the next two sections.

On the negative side, we have seen problems with Bowlby's view of attachment as a template (pattern) for future relationships. This would lead us to expect children to form similar relationships with others, *but* the similarities among a child's various relationships are actually quite low (Main & Weston, 1981). Evidence links attachment style to later relationships (e.g. Hazan & Shaver, discussed above) but this is not a universal finding. For example, Howes, Matheson, and Hamilton (1994) found that parent–child relationships were not always positively correlated with child–peer relationships. In addition, even if there are positive correlations between the main attachment relationship and later relationships, there are other ways to explain this. Perhaps some infants are simply better than others at forming relationships. Children who are appealing to their parents are likely to be appealing to other people, so that a child who does well in one relationship is likely to do well in others (Jacobson & Wille, 1986).

There have been various other criticisms of Bowlby's approach, such as his views on a critical period for the development of attachment (discussed earlier, see page 107), his argument about bad homes versus good institutions (see page 122), and perhaps most fundamentally research related to the effects of separation (discussed in the next section).

One final point we should note regards the evolutionary argument, which is not accepted by everyone. It is a *post hoc* (after the fact) assumption rather than proven fact. In other words, we are making the judgement looking backwards and arguing that a behaviour must be adaptive because it persists. We cannot *know* that natural selection works, but we assume that it is likely. Perhaps the value of a behaviour that endures is simply neutral rather than positive, and that is why it has remained.

Quantity or quality?

Whether children form one or multiple attachments, the question remains as to *why* they become attached to any caregiver. Is it simply because of the time spent with a person, i.e. *quantity* of care, or is it more related to the *quality* of care that is received?

Quantity of care

A study by Fox (1977) looked at the effects of time on the closeness of attachment between mother and child. This study involved children on a Kibbutz, a kind of Israeli farming community where many things are shared including infant care. The children spent most of their time in an infant house being cared for by a nurse or *metapelet*, and visiting their parents every evening. Fox found the infants were nevertheless most strongly attached to their mothers, possibly because the *metapelets* had to divide their attention among many children.

The great majority of children who spend the majority of their waking days away from their parents in day care nevertheless remain attached to their parents, as we will see later in Section 10. Perhaps children become most attached to the person who feeds them. Harlow's research (1959, discussed below) strongly suggested that feeding has nothing whatsoever to do with attachment, *but* this evidence is from non-human animals. In this study, rhesus monkeys were "fed" by wire "mothers", but seemed to be more attached to the cloth-covered "mother". The study by Schaffer and Emerson (see page 91) also found that infants were *not* most attached to the person who fed them.

Attachment in infant monkeys. To test whether monkeys prefer the activity of feeding to that of bodily comfort, Harlow (1959) arranged for very young rhesus monkeys to be taken from their mothers and placed in cages with two surrogate (or substitute) mothers, as shown in the picture. One of the "mothers" was made of wire and the other was covered in soft cloth. Milk was provided by the wire mother for some of the monkeys, whereas it was provided by the cloth mother for the others. The monkeys spent most of their time clinging to the cloth mother even when she didn't supply milk. The cloth mother provided "contact comfort",

The monkeys in Harlow's study appeared to be more attached to a cloth-covered artificial "mother" than to a wire version.

which was clearly preferable. If the monkeys were frightened by a teddy bear drummer they ran to their cloth mother.

However, the monkeys didn't develop into normal adults, as later in life they were either indifferent or abusive to other monkeys, and had difficulty with mating and parenting. This shows that contact comfort is preferable (but not sufficient) for healthy development.

Harlow conducted various further studies to investigate the effects of deprivation. Harlow and Harlow (1962) raised monkeys for lengthy periods in total isolation. When they were placed with other monkeys they remained withdrawn and extremely fearful. In comparison, monkeys raised with a cloth "mother" were much more able to engage in social activity. This shows that the cloth mother was better than nothing.

In another experiment, four young monkeys were raised on their own, without any "mother". They spent the first few months huddled together but gradually developed more independence and finally appeared to have suffered no ill-effects. This suggests that the infant–infant affectional bond can be just as effective as mother–infant. (See Freud & Dann's study on page 124 for more on the effects of infant–infant bonding.)

Monkeys usually live in quite large groups and their natural environment is a highly social one. Thus, Harlow's studies could be criticised on two grounds: (1) modern ethical considerations would make this experimental approach hard to justify, and (2) the studies could also be methodologically flawed as the rhesus monkeys were reared in isolation. After the experiments were completed, the monkeys exhibited severely disturbed behaviour. Such a study would not be allowed today because of the stricter **ethical guidelines** for research using non-human participants. The baby monkeys were doubly deprived of both maternal care *and* the company of others, and as such we cannot be certain whether their maladjustment was due to maternal deprivation or social deprivation, or both.

Although the wire mother on the left is where the baby monkey receives his food, he runs to the cloth mother for comfort when he is frightened by the teddy bear drummer (Harlow, 1959).

? Why should one be cautious in using results from animal studies to explain human behaviour?

Quality of care

Harlow's research pointed to another possibility. The monkeys' only attachment was with a mother who offered contact comfort but not interaction. These monkeys grew up to be quite maladjusted. Perhaps it is the *responsiveness* of the caregiver that is important. This could explain why the children on the Kibbutzim remained most strongly attached to their mothers, as they invested in a more intense emotional relationship during the quality time they had with their infants. Schaffer and Emerson (1964) also found that responsiveness from caregivers was

> **KEY TERM**
>
> **Ethical guidelines**: a written code of conduct designed to aid psychologists when designing and running their research. The guidelines set out standards of what is and is not acceptable. The code focuses on the need to treat participants with respect and to not cause them harm or distress. For example, the BPS code of conduct advises of "the need to preserve an overriding high regard for the well-being and dignity of research participants" (BPS, 1993).

■ **Activity:** List all the theories of attachment covered in this section. For each of them, suggest how the following questions would be answered: Why do attachments form? With whom are attachments formed? What is the major drawback of this explanation?

important. In their study, well-attached infants had mothers who responded most quickly to their demands (high responsiveness) and who offered the child the most interaction. The infants who were weakly attached had mothers who failed to interact.

Ainsworth, Bell, and Stayton (1974) proposed a **caregiving sensitivity hypothesis**, suggesting that it is the *quality* of the relationship that matters most of all. Attachment depends on the warm and loving responsiveness of the mother figure. There is considerable support for this. For example, Ainsworth et al. (1971) found that mothers who responded to their infants in a sensitive manner had securely attached children whereas mothers who were less responsive had insecurely attached children. Isabella, Belsky, and Von Eye (1989) also found that those mothers and infants who tended to be responsive to each other at one month were more securely attached to each other at twelve months; those who had a more one-sided pattern of interaction tended to have insecure relationships.

SECTION SUMMARY

What is attachment?

❖ Attachment is a close emotional relationship between two persons. It is characterised by:
– Seeking proximity to the attachment figure.
– Being distressed on being separated from the attachment figure.
– Experiencing pleasure at being reunited with the attachment figure.
– A general orientation towards the attachment figure.
❖ Attachment is adaptive in that:
– In the short term, it provides survival.
– In the long term, it is important for further adult relationships.

Stages in the formation of attachment

❖ Bowlby described four phases of attachment formation.
❖ Schaffer and Emerson suggested that attachment took place in three phases:
1. Asocial phase.
2. Phase of indiscriminate attachments.
3. Phase of specific attachments.
❖ The onset of a specific attachment is signified by separation and stranger anxiety.
❖ There is some debate as to whether infants are asocial in the early phase, for research has shown that babies can distinguish between familiar and unfamiliar faces.

The variety of attachments

❖ Individuals differ in terms of the quality of their attachment.
❖ Using the Ainsworth Strange Situation, different attachment types have been identified:
– Secure attachments.
– Insecure attachments, which may be anxious avoidant or anxious resistant.

❖ These individual differences could be due to:
  – Differences in temperament (according to Kagan).
  – Different parenting.
❖ Although the Strange Situation procedure has been found to be reliable and valid (but perhaps lacking external validity) there are concerns with the research:
  – It may be measuring infants' different relationships rather than a fixed feature of their personality.
  – Security of attachment could be explained in terms of innate temperament.
  – Separation may be constructed differently in different cultures and therefore the research may be culturally specific.

❖ Cross-cultural studies of secure and insecure attachment find general agreement for the classification of attachment types.
❖ However, there are questions about the validity of the Strange Situation assessment. The same behaviour (e.g. separation) may mean something different in different cultures, which invalidates the procedure.

Cross-cultural studies

❖ There are several major theories of attachment:
  – The psychodynamic approach.
  – Learning theory.
  – Social learning theory.
  – Bowlby's theory of attachment.

Explanations of attachment

❖ This suggests that attachment to the mother (the first love object) occurs because the mother gives pleasure to the infant through feeding.
❖ This approach has been criticised in that:
  – Babies can attach to others who do not meet their need for food.
  – Research on rhesus monkeys has shown that attachment to a cuddly mother was more important than food.
❖ The same criticisms can be made of learning theory.

The psychodynamic approach

❖ This also suggests that attachment occurs through feeding in that the infant associates food (a primary reinforcer) with the mother (secondary reinforcer).
❖ It is thought that the carer and infant engage in mutually reinforcing behaviour.
❖ However, learning explanations are reductionist and we know that feeding alone cannot explain attachment.

Learning theory

❖ Suggests that attachment and other relationships are learned through observation and imitation.

Social learning theory

❖ This theory is of enduring importance.
❖ Bowlby suggested that infants are most attached to a primary caregiver (monotropy) who is at the top of a hierarchy. This is important for healthy social development.
❖ He argued that attachment is:
  – innate,
  – adaptive,
  – reciprocal.

Bowlby's theory of attachment (monotropy)

❖ He suggested the primary attachment relationship:
  – Creates proximity-seeking behaviour.
  – Provides an internal working model for other relationships.
  – Offers a secure base for exploration.
  – Is important for healthy emotional development.
❖ Social releasers, like smiling, are a fundamental part of the attachment process.
❖ Attachment takes place at a critical or sensitive period. This idea has been linked to the notion of imprinting in other species.
❖ Bowlby's theory has been criticised in that:
  – Multiple attachments may be healthier than monotropy.
  – He may have overestimated the importance of the internal working model.
  – The negative effects of a lack of an attachment figure may be reversible.
  – There may not be a critical period for attachment.
❖ More generally, the claims made for imprinting have been criticised:
  – It is probable that imprinting describes a kind of learning that takes place most easily, but not exclusively, during a certain stage of development.
  – There is mixed support for the skin-to-skin hypothesis: infants have a sensitive period during which attachment bonds form more easily, perhaps because of a hormonal surge.
❖ Despite these criticisms, Bowlby's research has had practical applications for the care of children in hospitals.

See pp.42–50 of the revision guide.

SECTION 9
DEPRIVATION AND PRIVATION

In the real world, circumstances such as divorce between parents or the death of a parent can disrupt the child's attachments, or even prevent them from being formed at all. If attachment is critical to healthy psychological development, then Bowlby's theory would predict that any disruption to this process should result in the opposite effect—unhealthy psychological development. One way of determining the validity of Bowlby's theory is to consider the effects of such disruption.

In this section, we will discuss the effects on the young child of being separated from one or more of the most important adults in his/her life. Most studies have focused on the long-term effects of deprivation. However, we will first consider some of the short-term effects.

Short-term Effects of Separation

Even fairly brief separation from a primary caregiver has severe emotional effects on the child. **Separation** can be distinguished from **deprivation**: separation involves distress when separated from a person to whom there is an attachment bond for a relatively short period of time, whereas deprivation occurs when a bond has been formed and is then broken for what are generally fairly long periods of time. Thus, separation is a mild form of deprivation.

One of the main predictions from Bowlby's theory is that young children might suffer severe emotional effects as a result of even short-term separation

Separation from the mother can have severe emotional effects on a child. The first stage of the child's response to the separation is known as protest: an intense period during which the child cries for much of the time.

from their primary caregiver. At the start of the 1950s, this view was somewhat controversial, and the necessary evidence was not available. However, as we will see, relevant evidence was published in 1952.

Robertson and Bowlby (1952) studied young children separated from their mother for some time, often because she had gone into hospital. They found that there were three stages in the child's response to separation, which led them to produce the protest-despair-detachment (PDD) model:

1. Protest, which is often very intense. The child cries much of the time, and sometimes seems panic-stricken. Anger and fear are present.
2. Despair, involving a total loss of hope. The child is often apathetic and shows little interest in its surroundings. The child often engages in self-comforting behaviour such as thumb-sucking or rocking.
3. Detachment, during which the child seems to behave in a less distressed way. If the mother or caregiver re-appears during this stage, she is not responded to with any great interest.

It used to be thought that children in the third stage of detachment had adjusted fairly well to separation from their mother. However, it seems that the calm behaviour shown by the child when its mother re-appears is a disguise for true feelings. Fortunately, most children re-establish an attachment to the mother over time.

The research of Robertson and Bowlby (1952) is important for various reasons. First, they were among the first researchers to study in detail the effects of short-term separation on young children. Second, they identified clearly the main stages in children's response to separation. Third, their research highlighted the importance of doing whatever possible to minimise the adverse effects of separation on young children.

> **?** What are the limitations of Robertson and Bowlby's (1952) study?

Evaluation of the PDD model

Barrett (1997) suggests that the PDD model doesn't take individual differences into account. For example, a securely attached child may show little initial protest and cope relatively well, whereas an avoidant child would be plunged more immediately into protest and despair and become quite disoriented.

Is it inevitable that short-term separation produces these negative effects? Robertson and Robertson (1971) suggest it isn't. In their own home, they looked after several young children separated from their mothers. To minimise any distress the children might experience, they ensured that the children became familiar with their new surroundings beforehand. They also tried to provide the children with a similar daily routine and discussed the children's mothers with them. This approach proved successful, with the children showing much less distress than most separated children. The Robertsons also studied other children who were separated from their mothers but who spent the time in a residential nursery. These children didn't cope as well—they received good physical care but lacked emotional care. The Robertsons said that the nursery children experienced **bond disruption** whereas the others did not because they were offered substitute mothering. Therefore, we might conclude that separation need not lead to deprivation, but it may do so if accompanied by bond disruption.

> **?** How might the findings from the Robertson and Robertson study be applied to helping children in institutional care?

Long-term Effects of Separation

Prior to the development of his theory of attachment, John Bowlby proposed the **maternal deprivation hypothesis** (1953), which focused more on the effects of deprivation.

Maternal deprivation hypothesis

According to this hypothesis, breaking the maternal bond with the child during the early years of its life is likely to have serious effects on its intellectual, social, and emotional development. Bowlby also claimed that many of these negative effects were permanent and irreversible. This theory was revolutionary when it was first proposed, as most professionals then felt that only adequate physical provision was necessary for healthy development.

In the early 1940s, it was recognised that children could suffer if separated from their mother for a long period of time. However, the extent of such suffering had not been clearly established. In addition, it was not fully appreciated that there could be long-term negative effects produced by separation from the mother. It was in this context that Bowlby's classic study of juvenile thieves had a major impact. Bowlby (1944) carried out his well-known study on clients from the child guidance clinic where he worked. He interviewed the children and their families, and gradually built up a record of their early life experiences. He found some children had experienced "early and prolonged separation from their mothers", and some of them were emotionally maladjusted. In particular, he diagnosed the condition of **affectionless psychopathy** in some of the children, a disorder involving a lack of guilt and remorse. Could it be that there was a link between this form of emotional maladjustment and early separation?

Bowlby focused on a group of children who had been referred to the clinic because of stealing (these were the juvenile thieves). He compared them with a control group of children, who had been referred to the clinic because of emotional problems but who hadn't committed any crimes. He found that 32% of the thieves were affectionless psychopaths lacking a social conscience, whereas none of the control children was an affectionless psychopath. Of the thieves diagnosed as affectionless psychopaths, 86% had experienced early separation (even if only for a week before the age of 5). In contrast, only 17% of the thieves without affectionless psychopathy had been maternally deprived.

This study by Bowlby is important for various reasons. First, the findings seemed to show that maternal deprivation can have very severe effects, including producing a lack of emotional development (affectionless psychopathy). Second, Bowlby's results suggested that early maternal deprivation could have negative effects that were still observable several years later. Third, the findings of this study led many other researchers to examine the relationship between children's early experience and their subsequent emotional development.

Other studies of institutionalisation conducted around the time of the Second World War are described next. All of this research pointed to the fact that early separations were associated with severe consequences.

Institutionalisation

Important evidence came from the work of Spitz (1945) and Goldfarb (1947). Spitz visited several very poor orphanages and other institutions in South

America. Children in these orphanages received very little warmth or attention from the staff, and had become apathetic. Many of these children seemed to suffer from **anaclitic depression**, a state involving resigned helplessness and loss of appetite. This was attributed to their lack of emotional care, and separation from their mothers. Spitz and Wolf (1946) studied 100 apparently normal children who became seriously depressed after staying in hospital—the children generally recovered well only if the separation lasted less than three months.

Goldfarb (1947) compared two groups of infants, who before fostering spent either only the first few months or three years at a poor and inadequately staffed orphanage. Both groups were tested at various times up to the age of 12. Those children who had spent three years at the orphanage did less well than the others on intelligence tests, were less socially mature, and more likely to be aggressive.

In the 1950s, orphanages in the UK gradually began to disappear and therefore research into separation was limited. More recently there has been a new opportunity to study orphans—children from Romania. For example, Rutter and the ERA Study Team (1998) have followed 111 Romanian orphans adopted in the UK before the age of 2. When the orphans first arrived in the UK they were physically and mentally underdeveloped, but by the age of 4 all of them had improved, presumably as a result of improved care. Those who were adopted latest showed the slowest improvements educationally and emotional development. However, reasonable recovery occurred given good subsequent care.

News reports in the 1980s highlighted deprivation in Romanian orphanages, with many children demonstrating anaclitic depression, having received basic sustenance but little human warmth or contact.

Evaluation. The findings reported here provide less support for the maternal deprivation hypothesis than Bowlby assumed. The institutional experience was deficient in several ways; the children were not simply deprived of maternal care but also suffered from a general lack of stimulation and attention. As a result, the findings may be due to absence of the mother (lack of emotional care) and/or poor institutional conditions (poor physical care).

There is, however, some evidence supporting the importance of emotional care. Widdowson (1951) recorded the case of a group of orphanage children who were physically underdeveloped, a condition called **deprivation dwarfism**. A regime of dietary supplements didn't lead to weight gain but a change in supervisor did. Their original supervisor had been harsh and unsympathetic. So improved emotional, rather than physical, care appeared to be the cause of their physical improvements. In addition, it is likely that most bed-wetting behaviour (enuresis) occurs as a result of emotional disturbance.

A further consideration of the effects of institutional care is given in Hodges and Tizard's (1989) Key Study (see pages 121–122).

> ### CASE STUDY: THE RILEY FAMILY
>
> Jean Riley (54) and her husband Peter (58) adopted two children from Romania who are now aged 17 and 9. Cezarina, when they first saw her, was cross-eyed, filthy, and about four years behind in her physical development. First Cezarina's physical problems had to be sorted out, but from then on she made good progress. However, Cezarina is "laid back" about things that seem important to Jean and Peter. Jean understands this attitude, though, because clearly examinations seem less important when a child has had to struggle to survive.
>
> According to Jean, Cezarina is bright, but needs to have information reinforced over and over again. She has also struggled to understand jokes and sarcasm, although this may be due to difficulties with learning the language. Jean sees Cezarina as naive and emotionally immature. Cezarina says herself that initially she was frustrated because she couldn't communicate. She does see herself as being different from other girls, although she likes the same things, such as fashion and pop music. Jean runs The Parent Network for the Institutionalised Child, a group for people who have adopted such children. Cezarina has partly recovered from her poor early experiences.
>
> (Account based on an article in Woman, 21 September 1998.) ■

Hospitalisation

When children have to be hospitalised for prolonged periods this may lead to the breaking of attachment bonds (deprivation) and later maladjustment. A study by Douglas (1975) analysed data collected as part of the National Survey of Health and Development, a longitudinal study of 5000 children born during one week in 1946 and assessed regularly up to the age of 26. Douglas found that children who had spent more than a week in hospital, or had experienced repeated admissions under the age of 4, were more likely to have behaviour problems in adolescence and to be poor readers. Quinton and Rutter (1976) also found that repeated hospital admissions were associated with later problems whereas children admitted only once rarely had later difficulties.

Evaluation. Clarke and Clarke (1976) suggested that this apparent relationship between hospitalisation and later difficulties may be due to general home problems. Children from disadvantaged homes could be more likely to need hospital treatment because of poor living conditions; their disadvantaged homes might explain the maladjustment as well. Therefore, the maladjustment might not be the result of separation.

There is another way to interpret Douglas's findings. The experience of being in hospital is likely to create anxiety, and the lack of caregiving at such a critical time may cause long-term problems. So it is not separation alone that has long-term effects but the anxiety created by the hospital situation, which is not helped by being alone. Bowlby et al. (1956) conducted a study of children with tuberculosis, all initially under the age of 4, who were hospitalised for long periods. The children spent between 5 and 24 months in a sanatorium outside London. They didn't receive substitute mothering by the hospital staff but most of them were visited weekly by their families (i.e. bond disruption was minimised). When the TB children were assessed later by their teachers and a psychologist, there were very few differences between them and their peers in terms of later intellectual development and emotional adjustment. So it would appear that hospitalisation doesn't inevitably have harmful effects, possibly as long as bond disruption is minimised.

Evaluation of the maternal deprivation hypothesis

The evidence examined here, in relation to institutionalisation and hospitalisation, suggests that early separations can have important consequences in certain circumstances but that this is not necessarily the case. The maternal deprivation hypothesis has similarities with the concept of imprinting and can therefore be subject to similar criticisms. There may be a sensitive period in the development of attachments but probably not a critical period, meaning that it is definitely preferable for strong attachments to occur early in life. However, it is not absolutely essential (as is implied by the notion of a critical period), because the damage caused by deprivation may be reversible.

The importance of the maternal deprivation hypothesis, and the research related to it, is that it changed our attitudes towards infant care and influenced the way children are looked after, in hospitals, in institutions, and at home. Thirty years *before* Bowlby, the behaviourist John Watson wrote a book called *Psychological care of infant and child* (1928) where he recommended that parents should avoid displays of affection towards their children. Now Western attitudes are considerably changed—children are now accompanied by their parents while they are in hospital, institutional care has been largely replaced by fostering, and child-centred child care is the rule.

The most major criticisms of the maternal deprivation hypothesis were put forward by Rutter (1972) in a book entitled *Maternal deprivation reassessed*, which we will consider next.

Distinguishing Separation, Deprivation, and Privation

Rutter pointed out that Bowlby had assumed that *all* experiences of deprivation were the same, whereas in fact there are some quite key differences. Children may experience very short-term separations, as in the Robertsons' studies, or they may have repeated and prolonged separations. Children may experience separation without bond disruption, as with Bowlby's sanatorium study, or have no adequate substitute maternal care. Finally, children may experience deprivation as a result of never having formed any attachments. Rutter suggested that there was a key difference between deprivation and privation. Deprivation occurs when a child has formed an important attachment, from which it is then separated; privation occurs when a child has never formed a close relationship with anyone. Many of Bowlby's juvenile delinquents had experienced several changes of home/principal caregiver during their early childhood. This indicated to Rutter (1981) that their later problems were due to privation rather than deprivation. Rutter argued that the effects of privation are much more severe and long lasting than those of deprivation.

One of the most thorough and detailed studies of privation was reported by Hodges and Tizard (1989; see Key Study below). It was a longitudinal study, with the progress of the children being studied over a period of several years. This study is of major importance because it showed that privation does *not* always have negative long-term consequences for the children concerned, provided they are brought up in a loving environment. It also revealed that children's own family environment is not necessarily the best place for them to be if their own family fails to provide the love they need.

KEY TERM

Privation: the lack of any attachments, as distinct from the loss of attachments (deprivation). This is due to the lack of an appropriate attachment figure. Privation is more likely than deprivation to cause permanent emotional damage or "affectionless psychopathy"; the condition diagnosed by Bowlby as involving permanent emotional damage.

Key Study: Long-term effects of privation

Hodges and Tizard's (1989) study into the effects of privation.

Aims: Hodges and Tizard aimed to investigate the permanence of long-term effects of privation (the state of a child who has never formed a close attachment with anyone) due to institutionalisation, including emotional and social effects in adolescence. They aimed to test BOTH Bowlby's claim that maternal deprivation would cause permanent emotional damage AND earlier contradictory research by Tizard, which suggested that the negative effects of privation could be reversed.

Procedure: Sixty-five children who had been taken into care before the age of 4 months formed an opportunity sample. This was a natural experiment, using a matched pairs design, as the institutionalised children were compared with a control group raised at home. It was a longitudinal study

? How does a natural experiment differ from a laboratory experiment?

(age on entering care to 16 years). Each child had been looked after on average by 24 different caregivers by the age of 2. By the age of 4 years, 24 had been adopted, 15 restored to their natural home, and the rest remained in the institution. The children were assessed at ages 4, 8, and 16 on emotional and social competence through interview and self-report questionnaires.

Findings: At age 4, the children had not formed attachments. By age 8, significant differences existed between the adopted and restored children. At age 8 and 16 most of the adopted children had formed close relationships with their caregivers and were as attached as the control group. These attachments were closer than those of the children restored to their natural homes, i.e. the adopted group showed better emotional adjustment. However, negative social effects were evident in both the adopted and restored children at school, as they were attention seeking and had difficulty forming peer relationships.

Conclusions: Some of the effects of privation can be reversed, as the children were able to form attachments in spite of their privation. However, some privation effects are long lasting, as shown by the difficulties the institutionalised children faced at school. This suggests a need for research into possible reasons why the adopted children fared better than the restored children (probably due to the presence of a loving environment) and the importance of high-quality subsequent care if the effects of privation are to be reversed. Hence there are practical implications for care home, adoption, and fostering practices.

Criticisms

- Problems of a longitudinal study include sample drop-off. Hodges and Tizard noted that the adopted children who remained in the study had shown better adjustment at age 4. In contrast, the restored children who remained in the study had shown more adjustment problems at age 4. What these findings mean is that the children remaining in each group over the course of the study differed from those who did not—this creates biased samples. This may have distorted the difference between the adopted and restored children, because the adopted children were better adjusted at the start of the study. Consequently, the findings may lack validity, which reduces their meaningfulness and generalisability.
- As this was a natural experiment, the independent variable (i.e. privation) could not be directly manipulated, and so cause and effect cannot safely be inferred. Thus, it cannot be said that privation *causes* long-term social and emotional effects, such as the difficulties the children had in forming peer relationships. All we can say with confidence is that privation plays some role in this effect, meaning that conclusions are limited.
- It is misleading to assume that restored children will *always* show less social adjustment than adopted children. What happens depends crucially on the reasons WHY the restored children were initially taken into care and on the amount of love and affection they receive when restored to their natural home.

Note: If the question asks for findings or conclusions only, you could include research by Rutter (1981, see p.121), Curtiss (1989, see p.123), and Freud and Dann (1951, see p.123).

? **How might we account for the different patterns of behaviour shown by adopted children and children who returned to their families?**

? **What are the disadvantages associated with conducting longitudinal research?**

? **How has the research of Hodges and Tizard added to our knowledge of the effects of deprivation?**

Studies of privation

A few researchers have looked at the effects of very extreme privation and isolation on children. It is surprising how resilient these children seem to be. Koluchová (1976) studied identical twins in Czechoslovakia who had spent most of the first seven years of their lives locked in a cellar. They had been treated very badly, and were often beaten. They were barely able to talk, and relied mainly on gestures rather than speech. The twins were fostered at about the age of 9 by a pair of loving sisters. By the time they were 14, their behaviour was essentially normal. By the age of 20, they were of above average intelligence and had excellent relationships with the members of their foster family (Koluchová, 1991).

Curtiss (1989) reported the case study of Genie, who spent most of her childhood locked in a room at her home in Los Angeles. She had had very little contact with other members of her family, and was discouraged from making any sounds. She was found in 1970 when she was 13½ years old. She had not been fed adequately, could not stand erect, and had no social skills. At that time, she did not understand language and could not speak. Genie was given a considerable amount of education and assistance in the years after she was found. Her ability to perform tasks that did not depend on language improved rapidly, and she reached normal levels on several perceptual tasks (Curtiss, 1989). Unfortunately, Genie's language skills failed to reach normal adult levels. She developed a fairly large vocabulary, but she generally spoke in short, ungrammatical sentences, and did not understand complex sentences. Her social skills remained limited, in part because her language was poor ("Only people who knew her well could understand much of what she was trying to say", Curtiss, 1989, p.125). In addition, she seemed uninterested in people (Rymer, 1993).

? What ethical issues might be involved in the case study of Genie? Do these outweigh any understandings gained from this study?

? In what way might Genie be described as suffering from affectionless psychopathy?

Case studies

Some of the studies of privation described in this chapter are case studies. The advantage of such research is that it produces rich data that can be used by a researcher to develop new theoretical ideas. Case studies can provide information about exceptional types of behaviour or performance that had been thought to be impossible.

However, we need to be very careful when interpreting the evidence from a case study. The greatest limitation is the typically low reliability. The findings that are obtained from one unusual or exceptional individual are unlikely to be repeated in detail when another individual is studied. Thus, it is often very hard to generalise from a single case study. Second, many case studies involve the use of lengthy, fairly unstructured interviews which may produce subjective information. Third, researchers generally only report some of the data they obtained from their interviews with the participant. They may be unduly selective in terms of what they choose to report or to omit.

Not all children who experience privation may experience permanent emotional damage. Freud and Dann (1951) provided evidence that young children who form strong attachments with other young children can avoid the severe damage resulting from privation. They studied six war orphans whose parents had been murdered in a concentration camp when they were only a few months old. The infants lived together in a deportation camp for about two years until the age of 3, and had very distressing experiences such as watching people being hanged. In this camp, they were put in the Ward for Motherless Children, and had very

Children in concentration camps experienced terrible early privation. The children in this picture are awaiting release from Auschwitz in January 1945. Freud and Dann studied six such children who only had each other for companions throughout their early lives.

limited contact with anyone other than each other. After the camp was liberated at the end of the Second World War, they were flown to England. When they were freed from the camp, the children had not yet developed speech properly, were underweight, and expressed hostility towards adults. However, they were greatly attached to each other. According to Freud and Dann (1951, p.131): "The children's positive feelings were centred exclusively in their own group . . . They had no other wish than to be together and became upset when they were separated from each other, even for short moments."

As time went by, the six children became attached to their adult carers. In addition, they developed rapidly at a social level and in their use of language. It is hard to say whether their early experiences had any lasting adverse effects. One of them (Leah) received psychiatric assistance, and another (Jack) sometimes felt very alone and isolated (Moskovitz, 1983). However, it would not be exceptional to find similar problems in six adults selected at random.

Evaluation of studies of privation

In sum, the evidence indicates that most of the adverse effects of maternal deprivation or privation can be reversed, and that children are more resilient than Bowlby believed. Much of the available evidence does not support Bowlby's (1951) argument that the negative effects of maternal deprivation could not be reversed or undone, and indicates that even privation does not always have permanent effects. Clarke and Clarke (1998) note that early experience represents "no more than an initial step on the ongoing path of life". In other words, for most people early experience is very much related to what happens later on. Bad experiences are often likely to be followed by more of the same. However, where severely bad experiences are followed by much better ones the outcome may well be good. (The Czech twins went to a loving home; unfortunately

Genie experienced a series of difficult carers, ending in a foster home where she was once again abused.) There is one set of children for whom this may not be true, children with reactive attachment disorder, as described in the box below.

It is important to consider the methodology of these studies. They are very small samples and it may not be reasonable to generalise from them. It is possible that the children were abnormal from birth—we only have a retrospective history of their experience and abilities. In fact, Genie's father thought she was retarded and that is why he locked her away.

Better evidence comes from Hodges and Tizard's longitudinal research (1989, see Key Study on pages 121–122). On the one hand, this study appears to support our conclusion that both deprivation and privation can be recovered from, given good subsequent care. However, Hodges and Tizard's research also suggests a rather different conclusion, which is that recovery is only possible within the context of a loving relationship. Hodges and Tizard found that those children who went on to have good relationships at home coped well at home but found relationships outside the home difficult. In some way, they lacked an adequate model for future relationships. This would appear to support Bowlby's attachment theory.

Reactive attachment disorder

Consider a child in the early months of life. The child is hungry, or wet. What does the child do? He or she screams out for attention, and in the rage expressed, the mother comes to the child's aid and feeds or changes the child. Day after day, week after week, the closeness of eye contact, touch, movements, and smiles creates a bond of trust between the child and its mother.

But what happens if this cycle is broken? What if the mother doesn't want to respond to the demanding needs of the child? What if there was an undiagnosed condition in the child, that was never appropriately responded to and comforted? In these instances, the child does not learn to trust, does not learn to bond, and proceeds on with the next lesson to learn in life.

This leads to a condition called "reactive detachment disorder". Children with attachment disorders have trouble trusting others. Trusting means to love, and loving hurts. They attempt to control everyone and everything in their world. Lack of a conscience appears to be caused by their lacking trust in anyone. They become so dependent on themselves, that they ignore the needs of others to the point that they will steal, damage, and destroy anything that they feel hinders their control. In short, they do not trust any caregiver or person in authority.

As a relatively new diagnosis to the **DSM-IV** manual, reactive attachment disorder is often misunderstood, and relatively unknown. All too often these individuals grow up untreated and become **sociopaths** without conscience and without concern for anyone but themselves. This condition was made popular by the academy award winning movie *Good Will Hunting*. But unlike the movie, the hero, or heroine, rarely drives off into the sunset to have a happy-ever-after life. More realistically, parental dreams are lost, and the children grow up uncaring and without social conscience.

(Adapted from http://members.tripod.com/~radclass/index.html)

EXAM HINT

For questions on privation select research carefully. On an APFCC question DO NOT use the case studies, such as Genie, particularly if procedures have been asked for, as case studies have limited detail of procedures. Instead use Hodges and Tizard's (1989) research.

Reasons for Deprivation

Rutter's main criticism of Bowlby was that he had muddled together various kinds of separation. In addition, Bowlby (1951) argued that deprivation was the *cause* of long-term difficulties; Rutter (1981) suggested that it might simply appear to be deprivation that was causing later difficulties, whereas in fact the difficulties were due to factors associated with the deprivation. For example, in the case of hospitalisation, as we have seen, the cause of maladjustment was probably poor living conditions rather than separation itself. The same may be true for the effects of maternal deprivation due to divorce. Maladjustment might be caused by the discord and stress surrounding divorce rather than any maternal deprivation, as Bowlby would have predicted.

To test this hypothesis, Rutter et al. (1976) conducted their own study of over 2000 boys living on the Isle of Wight, aged between 9 and 12, who were questioned and their families interviewed. Rutter et al. looked at the relationship between separation and delinquency and found that if the separation was due to the physical illness or death of the mother, there was no correlation or association with delinquency. However, if it was due to psychiatric illness or discord within the family, then the boys were *four* times more likely to become delinquent. Thus, it is mostly family discord (rather than separation as such) that causes difficulties and maladjustment in children.

This finding was supported by Cockett and Tripp (1994). They found that children from homes where there was conflict suffered in terms of health, school performance, and **self-esteem** when compared with children who experienced minimal conflict at home.

Separation, Deprivation, and Privation: A Conclusion

? **Try to recall all three of Rutter's criticisms.**

Rutter made two important qualifications to Bowlby's maternal deprivation hypothesis. First, he argued that Bowlby had failed to distinguish clearly between deprivation and privation. Second, Bowlby exaggerated the extent to which deprivation was *directly* responsible for the problems later experienced by deprived children. A third point was that most children recover quite well and perhaps we should consider why some children are quite resilient whereas others never recover.

Ultimately, Rutter's contribution was not to cause people to reject Bowlby's hypothesis but to change its emphasis. Maternal deprivation should be seen as a "vulnerability factor" (Brown & Harris, 1978) that raises the likelihood of a child becoming disturbed, not a factor which means that maladjustment is bound to follow.

> **EXAM HINT**
> Essay questions may be on deprivation and privation OR may stipulate one or the other. Whilst this should change the focus of your essay slightly, do not panic. If the essay is on privation you can still use Bowlby's "44 juvenile thieves" study as evidence. Remember that Rutter (1972) made the criticism that Bowlby didn't distinguish between deprivation and privation, and in fact some of the juveniles did suffer from privation. You can then use Rutter et al.'s (1976) Isle of Wight study, and Hodges and Tizard's (1989) research to further weigh-up the effects of privation.

SECTION SUMMARY

Definitions

❖ Privation: a complete lack of early attachments.
❖ Deprivation: arises from disruption of earlier bonds resulting from separation from the carer.

❖ The short-term effects of deprivation have been described in the PDD model as:
  – protest,
  – despair,
  – detachment.

❖ However, there are some key variables that affect how children respond. These include:
  – The age of the child when separation occurs.
  – The gender of the child, in that males are thought to be more vulnerable.
  – The attachment style of the child.
  – The resilience of the child.
  – How the child is prepared for the separation.

The short-term effects of deprivation

❖ These were predicted by Bowlby's maternal deprivation hypothesis. He used evidence from a range of sources including:
  – the 44 juvenile thieves study;
  – studies on institutionalisation;
  – studies on hospitalisation.

❖ From this research, Bowlby suggested that the long-term effects of separation included:
  – Affectionless psychopathy: a disorder involving a lack of guilt and remorse.
  – Anaclitic depression: a state involving resigned helplessness and lack of appetite.
  – Deprivation "dwarfism": a condition where children are physically underdeveloped, due to emotional rather than physical deprivation.
  – Intellectual "retardation".

❖ Prolonged early hospitalisation can also lead to the breaking of attachment bonds and cause maladjustment, although both hospitalisation and maladjustment could be due to poor living conditions, and not a result of separation.

❖ Minimising bond disruption may help children cope with the anxiety of hospitalisation and thus avoid subsequent maladjustment.

The long-term effects of deprivation

❖ Rutter suggested that Bowlby confused correlation or association with causation, and that other variables such as poverty or family discord could contribute to the findings.

❖ From his research, Rutter suggested that the following variables could also influence the effects of long-term separation:
  Personal variables:
  – Gender: in that males are more vulnerable.
  – Age: in that children are more vulnerable between 6 months and 4 years.
  – Temperament: in that previously withdrawn and aggressive children are thought to suffer most.
  – Earlier relationships: in that if the child has experienced good multiple attachments he/she will be less vulnerable.

Variables that can influence deprivation

External or situational variables:
- – The number of previous separations and how they were experienced.
- – The presence of siblings.
- – The type of substitute caring provided.

The effects of privation

❖ Rutter distinguished between different kinds of separation and suggested that the complete lack of early attachments (privation) *may* have permanent consequences.

❖ Research into privation has come largely from case studies. For this reason they are sometimes difficult to interpret.

Are the effects of privation permanent?

❖ Hodges and Tizard have suggested that emotional recovery from privation is possible within the context of a supportive relationship.

❖ Children with reactive attachment disorder appear to be permanently affected by early privation.

See pp.51–57 of the revision guide.

SECTION 10—CRITICAL ISSUE DAY CARE

Some people interpreted Bowlby's maternal deprivation hypothesis as meaning that **day care** was a bad thing. Separation would harm the child's emotional development if he/she spent time away from a primary caregiver. However, this is only an interpretation put on Bowlby's views. Bowlby himself didn't specifically suggest that women should stay at home to look after their children. However, it seemed logical to argue that, if absent mothers create unhappy children, then mothers need to be present full-time. It is even possible that Bowlby's views were popularised by the post-war government to encourage women to stay at home— a cheaper alternative than having to provide universal child-care facilities. Bowlby himself argued that the quality of substitute care that is offered should be improved, as exemplified in the research he did with the Robertsons.

On the other side of the coin, there were those who argued for the *benefits* of day care, at least for *certain* children. In America in the 1960s there was a move towards providing pre-school care for disadvantaged children to enable them to start school on a par with their more middle-class peers. The best-known project of this kind was called Headstart, which involved half a million children in its first year. Kagan, Kearsley, and Zelazo (1980) asked whether there wasn't some kind of dual standard: lower-class children might benefit from day care as a source of intellectual enrichment, whereas middle-class children would be harmed because of maternal deprivation.

Many parents have to work for economic reasons, and some wish to because they otherwise feel trapped at home, so the question of the effects of day care is of great practical concern. We have seen that there are arguments for and against it. We will now consider how much day care affects the social and cognitive development of children and then ask what can be done to improve its quality.

Kinds of Day Care

There are many different kinds of day care. We will consider pre-school children and two main forms of care: day nurseries and childminding.

KEY TERM

Day care: this refers to care that is provided by people other than the parent or relatives of the infant. It can take different forms, for example, nurseries, childminders, play groups, etc. It is distinct from institutionalised care, which provides permanent substitute care; day care is a temporary alternative to the caregiver.

Day nurseries

Kagan et al. (1980) studied nursery care by setting up their own nursery school in Boston. The school had a fairly mixed intake from middle- and lower-class families and from various ethnic groups. The staff at the school each had special responsibility for a small group of children, thus ensuring close emotional contact. The study focused on 33 infants who attended the nursery full-time from the age of 3½ months who were compared with a matched home control group. Kagan et al. assessed the children throughout the two years they were at the nursery school. The researchers measured attachment, cognitive achievements, and general sociability, finding no consistently large differences between the nursery and home children. They did, however, find large individual differences among all the children, not related to the form of care, which may be due to temperamental or home factors, or both.

A larger-scale longitudinal study of day nurseries was conducted by Andersson (1992) in Sweden. Over 100 children of a starting age of 3–4 years were studied from both lower- and middle-class homes as well as single-parent families. At the start of the study, the age they first started in day care was recorded. The children were assessed at age 8 and 13, where cognitive and socioemotional competence were rated by their classroom teachers and IQ test data were collected. Andersson found that school performance was rated highest in those children who entered day care before the age of 1 and was lowest for those who did not have any day care, suggesting that day care may be beneficial. However, as children who entered day care before the age of 1 came from families with higher socioeconomic status, the good school performance could be explained by coming from a well-educated family.

A similar study looking at children in Texas (Vandell & Corasaniti, 1990) found that children with extensive child-care experiences from infancy were rated by parents and teachers as having poorer peer relationships and emotional health. The different results may be due to the different infant-care practices in both cultures. In Sweden, a substantial part of the infant's first year is spent with one or both parents due to a special parental leave system, thus allowing stronger attachments to be formed at home. In addition, day care in Sweden is given a great deal of financial support from the government and therefore may be of a generally higher quality than in the US, as it tends to offer very low staff/child ratios and carers are highly trained. Texas, on the other hand, has very low official requirements for child-care facilities. This emphasises the point that it is quality of care that should concern us, rather than the question of whether or not day care is a good thing. Andersson's study at least shows that high-quality care has no negative effects, and it seems that some children *benefit* from receiving day care from a young age.

Operation Headstart in the USA also involved day care. The programme was designed to reverse the effects of what was seen as social disadvantage by providing intensive pre-school education for certain children. When the children did start school, they showed IQ gains in comparison to those disadvantaged children who had not attended

Children attending nursery school are more likely to develop proper social behaviour in relation to other infants.

? Why do you think that it might be significant that the staff at the Boston school had responsibility for a small number of children, and maintained close emotional contact with them?

? Andersson's research was conducted in Sweden. How well do you think the findings can be applied to our culture?

Once they start school, children who have attended pre-school classes can have a range of advantages over children who have not.

? How might you use this evidence to advise parents on which form of child care to use?

day-care programmes. However, these differences soon disappeared. Later studies of the same children did find benefits, for example Lazar and Darlington (1982) reported that in adolescence the Headstart children were less likely to be placed in special classes, were more likely to go to college and, in terms of social benefits, were less likely to need welfare assistance or become delinquent. This evidence is important because, aside from the potential detrimental effects of day care, there can be some benefits, although they are not very clear or certain. The lack of large-scale success may be due to the variety of other factors that influence children's scholastic success. The Headstart effects were stronger when the pre-school programme was followed by later interventions.

Childminders

Childminding is an alternative form of day care which some parents prefer because it is more similar to the care that a child might get in their own home. Or at least it appears to be more similar. Mayall and Petrie (1983) studied a group of London children aged under 2 and their mothers and childminders. They found that the quality of care offered to these children varied considerably. Some childminders were excellent but others provided a rather unstimulating environment and the children in their care didn't thrive.

Bryant, Harris, and Newton (1980) also studied childminding and found that some of the children were actually disturbed. Many minders felt they didn't have to form emotional bonds with the children or stimulate them, and they rewarded quiet behaviour, therefore encouraging passivity and under-stimulation.

Effects on Social and Cognitive Development

Social development

Child care may affect **sociability**—either positively or negatively. Various studies of social development have found that children who go more often to a day nursery become more active, outgoing, and playful, and less aggressive. For example, Shea (1981) videotaped 3- and 4-year-olds in the playground during their first 10 weeks at nursery school, and found that sociability increased over that time. The children's behaviour was assessed on five dimensions: aggression, rough-and-tumble play, frequency of peer interaction [interaction with children of the same age], distance from the teacher, and distance from the nearest child. There were clear indications that the children became more sociable over time. There was a decrease in the distance from the nearest child and in aggression, and an increase in rough-and-tumble play, frequency of peer interaction, and in distance from the teacher. The increases in sociability were greater in those attending the nursery school for five days a week than in those attending for only two days, indicating that it was the experience of nursery school rather than maturation that was producing most of the changes.

Clarke-Stewart, Gruber, and Fitzgerald (1994) also found that peer relationships were more advanced in day-care children. This study looked at 150 children from Chicago, aged between 2 and 3 and from various social backgrounds. The children in day care had more advanced peer relationships due, no doubt, to their extensive experience coping with peers in the day-care setting. They learned earlier how to cope in social situations and how to negotiate with peers. This is useful experience for later years at school.

However, this is not true for all children. When children are shy and unsociable, the nursery experience can be threatening, which may have a negative effect on their school career (Pennebaker et al., 1981). The effect of day care on emotional development can be significant. Bowlby said there would be irrevocable harm if infants are separated from a primary caregiver, and there is some support for this. For example, Belsky and Rovine (1988) found that there was an increased risk of an infant developing insecure attachments if they were in day care for at least four months and if this had begun before their first birthday. Also Sroufe (1990) believed that the first year of life was vital for mother–child attachment and therefore day care should be delayed until the second year.

However, there is also considerable evidence that day care does *not* affect emotional development. Clarke-Stewart et al. (1994) investigated the relationship between time spent in day care and quality of attachment in over 500 children. They found that 15-month-old children who experienced "high-intensity" child care (30 hours or more a week from age 3 months) were no more distressed when separated from their mothers in the Strange Situation than "low-intensity" children (less than 10 hours a week). This suggests that attachment was *not* affected by the experiences of separation. Roggman et al. (1994) also found no ill-effects from early day care when they looked at behaviour in the Strange Situation. They compared infants cared for at home with those who attended day care before the age of 1. Both groups were equally securely attached to their mothers.

Cognitive development

There is much evidence that day care can have positive effects on **cognitive development** for *all* children. For example, Burchinal, Lee, and Ramey (1989) found that children entering school who had been in day care had higher IQs than those who had been at home with their mothers, suggesting that children benefit from the extra stimulation. Broberg et al. (1997), in a study of 146 Swedish children, compared children in day care, those looked after by a childminder, and those who stayed at home. When these children were assessed at the age of 8, the day-care children were consistently better on verbal and mathematical tests. Moreover, the longer the children had been in day care the higher their scores. Childminding again came out worst. Andersson's study (see page 129) found that all children, but especially boys, benefited from day care in terms of school achievement, in particular if they started before the age of 1 year. Clarke-Stewart et al. (1994) also found that children in day care had benefited from their enhanced amount of educational stimulation, although there was evidence that being in day care for more than six hours a day was not good for such young children.

On the other hand, Tizard (1979) found evidence that, irrespective of social class, the conversations between mother and child were more complex than between nursery teacher and child. Teachers had fewer exchanges and elicited less from the children, which may be due to the teacher's inevitably divided

? **What special ethical considerations should be taken into account when conducting work with young children?**

KEY TERM

Cognitive development: the development of the child's mental processes such as thought, reasoning, and memory. IQ tests and the child's academic performance at school are used to assess cognitive development. Cognitive development is determined by an interaction of biological predisposition and the environment.

EXAM HINT

The effects of day care may be social or cognitive. The biggest mistake made on day care questions is writing about cognitive when the question is on social and vice versa, so be clear on which is which. Know a minimum of three pieces of research evidence for each, which cover both positive and negative effects.

- Social:
  - Sociability: Shea (1981)
  - Peer relations: Clarke-Stewart et al. (1994)
  - Ability to form relationships: Belsky and Rovine (1988)
- Cognitive:
  - IQ achievement: Burchinal et al. (1989)
  - School performance: Andersson et al. (1992)
  - Conversational differences: Tizard (1979)

attention and less intimate relationship with the child. Such differences in conversation could be expected to affect cognitive progress.

Individual differences

It is worth considering the fact that some children may benefit from day care whereas others don't, and that this will be related to individual differences. Egeland and Hiester (1995) studied about 70 children, around half of whom entered day care before the age of 1 and the rest remained at home with their mothers. All the children came from poor backgrounds. The children were assessed at age 1 and again at 3½ years, using the Strange Situation procedure. Day care appeared to have a negative effect for secure children and a positive one for insecure children.

This may be because insecurely attached children *needed* compensatory education, and therefore benefited from day care, whereas the securely attached children didn't need this extra attention and therefore the separation effects alone were apparent. Later reports on socioemotional development found no differences in the two groups. These findings suggest, again, that what appears to matter is not the day-care experience but the *conditions* under which it may be positively beneficial.

Another study focused on differences in the mothers. The National Institute of Child Health and Human Development (NICHD) Study of Early Child Care (1997) examined over 1000 infants and their mothers at age 6 months and again at 15 months. The mothers were interviewed and the infants were observed at home and, where possible, in day care. There were no differences between the two groups in terms of emotional adjustment but those infants whose mothers were low in sensitivity/responsiveness were less secure if they were experiencing poor day-care arrangements. So the two factors—maternal sensitivity and poor-quality care—did affect development.

Recommendations for Improved Day Care

When day care is associated with a poor outcome this may be related to the *quality* of care rather than separation. Bowlby's arguments, as we have mentioned, could be interpreted as favouring *improved* child care. He suggested that separation could be compensated for by adequate bond substitution, where the child's emotional needs are placed foremost. For many parents there is little choice about day care—it is an economic necessity. Andersson's descriptions of high-quality child care in Sweden suggest that we need to develop higher-quality care worldwide. Schaffer (1998) felt that we need to focus on *consistency* of care (as well as quality) to improve day care.

Consistency of care

A number of the studies we have already examined point to the importance of consistency of care. For example, in Hodges and Tizard's study of institutional care (1989, see Key Study on pages 121–122), one of the reasons the children did not form attachments was because they had an average of 50 different caregivers before the age of 4. In contrast, in Kagan et al.'s study of day care, one of the key criteria was that the children received consistent emotional support. The NICHD

? Do you think the fact that all the children came from poor backgrounds may have biased Egeland and Hiester's results?

? What method was probably used by the NICHD to assess emotional adjustment?

study (1997) reported that the highest infant-to-caregiver ratio should be 1:3 in order to ensure that infants had sensitive and positive interactions. In order to improve consistency, a day-care facility needs to find some way of ensuring minimal turnover of staff, and to arrange that each child is assigned to *one* specific individual who is more or less constantly available and feels responsible for that child. It may also be important to establish consistent routines and physical environments.

Quality of care

Schaffer notes that it is very difficult to define "quality of care" although we can identify some features of day care that contribute to it. One important characteristic of high-quality care is the amount of verbal interaction between caregiver and child. We have already noted Tizard's (1979) evidence that mothers had more complex conversations with their children than teachers did, as teachers have to divide their attention.

A second way to improve the quality of day care is by increasing the availability of suitable toys, books, and other playthings. Sufficient stimulation is clearly important for cognitive development.

Third, and perhaps most important, is the issue of providing sensitive emotional care. The NICHD study found that just over a quarter of the infant care providers gave highly sensitive infant care, half of them provided moderately sensitive care, but worryingly a fifth of the caregivers were "emotionally detached" from the infants under their care. Where day care lacks emotional involvement we have seen that infant development will suffer.

Interaction with other children at nursery school provides social experience useful in later school life.

It may be possible to improve the quality of care that is offered by day-care providers. Howes, Galinsky, and Kontos (1998) found that a modest intervention programme, providing caregivers with in-service training to increase their sensitivity, did improve the attachment security of children within child care. Six months after training Howes et al. found the children (aged around 2 years) had become more secure and the caregivers were rated as more sensitive. There was a control group of caregivers who received no training. The attachment of the children in their care and their own sensitivity remained unchanged.

The effects of separation on parents

An important issue that is frequently overlooked is the two-way nature of the separation. Parents may themselves suffer when separated from their children, which may affect their ability to give quality care when they are with them. Harrison and Ungerer (2002) studied families in which the mother had gone back to paid work during the first year of her infant's life. Infants were most likely to be securely attached to their mothers at 12 months when their mother was strongly committed to work and had little anxiety about using non-family child care than when the mother was not committed to work and had anxieties about child care. To reduce mothers' feelings of anxiety or guilt, it may be helpful to provide more interlinking between home and day care, for example providing workplace nurseries.

Furthermore, it might help to relieve some of the guilt experienced by mothers to recognise that day care is *not* necessarily associated with negative effects. For some children there are actually benefits of having parents who work. For example, Brown and Harris (1978) found that women who don't work and have several young children to care for are more likely to become seriously depressed. Shaffer (1993) reported that children of working mothers tend to be more confident in social settings. It might be that going out to work enables some women to be *better* mothers.

SECTION SUMMARY

Types of day care

❖ Day care embraces a wide range of activities such as:
  – day nurseries,
  – childminding.
❖ Any discussion on the effects of day care needs to consider what type of day care is being provided, and individual differences between children.
❖ Day nurseries are thought to offer a good standard of care, while childminding varies greatly between different child minders.

The effects of day care on social and emotional development

❖ The effects of day care on social and emotional development are contradictory in that:
  – Many children benefit from attending day care in that they become more sociable.
  – Shy children, and insecurely attached children, do not thrive in day care.
  – Day care may lead to some children becoming more aggressive.
❖ However, children seem to be attached to their primary caregivers, whether or not they are in day care.

The effects of day care on cognitive development

❖ These depend very much on whether the cognitive stimulation provided at day care is an improvement on that provided at home.
❖ Individual differences have an effect: those who are insecurely attached and lacking in cognitive stimulation at home may benefit, as well as those whose mothers lack sensitivity.
❖ Day care has been shown to improve cognitive development in disadvantaged children, especially where intervention continues throughout childhood.

Improving the quality of day care

❖ The quality of day care can be improved by providing:
  – Consistent care.
  – Better interaction with infants.
  – Carers who are sensitive to the children's needs—possibly enhanced by in-service training.
  – Stimulating environments.
  – More caregivers: children receive less personal attention and therefore less stimulation when having to share the attention of a caregiver.

❖ The effects of day care separation on parents should not be overlooked, if primary caregivers are to continue to give quality care when they are with their children and to minimise bond disruption.

See pp.58–62 of the revision guide.

You have reached the end of the chapter on developmental psychology. Developmental psychology is an approach or perspective in psychology. The material in this section has exemplified the way that developmental psychologists explain behaviour. They look at behaviour in terms of the way that people change as they grow older, and the forces which create this change. Many of the changes, as we have seen, are due to inherited factors (nature). However, a major contribution also comes from the influence of other people and the physical environment (**nurture**). Development doesn't stop when you leave childhood, it continues through the lifespan. If you go on to study psychology, you will consider this wider area of developmental, or lifespan, psychology.

FURTHER READING

Chapter 6 in M. Harris and G. Butterworth (2002) *Developmental psychology: A student's handbook* (Hove, UK: Psychology Press) contains a good account of the development of attachment behaviour. An accessible account of early development is provided by J.C. Berryman, D. Hargreaves, M. Herbert, and A. Taylor (1991) *Developmental psychology and you* (Leicester, UK: BPS Books). The early development of sociability and attachment is discussed fully in Chapter 11 of D.R. Shaffer (1998) *Developmental psychology: Childhood and adolescence (5th Edn.)* (Pacific Grove, CA: Brooks/Cole). Studies of day care and other attachment issues are considered in H.R. Schaffer (1998) *Making decisions about children (2nd Edn.)* (Oxford, UK: Blackwell).

REVISION QUESTIONS

The examination questions aim to sample the material in this whole chapter. For advice on how to answer such questions refer to Chapter 1, Section 2.

Whenever you are asked to describe a study try to include some or all of the following details: research aim(s), participants, research method (e.g. experiment or observation), procedure, findings, and conclusion.

You will always have a choice of two questions in the AQA AS-level exam and 30 minutes in which to answer the question you choose:

Question 1 (AQA, 2004)
a. Explain what is meant by the terms "secure attachment" and "insecure attachment" (6 marks)
b. Outline the findings **and/or** conclusions of research into the effects of day care on cognitive development. (6 marks)
c. Outline and evaluate research (theories **and/or** studies) into privation. (18 marks)

Question 2
a. Explain what is meant by the terms "deprivation" and "privation". (3 marks + 3 marks)
b. Outline one psychological explanation of attachment. (6 marks)
c. "Some mothers choose to stay at home and look after their children while other mothers have little choice in the matter and may feel quite worried about the effects of day care." To what extent does day care affect the social **and/or** cognitive development of children? (18 marks)

Physiological psychology is an approach or perspective in psychology, and it is concerned with explanations of behaviour that refer to the body systems—cells, muscles, blood, hormones, and the nervous system. There is no doubt that much of human behaviour can be explained in terms of our body systems, or physiology. However, it may not be possible to explain higher activities such as problem solving in this way. Even a relatively "basic" behaviour, such as emotion, might seem rather simplistic when described in terms of the flow of hormones and heart rate. For this reason, psychologists often combine physiological explanations with psychological or sociological ones—this is called the biopsychosocial approach.

SECTION 11
Stress as a bodily response p.137

Stress is a healthy and adaptive response to certain situations. How does the body react to stress? What are the effects of prolonged stress on the body?

Specification content: The body's response to stressors (e.g. pituitary–adrenal system), the General Adaptation Syndrome (Selye). Research into the relationship between stress and cardiovascular disorders and the effects of stress on the immune system.

SECTION 12
Sources of stress p.151

What are the main sources of stress in modern life? Why do different people respond quite differently to stressful situations?

Specification content: Research into sources of stress, including life changes (e.g. Holmes & Rahe), and workplace stressors (e.g. Johansson, Marmot). Individual differences in modifying the effects of stressors, including the role played by personality (e.g. Type A behaviour, hardy personality) and gender (e.g. physiological reactivity, social support).

SECTION 13—CRITICAL ISSUE
Stress management p.171

The study of stress can be used to suggest ways of managing stress. Physiological methods include using drugs or biofeedback; psychological approaches include Meichenbaum's stress inoculation therapy and Kobasa's concept of increasing hardiness.

Specification content: Methods of managing the negative effects of stress, including physiological (e.g. drugs, biofeedback) and psychological approaches (e.g. stress inoculation, increasing hardiness). The strengths and weaknesses of methods of stress management.

PHYSIOLOGICAL PSYCHOLOGY:
Stress

Stress is an example of a behaviour and experience that can be explained in physiological and psychological terms. It is something with which most of us are all too familiar. If the media are to be believed, the pressures of everyday life are so great that most of us are highly stressed much of the time. No-one denies that millions suffer from stress, but people may have become too concerned about it. Indeed, we may be in danger of becoming stressed because we can't stop thinking about stress! In this chapter we consider the processes involved in stress and the management of stress.

SECTION 11
STRESS AS A BODILY RESPONSE

Defining Stress

We will make a start by considering the meaning of the term **stress**. Selye (1950) defined it as "the nonspecific response of the body to any demand". In other words, stress is a generalised reaction to a demand placed on the body. Interestingly, the term "stress" had not been used in relation to behaviour until Selye (1936) suggested using it to describe what happened when an organism was exposed to a noxious (unpleasant) stimulus. Thus, stress refers to our reactions (e.g. behavioural; physiological) to be exposed to a stressful situation. It is *really* important to note that the way psychologists use the term "stress" is *not* exactly the way we often use it in everyday life. For example, we say, "I'm under so much stress!", in which the word "stress" refers to the excessive demands we face and not our response to those demands. In psychology-speak, we should say, "I'm exposed to too many stressors!", as we will see in the next paragraph.

"Demands" are called **stressors**—events that throw the body out of balance and force it to respond, such as environmental factors like work overload, noise, cold, pain, or viruses. The stress response is useful in situations where an animal needs to react quickly, for example when a mouse sees a cat. Stress results in arousal, which makes the animal ready to respond in situations that threaten survival. A stress response is an **innate**, defensive, and **adaptive** reaction that promotes survival.

There are other situations where stressors require a less immediate response, such as when you know you have to get an assignment done by the following

KEY TERMS

Stress: a state of psychological and physical tension produced, according to the transactional model, when there is a mismatch between the perceived demands of a situation (the stressor[s]) and the individual's perceived ability to cope. The consequent state of tension can be adaptive (eustress) or maladaptive (distress).

Stressor: an event that triggers the stress response because it throws the body out of balance and forces it to respond. For example, life changes (e.g. divorce, bereavement), daily hassles (e.g. traffic, lost keys), workplace stressors (e.g. role strain, lack of control), and environmental stressors (e.g. noise, temperature, overcrowding). Stressors are not objective in that they do not produce the same response in all people, as this depends on the individual's perception of the stressor. Thus, nothing is a stressor unless it is thought to be so!

day and feel psychologically stressed (or distressed) as a result. This stress response is important because it makes you feel physiologically aroused, and this should increase your motivation and concentration. However, there are times when the stress response has the opposite effect, as we shall see.

The Role of the Autonomic Nervous System

In order to understand stress as a bodily response, we first need to understand the physiology of arousal (the response to stress), which basically involves the **autonomic nervous system (ANS)**. Your nervous system is divided into two main sub-systems:

- The **central nervous system (CNS)**: the brain and the spinal cord.
- The **peripheral nervous system (PNS)**: all the other nerve cells in the body.

The PNS is further subdivided into:

- The **somatic nervous system**—concerned with voluntary movements of skeletal muscles (those attached to our bones).
- The **autonomic nervous system**—concerned with involuntary movements of non-skeletal muscles (e.g. those of the heart).

The ANS is a largely *automatic* or self-regulating system, which means that it responds with little or no conscious thought on your part. It is concerned with many vital functions such as breathing and digestion.

Sympathetic and parasympathetic systems

The ANS has two general functions: to activate internal organs, and to save energy. These two functions are represented by what are called "branches" of the ANS:

The stress response is important for survival. An animal that does not feel stress when being pursued by a predator is not likely to survive because it does not become mobilised to respond.

- The **sympathetic branch** activates internal organs in situations needing energy and arousal, such as for "fight or flight". The sympathetic nervous system produces increased heart rate, reduced activity within the stomach, pupil dilation or expansion, and relaxation of the bronchi of the lungs.
- The **parasympathetic branch** is involved when the body is trying to conserve and store resources. It monitors the relaxed state, and promotes digestion and **metabolism**. The parasympathetic nervous system produces *opposite* effects to the sympathetic nervous system. Thus, it produces decreased heart rate, increased activity within the stomach, pupil contraction, and constriction of the bronchi of the lungs.

The sympathetic and parasympathetic nervous systems often operate in opposition (antagonistically) to each other. For example, heart rate will tend to be high if there is more sympathetic nervous system activity, and low if parasympathetic activity is greater. Sometimes, however, the two systems need to work cooperatively together to achieve a goal. For example, consider sex in the male. Parasympathetic activity is needed to obtain an erection, whereas sympathetic activity is needed for ejaculation.

Endocrine system

The ANS achieves its effects via the **endocrine system**, which consists of various ductless glands. Most importantly, the endocrine glands secrete **hormones** into the bloodstream—these hormones control ANS activity.

Activities of the autonomic nervous system	
Sympathetic branch	**Parasympathetic branch**
Increased heart rate	Decreased heart rate
Reduced activity within the stomach	Increased activity within the stomach
Saliva production is inhibited (mouth feels dry)	Saliva production increased to aid digestion
Pupil dilation or expansion	Pupil contraction
Relaxation of the bronchi of the lungs	Constriction of the bronchi of the lungs
Glucose is released	Glucose is stored

Nervous system	Endocrine system
• Consists of nerve cells	• Consists of ductless glands
• Acts by transmitting nerve impulses	• Acts by release of hormones
• Acts rapidly	• Acts slowly
• Direct control	• Indirect control
• Specific localised effects of neurotransmitters	• Hormones spread around the body
• Short-lived effects	• Hormones remain in the blood for some time

Hormones can have dramatic effects on our behaviour and emotions, especially stress, which can be regarded in part as an emotional reaction to stressors. Most hormones are slow acting because they are carried around the body relatively slowly by the bloodstream. The effects of hormones last for some time but typically gradually diminish as the situation becomes less stressful.

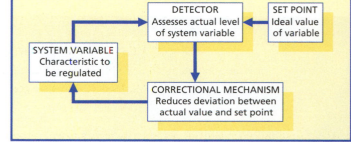

Homeostasis

The body's internal environment generally remains almost constant in spite of large changes in the external environment. This "steady state" or **homeostasis** is the result of ANS activity and is a fundamental part of the stress response. When an individual is placed under stress, the body strives to return to its normal, steady state as soon as possible. The normal body state is controlled by the parasympathetic branch storing and conserving energy. The sympathetic branch produces arousal which is necessary to deal with emergencies.

What we strive for is a *balance* between parasympathetic and sympathetic activity.

Central heating systems have similar regulatory mechanisms to the body's homeostatic mechanism. Both are designed to regulate temperature. The thermostat is set to the chosen temperature, and it detects deviations between the actual and chosen temperatures. When the temperature falls too low, the boiler of the central heating system is activated to restore the chosen temperature.

Bodily Responses to Stress

It is now time to focus more directly on the ways in which the body responds to stressors, which are events imposing demands on us. It is of key importance to note that stress (our reaction to a stressor) involves an immediate shock response, which is followed by a countershock response. The first or shock response depends mainly on the sympathetic adrenal medullary system (SAM), whereas the second or countershock response involves the hypothalamic–pituitary–adrenocortical axis (HPA). We will consider each of these systems in turn.

Sympathetic adrenal medullary system

The initial response to shock involves the sympathetic adrenal medullary system (SAM). In essence, activity in the sympathetic branch of the autonomic nervous system stimulates the adrenal medulla, which forms part of the **adrenal glands**. The adrenal medulla secretes the hormones **adrenaline** and **noradrenaline** (Americans call these epinephrine and norepinephrine, respectively). These hormones lead to increased arousal of the sympathetic nervous system and reduced activity in the parasympathetic nervous system.

Effects of SAM activity

Heightened activity of the SAM prepares us for "fight or flight". More specifically, there are the following effects: an increase in energy; increased alertness; increased blood flow to the muscles; increased heart and respiration rate; reduced activity in the digestive system; and increased release of clotting factors into the bloodstream to reduce blood loss in the event of injury. Adrenaline and noradrenaline increase the output of the heart, which can cause an increase in blood pressure.

Evaluation

SAM activity forms an important part of the stress response. It is an appropriate reaction of the body, because it prepares us for fight or flight. However, SAM activity is not *only* associated with stress. For example, we have elevated levels of adrenaline and noradrenaline when we are concentrating hard on a task. There is also the issue of how we *perceive* our internal **physiological** state. Sometimes we perceive heightened activity in the SAM as indicating that we are stressed, but sometimes we interpret such activity as meaning that we are excited or stimulated.

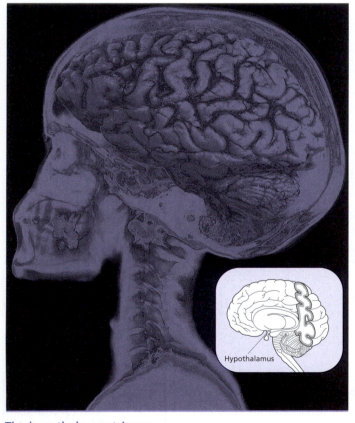

The hypothalamus triggers off the stress response. It is located at the base of the brain.

Hypothalamic–pituitary–adrenocortical axis

If someone is exposed to any given stressor for several hours or more, activity within the sympathetic adrenal medullary system increasingly uses up bodily resources. As a result, there is a countershock response designed to minimise any damage that might be caused. As mentioned earlier, this countershock response involves the hypothalamic–pituitary–adrenocortical axis (HPA), the details of which are discussed below.

The glands of the endocrine system are distributed throughout the body. Most of the system is controlled by the **hypothalamus**. It is a small structure at the base of the brain producing hormones (e.g. corticotropin releasing factor or CRF) which stimulate the anterior **pituitary gland**. The anterior pituitary gland releases several hormones. However, the one of most importance is **adrenocorticotrophic hormone (ACTH)**. ACTH stimulates the adrenal cortex, which forms part of the adrenal glands. The adrenal cortex produces various glucocorticoids, which are hormones having effects on **glucose** metabolism. The key glucocorticoid with respect to stress is **cortisol**, which is sometimes called the "stress hormone" because excess amounts are found in the urine of individuals experiencing stress.

Effects of HPA activity

- Good effect: Cortisol is important for coping with long-term stress, because it maintains a steady supply of fuel.
- Good effects: The secretion of cortisol and other glucocorticoids during the countershock response has various useful functions:
  (i) The glucocorticoids help to conserve glucose for neural tissues.
  (ii) The glucocorticoids elevate or stabilise blood glucose concentrations.
  (iii) The glucocorticoids mobilise protein reserves.
  (iv) The glucorticoids conserve salts and water.
- Good effect: Cortisol is important in reversing some of the body's initial responses to stress, and thus putting bodily systems into a balanced state (Gevirtz, 2000).
- Bad effects: "The blood still has elevated levels of glucose (for energy) and some hormones (including adrenaline and the pituitary hormone ACTH), and the body continues to use its resources at an accelerating rate. Essentially, the organism remains on red alert" (Westen, 1996, p.427).
- Bad effect: The anti-inflammatory action of glucocorticoids slows wound healing.
- Bad effect: Glucocorticoids suppress the immune system, which has the task of protecting the body against intruders such as viruses and bacteria. When immune responses are low, we are more likely to develop a disease (see Kiecolt-Glaser et al., 1984, 1995, discussed later in the chapter).

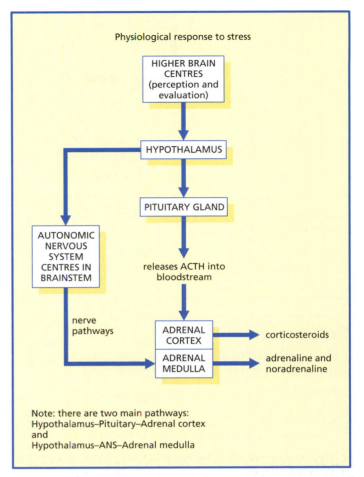

Physiological response to stress

Note: there are two main pathways:
Hypothalamus–Pituitary–Adrenal cortex
and
Hypothalamus–ANS–Adrenal medulla

Evaluation

As we have seen, the HPA is of value in reducing many of the effects of the first or shock response to stress. We can see this by considering people without adrenal glands who cannot produce the normal amounts of glucocorticoids. When exposed to a stressor, they must be given additional quantities of glucocorticoid to survive (Tyrell & Baxter, 1981). However, the beneficial effects of HPA activity are achieved at considerable cost, and the HPA cannot continue indefinitely at an elevated level of activity. If the adrenal cortex stops producing glucocorticoids, this eliminates the ability to maintain blood glucose concentrations at the appropriate level.

We have discussed the SAM and HPA as if they were different systems. This is basically correct, but note that the two systems do *not* operate in complete independence of each other. As Evans (1998, p.60) pointed out, "At the level of

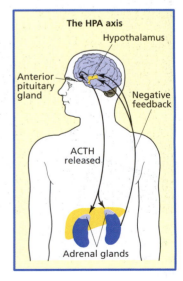

The HPA axis

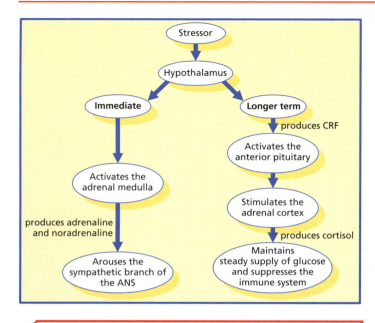

the central nervous system, the crucially important SAM and HPA systems can be considered as one complex: they are as it were the lower limbs of one body."

The General Adaptation Syndrome

Hans Selye (1936, 1950) conducted much research into stress from the 1930s until he died in 1982. In fact, he first popularised the term "stress", which had not been used previously as a psychological concept.

In 1936, Selye published his first article on the effects of stress, reporting an experiment with rats. When he exposed the rats to "acute nocuous [harmful] agents" (including cold, surgical injury, excessive exercise, severing the spinal cord, or sub-lethal doses of various drugs!), a typical syndrome appeared (discussed below). The same symptoms appeared in response to all of the stimuli, so they were all presumably due to the more general state of what he called "stress".

It is impossible to read Selye's account without wincing at the treatment received by the experimental rats. This is an example of an earlier period in psychology when researchers were less sensitive to the effects they were having on their participants.

Selye argued that stress can be adaptive in the short term, because it enables us to cope with environmental demands (fight or flight). However, the body's reaction to long-term or prolonged stress can be very damaging. Selye noticed that rats and hospital patients all seemed to show a similar pattern of bodily response. He called this pattern the **General Adaptation Syndrome (GAS)**, because it represented the body's attempt to cope in an adaptive way with stress. He argued that the GAS consisted of three stages (alarm reaction; resistance; and exhaustion). After the initial alarm reaction, the individual adapts and returns to normal functioning. It is only after prolonged stress that exhaustion occurs. In such extreme cases, stress-related illnesses can develop (see later).

The three stages of the GAS are described below:

1. *Alarm reaction stage*: This involves increased activity in the sympathetic adrenal medullary system (SAM) and the hypothalamic–pituitary–adrenocortical axis (HPA). However, Selye emphasised the role of the HPA in his account. According to Selye, the alarm reaction develops 6–48 hours after stress (e.g. injury), and includes loss of muscular tone, drop in body temperature, and decrease in size of the spleen and liver.
2. *Resistance stage*: This is the stage of adaptation, and also involves activity in the HPA. The body is adapting or fitting in with the demands of the environment. However, as this stage proceeds, the parasympathetic nervous system (which is involved in energy-storing processes) requires more careful use of the body's resources in order to cope. The system is being taxed to its limits. This stage is initially marked by an increase in the size of the adrenal glands and a decrease in some pituitary activity, such as the production of growth hormone. If the stress is not too great (e.g. slight injuries), then the body returns to a near-normal state.
3. *Exhaustion stage*: When stress is very prolonged, the physiological systems used in the previous two stages eventually become ineffective. The initial autonomic nervous system symptoms of arousal re-appear (increased heart rate, sweating, and so on). In extreme cases, the damaged adrenal cortex leads to failure of the parasympathetic system (metabolism and storage of energy) and collapse of the body's immune system. Stress-related diseases (e.g. high blood pressure, asthma, heart disease) become more likely.

> **KEY TERM**
>
> **General Adaptation Syndrome (GAS)**: the body's non-specific response to stress that consists of three stages: the alarm reaction, when the body responds with the heightened physiological reactivity of the "fight or flight" response to meet the demands of the stressor; resistance, when the body tries to cope with the stressor and outwardly appears to have returned to normal but inwardly is releasing high levels of stress hormones; and exhaustion, where resources are depleted and the body's defence against disease and illness is decreased.

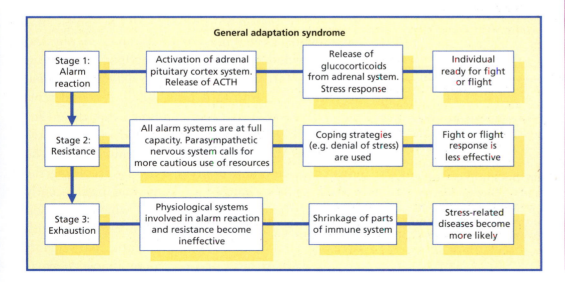

? Why do you think the work of Selye has been so influential to the study of stress?

EXAM HINT

If you are asked to outline two ways the body responds to stress and you struggle with the biology of the dual-stress response (see pages 139–142) you can describe:

- The "fight or flight" response.
- The General Adaptation Syndrome (GAS).

However, the disadvantage of choosing this answer over the dual-response, is that there is more to write on GAS so bear this in mind given the tight time conditions!

? What are the weaknesses of Selye's work in terms, for example, of the methodology or the ethics?

EXAM HINT

The three stages of the General Adaptation Syndrome ARE (note the mnemonic!)

Alarm reaction
Resistance
Exhaustion

Remember that individual differences can be used as a criticism of the GAS. The perception of stress and reaction to it are so varied. The "mismatch definition of stress" should be used to illustrate perception as it shows we are only as stressed as we perceive ourselves to be. Personality, gender, and cultural differences are rarely accounted for by research.

KEY TERM

Life changes: life changes require some degree of social readjustment or alteration in the individual's current life patterns (life change), which is the response to a significant life event. For example, death, divorce, a change of job, marriage, vacation, or Christmas. Each life event is assigned a life change unit (LCU) based on how much readjustment the change would necessitate. The adaptation needed to cope with the life change absorbs energy, and so depletes the body's resources, and thus life changes are a source of stress.

Evaluation of the General Adaptation Syndrome

Selye carried out pioneering research to identify major components of the stress response. For example, he correctly focused on what is now called the HPA system and on the importance of the glucocorticoids. Another key contribution was that he alerted medicine to the importance of stress in disease. Previous researchers had not properly appreciated the damaging effects of prolonged exposure to stress.

There are several limitations with Selye's research. First, he did not pay much attention to the SAM system, and he didn't understand fully the relationship between the HPA and SAM systems. Second, Selye exaggerated when he claimed that stress *always* produces the same physiological pattern. For example, Mason (1975) compared the reactions to stressors varying in the degree of how much fear, anger, or uncertainty they created. The various stressors produced *different* patterns of adrenaline, noradrenaline, and cortisol secretion. Third, Selye has been criticised for using non-human animals to support his research on human responses to stress. This may explain why his model overemphasises physiological factors at the expense of psychological factors (e.g. the role of emotional and cognitive factors in stress). Fourth, Selye assumed that people respond in a *passive* way to stressors. However, Mason (1975) argued that there is an active process of psychological appraisal when people confront a stressor. Symington et al. (1955) compared the physiological responses of two groups of dying patients, some of whom remained conscious and some of whom were in a coma. There were many more signs of physiological stress in the patients who remained conscious, presumably because they engaged in stressful psychological appraisal of their state.

Stress and Physical Illness

The research by Selye pointed to the importance of stress as a factor in physical illness. Stress has subsequently been linked with a range of physical illnesses including headaches, infectious illness (e.g. influenza), cardiovascular disease, diabetes, asthma, and rheumatoid arthritis (Curtis, 2000). A considerable body of research evidence supports this view. For example, Cohen, Tyrrell, and Smith (1991) gave participants nasal drops containing cold viruses. The researchers determined stress levels by recording the number of **life changes** an individual had recently experienced and also the extent to which they "felt out of control", both of which are associated with increased stress (see Section 12). Those participants with the highest level of stress were almost *twice* as likely to develop colds as those with the lowest level, suggesting a strong link between stress and illness.

What roles are played by the sympathetic adrenal medullary system (SAM) and the hypothalamic–pituitary–adrenocortical axis (HPA) in determining the effects of stress on our physical health? As yet, we cannot provide a clear and detailed answer, in part because stressors typically lead to activity in both systems. However, excessive activity of the SAM system probably causes wear and tear to the cardiovascular system. This would have the effect of increasing the probability of developing some form of heart disease. It is probable that the HPA has a greater role than the SAM in the development of physical disease. A key aspect of the HPA is the production of glucocorticoids (e.g. cortisol), and they have the unfortunate effect of impairing the functioning of the immune system. The issue of the effects of stress on immune functioning is discussed below.

> Speaking of an alcoholic's two sons: "One was a teetotaller and the other was a drunk. When asked to explain their drinking habits, both replied, 'With a father like that, what do you expect?' This illustrates perhaps the most important moral we can draw from stress research: that it is not what we face but how we face it that matters . . . We do have limited control over ourselves. It is the exercise of this control, or the lack of it, that can decide whether we are made or broken by the stress of life." (Selye, 1980, p.143)

Stress and ulcers

There is evidence that stress may be a causal factor in stomach ulcers, as first described by Brady (1958), whose research is discussed shortly. Stress often increases the secretion of hydrochloric acid, which plays a role in the development of some ulcers. Stress also weakens the defences of the gastrointestinal tract against this acid, thereby permitting gastric ulcers to develop (Pinel, 1997).

Brady (1958) linked high levels of stress to increased hormone production and the development of ulcers. In an early study, he placed monkeys in "restraining chairs" and conditioned them to press a lever. They were given shocks every 20 seconds unless the lever was pressed during the same time period. This study came to an abrupt halt when many of the monkeys suddenly died from ulcers caused by raised gastrointestinal hormone levels. The crucial question was whether the ulcers were due to the electric shocks or to the stress. To test this, Brady and his colleagues used yoked controls. One monkey, called the "executive", was responsible for controlling the lever and received the shocks, while at the same time a second monkey received the shocks but had no control over the lever. Thus, only the "executive" monkey had the psychological stress of deciding when to press the lever, but both monkeys received the shocks.

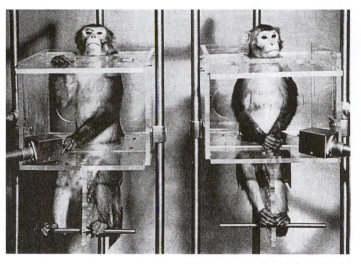

The executive monkey (left) and his yoked control (right). Both animals received shocks at regular intervals but only the executive had control, and only the executive developed the ulcers.

After 23 days of a 6 hours on, 6 hours off schedule, the executive monkey died due to a perforated ulcer. Initially, Brady thought that stress might be related to the reinforcement schedule. He tried various routines, such as 18 hours on and 6 hours off, or 30 minutes on, 30 minutes off, but no monkeys died. He then tested the stomachs of executive monkeys on a 6 hours on, 6 hours off schedule, and found that stomach acidity was greatest during the rest period. Brady concluded that it was clearly stress, not the shocks, that created the ulcers. The greatest danger occurred when the sympathetic arousal stopped and the stomach was flooded with digestive hormones, which is a parasympathetic rebound associated with the hypothalamic–pituitary–adrenocortical axis (HPA).

This study suggested that too much stress at work can lead to ulcers. Brady's findings were supported in a study by Weiner et al. (1957) using army recruits. Prior to basic training, the soldiers were tested and classed on the basis of their release of digestive enzymes as over-secretors or under-secretors. After four months of stressful training, 14% of the over-secretors had developed ulcers, whereas none of the under-secretors had. This suggests not only that the same principles apply to humans, but also that individual differences may be important in view of the fact that not *all* of the over-secretors developed ulcers.

Stress and hypertension

Perhaps the best known link is between stress and cardiovascular (heart) disease. **Hypertension** occurs when a person has raised blood pressure consistently for several weeks or more. It is a major risk factor for coronary heart disease (CHD). Hypertension is caused by a variety of factors such as obesity, too much salt, coffee (caffeine), or alcohol, lack of exercise, inherited predispositions, and psychosocial factors such as stress, anger, and hostility. Cobb and Rose (1973) produced evidence of a link between stress and hypertension in a study of men working as air traffic controllers and airmen. The researchers analysed annual medical records and found that hypertension rates were several times higher in the air traffic controllers than in the airmen. In addition, those controllers working in airports with greater traffic density had higher levels of hypertension.

Stress and coronary heart disease

Studies of coronary heart disease (CHD) itself have also implicated stress, most notably a study by Friedman and Rosenman (1959, 1974, discussed later, see Key Study on page 163). They found that individuals who cope least well with stress (**Type A**) are much more likely than other personality types to experience CHD.

How does stress cause illness?

As we have seen, there is good evidence that stress can increase the chances of someone becoming ill. There are *two* major ways in which stress can cause illness:

1. Directly, by reducing the body's ability to fight illness.
2. Indirectly, by leading the stressed individual to adopt an unhealthy lifestyle (e.g. increased smoking and drinking).

Direct effects of stress on the immune system

There is increasing evidence that stress can cause illness by impairing the workings of the **immune system**. This system acts like an army, identifying and killing any intruders to the body. It consists of cells distributed throughout the body that fight disease. The immune system cells, known as white blood cells or

---

? What ethical objections could be raised in connection with this study?

KEY TERM

Immune system: a system of cells (white blood cells) within the body that is concerned with fighting disease. The white blood cells, called leucocytes, include T and B cells and natural killer cells. They help prevent illness by fighting invading antigens such as viruses and bacteria.

leucocytes, fight any bacteria or viruses that are attempting to invade the body. There are various types of leucocytes such as T cells, B cells, and natural killer cells.

The reason AIDS has such a disastrous effect is because HIV attacks T-helper cells and this cripples the immune system.

Psychoneuroimmunology

The field of research that investigates the link between stress and other psychological states is called **psychoneuroimmunology** (PNI). One of the first studies to demonstrate immunosuppressive effects (something that suppresses the immune system) of stress was conducted by Riley (1981) using mice. Stress was created by placing the mice on a turntable rotating at 45 rpm (the speed of an old "single" vinyl music record). Riley measured the lymphocyte count of the mice over a five-hour period and found a marked decrease. Thus, their immune response was suppressed, presumably by the stress of sitting on the revolving disc. In a later study, Riley studied the link between stress and tumour growth by implanting cancer cells in mice. One group had 10 minutes of rotation per hour for three days (high-stress condition), whereas another group had no stress. Tumour growth stopped in the no-stress group, presumably because their intact immune systems were able to control it, whereas the "stressed" mice developed large tumours as a result of their low levels of lymphocytes.

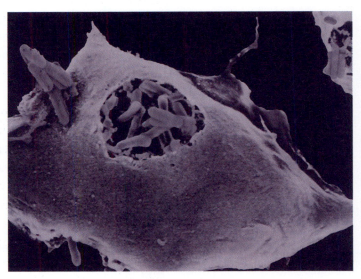

Like some monster in a movie, some cells of the immune system kill "invaders" by engulfing them. In the photograph a macrophage cell is engulfing *M. Tuberculosis* bacteria.

The above research has been supported by studies with humans. For example, Schliefer et al. (1983) looked at the functioning of the immune system in the husbands of women who died from breast cancer. The husbands' immune systems functioned less well after their wives had died than before, showing the impact of bereavement on the immune system.

Further evidence of the immunosuppressive effects of stress. By the early 1980s, it was generally accepted that stress can have various negative effects on people, including making them more vulnerable to physical illness and psychological disorders. However, there was not much evidence concerning *how* stress had these effects. Some light was shed on this issue by Kiecolt-Glaser et al. (1984), who studied human responses to stress by using a naturally occurring stressful situation with which you will be familiar—examinations. They took blood samples from medical students. Samples were taken one month before their final examinations and again on the first day of their final examinations, after the students had completed two of their examinations. A key finding was that natural killer cell activity *decreased* between the two samples. This finding suggests that stress is associated with a reduced response of the immune system.

Kiecolt-Glaser et al. (1984) also collected questionnaire data on both sampling occasions, obtaining information on psychiatric symptoms, loneliness, and life events. They did this because some theories suggest that all of these factors are associated with increased levels of stress. Immune responses were especially weak in those students who reported feeling most lonely, as well as in those experiencing stressful life events or psychiatric symptoms such as depression or anxiety.

This study by Kiecolt-Glaser et al. (1984) suggested that stress could have negative effects on people by producing a lowered immune response. In addition, several other psychological factors (e.g. psychiatric symptoms; life events) were also associated with impaired functioning of the immune system.

Further evidence was reported several years later by Kiecolt-Glaser et al. (1995; see Key Study below). They used a very different stressor (long-term caregiving to a relative with Alzheimer's disease) and a different measure of reduced functioning of the immune system (speed of wound healing). Their findings support those of Kiecolt-Glaser et al. (1984) in finding that stressors can have adverse effects on the immune system.

Key Study: Stress and the immune system

Kiecolt-Glaser et al. (1995) on slowing of wound healing by psychological stress.

Aims: Kiecolt-Glaser et al. aimed to test the hypothesis that psychological stress (looking after a relative with Alzheimer's disease) can cause damage to the immune system (in the form of slowing of wound healing). This hypothesis was based on previous research suggesting that the functioning of the immune system can be damaged by various forms of stress.

Procedure: There were two groups: (1) caregivers who were women looking after a relative with Alzheimer's disease; and (2) control participants who were women matched in age and family income with the caregivers. The caregivers (who had on average been looking after a relative for almost 8 years) scored much higher on a perceived stress scale than did the controls. The functioning of the immune system was studied by creating a small wound on the forearm close to the elbow; this is known technically as a punch biopsy. The time taken for the wound to heal was assessed by photographing the wound regularly and by observing the response to hydrogen peroxide (an absence of foaming indicated healing). A small amount of blood was obtained for analysis before the punch biopsy took place.

Findings: The key finding was that the time taken for the wound to heal was significantly longer for the caregivers than for the controls. The healing time averaged 48.7 days for the caregivers and 39.3 for the controls. In addition, the caregivers had a larger average wound size than the controls, especially during the first few days after the wound had been created. Analysis of the blood collected from the participants revealed that the caregivers produced significantly less interleukin-1β than controls under certain conditions. This may be important because interleukin-1β seems to play a role in speeding up wound healing.

Conclusions: The findings show that high levels of psychological stress can damage the functioning of the immune system as indicated by a slowing of wound healing and an increase in the size of the wound. It is possible (but by no means certain) that the slower rating of wound healing in caregivers than controls is due in part to their lower levels of interleukin-1β.

[?] This was a natural experiment. What are the advantages and disadvantages of such research?

[?] How well do you feel these results would generalise to all humans?

Criticisms

- The fact that the experimenters created the same wound in all the participants means they could observe effects of stress on the immune system in a controlled way.
- The finding that stress slows down wound healing may have important implications for recovery from surgery.
- The groups of caregivers and controls may have differed in ways other than the level of psychological stress; for example, more caregivers were on medication, and this may have affected their immune system.
- The role of interleukin-1β in wound healing is somewhat speculative, and Kiecolt-Glaser et al. had no *direct* evidence that it was relevant.
- It was a small and preliminary study with only 13 participants in each group, and so the study needs to be repeated with a larger sample.

Evaluation of stress and illness

There is good evidence that stress can directly produce changes in the immune system, and there is also reasonable evidence that stress can directly increase the probability that individuals develop various physical illnesses. However, there are several limitations with this evidence. First, as Bachen, Cohen, and Marsland (1997) concluded, "It is not yet clear that either the nature or magnitude of immunological change found in PNI [psychoneuroimmunology] research bears any relevance to increased disease susceptibility." In other words, there *are* genuine effects of stress on immune system functioning, but these effects are typically rather small. Indeed, the functioning of the immune system in most stressed individuals is actually within the normal range! If the effects on the immune system are so limited, how can such effects increase an individual's chances of developing, say, coronary heart disease?

Second, the immune system is extremely complex, and so it is very hard to assess the quality of an individual's immune system. As a result, it is a gross oversimplification to say that stress impairs immune system functioning simply because there are effects of stress on certain small parts of the immune system. Research by Evans, Clow, and Hucklebridge (1997) into PNI found the assumption that stress suppresses the immune system is too simple. They suggested that individual measures of the state of the immune system during stress may vary with the type of stress, its duration, and even its timing.

Third, the effects of stress on the immune system depend on the duration of the stressor. So far we have considered the effects of *long-term* stress on the immune system, and we have seen that aspects of its functioning are often reduced by such stress. However, the effects are rather different with *short-term* stress, and can include an improvement in at least some aspects of immune system functioning. For example, Delahanty et al. (1996) looked at the effects of short-term stress under laboratory conditions. Their participants performed a mental arithmetic task with harassment, immersed their hand in cold water at 3°C, or read magazines. There was *greater* natural killer cell activity during the two stressful tasks than during the control task of reading magazines, suggesting enhanced functioning of at least one part of the immune system.

SECTION SUMMARY

What is stress?

❖ Stress is an innate, defensive response to situations that threaten survival.
❖ The bodily response to stress can be explained by looking at:
  – The role of the autonomic nervous system and
  – The hypothalamic–pituitary–adrenocortical axis.
❖ However, the beneficial effects of activity in this system (described below) are achieved at much cost, and it cannot continue indefinitely at an elevated level of activity.
❖ Continued stress can deplete our resources and may lead to illness.

The autonomic nervous system (ANS)

❖ The ANS is concerned with involuntary movements and vital bodily functions, and is automatic.
❖ It is divided into two branches:
  1. The sympathetic branch, which activates internal organs for flight or fight.
  2. The parasympathetic branch, which conserves energy and promotes metabolism.
❖ These two branches often operate in opposition to each other and maintain homeostastis.
❖ The ANS achieves its effects via the endocrine system which produces hormones.
❖ In stress situations, the immediate shock response arouses the sympathetic branch which prepares the individual for flight or fight.
❖ This is followed by the countershock response which is designed to minimise any damage caused by the shock response. It involves the hypothalamic–pituitary–adrenocortical axis and seeks to return the body to its parasympathetic state.

The hypothalamic–pituitary–adrenocortical axis

❖ The hypothalamic–pituitary–adrenocortical axis governs the stress response in that:
  1. The hypothalamus directs ANS activity via the corticotrophic releasing factor (CRF).
  2. CRF stimulates the anterior pituitary and this triggers the release of hormones in the endocrine system (which is a group of ductless glands).
  3. The pituitary hormone ACTH stimulates the adrenal cortex, which produces adrenaline and nonadrenaline.
  4. Both of these are released as a response to stress, and they then create sympathetic arousal (which includes raised heart rate and sweating).
  5. The adrenal cortex also releases hormones such as cortisol which result in parasympathetic activity such as suppression of the immune system.

The General Adaptation Syndrome

❖ Selye proposed the General Adaptation Syndrome, which is a model of how the stress response adapts physiological systems to a stressor.
❖ It has three stages:
  1. alarm reaction,
  2. resistance,
  3. exhaustion.
❖ Eventually resources become depleted and illness ensues.

❖ Seyle's model highlighted the importance of stress in illness but failed to adequately account for situational and individual differences that need to be considered when exploring any link between stress and illness.

❖ The relationship between stress and physical illness is extremely complex. Caution is needed before generalising from animal research to humans, and inferring causation from correlational studies needs to be avoided.

❖ However, research has suggested that stress can cause colds, gastric ulcers, and cardiovascular disorders.

❖ Stress may cause illness *directly* by affecting the workings of the immune system (the activity of lymphocytes, natural killer cells, endorphins). The field that investigates this is called psychoneuroimmunology (PNI), but the approach has been criticised for being oversimplified.

❖ Stress may cause illnesses *indirectly* by affecting people's life style in that they might drink or smoke more, or take less care of themselves.

The relationship between stress and illness

See pp.66–75 of the revision guide.

SECTION 12
SOURCES OF STRESS

An alternative way to consider stress is to examine the factors that cause stress—potential stressors. The study by Kiecolt-Glaser et al. (1984) indicated that individuals are often exposed to more than one stressor at any time. In this section, we will consider some of the most important stressors: life events and daily hassles; and work-related stressors, including environmental stressors such as overcrowding, temperature, and noise.

In addition to having many sources of stress, we should also consider that there are many different responses to stress. At the beginning of the last section, we considered Selye's definition of stress: "the nonspecific response of the body to any demand". However, this definition suggests there is only *one* kind of stress response, whereas in fact there are *many* responses to stress, e.g. anxiety, depression, anger, and even happiness (Selye called this last form of response "eustress"). The nature of the stress response depends on various other factors—what we might loosely term "the situation". Selye's definition does not consider adequately the different sources of stress and responses to it.

Cox (1978) proposed a **transactional model** that described stress in terms of an interaction between the individual and his/her environment. Cox proposed that stress is experienced when the perceived demands of the environment are greater than the individual's perceived ability to cope. The use of the term "transaction" refers to the *interaction* between the individual and the environment.

Cox's transactional model can explain why learners find driving stressful whereas experienced drivers don't. The learner has limited ability to meet the demands of handling a car in traffic, which means that the demands of the environment are greater than their perceived ability to cope. For experienced drivers the perceived demands of the environment are less than their perceived ability to cope.

Changes can be stressful, even the usually pleasant ones associated with going on holiday.

LIFE EVENTS		
Rank	**Life Event**	**Stress Value**
1	Death of a spouse	100
2	Divorce	73
3	Marital separation	65
4	Jail term	63
5	Death of a close family member	63
6	Personal injury or illness	53
7	Marriage	50
8	Fired at work	47
9	Marital reconciliation	45
10	Retirement	45
13	Sex difficulties	39
23	Son or daughter leaving	29
38	Change in sleeping habits	16
40	Change in eating habits	15
41	Vacation	13
42	Christmas	12
43	Minor violations of the law	11

Adapted from Holmes, T., & Rahe, R. (1967). The social readjustment rating scale. *Journal of Psychosomatic Research, 11*, 213–218.

Some people who spend a lot of money on the National Lottery have received stress counselling because their failure to win is making them poor; others receive counselling because of the stress associated with winning large sums of money!

Life Events

Two medical doctors, Holmes and Rahe (1967), were the first to record the effects of **life events** in a systematic way. They observed that patients often experienced several life events in the months before the onset of illness, and that these life events seemed to be associated with stress and poor health. In particular, these life events could be characterised as involving change from a steady state, such as getting divorced or moving house. Even positive events, such as getting married or going on holiday, seemed to be associated with stress. They suggested that the changes associated with major life events absorb "psychic [mental] energy", leaving less available for other matters such as physical defence against illness.

In order to demonstrate these associations or correlations between life events, stress, and illness, Holmes and Rahe first needed some method of measuring life events. Accordingly, they developed the Social Readjustment Rating Scale (SRRS) by examining 5000 patient records and making a list of 43 life events that seemed to precede illness. Nearly 400 participants were asked to rate each item in terms of the amount of stress it produced, and an arbitrary value of 500 was assigned to marriage as a reference point. The results were averaged and divided by 10 to get a measure of the individual events in terms of life change units (LCUs), representing the degree of stress caused by events. Holmes and Rahe had tested various sub-groups to see if the ratings were consistent, e.g. male and female, single and married, black and white, younger and older respondents. As there was strong agreement between different groups, it seemed that the SRRS was a valid measure for all types of people. The final scale consisted of 43 items or events, some of which are shown in the table. Total life events scores could be calculated by adding up the LCUs for each event ticked on the scale. The evidence from numerous studies using the Social Readjustment Rating Scale is that people who have experienced events totalling more than 300 LCUs over a period of one year are at greater risk than other people for a wide range of physical and mental illnesses. These illnesses include heart attacks, diabetes, TB, asthma, anxiety, and depression (Martin, 1989). However, the associations or correlations between LCUs and susceptibility to any particular illness tend to be rather low, indicating only a weak association between life events and illness.

Using the SRRS

Research by Holmes and Rahe (1967) using the Social Readjustment Rating Scale suggested that life events were associated with various physical illnesses.

The notion that the stressful experiences we have in life can have effects on our physical health is an important one, because it means we should not look only for physical causes of physical illnesses. Several researchers, including Rahe, Mahan, and Arthur (1970; see Key Study below), carried out more detailed studies to try to obtain stronger support for the above notion. They found a small but significant positive correlation or association between LCUs and physical illness. Rahe and Arthur (1977) provided support for the findings of Rahe et al. (1970). They found an increase of various psychological illnesses, athletic injuries, physical illness, and even traffic accidents, when LCUs were raised.

? **What are the main reasons why some life events are much more stressful than others?**

Key Study: Life changes

Rahe et al.'s (1970) study of the correlation between life events and susceptibility to stress-related illnesses.

Aims: Rahe et al. aimed to test the hypothesis that the stress of life events was correlated or associated with illness. This hypothesis aimed to test findings by Holmes and Rahe (1967), who had observed that patients tended to have experienced critical life events in the months prior to the onset of illness.

Procedure: An investigation of 2500 male US naval personnel took place over a period of six months. A self-report questionnaire measured the number of life events, which was based on the Social Readjustment Rating Scale (SRRS) constructed by Holmes and Rahe. This consisted of 43 life events, which are defined as positive or negative events that disrupt normal routines and so require social readjustment. Each life event had assigned to it a value (or life change unit, LCU) based on how much readjustment the event would necessitate. Participants were asked to indicate how many of the life events they had experienced in the past six months. A total life change unit score (stress score) was calculated for each participant by adding up the LCUs of each life event. A health record was also kept of each participant during the six-month tour of duty. A correlational analysis was carried out to test the association between total LCUs and incidence of illness.

Findings: A significant positive correlation of +0.118 was found between the total LCU score and illness (as total LCUs increased so did incidence of illness). The direction of the correlation was positive and the strength of the relationship was weak. The association was small but significant.

Conclusions: The findings suggest that the stress of life events is correlated with physical illness. The correlation appears weak: if the total LCU score was always associated with illness a perfect positive correlation of +1.0 would have been found. If there were no association the correlation coefficient would have been 0. The correlation coefficient of +0.118 is fairly small, but in a sample of 2500 this is a significant correlation. Implications include the importance of using stress management techniques when experiencing life events.

Criticisms

- This study used the correlational method. As a consequence, cause and effect cannot be inferred, because causation can only be inferred when an IV has been directly manipulated. Thus, it cannot be said that life events cause illness, and so conclusions are limited.

- In many cases, it is likely that illness helped to cause certain life events rather than that life events helped to cause illness. For example, two of the life-event items on the SRRS are change in eating habits and change in sleeping habits, and it is perfectly possible that physical illness would produce such changes. Thus, the direction of effect is not clear.
- The sample was biased because only American men were investigated. Thus, the sample was ethnocentric (as only one culture was sampled) and androcentric (as only males were sampled). The fact that such a restricted sub-group was sampled means the findings are not representative of the wider population (e.g. other cultures; women). The findings may not even be representative of the target population, as a random sample of American naval men was not taken. Thus, the research may lack external validity.

Note: It is tempting to criticise the SRRS, because it has many limitations. However, it is better to focus on criticisms of this piece of research rather than the general criticisms of the SRRS.

Note: If the question asks for findings or conclusions only, you could include research by Rahe and Arthur (1977, see p.153).

Why is the study by Rahe et al. (1970) important? First, it provided some of the first evidence that there is a genuine association between stressful life events and physical illness. Second, the study was an improvement on previous research, in that careful records of physical illness were kept over a six-month period. Third, the fact that physical health was assessed *after* the life events increases the chances that the life events were helping to cause problems with physical health, rather than the other way around.

Evaluation of the SRRS evidence

The major importance of the Social Readjustment Rating Scale (and the research associated with it) is that it represented a major breakthrough. It is now generally accepted that life events of various kinds influence our psychological well-being and our physical and mental health. While these ideas had been proposed previously by other psychologists, the development of the SRRS meant that it was easy to carry out research to test these ideas. This in turn has led to a clearer understanding of the ways in which life events affect us.

There are various limitations with the SRRS and research based on it. First, the research is correlational, so it is not clear whether life events have *caused* some stress-related illness, or whether it was stress that caused the life events. For example, stress may cause a change in eating habits, rather than a change in eating habits causing stress. Other variables may also be involved. Certain individuals may find life events threatening because they have vulnerable personalities, and they may become ill due to their personality rather than the life events themselves. Individual differences in coping skills and in past experience influence the extent to which a potentially stressful event will affect you (the issue of individual differences is explored later in this section).

Second, the impact of most life events depends on the precise situation. For example, marital separation may be less stressful for someone who has already established an intimate relationship with another person. Some measures take account of the *context* in which people experience life events. This is true of the Life Events and Difficulties Schedule (LEDS; see Harris, 1997). For example, consider the life event of losing your job. That is much more likely to create stress if you have no other source of money and very poor job prospects than if you have a million pounds in the bank and excellent prospects of finding a very good job in the near future. It is important to take subjective interpretation into account— it is not the events themselves but their meaning for us that is important. Cohen (1983) developed a "perceived stress scale" to assess this.

Third, the assumption that desirable life events can cause stress-related illnesses has not attracted much support (Martin, 1989). In addition, the SRRS tends to muddle together different kinds of life events, e.g. those over which you have some control and those you do not. The latter may be more stressful.

Fourth, the data on life events were collected some time after they had occurred. This can cause unreliability, and there is evidence that relatively minor life events can be forgotten within a period of a few months, and stressful events exaggerated once an illness diagnosis is made.

Fifth, it has often been assumed that almost any serious life event can help to produce almost any type of illness. This has led to a relative ignoring of more *specific* effects. For example, Finlay-Jones and Brown (1981) found that anxious patients were more likely than depressed patients to have experienced danger events (involving future threats), whereas depressed patients were more likely to have experienced loss events (involving past losses). It would be useful to have more such studies.

Daily hassles

Anita DeLongis and her co-workers (1982) were critics of the life events approach, because of the various problems just outlined, and because most people experience major life events very infrequently. Most importantly, they felt that these studies had found at best a very weak correlation or association between life events and illness. In reality, according to DeLongis et al., it is the ongoing stresses and strains of daily living, what we generally call "hassles" (e.g. being caught in traffic jams; discovering the computer has lost your work), that determine the extent to which a person feels stressed. Therefore, this would lead us to expect a stronger correlation between hassles and physical illness than was found for life events.

? Why might daily hassles be a better measure of stress than life events?

DeLongis et al. (1982) compared the two measures: a life events scale and their own hassles scale, to see which was a better predictor of later health problems. They also considered how "uplifts"—events that make you feel good— affect health. Participants were asked to complete four questionnaires once a month for a year:

- Hassles scale (117 hassles, e.g. concerns about weight, rising prices, home maintenance, losing things, crime, and physical appearance).
- Uplifts scale (135 uplifts, e.g. recreation, relations with friends, good weather, job promotion).
- Life events questionnaire (24 major events).
- A health status questionnaire covering overall health status, bodily symptoms, and energy levels.

? Can you think of some examples of "hassles"? Some ideas are given in the activity on the next page.

There were 100 participants aged between 45 and 64, who were predominantly well educated and had high incomes. DeLongis et al. found that both the

■ **Activity:** You could conduct your own research into the effects of stress and illness using your own daily hassles index. Some examples are given below from an index that was designed specifically for college students. Illness can be assessed by, for example, checking absenteeism or asking people to keep a diary for a short period.

Hassles scale
Assess yourself by indicating how often each item irritates you, by entering a number between 1 and 10 in the box, where 10 = frequently, 5 = sometimes, and 0 = almost never.

Example items:

☐ Parking problems around campus
☐ Library too noisy
☐ Too little money
☐ Not enough close friends
☐ Conflicts with family
☐ Writing essays

☐ Careless bike riders
☐ Too little time
☐ Boring teacher
☐ Room temperatures
☐ Too little sleep
☐ Fixing hair in the morning

Adapted from Schafer, W. (1992), *Stress management for wellness* (2nd Edn.). New York: Harcourt Brace Jovanovich.

frequency and intensity of hassles were significantly correlated with overall health status and bodily symptoms, yet daily uplifts had little effect on health. They failed to find a relationship between life events and health during the study, although there was a relationship for life events recorded for the two years before the study.

Evaluation of the hassles approach

When DeLongis et al. investigated the relationship between hassles and physical health, as well as uplifts and physical health they found a slightly better correlation than that for life events and health. However, the scale suffered from similar problems to the SRRS, e.g. the same hassle can be experienced in a different way on two occasions, and individual differences affect the extent to which a hassle is stressful or not.

DeLongis et al.'s approach managed to avoid the problem of the relevance of major life events but it still overlooked many chronic "ongoing" sources of stress, such as poor housing, low incomes, strains of family life, unsatisfying work, and so on. Health is probably affected by all three: hassles, chronic situations, and life changes.

Another problem is that the same factors that are a hassle to one person may actually be an uplift to another, or might mean different things to the same person on different occasions. For example, a traffic jam may sometimes give you time to relax, whereas at other times it seems highly stressful. For this reason DeLongis, Folkman, and Lazarus (1988) later produced a single "Hassles and Uplifts Scale" where respondents could indicate the strength of a factor either as a hassle or an uplift.

A further problem of the 1982 study concerns the original sample, which was of people aged over 45, as this sample bias may have affected the results. Khan and Patel (1996) found that older people tended to have less severe (and fewer) hassles than younger people.

In general this makes these "scale" approaches to stress of somewhat limited usefulness. It is not possible to identify a global set of events, large or small, to

EXAM HINT
Daily hassles are not life events, and therefore the research by DeLongis et al. should not be used to answer questions on life changes or events, except as a means of evaluation.

provide a clear link with subsequent stress. It may be more profitable to focus on particular "hassles" such as overcrowding, noise, and so on.

Work-related Stress

Both the pressures of work and the work environment itself (e.g. noise) are potential **workplace stressors** that should be considered. These include job insecurity, overcrowding, organisational change, interpersonal conflicts, sexual harassment, punitive management, lack of control, underutilisation of skills, responsibility for others, excessive workload, shift work, lack of support, and a dangerous, unpleasant, or uncomfortable work environment. For example, many non-smokers find it very unpleasant to work in a smoky environment. More generally, we might expect that individuals whose work environment is unpredictable or uncontrollable might experience more stress than those whose work environment is reasonably predictable and under their control.

Johansson, Aronsson, and Lindstroem (1978) compared two groups of workers in a highly mechanised production industry. One group was identified as high-risk because what they did had the following features: repetitive work; machine regulation of the pace of their work; physical constraints; and requirement to attend continuously. In contrast, the low-risk group carried out their work under more flexible conditions. At work, the high-risk group produced higher levels of adrenaline and noradrenaline (both involving activity in the sympathetic nervous system) than did the low-risk group, suggesting that they experienced more need to mobilise their physiological coping resources. This may help to explain why members of the high-risk group had higher levels of absenteeism and more psychosomatic illness (physical problems thought to be influenced by psychological factors, e.g. hypertension).

The effects of work-related stressors include absenteeism, high job turnover, alcohol and drug abuse, and poor work performance. An extreme stress response is **burnout**, in which the individual workers can no longer function effectively. Maslach and Jackson (1982) measured burnout in terms of three psychosocial components:

1. *Emotional exhaustion.* Working with people, and particularly those who are in difficulty, is a strain on psychic resources.
2. *Depersonalisation.* Both worker and client deindividuation, a sense of losing individual identity.
3. *Perceived inadequacy.* The worker experiences low job satisfaction because he/she feels his/her efforts fail to produce the desired results.

In what follows, we will consider some of the main work stressors in some detail. Bear in mind that all good employers strive to reduce work stress in order to have a contented and productive work force. Also bear in mind that some workers in Britain have successfully sued their companies for exposing them to high levels of stress causing illness.

Noise

Many people claim that they can concentrate reasonably well no matter what the noise levels are like. Research has found this is true to some extent. However,

KEY TERM

Workplace stressor: Factors in the work environment or aspects of the job that cause stress. For example, overcrowding, noise, and temperature are factors in the environment. Lack of control, interpersonal relationships, role ambiguity, and work overload are all examples of work pressures that cause stress.

You may think you can work just as well with background noise, but psychological research suggests that there are some psychic costs and it may contribute to your stress levels.

Glass, Singer, and Friedman (1969) examined whether people may just *appear* to cope by incurring a psychic cost and being left with fewer available resources. To test this hypothesis, they arranged for 60 undergraduate students to complete various cognitive tasks (e.g. word searches) under one of five conditions: loud or soft noise, played at random (unpredictable) or fixed (predictable) intervals, or no noise. During the task, physiological arousal was measured using the galvanic skin response (GSR, a measure of autonomic arousal or stress). Afterwards, the participants were asked to complete four puzzles, two of which were unsolvable. Frustration (stress) was measured in terms of the length of time that participants participated in these tasks.

The participants adapted to the noise. In the predictable noise condition, they made fewer errors and had lower GSR and higher task persistence than did participants in the unpredictable noise condition. Those in the no-noise condition made even fewer errors. These findings suggest that unpredictable noise has the greatest effect, but even predictable noise creates some stress. Glass et al. suggested that this is because we can "tune out" constant stimuli while still attending to a task. However, unpredictable stimuli require continuous attention, which reduces our ability to cope with them. Therefore, noise (especially unpredictable noise) is a stressor.

Predictability and controllability

There are two important features of noise effects: predictability and controllability. In a further study, Glass et al. (1969) arranged for participants to listen to random noise while performing the same tasks as before. There were two conditions: (1) each participant was given a button to press so she could control the noise (the participants were all female); and (2) the noise couldn't be controlled. Participants in the button condition were significantly more persistent on the unsolvable tasks than those given no control over the noise. What is interesting is that no-one in the condition where they had control actually switched the noise off—presumably the greater sense of control increased the individual's ability to cope, which reduced anxiety. An everyday example of this would be if you find noise coming from your home more bearable than noise coming from next door—you probably have much more control over noise in your own home than in someone else's.

Earlier in the chapter, we discussed a study by Cohen et al. (1991) on stress and the common cold. They found that those participants who felt their lives were unpredictable and uncontrollable were twice as likely to develop colds as those who experienced little stress.

In a replication of Glass et al.'s (1969) research, Gardner (1978) found no negative effects of unpredictability. However, he realised he had asked his participants to sign a consent form saying that they understood their rights as a participant. This led him to wonder if this had given them a sense of control not present in the original study. He tested this notion by giving the consent forms to

? What comments might you make on the ethics of Gardner's study?

only half of the participants. Those without consent forms experienced stress, whereas those with consent forms did not.

Earlier in the chapter, we considered the study by Brady (1958) on stress in "executive" monkeys (see page 145). This indicated how the stress related to making decisions might be linked to physical illness (e.g. gastric ulcers). This is in apparent contrast with the findings from Glass et al. (just described) and this next classic study by Ellen Langer and Judith Rodin. Why is there a difference? We can't be sure. However, it is possible that Brady's executive monkeys were stressed by the *responsibility* they had for preventing

Elderly people moved from their own homes into nursing homes may experience a decline in their health due to changes in their routines or the sense of losing control.

something really unpleasant (i.e. electric shocks). Thus, control is generally associated with reduced stress, but not if it is accompanied by worrying responsibilities.

Older people often experience a decline in their health when they begin living in a home for the elderly. Langer and Rodin (1976) questioned whether a key factor might be loss of control, by studying residents in a nursing home. At the start, all the residents were similar in psychological and physical health, and had similar socio-economic status. Residents on Floor 1 formed the "responsibility induced" group. They were allowed to make certain decisions such as how to arrange their rooms, when they went to see films, and whether to receive visitors or not. Residents on Floor 2 formed the "traditional" group. They had their rooms arranged for them, had to see films when they were scheduled, and had all other choices made for them.

When the nurses were asked to rate the participants, 71% of the traditional group were classified as "more debilitated", whereas 93% of the responsibility induced group were classified as "improved". In addition, the responsibility induced group saw more films, and rated themselves as more active and happier. This was still the case 18 months later. Mortality or death rates also differed between the two groups. In a follow-up, only 15% of the responsibility induced group had died, whereas twice as many of the other group had died. It is possible that higher death rates may be associated with less efficient immune systems.

There are some limitations with this study. Many of the outcome measures involved subjective (and possibly biased) judgements. For example, the nurses knew which group each of the participants belonged to, and this may have influenced their assessments. It is also possible that nurses treated the residents on each floor differently, which could help to account for the different health outcomes.

? In these studies responsibility was taken to be equivalent to control.

Do you think that responsibility is the same as control?

Control vs lack of control

Is **control** or lack of control associated with higher stress? The evidence discussed so far has revealed rather mixed findings. In order to answer this question more fully, we could consider the amount of control that people have at work. This makes sense for two reasons. First, millions of people spend 40 hours or so every week at work, and so the conditions in which they work

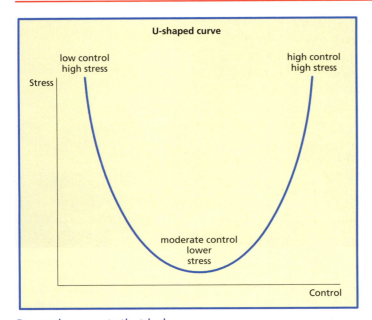

U-shaped curve

low control
high stress

high control
high stress

Stress

moderate control
lower
stress

Control

Research suggests that lack of control may lead to stress (e.g. Glass et al.) but also that high control may create stress (Brady). This is a curvilinear relationship as shown in the graph.

are likely to have a significant impact on their stress levels. Second, the amount of control that individual workers have at work varies enormously: some workers have almost total control over their work, whereas others have practically no control at all.

Some of the above considerations led Marmot et al. (1997; see Key Study below) to study employees in the civil service in a longitudinal study. Workers on the lowest employment grades were much more likely to die of a heart attack than those on the most senior grades, and were also more likely to suffer from cancer, strokes, and gastrointestinal disorders. Marmot et al. concluded that low control at work (found among the workers on the lowest employment grades) is associated with higher stress.

Key Study: Workplace stressors

Marmot et al.'s (1997) study of the association between workplace stress and stress-related illness.

Aims: This particular investigation aimed to investigate the negative correlation or association between job control and stress-related illness in male and female civil servants. The hypothesis that job control is negatively correlated with stress-related illness was assumed to apply to several different illnesses. This was part of the Whitehall studies where a number of different psychosocial characteristics of work were investigated to test their association with illness.

Procedure: A sample of 10,308 civil servants aged 35–55 (6895 men—67%, and 3413 women—33%) were investigated in a longitudinal study over three years. Research methods included questionnaires and observation. Job control (an aspect of workplace stress) was measured through both a self-report survey and by independent assessments of the work environment by personnel managers. Job control was assessed on two occasions, three years apart. Records were also kept of stress-related illness. A correlational analysis was carried out to test the association between job control and stress-related illness.

Findings: Participants with low job control were FOUR times more likely to die of a heart attack than those with high job control. They were also more likely to suffer from other stress-related disorders such as cancers, strokes, and gastrointestinal disorders. These findings were consistent on both occasions that job control was measured and the association was still significant after other factors, such as employment grade, negative attitude to employment, job demands, social support, and risk factors for coronary heart disease (CHD) had been accounted for.

Conclusions: The findings seem to show that low job control is associated with high stress, as indicated by the number of stress-related illness. There is an inverse (opposite) social gradient in stress-related illness among British civil servants: as job control decreases so illness increases. In other words, the variables are negatively correlated. Implications include the responsibility of employers to address lack of job control as a source of stress and illness. Giving employees more autonomy (freedom) and control may decrease stress-related illness, which would increase the efficiency, productivity, and general well-being of the workforce.

Criticisms

- The self-report method is vulnerable to investigator effects and participant reactivity bias (effects due to the fact that the participants were aware they were being observed). The questions may give cues as to the aim of the research and so create an expectancy effect. The participants may have guessed that an association between job control and stress-related illness was being looked for, and so reported low job control if suffering from illness and high job control if not. Similarly, the observations made by the personnel managers could be biased by an expectancy effect.
- Weaknesses of the correlational method mean that there is no control over job control as a variable, which makes interpretations difficult as cause and effect cannot be inferred (causation can *only* be inferred when an independent variable has been directly manipulated). Thus, it cannot be said that low job control causes stress-related illness; only that an association can be inferred. It is possible that workers whose health is poor are less likely than healthy workers to achieve career success and to have jobs offering good control. The lack of control over the independent variable (i.e. job control) means that other factors (e.g. personality; coping skills) may be involved in the correlation or association.
- The jobs performed by those high and low in job control differed in several ways other than simply control. For example, those having high levels of job control generally earn more money, have more interesting jobs, have more opportunity for interpersonal contact, and so on than those having low levels of job control. The researchers tried to take account of some of these factors, but we simply don't know which of these various factors is most closely associated with heart disease.

Note: If the question asks for findings or conclusions only, you could include research by Shirom (1989, see p.162), and Margolis and Kroes (1974, see p.162).

The study by Marmot et al. (1997) is important for various reasons. First, it provided striking evidence that the amount of control we have at work can have large effects on physical health. Second, the study showed that what happens in the workplace can sometimes cause high levels of stress. Third, the study strongly suggests that it is important to provide workers with a reasonable amount of control over their work activities if they are to remain healthy. However, note that those workers at the most senior levels had more prestigious jobs than those on the lowest grades, they earned more money, and they had more interesting work to do. Thus, it is hard to be sure that the difference in amount of illness between the two groups was only due to differences in control at work.

Role conflict

Organisational demands (e.g. higher productivity, reduced work bills) may be in direct conflict with the needs of the workers, who may be highly resistant

EXAM HINT

If you are asked to outline two sources of stress, you could describe life changes and workplace stressors. Use research evidence in brief to support your answer:

- Life changes: can absorb "psychic energy" and require psychological adjustment. See Holmes and Rahe (1967) on the development of the SRRS, and Rahe et al.'s (1970) finding of a +0.118 correlation between stress and illness in naval officers.
- Workplace stressors: these can include job insecurity, organisational change, interpersonal conflicts, lack of control. See the Marmot et al. (1997) Key Study on lack of control.

to the idea of working longer hours for smaller rewards. This creates **role conflict** and stress for the individual. If individuals don't accept organisational demands, they may lose their jobs. However, if they do accept them, this may conflict with other demands from their family, or they may fear for their health. Shirom (1989) found there was a significant correlation between perceived role conflict and coronary heart disease. However, this was only the case for middle management (white-collar workers) but not for blue-collar workers (the "shop floor"). Margolis and Kroes (1974) found that foremen were seven times more likely to develop gastric ulcers than shop-floor workers, suggesting more role conflict for those in greater control.

Individual Differences

In our discussion of factors cuasing stress, we have seen that a key consideration is the way that different individuals react—everyone responds differently. Psychologists call this **"individual differences"**. These may be innate temperamental, due to heredity, or the differences may be explained in terms of learning—through conditioning or by modelling one's behaviour on others. Or differences may be related to cultural styles of coping that are also learned, e.g. the Japanese try to accept problems, whereas Westerners take control and try to change stressful situations (Wade & Tavris, 1993).

Personality: Types A, B, and C

As recently as the 1950s, there was very little scientific evidence suggesting that physical illnesses such as heart disease might be influenced by psychological factors. Many people suspected there was a link between stress and physical illness, but the view in the medical profession was that we should seek physical causes for physical illnesses. It was in this context that two cardiologists, Meyer Friedman and Ray Rosenman carried out their well-known research to show that heart disease depends on individual differences in vulnerability to stress.

Friedman and Rosenman (1959) introduced a new "typology" to psychology in the 1950s. They proposed that there were *two* important personality types:

- Type As are competitive, ambitious, impatient, restless, and pressured.
- Type Bs lack these characteristics and are generally more relaxed.

Subsequently, various researchers (e.g. Morris et al., 1981) added a further personality type to the list:

- Type Cs are nice, industrious, conventional, sociable but tend to be repressed and react to stress or threat with a sense of helplessness.

There is a long history of "types" in psychology. The Greeks said there were melancholic types and phlegmatic types, due to the production of too much of a particular "humour" or bodily fluid, e.g. melancholics had an overproduction of black bile (melan = black, coln = bile), leading to a sad, depressed individual.

Evidence for the effect of personality on stress

Friedman and Rosenman (1959, 1974, see Key Study below) argued that individuals with the Type A pattern are more stressed than Type B individuals, and so are more likely to suffer from **cardiovascular disorders**. To test their hypothesis they set up a long-term study of men, called the Western Collaborative Group Study. They found strong evidence of the predicted association.

? Bearing in mind the characteristics of a Type A person, what types of careers would most suit such a personality type?

Key Study: Stress and cardiovascular disorders

Friedman and Rosenman's (1974) study of the association between Type A behaviour and coronary heart disease.

Aims: Friedman and Rosenman aimed to test the hypothesis that Type A individuals (a high-stress personality type) were more likely to develop coronary heart disease (CHD) than Type Bs (relatively relaxed individuals). This was testing their observations as cardiologists that their patients displayed a common behaviour pattern consisting of three key components: impatience, competitiveness, and hostility. Thus, a positive correlation between Type A behaviour pattern and CHD was sought.

Procedure: A self-selected sample of nearly 3200 Californian men aged between 39 and 59 years was used. This was a prospective, longitudinal study, as the participants were healthy at the outset in 1960 and were assessed over a period of 8½ years. Part one of the study included a structured interview and observation, which assessed personality type and current health status. Personality type was determined by the amount of impatience, competitiveness, and hostility reported and observed during the structured interview and from their answers to questions. On the basis of the structured interview, participants were classified as A1 (Type A), A2 (not fully Type A), X (equal amounts of Type A and Type B), or B (fully Type B). Part two of the study was the follow-up 8 years later when incidence of CHD was recorded. A correlational analysis was carried out to test the association between Type A/B behaviour pattern and CHD.

Findings: Of the original sample of 3200, 257 participants had developed coronary heart disease (CHD) during the 8½; years, 70% of whom had been classified as Type A. This was nearly twice as many as were Type B, even when other factors (e.g. blood pressure, smoking, obesity) known to be associated with heart disease were taken into account. Compared to Type Bs, Type As were found to have higher levels of adrenaline and noradrenaline (both associated with stress) and cholesterol. A significant but moderate correlation was found between personality type and coronary heart disease.

Conclusions: The research shows that Type A behaviour pattern is fairly strongly linked to CHD. Friedman and Rosenman concluded that the Type A behaviour pattern increases the individual's experience of stress, which increases physiological reactivity, and that in turn increases vulnerability to CHD. The high levels of the stress hormones suggest that they do experience more stress than Type Bs. The stress response inhibits digestion, which leads to the higher level of cholesterol in the blood, and this places Type As at risk of CHD. Implications include the need to reduce the "harmful" Type A characteristics.

? What are the methodological strengths and weaknesses of this study?

KEY TERM

Cardiovascular disorders: these are disorders of the cardiovascular system, which includes the heart and its supporting systems. An example is atherosclerosis, which is the thickening of the arteries due to high levels of cholesterol in the bloodstream. Another disorder is hypertension or high blood pressure, which puts pressure on the heart as it has to work harder to beat at high pressure.

Criticisms

- Type A behaviour pattern consists of a number of characteristics and so the variable Type A lacks precision: does it make much sense to assign everyone in the world to only four categories? It is too broad to be useful, because it is not clear *which* aspect of Type A is most strongly associated with CHD. Consequently, the research lacked **internal validity**, as it did not precisely measure what it set out to. Later research by Matthews et al. (1977), who re-analysed the data, found that the hostility component of Type A correlated highest with CHD. Thus, hostility, rather than Type A in general, may explain the findings.
- Weaknesses of the correlational method mean that there is no control over Type A/B behaviour as a variable, which makes interpretations difficult. For example, rather than causing physiological reactivity, the Type A behaviour pattern may be a response to heightened physiological reactivity in some individuals. Thus, the direction of effect can be questioned: does Type A result in increased physiological reactivity or is Type A a result of high levels of physiological reactivity, which may be genetically determined? Most importantly, cause and effect cannot be inferred, as the variables are not under the control of the researcher (causation can only be inferred when an independent variable has been directly manipulated). Thus, it cannot be said that Type A *causes* coronary heart disease and so conclusions are limited.
- It has proved fairly difficult to repeat the findings of Friedman and Rosenman (1974), as is discussed shortly. Indeed, there are several later studies in which the correlation between personality type and coronary heart disease was non-significant. These later findings cast doubt on the notion that coronary heart disease depends in part on the Type A personality.

Note: If the question asks for findings or conclusions only, you could include research by Matthews et al. (1977, see above) and Ganster et al. (1991, see below).

? Do you think that the study may have affected the lives of the men taking part? How might that be an ethical issue?

The research of Friedman and Rosenman (1974) is still regarded as important for various reasons. First, they provided some of the earliest scientific evidence that the occurrence of a physical illness such as heart disease can depend on individual differences in personality. Second, this study led to a huge amount of research on the effects of stress on the immune system and various physical illnesses. Third, the study persuaded many people to change their lifestyle so as to have healthier and longer lives.

Ganster et al. (1991, p.145) pointed out that it has often been assumed that "chronic elevations of the sympathetic nervous system (in Type As) lead to deterioration of the cardiovascular system". They put their participants into stressful situations and recorded various physiological measures such as blood pressure and heart rate. Only the hostility component of Type A was associated with high levels of physiological reactivity. These findings, when combined with those of Matthews et al. (1977), suggest that high levels of hostility produce increased activity within the sympathetic nervous system, and this plays a role in the development of CHD.

The findings of Friedman and Rosenman (1974) were confirmed in another large-scale longitudinal study which involved both men and women, the

KEY TERM

Internal validity: the validity of an experiment in terms of the context in which it is carried out. Concerns events within the experiment as distinct from external validity.

Framingham Heart Study (Haynes et al., 1980). However, some researchers have failed to find any relationship between Type A and CHD. This has led some psychologists to doubt the importance of the Type A behaviour pattern as a factor in causing heart disease. However, Miller et al. (1991) reviewed the literature. They found that many of the negative findings were obtained in studies using self-report measures of Type A behaviour, which may assess Type A inaccurately. Studies using the structured interview (which was used by Friedman and Rosenman, 1974) with initially healthy populations reported a mean correlation of +0.33 between Type A behaviour and CHD, supporting the initial finding of a moderate relationship between the two variables.

One problem for any study is that as soon as an individual knows they are at risk of CHD they may engage in behaviours to modify that risk, such as giving up smoking or taking more exercise. This may create lower long-term correlations between Type A and CHD.

The evidence has been applied successfully, for example Friedman, Tordoff, and Ramirez (1986) reported on the Recurrent Coronary Prevention Project which aimed to modify Type A behaviour and so reduce CHD in participants who had experienced a heart attack. At a five-year follow-up, those participants who had taken part in a behaviour modification had fewer second heart attacks than those who received counselling or no treatment.

Other research has looked at a possible link between Type C (conventional and tending to experience helplessness when stressed) and cancer. Morris et al. (1981) proposed that the likelihood of developing cancer may be related to Type C behaviour because such individuals tend to deal with stressful events by repressing their emotions. To study this, Morris et al. interviewed 50 women being tested to see if a breast lump was malignant (cancerous) or benign (non-cancerous). The patients were assessed to determine their typical patterns of emotional behaviour using questionnaires and interviews. Morris et al. found that those found to have a malignant lump had reported that they both experienced and expressed far less anger than those with a benign tumour. This supports the idea of a link between cancer and the suppression of anger. Emotional suppression is associated with increased stress, lowered effectiveness of the immune system, and illness.

Supporting evidence was given in a study by Thomas and Duszynski (1974) who followed 1000 medical students over 15 years. They found that those who developed cancers also reported less family closeness. This may be due to stress, because people with poor social support systems suffer greater stress.

CASE STUDY: DON'T LET IT GET YOU DOWN

"Comfort always, cure rarely" is an old medical motto. And it may be nearer the truth than modern medicine would like to admit. Perhaps if patients were less depressed and more optimistic they might be more likely to recover from stressful operations.

In one study of 100 patients about to undergo bone marrow transplants for leukaemia it was found that 13 of the patients were severely depressed. Of these patients 12 had died within a year of the operation (92%) whereas only 61% of the not-depressed died within two years of the study.

Other research has looked at the effects of pessimism and found this to be the biggest single predictor of death from a heart attack. 122 men were evaluated for pessimism or optimism at the time they had a heart attack. Eight years later their state of mind was found to correlate with death more highly than any of the other standard risk factors such as damage to the heart, raised blood pressure, or high cholesterol levels. Of the 25 men who were most pessimistic, 21 had died whereas only 6 of the most optimistic 25 had died.

Peterson, Seligman, and Valliant (1988) studied optimists and pessimists. They suggested that pessimists tended to explain setbacks in their lives as the result of things within their personality that were unchangeable. In contrast, optimists tended to explain setbacks as the result of things arising from situations within their control, but which were not their own fault. Peterson et al. rated a number of Harvard undergraduates for pessimism and optimism on the basis of essays they wrote about their wartime experiences. After an interval of more than 20 years, the pessimists (aged 45) were more likely to be suffering from some chronic disease.

(Adapted from Goleman, 1991.) ∎

Hardiness

Kobasa (1979) argued that people differ considerably in their ability to cope with stressors. She used the term **hardiness** to describe a cluster of **traits** possessed by those people best able to cope with stress. According to Kobasa, "hardy" individuals have the following characteristics:

- *Commitment.* They are more involved in what they do and have a direction in life. They find meaning in their work and personal relationships.
- *Challenge.* They view potentially stressful situations as a challenge and an opportunity, rather than a problem or a threat.
- *Control.* They have a stronger sense of personal control. They feel they can influence events in their lives.

Kobasa's view was supported by a large-scale study Kobasa, Maddi, and Puccetti (1982) undertook with highly stressed male managers for a large company. Those with high scores on hardiness, and who also exercised a lot, had the least illness. In another study (Kobasa et al., 1985), male executives in stressful jobs were interviewed and followed up a year later. Three factors—hardiness, exercise, and social support—were found to be important factors in their health, with hardiness playing the biggest role.

However, Funk (1992) criticised the model on the grounds that hardiness is quite difficult to assess. Another criticism is that white, middle-class males were the main participants. Finally, the data are correlational and the conclusions presumed that hardiness is the causal factor in health. It is also possible that people who are ill find it harder to be psychologically hardy. On the positive side, the concept of hardiness has been used as a means of coping with stress (as we will see later).

? Do you think there are likely to be cultural differences in the prevalence of Type A and B individuals (i.e. between individualistic and collectivistic cultures)?

Gender

In most countries, women live longer than men on average. Part of the reason may be that women cope better with stress. How might this happen? First, there may be gender differences in physiological responses to stressors. Second, there may be gender differences in life style reflecting different ways of handling stressful situations. Third, there may be gender differences in the behaviour produced in stressful situations (e.g. seeking and obtaining social support).

So far as physiological responses are concerned, Stone et al. (1990) found that women showed smaller increases in blood pressure than men when performing stressful tasks. Similarly, Frankenhaeuser et al. (1976) found that boys showed a faster increase in stress hormones than did girls when taking an examination. In addition, the level of stress hormones returned to normal faster in girls than in boys. These findings may mean that the sympathetic adrenal medullary system and the hypothalamic-pituitary-adrenocortical axis (discussed earlier) are more responsive in males than in females. Alternatively, boys may *perceive* examinations as more threatening than do girls, with this perception influencing the bodily response.

There are other important physiological differences between men and women. Hastrup, Light, and Obrist (1980) tested women's cardiovascular (heart) reactions. The women had lowered stress responses at the time in their menstrual cycle when their oestrogen levels were highest. This suggests that the hormone oestrogen may have helped them to cope. This finding may help to explain gender

Gender differences in life style, behaviour, and physiological responses to stress may contribute to women living longer than men.

differences in atherosclerosis, which is a disease of the large and intermediate-sized arteries. This disease causes strokes as well as coronary heart disease, and accounts for nearly half of all deaths in the UK. Men in their early and mid-adult years are several times more likely than women to develop atherosclerosis. According to Guyton and Hall (2000, p.789), "Male sex hormones might be atherogenic [causing atherosclerosis] or, conversely, female sex hormones might be protective." The incidence of atherosclerosis in women after the menopause approaches that of men of the same age, which fits with the notion that female sex hormones (e.g. oestrogen) help to protect women.

So far as life style is concerned, men used to be much more likely than women to smoke and to drink heavily (Ogden, 2000). For example, in the UK in 1992, nearly 30% of men were found to be heavy drinkers of alcohol compared to just over 10% of women. These responses to stress both have the effect of shortening life expectancy. However, the incidence of smoking is now very similar in men and women, and heavy drinking (including binge drinking) has become more common among young women than was the case in the early 1990s. These changes may eventually produce a narrowing of the gap in life expectancy between men and women.

Taylor et al. (2000) claimed that there are major gender differences in hormonal activity *and* in behaviour in stressful situations. They argued (with much supporting evidence) that men are more likely than women to respond to stressful situations with a "fight-or-flight" response, whereas women generally respond with a "tend-and-befriend" response. Women handle stressful situations by protecting and looking after their children (the tend response) and by actively seeking social support from others (the befriend response). Research by Repetti (discussed by Taylor et al., 2000), was summarised as follows by Taylor et al.:

When the typical father in the study came home after a stressful day at work, he responded to stress by wanting to be left alone . . .; when office-related stress was particularly acute, a typical response would be to react harshly or create conflict with his wife or children. When the typical mother in the study came home from work bearing stress, she was more likely to cope with her bad day by focusing her attention on nurturing her children. This difference in seeking social support during stressful periods is the principal way men and women differ in their response to stress.

Taylor et al. (2000) argued that the tend-and-befriend response in women is an effective way for women with several children to cope with life's stressors. They emphasised the role of oxytocin, which is a hormone secreted [released] by men and women in response to stress. Oxytocin makes people less anxious and more sociable. Its effects are reduced by male sex hormones but are increased by the female hormone oestrogen. Overall, these gender differences may explain why men are more likely than women to develop "certain stress-related disorders, including hypertension, aggressive behaviour, or abuse of alcohol or hard drugs. Because the tend-and-befriend regulatory systems may . . . protect women against stress, this bio-behavioural pattern may provide insights into why women live an average of seven and a half years longer than men" (Taylor et al., 2000). However, note that men sometimes show the tend-and-befriend response, and women sometimes show the fight-or-flight response.

? Do you think Taylor et al.'s findings would be true of every culture?

Culture

Cultural differences are the third kind of individual difference modifying the effects of stressors. The term "culture" refers to the rules, morals, and social practices of a group of people. "Culture" does *not* describe the people themselves but the ways in which they interact with each other. These learned ways of interacting influence how individuals respond to stressors. Some cultural groups may experience less stress because they have healthier social practices. Weg (1983) studied the Abkarzians living in Georgia, a part of the former USSR. They are remarkable for their longevity: 400 per 100,000 live beyond the age of 100, compared to 3 per 100,000 in the UK or USA. Weg (1983) argued that there were several reasons for this long life span, including low stress levels, a high level of social support, a diet low in saturated fat and meat and high in fruit and vegetables, genetic factors, and an avoidance of alcohol and cigarettes. Probably most (or all) of these factors contribute to the longevity of the Abkarzians.

Stress is believed to be partly responsible for essential hypertension, which is high blood pressure for which there is no obvious cause. According to Anderson et al. (1989), "The higher prevalence of essential hypertension in black than in white populations in Westernised societies is a consistent finding." This may occur because black people are more likely than white people to respond to stressful situation with suppressed anger. Support for this view was obtained by Gentry et al. (1981). They found that suppressed anger was associated with especially large increases in blood pressure for black people living in stressful situations.

High blood pressure is a risk factor for coronary heart disease, and so the above findings may help to explain why black Americans are more likely to suffer from heart disease than white Americans or black Africans. Another possibility is that genetic selection took place on board slave ships travelling to America: individuals who could retain water better were more likely to survive, thus creating a unique genetic group. The same genes that are responsible for water retention also lead to salt retention, which is related to high blood pressure (Cooper, Rotimi & Ward, 1999).

We can also explain the above differences between black Americans and both white Americans and black Africans in terms of psychosocial factors. Anderson (1991) discussed *acculturation stress*, which is caused when minorities try to adopt the majority values, norms, and life style. He found that African-Americans suffered more physical and mental ill-health than white Americans. They also experience more life events, hassles, and racism. Black Americans may experience greater stress as a result of prejudice, lower education, lower use of medical care, lower job status, and so on. Cooper et al. (1999) looked at rates of high blood pressure in black Americans and black Africans, and found that blood pressure was highest in urban societies. This supports the view that high blood pressure may be due to social rather than to biological factors.

We can distinguish between individualistic cultures (in which a sense of personal identity and responsibility is valued), and collectivistic cultures (in which the emphasis is on the group rather than the individual). Social support (which reduces the stress response in difficult situations) should be more available in collectivistic cultures than in individualistic ones. Evidence that individualism–collectivism influences coping with stressful situations was reported by Bailey and Dua (1999). They compared Asian students and Anglo-Australian students in

Australia with respect to the use of collectivistic coping strategies (e.g. seeking social support) and individualistic coping strategies (e.g. working out what to do on one's own). Asian students recently arrived in Australia made much more use of collectivistic coping strategies than did the Anglo-Australian students, who preferred individualistic coping strategies. A direct influence of culture on coping with stress was shown in the finding that the longer that Asian students remained in Australia (a very individualistic culture), the more use they made of individualistic coping strategies.

Evaluation of individual differences in stress

The effects of stressors on people's physiological stress responses, their behaviour, and their physical well-being all depend on personality, on gender, and on culture. However, there are several limitations with the available research. First, the evidence is basically correlational (e.g. there is an association between having a Type A personality and suffering from coronary heart disease). We cannot use such correlational evidence to show there are causal effects of individual differences on stress responses. For example, it is possible that being exposed to stress alters someone's personality, as well as their personality influencing how affected they are by stress.

Second, the issues involved are very complicated, and so no simple conclusions can be drawn. For example, women differ from men in their physiological reactions to some stressful situations, in their hormonal responses, and in their chosen coping strategies. Most of these differences suggest that women cope better than men with stressful situations. However, Miller and Rahe (1997) found that women report *more* stress than men in response to several life events, including the death of a close family member, a major illness, and the loss of a job. As yet, we have an incomplete picture of the ways in which individual differences influence our responses to stressors.

Third, most research has involved categorising people in various ways. Individuals are categorised as Type A, Type B, or Type C; they are categorised as men or women; and they are categorised as belonging to a particular culture. Those categorised as Type A do not *all* respond in the same way to stressors, neither do those categorised as women, or as white Americans. Use of such categories is valuable, but oversimplifies a complex reality.

> **EXAM HINT**
> Note that the question may not say "individual differences". Instead it might be "Outline two factors that modify the effects of stress". Remember this question and that two of the individual differences, personality, gender, and culture should be your answer.

SECTION SUMMARY

❖ There are many different sources of stress and different responses to stress.
❖ Cox's transactional model of stress focuses on the imbalance between the perceived demands of the environment and the individual's perceived ability to cope.
❖ Sources of stress include life events, daily hassles, and work stress.

❖ Life events may be a source of stress because they involve change that uses psychic energy.
❖ Holmes and Rahe were the first to record the effects of life events in a systematic way. They developed the SRRS (Social Readjustment Rating Scale) which has been used to measure life change units (LCUs).

Life events

❖ Research into life events has demonstrated a small but significant correlation between life change units (LCU) and physical illness. However, this research has been criticised in that:
- Correlations do not establish cause and effect—we do not know that life events *caused* the illness.
- Individuals may differ markedly in their perception of life events.

❖ An alternative is to look at daily hassles—the ongoing stressors of daily life.

Workplace stressors

❖ Johansson et al. (1978) and Marmot et al. (1997) both conducted research into workplace stressors.

❖ Work place stress includes environmental factors such as:
- overcrowding,
- heat,
- pollution,
- noise.

❖ Overcrowding creates stress in both humans and animals, although other factors might moderate these effects. People do not always become aggressive in overcrowded situations.

❖ Heat, pollution, and noise may also make people become aggressive, although some people can "tune" these things out.

❖ Unpredictable noise requires vigilance and reduces our psychic energy, so enhancing feelings of stress.

❖ Other factors causing stress in the workplace include:
- too much control,
- too little control,
- role conflict,
- shift work,
- interpersonal relationships.

❖ The relationship between these various factors is complex.

❖ Burnout is an extreme effect of work-related stress.

Individual differences in modifying the effects of stressors

❖ Not everyone reacts to stress in the same way. Individual differences are important when considering the effects of stressors.

❖ Key variables to consider include:
- *Personality*: Type A individuals cope less well with stress and are more likely to suffer from coronary heart disease. Type B individuals are more relaxed. Type C individuals may be more prone to cancer because they respond to stress by suppressing their emotions.
- *Hardiness*: Hardy individuals cope better with stress than those who are not hardy.
- *Gender*: Women have smaller physiological reactions than men to some stressful situations. They tend to respond to stressful situations with a tend-and-befriend response, whereas men show a fight-or-flight response. The effects of oxytocin (which makes people less anxious) are reduced by male sex hormones but increased by female sex hormones.
- *Culture*: Some cultural practices may reduce stress and increase longevity. Black Americans may have more essential hypertension than white Americans which may be because of psychosocial factors, or because they are more likely to respond to stressful situations with suppressed anger.

See pp.76–80 of the revision guide.

SECTION 13—CRITICAL ISSUE
STRESS MANAGEMENT

Stress research is important because it can help us manage our own, and others' stress reactions. This is an increasingly important application at a time when everyone appears to feel over-stressed.

There are many approaches to reducing stress levels. One way to classify these is in terms of whether they are physiological or psychological methods. **Physiological approaches to stress management** include the following:

Research into stress management leads to ways in which we can deal with our stress.

1. *Biofeedback*. A technique to learn how to control involuntary muscles, or voluntary muscles that are not normally controlled, such as those involved in blood pressure and heart rate. The aim is to reduce autonomic nervous system (ANS) activity, and thus the bodily sensations associated with stress. In turn, this will reduce the consequent effects of stress in terms of illness.

2. *Anti-anxiety drugs*. The body produces hormones and neurotransmitters (substances transmitting information between nerves and cells). Manufactured drugs such as Valium can be used to mimic or intervene in the natural body processes but have side effects, such as addiction to the drugs or drowsiness.

Psychological approaches to stress management include:

1. *Cognitive therapies*. This form of **psychotherapy** aims to change the way that people think about their problem and thus to alter the effects of the problem itself. Two examples are stress inoculation treatment and increasing hardiness.

2. *Social support* from friends and family.

Lazarus and Folkman (1984) made a distinction between problem-focused and emotion-focused strategies of **stress management**. Stress can be managed by: tackling the problem itself (problem-focused)—psychological methods; or by reducing the stress response (emotion-focused)—physiological methods.

Another distinction between "coping" with stress and "managing" it is that most of us try to get on and cope as best we can, but the concept of "management" suggests the use of techniques to overcome chronic problems, or tackle stress before it occurs.

> **EXAM HINT**
>
> If you are asked to outline one method of stress management, you could select one from:
>
> - Biofeedback (a physiological approach)
> - Anti-anxiety drugs (a physiological approach)
> - Stress inoculation (a psychological approach)
> - Hardiness training (a psychological approach).

> **KEY TERMS**
>
> **Physiological approaches to stress management**: techniques that try to control the body's response to stress by reducing physiological reactivity. For example, anti-anxiety drugs decrease the "fight or flight" response such as high blood pressure, increased heart rate, etc. Biofeedback is another technique, which works by training the participant to recognise their heightened physiological reactivity and reduce it through relaxation exercises.
>
> **Psychological approaches to stress management**: techniques that try to control the cognitive, social, and emotional responses to stress. They attempt to address the underlying causes of stress, such as faulty thinking and disproportionate emotional responses (overreactions and underreactions). Psychological techniques work by changing the person's perception of the stressor and/or increasing the individual's perception of control.
>
> **Stress management**: stress management is the attempt to cope with stress through reduction of the stress response. This may be aimed at the physiological effects of stress (e.g. anti-anxiety drugs or biofeedback) and the psychological effects of stress (e.g. stress inoculation training or hardiness training). Stress management is often based on changing the person's perception of the stressor and/or increasing the individual's perception of control.

People learn to use biofeedback techniques to control normally involuntary bodily functions such as heart rate. The technique may involve a machine that monitors relevant bodily functions and produces visual or auditory signals. Through relaxation, the individual learns to alter the rate of these signals and thus control the involuntary functions.

People who practise yoga have been reported to be able to slow their heartbeat down sufficiently for them to survive in a sealed booth long after most people would have suffocated to death. They use relaxation to control their bodily systems.

Biofeedback

Biofeedback, "a technique for transforming some aspect of physiological behaviour into electrical signals which are made accessible to . . . awareness (usually vision or audition)" (Gatchel, 1997, p.198), is often used to reduce stress. An individual is attached to a machine producing feedback about some physiological activity (thus, biofeedback), such as an auditory or visual signal to indicate whether his/her heart rate is too high or about right. The individual is also trained in techniques to reduce physiological aspects of stress, e.g. relaxation training, part of which involves breathing in a regular and calm way, to bring the physiological activity under control. Humans can even learn to control their brain-waves, using electroencephalogram (EEG) biofeedback.

The key feature is that these physiological activities are ones we are not normally able to control. They either involve involuntary muscles (not under voluntary control), or voluntary muscles that are not usually controlled at a conscious level. The muscles involved with the ANS are automated specifically because they control forms of behaviour that need to function without our conscious involvement. This makes it seem unlikely that we would be able to exert voluntary control over processes such as blood pressure.

In fact, biofeedback probably doesn't involve learning *direct* control of, for example, heart rate and blood pressure. Control is exerted *indirectly*. For example, breathing deeply, using methods of relaxation, or simply moving around can produce changes in various physiological measures. And indeed biofeedback has been found to produce short- and long-term reductions in heart rate, blood pressure, skin temperature, and brain-wave rhythms.

Biofeedback training involves three stages:

1. Developing an awareness of the particular physiological response (e.g. heart rate).
2. Learning ways of controlling that physiological response in quiet conditions. This can include providing rewards for successful control in addition to feedback.
3. Transferring that control into the conditions of everyday life.

Supporting evidence for biofeedback

Neal Miller and his colleagues conducted extensive research in the 1960s and 1970s showing that ordinary people can learn to control their involuntary physiological systems. In one of the early experiments, Miller and DiCara (1967) demonstrated that rats were able to learn how to control their cardiac muscles using operant conditioning techniques, although subsequent research has not been able to replicate this.

Other research support comes from work done by Dworkin and Dworkin (1988) with teenagers who were suffering from curvature of the spine (scoliosis).

The teenagers successfully used biofeedback techniques to learn how to control the muscles of their spine and thus alter their posture and overcome the disorder. Holroyd and French (1994) reported on the findings from several clinical studies on sufferers from tension headaches. Biofeedback providing information about muscle tension led to an average reduction of 46% in the number of headaches reported. Biofeedback has also been used to successfully treat migraine headaches and Reynaud's disease (a vasoconstrictive disorder resulting in constricted blood flow to the fingers or toes) (Curtis, 2000). Some doctors even claim to use biofeedback techniques successfully with asthma and high blood pressure, although there is considerable controversy about the success rates (Wade & Tavris, 1993).

How does biofeedback work?

Learning involuntary control may happen by means of operant conditioning. The ANS responds to rewards and reinforcement, so that autonomic responses that are reinforced occur more frequently. However, the research hasn't been replicated, which casts doubt on this explanation.

Another possibility is that biofeedback results in a restoration of homeostasis because it involves relaxation. Stress may disrupt the normal functioning of the body and mean that it is difficult to maintain homeostasis. Without this natural system of regulation, various physiological activities are out of control—high blood pressure, intestinal distress, and pain can develop. Relaxation (biofeedback) may help the body return to its normal state of balance or homeostasis.

Another possibility is that biofeedback gives people the perception that they have control over their bodies and themselves. Holroyd et al. (1984) found that biofeedback providing information about muscle tension was associated with a reduction in tension headaches. However, they also found that participants who *falsely* believed they were reducing muscle tension through biofeedback experienced fewer headaches! Thus, the beneficial effects of biofeedback may work through perceptions of control in addition to (or even instead of) effects on physiological processes.

The famous escapologist Harry Houdini used biofeedback in some of his feats. For example, he managed to escape when he was securely shackled, with his clothes and body having been searched thoroughly to ensure he was not hiding any keys. How did he do it? He held a key suspended in his throat, and regurgitated it when no-one was looking. The natural reaction to having an object stuck in your throat is to gag. However, Houdini had spent hours practising until he was able to control his gag reflex.

Evaluation of biofeedback

Biofeedback has produced significant long-term reductions in stress in everyday life, even though it is likely that people have no *direct* feedback about their current physiological state. However, caution is needed when considering the evidence—it is hard to *interpret* the beneficial effects of biofeedback. Relaxation training is often given along with the biofeedback, making it hard to tell whether it is the biofeedback or the relaxation training that is more effective. Biofeedback may lead to benefits by producing a sense of control rather than through purely physiological mechanisms (Holroyd et al., 1984). Gatchel (1997, p.199) commented that, "There have been claims for the therapeutic efficacy of biofeedback which have been grossly exaggerated and even wrong."

However, we should consider the effects of individual differences. Biofeedback may be more successful with some people than others, such as with children rather than adults. Attanasio et al. (1985) studied a biofeedback programme that reduced muscle-contraction headaches. They found that children benefited more than adults, possibly because the children were more enthusiastic and less

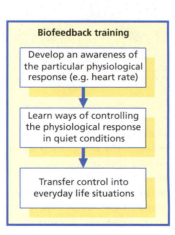

Biofeedback training

Develop an awareness of the particular physiological response (e.g. heart rate)

Learn ways of controlling the physiological response in quiet conditions

Transfer control into everyday life situations

CASE STUDY: BIOFEEDBACK IS BACK

Imagine having hands so sensitive to cold that each winter they would swell and split open. Just grabbing a carton of milk out of the refrigerator makes them whiten and throb with pain. Then imagine learning to raise the temperature in your hands to the extent that you could put them into a bucket of ice without discomfort. This is a dramatic example of what biofeedback training can accomplish for certain medical problems such as Reynaud's disease, a circulatory disorder that can cause its victims extreme discomfort and debilitation, and sometimes even requires limb amputation.

Biofeedback training as a tool for relaxation and stress reduction enjoyed a brief surge of popularity following its inception in the late 1960s, but then largely slipped out of the public view during the 1970s and 1980s. Now biofeedback is making a quiet comeback, this time in mainstream medicine. Several decades of clinical experience (and hundreds of published studies) support the use of biofeedback training in many common medical problems, such as incontinence, anxiety, hypertension, migraine, circulatory problems, irritable bowel syndrome, pain control, and bed wetting.

How biofeedback works

Every time you scratch an itch, grab a snack when you're hungry, or use the bathroom when you feel the urge, you are responding to biofeedback cues from your body about your physiologic state. With biofeedback training, however, you are cued by sensors attached to your body. These sensors measure "invisible" parameters like your heart rate, the temperature of your extremities, the muscle tension in specific muscle groups. This information is conveyed by visual displays or sounds. Using imagery and mental exercises, you learn to control these functions, using the feedback provided by the sensors as a gauge of success. With practice, you can learn to "tune in" without instrumentation, and control these functions at will during ordinary life.

For example, in a training session to "warm up" your hands and feet, you might imagine basking in the sun on a beach while listening to a script like "I feel warm . . . my hands are growing warm and heavy . . ." Both the image and the script would be tailored to you personally to evoke a vivid and relaxing mental image. After your training session, you'd be sent home with this script on audiotape and small thermometers to use for your biofeedback.

The major advantages of biofeedback are that it is non-invasive, has virtually no side effects, and is effective over the long term. The major disadvantage is that it requires effort, commitment, and involvement on the part of patients.

(Adapted from Lisa H. Underhill, 1999, http://bewell.healthgate.com/healthy/mind/1999/biofeedback/index) ∎

---

sceptical. This more positive attitude would make them more willing to try hard to succeed.

Anti-anxiety Drugs

Another way of reducing people's level of stress is by giving them anti-anxiety drugs. This is directly related to our understanding of the body's responses to stress, which we considered in Section 9. The body produces chemicals (hormones) that create anxiety, which can be countered using other chemical substances (i.e. drugs) that reduce anxiety. Several different types of drugs work via different mechanisms.

Beta blockers

Among the drugs used to reduce stress and anxiety are the beta blockers, which reduce activity in the sympathetic nervous system. Beta blockers have a direct action on the heart and circulatory system, thereby decreasing heart rate and lowering peripheral blood pressure. Their effects are on the body, and they do *not* have direct effects on brain activity. Beta blockers have proved useful in reducing blood pressure and in treating patients with heart disease. For example, Lau et al. (1992) considered the findings from numerous studies in a meta-analysis (combining data from several studies). They found that beta blockers reduced the risk of death by about 20% in patients suffering from heart disease. Beta blockers

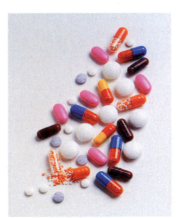

Stress can be treated with anti-anxiety drugs such as Valium that reduce the effects of stress but not the problems that cause it. Such drugs often have undesirable side effects.

have been used successfully to reduce performance anxiety and to enhance performance in musicians and public speakers (Taylor, 1995). An advantage of beta blockers is that there are no problems of dependence.

Are there any problems with the use of beta blockers? They target symptoms rather than causes of anxiety and stress, and so provide only temporary improvement. In addition, there are various side effects, including cold extremities, fatigue, nightmares, and hallucinations.

Benzodiazepines

Drugs can intervene in natural processes by controlling the action of neurotransmitters. **Benzodiazepines** such as Valium and Librium increase the activity of the neurotransmitter **GABA**, which decreases **serotonin** activity, which in turn reduces arousal. They are very effective at reducing anxiety, and are used by hundreds of millions of people around the world.

In spite of the effectiveness of the benzodiazepines, they have several unwanted side effects, all linked to low levels of serotonin: they often have sedative effects, and can make people feel drowsy; they can cause cognitive and memory impairments; they sometimes lead to feelings of depression; and they can interact unpredictably with alcohol (Ashton, 1997). Individuals taking benzodiazepines are therefore more likely to be involved in accidents. Many people become dependent on benzodiazepines, and their sudden removal can lead to a return of the initial symptoms of intense stress and anxiety.

A more recent anti-anxiety drug, **buspirone**, offers some advantages over benzodiazepines. It is a serotonin agonist, meaning that it helps or "facilitates" the effects of serotonin. It does not have the sedative effects of benzodiazepines, and there are no withdrawal symptoms. However, buspirone produces other side effects such as headaches and depression (Goa & Ward, 1986).

Evaluation of anti-anxiety drugs

Anti-anxiety drugs can be very effective at reducing intense feelings of stress. However, they don't address the problems that are causing the stress, i.e. they are emotion-focused.

Drugs can also have unfortunate side effects. The recommendation is that the benzodiazepines should generally be limited to short-term use of no more than four weeks (Ashton, 1997), that they should only be given to individuals with severe anxiety symptoms, and that they should be given in the minimal effective

> **EXAM HINT**
>
> If you choose to discuss physiological approaches in the essay question, remember:
>
> - They generally work better than a psychological approach if the individual is highly stressed and assessment and focusing would be difficult.
> - A key strength is the multi-dimensional approach, e.g. hardiness training and stress inoculation therapy combine cognitive and behavioural approaches.

CASE STUDY: SEROTONIN AND ECSTASY

If you have heard of serotonin, it is probably because you have read articles about the antidepressant Prozac, which increases levels of serotonin in the brain. Less well known is the fact that the ecstatic "rush" experienced by users of the drug Ecstasy is a result of a dramatic increase in serotonin levels in the brain.

Ecstasy causes long-term damage because it is thought to kill serotonin receptors. People with low levels of serotonin are thought to suffer from a host of problems including depression, impulsive violence, eating disorders, and sleep problems.

(Taken from Oliver James, 1997, Serotonin: A chemical feel-good factor. *Psychology Review, 4*, 34.) ■

? **To what extent can patients give fully informed consent to taking medication?**

doses. Individuals who have become dependent on benzodiazepines should have their dosage reduced gradually. The good news is that about 70% of dependent users of benzodiazepines, who are motivated to give them up, manage to do this for periods of several years or more (Ashton, 1997).

Cognitive Therapies

Psychologists and psychiatrists have developed a huge assortment of psychological treatments for abnormal behaviours, some of which are designed especially for stress disorders. **Cognitive therapies** are especially appropriate for dealing with stress. Their aim, in general, is to replace negative and irrational thoughts (e.g. "I am totally incompetent") with positive and rational ones (e.g. "I can achieve many things if I try hard enough"). The assumption behind the cognitive approach is that it is the way one thinks about the problem that is **maladaptive**. If one can be trained to restructure one's thinking and self-beliefs, the problem itself may simply disappear.

Stress inoculation training

Meichenbaum (1977, 1985), arguing that we should use cognitive therapy *before* a person becomes very anxious or depressed rather than afterwards, developed stress *inoculation* training, a form of coping and management. There are three main phases in **stress inoculation training**:

1. *Assessment*: the therapist discusses the nature of the problem with the individual, and solicits the individual's perception of how to eliminate it.
2. *Stress reduction techniques*: the individual learns various techniques for reducing stress, such as relaxation and self-instruction, by using coping self-statements (see box on page 177 for examples).
3. *Application and follow-through*: the individual imagines using the stress reduction techniques learned in the second phase in difficult situations, and/or engages in role play of such situations with the therapist, before using the techniques in real-life situations.

Empirical support

Meichenbaum (1977) compared his stress inoculation technique to other forms of treatment, such as desensitisation, where patients are gradually introduced to the object of their fear while being taught how to relax. In order to compare the two forms of therapy, he treated individuals suffering from both snake phobia and rat phobia. Each patient received treatment for only one phobia, using one of the two methods. Both forms of treatment were effective in reducing or eliminating the phobia that was treated, and stress inoculation also greatly reduced the

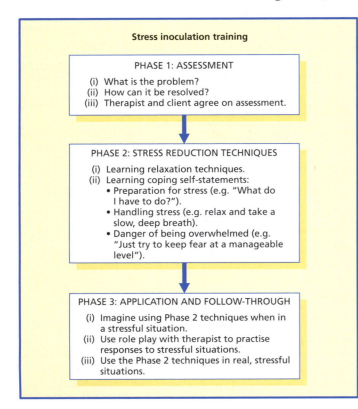

Stress inoculation training

PHASE 1: ASSESSMENT

(i) What is the problem?
(ii) How can it be resolved?
(iii) Therapist and client agree on assessment.

PHASE 2: STRESS REDUCTION TECHNIQUES

(i) Learning relaxation techniques.
(ii) Learning coping self-statements:
 • Preparation for stress (e.g. "What do I have to do?").
 • Handling stress (e.g. relax and take a slow, deep breath).
 • Danger of being overwhelmed (e.g. "Just try to keep fear at a manageable level").

PHASE 3: APPLICATION AND FOLLOW-THROUGH

(i) Imagine using Phase 2 techniques when in a stressful situation.
(ii) Use role play with therapist to practise responses to stressful situations.
(iii) Use the Phase 2 techniques in real, stressful situations.

non-treated phobia. The implication is that self-instruction easily generalises to new situations, which makes it more useful than very specific forms of treatment.

Evaluation of stress inoculation training

Stress inoculation is fairly effective in reducing the stress experienced in *moderately* stressful situations. However, it is of less value when treating individuals who are highly stressed or exposed to very stressful situations. Individuals differ in how easy they find it to use coping self-statements in stressful situations.

Hardiness training

One way to describe individual differences in stress responses is in terms of hardiness (see page 166). Kobasa (1986) suggested that hardiness could form the basis of a form of stress management programme—by increasing our hardiness, we decrease our sense of stress. Her programme consists of three techniques:

1. *Focusing.* Focus on physical signs of stress and be aware when further attention is needed.
2. *Reconstructing stress situations.* Think about recent stressful situations and note how it might have turned out both better and worse—becoming aware that things could have been worse enables you to feel more positive.
3. *Compensating through self-improvement.* If you are affected by a stressor that cannot be changed or avoided then it may be helpful to take on another challenge that can be mastered—this reassures you that you can cope.

Evaluation of hardiness training

Sarafino (1990) reports that people who have followed the kind of programme just outlined do score higher on a test of hardiness, report feeling less stressed, and have lower blood pressure than before.

Fischman (1987) taught a small number of executives these strategies and they had greater job satisfaction, fewer headaches, and better sleep patterns. However, the study was done on a small scale and there was no follow-up, so results may have been due to increased attention and communication only.

Examples of coping self-statements used in Meichenbaum's stress inoculation training

Preparing for a stressful situation:
  What is it you have to do?
  You can develop a plan to deal with it.
  Just think about what you can do. That's better than getting anxious.
  Maybe what you think is anxiety is in fact eagerness to confront it.

Confronting and handling a stressful situation:
  Just "psych" yourself up—you can meet this challenge.
  One step at a time, you can handle the situation.
  This tenseness can be an ally, a cue to cope.
  Relax; you're in control. Take a slow deep breath. Ah, good.

Coping with the feeling of being overwhelmed:
  When fear comes, just pause.
  Keep the focus on the present; what is it you have to do?
  You should expect your fear to rise.
  It's not the worst thing that can happen.

Reinforcing self-statements:
  It wasn't as bad as you expected.
  Wait until you tell your therapist about this.
  You made more out of the fear than it was worth.
  You did it!

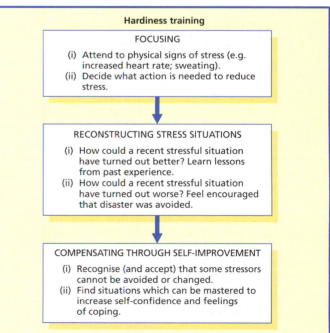

Hardiness training

FOCUSING

(i) Attend to physical signs of stress (e.g. increased heart rate; sweating).
(ii) Decide what action is needed to reduce stress.

RECONSTRUCTING STRESS SITUATIONS

(i) How could a recent stressful situation have turned out better? Learn lessons from past experience.
(ii) How could a recent stressful situation have turned out worse? Feel encouraged that disaster was avoided.

COMPENSATING THROUGH SELF-IMPROVEMENT

(i) Recognise (and accept) that some stressors cannot be avoided or changed.
(ii) Find situations which can be mastered to increase self-confidence and feelings of coping.

Social support is one of the psychological approaches to reducing stress levels.

Some studies offer limited support, such as Ganellen and Blaney (1984) who found that hardiness training only works in conjunction with social support. Some research offers no support, such as Schmied and Lawler (1986) who found no relationship between hardiness and illness in female secretaries. The original research was based on an all-male population and may not generalise to women.

Social Support

It has often been claimed that social support can help to provide protection against stress. Kiecolt-Glaser et al. (1984) found that students who had more social support suffered less reduction of their immune responses prior to university examinations. Before discussing further evidence, however, we need to consider definitions of social support. Schaefer et al. (1981) argued that the term social support has two rather different meanings, with very different effects on health and well-being:

1. *Social network*: the number of people who are available to provide support—unrelated to well-being. It can even be negatively related to well-being, because it is very time-consuming and demanding to maintain a large social network.
2. *Perceived support*: the strength of social support that can be provided by these individuals—positively related to health and well-being.

The extent of a person's social network and their perceived sense of support are positively correlated.

Studies of social networks and perceived support

The importance of perceived social support was shown by Brown and Harris (1978). They found that 61% of severely depressed women had experienced a very stressful life event in the previous nine months, compared with only 25% of non-depressed women. Many women managed to cope with severe life events without becoming depressed. Of those women who experienced a serious life event, 37% of those without an intimate friend became depressed, against only 10% of those who did have a very close friend.

The effects of both social networks and perceived support on physical well-being were examined by Nuckolls, Cassel, and Kaplan (1972) in a study of pregnant women. They made use of a general measure of "psychosocial assets" including measures of social network and perceived support. Women exposed to many stressful life events were much more likely to have medical complications

■ **Activity:** Cohen et al. (1991) have continued their research on colds. They asked participants to list how many of 12 intimate social roles they engaged in, for example as a parent, spouse, child, or close friend. Those who reported fewer than three roles were four times more likely to catch a cold when exposed to the virus under experimental conditions, than those with six or more social roles.

You might try a similar study by asking people to list their social roles and also answer a questionnaire about recent illness (illness can be assessed in terms of, for example, time off work).

during pregnancy if they had low psychosocial assets.

Tache, Selye, and Day (1979) found that cancer was more common among adults who were divorced, widowed, or separated than among those who were married. The most likely explanation is that those who were not married were more stressed because of a lack of social support. However, it is hard to establish causal relationships from such data—perhaps those who were divorced or separated were more vulnerable to stress, which played a role in the collapse of their marriages.

Individual Differences

Individuals show consistent differences in the coping strategies they use to handle stressful situations. Endler and Parker (1990) devised the Multidimensional Coping Inventory to assess three major coping strategies:

- *Task-oriented strategy*: involves obtaining information about the stressful situation and alternative courses of action, deciding priorities, and dealing with the stressful situation.
- *Emotion-oriented strategy*: can involve efforts to maintain hope, controlling one's emotions, venting feelings of anger and frustration, or accepting the situation.
- *Avoidance-oriented strategy*: involves denying or minimising the situation, conscious suppression of stressful thoughts, and self-protective thoughts.

Individuals who are high in the personality dimension of trait anxiety, and so experience much stress and anxiety, tend to use the emotion-oriented and avoidance-oriented strategies rather than the task-oriented strategy (Endler & Parker, 1990). However, those with Type A behaviour have a strong tendency to use the task-oriented strategy, even when it is inappropriate (Eysenck, 1994).

Which strategy is most effective in reducing stress? The effectiveness of any coping strategy depends on the nature of the stressful situation, e.g. task-oriented coping tends to be most effective when the individual has the resources to sort out the stressful situation, whereas emotion-oriented coping is preferable when the individual cannot resolve the situation (Eysenck, 1994). So individual differences are important but so is the context surrounding the stress situation.

EXAM HINT

If you choose to discuss psychological approaches in the essay, think about the following positive points:

- They are less invasive and do not have side effects.
- The psychological techniques may tackle causes better than the physiological techniques as faulty cognitions may well be the underlying cause of stress given that perception (a cognitive process) is fundamental to the experience of stress.

However, be aware of the following issues:

- A patient in denial may not benefit much from such an approach as the focusing and assessment require the patient to have a high level of self-insight. So they may work better for some patients than others.
- The techniques require commitment and a belief in the approach to be effective. Failure rates may be due to a lack of motivation or belief in the technique. For example, some people may have difficulty using the self-coping statements, as they may find them ridiculous!

Avoidance-oriented strategy

■ **Activity:** Try to classify each of the stress management techniques in this section in terms of whether they are a task-, emotion-, and/or avoidance-oriented strategy.

How well does this classification scheme work?

■ **Activity:** Find out from other people which kind of stress management strategy they prefer to use. You might try to devise a suitable questionnaire to collect these data. Are there differences in people who, say, prefer a task-oriented strategy to an emotion-focused one? Do people who experience a lot of stress prefer one strategy more than another, in comparison with people who experience very little stress? Do people vary their strategies depending on the situation? What kinds of strategies are best for which situations?

SECTION SUMMARY

Methods of managing stress

- ❖ Stress can be reduced using physiological methods and psychological methods.
- ❖ Stress management may be problem focused or emotion focused.
- ❖ There is also a difference between coping with stress and managing it!

Physiological methods of reducing stress

These can include:

- ❖ Biofeedback
  - This has been used to give individuals feedback about the action of involuntary muscles or voluntary muscles that are not usually under conscious control.
  - It works in the short term due to operant conditioning, by relaxation, which impacts on involuntary physiological functions, or by restoring homeostasis.
  - It is less clear that biofeedback can produce long-term reductions in stress in everyday life.
- ❖ Anti-anxiety drugs
  - Beta blockers: These cause changes in the circulatory system. They have no dependence problems but can have some side effects.
  - Benzodiazepines: These increase the activity of the neurotransmitter GABA which inhibits activation throughout the nervous system by reducing, for example, serotonin levels. They also have undesirable side effects, and their sudden removal can lead to intense anxiety.
  - Buspirone: This is a newer drug which does not have the sedative effects of the other drugs, but it can produce headaches and depression.
- ❖ These physiological methods tend to be focused on reducing the emotion accompanying stress, in that they reduce feelings of panic.
- ❖ Criticisms of physiological methods of reducing stress include:
  - It is not entirely clear whether biofeedback produces long-term reductions in stress in everyday life.
  - The side effects of drugs may be unpleasant.
  - These methods do not address what might be causing the stress in that they focus on the symptoms of stress. Anti-anxiety drugs should be used for short periods of time on low doses.

Psychological methods of reducing stress

- ❖ Cognitive therapies aim to treat the way an individual thinks about the problem and thus alter their ability to cope. They can include:
  - Stress inoculation training: a scheme to manage stress before it becomes a problem. Participants are taught to use coping self-statements which may generalise to other situations.
  - Hardiness training: Individuals are taught to become more "hardy" by focusing on the stress response, seeing the positive side of any stress situation, and taking on other challenges where one can experience success.
- ❖ Perceived social support is a further way of coping with stress.

See pp.81–86 of the revision guide.

Individual differences in stress management

- ❖ Individual differences are an important consideration with respect to managing stress.
- ❖ Different individuals will find it different strategies to be successful.

❖ The Multi-dimensional Coping Inventory offers a means of assessing which strategies will suit which individuals.

❖ Psychological methods have proved successful for managing less intense stress, although some people find it difficult to put these methods into practice.

Strengths and weaknesses of psychological methods of stress management

> You have reached the end of the chapter on physiological psychology. Physiological psychology is an approach or perspective in psychology. The material in this chapter has exemplified the way that physiological psychologists explain behaviour. They look at behaviour in terms of the way the bodily systems work (for example, nerves and hormones, parts of the brain and bodily organs). This is often regarded as a "reductionist" approach because it reduces complex behaviour and experiences to simpler processes and explanations.

FURTHER READING

There is good coverage of stress research in J. Ogden (2000) *Health psychology: A textbook (2nd Edn.)* (Buckingham: Open University Press). E.P. Sarafino (1990) *Health psychology* (New York: John Wiley & Sons) discusses many aspects of stress and stress management, as does A. Curtis (2000) *Health psychology* (London: Routledge).

REVISION QUESTIONS

The examination questions aim to sample the material in this whole chapter. For advice on how to answer such questions refer to Chapter 1, Section 2.

Whenever you are asked to describe a study try to include some or all of the following details: research aim(s), participants, research method (e.g. experiment or observation), procedure, findings, and conclusion.

You will always have a choice of two questions in the AQA AS-level exam and 30 minutes in which to answer the question you choose:

Question 1 (AQA, 2004)
a. (i) Outline *one* psychological method of stress management (e.g. increasing hardiness, stress-inoculation). (3 marks)

   (ii) Outline *one* strength of the psychological method of stress management you have identified in (i). (3 marks)

b. Outline findings of research (theories *and/or* studies) into workplace stressors. (6 marks)

c. Outline and evaluate research (theories *and/or* studies) into life changes as a source of stress. (18 marks)

Question 2
a. Outline the main features of Selye's General Adaptation Syndrome. (6 marks)

b. Describe the findings and conclusions of *one* study into the relationship between stress and physical illness. (3 marks + 3 marks)

c. Consider the extent to which individual differences modify the effects of stressors. (18 marks)

Individual differences is an approach or perspective in psychology. The study of individual differences is literally the study of the ways that individuals differ in terms of their psychological characteristics. Individuals differ *physically* in terms of, for example, height and hair colour. They differ psychologically in terms of intelligence, aggressiveness, willingness to conform, masculinity and femininity, and just about every other behaviour you can think of. An important individual difference is the degree to which a person is mentally healthy. This is specifically referred to as the study of abnormal or atypical psychology.

SECTION 14
Defining psychological abnormality p.183

This section explores the question "What is abnormality?" by looking at various possible definitions. What are the limitations of these definitions of abnormality?

Specification content: Definitions of abnormality: Statistical infrequency, deviation from social norms, failure to function adequately, and deviation from ideal mental health. Limitations associated with these definitions of psychological abnormality (e.g. cultural relativism).

SECTION 15
Biological and psychological models of abnormality p.193

It may be possible to explain mental disorders in the same way that we explain physical illnesses—in terms of biological or physical causes. This is called the biological (or medical) model. Or we might use psychological explanations, such as those based on learning theory (the behavioural model), or on Freud's views (a psychodynamic model), or using a cognitive approach. What are the implications of these models for treatment?

Specification content: Assumptions made by biological (medical) and psychological (including psychodynamic, behavioural, and cognitive) models of abnormality in relation to the causes of abnormality.

SECTION 16—CRITICAL ISSUE
Eating disorders p.208

Do the models of abnormality discussed explain what causes eating disorders? How does anorexia nervosa differ from bulimia nervosa, and how are they similar?

Specification content: The clinical characteristics of anorexia nervosa and bulimia nervosa. Explanations of these disorders in terms of biological and psychological models of abnormality, including research studies on which these explanations are based.

INDIVIDUAL DIFFERENCES:
Abnormality

6

This chapter explores one topic in the study of individual differences—abnormality. What is **abnormality**?

To treat patients with mental disorders clinicians need to distinguish between normal and abnormal behaviour, but first they need to define abnormality. Mental disorder has been likened to physical illness—having a cold is an abnormal and undesirable state. We will investigate this definition in this chapter.

Why do some people have mental disorders and others don't? Is an eating disorder "caught" in the same way that you catch a cold? We will explore mental abnormality and its potential undesirability in this chapter.

Most of our definitions of abnormality and our explanations for mental disorders are based on Western beliefs. In recent years, however, there has been a growing recognition that it is very important to take account of cultural and sub-cultural differences. This chapter examines ALL of these issues and finally looks at them in the context of one group of mental disorders—eating disorders.

SECTION 14
DEFINING PSYCHOLOGICAL ABNORMALITY

What is Abnormality?

The term "abnormal" is defined as "deviating from what is normal or usual". What, then, is meant by the term "normal"? Conforming to a standard of some sort. But how do we establish the standard? Several approaches will be considered here.

1. A standard can be defined in statistical terms—what most people are doing.
2. The standard can be defined in social terms—what is considered socially acceptable/deviant.
3. We might use the standard of "adequate functioning"—being able to cope with daily life.
4. There is the concept of **ideal mental health**—a state of contentment we all strive to achieve.

Statistical Infrequency

The statistical approach is based, not surprisingly, on the idea that certain behaviours are statistically rare in the population. Consider, for example, trait anxiety

> **KEY TERM**
>
> **Abnormality**: behaviour that is considered to deviate from the norm (statistical or social), or ideal mental health. It is dysfunctional because it is harmful or causes distress to the individual or others and so is considered to be a failure to function adequately. Abnormality is characterised by the fact that it is an undesirable state that causes severe impairment in the personal and social functioning of the individual, and often causes the person great anguish depending on how much insight they have into their illness.

Statistical deviation from a normal distribution

If you measure any aspect of human behaviour, such as height or intelligence or aggressiveness, you should find that people with varying degrees of the behaviour are normally distributed around the mean. For example, there are a lot of people who are "averagely" tall or aggressive, whereas there are very few who are very small or highly aggressive. The shape of this distribution is shown in the figure on the right. The majority of individuals are clustered round the mean, which is why the curve is highest at this point. The further away you go from the mean, the fewer individuals there are. There are as many people above and below the mean. In other words (theoretically) there are as many non-aggressive as there are very aggressive people, and as many people who are taller than average as there are people who are shorter than average. Furthermore, we can specify the percentage of people who are within one or two **standard deviations** of the mean (this concept is explained further in Chapter 8 Section 22). Basically, a standard deviation is a measure of "average" distance from the mean. A very unusual behaviour will be more than 2 standard deviations from the mean, that is it will be found in less than 5% of the population. With reference to the normal curve in the figure, you can see that only very few people are in the "tail" regions.

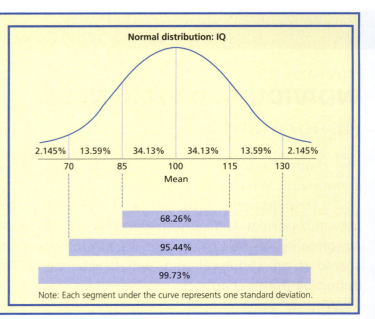

Normal distribution: IQ

2.145% 13.59% 34.13% 34.13% 13.59% 2.145%
70   85   100   115   130
                Mean

68.26%

95.44%

99.73%

Note: Each segment under the curve represents one standard deviation.

(the tendency to experience high levels of anxiety) as assessed by Spielberger's State-Trait Anxiety Inventory. The mean score for trait anxiety is about 40. Only 2% of the population will obtain a score higher than 55, so these people can be regarded as abnormal, in the sense that their scores deviate from the great majority of the population. We can express this concept of deviation from the majority in terms of the **normal distribution**, which is discussed in the box above.

Limitations of the statistical approach

? **In what ways are you abnormal?**

There are problems with this approach. In terms of a trait such as anxiety, we would expect to find a normal distribution of that trait within any population. Most people cluster around the mean score with just a few scoring very high or very low. An "abnormally" high score on trait anxiety would suggest that treatment might be helpful. A low score on trait anxiety (scores of 25 or less) would also be statistically abnormal, but hardly indicates clinical abnormality—it might even be quite desirable.

So the concept of **statistical infrequency** in relation to abnormality communicates an important meaning but doesn't permit us to identify what behaviours require treatment, i.e. it overlooks *desirability*. Some statistically abnormal behaviours are undesirable, e.g. high trait anxiety, whereas others are quite desirable, e.g. low anxiety, or genius. To treat mental disorder we need a definition to encompass behaviours that are *not only* statistically rare *but also* undesirable and damaging.

A second problem with the statistical approach is deciding by how much a behaviour must deviate from the norm before it will be considered abnormal. Statistical definitions rely on an arbitrary cut-off point, which might be in terms of standard deviations. A third problem is that our cut-off point might not apply to another cultural group where anxiety is rather differently distributed. A fourth problem with statistical definitions is that they are related to a standard set by a particular population, which may not apply to people in different age groups or cultures. On the positive side, the statistical approach is less affected by value judgements than some of the other approaches we will look at. A fifth problem is that we sometimes find that behaviours are not rare at a given time in a particular culture even thought they are clearly "abnormal" in the sense of being undesirable. A clear example was the genocide in Rwanda several years ago.

Deviation from Social Norms

An important part of what is missing from the statistical approach to abnormality is any consideration of the *impact* of an individual's behaviour on others. A different approach is that people who behave in a socially deviant and apparently incomprehensible way should be regarded as abnormal.

The social norms approach also allows us to account for desirability of a behaviour, both for the individual and for society as a whole. Deviation from social norms is abnormal and undesirable. Many people labelled as clinically abnormal do behave in a socially deviant way, e.g. anti-social personality disorder describes individuals who lack a conscience and behave aggressively towards others because they feel no guilt. Consider also the Case Studies described below and on the following page.

Limitations of the social deviance approach

There are many problems with this approach. Here are a few:

1. The concept of social deviancy is related to moral codes or standards, subjectively defined by a society, and these vary with prevailing social attitudes. For example, until fairly recently in Britain it was unacceptable to have a child out of wedlock. Single

Moral codes

The subjective judgements we make when deciding whether or not a particular form of behaviour is normal are derived from the moral codes or standards that we have observed in the behaviour of significant others. We never become entirely independent in our moral thinking. Even as adults our thinking about morality often refers to a collective understanding of the right way to behave in a given situation. Someone who demonstrates a deviation from this may be perceived as either "mad" or "bad".

KEY TERM

Deviation from social norms: behaviour that does not follow socially accepted patterns; violation of them is considered abnormal. These unwritten social rules are culturally relative and era-dependent. For example, homosexuality was once illegal and considered to be a mental disorder because it deviated from the social norm. Now there are campaigns for gay marriages to be recognised and afforded the same benefits as heterosexual marriages, and this shows the extent to which this definition of abnormality is subject to change.

CASE STUDY: SIMON, AN ACUTE SCHIZOPHRENIC

Simon lived at home with his parents. Over some months his parents had become increasingly concerned about his behaviour. He had grown reclusive, spending a lot of time in his room, and he had lost contact with his friends. His parents feared he might be taking drugs. They decided to call the doctor when they found that he had scratched the words "good" and "evil" on his arms, along with other unusual symbols. The GP was also concerned and contacted a psychiatrist who visited Simon at home. Simon at first pretended to be out. After some negotiation, he agreed to let the psychiatrist in. Initially, Simon was very suspicious and denied that there was a problem. Eventually, he told the psychiatrist that he was very worried about all the evil in the world, and had discovered that he could tell whether people were good or evil just by looking at them. He described receiving messages from the radio and TV.

The psychiatrist was concerned when Simon said that he left the house at night to look for evil people,

believing it was his duty to fight them. The psychiatrist found that Simon's bedroom was painted black and the curtains were taped shut. The walls were covered with crucifixes and mystical symbols, and Simon slept with a large knife near his bed in case he was confronted by evil people at night.

Simon was asked if he was willing to be admitted to a local hospital. He refused, saying he did not need help. The psychiatrist was sufficiently concerned about the possible risks to Simon or others that he arranged for Simon to be admitted under the Mental Health Act. For the first few weeks in hospital, Simon continued to claim that he was not ill and did not need treatment. Drug therapy resulted in significant improvements and he eventually returned home, continuing with his medication.

(Adapted from J.D. Stirling & J.S.E. Hellewell, 1999, *Psychopathology*. London: Routledge.) ■

CASE STUDY: SARAH: A CASE OF AGORAPHOBIA

Sarah, a woman in her mid-thirties, was shopping for bargains in a crowded department store during the January sales. Without warning and without knowing why, she suddenly felt anxious and dizzy. She worried that she was about to faint or have a heart attack. She dropped her shopping and rushed straight home. As she neared home, she noticed that her feelings of panic lessened.

A few days later she decided to go shopping again. On entering the store, she felt herself becoming increasingly anxious. After a few minutes she had become so anxious that a shopkeeper asked her if she was alright and took her to a first aid room. Once there her feelings of panic became worse and she grew particularly embarrassed at all the attention she was attracting.

After this she avoided going to the large store again. She even started to worry when going into smaller shops because she thought she might have another panic attack, and this worry turned into intense anxiety.

Eventually she stopped shopping altogether, asking her husband to do it for her.

Over the next few months, Sarah found that she had panic attacks in more and more places. The typical pattern was that she became progressively anxious the further away from her house she got. She tried to avoid the places where she might have a panic attack but, as the months passed, she found that this restricted her activities. Some days she found it impossible to leave the house at all. She felt that her marriage was becoming strained and that her husband resented her dependence on him.

Clearly Sarah's behaviour was abnormal, in many of the ways described in the text. It was statistically infrequent and socially deviant. It interfered with her ability to function adequately, both from her own point of view and from that of her husband. She did not have many of the signs of mental healthiness.

(Adapted from J.D. Stirling & J.S.E. Hellewell, 1999, *Psychopathology*. London: Routledge.) ■

Sitting in the road may be considered an abnormal behaviour in our society, but it is acceptable to those involved in a road protest.

women who became pregnant were seen as social deviants and some were even locked up in psychiatric institutions as a result. Early in the 20th century, in Russia, individuals who disagreed with the communist government were called dissidents. Their attitudes were seen as symptoms of mental derangement and they were confined in mental hospitals. Using social deviancy to establish a standard allows serious abuses of human rights to occur. Szasz (1960) suggested that the concept of mental illness is a myth, used by the state as a means of control. It is certainly open to such abuse.

2. Social deviance is defined by the context in which a behaviour occurs. Wearing very few clothes is acceptable on a beach but not in the high street. Cultural context is also important, e.g. the Kwakiutl Indians engage in a special ceremony in which they burn valuable blankets to cast shame on their rivals. If someone in our society deliberately set fire to his/her most valuable possessions, they would be regarded as very odd or mentally ill (Gleitman, 1986). Even within societies there are sub-cultural differences in relation to, for example, different religious groups that have different norms, such as Mormons who believe it is acceptable to have several wives.

3. Social deviancy is not necessarily a bad thing. Some people are socially deviant because they have chosen a non-conformist lifestyle; others because their behaviour is motivated by high principles. For example, consider those

"deviants" in Nazi Germany who spoke out against the atrocities that were being committed.

The fact that social deviance should be rejected as the *only* criterion of abnormality doesn't mean it is entirely irrelevant. After all, people derive much of their pleasure in life from their interactions with other people. As a result, most people find it important for a contented existence to avoid behaving in socially deviant ways that bemuse or upset others.

Abnormal behaviour...?

Failure to Function Adequately

The next possible way of defining abnormality is as a **failure to function adequately**. Most people who seek psychiatric help are suffering from a sense of psychological distress or discomfort (Sue et al., 1994). We could say that this recognition of not functioning adequately could act as a standard of abnormality.

In most societies, we have expectations about how people should live their lives and how they should contribute to the social groups around them. When an individual cannot meet these obligations then both we and they usually feel they are not functioning adequately. Rosenhan and Seligman (1989) suggested that the concept of distress and failure to function can be extended to encompass a number of behaviours.

According to Rosenhan and Seligman (1989), the most suitable approach to defining mental abnormality may be to identify a set of seven abnormal characteristics. Each of these on its own may not be sufficient to cause a problem but, when several are present, then they are symptomatic of abnormality. The fewer features displayed, the more an individual can be regarded as normal. This approach enables us to think in terms of *degrees* of normality and abnormality, rather than whether or not a behaviour or person is abnormal.

...Not when rescuing a cat!

- *Suffering.* Most abnormal individuals report that they are suffering, and so this is a key feature of abnormality. But nearly all normal individuals grieve and suffer when a loved one dies, and some abnormal individuals (e.g. psychopaths or those with anti-social personality disorder) treat other people very badly but don't suffer themselves.
- *Maladaptiveness.* Maladaptive behaviour prevents an individual from achieving major life goals such as enjoying good relationships with other people or working effectively. Most abnormal behaviour is maladaptive in this sense. But it can be due, instead, to a lack of relevant knowledge or skills.
- *Vividness and unconventionality of behaviour.* The ways in which abnormal individuals behave in various situations differ substantially from most people. But the same is true of non-conformists.
- *Unpredictability and loss of control.* Abnormal individuals' behaviour is often very variable and uncontrolled, and is inappropriate. But most people can sometimes behave like this (e.g. after binge drinking).
- *Irrationality and incomprehensibility.* A common feature of abnormal behaviour is that it isn't clear *why* anyone would choose to behave in that way. But we might simply not know the reasons for it.
- *Observer discomfort.* Those who see these unspoken rules of social behaviour being broken by others often experience some discomfort. But observer discomfort may reflect cultural differences in behaviour and style rather than abnormality.

■ **Activity:** The seven features of abnormality

Imagine a continuum from extremely abnormal behaviour at one end to normality at the other. At what point does our behaviour become unacceptable? Bearing in mind Rosenhan and Seligman's definitions, consider the experiences described below. For each one describe what would be acceptable behaviour and what would be regarded as abnormal. For example, what kind of expression of grief would go beyond the bounds of normality?

Suffering: Grief at the loss of a loved one.

Maladaptiveness: Disregard for one's own safety, e.g. taking part in extreme sports.

Vividness and unconventionality: Tattooing or body piercing.

Unpredictability and loss of control: Losing one's temper.

Irrationality and incomprehensibility: Remaining friendly towards someone who is hostile.

Observer discomfort: Laughing at inappropriate times, e.g. when someone is describing a sad event.

Violation of moral and ideal standards: Removing one's clothes to sunbathe on the beach.

- Are the criteria we use influenced by our cultural and personal backgrounds?
- Try to think of other examples for each standard.

- *Violation of moral and ideal standards.* Behaviour may be judged to be abnormal when it violates established moral standards. But the majority of people may fail to maintain those standards, which may be out of date or imposed by minority religious or political leaders. For example, various common sexual practices are illegal in some parts of the United States.

One serious problem with Rosenhan and Seligman's features is that most of them involve making subjective judgements. For example, behaviour causing severe discomfort to one observer may have no effect on another observer, and behaviour that violates one person's moral standards may be consistent with another person's moral standards. Another problem with some of the features is that they also apply to people who are non-conformists or who simply have their own idiosyncratic style. However, there are no clear objective measures of abnormality that we can use.

Limitations of the "failure to function" approach
The main problem with this way of defining abnormality is that not all people who experience mental disorder are aware of their failure to function, e.g. people with schizophrenia often deny they have a problem (see the Case Study on page 185). It *is* distressing to others, who may be able to judge that the individual is not functioning adequately and seek help on their behalf.

On the positive side, it is relatively easy to assess the consequences of dysfunctional behaviour, such as absenteeism from work, to measure the level of functioning. However, value judgements are still required, so the "failure to function adequately" model is tied to the social deviancy one.

The model does recognise the individual's subjective experience but, inevitably, such judgements are made by others and are influenced by social and cultural beliefs and biases.

Deviation from Ideal Mental Health

If we take the view that abnormality is related to the lack of a "contented existence" then we might seek a definition in terms of **deviation from ideal mental health.**

KEY TERM

Deviation from ideal mental health: deviation from optimal psychological well-being (a state of contentment that we all strive to achieve). Deviation is characterised by a lack of positive self-attitudes, personal growth, autonomy, accurate view of reality, environmental mastery, and resistance to stress; all of which prevent the individual from accessing their potential, which is known as self-actualisation.

This is the view put forward by **humanistic psychologists**, such as Carl Rogers and Abraham Maslow. They both felt that **self-actualisation** (fulfilment of one's potential) was a key standard and goal for human endeavour.

Rogers (1959) was the founder of **client-centred therapy**, or counselling. He believed that maladjustment or abnormal development occurred because a child received conditional love from his/her parents. What that means is that the child will only receive love from his/her parents if he/she behaves in certain ways. The resulting conflict between the self-concept and the ideal self means the individual will try to be someone else in order to receive the love they want. Healthy psychological development occurs through receiving *unconditional* positive regard from significant others (love is given regardless of the child's behaviour). This leads to high **self-esteem** and self-acceptance. It frees the individual from seeking social approval and enables him/her to seek self-actualisation.

According to Rogers, young children should receive unconditional positive regard from their parents.

Maslow (1954) was interested in the factors driving or motivating individuals. He claimed that we seek first to have our basic needs satisfied, e.g. hunger, safety. Then people are "driven" by "higher" motives, e.g. love, belonging, and knowledge. The highest motive of all is to seek self-actualisation (see diagram below).

Humanists wanted to define the ultimate goals of human behaviour. Normal people would strive for these goals; abnormality results from a failure to achieve them.

Jahoda (1958) argued that the concepts of abnormality and normality were useless because their definition varies as a function of the group or culture we are considering. She suggested it was preferable to identify the criteria for positive mental health and then look at the frequency of their distribution in any population. Jahoda tried to identify common concepts that were used when describing mental health, and proposed that there were six categories that **clinicians** typically related to mental health:

1. *Self-attitudes*. High self-esteem and a strong sense of identity are related to mental health.
2. *Personal growth*. The extent of an individual's actual growth, development, or self-actualisation is important.
3. *Integration*. This is a "synthesising psychological function", integrating the above two concepts. It can be assessed in terms of the individual's ability to cope with stressful situations.
4. *Autonomy*. The degree to which an individual is independent of social influences.
5. *Perception of reality*. A prime factor in mental healthiness. Individuals with good mental health don't need to distort their perception of reality, and demonstrate empathy and social sensitivity.
6. *Environmental mastery*. The extent to which an individual is successful and well adapted, including ability to love, adequacy at work and play, and in interpersonal relations, efficiency in meeting situational requirements, capacity for

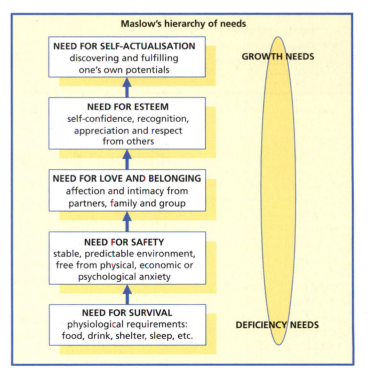

Maslow's hierarchy of needs

NEED FOR SELF-ACTUALISATION
discovering and fulfilling one's own potentials

NEED FOR ESTEEM
self-confidence, recognition, appreciation and respect from others

NEED FOR LOVE AND BELONGING
affection and intimacy from partners, family and group

NEED FOR SAFETY
stable, predictable environment, free from physical, economic or psychological anxiety

NEED FOR SURVIVAL
physiological requirements: food, drink, shelter, sleep, etc.

GROWTH NEEDS

DEFICIENCY NEEDS

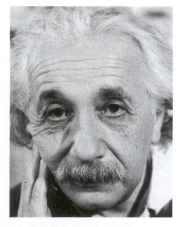

Maslow characterised Einstein as a famous individual who demonstrated "self-actualisation"—including characteristics such as self-acceptance, resistance to cultural influences, empathy, and creativeness.

adaptation and adjustment, and efficient problem solving. Many of us probably don't succeed in all these areas!

This approach has the benefit of being positive. It seeks to identify the characteristics that people need to be mentally healthy rather than identifying the problems, so it could be translated into useful therapeutic aims (treatment goals).

However, it may not provide useful criteria for identifying what constitutes abnormality. A psychological scale that measures psychological concepts, e.g. a person's self-esteem, can never be an objective measurement.

Also, any set of values is inevitably bound to culture and historic period. Many psychologists (e.g. Oyserman et al., 2002) draw a distinction between individualistic cultures and collectivistic societies. Individualistic cultures (e.g. Britain; United States) emphasise independence and personal control whereas collectivistic societies (e.g. China; Japan) focus on interdependence and considering oneself as a member of a group. Jahoda's list of mentally healthy behaviours such as autonomy and personal growth makes more sense in individualistic cultures than in collectivistic ones.

Limitations of the ideal mental health approach

One advantage of this approach is that it focuses on positive characteristics—on health rather than illness. However, the criteria used are hard to define—they are abstract ideals and related to our particular culture. Not all societies feel that these are the ultimate aims for psychological health. As we have seen, **collectivistic** societies strive for the greater good of the community rather than for self-centred goals.

These vague criteria are also difficult to measure. How can we rate positive interpersonal relations or self-acceptance? Finally, we should consider the fact that these "healthy behaviours" are ideals. Very few people ever achieve them, so many of us would be classed as abnormal.

> **EXAM HINT**
>
> You need to be able to describe each definition of abnormality in sufficient detail for 3 marks:
>
> - *Statistical infrequency*: Make sure you can use the normal distribution.
> - *Deviation from social norms*: Remember these are culturally relevant and era dependent.
> - *Failure to function adequately*: Be able to include some (not necessarily all) of Rosenhan and Seligman's criteria for failure to function, e.g. personal distress, observer discomfort, and maladaptiveness.
> - *Deviation from ideal mental health*: Consider Jahoda's criteria for ideal mental health, e.g. positive self-attitudes, autonomy, perception of reality.

Cultural Relativism

A core limitation to all the definitions of abnormality we have examined is the extent to which they are culturally specific. The concept of **cultural relativism** means that value judgements are *relative* to individual cultural contexts and we cannot make absolute statements about what is normal or abnormal in human behaviour. For example, dhat syndrome is a culture-bound sex neurosis of males of the Indian subcontinent. Sufferers have multiple somatic complaints, and blame their physical and mental exhaustion on the presence of semen in their urine. The origins of this lie in the Hindu belief that semen is produced in the blood, and that the loss of semen will result in illness. Chadda and Ahuja

(1990) examined a number of patients with dhat and concluded they were suffering from either neurotic depression or anxiety neurosis. Thus, a single underlying disorder (e.g. depression) may be expressed in different ways from one culture to another.

As we have seen, notions of abnormality vary from one culture to another, and within the same culture at different periods in history. For example, the way in which homosexuality is regarded has altered over successive editions of DSM (*Diagnostic and Statistical Manual of Mental Disorders*). This is the system used to classify mental illness in America and is used by clinicians to diagnose mental disorders. In DSM-II, which was published in 1968, homosexuality was classified as a sexual deviation. In DSM-III, published in 1980, homosexuality was no longer categorised as a mental disorder, but there was a new category of "ego-dystonic homosexuality", used only for homosexuals wishing to become heterosexual. In DSM-III-R, this last category had disappeared, but one of "sexual disorder not otherwise specified", with "persistent and marked distress about one's sexual orientation" was inserted. This remains the case in **DSM-IV**. However, even today many people still view homosexuality as an aberrant mental state.

Homosexuality ceased to be categorised as a mental disorder in the 1980 edition of DSM.

The importance of the cultural context can be seen if we return to the seven features of abnormality proposed by Rosenhan and Seligman (on page 187). Many of the features refer to behaviour defined by the social norms or expectations of the culture. So abnormality has a somewhat different meaning across cultures, e.g. hallucinations are considered normal in certain situations in some societies, whereas in the West they are seen as a manifestation of a mental disorder (Sue et al., 1994).

However, some features identified by Rosenhan and Seligman are universal indicators of undesirable behaviour—both for the individual concerned and those around them, e.g. failure to eat, chronic depression, fear of going outdoors, and anti-social behaviour. So there are some universal indicators of abnormality.

> **EXAM HINT**
> - You are most likely to be asked to give ONE criticism of any of the definitions of abnormality, however as there are many you should know at least two to be fully prepared for all possible types of question. You must be able to ELABORATE the criticism sufficiently for 3 marks.
> - Culture bias works well for all four definitions. However, be cautious in using this for statistical frequency as it is the statistical norm (the measurement) that is culturally relative, rather than people's views in different cultures.
> - Use examples of social norms changing across cultures and examples of how the criteria in failure to function and ideal mental health can be viewed differently across cultures to make sure your answer is DETAILED and FOCUSED on the definition specified in the question.

Conclusions

Concepts differ very much in their precision. "Abnormality" is an imprecise concept. Abnormal behaviour can take different forms, and can involve different features. Moreover, there is no *single* feature that can always be relied on to distinguish between normal and abnormal behaviour. What is needed is to identify the main features that are *more likely* to be found in abnormal than in normal individuals. The seven features proposed by Rosenhan and Seligman (1989) may offer a

> **Labels and symptoms**
>
> Imagine that you are in a situation where you have been wrongly diagnosed as suffering from a mental disorder such as schizophrenia. How would you react to such a situation? Would you be incredulous? Furious? Tearful? Shocked and withdrawn? How could all those emotions be interpreted by those people whose job it is to assess your mental condition?

combined and realistic approach. The more of these features possessed by an individual, the greater the likelihood that he/she will be categorised as abnormal.

SECTION SUMMARY

The statistical infrequency approach

❖ This is one way of defining abnormality. According to this approach abnormality can be defined in terms of behaviour or beliefs that are statistically rare in a population.

❖ The normal distribution is one way to describe a statistical distribution.

❖ While this approach suffers less from value judgements than the other approaches it has been criticised as follows:

  – It does not distinguish between desirable deviation and undesirable deviation.

  – It doesn't define at what level or percentage statistical deviancy is decided.

  – It doesn't allow for cultural and sub-cultural differences.

Deviation from social norms

❖ This is another way of defining abnormality. Social groups have norms of what is considered to be socially acceptable behaviour. Deviation from these is abnormal and undesirable.

❖ This approach has been criticised as follows:

  – The perception of deviance may change over historical time and what is socially deviant varies across cultures with ethnic or religious differences.

  – The definition ignores the role of social context. In some cases it may be desirable to be socially deviant.

  – The concept of social deviance could lead to an abuse of human rights.

Failure to function adequately

❖ The third approach suggests that abnormality can be defined in terms of an inability to function adequately in day-to-day life and social interactions.

❖ An absence of distress and the ability to function are standards of normal behaviour.

❖ This approach has the benefit of taking the individual's experience into account. However it has been criticised as follows:
  - How do we determine whether a person is functioning adequately?
  - Not all those with mental disorders are aware of their own distress or dysfunction.
  - The definition raises concerns about cultural bias and subjectivity as judgements by others on their behalf may be biased.
  - Rosenhan and Seligman have extended the "failure to function" model to cover seven features associated with abnormality, but these again rely on making subjective judgements.

❖ Another approach suggests that abnormality can be defined in terms of deviation from ideal mental health.

Deviation from ideal mental health

❖ Humanistic psychologists consider the factors that may be important for normal development such as unconditional positive regard. They also see self-actualisation as an ultimate goal.
❖ However, this approach has been criticised as follows:
  - The approach is based on abstract and culturally relative ideals, not shared by collectivist societies. There are cultural variations in how to identify psychological health.
  - Unlike physical health, it is difficult to measure psychological health.

❖ Cultural relativism is a problem in all four of the approaches described. The definitions inevitably refer to some subjective, culturally determined set of values.

Limitations with all these approaches

❖ However, there are also cultural universals—behaviours such as anti-social behaviour or chronic depression are universally viewed as abnormal and undesirable.

See pp.90–93 of the revision guide.

❖ The resolution may lie in using a combined approach that focuses on which features are more likely to be associated with abnormality.

SECTION 15
BIOLOGICAL AND PSYCHOLOGICAL MODELS OF ABNORMALITY

A different way to approach abnormality is to consider explanations of *why* it happens. Several models of abnormality have been put forward over the years. These models have been very influential, because the form of treatment for any given mental disorder is based in part on our understanding of the causes of that disorder.

The dominant model, at least until fairly recently, was the **biological (medical) model**, where mental disorders are regarded as illnesses. Most **psychiatrists** accept this model, whereas most clinical psychologists reject it in favour of psychological models. There are also numerous psychologically based models of abnormality, focusing on different factors and/or attitudes to life. It is probable that each of the models is partially correct, and that a full understanding of the origins of mental disorders requires us to combine information from all of them. Here we will focus

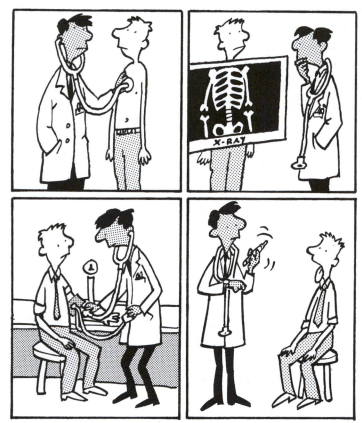

Results of medical tests provide more precise information than is available to psychiatrists and clinical psychologists.

One way to investigate the genetic cause of mental disorders is to look at genetically related individuals. If relatives of a person with a mental disorder are found also to suffer from it, then this suggests a genetic basis for the mental disorder.

on the four most important ones: biological, psychodynamic, behavioural, and cognitive models.

The Biological Model

The essence of the biological (medical) model is that "abnormal behaviours result from physical problems and should be treated medically". In other words, mental disorders are illnesses with a physical cause, so we should approach mental disorders from the perspective of medicine.

There are four kinds of medical explanation that can be used to explain the cause of abnormality.

Infection

Germs or micro-organisms such as bacteria or viruses are known to produce disease states. Many common physical illnesses are caused in this way, such as measles and influenza. Some mental illnesses have also been linked to known micro-organisms. However, this approach doesn't make much sense, because most mental disorders don't form distinct syndromes nor do they have one cause. But this is the aim of the medical approach—if we can diagnose a syndrome then we might find a cure. The one relies on the other. For example, micro-organisms have been suggested as a cause of schizophrenia. Barr et al. (1990) found there was increased incidence of schizophrenia in children whose mothers had flu when they were pregnant, thereby suggesting that the cause of the disorder might be a disease. However, this approach to schizophrenia is not generally regarded as useful.

Genetic factors

Individuals may inherit predispositions to certain illnesses. These predispositions are carried on **genes** which pass from one generation to the next. One way to demonstrate the inheritance of mental disorder is by looking at patterns of such disorders within families or within twin pairs. If a disorder is caused genetically then we would expect individuals who are closely related to be more likely to have it, especially when they have been reared apart (i.e. there are no shared environmental influences). However, individuals within a family who are closely related are likely to have more similar environments (e.g. living in the same home) than those who are not closely related. That can make it hard to decide whether the presence of a given mental disorder in two closely related individuals is due to the similarity in their genes or to the similarity in their environment.

In spite of the complexities, there is reasonable evidence that genetic factors are involved in many mental disorders. For example, Kendler et al. (1985) found that relatives of people with schizophrenia were 18 times more likely to be diagnosed with schizophrenia than is normal. Kendler et al. (1991; see page 212) discovered that genetic factors play a role in the development of bulimia nervosa.

Another way to study **genetic** influences is actually to identify particular genes and show they are more likely to be present in individuals with a disorder than in individuals without the disorder. This is more informative than simply showing that genetic factors are involved in producing a given disorder. **Gene-mapping** studies have found specific genes that may be implicated in particular disorders. For example, Berrettini (2000) linked bipolar disorder (a disorder in which there are depressive and manic [elated] episodes) to genes on chromosomes 4, 6, 11, 12, 13, 15, 18, and 22.

? How might research on gene-mapping be of use when counselling prospective parents?

Biochemistry

A third possible cause of abnormality lies in the patient's **biochemistry**. For example, several theorists have argued that one of the factors involved in schizophrenia is an excessive amount of dopamine, a chemical substance in the brain. However, research has only identified *correlations* between the disorder and the raised biochemical levels. What this means is that we cannot be certain whether the excessive amount of dopamine is *cause* or *effect*. It is possible that having schizophrenia causes dopamine levels to rise rather than excessive dopamine levels playing a role in the onset of schizophrenia.

Some evidence that biochemical changes can have significant effects on the symptoms of abnormality comes from drug studies using patients. For example, it has been suggested that depression is associated with low levels of the neurotransmitter serotonin. Prozac, a well-known drug that increases serotonin activity, has been found to reduce significantly the symptoms of depression (Hirschfeld, 1999). This is consistent with the hypothesis that abnormal levels of serotonin play a role in producing depression.

Neuroanatomy

A fourth possible cause lies in **neuroanatomy**—the structure of the nervous system. For example, post-mortem [after death] studies of people with schizophrenia show that their brains differ from those of normal individuals. Again, we cannot be certain whether schizophrenia caused the neuroanatomical changes or whether the differences were the cause of the mental disorder. However, neuropathology (abnormal neuroanatomy) has been found in recently diagnosed untreated schizophrenic patients, suggesting that there is a link between neuropathology and schizophrenia.

Evaluation of the biological model

The biological (medical) model has had an enormous influence on the terms used to refer to mental disorders and their treatment. As Maher (1966, p.22) pointed out, deviant behaviour

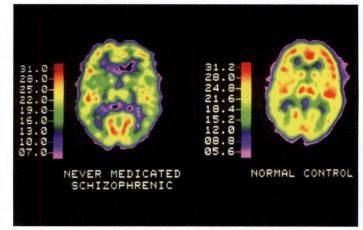

NEVER MEDICATED SCHIZOPHRENIC   NORMAL CONTROL

PET scans of a normal (right) and schizophrenic human brain.

is termed pathological and is classified on the basis of symptoms, classification being called diagnosis. Processes designed to change behaviour

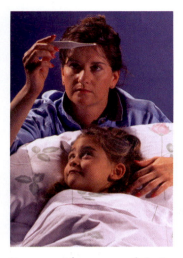

It may not be appropriate to think that mental illnesses are the same as physical ones.

are called therapies, and are [sometimes] applied to patients in mental hospitals. If the deviant behaviour ceases, the patient is described as cured.

The biological model approach is clearly successful in the case of some psychological conditions, e.g. phenylketonuria (PKU), a cause of mental retardation, can be simply and effectively treated by physical means. This is a condition where an individual is born with an inability to metabolise (process) the amino acid phenylalanine. As a result, the concentration of phenylalanine increases, and there is permanent brain damage. In addition, there are usually seizures and behaviour problems. PKU is preventable if it is detected early enough. Infants are given a special diet low in phenylalanine and this has proved very successful in preventing the development of PKU.

But how useful is the biological model approach to most mental disorders? It has the merit of being based on well-established sciences such as medicine and biochemistry. Some forms of mental disorder can be understood from the perspective of the biological model, and numerous mental disorders are caused *in part* by genetic factors. Drug therapies based on the biological model have often proved effective, in at least reducing symptoms.

On the negative side, there is generally only a loose analogy between physical and mental illness. It is easier to establish the causes of most physical illnesses than mental ones, and symptoms of mental disorders are often more subjective. The biological model seems to apply much better to some mental disorders (e.g. schizophrenia) than others (e.g. phobias).

One important difficulty is knowing whether any biological difference between individuals with a mental disorder and those without such disorder is a by-product of the disorder or a direct cause.

Another criticism is that the focus within the biological model is on physical symptoms, rather than psychological and social factors (such as anxiety and isolation) and so the application of medical principles is inappropriate.

One of the biggest critics of the medical approach, Thomas Szasz, suggested that mental illnesses were more appropriately described as "problems in living" rather than as disease, and states:

It is customary to define psychiatry as a medical specialty concerned with the study, diagnosis, and treatment of mental illnesses. This is a worthless and misleading definition. Mental illness is a myth. Psychiatrists are not concerned with mental illnesses and their treatment . . . In actual practice they deal with personal, social and ethical problems in living. I have argued that, today, the notion of a person "having a mental illness" is scientifically crippling. It provides professional assent to a popular rationalization, namely that problems of living . . . expressed in terms of so called psychiatric symptoms are basically similar to bodily diseases . . . We must recast and redefine the problem of "mental illness" so that it may be encompassed in a morally explicit science of man (1960, p.269).

Szasz's objections to the medical or biological model are not made very clear in the above quotation (as you

> **Assumptions of the biological model**
> - All mental disorders have a physical cause (micro-organisms, genetics, biochemistry, or neuroanatomy).
> - Mental illnesses can be described in terms of clusters of symptoms.
> - Symptoms can be identified, leading to the diagnosis of an illness.
> - Diagnosis leads to appropriate physical treatments.

will probably agree!), so I will try to clarify what he had in mind. First, he pointed out that we generally don't hold someone responsible if they have a physical illness and we tend to do the same if they have a so-called mental illness. He felt this was very undesirable ethically, because it stops people accepting responsibility for themselves and for their own lives. Second, putting a label on someone (e.g. "You're a schizophrenic") can create problems for the individual concerned. People who are identified as suffering from a mental illness are often rejected by others in the same way as someone who is identified as a criminal or prostitute. In Szasz's view, it is unfair to add to someone's problems in this way.

Ethical implications of the biological model

We could turn Szasz's argument on its head. The notion that individuals with mental disorders are suffering from an illness could be regarded as ethically desirable, because it suggests that they are not responsible for their condition and so should not feel guilty. However, it may be undesirable to encourage individuals with mental disorders to hand over complete responsibility for their recovery to experts trained in treating "mental illness".

The notion that genetic factors often play a significant role in the development of mental disorders raises ethical issues. The relatives of an individual diagnosed as suffering from such a disorder may well become very anxious, which could greatly increase their chances of developing the disorder. On the other hand, it could be regarded as unethical not to provide full and accurate information to the relatives! For example, if they are at high risk of developing an anxiety disorder, they could take action to reduce the risk by trying to have a predictable and safe existence.

Many of the forms of treatment based on the biological model raise important ethical issues. Drugs can have serious side effects and lead to drug dependence. However, a failure to use drugs may increase the suffering of those with mental disorders.

Finally, most people would argue that the best approach to diagnosis is to take account of all the factors that might be relevant, including environmental factors such as close relationships and employment. It could be regarded as unethical to focus exclusively on biological factors.

> ### ECT and psychosurgery
>
> Some forms of treatment based on the biological model include fairly drastic methods such as electroconvulsive therapy (ECT) and brain surgery. However, ECT is not the barbaric treatment it once was. Patients are given sedatives before treatment and then brief shocks are applied to the non-dominant hemisphere of the brain. The treatment has been found to be successful for patients suffering from chronic depression, and long-term side effects are unusual (Stirling & Hellewell, 1999).
>
> Brain surgery (psychosurgery) is used in extremely rare conditions, where no other treatment seems appropriate. Sections of the brain are removed or lesions are made separating regions of the brain. The technique was first pioneered by Antonio Egas Moniz (1937) who performed prefrontal lobotomies, in which fibres running from the frontal lobes to other parts of the brain were cut. Lobotonies typically make patients calmer, but side effects include apathy, diminished intellectual powers, impaired judgement, and even coma and death. In view of the dangers of lobotomies, it is ironic that Moniz was shot by one of his own lobotomised patients!

The Psychodynamic Model

The term "psychodynamic" refers to a group of explanations that try to account for the *dynamics* of behaviour, or the forces that motivate it. Sigmund Freud's theory is the best-known example, and he has probably been the most influential person in the history of clinical psychology. His view was that mental illness didn't have a physical origin. Instead he suggested that it arises out of unresolved, unconscious conflicts which form in early childhood.

Sigmund Freud, 1856–1939.

Defence mechanisms

Another example of a defence mechanism is reaction formation, e.g. in an adult who has developed a fear of close, intimate relationships due to a disappointment or hurt experienced during childhood. As a consequence, when this adult meets someone to whom they feel a strong attraction, they may consciously experience the opposite emotion of dislike, or even hatred.

KEY TERM

Defence mechanisms: strategies used by the ego to defend itself against anxiety.

To understand this we need to look again briefly at Freud's theory of personality development (see Chapter 2, Section 4). Freud argued that the mind is divided into three parts: the id, the ego, and the superego, which are often in conflict with each other.

The **psychodynamic model** proposed by Freud was based on his theory of **psychosexual development**. The child passes through a series of stages (oral, anal, phallic, latency, and genital). Major conflicts (or excessive gratification) at any of these stages can mean that the child spends an unusually long time at that stage of development (known as **fixation**). Conflicts cause anxiety, and the ego defends itself against anxiety by using several defence mechanisms to prevent traumatic thoughts and feelings reaching consciousness. These defence mechanisms include **repression**, displacement, **projection**, and denial.

According to Freud, mental disorders can arise when an individual has unresolved conflicts and traumas from childhood. Defence mechanisms may be used to reduce the anxiety caused by such unresolved conflicts, but they act more as sticking plaster than as a way of sorting out an individual's problems.

CASE STUDY: ANNA O

Freud's theory was largely based on the observations he made during consultations with patients. He suggested that his work was similar to that of an archaeologist, who digs away layers of earth before uncovering what he or she was seeking. In a similar way, the psychiatrist seeks to dig down to the unconscious and discover the key to the individual's personality dynamic.

"Anna O. was a girl of twenty-one, of a high degree of intelligence. Her illness first appeared while she was caring for her father, whom she tenderly loved, during the severe illness which led to his death. The patient had a severe paralysis of both right extremities, disturbance of eye-movements, an intense nausea when she attempted to take nourishment, and at one time for several weeks a loss of the power to drink, in spite of tormenting thirst. She occasionally became confused or delirious and mumbled several words to herself. If these same words were later repeated to her, when she was in a hypnotic state, she engaged in deeply sad, often poetically beautiful, day dreams, we might call them, which commonly took as their starting point the situation of a girl beside the sick-bed of her father. The patient jokingly called this treatment 'chimney sweeping'.

Dr. Breuer [Freud's colleague] soon hit upon the fact that through such cleansing of the soul more could be accomplished than a temporary removal of the constantly recurring mental 'clouds'.

During one session, the patient recalled an occasion when she was with her governess, and how that lady's little dog, that she abhorred, had drunk out of a glass. Out of respect for the conventions the patient had remained silent, but now under hypnosis she gave energetic expression to her restrained anger, and then drank a large quantity of water without trouble, and woke from hypnosis with the glass at her lips. The symptom thereupon vanished permanently.

Permit me to dwell for a moment on this experience. No one had ever cured an hysterical symptom by such means before, or had come so near understanding its cause. This would be a pregnant discovery if the expectation could be confirmed that still other, perhaps the majority of symptoms, originated in this way and could be removed by the same method.

Such was indeed the case, almost all the symptoms originated in exactly this way, as we were to discover. The patient's illness originated at the time when she was caring for her sick father, and her symptoms could only be regarded as memory symbols of his sickness and death. While she was seated by her father's sick bed, she was careful to betray nothing of her anxiety and her painful depression to the patient. When, later, she reproduced the same scene before the physician, the emotion which she had suppressed on the occurrence of the scene burst out with especial strength, as though it had been pent up all along.

In her normal state she was entirely ignorant of the pathogenic scenes and of their connection with her symptoms. She had forgotten those scenes. When the patient was hypnotized, it was possible, after considerable difficulty, to recall those scenes to her memory, and by this means of recall the symptoms were removed."

(Adapted from Sigmund Freud, 1910, The origin and development of psychoanalysis. *American Journal of Psychology, 21*, 181–218.) ■

As we have seen, Freud assumed that most adult mental disorders have their roots in either childhood experiences or personality development in childhood. The evidence is mixed, but there is some support for this assumption. Kendler et al. (1996) considered the role of childhood experiences. They studied adult female twins who had experienced parental loss through separation in childhood. These twins showed an above-average tendency to suffer from depression and alcoholism in adult life. Caspi et al. (1996) considered the role of childhood personality in subsequent problems. They studied 3-year-olds and then carried out a follow-up 18 years later. Children who had an inhibited personality at the age of 3 tended to be depressed at the age of 21. Children who were under-controlled and impulsive at the age of 3 were more likely to have developed anti-social personality disorder by the time they reached 21.

Evaluation of the psychodynamic model

The psychodynamic model proposed by Freud was the first systematic model of abnormality that focused specifically on *psychological* factors as the cause of mental disorder and on psychological forms of treatment. Before Freud, nearly all explanations of mental illness were in terms of physical causes or ideas such as possession by evil spirits. Psychoanalysis paved the way for later psychological models. Another advantage is that it identified traumatic childhood experiences as a factor in the development of adult disorders, an assumption for which there is good evidence (Barlow & Durand, 1995). More generally, the notion that childhood experiences and childhood personality development play a role in adult mental disorder has received some support (e.g. Caspi et al., 1996; Kendler et al., 1996). Note, however, that finding that there is an association between having had a troubled childhood and adult mental disorder does not prove that the troubled childhood helped to *cause* the adult mental disorder.

A great weakness of the psychodynamic model as put forward by Freud was the relative lack of interest in the *current* problems his patients were facing. Even if childhood experiences stored in the unconscious play a part in the development of mental disorders, that does not mean that adult experiences can be ignored. Modern psychodynamic therapy has evolved from Freud's approach, but has more emphasis on current problems.

Also, Freud tended to focus too much on sexual factors as the cause of mental disorders, whereas interpersonal and social factors are regarded as important by most psychodynamic therapists nowadays. Most modern psychodynamic therapists believe that sexual problems are a *result* of poor relationships with others rather than a cause of disorder.

The psychodynamic model is not based on a solid foundation of scientific research. Freud's theoretical

Positive aspects of the Freudian approach

Freud's work is often criticised, and it is true that it is difficult to verify the workings of the subconscious mind through scientific investigations. However, post-Freudian study of the importance of subjective feelings and experience has been a major undertaking in both psychology and other dissociated fields such as creative writing, literary theory, and art history. Freud's ideas about the importance of the subconscious mind were one of the most profound influences on human thought of the 20th century, leading to in-depth questioning of human motives and intentions. It is hard for us to think about the world without employing Freudian concepts.

> **Assumptions of the psychodynamic model**
> - Much of our behaviour is driven by unconscious motives.
> - Childhood is a critical period in development.
> - Mental disorders arise from unresolved, unconscious conflicts originating in childhood.
> - Resolution occurs through accessing and coming to terms with repressed ideas and conflicts.

views emerged mainly from his interactions with patients in the therapeutic situation—a weak form of evidence probably contaminated by his biases and preconceptions.

In sum, the psychodynamic approach is limited because it tends to ignore genetic factors involved in the development of mental disorders. In its original form, the patient's current concerns and interpersonal relationships were de-emphasised, and there was undue focus on childhood experiences and sexual problems. In practice, the psychodynamic model has been applied mainly to patients suffering from anxiety disorders or depression rather than from severe disorders such as schizophrenia.

Ethical implications of the psychodynamic model

One of the implications of the psychodynamic model is that individuals are not really responsible for their own mental disorders, because these disorders depend on unconscious processes. However, the notion that adult mental disorders have their basis in childhood experiences suggests that parents or other caregivers are at least partially to blame. This can easily cause them distress, if they are led to believe that they are responsible for their child's disorder.

Very serious ethical issues are raised by numerous recent cases of **false memory syndrome**. In these cases, patients undergoing psychotherapy have made allegations about childhood physical or sexual abuse that have sometimes turned out to have no basis in fact. However, note that this is a very controversial area, and many memories of abuse are undoubtedly genuine.

Freud argued that males and females have their own biologically determined sexual natures, and anxiety disorders or depression can develop when the natural course of their sexual development is thwarted. This approach is dubious, in that it ignores the importance of cultural differences in sexual attitudes and behaviour. It is also very sexist in its emphasis that behavioural differences between men and women stem from biology rather than from social and cultural factors.

The Behavioural Model

The **behavioural model of abnormality** was developed out of the behaviourist approach to psychology put forward mainly by John Watson and B.F. Skinner. According to this model, individuals with mental disorders possess **maladaptive** forms of behaviour, which have been learned. Most of the learning takes the form of classical conditioning or operant conditioning (see Chapter 2, Section 4).

Classical conditioning

Classical conditioning is a form of learning first demonstrated by Pavlov. In essence, a neutral or conditioned stimulus (e.g. a tone) is paired repeatedly with a second or unconditioned stimulus (e.g. presentation of food). After a while, the natural or unconditioned response to the second or unconditioned stimulus (e.g. salivation) comes to be made in response to the neutral stimulus when it is

John Watson, 1878–1958.

> **Classical conditioning**
> - Unconditioned stimulus (US) e.g. food → causes → reflex response e.g. salivation.
> - Neutral stimulus (NS) e.g. bell → causes → no response.
> - NS and US are paired in time (they occur at the same time).
> - NS (e.g. bell) is now a conditioned stimulus (CS) → which produces → a conditioned response (CR) [a new stimulus–response link is learned, the bell causes salivation].
>
> **Operant conditioning**
> - A behaviour that has a positive effect is more likely to be repeated.
> - Positive and negative reinforcement (escape from aversive stimulus) are agreeable.
> - Punishment is disagreeable.

presented on its own, and this learned response is known as the conditioned response.

John B. Watson and Rosalie Rayner (1920) showed in a classic study that emotions could be classically conditioned in the same way as any other response is conditioned. Their participant was an 11-month-old boy called "Little Albert", an orphan living in a hospital. At the start of the experiment, Watson and Rayner established that items such as a white rat, a rabbit, and white cotton wool provoked no fear response. In other words, they could all be regarded as neutral or conditioned stimuli. Watson and Rayner then induced a fear response (unconditioned response) by striking a steel bar with a hammer (unconditioned stimulus), which startled Albert and made him cry. Next, they gave him a white rat to play with and, as he reached out to touch it, they struck the bar to make him frightened. They repeated this three times, and did the same a week later. After this, when they showed the rat to Albert he began to cry, rolled over, and started to crawl away quickly. Classical conditioning had occurred, because the previously neutral or conditioned stimulus (i.e. the rat) produced a conditioned fear response.

CASE STUDY: JOHN WATSON

At the time the "Little Albert" study was conducted, Watson was a major figure in behaviourism and psychology. In 1913 he published a key paper arguing that psychology had to throw out introspection as a research method, and dismiss vague concepts such as "the mind" in order to become a respectable science. Psychologists, he suggested, should instead focus on observable, directly measurable behaviours. In short, he was largely responsible for founding the behaviourist movement, drawing on the ideas of Pavlov.

At the time he was the Professor of Psychology at Johns Hopkins University, Baltimore, USA, where he conducted research into animal behaviour until 1918 when he turned his attention to conditioning infants. However in 1920 he was involved in a rather sensational divorce as a result of his affair with his research assistant Rosalie Rayner, whom he subsequently married. This led him to resign from his job and he went into the advertising business. He continued to have an interest in psychology, publishing a book on infant and child care, but for the most part devoted himself entirely to business where he applied the principles of behaviourism to the world of advertising. In fact he probably was the first applied psychologist and had an extremely successful second career. ■

Watson and Rayner taught a boy ("Little Albert") to fear white fluffy objects by striking a metal bar (unconditioned stimulus) every time he touched the previously unfeared object (neutral stimulus). Thus, they demonstrated that fears could be learned through classical conditioning.

Watson and Rayner found that, now, the sight of any object that was white and furry, such as a white fur coat and a Father Christmas beard, provoked a fear response. This is called **generalisation**—Albert had learned to generalise his fear of the white rat to other similar objects. They intended to "recondition" Albert to eliminate these fearful reactions but he was taken away from the hospital before this could happen.

It is possible that Little Albert developed a phobia, which is an extreme fear causing the individual concerned to avoid the feared stimulus. Mowrer (1947) developed a two-process theory to explain the origin of phobias (extreme fears causing the individual to avoid the feared stimulus). The first stage involves classical conditioning (e.g. linking the white rat and the loud noise). Then the second stage involves operant conditioning. What happens here is that avoidance of the phobic stimulus reduces fear and this reduction in fear is reinforcing or rewarding. It should be noted that **specific phobia**, in which there is an extreme fear reaction to a specific type of stimulus such as snakes or spiders, is recognised as a mental disorder, even though it is generally nothing like as serious as most other mental disorders.

There are various problems with this approach to phobias. It has been found difficult to repeat the findings on Little Albert when attempts were made to condition people to fear neutral stimuli by pairing them with unpleasant ones in the laboratory (Davison & Neale, 1996). In addition, research into phobias has found that many phobics have *not* had prior traumatic experiences with the objects (e.g. snakes) of which they are frightened. Menzies and Clarke (1993), in a study on child participants suffering from water phobia, found only 2% of them reported a direct conditioning experience involving water. DiNardo et al. (1988) found that about 50% of dog phobics had become very anxious during an encounter with a dog, which seems to support conditioning theory. However, about 50% of normal controls without dog phobia had also had an anxious encounter with a dog!

? Try to use classical conditioning to explain some other abnormal behaviour.

Social learning theory

Operant conditioning involves learning a new response because that response has previously resulted in a reward or reinforcement. Bandura (1986) further developed conditioning theory by arguing that **observational learning** or modelling is important—learning by imitating the behaviour of someone else. Observational learning is especially likely to influence behaviour when the other person's behaviour is rewarded or reinforced (vicarious reinforcement).

Observational learning may be relevant to several mental disorders, e.g. Mineka et al. (1984) found that monkeys could develop snake phobia simply by watching another monkey experience fear in the presence of a snake. We might assume that the same principles apply to humans. Some evidence that they do was reported by Bandura and Rosenthal (1966). Participants observed someone responding to

Reinforcement increases the likelihood that the behaviour will be repeated...

a buzzer by pretending to be in pain (e.g. twitching; shouting). After the participants had observed this reaction several times, they experienced a fear reaction whenever they heard the buzzer.

Evaluation of the behavioural model

The basic concepts in the behavioural model (e.g. stimulus; response; reinforcement; modelling) are easier to observe and to measure than the concepts emphasised in other models. Conditioning experiences may play a role in the development of some mental disorders (e.g. phobias). However, we need to be very careful about applying laboratory findings (e.g. on Little Albert) to the real world. As Comer (2001, p.63) pointed out, "There is still no indisputable evidence that most people with psychological disorders are victims of improper conditioning." The sad fact is that we are rarely in a position to know for sure the details of the learning experiences of anyone suffering from a mental disorder, and this makes it hard to test the behavioural model thoroughly.

The behavioural model exaggerates the importance of environmental factors in causing disorders, and minimises the role played by genetic factors. So it is of little value in explaining disorders such as schizophrenia that are likely to have a genetic basis. The behavioural model also minimises the role played by internal processes (e.g. thinking; feeling). This makes it more relevant to disorders with easily observed behavioural symptoms (e.g. the avoidance of certain stimuli in phobics) rather than to disorders with few clear behavioural symptoms (e.g. generalised anxiety disorder in which the main symptom is excessive worrying).

Those who favour the behavioural model are correct in assuming that the experiences people have in life, including the forms of conditioning to which they have been exposed, play a part in the development of mental disorders. However, conditioning is generally less important in humans than in the animal species studied in the laboratory by behaviourists.

In general terms, the behavioural model is oversimplified and rather narrow in scope. On the basis of the available evidence, it seems that only a small fraction of mental disorders depend to any great extent on the individual patient's conditioning history.

> **Assumptions of the behavioural model**
> - All behaviour is learned, and maladaptive behaviour is no different.
> - This learning can be understood in terms of the principles of conditioning and modelling.
> - What was learned can be unlearned, using the same principles.
> - The same laws apply to human and non-human animal behaviour.

Ethical implications of the behavioural model

The behavioural model has some advantages from the ethical perspective:

1. It is assumed that mental disorders result from maladaptive learning and thus should not be regarded as "illnesses".
2. The focus on each individual's particular experiences and conditioning history means that the behavioural model is sensitive to cultural and social factors.
3. The behavioural approach tends to be non-judgemental, in the sense that treatment is recommended only when an individual's behaviour causes severe problems to that person or to other people.
4. It is assumed within the behavioural model that abnormal behaviour is determined mainly by environmental factors—so individuals who develop mental disorders should not be held responsible for those disorders.

? Behavioural approaches to the treatment of mental disorders have been successful but they assume that the patient and therapist share the same goals for behaviour. In what way might such treatments be seen as "social manipulation"?

There are ethical problems with some of the forms of treatment based on the behavioural model. Aversion therapy involves giving very unpleasant stimuli (e.g. electric shocks and nausea-inducing drugs) to patients in order to stop some undesirable form of behaviour, such as drinking in alcoholics. There has been much controversy about the morality of causing high levels of pain and discomfort. Most forms of treatment focus mainly on changing behaviour, and it could be argued that it is dehumanising to neglect the patient's internal experiences and feelings. Therapies derived from the behavioural model can be seen as manipulative.

The Cognitive Model

The central notion in the cognitive model is that individuals suffering from mental disorders have distorted and irrational thinking—rather than maladaptive *behaviour*, as in the behavioural model. Warren and Zgourides (1991) pointed out that many of these thoughts have a "must" quality about them, e.g: "I *must* perform well and/or win the approval of others, or else it's awful", "You *must* treat me fairly and considerately and not unduly frustrate me, or it's awful", "My life conditions *must* give me the things I want easily and with little frustration . . . or else life is unbearable." These distorted thoughts can play an important role in the development of mental disorders.

In practice, the cognitive model has been applied most often to patients suffering from anxiety and depression. There is reasonable evidence that such patients do have irrational thoughts. For example, Newmark et al. (1973) found that 65% of anxious patients (but only 2% of normals) agreed with the statement "It is essential that one be loved or approved by virtually everyone in his [sic!] community" The statement "One must be perfectly competent, adequate, and achieving to consider oneself worthwhile" was agreed to by 80% of anxious patients compared with 25% of normals.

Nearly everyone agrees that anxious and depressed patients have distorted views and attitudes about themselves and the world around them. For example, Beck (1976) used the term **cognitive triad** to refer to the typical unrealistically negative thoughts of depressed patients in the three areas of themselves, the world, and the future. The crucial issue (and one that is still not resolved) is whether the distorted and unrealistic thoughts of patients with various mental disorders actually played a part in the development of the mental disorder. It is entirely possible that patients only have these unrealistic thoughts *after* they have developed an anxiety disorder or depression.

Some support for the notion that unrealistic thoughts may occur *before* a disorder develops and may play a part in its occurrence was reported by Lewinsohn et al. (2001). They identified one group of adolescents who had unrealistic negative thoughts at

? Think of an occasion when you felt helpless or worthless. Could you try to re-interpret the occasion in a more positive way?

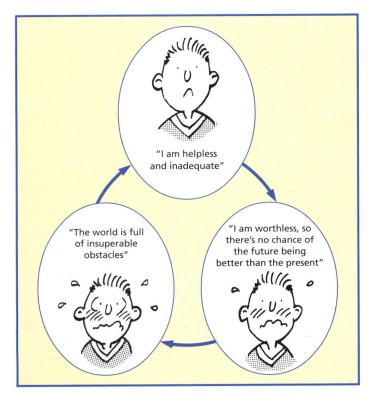

"I am helpless and inadequate"

"The world is full of insuperable obstacles"

"I am worthless, so there's no chance of the future being better than the present"

the start of the study and another group who did not. Lewinsohn et al. then had a look 12 months later to see how many of these adolescents had developed depression. Those who had had unrealistic negative thoughts 12 months earlier were significantly more likely to have become clinically depressed than those whose thoughts one year earlier were realistic. These findings don't prove that unrealistic negative thoughts help to cause depression, but they are entirely consistent with that possibility.

Evaluation of the cognitive model

The **cognitive model of abnormality** has become very influential in recent years. Distorted and irrational beliefs are very common among patients with mental disorders, and seem to be of central importance in anxiety disorders and depression (Beck & Clark, 1988). Distorted beliefs are also found in other mental disorders (e.g. bulimia nervosa and anorexia nervosa, discussed later), but most of the focus in the cognitive model has been on anxiety and depression. It is generally not clear whether distorted beliefs help to cause the disorder, or whether they are merely a consequence of having a mental disorder. However, the findings of Lewinsohn et al. (2001) suggest that distorted beliefs may play a part in the development of depression.

The cognitive approach grew out of a dissatisfaction with the behavioural model and its focus on external factors only. The cognitive model emphasises internal, mental influences and the power of the individual to shape their own thinking. In recent years, there have been attempts to *combine* the behavioural and cognitive models. According to this cognitive-behavioural model, mental disorders involve maladaptive behaviour as well as distorted thoughts and beliefs.

On the negative side, the cognitive approach to abnormality is rather limited. Genetic factors are ignored, and little attention is paid to the role of social and interpersonal factors or of individuals' life experiences in producing mental disorders. In addition, the cognitive model has been applied mainly to anxiety disorders and depression, even though it would seem to have some relevance for various other disorders.

> **Assumptions of the cognitive model**
> - Maladaptive behaviour is caused by faulty and irrational cognitions.
> - It is the way you think about a problem, rather than the problem itself, that causes mental disorder.
> - Individuals can overcome mental disorders by learning to use more appropriate cognitions.
> - Aim to be positive and rational.

Ethical implications of the cognitive model

According to the cognitive model, individuals with mental disorders have distorted thoughts and beliefs, and so the disorders are mainly their own fault. That notion raises various ethical issues. First, patients may find it stressful to accept responsibility for their mental disorder. Second, it may be unfair to "blame" individuals for their mental disorder, because others around them may be mainly responsible. It is suggested that the root of maladaptive experiences may be childhood experiences. Third, the negative thoughts and beliefs of those with mental disorders are often entirely rational, and reflect all too accurately the unfortunate

> **EXAM HINT**
> All of the models of abnormality can be evaluated as:
>
> - *Reductionist* because they are oversimplified and ignore other explanations.
> - *Deterministic* because they ignore the free will of the individual to control their own behaviour.
>
> Each of these can be further elaborated for 3 marks so do this for each model or choose alternative criticisms but make sure you elaborate for 3 marks.

circumstances in which a person is living. Attempts to put the blame on to the patient may inhibit efforts to produce desirable changes.

The Multi-dimensional Approach

At the beginning of this section, we noted that some models are appropriate for some disorders but not others, that each model is partially correct, and that a full understanding of the origins of mental disorders requires us to combine information from all the models. This is called a multi-dimensional approach. One way to express this is in terms of the **diathesis–stress model**. According to this model, the occurrence of psychological disorders depends on two factors:

1. Diathesis: a genetic vulnerability or predisposition to disease or disorder.
2. Stress: some severe or disturbing environmental event.

The key notion in this model is that both diathesis (genetic vulnerability), *and* stress are necessary for a psychological disorder to occur.

This would explain why, when one identical twin develops a disorder, their twin doesn't always go on to develop the disorder—because an environmental trigger is required. The diathesis–stress model also explains why one individual might have a disorder but a sibling, who has shared the same childhood experiences, does not develop the disorder—as they are genetically different, only one had the genetic vulnerability.

SECTION SUMMARY

The models of abnormality

❖ There are five major models of abnormality, each of which provides explanations for the treatment of mental disorders. They are:
  - Biological (medical) model
  - Psychodynamic model
  - Behavioural model
  - Cognitive, and now cognitive-behavioural, model
  - Diathesis–stress model

❖ These models are not mutually exclusive, and all of them have contributed to our understanding of the causes of mental disorders.

The biological model of abnormality

❖ This model suggests that the causes of mental disorders resemble those of physical illnesses.

❖ Clusters of symptoms can be identified and a diagnosis made, followed by suitable treatment.

❖ There is some evidence that the following may account for mental disorders:
  - genetics,
  - biochemistry,

- neuroanatomy,
- infections.

❖ While this approach has received some scientific support and has contributed to treatments it has been criticised in that:
  - It focuses on symptoms rather than the person's thoughts and feelings.
  - It is less appropriate for disorders with psychological symptoms such as eating disorders.
  - There is some debate as to whether mental disorders are the same as physical illnesses.
  - The treatments based on the medical model (e.g. drugs, ECT, and psychosurgery) may have unpleasant side effects and their efficacy has been challenged.

The psychodynamic model of abnormality

❖ This model suggests that the causes of mental disorders arise from unresolved unconscious conflicts and traumas of early childhood and in problems with personality development.
❖ Whilst this model has offered insights into anxiety disorders and changed the perception of mental illness, it has been criticised in that:
  - It is difficult to disprove and thus has been criticised for being unscientific.
  - It may focus too much on the past, rather than the present.
  - It may focus too much on sexual problems rather than interpersonal and social issues.
  - It raises ethical concerns about the problems of false memory syndrome, sexism and parental blame.

The behavioural model

❖ This model suggests that mental disorders are caused by learning maladaptive behaviour via conditioning or observational learning.
❖ This model offers people with mental disorders hope, in that it implies their behaviour can be changed—anything that is learned can be unlearned using the same techniques.
❖ The approach is most suited to explaining and treating those disorders that emphasise external behaviours, e.g. phobias.
❖ Ethically, there are advantages such as the lack of blame attached to a person with a mental disorder, however it has been criticised in that:
  - It is somewhat oversimplistic and ignores individual differences.
  - It is based on animal research.
  - The treatments developed from this model can be painful and manipulative (e.g. aversion therapy).

The cognitive model

❖ This model suggests that mental disorders stem from distorted and irrational beliefs, and there is no doubt that patients with anxiety disorder and depression have distorted negative beliefs.
❖ However, this model has been criticised in that:
  - It is not always clear whether the distorted thinking is an effect of the disorder, or the cause.
  - Another issue is that the cognitive model has mainly been applied to anxiety and depression, and its relevance to other mental disorders is largely unknown.
  - It implies that individuals are somehow to blame for their problems.

See pp.94–100 of the revision guide.

The diathesis–stress model

❖ More recently a cognitive-behavioural model has been suggested, blending the cognitive and behavioural approach.

❖ This model offers a multi-dimensional approach.
❖ It suggests that individuals may have a genetic vulnerability (diathesis) which can be triggered by environmental factors (stress).

SECTION 16—CRITICAL ISSUE
EATING DISORDERS

There are several **eating disorders**. The most common (discussed in detail here) are anorexia nervosa and bulimia nervosa. Other, considerably rarer, eating disorders include:

? What could be the reasons for the increased incidence of eating disorders in recent years?

- *Rumination disorder*: partially digested food is regurgitated and then swallowed for a second time.
- *Pica*: non-food substances such as sand, leaves, or string are eaten.

As we will see, there has been a large increase in the number of people suffering from eating disorders over the past 20 years or so. Barlow and Durand (1995) even described it as an epidemic.

Characteristics of the Disorders

Anorexia nervosa
One of the two main eating disorders identified by DSM-IV (a system for classifying mental disorders developed in the United States) is **anorexia nervosa**. According to DSM-IV, there are four criteria for anorexia nervosa:

- *Weight*. A body weight that is less than 85% of that expected.
- *Anxiety*. Intense fear of becoming fat in spite of being considerably underweight.
- *Body-image distortion*. Either by exaggerating the importance of body weight or by minimising the dangers of being considerably underweight.
- *Amenorrhoea* (the absence of menstruation in females). The absence of three or more consecutive menstrual cycles is an indication.

Over 90% of patients with anorexia nervosa are female, and the age of onset is typically during adolescence. There has been an increase in the frequency of anorexia nervosa in Western societies in recent decades (Cooper, 1994). This probably reflects the growing media emphasis on slimness. Anorexia nervosa used to be very rare among black people in

KEY TERMS

Eating disorder: a dysfunctional relationship with food. The dysfunction may be gross under-eating (anorexia), binge–purging (bulimia), over-eating (obesity), or healthy eating (orthorexia). These disorders may be characterised by faulty cognition and emotional responses to food, maladaptive conditioning, dysfunctional family relationships, early childhood conflicts, or a biological and genetic basis, but the nature and expression of eating disorders show great individual variation.

Anorexia nervosa: an eating disorder characterised by the individual being severely underweight; 85% or less than expected for size and height. There is also anxiety, as the anorexic has an intense fear of becoming fat and a distorted body image. The individual does not have an accurate perception of their body size, seeing themselves as "normal", when they are in fact significantly underweight, and they may minimise the dangers of being severely underweight.

the United States, but has shown signs of a marked increase (Hsu, 1990). Within Western cultures, it is more common in middle-class than working-class individuals. It is potentially a very serious disorder, with the self-imposed near-starvation causing death in about 5% of sufferers.

Bulimia nervosa

The other main eating disorder discussed in DSM-IV is bulimia nervosa. According to DSM-IV, bulimia nervosa (purging type) is defined by the following four criteria:

- *Binge*. Numerous episodes of binge eating, in which much more food is eaten within a two-hour period than most people would consume in that time; the eater lacks control over his/her eating behaviour.
- *Purge*. Frequent inappropriate compensatory behaviour to prevent weight from being gained, e.g. self-induced vomiting, and misuse of laxatives, enemas, and/or diuretics. (Note that the non-purging type of this disorder involves excessive exercise and/or going without meals as compensatory behaviour.)
- *Frequency*. Binge eating and inappropriate compensatory behaviour occur at a rate of twice a week, or more, over a three-month period.
- *Body image*. Self-evaluation depends excessively on shape and weight.

CASE STUDY: AN EATING DISORDER

At the age of 12, JC had weighed 115 pounds and had been teased by friends and family for being "podgy". At first JC had started to restrict her food intake by eating less at meal times, becoming selective about what she ate, and cutting out snacks between meals. Initially, JC's progressive weight loss was supported by her family and friends. However, as she began to lose pounds she would set herself new targets, ignoring feelings of hunger by focusing on each new target. In her first year of dieting JC's weight dropped from 115 pounds to 88 pounds. Her initial goal had been to lose 10 pounds. JC's periods stopped shortly after she started her regime, her appearance changed dramatically, and in the second year of her regime her weight loss was considered to be out of control. Her personality had also changed, and she was not the active, spontaneous, and cheerful girl she had been before dieting. Her girlfriends were less enthusiastic about coming over to her house, because JC would be stubborn and argumentative, designing strict programmes of activities for them to carry out.

JC's family had asked their GP for help. He had been alarmed at JC's appearance and designed a high calorific diet for her. However, JC believed that there was something inside her that would not let her gain weight. She would pretend to eat, often listing food she claimed to have eaten which had in fact been flushed down the toilet, or would not swallow food she put in her mouth. JC admitted that when she felt down over the past two years she would still feel driven to lose weight, and as a result would go on walks, run errands, or spend long periods of time keeping her room immaculate. (Adapted from Leon, 1984.) ∎

There has been a dramatic increase in the number of patients in Western countries being treated for bulimia nervosa. About 4% of women receive treatment for this condition, compared to about 1% for anorexia nervosa (Andreasen & Black, 2001). Like anorexia, bulimia is very much more common in females than in males, with only 10% as many men as women having the condition. Bulimia nervosa resembles anorexia nervosa in that both disorders are far more common in Western societies than elsewhere in the world, and they occur more often in middle-class than working-class families.

The self-induced vomiting found in most bulimics can produce a variety of medical effects, e.g. it can damage the teeth by eroding dental enamel. It can also change the levels of sodium and potassium in bodily fluids, which can be life threatening.

Anorexia and bulimia

In spite of the similarities between them, there are some important distinctions between anorexia and bulimia. First, bulimia nervosa is far more common in Western society than anorexia nervosa. Second, nearly all patients with bulimia nervosa are within about 10% of their normal weight, whereas anorexic patients by definition are at least 15% below their normal weight. Thus, anorexia tends to be the more serious disorder. Third, bulimics are generally more concerned

KEY TERM

Bulimia nervosa: an eating disorder in which excessive (binge) eating is followed by compensatory behaviour such as self-induced vomiting or misuse of laxatives. It is often experienced as an unbreakable cycle where the bulimic impulsively overeats and then has to purge to reduce anxiety and feelings of guilt about the amount of food consumed, which can be thousands of calories at a time. This disorder is not associated with excessive weight loss.

In the eating disorder bulimia nervosa, sufferers consume much more food over a short period than most people would and compensate by making themselves vomit or by taking laxatives.

than anorexics about being attractive to other people, and are more involved with other people. Fourth, bulimics are more likely than anorexics to have a history of mood swings.

What causes anorexia nervosa and bulimia nervosa? In the last section we looked at the various models of abnormality. We can now apply these models to the specific problems of anorexia and bulimia. We will look at the two eating disorders simultaneously. Explanations apply to both eating disorders unless otherwise stated.

The Biological Approach

Infection
It is possible that physical illness may act as a precipitating factor in eating disorders. Park, Lawrie, and Freeman (1995) studied four females suffering from anorexia nervosa, all of whom had had glandular fever or a similar disease shortly before the onset of the eating disorder. Park et al. (1995) argued, rather speculatively, that the physical disease may have influenced the functioning of the **hypothalamus**, and this caused homeostatic imbalances (see page 139).

Evaluation: Infection
Park et al.'s (1995) research fails to establish a causal link between anorexia nervosa and glandular fever as they used a small sample size, and most people who have had glandular fever do not go on to develop anorexia nervosa.

Genetic factors
There is increasing evidence that genetic factors play a part in the development of eating disorders—relatives of sufferers are about four or five times more likely to have an eating disorder (e.g. Strober & Humphrey, 1987). This increased probability is true of the relatives of those with bulimia and anorexia.

Genetic vulnerability and twin studies
Another line of evidence for genetic factors comes from twin studies. **Monozygotic (MZ) twins** (also known as identical twins) share exactly the same genes whereas **dizygotic (DZ) twins** (also known as fraternal twins) have the same genetic relatedness as any siblings (about 50%). How can we use information from identical and fraternal twins to decide how important genetic factors are in eating disorders? If an eating disorder is inherited then we would expect to find more cases of MZ twins both having the disorder than non-identical DZ twins. Both kinds of twins will usually share a similar environment—they both shared the same womb and they are both generally share similar experiences as they grow up. So the main differences between MZ and DZ twins are in terms of their degree of genetic similarity.

What does all this mean in practice? In twin studies, researchers look at **concordance rates**, the extent to which a certain trait in both twins is in "concord" or agreement. If genetic factors are important, then the concordance rate for identical or MZ twins should be much higher than the concordance rate for fraternal or DZ twins. Studies using this approach were carried out by Holland et al. (1988, see Key Study) on anorexics and by Kendler et al. (1991) on bulimics.

EXAM HINT
Comparing and contrasting anorexics and bulimics:

- Similarities between sufferers: distorted body image, obsessive thinking, dysfunctional eating behaviour.
- Differences between sufferers: weight, eating patterns, age of onset.

CASE STUDY: THE LIFE OF A BULIMIC

Julie's life is food. In her dingy bedsit there is scarcely space to move around among the empty drinks cans, crisp packets, piles of clothes, and ornaments. Her fridge is stuffed to overflowing with different kinds of chocolates. Eating occupies many hours of her day but you wouldn't think it to look at her. She is a tiny thing, and when she pushes her sleeves up she reveals wrists no larger than sparrow's legs. For the best part of 20 years she has been trapped in an eating and vomiting cycle. At her lowest weight of four stone she found work as a dancer in a freak show.

Breakfast starts her day. "Half a box of cereal, two pints of milk, half a large sliced and buttered loaf which I eat with a packet of bacon or ham, about three eggs and sausages. I eat the other half of the sliced loaf with butter and marmalade. I drink cooking oil with all my meals to wash the food down. After I've finished that I have a brief pause, then I need some chocolate. I eat until I can't breathe."

Then she trips out to the bathroom to collect a square plastic washing-up bowl, and begins the process of bringing up all that food. When she has finished the bowl is full. Then there is a fleeting release from the self-loathing and the yearning for food which has nothing to do with hunger.

She had a boyfriend, another bulimic, who recently died. "I need someone to love but it's too difficult with ordinary men." She loved her father until, at the age of 10, he developed schizophrenia. "From then on it was as if he hated me." It was soon after that that she started bingeing. She made herself sick and then tried to tell her mum, who could only cope by pretending it wasn't happening. Julie attempted suicide three times before the age of 19 and was then placed in a mental hospital and drip-fed. She says she now wouldn't go back even to save her life, and recognises that she will probably die soon.

On Sundays she visits her mum who lives close by but otherwise she goes out very little. When we met she was planning a birthday treat for herself. "I get a birthday cake, little fairy cakes and biscuits and lemonade—all the things I had as a child for parties—and then I binge by myself."

(Adapted from Angela Neustatter in the *Daily Telegraph*, 7 March 1998.) ■

Key Study: Biological explanations of anorexia

Holland et al.'s (1988) study of genetic vulnerability in anorexics.

Aims: Holland et al. aimed to investigate whether there was a higher concordance rate of anorexia nervosa for monozygotic (MZ) than dizygotic (DZ) twins. This study was based on previous research, which suggested that abnormality might have a genetic basis. A difference was sought between MZ and DZ twins, because MZ are 100% genetically identical whereas DZ have only 50% of their genes in common. Thus, there should be higher concordance rate for MZ than DZ twins if there is a genetic basis to anorexia nervosa.

Procedure: An opportunity sample of 34 pairs of twins (30 female and 4 male) and one set of triplets was selected because one of the pair (or triplets) had been diagnosed with anorexia. This was a natural experiment, as the independent variable (genetic relatedness) is naturally occurring and cannot be controlled by the experimenter. A physical resemblance questionnaire established genetic relatedness, that is, whether the twins were MZ or DZ (16 were MZ and 14 were DZ). MZ twins typically have greater physical resemblance but if there was any uncertainty a blood test was carried out. This was a longitudinal study, with the researchers checking over time to establish whether the other twin went on to develop anorexia (the dependent variable). A clinical interview and standard criteria were used for diagnosis of anorexia.

Identical twins offer the opportunity of conducting a natural experiment. They are the same genetically so any differences in their behaviour should be due to the environment. However, they usually share the same environment as well.

Findings: A significant difference was found between the concordance rates for identical (MZ) and fraternal (DZ) twins: there was a much higher concordance rate of anorexia for MZ (56%—9 of 16) than DZ (7%—1 of 14)

What explanations can account for the differences between MZ and DZ twins?

twins. Further findings were that in three cases where the non-diagnosed twin did not have anorexia they were diagnosed with other psychiatric illnesses, and two had minor eating disorders.

Conclusions: The results suggest a genetic basis for anorexia and general psychiatric illness. The fact that the percentage for MZ twins was well below 100% indicates that genes are not wholly responsible. Thus, genes can provide a predisposition, i.e. they make the individual vulnerable but do *not* directly trigger the disorder. Implications include the need to identify the precipitating factors, i.e. environmental triggers, which interact with the genetic predisposition.

Criticisms

- The study ignores the role of environmental factors or nurture in causing anorexia. The environment certainly plays a role, because the concordance rate was only 56% for MZ twins. This would have to be 100% if anorexia were exclusively due to genetic factors. Furthermore, the 56% concordance may be due in part to environmental factors. MZ twins often experience a more similar environment and are treated more similarly than DZ twins because they look and behave more alike. This *doesn't* account for the considerable difference found between MZ and DZ twins, but it does show it is hard to separate out the influence of nature and nurture or environment. Thus, it is oversimplified and **reductionist** to consider only ONE factor, genes, as a basis for anorexia.
- This natural experiment lacks control of the variables. The IV, genetic relatedness, is not isolated, as multiple other factors (confounding variables) may be implicated, e.g. environmental factors (as identified above), individual-specific experiences, and socio-economic factors. Consequently, internal validity is low, as factors other than the IV may have resulted in anorexia. Also the IV is not controlled and so causation cannot be inferred. This means conclusions are limited as it cannot be said that genes cause anorexia—at best they are strongly implicated.
- This study is limited because it was carried out in a Western society. Anorexia is much more common in Western societies than other parts of the world, presumably because of the emphasis on the desirability of thinness (especially in women) in Western societies. These cultural factors are very important, but were not considered by Holland et al.

Note: If the question asks for findings or conclusions only, you could include research by Strober and Humphrey (1987, see p.210), Park et al. (1995, see p.210), and Barlow and Durand (1995, see p.208), and Garfinkel and Garner (1982, see p.221), all of which offer further insights into biological explanations.

Why is this study by Holland et al. important? First, it provides strong evidence that genetic factors are involved in the development of anorexia nervosa. Second, the evidence that genetic factors play a major role in anorexia nervosa led other researchers to carry out twin studies on eating disorders, most of whom obtained similar findings. Third, the finding that the concordance rate for MZ pairs was 56% rather than 100% provides strong evidence that environmental factors are also important.

Kendler et al. (1991) did a similar twin study to Holland et al. (1988) except that they focused on bulimia in female twins. They investigated whether there was a higher concordance rate or level of agreement for bulimia nervosa in MZ or identical twins than in DZ or fraternal twins. The study made use of a sample of 2163 female twins in which at least one of the pair had been diagnosed with bulimia. Their key finding was that the concordance rate for MZ twins was 23%, whereas it was 9% for DZ. This difference (although not large) was statistically significant. These results suggest that genetic factors play some part in bulimia, but the evidence is less strong than for anorexia. The fact that the concordance rate for MZ twins was only 23% means that environmental factors are much more important than genetic ones in accounting for bulimia. Note that this study was carried out in a Western society, and so the findings may well not generalise to other cultures.

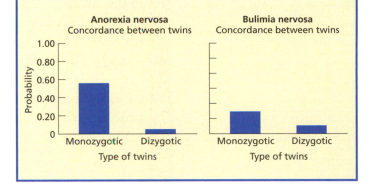

Holland et al. (1988) and Kendler et al. (1991) studied anorexia and bulimia in twins.

Why is this study by Kendler et al. important? First, it provides good evidence that the development of bulimia nervosa depends in part on genetic factors. Second, the findings are important because they suggest that genetic factors are much less important in the development of bulimia than in the development of anorexia. Thus, attempts to reduce the number of sufferers from bulimia need to focus on identifying the main aspects of the environment that play a part in triggering the disorder.

Evaluation: Genetic factors

On the face of it, these findings suggest that genetic factors play a part in the development of eating disorders, especially anorexia nervosa. But not *all* MZ twins had the disorder, so factors other than inherited genes are important. It may be that genes *predispose* individuals to develop the disorder, creating a **genetic vulnerability**, as suggested by the diathesis–stress model.

Another argument against the genetic explanation taken on its own refers to the recent dramatic increase in the number of people suffering from eating disorders. This cannot be explained in genetic terms alone, because there haven't been major genetic changes over the past 20–30 years.

Biochemical factors

Serotonin, a **neurotransmitter** implicated in a number of behaviours such as arousal, aggressiveness, and sleep, may be involved in some cases of both bulimia and anorexia. Fava et al. (1989) reported links between anorexic behaviour and changes in the levels of serotonin and noradrenaline (also related to arousal and stress). Eating large amounts of starchy foods containing carbohydrates can increase serotonin levels in the brain, and this may improve mood in those who have low serotonin levels. Bulimics often display low levels of serotonin (e.g. Carrasco et al., 2000). The finding that low serotonin levels are associated with bulimia doesn't necessarily mean that serotonin levels are involved in its development. It could well be that the development of bulimia leads to a reduction in serotonin activity.

One suggestion is that eating large amounts of starchy food may increase serotonin levels and improve mood in individuals suffering from an eating disorder.

Finally, it has also been suggested that the link between anorexia and amenorrhoea (absence of menstruation in females) is because of an underlying problem with the endocrine system, which is responsible for producing hormones such as those that govern the menstrual cycle.

Evaluation: Biochemical factors

The problem with the starchy food explanation is that patients with bulimia nervosa don't seem to focus specifically on foods containing carbohydrates when they binge (Barlow & Durand, 1995). Any endocrine imbalance in anorexics may be an effect rather than a cause of their eating disorder. This is probably more likely, as menstruation is known to be affected by periods of emotional upset or privation (Russell, 1972). In similar fashion, the low levels of serotonin often found in patients with eating disorders may occur as a consequence of having an eating disorder rather than as a factor helping to produce the eating disorder in the first place.

Barlow and Durand (1995, p.319) concluded, "The consensus is that some neurobiological and endocrinological abnormalities do exist in eating disorders, but they are a *result* of semi-starvation or a binge–purge cycle, rather than a cause."

The Psychodynamic Approach

There have been various psychodynamic approaches to anorexia nervosa.

Sexual development

The fact that the disorder generally emerges in adolescent girls has suggested to some psychodynamic theorists that anorexia is related to the onset of sexual development and sexual fears, such as increasing sexual desires or a fear of becoming pregnant, even a fear of "oral impregnation" (becoming pregnant orally). If eating is linked to getting pregnant, then semi-starvation will prevent pregnancy. Not eating also results in amenorrhoea (absence of menstruation), also preventing pregnancy because ovulation stops.

A somewhat different psychodynamic account, still focused on sexual development, is based on the notion that anorexia nervosa occurs in females who have an unconscious desire to remain pre-pubescent. Their weight loss prevents them from developing the body shape associated with adult females, and thus allows them to preserve the illusion that they are still children.

There is evidence that at least some people with eating disorders were sexually abused as children. This may lead them to reject and destroy their own bodies, and would support a link between eating disorders and sexual development. However, note that these ideas have been applied to anorexia rather than to bulimia.

Evaluation: Sexual development

One problem with these ideas is that it is extremely difficult to prove or disprove them. In addition, not all people who have been sexually abused go on to develop an eating disorder and not all people with eating disorders have been sexually abused.

Family systems theory

Minuchin, Rosman, and Baker (1978) developed the notion that the family may play a key role in the development of anorexia nervosa, although it is possible that it could also be applied to bulimia. The family of an anorexic is characterised by **enmeshment**, meaning that none of the members of the family has a clear identity because everything is done together. Such families impose great constraints on children, because they are not allowed to become independent. According to psychodynamic theory, adolescence is the fifth phase of psychosexual development, and is a time of developing independence. Blos (1967) suggested that adolescence was like a second period of individuation. The first took place when the infant became a self-reliant toddler. A child growing up in an enmeshed family may be denied this "reindividuation" and rebel against its constraints by refusing to eat. In other words, if an adolescent feels unable to assert himself/herself within the family, then one way of gaining control is by developing an eating disorder.

Minuchin et al. (1978) also argued that enmeshed families find it hard to resolve conflicts. In psychodynamic theory, this would create anxieties that are dealt with by ego-defences. Parents may cope with their anxieties by attending to the symptoms of their anorexic child, so the "ill" child plays an important role in the family dynamic. In other words, it is as if the other family members "need" the adolescent to develop an eating disorder so they can continue to have an important role in his/her life.

There is some evidence for high levels of parental conflict within the families of anorexics (e.g. Kalucy, Crisp, & Harding, 1977). Hsu (1990) reported that families with an anorexic child tend to be ambitious, to deny or ignore conflicts, and to blame other people for their problems. Family conflicts have also been identified in families with a child who shows signs of bulimia as well as anorexia. Such families have more negative and fewer positive interactions than families with a normal adolescent (Humphrey et al., 1986).

Evaluation: Family systems theory

There are several problems with this explanation. (1) These parental conflicts may be more a result of having an anorexic child than a cause of anorexia. (2) These conflicts have occurred in families throughout history and therefore this explanation cannot account for the recent increase in eating disorders. (3) It doesn't explain why many more girls suffer from eating disorders than boys or why the disorder occurs during adolescence.

Struggle for autonomy

Some of the drawbacks to family systems theory are overcome in the model proposed by the psychoanalyst Hilda Bruch (1971, see Case Studies on the following page). She analysed 64 anorexic patients (55 females and 9 males) and proposed that individuals with anorexia nervosa are engaged in a struggle for their own sense of identity and autonomy, and are in conflict with their parents, especially their mother. A prime characteristic of the mothers was that they didn't provide appropriate responses to child-initiated expressions of need, e.g. children were offered food only at the "correct time" or when the mother felt hungry. Food was often used as a means of providing comfort or compensation. So food became not only the currency of affection but also was a battle-ground for dominance.

? Psychodynamic theories cannot explain why adolescent girls are most likely to suffer from eating disorders but can they account for cultural differences?

CASE STUDY: ANOREXICS

Hilde Bruch (1971) developed a theory of anorexia based on her experience in treating such patients. The cases below are adapted from her records:

Case 1

A 12-year-old girl from a prominent upper-class family was seen when her mother consulted the psychiatrist about an older sister who was obese. The mother felt that she wanted to punish this daughter for being overweight, but spoke in glowing terms about her younger daughter who in every way was an ideal child. Her teachers would refer to her as the "best balanced" girl in the school, and relied on her helpfulness and kindness when another child was having difficulty making friends.

Later, when the anorexia developed, it became apparent to what extent the anxious and punitive behaviours of the mother had affected the way the younger daughter felt and thought about herself. She had become convinced that being fat was most shameful. As she began to put on weight in puberty, she felt horrified and that, if she was to retain respect, she would have to maintain her thinness. This led her to go on a starvation regime. At the same time she also began to realise that she didn't have to be an ideal daughter and do what others expected of her, but she could be the master of her own fate.

Case 2

A mother sought psychoanalytic treatment because she had become depressed. Her daughter was her one great satisfaction in life. The girl (aged 14) had always been a happy child who had no problems. She had a governess, but the mother fed the daughter herself, making a special effort to provide good food and tastefully present it.

Shortly after the mother had consulted the psychiatrist the daughter became anorexic, having started to get plump. When she visited the psychiatrist her version of childhood was the exact opposite of her mother's account. She remembered it as a time of constant misery and that she could never have what she wanted but always had to have exactly what her mother wanted. She knew her mother had talked about what she should be eating with their doctor, and this made her feel that every bite that went into her mouth was watched. The concern about her fatness was reinforced by her father's excessive attention to appearance. Theirs was a wealthy home and there were always lavish arrays of food. Her father showed his superiority by eating very little and making snide remarks about people who ate too much.

When the girl became plump at puberty she tried to outdo her father's haughty control. She felt she owed it to him to remain slim and aristocratic. Her life was dominated by trying to satisfy her father. She did well at school but was haunted by the fear of being found out to be stupid. She described her life as "I never deserved what they gave me" and that she was "worthless". Keeping her weight as low as possible was her only way of proving herself to be "deserving" and having "dignity".

(Adapted from H. Bruch, 1971, Family transactions in eating disorders. *Comprehensive Psychiatry*, 12(3), 38–248.) ■

? Case studies are often used as a way of understanding unusual behaviours. What are the advantages and limitations of using this method of research?

Evaluation: Struggle for autonomy

The problem with Bruch's approach, as with many psychoanalytic explanations, is that the evidence lacks objectivity. It is an interpretation of the facts from only one particular perspective. While it is an interesting interpretation, it is extremely difficult to test, and the anorexic patient may agree with the therapist because they want to be liked, rather than believing the interpretation to be true.

The Behavioural Approach

Conditioning theory

We can explain anorexia nervosa using the principles of **classical conditioning**. According to Leitenberg, Agras, and Thomson (1968), anorexics may have learned to associate eating with anxiety, because eating too much makes people overweight and unattractive. Therefore they seek to lose weight to reduce their anxiety. Weight loss is associated with relief from an unpleasant or aversive stimulus.

The second part of the process can be explained in terms of **operant conditioning**. Food avoidance can be rewarding or reinforcing, because it is a good way of gaining attention. It can also be rewarding or reinforcing in that those who are slim are more likely to be admired by other people.

A behaviourist approach can also be applied to bulimia nervosa. According to Rosen and Leitenberg (1985), bingeing causes anxiety, and the subsequent vomiting or other compensatory behaviour reduces that anxiety. This reduction in anxiety is reinforcing and helps to maintain the cycle of bingeing followed by vomiting.

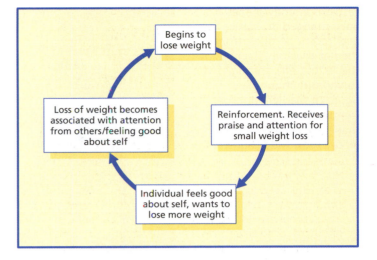

Evaluation: Conditioning theory

The behaviourist approach helps to provide some of the reasons why anorexics and bulimics maintain their disorders. There has been some success in using behavioural therapies as a means of treating bulimia (Hallstein, 1965), e.g. rewarding clients when they attain and maintain certain target body weights. This would suggest that rewards may be part of the cycle. However, conditioning alone does not account for individual differences in vulnerability to eating disorders.

? **Could conditioning theory be used to explain cultural differences?**

Social learning theory

One of the most striking facts about both bulimia and anorexia is that they are considerably more common in Western than in non-Western societies (Cooper, 1994). Indeed, eating disorders may well be more strongly specific to certain cultures than any other psychological disorders. This can be explained in terms of the role models available to young women. In our society, women see other women rewarded for looking slim in terms of the attention and admiration they receive. According to social learning theory, this will lead many women to imitate this rewarded behaviour by striving to be slim. Learning to change our behaviour by observing others being rewarded is known as vicarious reinforcement. Social learning theory also predicts that we are most likely to imitate people we admire and identify with.

More than half of Miss America contestants are 15% or more below their expected body weight—meeting one of the criteria for anorexia nervosa! Further evidence to support the importance of Western role models in the development of eating disorders was reported by Nasser (1986), who compared Egyptian women studying in Cairo and in London. None of the women studying in Cairo developed an eating disorder, in contrast to 12% of those studying in London. Lee, Hsu, and Wing (1992) noted that bulimia was almost non-existent among the Chinese in Hong Kong and suggested that this can largely be explained in terms of socio-cultural differences.

Chinese girls are usually slim, and therefore don't share the Western "fear of fatness" that can lead to excessive dieting behaviour. The Chinese regard thinness as a sign of ill-health rather than the Western view that it is a sign of self-discipline and economic well-being. Obesity is not seen as a sign of weak control or moral impairment, as it is in the West; instead excessive weight gain is seen as a sign of health and prosperity.

Chinese attitudes towards food are also different. The Chinese diet is generally low in fat and high in fibre, whereas Westerners prepare a lot of fattening foods and then feel shame about eating them. In Western culture, there is a strong tendency to feel guilty about eating too much, whereas the Chinese have no need to practise restraint.

Fashions in body shapes have changed dramatically over recent decades; from the flat-chested "flapper" of the 1920s (left), through the curvaceous "hour-glass" figure of Marilyn Monroe (centre) to the "waif-like" shape epitomised by the model Jodie Kidd (right).

Bulimia is almost non-existent in Chinese women. Lee et al. (1992) suggested this is due to socio-cultural differences.

? What cultural differences are identified in Lee et al.'s research?

What explanations can you suggest for these cultural differences?

Lee et al. suggest a further difference between the two cultures in terms of role conflict. Western women experience role conflicts between home and career, and their inner and outer selves. This may result in low self-esteem and ambivalence towards oneself. Chinese women live in a society where their success is more related to "traditional" values such as success within the family rather than a good personal appearance or career accomplishment.

The media attention given to bulimia in the Western world may provide individuals with the idea that self-induced vomiting is an effective method of weight control, and provide them with specific information about how to do it. The lack of publicity for such methods in Hong Kong may explain why the method is not favoured. In addition there is a traditional belief among the Chinese that wasting food by vomiting will lead to bad luck and severe punishment by the gods.

Lee et al. conclude that the rarity of bulimia nervosa in Hong Kong is related mainly to the absence of the relevant sociocultural factors.

Why is it that adolescent girls are most likely to suffer from eating disorders? The cultural pressures are greatest on adolescent girls for two reasons. One reason is that most of them have reached the stage at which they want to appear attractive to boys. The other reason is that most of the weight girls gain after puberty is in the form of fat tissue, which makes it harder for them to match the ideal shape.

It has often been argued that social and cultural factors are very important in the development of eating disorders such as anorexia and bulimia. However, the fact that far more women than men suffer from eating disorders suggests that social pressure emphasising the desirability of thinness is much stronger for women than it is for men. An important study designed to examine some of these issues was reported by Behar et al. (2001, see Key Study below). Their key finding was that the cultural pressures towards thinness in women have more impact on individuals who adopt the female gender role than on those who do not.

Key Study: Psychological explanations of anorexia and bulimia

Behar et al.'s (2001) study of a psychological explanation for the eating disorders anorexia and bulimia.

Aims: Behar et al. aimed to investigate the effect of gender identity on eating disorders to test behavioural explanations that gender differences exist because women experience more pressure to be thin than men do. For example, women are presented with more "idealised" body images in the media. The hypothesis is that the existence of these role models can lead to the development of eating disorders if women model themselves on these examples of female "perfection". Thus, Behar et al. aimed to see if acceptance of the female gender role, as indicated by feminine gender identity, was higher in females with eating disorders than in controls.

Procedure: A total of 126 participants—63 patients with eating disorders (anorexia and bulimia) and 63 comparison subjects—were selected. This was a natural experiment as the independent variable (presence/absence of eating disorder) could not be controlled by the experimenter. Further procedures included a structured clinical interview for diagnosis of eating disorders using standardised (DSM-IV) criteria, and a self-report survey to measure gender identity (the Bem Sex Role Inventory: BSRI), which is accepted as a valid measure of gender identity.

? What are the limitations of this study?

Findings: Significant differences were found in gender identity. More eating disorder patients were classified as feminine gender identity: 43% compared to only 23.8% of controls. In contrast, more controls were classified as androgynous (showing a mixture of feminine and masculine traits): 31.7% of controls compared to only 19% of patients. In addition, more controls were classified as undifferentiated (not fitting the masculine, feminine, or androgynous category): 43% compared to 27% of patients.

? How important is gender identity in the development of eating disorders?

Conclusions: Feminine gender identity was significantly more common in eating disorder patients than "normal" controls. This supports the behavioural explanation for eating disorders, i.e. that women face greater pressure than men from society (in particular the media) to conform to "idealised" body images. These pressures may place them at greater risk for eating disorders. Implications include the positive aspects of androgyny as a defence against eating disorders.

Criticisms

* The study ignores the role of genetic factors in causing eating disorders, even though there is strong evidence for genetic involvement. It is hard

to separate out the influence of nature and nurture, but it is oversimplified and reductionist to consider only ONE explanation (the behavioural account) as a basis for eating disorders when there are many other explanations, e.g. biological, cognitive, and psychodynamic.

- This is not a true experiment; it is a natural experiment. This means the independent variable (presence/absence of an eating disorder) was not under the control of the experimenter. Causation cannot be inferred if the independent variable is not directly manipulated, and so it cannot be said that eating disorders and gender identities are causally related. Gender identity was measured only *after* eating disorders had developed, even though it was assumed that gender identity leads to eating disorders. It would be preferable to carry out a prospective study in which gender identity was assessed *before* eating disorders had developed. This would rule out the possibility that having an eating disorder changes gender identity.

- This study was carried out in a Western society, and eating disorders are far more common in Western societies than in non-Western ones. There is probably less of an association between feminine gender identity and eating disorders in non-Western societies than in Western ones, but this study doesn't provide any relevant evidence.

Note: This research investigated anorexia and bulimia and so could be used as a psychological study of either disorder. Remember to focus on the disorder asked for in the question. Indicate that it was an investigation of *both* eating disorders and so offers insight into anorexia and bulimia, but then refer to the disorder specified in the question for the rest of your answer.

Note: If the question asks for findings or conclusions only, you could include research by Lee et al. (1992, see p.218), Cooper (1994, see p.217), and Nasser (1986, see p.217), all of which offer further insights into behavioural explanations.

Why is this study by Behar et al. important? First, it represents a systematic attempt to shed light on the issue of the kind of woman who is likely to be most vulnerable to the development of an eating disorder. Second, the study suggests that it is important to distinguish between actual gender (female vs male) and gender identity. The susceptibility to develop an eating disorder may depend more on feminine gender identity than on gender itself. However, this study is only correlational, and so we cannot be confident that feminine gender identity plays a role in causing eating disorders. It is also possible that having an eating disorder increases the tendency to adopt a feminine gender identity.

Evaluation: The role of models

Social learning theory can explain many features of the disorders, such as the increased prevalence in recent years and in Western society. It can also explain age and gender effects, as well as why eating disorders are increasing in men (as a result of changing stereotypes).

However, cultural factors *cannot* be the only reason for the occurrence of eating disorders. The great majority of young women exposed to cultural pressures towards slimness do not develop eating disorders. It is only young women who are already vulnerable who are likely to be greatly affected by such pressures.

? Why do you think there were fewer anorexics in Victorian Britain than now?

The Cognitive Approach

Distortion of body image

The distorted views about body shape and weight that sufferers from eating disorders typically have are known as *cognitive biases*. In order to assess anorexics' perception of their own body size, they can be exposed to an image-distorting technique designed to provide information about their perception of their whole body. Garfinkel and Garner (1982) found that anorexic patients typically overestimate their body size. It has also been shown that this overestimation is greater than that found in controls.

Bulimic patients also have distorted beliefs. In spite of the fact that they are typically not overweight, patients with bulimia usually show a substantial *discrepancy* between their estimation of their actual body size and their desired body size (Cooper & Taylor, 1988). This discrepancy arises both because they overestimate their actual body size *and* because their desired body size is smaller than average. McKenzie et al. (1993) found that bulimics mistakenly believe that eating a small snack has a noticeable effect on their body size.

Distorted beliefs about body size are found even among those not suffering from an eating disorder. Fallon and Rozin (1985) asked males and females to indicate their ideal body size and the body size that would be most attractive to the opposite sex. Females rated their ideal body weight as significantly *lower* than the weight males thought most attractive, whereas males rated their ideal body weight as *higher* than the weight women found most attractive. These differences place extra pressure on females to be slim.

Another feature of the cognitive make-up of patients with bulimia and anorexia is the tendency towards perfectionism, which involves a strong desire to achieve excellence. We might expect that individuals high in perfectionism would be very likely to strive to have an unrealistically slim body shape. Steinhausen (1994) found that females with bulimia and anorexia showed clear signs of perfectionism.

One of the most important findings in the research on eating disorders such as bulimia is that there are very large differences from culture to culture in the numbers of women suffering from such disorders. In general terms, women living in Western cultures are most at risk, and those living in non-Western countries are

Even when sufferers from anorexia nervosa are significantly underweight, they continue to fear becoming fat.

least at risk. In spite of the importance of carrying out cross-cultural studies on eating disorders, relatively few such studies have been done so far. One exception is a study by Jaeger et al. (2002). They had the good idea of considering cross-cultural differences in factors (e.g. body dissatisfaction) that may well be of relevance in the development of bulimia. They sampled 1751 medical and nursing students across 12 countries, including a mixture of Western and non-Western ones. A self-report method was used to obtain data on body dissatisfaction, self-esteem, and dieting behaviour. Body mass index (BMI), which provides an indication as to whether someone is overweight or underweight, was also measured. A series of 10 body silhouettes, designed to be as culture-free as possible, were shown to the participants to assess body dissatisfaction.

The key finding was that the most extreme body dissatisfaction was found in Mediterranean countries, followed in order by northern European countries, countries in the process of Westernisation, and finally non-Western countries, which had the lowest levels of body dissatisfaction. This is an important finding, because there is a reasonably close relationship between a country's level of body dissatisfaction and its level of bulimia and other eating disorders. Jaeger et al. found that body dissatisfaction was the most important factor in most countries in influencing dieting behaviour. Of interest, body dissatisfaction was *independent* of self-esteem and body mass index—those with the greatest body dissatisfaction were very often not, in fact, overweight. Note, however, that the participants were all medical or nursing students, and so weren't representative of the countries from which they came.

Why are Jaeger et al.'s findings important? First, it is one of the few systematic cross-cultural studies on eating disorders, and a wide range of Western and non-Western countries was sampled. Second, Jaeger et al. obtained reasonable evidence that body dissatisfaction may be an important vulnerability factor for eating disorders such as bulimia—it predicts dieting behaviour, and is greatest in those countries with the greatest numbers of sufferers from eating disorders. Third, the fact that body dissatisfaction was independent of body mass index suggests that vulnerability to eating disorders depends much more on subjective factors (i.e. how satisfied a person is with their body shape) than on objective factors (i.e. actually being overweight). Fourth, there is the worrying implication that there may be a major increase in bulimia in countries currently in the process of Westernisation.

Evaluation: Cognitive approach

We know that most patients with anorexia nervosa and bulimia nervosa have strong cognitive biases that, for example, lead them to overestimate their own body size. What is unclear is whether these cognitive biases exist *before* the onset of eating disorders, playing a part in their development, or whether they only develop *afterwards*, in which case they cannot be a causal factor. There is very little research that is of relevance. However, the cognitive approach is potentially of value in helping to explain why eating disorders are so much more common in Western societies than elsewhere. It seems reasonable to assume that the media emphasis on the desirability of thinness in women in Western societies helps to create cognitive biases. The findings of Jaeger et al. (2002) seem consistent with that viewpoint.

Body image is a powerful factor in how people feel about themselves. In a climate in which extreme thinness is presented as the "ideal", curvaceous singer Beyonce projects a positive body image.

Evaluation of the Different Approaches

You probably feel that there is a bewilderingly large number of attempts to explain the major eating disorders. What conclusions can we draw from these theories? First, there is no doubt that several factors play a part in the development of anorexia and bulimia, with *all* the main theoretical approaches contributing something to our understanding. Second, some factors are more important than others. Anorexia and bulimia are much more common in Western cultures than elsewhere in the world, which suggests strongly that social and cultural factors are particularly important. Cultural differences in body dissatisfaction may be important here (Jaeger et al., 2002). In contrast, it has proved difficult to show that the development of eating disorders depends much on the factors identified within the psychodynamic approach. Third, while the same factors seem to be involved in the development of bulimia and anorexia, the *relative* importance of some factors differs between the two disorders. In particular, genetic factors are of major importance in the development of anorexia, but are less important in the development of bulimia.

> **EXAM HINT**
> Exam questions usually specify whether they require biological or psychological, anorexia or bulimia content. So you should prepare an answer for all of the possibilities rather than rely on being given a choice between anorexia and bulimia, or biological and psychological.

SECTION SUMMARY

❖ Anorexia nervosa is typified by:
- low body weight (being less than 85% of expected weight);
- anxiety;
- an unrealistic body image;
- amenorrhea.

❖ It is a disorder found mostly in young women in Western and middle-class culture, and has increased in the last 20 years.

The clinical characteristics of anorexia nervosa

❖ Bulimia nervosa is typified by:
- body weight being usually within 10% of normal weight;
- episodes of binge eating and purging;
- lack of control over eating when bingeing;
- self evaluation depending excessively on body shape.

❖ Sufferers may also have been anorexic.

❖ The condition is also increasing in Western society as well as elsewhere.

The clinical characteristics of bulimia nervosa

❖ This approach considers the possibility of infection which is an unlikely cause of eating disorders. It also focuses on:
- genetic vulnerability—by looking at twin studies;
- environmental factors;
- biochemical factors such as endocrine dysfunction and changed hormone levels.

❖ This approach has been criticised in that:
- There is not a 100% concordance rate for monozygotic twins.
- Changes in biochemistry may be the result of the disorder, rather than the cause.

The biological approach as an explanation for eating disorders

– Care needs to be taken before generalising research findings based on animals to humans.

The psychodynamic approach as an explanation for eating disorders

❖ This approach focuses on:
  – Eating disorders act as a means of avoiding sexual maturity.
  – Minuchin's family systems theory which suggests anorexia develops as a result of enmeshed family dynamics.
  – Bruch's view that anorexia is related to mother–daughter conflicts over dominance and autonomy.
❖ This approach has been criticised in that:
  – It lacks objective support.
  – It blames the mother for the daughter's disorder.
  – It does not explain why there has been an increase in the incidence of anorexia.

The behavioural approach as an explanation for eating disorders

❖ This approach outlines anorexia as the result of conditioning. It focuses on:
  – Classical conditioning: eating food is associated with anxiety.
  – Operant conditioning: individuals are given positive reinforcement for being slim.
  – Social learning theory: young women are rewarded for being slim and imitate cultural role models.
❖ The success of behaviour modification therapy supports these explanations.
❖ While this approach can explain features of the disorder such as cultural specificity and the increasing incidence of eating disorders, it has been criticised in that:
  – It doesn't explain why some women develop the disorder, but others do not.

The cognitive approach as an explanation for eating disorders

❖ This approach focuses on:
  – Distorted cognitions about body image.
❖ However this approach can be criticised in that:
  – Cognitions may be an effect of the disorder, rather than the cause.

See pp.101–106 of the revision guide.

> You have reached the end of the chapter on individual differences. Individual differences is an approach or perspective in psychology. The material in this chapter has exemplified this approach in so far as abnormal behaviour is one of the ways that individuals vary. Individual differences can be explained in terms of biological (physiological), behaviourist (learning theory), psychoanalytic, and cognitive explanations. All of these explanations have also appeared elsewhere in this book and are important "tools" for explaining behaviour.

FURTHER READING

The various models of abnormality are discussed fully in P.C. Kendall and C. Hammen (1998) *Abnormal psychology (2nd Edn.)* (Boston: Houghton Mifflin). The evidence on causal factors in mental disorders is discussed in D.H. Barlow and V.M. Durand (1995) *Abnormal psychology: An integrative approach* (New York: Brooks/Cole). The other topics in this chapter are covered in an accessible way in R.P. Halgin and S.K. Whitbourne (1997) *Abnormal psychology: The human experience of psychological disorders* (Madison, WI: Brown & Benchmark). Another textbook with good coverage of most mental disorders is R.J. Comer (2001) *Abnormal psychology (4th Edn.)* New York: Worth.

REVISION QUESTIONS

The examination questions aim to sample the material in this whole chapter. For advice on how to answer such questions refer to Chapter 1, Section 2.

Whenever you are asked to describe a study try to include some or all of the following details: research aim(s), participants, research method (e.g. experiment or observation), procedure, findings, and conclusions.

You will always have a choice of two questions in the AQA AS-level exam and 30 minutes in which to answer the question you choose:

Question 1 (AQA, 2004)
a. (i) Outline **one** assumption of the behavioural model in relation to the causes
    of abnormality. (3 marks)
  (ii) Outline **one** assumption of the cognitive model in relation to the causes
    of abnormality. (3 marks)
b. Explain how cultural relativism limits **two** definitions of abnormality. (3 marks + 3 marks)
c. Describe **one** explanation of eating disorders and evaluate this explanation
  using research studies and/or alternative explanations. (18 marks)

Question 2
a. Describe three characteristics of anorexia nervosa. (2 + 2 + 2 marks)
b. Outline the assumptions of the biological (medical) model of abnormality
  in terms of its view on causes of abnormality. (6 marks)
c. "Individuals who are described as abnormal are not that different from the
  rest of us." Outline and evaluate attempts to define psychological abnormality. (18 marks)

Social psychology is an approach or perspective in psychology. "Social" refers to any situation involving two or more members of the same species. Social psychologists are interested in the way people affect each other. Social psychology differs from sociology in that it places greater emphasis on the individual as a separate entity; sociologists are interested in the structure and functioning of groups, whereas social psychologists look at how these processes influence the individual members of a social group.

SECTION 17
Majority and minority influence p.227

Individuals show conformity when they behave as expected by other members of a group. Conforming to the norms of the group is majority influence, but there are also cases where a minority can influence the behaviour of a group. Why do people yield to both majority and minority influence?

Specification content: Research studies into majority (conformity) and minority influence. Explanations of why people yield to majority and minority influence.

SECTION 18
Obedience to authority p.243

Individuals show obedience to authority when they unthinkingly follow the orders of authority figures. Why do people show obedience to authority? What are the explanations of the psychological processes involved in obedience? What makes some people resist obedience?

Specification content: Research studies into obedience to authority. Issues of internal and exernal validity associated with such research. Explanations of why people obey, and how people might resist obedience.

SECTION 19—CRITICAL ISSUE
Ethical issues in psychological research p.261

What is deemed to be acceptable in terms of psychological research on human behaviour? This section considers the use of deception, informed consent, and protection from psychological harm, in the context of social influence research. How do psychologists deal with these issues?

Specification content: Ethical issues surrounding the use of deception, informed consent, and the protection of participants from psychological harm, including the relevance of these issues in the context of social influence research. Ways in which psychologists deal with these issues (e.g. through the use of ethical guidelines, ethical committees).

SOCIAL PSYCHOLOGY:
Social Influence

7

This chapter explores one topic in social psychology—social influence. What we say, and what we do are very much influenced by other people. **Social influence** "involves the exercise of social power by a person or group to change the attitudes or behaviour of others in a particular direction" (Franzoi, 1996).

This chapter examines three of the most common kinds of social influence: majority influence, minority influence, and obedience, as well as one critical issue that is related to studies of social influence. **Majority influence** is when a majority within a group changes the expressed attitudes or behaviour of a minority. **Minority influence** is when a minority within a group changes the attitudes or behaviour of the majority. **Obedience** involves behaving as instructed, usually in response to individual rather than group pressure.

SECTION 17
MAJORITY AND MINORITY INFLUENCE

Conformity (which typically takes the form of majority influence) can be defined as yielding to group pressures in terms of our expressed attitudes or behaviour, something that nearly all of us do at least some of the time. For example, if all your friends think a film is wonderful, you may pretend to agree with them rather than saying how unimpressed you were with the film. Majority influence occurs much more often than most people imagine.

KEY TERMS

Social influence: the influence of a group (majority influence) or individual (minority influence or obedience) to modify the thinking, attitudes, and/or behaviour of others. For example, fashion trends are a consequence of majority influence; political and religious leaders are an example of minority influence; and complying with the demands of an authority figure, such as an employer, is an example of obedience.

Majority influence: this occurs when people adopt the behaviour, attitudes, or values of the majority (dominant or largest group) after being exposed to their values or behaviour. In this sense they publicly yield to group pressure (compliance), although in some cases they yield privately (internalisation). The majority is able to influence because of other people's desire to be accepted (normative) or their desire to be right (informational).

Minority influence: a majority being influenced to accept the beliefs or behaviour of a minority. This usually involves a shift in private opinion, as the majority needs to accept the minority as "right" if they are to reject the dominant majority. This private change involves a process conversion, which is more likely to occur when the minority is consistent and flexible, as this is more persuasive.

Even the most independent of individuals can feel the need to conform under social pressure from peers.

Is Majority Influence Undesirable?

As you read about the research on majority influence, you may think that it is undesirable. That is often true. For example, Rodney King, a black man, was assaulted by four Los Angeles police officers. The assault was videotaped by a local resident, and shown in court to the jurors. In spite of the fact that this videotape seemed to show that Rodney King was a victim of police brutality, the police officers were acquitted. Afterwards, one of the jurors, Virginia Loya, admitted she had changed her vote from guilty to not guilty because of pressures to conform to the views of the other jury members, while remaining unconvinced of their views. In spite of examples like the Rodney King case, it is not clear that majority influence or conformity is always undesirable. Collins (1970, p.21) pointed out:

It would be a mistake to oversimplify the question and ask whether conformity is good or bad. A person who refused to accept anyone's word of advice on any topic whatsoever ... would probably make just as big a botch of his [or her] life ... as a person who always conformed and never formed a judgement on the basis of his [or her] own individual sources of information.

On the other hand, there are probably many more cases where majority influence leads to desirable and even necessary behaviour. People live together and abide by social rules in order to facilitate their interactions—think of traffic on the road. We also know that other people possess useful knowledge about the world, and it is often sensible to take account of what they say. In addition, we want to be liked by other people, and to fit into society.

In a very early psychology experiment, Jenness (1932) asked students to estimate the number of beans in a bottle and then arranged for them to discuss their guesses with a group. Later, when they were asked to give their estimates again, he found that their individual judgements had converged towards the group estimate. What happened was that the students allowed the *perceived* superior knowledge of others to influence their estimates. This effect is known as **informational social influence** and is demonstrated in a classic study by Sherif.

The first major study of majority influence or conformity was carried out by Muzafer Sherif (1935), who made use of what is known as the **autokinetic effect**. If we look at a stationary spot of light in a darkened room, very small movements of the eyes make the light seem to move. The participants were first of all tested one at a time, and then in small groups of three. They were asked to say how much the light seemed to move, and in what direction. Each participant rapidly developed his/her own personal norm. This norm was stable but varied considerably between individuals. When three individuals with very different personal norms were then put together into a group, they tended to make

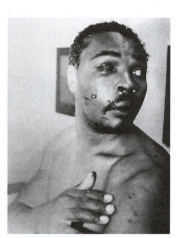

Group decisions can lead people to deny the evidence in front of their eyes. This picture shows Rodney King, victim of a videotaped beating by Los Angeles police officers in 1992. The police officers involved were acquitted.

judgements that were very similar. So a group norm rapidly replaced the personal norms of the members of the group, indicating the existence of social influence.

Sherif (1935) also used a condition in which individuals started the experiment in groups of three, and then were tested on their own. Once again, a group norm tended to develop within the group. When the members of the group were then tested on their own, their judgements concerning the movement of the light continued to reflect the influence of the group.

Asch (1951, 1956; see Key Study below) wondered whether there would be majority influence when the right answer was obvious but the majority gave the wrong answer. His notion that individuals are most likely to give way to pressure when several people are united against them is reminiscent of the old Spanish saying, "If three people call you an ass, put on a bridle!"

Norms are a set of rules established by the behaviour of a group of people. Conforming to group norms is a part of group membership. At a football game, different people are conforming to different norms—the home team has prescribed behaviours (clothes, songs, slogans), and so has the away team (such as unwritten "rules" for how to behave at an away match).

Key Study: Majority influence

Asch's (1951) study on majority influence.

Aims: To determine whether a majority can influence a minority even when the situation is unambiguous. Asch aimed to find out if the effects of majority influence that had previously been found in situations in which the stimulus was ambiguous are so great that they are still present when it is apparently obvious that the majority have responded incorrectly.

Procedure: Asch set up a situation in which seven people all sat looking at a display. In turn, they had to say out loud which one of the three lines A, B, or C was the same length as a given stimulus line X (see illustration on the right). All but one of the participants were confederates of the experimenter, and on some "critical" trials the confederates were instructed to give the same wrong answer unanimously. The one genuine participant was the last (or the last but one) to offer his/her opinion on each trial. The performance of participants exposed to such group pressure was compared to performance in a control condition in which there were no confederates.

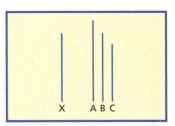

Findings: On the critical trials where the confederates gave the same wrong answer, the genuine participants also gave the wrong answer on approximately 37% of these trials. This should be compared against an error rate of only 0.7% in the control condition. Many of the participants who gave wrong responses indicated that they had yielded to majority influence because they didn't want to stand out. Individuals who gave only correct answers said that they were either confident in the accuracy of their own judgement or focused on doing the task as directed (i.e. being accurate and correct).

Conclusions: A majority can influence a minority even in an unambiguous situation in which the correct answer is obvious (as was shown by the almost perfect performance in the control condition). Asch showed

? Asch's participants weren't told the true nature of the study. Was this ethical?

convincingly that group pressures to conform in terms of majority influence are much stronger than had been thought previously. However, on about two-thirds of the crucial trials, the genuine participant gave the correct answer, so many people managed to resist majority influence.

Criticisms

* Asch's results may be explained in terms of the fact that the study took place in America in the 1950s, a time when conformity was high and "doing your own thing" was less socially acceptable. However, Asch's basic findings have been repeated several times more recently in various cultures.
* The research raises important ethical issues. Asch's participants didn't provide fully informed consent, because they were misled about key aspects of the experimental procedures (e.g. presence of confederates). In addition, they were placed in a difficult and embarrassing position.
* Asch's situation was limited in that he only assessed conformity among strangers. In fact, majority influence has been found to be even greater among friends than among strangers (Williams & Sogon, 1984).
* Asch obtained some relevant evidence from questioning his participants, but he didn't really explain exactly *why* there was so much majority influence. He also didn't explain why there were individual differences in the tendency to submit to majority influence.

? Asch carried out his research in the United States. Why might the findings be different in other cultures?

? What does Asch's study tell us about non-conformity?

Refer back to the case of Kitty Genovese (see Chapter 2, Section 3), who was fatally stabbed, despite there being 38 witnesses to the attack. The reason no one answered her pleas for help can be explained in terms of conformity and informational social influence. The fact that each individual did nothing sent a message to the others that everything was OK and there was no need to do anything. Everyone conformed to the behavioural norm of the majority by not acting (Rosenthal, 1964).

Asch (1956) extended his earlier research. He manipulated a number of aspects of the situation to understand more fully the factors underlying conformity in terms of majority influence. For example, he found that the majority influence increased as the number of confederates went up from one to three, but there was no increase between three and sixteen confederates. Another important factor was whether the genuine participant had a supporter in the form of a confederate who gave the correct answer on all trials, and who gave his answers before the genuine participant. Asch (1956) found that the presence of such a supporter produced a dramatic drop in majority influence. Participants who had a supporter showed majority influence on only 5% of the trials, which is a dramatic reduction from the 37% found by Asch (1951) when there was no supporter.

In the case of Asch's research, participants were not following informational social influence because they did not need guidance on the "information". It is more likely that they were responding to **normative social influence**, responding to group **norms** because they want to be liked and a part of the group.

Informational and normative social influence

Deutsch and Gerard (1955) were the first to identify these two explanations for majority influence:

* *Informational social influence*: Majority influence due to the *perceived* superior knowledge or judgement of others, as in Sherif's (1935) study. It tends to lead to a change in private opinion.

- *Normative social influence*: Majority influence due to wanting to be liked by the other members of the group, and to avoid being rejected. This played an important part in Asch's (1956) research, and may have played some part in Sherif's (1935) study. It is not likely to change private opinion; it affects public opinions.

? What is the difference between informational and normative social influence?

Three more reasons for majority influence or conformity

As we have seen, majority influence can be related to the extent to which an individual changes their private and/or public opinion. Kelman (1958) has used this distinction to outline three different kinds of majority influence or conformity:

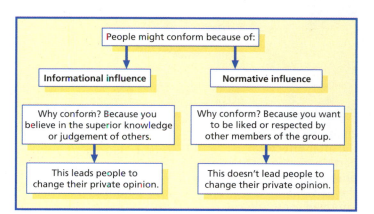

1. **Compliance** (or group acceptance) involves accepting the views of the majority despite not really agreeing with them. As the majority influence is only superficial, compliance stops when there are no group pressures to conform, so it is not "true conformity". Normative social influence is a kind of compliance.

2. **Identification** (or group membership) occurs when someone shows majority influence with respect to the demands of a given role in society, conforming to what is expected of them, as seen in the behaviour of nurses, traffic wardens, and air hostesses, regardless of how they may actually be feeling. Zimbardo's prison study (see below) is an example of this kind of majority influence. The individual identifies with a role and this leads to conformity to a norm. There may still be no change to personal opinion.

? Which of these are examples of "true conformity"?

3. **Internalisation** (or acceptance of group norms) occurs when someone shows majority influence because they are really in agreement with the views of those who are seeking to influence them—the individual is being persuaded to do something he/she really wants to do. There is no external pressure to conform. Personal opinion *does* change because the new norms are internalised.

? Do some individuals and groups have more influence over you than others? If so, why do you think this might be the case?

The Stanford prison experiment

In the 1960s, there were numerous reports of problems in American prisons. Many of these reports referred to brutal attacks by prison guards on the prisoners in their care. Why did this brutality occur? One possibility is that those who choose to put themselves into a position of power by becoming prison guards tend to have aggressive or sadistic personalities. A different possibility is that the behaviour of prison guards is due mainly to the social environment of prisons, including the rigid power structure that is found in them. These can be regarded as **dispositional** and **situational explanations** respectively.

Philip Zimbardo (1973) studied this key issue in what is generally known as the "Stanford Prison Experiment", because it was conducted in the basement of the psychology department at Stanford University. Emotionally stable individuals agreed to act as "guards" and "prisoners" in a mock prison. Zimbardo wanted to see whether the hostility found in many real prisons would also be found in his mock prison. If hostility were found in spite of not using sadistic guards, this would suggest that it is the power structure that creates hostility.

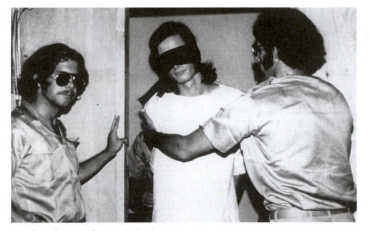

Zimbardo tried to minimise the after-effects of participation in his Stanford prison experiment by asking the participants to sign an informed consent form before the experiment began. Even so, some of the mock guards became very aggressive during the experiment, and four of the mock prisoners had to be released early.

? Are you surprised by the findings from the Stanford prison experiment?

? How can the concept of "demand characteristics" be used to explain the behaviour of the participants in this study?

What happened? The events in the prison were so unpleasant and dangerous that the entire experiment had to be stopped after 6 days instead of the intended 14 days! Violence and rebellion broke out within two days of the start. The prisoners ripped off their clothing, and shouted and cursed at the guards. In return, the guards violently put down this rebellion by using fire extinguishers. They also played the prisoners off against each other, and harassed them almost constantly. One prisoner showed such severe symptoms of emotional disturbance (disorganised thinking, uncontrollable crying, and screaming) that he had to be released after only one day. On the fourth day, two more prisoners showed symptoms of severe disturbance and were released. Changes were observed over time. The prisoners became more subdued and submissive, often slouching and keeping their eyes fixed on the ground. At the same time, the use of force, harassment, and aggression by the guards increased steadily day by day, and were clearly excessive reactions to the submissive behaviour of the prisoners. For example, the prisoners were sleep deprived, put in solitary confinement, and had to clean the toilets with their bare hands.

Why is the Stanford prison experiment important? First, it seemed to show that brutality and aggression in prisons is due far more to the power structure than to the personality of the guards, in view of the fact that the guards were selected on the basis of being emotionally stable. It could still be the case, of course, that real prison guards are more sadistic than other people. Second, the situation within the mock prison had such a strong influence that there were progressive increases in the amount of aggressive behaviour shown by the guards over time. Third, the study showed how expectations or stereotypes about the kinds of behaviour expected of guards and prisoners influenced the actions of the participants.

One important issue concerning the Stanford Prison Experiment is that the artificial set-up may have produced participant reactivity bias. In other words, the guards and prisoners may have been play-acting rather than genuinely conforming to their roles. The guards afterwards reported that they were influenced by the film *Cool Hand Luke*, which stereotyped prison guards as tough and aggressive. However, it is unlikely that only play-acting was involved. The fact that the guards didn't initially behave in an aggressive way suggests that the situation itself was an important factor in influencing their behaviour. In addition, the physical abuse and harassment shown by the prison guards went far beyond what would have been expected from mere play-acting. Although acting is most likely in the presence of an audience, Zimbardo (1973) found that harassment of prisoners was greater when individual guards were alone with solitary prisoners or out of range of the recording equipment being used in the experiment.

Many critics have argued forcefully that it was not ethically acceptable to expose people to the degradation and hostility they experienced in the Stanford Prison Experiment, even with their informed consent. Was it reasonable for Zimbardo to stand by while the guards forced prisoners to clean toilets with their bare hands, hosed them with fire extinguishers, and made them do push-ups with a guard standing on their back? Savin (1973) argued that the mock prison was a "hell". In reply, Zimbardo pointed out that he had tried to reduce any negative effects on the participants by holding day-long debriefing sessions, in which the moral conflicts posed by the study were discussed. He also pointed out that most of the participants accepted afterwards that they had benefited from the experience of taking part in the experiment.

How does this experiment relate to other research on majority influence and obedience? In our everyday lives, we often show majority influence by acting out a role in the way expected by society. This is known as identification, and was shown by the guards and the prisoners, who conformed closely to the ways we might expect them to behave.

In addition, the guards all tended to behave in similar ways to each other, and the same was true of the prisoners. This indicates a conformity effect, and may reflect the participants' need to be accepted by their fellow guards or prisoners.

Obedience to authority was also clearly at work. There was a definite power structure in the prison, with the guards having the power to force the prisoners to behave in ways they did not want to. This corresponds closely to the kinds of obedience to authority observed by Milgram (discussed later).

Wearing a uniform may lead individuals to conform to an expected role, as they did in Zimbardo's prison study.

Minority Influence

Nearly all the early research on social influence focused on the ways in which the majority can influence the thinking and behaviour of a minority. This happened at least in part because social psychologists assumed it was very hard for a minority to have any real influence on the majority. However, Moscovici disagreed with that assumption, and it is certainly true that minorities such as revolutionary groups and leaders have sometimes changed the course of history. Moscovici conducted his own research (Moscovici, Lage, & Naffrenchoux, 1969, see Key Study below) and showed that individuals will indeed conform to a minority on an Asch-like task. The rates were lower than in Asch's experiment but there was a significant amount of conformity.

Key Study: Minority influence

Moscovici et al.'s (1969) study of minority influence.

Aims: To determine whether a minority can influence a majority of naive participants, and thus reverse the usual direction of social influence. Moscovici et al. aimed to determine the conditions necessary for this to occur, in particular, the necessity for the minority to be consistent in their opinions.

Procedure: The participants were pre-tested to check for colour blindness. A laboratory experiment was carried out, in which participants were randomly allocated to either a consistent, inconsistent, or control condition. Each condition involved six participants being present at the same time: four naive participants (the majority), and two confederates (the minority). Participants were asked to describe the colour of 36 slides, all of which were blue, but which varied in brightness due to different filters. In the *consistent* condition, the two confederates described all 36 slides as green. In the *inconsistent* condition, the two confederates described 24 of the 36 slides as green and the remaining 12 slides as blue. In the control

EXAM HINT

Sometimes the exam question asks for "psychological processes". Don't let this throw you—just read it as explanations! Most students have no difficulty with majority influence (normative and informational) and obedience (agentic state, authoritarian personality, or power of authority) but struggle when it comes to minority influence so read on and learn to make sure there are no gaps in your knowledge.

? How do the results of this study compare with the studies that looked at majority influence?

? To what extent can we generalise about human behaviour from these studies?

condition, there were no confederates. Minority influence was measured by the percentage of naive participants who yielded to the confederates by calling the blue slides green.

Findings: In the consistent condition, 8.42% of the participants answered "green" and 32% conformed at least once. In the inconsistent condition, 1.25% of the participants answered "green". In the control condition, only 0.25% of the participants answered "green". Thus, the consistent condition showed the greatest yielding to minority influence. In a follow-up study, both experimental groups were more likely to report ambiguous blue/green slides as green compared to the control group.

Conclusions: A minority can have influence over the majority, and this minority influence is more effective when the minority is consistent. The fact that minorities are more persuasive when they are consistent has implications for people in leadership positions who are hoping to influence the majority.

Criticisms

- The research lacked experimental realism, since the experimental set-up was not very believable. The slide test was artificial and may have yielded demand characteristics because it was not believable. Thus, the research may lack internal validity, as the conversion (private change of opinion) may not have been a genuine effect. It may have been due to demand characteristics (the cues that revealed conversion was expected).
- The research lacked mundane realism, that is, the research set-up had no relevance to real life. It took place in a controlled environment with an artificial task that is not representative of minority influence in real-life social situations. Identifying the colour of a slide is trivial compared to real-life instances of minority influence such as the views of political leaders or decision making by juries. Consequently, the findings have low external validity as they cannot be generalised to real-life settings. Indeed, real-life studies often (but by no means always) show very little impact of minorities on issues of importance.
- Moscovici et al. focused on the distinction between the majority and the minority. In the real world, the distinction is more complex, because minorities typically have less power and status than majorities. This may be the reason why minorities rarely prevail in the real world.

Note: If the question asks for findings only, you could include research by Nemeth et al. (1974, see p.235).

Why is it important for a minority to be consistent in their responses if they are to produce minority influence? Suppose you are in a group, and someone consistently expresses a point of view that differs from that of everyone else in the group. You would probably interpret that person's behaviour as indicating that they were expressing their genuine beliefs. As a result, their views deserve to be taken seriously.

Why is the study by Moscovici et al. (1969) important? First, it was one of the first studies to show that a minority can change the behaviour of the majority. Second, the study showed clearly that a minority has to be consistent in its behaviour if it is to influence the majority. Third, the research of Moscovici and colleagues led to much important research on the issue of whether the nature of the influence of minorities on majorities was the same as the nature of the influence of majorities on minorities.

Nemeth, Swedlund, and Kanki (1974) confirmed that consistency is necessary for a minority to influence the majority, *but* it is not always sufficient. They essentially replicated the study by Moscovici et al. (1969). However, their participants could respond with all of the colours they saw in the slides rather than only a single colour. There were three main conditions:

1. The two confederates of the experimenter said "green" on half of the trials and "green-blue" on the other half in a random way.
2. As (1), except that the confederates said "green" to the brighter slides and "green-blue" to the dimmer slides, or vice versa.
3. The two confederates said "green" on every trial.

Nemeth et al. found that nearly 21% of the responses of the majority were influenced in condition 2, but the minority had no influence at all in conditions 1 and 3. The minority had no effect in condition 1 because it did not respond consistently. The minority in condition 3 did respond consistently, but its refusal to use more complex descriptions of the stimuli (e.g. "green-blue") made its behaviour seem rigid and unrealistic.

Moscovici (1976, 1980) claimed that Asch and others had put too much emphasis on the notion that the majority in a group has a large influence on the minority. He felt a minority could influence the majority. In fact Asch agreed with Moscovici, and believed that this was potentially a more valuable issue to study (reported by Spencer & Perrin, 1998).

Moscovici drew a distinction between compliance and conversion. As we saw earlier, compliance involves *superficial* (but not internal or private) changes in expressed attitudes or behaviour in response to social influence. In contrast, **conversion** involves internal and private changes in attitudes in a majority due to minority influence. Individuals might still appear to go along with the majority (for the sake of their safety!) but privately their opinions have changed. According to Moscovici, majority influence typically involves compliance or superficial agreement by the minority. In contrast, minority influence typically involves conversion or genuine agreement by the majority.

Explaining the minority effect

Moscovici (1985) argued that conversion is most likely to occur under certain conditions:

1. *Consistency.* The minority must be consistent in their opinion.
2. *Flexibility.* The minority must not appear to be rigid and dogmatic.
3. *Commitment.* A committed minority will lead people to rethink their position—this is conversion.
4. *Relevance.* The minority will be more successful if their views are in line with social trends.

An important real-life example of a minority influencing a majority was the suffragette movement in the early years of the 20th century. A relatively small group of suffragettes argued strongly for the initially unpopular view that women should be allowed to vote. The hard work of the suffragettes, combined with the justice of their case, finally led the majority to accept their point of view.

? **What is the difference between compliance and conversion?**

EXAM HINT

The two main explanations for minority influence you can bring into an answer are:

- Conditions for conversion (Moscovici): consistency, flexibility, commitment, relevance.
- Social impact theory: strength, status and knowledge, immediacy.

He also suggested some behavioural styles that minorities should have if they want to exert an influence. These include being consistent in order to demonstrate certainty, convey an alternative view, disrupt the norm, and draw attention to views. Also, they should avoid being too dogmatic, should act on principles rather than just talking about them, should make sacrifices to maintain the view they hold. It also helps if they are similar in terms of age, class, and gender to the people they are trying to persuade.

History is full of cases of individuals and minority groups who have finally managed to persuade the majority of their rightness of their views. In Britain, for example, there was the suffragette movement in the early years of the twentieth century. The suffragettes' campaign to give the vote to women as well as to men was initially ignored by the government of the day. Eventually, however, their high level of commitment and consistency in expressing their views (combined with the clear rightness of their position) led to success. Indeed, it is hard nowadays to imagine a time in which half the adult British population was not allowed to vote in so-called democratic elections!

Majority and Minority Influence

Might it be possible to explain both majority and minority influence with the same theory? The research examined so far contains a contradiction. Asch found that once there were more than three people behaving in a certain way, majority influence was fairly likely; yet an individual with a partner, i.e. a minority of two, can resist a majority. Thus, the number of other people behaving in a particular way leads to conformity but can also lead to anti-conformity, so conformity cannot be explained simply in terms of number of people present.

? **In fact minority influence is probably of more importance than majority influence in terms of social change. Can you think of an example where a minority of one changed the course of human history?**

Social impact theory

Latané and Wolf (1981) proposed **social impact theory**, which offers a more complex explanation and can account for both majority and minority influence (as well as being a general explanation for social behaviour). According to this theory, an individual's behaviour in any situation can be predicted in terms of three factors:

- *Strength*. This is determined by, for example, numbers of people present, or the consistency of the message. Hearing the opinion of a group of friends, who may not all be in close agreement, would be similar in strength to one person, such as a politician, forcefully delivering a message every night on television.
- *Status and knowledge*. People will be equally influenced by a lot of amateurs or one independent expert. The same would apply to individuals who have greater status—you need fewer of them to make the same impact.
- *Immediacy*. The closer you are to the influencer (physically, i.e. face-to-face vs radio, or psychologically, i.e. a close friend vs acquaintance), the more effect their message will have.

The effect of social influence in any situation is a combination of all three factors and, for each factor, a question of degree. In some situations this would lead to majority influence (e.g. where strength in terms of number is high, and status and immediacy may be low). In other situations, a minority influence would occur (e.g. where strength in numbers is low but the person saying the message has high status and consistency).

Evaluation of social impact theory

The attractiveness of this theory is that it can account for many different kinds of social behaviour. It can explain majority and minority influence, as in Asch's studies where there was conformity to the majority, but also dissension from the majority when a co-dissenter was present (minority influence). The theory offers a way of explaining *both* majority and minority influence using the same terms of social impact.

Other suggested theories

Other theories that have been suggested to explain minority influence include the **dissociation** model of minority influence and the self-categorisation theory. The dissociation model was developed by Mugny and Perez (1991). It states that minority ideas are taken up, but are often dissociated from the people with whom the ideas originated, especially if they are disliked. By dissociating themselves from the minority group, the majority avoids any identification with them.

David and Turner (1996) suggested the self-categorisation theory, in which minority ideas are unlikely to be taken up if they are seen as originating from an "out-group" (a group against which we define ourselves, as it is perceived as having different values and beliefs from us). However, if the minority views stem from an "in-group" they are more likely to be taken up, as we perceive that we share values and beliefs with members of an in-group. In other words, our relationship towards members of the minority is very important in determining whether we allow ourselves to be influenced by them.

Differences between majority and minority influence

We have seen that minorities can influence majorities, as well as majorities influencing minorities. However, there are various differences between these two types of influence. First, it is often the case that the influence of minorities on majorities is mainly in the form of private rather than public agreement, with the opposite pattern being found when majorities influence minorities. However, we shouldn't exaggerate this difference. As Smith and Mackie (2000, p.371) concluded, "By and large, majorities and minorities achieve influence by pulling the same levers."

Second, the influence of majorities often stems from the sheer number of individuals in the majority, whereas the influence of minorities is more likely to depend on the status and/or knowledge of minority members.

Third, the influence of minorities is more often indirect than the influence of majorities. For example, majorities may accept the ideas of the minority but only after disassociating or breaking the link between the ideas and those responsible for suggesting them.

Important Influences on Majority and Minority Influence

We can further explain social influence in terms of individual differences. Different people conform differently because of situational factors (such as culture) or dispositional factors (such as personality).

> ■ **Activity:** The true nature of a theory is that it can account for the facts. Can social impact theory do this? Try to use it to explain one of the studies in this chapter, for example the variations of Asch's research.

> **EXAM HINT**
> You might be asked to describe the differences between majority and minority influence. You could focus on the following:
> - Compliance vs conversion.
> - Immediacy vs takes place slowly.
> - High need for approval vs low need for approval.

Are we more likely to assume that this man is sleeping rough because of situational factors (he's been taken ill, forgotten his house keys) or dispositional factors (he can't keep a job, he's drunk and rowdy in accommodation, for example)?

? Why might engineering students be less likely to conform in these kinds of studies than other students?

? What are some of the limitations of cross-cultural studies?

? Why do you think students were less likely to conform (28%) than non-students (37%)?

When Asch's study was replicated, cross-cultural differences emerged.

Cultural factors

One of the possible limitations of Asch's work on majority influence and conformity is the cultural background of the participants. The study was carried out in the United States, so the results may not generalise to other, less conformist cultures. It was also culturally biased in terms of the historical period during which it took place—the late 1940s and early 1950s, before it became fashionable to "do your own thing".

Historical differences

Perrin and Spencer (1980), in a repeat of Asch's study in England in the late 1970s, found very little evidence of majority influence, leading them to conclude that the Asch effect was "a child of its time". However, the low level of majority influence in their study may have occurred because they used engineering students who had been given training in the importance of accurate measurement and therefore had more confidence in their own opinions. Smith and Bond (1993) carried out an analysis of a number of studies that had used Asch's task in the United States. They concluded (1993, p.124) that: "Levels of conformity in general had steadily declined since Asch's studies in the early 1950s." However, the above findings of Perrin and Spencer (1980) are unusual in showing so little evidence of majority influence.

Perrin and Spencer (1980) carried out two more studies on cultural factors in majority influence. In one study, the participants were young men on probation. Mixed in with these true participants were some confederates of the experimenter primed to give the wrong answers. The level of conformity shown was about the same as in the Asch studies. In the other study, the participants and the confederates were both young unemployed men with Afro-Caribbean backgrounds. Once again, conformity levels were comparable to those reported by Asch (1951).

Studies in other countries

There have been over 20 other cross-cultural studies of majority influence using Asch's experimental design. The findings from these studies were summarised by Smith and Bond (1993). Asch (1951) found that students gave the wrong answer on 37% of the conformity trials. The average figure in Smith and Bond's **meta-analysis** (combining data from many studies) was about 30% for the other

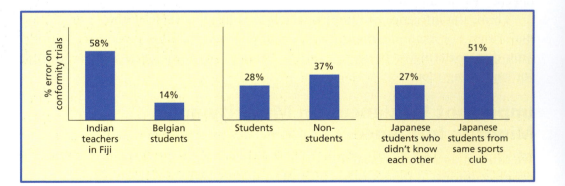

studies carried out in several parts of the world. The highest figure was 58% wrong answers for Indian teachers in Fiji, and the lowest figure (apart from Perrin & Spencer, 1980) was 14% among Belgian students.

Individualism and collectivism

In general terms, it is possible to distinguish between **individualistic** and **collectivistic** societies. Individualistic societies, such as the United Kingdom and the United States, emphasise the desirability of individuals being responsible for their own well-being and having a sense of personal identity. In contrast, collectivistic cultures (e.g. China) emphasise the priority of group needs over individual ones, and value the feeling of group identity. One would expect individuals to be less susceptible to majority influence in individualistic societies. This hypothesis was supported by Smith and Bond (1993) in a further meta-analysis on 133 Asch-type studies drawn from 17 countries.

Deindividuation

Deindividuation is another factor that may affect the amount of majority influence. The term refers to the loss of a sense of personal identity that can occur when we are, for example, in a crowd or wearing a mask. Zimbardo (1969) conducted a Milgram-type obedience experiment (Milgram's experiment is described later in the Key Study on page 244). Female participants were told to give electric shocks to other women. Deindividuation was produced in half of the participants by having them wear laboratory coats and hoods that covered their faces, and the experimenter addressed them as a group rather than as individuals. The intensity of electric shocks given by the deindividuated participants was twice as great as those given by participants who wore their own clothes and were treated as individuals. Why was this? Presumably the deindividuated participants felt more able simply to follow the experimenter's instructions, conforming to the stereotypical role of obeying a person in authority.

Johnson and Downing (1979) were not convinced that deindividuation was really responsible for the findings of Zimbardo. They pointed out that the clothing worn by the deindividuated participants resembled that worn by the Ku Klux Klan (a secret organisation in the United States which carried out many violent acts against American black people). Johnson and Downing found that deindividuated individuals dressed as nurses actually gave fewer electric shocks than did those who wore their own clothes. So the participants in both studies were still showing conformity to a role.

Uniforms, such as those worn by nurses, increase an individual's sense of anonymity and make it more likely that they will conform to the role associated with the uniform.

? If you feel deindividuated, do you think this makes you more or less likely to conform to group norms or to follow orders?

Johnson and Downing (1979) pointed out the similarity between the clothes of Zimbardo's deindividuated participants and another uniform, that of the Ku Klux Klan.

Personality

Some people are more conformist than others, due either to their biology or their experience. Students made errors on 28% of crucial trials in the Asch task, vs 37% for non-students. This may be because students learn to be more independent in their thinking than non-students, or their higher level of intelligence may make them more confident in their opinions.

Desire for personal control may be important as well. Burger and Cooper (1979) asked participants to rate a set of cartoons in terms of their funniness in the presence of a confederate who was expressing his own opinion. Participants who had previously measured high in terms of their desire for personal control were less influenced by the confederate. Some studies have found gender differences, with women being more subject to majority influence than men (Eagly & Carli, 1981). However, Eagly (1978) suggested this may be because women are more oriented towards interpersonal goals and therefore *appear* to be more conformist in experimental situations.

Finally, research by Adorno et al. (1950) produced evidence that some individuals become more conformist as a result of the kind of parenting they receive. This research is described later on page 254. Such people have an authoritarian personality involving hostility towards others and rigid beliefs.

Non-conformity—reactance

Some people express their sense of personal control by displaying **reactance**, reacting against attempts to restrict personal choice. Venkatesan (1966) demonstrated this in a study where a group of students were asked to select their favourite suit (they were all identical!). The true participant made their choice last and tended to conform to majority opinion (remember that the situation was ambiguous) *except* when everyone strongly favoured the same suit. Then the

? Driving down the wrong side of the road is an example of nonconformity (as well as downright foolishness). Can you think of other examples where conformity is desirable?

? Consider how you might use social impact theory to explain Venkatesan's study.

CASE STUDY: GROUPTHINK

Conformity to group opinion has many important applications, such as in juries and in the management committees of large organisations. The way individuals behave in these groups is likely to matter a lot. Janis (1972) coined the term **"groupthink"** to describe how the thinking of people in these situations is often disastrously affected by conformity.

Janis was describing the "Bay of Pigs" disaster to his teenage daughter and she challenged him, as a psychologist, to explain why such experts could make such poor decisions. (The Bay of Pigs invasion took place in 1961. President Kennedy and a group of government advisers made a series of bad decisions which resulted in this extremely unsuccessful invasion of the Bay of Pigs in Cuba—disastrous because 1000 men from the invasion force were only released after a ransom payment of fifty-three million dollars-worth of food and medicine, and

also because ultimately the invasion resulted in the Cuban missile crisis and a threat of nuclear war.) Janis suggested that there are a number of group factors that tend to increase conformity and result in bad decision-making:

- Group factors. People in groups do not want to be ostracised, they want to be liked and therefore tend to do things to be accepted as one of the group.
- Decisional stress. A group feels under pressure to reach a decision. To reduce this sense of pressure they try to reach the decision quickly and with little argument.
- Isolation. Groups often work in isolation which means there are no challenges to the way they are thinking.
- Institutional factors. Often people who are appointed to higher positions are those who tend to conform, following the principle that a good soldier makes a good commander. ■

participant tended to go for a different choice—the participant may have felt strong pressure to conform and reacted by asserting their independence.

Ethical Issues Raised by Majority and Minority Influence Research

There is a section of this chapter (see pages 261–272) dealing with ethical issues of relevance to all psychological research, and the main issues are all shown on page 269. However, here we will consider ethical issues of particular importance with respect to research on majority and minority influence. Four such issues will be discussed:

1. *Lack of informed consent*: A key feature of ethical research is that the participants should be given full information about what is involved in an experiment or other study *before* they are asked to agree to take part. This is known as informed consent, and it was lacking in the studies carried out by Asch and by Moscovici et al. The participants were totally unaware of the fact that most (or all) of the other participants were confederates of the experimenter, and had been told beforehand how to respond on each trial. However, the experiments wouldn't have made any sense if the participants had known this beforehand, because they wouldn't have experienced any pressure to go along with the majority or minority.

2. *Deception*: A point that is closely related to the first one is that it is generally unethical to deceive participants about the purpose of the study. Participants in the studies by Asch and by Moscovici had no idea that their purpose was to study social influence or conformity.

3. *Withdrawal from the study*: It is now regarded as very important that participants in any study are told beforehand that they can withdraw from it at any point and without giving a reason. At the time that Asch was carrying out his studies, participants were rarely told this. As a result, many of them probably suffered unnecessarily because they felt it would be very awkward and embarrassing to withdraw from the experiment.

4. *Protection of participants*: It is very important ethically for researchers to ensure that participants are protected from psychological and physical harm. There are real doubts whether that was the case with Asch's studies. Observations of the participants indicated that many of them experienced considerable conflict and embarrassment in deciding whether to report what they saw or to go along with majority influence. Bogdonoff et al. (1961) found that participants in an Asch-type study had greatly increased levels of physiological arousal, strongly suggesting that they experienced a high level of stress.

Very similar issues are raised by Zimbardo's Stanford Prison Experiment. Zimbardo's participants had given informed consent in that they were told ahead of time that there were be invasion of privacy, loss of some civil rights, and harassment. However, they probably didn't expect the level of humiliation and degradation to which they were actually exposed. Indeed, as you may remember, this experiment was stopped early because the levels of abuse directed at the mock prisoners were obviously becoming unacceptable.

SECTION SUMMARY

Conformity

❖ Conformity in the form of majority or minority influence is often (but not always) desirable.

Research studies into majority influence

❖ Conformity, in the form of majority influence, occurs when people adopt the behaviour, attitudes, or values of the majority or dominant group.

❖ Classic research studies include the work of Asch, Sherif, and Zimbardo.

❖ From these studies the following explanations of conformity have been given:
  – Informational social influence: People conform to gain information or because they lack relevant information and are uncertain about what to do.
  – Normative social influence: People conform to be liked or to avoid ridicule.
  – People conform to perceived social roles.

❖ Only informational social influence is likely to change private opinion.

❖ Conformity may be the result of:
  – Compliance: Group acceptance.
  – Identification: Group membership.
  – Internalisation: Acceptance of group norms and the changing of private opinions.

Minority influence

❖ Minority influence occurs when the minority changes the beliefs and opinions of the majority group.

❖ Individuals often comply with the majority whereas they are converted by the minority.

❖ The likely conditions for minority influence include:
  – consistency,
  – flexibility,
  – commitment,
  – relevance of minority argument.

Research studies into minority influence

❖ Moscovici suggested that minority influence and majority influence work in different ways:
  – Majority influence is the result of compliance.
  – Minority influence is the result of conversion.

❖ However, Latané and Wolf suggest that minority influence and majority influence work in similar ways. Their Social Impact Theory, which can be used to explain both majority and minority influence, suggests that social influence can be related to:
  – strength,
  – number and status,
  – immediacy.

See pp.111–119 of the revision guide.

Explanations of why people yield to majority and minority influence

❖ We can further explain majority and minority influence in terms of the factors that influence it.

❖ People differ in the extent of their conformity as a result of:
  – situational factors: e.g. cultural and historical factors;
  – gender;
  – dispositional factors: self esteem, the need for personal control.

❖ Non-conformity can be explained in terms of reactance.

SECTION 18
OBEDIENCE TO AUTHORITY

This section is concerned with **obedience to authority**. What is obedience? According to Franzoi (1996, p.259), "Obedience is the performance of an action in response to a direct order. Usually the order comes from a person of high status or authority."

In nearly all societies, certain people are given power and authority over others. In our society, for example, parents, teachers, and managers are invested with varying degrees of authority. Most of the time, this doesn't cause any problems. If the doctor tells us to take some tablets three times a day, we accept that he/she is the expert. If the school crossing attendant says "Cross now" it would be foolish not to obey—except if you could see a car approaching. The desirability of obeying authority is related to the reasonableness of their commands.

Obedience to Unjust Commands

An issue that has been of interest to psychologists for many years is to work out how far most people are willing to go in their obedience to authority. What happens if you are asked by a person in authority to do something that you think is wrong? The lesson of history (e.g. Nazi Germany) seems to be that many people are willing to do terrible things when ordered to do so.

Many people argue that only sadistic or psychopathic individuals would be so obedient to authority as to be prepared to do appalling things to another human being. Other people argue that most of us would probably be prepared to treat someone else very badly if ordered to do so by an authority figure. The famous (some would say infamous!) research of Stanley Milgram was designed to find out how far most people are willing to go to obey an authority figure. Milgram's first study was conducted in 1963 at the prestigious Yale University (see Key Study overleaf).

Why is Milgram's research so important? First, he obtained remarkable evidence that people are much more prepared to obey an authority figure than had been generally assumed. Second, he showed that people will do terrible things to someone else (e.g. possibly giving them fatal shocks) provided that someone else (in this case the experimenter) accepts responsibility. Third, the findings suggest that perfectly ordinary and normal people can be persuaded to do things that are clearly wrong. Fourth, while it may seem from the findings that many people are content to administer very painful electric shocks to someone else, the fact that so many of the participants were in a state of distress indicates that most people have a good moral sense.

How does obedience differ from conformity?

Both obedience and conformity involve social pressure. In obedience the pressure comes from behaving as you are instructed to do, whereas in conformity the pressure comes from group norms. A further distinction can be made in terms of the effects on private opinion. Obedience is more likely to involve public behaviour only.

Research on obedience to authority differs in at least three ways from research on conformity. First, the participants are ordered to behave in certain ways rather than being fairly free to decide what to do. Second, the participant is of lower status than the person issuing the orders, whereas in studies of conformity the participant is usually of equal status to the group members trying to influence him or her. Third, participants' behaviour in obedience studies is determined by social power, whereas in conformity studies it is influenced mostly by the need for acceptance.

KEY TERM

Obedience to authority: behaving as instructed, usually in response to individual rather than group pressure. This usually takes place in a hierarchy where the person issuing the order is of higher status than the person obeying the order. Obedience occurs because the individual feels they have little choice; they cannot resist or refuse to obey. It is unlikely to involve a change in private opinion.

EXAM HINT

You might be asked to describe the differences between obedience and conformity. You could focus on the following:

- Hierarchy vs equal status.
- Explicit vs implicit.
- Embrace as an explanation of behaviour vs reject as an explanation of behaviour.

Unquestioning obedience to authority may have catastrophic consequences. The picture shows survivors of the Auschwitz concentration camp at the end of the war in 1945, following a decade of persecution, imprisonment, and genocide.

Milgram (1974) carried out several variations on his basic experiment. He found there were two main ways in which obedience to authority could be reduced. The first was to increase the obviousness of the learner's plight. This was studied by comparing obedience in four situations differing in the obviousness of the learner's plight (the percentage of participants who were totally obedient is shown in brackets):

- *Remote feedback*: The victim couldn't be heard or seen (66%).
- *Voice feedback*: The victim could be heard but not seen (62%).

Key Study: Obedience

Milgram's (1963) study on obedience to authority.

Aims: Milgram aimed to investigate how willing participants were to obey authority when asked to inflict pain on another person. He also aimed to see whether he could set up a situation in which participants were more obedient to authority than was generally believed to be the case.

Procedure: Forty male volunteers (a self-selected sample) took part in a controlled observational study, which they were deceived into thinking was a test of learning. The naive participant was always assigned the role of "teacher" and a middle-aged confederate, Mr Wallace, played the role of "learner". Mr Wallace was said to have a heart condition. A word association test was the learning task, and the naive participant was instructed to deliver an electric shock to the learner for each incorrect answer. The teacher and learner were in separate rooms with no voice contact. The measure of obedience was the strength of the electric shock administered by the participants, which was on a scale of 15 to 450 volts with 15-volt increments for each wrong answer. The participants understood that the highest levels of shock might be fatal, especially to a man with a heart condition. The participants didn't know until the end of the experiment that no shocks were actually administered.

Findings: All participants gave shocks up to the 300-volt level, and 65% of participants continued to the highest level, 450 volts. This completely contradicted the predicted results that 3% or less would reach 450 volts. There were marked effects on the naive participants' behaviour, with most showing signs of extreme tension. For example, they trembled, sweated, stuttered, groaned, dug their fingernails into their flesh, and three had uncontrollable seizures.

Conclusions: The research showed that obedience to authority is due more to situational factors (the experimental setting, the status of the experimenter, and the pressure exerted on the participant to continue) than to "deviant" personality. Implications include the relevance of this research to the real-life atrocities of the Second World War, and the need to identify ways of preventing people from showing misplaced obedience to authority.

? Milgram's study is invariably described as an "experiment". Why might this be more correctly described as a "controlled observational study"?

? Do most people simply obey authority in a rather mindless way?

Criticisms

- Orne and Holland (1968) claimed that the research lacked experimental realism, meaning that the experimental set-up was simply not believable. They thought the participants were alerted to the fact that the electric shocks were not real, because electric shocks were not a credible punishment for making a mistake on a test. Thus, the research lacked internal validity, as the obedience was not a genuine effect. However, the participants' stress reactions contradict this.
- Orne and Holland (1968) also claimed that the research lacked mundane realism. The research set-up is unlike real life as it was an artificial, controlled, environment. Consequently, the findings have low external validity as they lack generalisability to real-life settings. However, experimental realism can compensate for a lack of mundane realism, which it could be argued is the case with this study.
- An additional limitation with Milgram's research is that he didn't provide a very clear explanation for the finding that about 35% of the participants refused to give the strongest electric shock. Milgram doesn't tell us what was different about them that allowed them to resist the pressures to be obedient.
- Milgram's research was extremely dubious ethically: he tried to prevent the participants from leaving the experiment and they were placed in a very stressful situation. It would be very difficult (or impossible) to carry out such a study nowadays in many countries. A key reason for this is that he totally failed to obtain informed consent from his participants—they simply didn't know what was in store for them. Ethical issues with this research are discussed further on page 250.

Note: If the question asks for findings or conclusions only, you could include research by Hofling et al. (1966, see p.249) and Bickman (1974, see p.248).

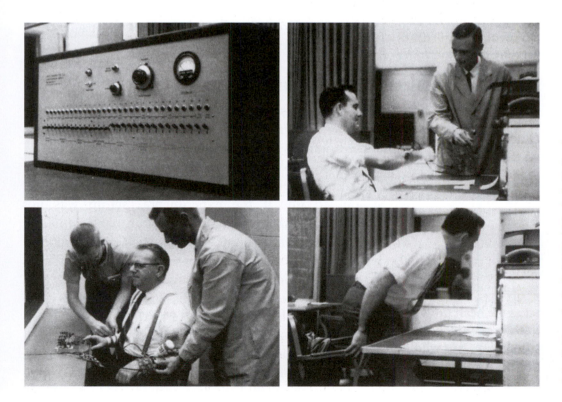

The photographs show the electric shock machine used in Milgram's classic experiment where 65% of the participants gave a potentially lethal shock to the "learner", shown in the bottom photograph. The learner was actually a confederate of the experimenter, a 47-year-old accountant called "Mr Wallace". The photographs show the experimenter (in the overall) and the true participant, the "teacher".

- *Proximity*: The victim was only one metre away from the participant (40%).
- *Touch-proximity*: This was like the proximity condition, except that the participant had to force the learner's hand onto the shockplate (30%).

Reducing obedience to authority was acheived by:

increasing the obviousness of the learner's plight…		reducing the authority or influence of the experimenter…	
victim not seen or heard	66%	at Yale University	65%
victim not seen but heard	62%	at a run-down office	48%
victim one metre away	40%	with experimenter sitting next to participant	65%
victim's hand placed on shock plate	30%	with experimenter giving orders via telephone	20.5%
		when confederates of experimenter refusing to give shocks	10%

Differences between obedience and conformity

OBEDIENCE	CONFORMITY
Occurs within a hierarchy. Actor feels the person above has the right to prescribe behaviour. Links one status to another. Emphasis is on power.	Regulates the behaviour among those of equal status. Emphasis is on acceptance.
Behaviour adopted differs from behaviour of authority figure.	Behaviour adopted is similar to that of peers.
Prescription for action is explicit.	Requirement of going along with the group is often implicit.
Participants embrace obedience as an explanation for their behaviour.	Participants deny conformity as an explanation for their behaviour.

The other main way in which obedience to authority could be lessened was to reduce the authority or influence of the experimenter in the following ways:

- Staging the experiment in a run-down office building rather than at Yale University (48%).
- Orders given by telephone rather than having experimenter sitting close to the participant (20.5%). (The effect of distance may help to explain why it is less stressful to kill people by dropping bombs from a plane than by shooting them at close range.)
- The experimenter was an ordinary member of the public rather than a white-coated scientist (20%).
- Giving the participant a confederate who refused to give shocks (10%).

Milgram's (1974) variations on the original study give us greater insight into the conditions under which people will obey unjust requests. They also show us something about independent behaviour because in many situations the majority of participants behaved independently.

The main criticisms of Milgram's research concern the lack of internal and external validity, and the contravention of ethical codes. We will consider these criticisms now.

Validity of Obedience Research

"Validity" refers to the extent to which something is true or valid. An experiment may produce a significant finding and "prove" the researcher's initial expectation, but this doesn't mean that the finding is "true" or "real".

There are several ways we can look at validity. One is **internal validity**, a measure of the extent to which the experimental design actually did the job it set out to do. If the experimental set-up was not believable then the participants probably wouldn't behave as they would normally do in such situations. It is called *internal* validity because it concerns what goes on inside the experiment.

The other form of validity is **external validity**, the extent to which the results of a study can be applied to other situations and other individuals. It is called external validity because it concerns issues outside the study. We will consider both of these forms of validity in relation to obedience research.

? What is the difference between internal and external validity?

KEY TERMS

Internal validity: the validity of an experiment in terms of the context in which it is carried out. Concerns events within the experiment as distinct from external validity.

External validity: the validity of an experiment outside of the research situation itself; the extent to which the findings of a research study are applicable to other situations, especially "everyday" situations.

Internal validity

To what extent did Milgram's participants actually believe they were giving electric shocks to the "learner"? Orne and Holland (1968) claimed that Milgram's experiment lacked **experimental realism** because the participants couldn't have believed in the set-up. For example, surely they would have questioned why the experimenter wasn't giving the shocks himself; why employ someone else if there wasn't some kind of subterfuge going on? However, in a replication of Milgram's experiment by Rosenhan (1969), nearly 70% of participants reported that they believed the whole set-up. Milgram's own response was that there is evidence that participants will believe and comply with almost anything. In a study conducted by Turner and Solomon (1962), participants were willing to be *given* strong shocks and therefore must have believed the experimental task. Coolican (1996) agrees with Milgram on the basis of film evidence which shows that the participants in Milgram's (and Asch's) studies were taking the situation very seriously and appeared to be experiencing real distress.

Orne and Holland also considered the question of **demand characteristics** in relation to internal validity. Demand characteristics are those cues in an experiment that "invite" participants to behave in certain predictable ways. One demand characteristic of *any* experiment is that participants should obey the experimenter's instructions. So, in Milgram's experiment, the reason the participants obeyed so completely was not necessarily because they were very obedient, but perhaps more because this is how one should behave in an experiment. This would lead us to conclude that the Milgram finding lacks validity—it tells us not about human obedience behaviour in general but only about how willing participants are to obey in experiments.

The Milgram experiment may also lack validity as a consequence of the fact that the participants behaved as they did because they had entered into a social contract with the experimenter. In exchange for payment ($4.50) participants would feel they should obey the instructions—their behaviour did not demonstrate obedience in the real world but only within a contractual relationship. They were told that they could leave and still be paid but, at the same time, the instructions "You must continue" must have made it quite difficult to leave. However, Milgram (1992) argued that experiments, in general, follow similar rules to social situations and in this sense they are true to life.

External validity

External validity concerns the extent to which we can generalise the findings of a study to other situations. Milgram conducted many variations of the original experiment and found many different levels of obedience (see earlier).

The main challenge to external validity in all of Milgram's research on obedience to authority is that it was carried out in laboratory situations, so we might not be able to generalise the findings to the real world. But consider the point, made earlier, that experiments are like real-life social situations. Another way to answer the external validity criticism is by reference to the distinction made between experimental and mundane realism (Carlsmith, Ellsworth, & Aronson, 1976). Any research set-up that is like real life can be said to have mundane realism in so far as it appears real rather than artificial to the participants. Some experiments lack mundane realism. However, experimental realism can compensate for this when the way the experiment is conducted is

? Why do you think that the setting in which the experiments took place made such a difference?

so engaging that participants are fooled into thinking the set-up is real rather than artificial.

Milgram argued that his study had both mundane realism, because the demands of an authority figure are the same whether the setting is artificial or occurring more naturally outside the laboratory, and experimental realism, because the experiment must have been highly engaging in order for the participants to behave in the way they did.

External validity can also be demonstrated through attempts to replicate the research in more natural situations, for example Leonard Bickman's (1974) study, which produced some similar findings to Milgram on obedience.

Bickman tested the external validity of Milgram's work by conducting an experiment in a more realistic setting, using New York pedestrians as participants. Three male experimenters (one dressed in a sports coat and tie, one dressed as a milkman, and one dressed in a guard's uniform that made him look like a police officer) gave one of three orders to the pedestrians:

1. Pointing to a bag on the street, "Pick up this bag for me."
2. Nodding in the direction of a confederate, "This fellow is overparked at the meter but doesn't have any change. Give him a dime."
3. Approaching a participant at a bus stop, "Don't you know you have to stand on the other side of the pole? This sign says 'No standing'."

? What ethical codes are infringed by Bickman's study?

Obedience can be related to the amount of perceived authority.

Bickman found that participants were more likely to obey the experimenter dressed as a guard than the milkman or civilian. This supports one of the variations of Milgram's findings, that obedience can be related to the amount of perceived authority. However, what Bickman asked participants to do was much more trivial than what was expected of participants in Milgram's research, and so may be of only partial relevance.

Perhaps the best-known replication of obedience research is a real-life study by Hofling et al. (1966) in which 22 nurses were phoned up by someone claiming to be "Dr Smith". He asked the nurses to check that a drug called Astroten was available. When the nurses did this, they saw on the bottle that the maximum dosage of this drug was supposed to be 10mg. When they reported back to Dr Smith, he told them to give 20mg of the drug to a patient.

There were *two* good reasons why the nurses should have refused to do as they were instructed. First, the dose was double the maximum safe dose. Second, the nurses didn't know Dr Smith, and they were only supposed to take instructions from doctors they knew. However, the nurses' training had led them to obey instructions from doctors. The nurses were more influenced by the clear power structure than by the two hospital regulations they were meant to obey. All but one did as instructed. When asked what other nurses would have done in the circumstances, they all predicted that others would *not* have obeyed the

? What are the main factors determining whether or not there is obedience to authority?

instructions. This provides evidence that the pressures to show obedience to authority are greater than most people imagine. The study raises important questions about hospital practices.

Many people suggest that Hofling et al.'s study had greater external validity than Milgram's. However, attempts to replicate Hofling et al.'s study have produced variable results. Rank and Jacobsen (1977) failed to replicate their findings, but Lesar et al. (1997) in a study on actual medication errors in American hospitals found that nurses typically carried out doctors' orders even when they had good reason for doubting the wisdom of those orders. In contrast, Milgram's main findings have been replicated dozens of times in other situations and other countries. And this is the criterion for external validity—that the finding should be replicable in other settings.

Cross-cultural support for external validity

Milgram's (1974) studies were carried out in the United States. It is important to know whether similar findings would be obtained in other cultures as a confirmation of the validity of the original findings. The relevant cross-cultural evidence has been collected by Smith and Bond (1993). Unfortunately, key aspects of the procedure varied from one culture to another, and so it is very difficult to interpret the cross-cultural differences in obedience. However, the percentages of participants willing to give the most severe shock were very high in several countries: 80% or higher in studies carried out in Italy, Spain, Germany, Austria, and Holland, suggesting substantial obedience to authority.

Ancona and Pareyson (1968) replicated the study in Italy, to find a total obedience rate of 80%, and Schurz (1985) studied Austrians and found the obedience rate to be 85%.

An interesting series of studies was conducted by Meeus and Raaijmakers (1995) in Holland, which gave support to the extent of obedience in another culture, as well as providing further insight into obedience to authority. Meeus and Raaijmakers told participants that the study was to see how job applicants would handle stress in an interview. The participant was given the role of being the interviewer, and the applicants were actually confederates of the experimenter. The interviewer was instructed to create stress for the interviewee, and was given a set of negative statements to do this, ranging from mild to utterly humiliating, such as "This job is too difficult for you."

At the time of the study, unemployment rates were very high in Holland and therefore the participants would have felt bad about making an interview more difficult for the person trying to get a job. Thus, we might expect them to refuse to obey. The confederates were instructed to start off behaving confidently but to gradually appear more and more distressed as the interviewer's statements became more humiliating, eventually pleading to the interviewer to stop interrupting, and finally refusing to answer any more questions. Nevertheless, 22 out of the total of 24 participants (interviewers) delivered all 15 "stress remarks". They clearly felt stressed themselves but attempted to hide this from the interviewee and act as if nothing was wrong, obeying the experimenter's authority and continuing with the task.

This experiment again demonstrates the willingness of individuals to obey even when both their stress and that of the receiver is apparent. The explanation for

Milgram's initial hypothesis was that German obedience during the Second World War was a facet of German culture. He was going to compare how Americans behaved with how Germans behaved but he found, to his astonishment, that Americans were extremely obedient—and therefore concluded that obedience was in human nature, not just German nature.

EXAM HINT

Issues of internal or external validity: You may be asked to define each of these terms or to explain why they are criticisms of Milgram's research. Also, the essay question might be on validity so make sure you can give evidence for and against the two types of validity.

? In what way does Meeus and Raaijmakers' study have greater validity than Milgram's study?

the high level of obedience may lie in the Dutch attitude to social institutions and their ways of relating to fellow citizens.

Ethical Issues Raised by Obedience Research

Let's start by noting that ethical issues apply to *all* psychological research, with the key general issues being discussed starting on page 261. When we as psychologists carry out an experiment, we must accept the responsibility to ensure that no psychological harm is done to our participants. There is now (quite rightly) much more concern about ethical issues in psychological research than used to be the case. One of the important results of this is widespread use of ethical guidelines so that anyone planning an experiment can see what is acceptable and what is unacceptable. A set of ethical guidelines for human research is given on page 269.

We turn now to Milgram's work, which raises some important ethical issues—issues that also apply to many other studies of obedience and conformity. In fact, it is almost true to say that Milgram's study has become more famous (or notorious) for the ethical issues it raised than for its findings related to obedience.

Protection from psychological harm

Baumrind (1964) was concerned that participants experienced a loss of self-esteem, dignity, and trust in authority, and it was a stressful experience for some. Milgram argued that the participants were fully debriefed, meaning that they were told in detail what the experiment had been about at the end of the experiment and any concerns they had were discussed sympathetically. In addition, psychiatric examination one year after the study revealed no sign of psychological damage.

Distress

Baumrind (1964) criticised Milgram for the severe distress he caused many, if not all, of his participants. Milgram's defence was that this effect was not anticipated nor was it deliberate. Prior to conducting the study he had surveyed opinion about how people would behave and had reason to expect very little obedience and therefore very little distress. However, this doesn't justify all the subsequent variations he conducted, which must have been equally stressful and were by then predictable as well. Both Zimbardo (1973) and Gamson, Fireman, and Rytina (1982, see page 256) stopped their studies because of their concerns for the participants.

Milgram also pointed out that the participants appeared to recover well afterwards, as evidenced in post-experiment interviews. Nearly 74% of the original participants said they were glad to have participated, and Milgram arranged for 40 of them to be interviewed by a psychiatrist who reported no signs that they had been harmed. The fact that very few complained afterwards could be explained in terms of denial, Freud's suggested ego-defence for dealing with anxiety. That is, in order for the participants to accept their own behaviour, they denied that there was anything to feel bad about.

Deception

The participants were not told in advance the true nature of Milgram's experiment, but simply that it was a test of punishment on learning using a word-association test. Also, they were deceived because they believed they were giving real electric shocks and that the confederate was another participant. Milgram (1992) has argued that the deception (or "illusion") was a necessary part of the experiment because, without it, the experiment would lack experimental realism. In addition, it wouldn't have worked at all—you wouldn't expect many people to object to giving *pretend* shocks to someone else! The value of the experimental findings (the end) justifies the method (means)—and ethics is a question of balancing ends and means. Brown (1986, p.6) says:

> As far as the ethics of research on human [participants] is concerned, I think Milgram is absolutely in the clear and deserves to be praised for doing research of the highest human consequence while showing great concern for the welfare of his [participants]. The slight personal risk involved is justified by the importance of the topic.

In addition, Milgram claimed that the fact that participants did not find fault with his procedures is a sufficient judgement of his deception. He debriefed the participants and 74% of them said they were glad that they had taken part in the study.

? What other reasons could there be for the fact that so many of Milgram's participants said they were glad to have taken part in the experiments? Might the fact that they were paid volunteers have had any effect on what they said they felt?

Lack of informed consent

Clearly where an experiment involves deception the participant is not in a position to provide informed consent, which is of central importance in ethical research. Informed consent involves telling participants in advance what they are going to be asked to do, what the purpose of the study is, and so on. The argument is that it is only fair to participants to let them know what they are letting themselves in for. Baumrind (1964) noted that in Milgram's experiment the participants weren't told that the study might cause conflict and distress, and so they were *not* in a position to give their informed consent. Milgram argued that while this was the case, the study helped people to review their value systems and made them aware of the destructiveness of obedience.

There are several ways to overcome the objections in relation to deception. One is to replace informed consent with presumptive consent, that is to obtain the views of other people about the acceptability of the experimental procedures. It is argued that if they felt it would be acceptable to take part, then we can *presume* that the actual participants would have felt this way if they had been asked. Milgram did obtain this form of consent from a group of psychiatrists as well as his students.

The second way to overcome objections about deception is to thoroughly debrief participants afterwards (providing full information about the study), offering them the opportunity to withdraw their data from the findings as a means of exercising some control over their participation. It is not on record whether Milgram did offer this to his participants but he did debrief them.

A third way is to use role-play, as Zimbardo did. Meeus and Raaijmakers (1995) claim that it is a viable alternative to the obedience experiment. In other words, the participants could have been asked to take part in a Milgram-type experiment having been told about the experimental manipulations and the absence of actual electric shocks. However, they would try to behave as they would have done in the absence of this knowledge. This would seem to eliminate

■ **Activity:** Imagine that you are one of twelve participants role-playing a jury, after viewing a video of a simulated event. Consider whether you would be more or less likely to find the accused guilty or innocent because:

(a) This is a pretend situation.
(b) You are:
    (i)   emotionally committed to the decision.
    (ii)   motivated to put forward personal views.
    (iii) in a position to empathise with the accused and/or victim.
    (iv) able to recall all the events.
    (v)   able to believe the situation to be real.
    (vi) able to feel the decision matters.

After considering these factors, do you think role play is a valuable research technique or an effective way to measure human behaviour?

the main ethical problems (because there would be full informed consent). The problem is to assess how useful the information obtained from a role-playing experiment would be. As Freedman (1969) pointed out, what we are likely to obtain from role-playing studies are "people's guesses as to how they would behave if they were in a particular situation."

The right to withdraw

A further ethical consideration is the participant's **right to withdraw** at any time. Baumrind (1964) observed that participants who wanted to withdraw were informed that they had no choice but to go on. Milgram argued that by persuading participants to remain, the power of the scientific establishment and authority figures was demonstrated, and he pointed out that they had not been physically detained.

Coolican (1990) claims that this was not really the case in Milgram's experiment. It appeared as if participants were able to withdraw at any time but in reality they were more or less ordered to continue. The experimenter had a script to follow. Each time the participant said he wanted to quit, the experimenter gave the next prompt or "prod": "Please continue", "The experiment requires that you continue", "It is absolutely essential that you continue", and "You have no other choice, you must go on". So participants were not really free to leave if that was what they wanted to do, although Milgram claims they were told at the beginning that they could leave and be paid regardless. In fact, a few participants *did* withdraw from Milgram's experiment in spite of all the pressure on them to remain.

Of central importance to current ethical guidelines is the emphasis that the rights and status of the participant are equal to those of the researcher (this is discussed in the next section). It has been argued that Milgram totally failed in this respect, because his research was specifically designed to see how far the researcher could exploit his superior position to compel participants to behave in ways in which they did not want to behave.

Conclusion relating to ethical issues

Erikson (1968) summed up Milgram's findings thus: it is "to man himself, not to 'the devil' belongs the responsibility for, and the control of, his inhumane actions". Aronson (1988) argued that there might have been no ethical objections if the findings had been less distasteful, and Milgram (1974) also suggested that the ethical concerns would have been reduced if the participants had disobeyed. So it is not that the method is unethical, but that the distasteful findings lead one to want to find some way to discredit them.

It is interesting to note that Hofling et al.'s (1966) nurse study could also be criticised for not following ethical guidelines. As the nurses were deceived, there was no informed consent, and they didn't have the right to withdraw.

Why Do People Obey?

People may obey authority because the situation they find themselves in somehow puts pressure on them to be obedient. Alternatively, Erikson concluded that people obey because obedience is a feature of human nature. Below we consider situational and personality/dispositional explanations of obedience.

Gross (1999) used the example of the Ik who are a society of hunter-gatherers now forced to live in a confined territory with few resources because of the changes that have occurred in their native Uganda. Their harsh living environment has forced them not to have many of the values that we Europeans hold. They are extremely selfish to the point of even depriving their own children of food. The conclusion is that, in certain situations, people are "forced" to behave in anti-social ways.

Situational explanations for obedience

Milgram (1974) identified three main features of the situation of his study that were conducive to obedience.

1. *A socially obedient environment* (**legitimate authority**). Our experience has taught us that authorities are generally trustworthy and legitimate.
2. *Graduated commitment.* The orders given by the experimenter moved gradually from the reasonable (small shocks) to the unreasonable (harmful shocks), and so it was hard for the participants to notice when they began to be asked to behave in an unreasonable way. Think of the "foot-in-the-door technique" used by salespeople—they start with a minor request, such as "Can I ask you a few questions?" (getting their foot metaphorically in the door) and then gradually make larger requests. Before you know it, you have bought some item you could not afford!
3. *Buffers.* **Buffers** are aspects of the situation that prevent the person from seeing the consequences of their actions. In Milgram's study, this occurred when the participants could not see the victim.

Personality/dispositional explanations for obedience

Adorno et al. (1950) felt that personality was a better explanation of obedience. Some people have an **authoritarian personality**, and are most likely to be obedient and also to be prejudiced. Such individuals have the following characteristics:

- Rigid beliefs in conventional values.
- General hostility towards other groups.
- Intolerance of ambiguity.
- Submissive attitudes towards authority figures.

Early experiences

Adorno et al. argued that childhood experiences play a key role in the development of the authoritarian personality. Harsh treatment causes the child to have much hostility towards his/her parents, but this remains unconscious, causing motivated forgetting, or what Freud called repression. The child seems to idealise his/her parents, and in later life acts in a submissive way towards authority figures. However, there is still much hostility lying below the surface, which is displaced onto non-threatening minority groups, in the form of prejudice. These

? Why do you think situational explanations may be more common in some cultures than others?

CASE STUDY: WAR CRIMINALS

After the Second World War, the Allies tried many of the high-ranking Nazi officers at Nuremberg. Adolf Eichmann argued that he had only been obeying orders. He said he was not the "monster" that the newspapers described but simply an ordinary person caught up in an extraordinary situation. Eichmann was described as having no violent anti-Jewish feelings (Arendt, 1963). The argument was that he was an autonomous individual who became agentic when he joined the SS and subscribed to the military code of obedience to those in authority. ■

characteristics of the authoritarian personality make people especially likely to obey the orders of an authority figure.

The F Scale

Adorno et al. devised a number of questionnaires relating to their theory. The most important questionnaire was the **F (Fascism) Scale**, designed to measure

---

Items from the F scale devised by Adorno et al.

Indicate whether you hold slight, moderate, or strong support OR slight, moderate, or strong opposition to the following:

"Obedience and respect for authority are the most important virtues children should learn."

"Most of our social problems would be solved if we could somehow get rid of the immoral, crooked, and feeble-minded people."

"What the youth needs most is strict discipline, rugged determination, and the will to work for family and country."

"Familiarity breeds contempt."

"Sex crimes, such as rape and attacks on children, deserve more than mere imprisonment, such criminals ought to be publicly whipped."

---

the attitudes of the authoritarian personality (look at the box on the left). Adorno et al. gave the test to about 2000 people and found that those who scored high on the F Scale also scored high on a scale that measured prejudice, thus confirming the validity of the scale. Milgram (1974) found that high scorers on the F Scale gave stronger shocks than low scorers when ordered to do so by an authority figure, thus suggesting that personality plays a part in determining obedience to authority. However, the fact that about two-thirds of participants in Milgram's experiments were fully obedient but far fewer people than that have an authoritarian personality means that this approach only provides a partial explanation.

Agentic state

Milgram (1974) argued that situational factors such as the ones discussed below played an important part in causing people to be obedient to authority. However, he also argued that there was another crucial factor. In our everyday lives, we are generally in the **autonomous state**, in which we are aware of the consequences of our actions and feel in control of our own behaviour. In the Milgram situation, in contrast, people were put into the **agentic state**. The key features of the agentic state is that people surrender their sense of responsibility to an authority figure and cease to act according to their conscience. The attitude of those in the agentic state is as follows: "I am not responsible, because I was ordered to do it." In essence, Milgram was arguing that we have an unfortunate tendency to do as we're told provided that the person doing the telling is an authority figure. He called this our "fatal flaw", and it is discussed more fully on page 258.

Resisting Obedience and Conformity

We have seen that social pressures to conform or to obey authority can exert powerful effects on people's behaviour. However, some people manage to resist

CASE STUDY: THE MY LAI MASSACRE

The My Lai massacre has become known as one of the most controversial incidents in the Vietnam War. On 14 December 1969 almost 400 Vietnamese villagers were killed in under 4 hours. The following transcript is from a CBS News interview with a soldier who took part in the massacre.

Q. How many people did you round up?
A. Well, there was about forty, fifty people that we gathered in the center of the village. And we placed them in there, and it was like a little island, right there in the center of the village, I'd say . . . And . . .
Q. What kind of people—men, women, children?
A. Men, women, children.
Q. Babies?
A. Babies. And we huddled them up. We made them squat down and Lieutenant Calley came over and said, "You know what to do with them, don't you?" And I said yes. So I took it for granted that he just wanted us to watch them. And he left, and came back about ten or fifteen minutes later and said, "How come you ain't killed them yet?" And I told him that I didn't think you wanted us to kill them, that you just wanted us to guard them. He said, "No. I want them dead." So—
Q. He told this to all of you, or to you particularly?
A. Well, I was facing him. So, but the other three, four guys heard it and so he stepped back about ten, fifteen feet, and he started shooting them. And he

told me to start shooting. So I started shooting, I poured about four clips into the group.
Q. You fired four clips from your . . .
A. M-16.
Q. And that's about how many clips—I mean, how many—
A. I carried seventeen rounds to each clip.
Q. So you fired something like sixty-seven shots?
A. Right.
Q. And you killed how many? At that time?
A. Well, I fired them automatic, so you can't—You just spray the area on them and so you can't know how many you killed 'cause they were going fast. So I might have killed ten or fifteen of them.
Q. Men, women and children?
A. Men, women and children.
Q. And babies?
A. And babies.

William Calley stood trial for his involvement in this massacre. His defence was that he was only obeying orders. Before the massacre Calley showed no criminal tendencies and afterwards he returned to a life of quiet respectability. His behaviour was that of a "normal" person. Kelman and Lawrence (1972) conducted a survey after the trial and found that half of the respondents said that it was "normal, even desirable" to obey legitimate authority. ■

the pressures to conform or to obey and thus exhibit **independent behaviour.** In all the studies reviewed so far, there were always some people who didn't obey or conform. Why did they remain in an autonomous state while others were apparently in an agentic state?

Situational factors

We will start by considering some of the reasons why some people refused to show complete obedience to authority in Milgram's studies. As Milgram (1974) pointed out, there are two main ways in which obedience to authority can be reduced. First, the harm being done to the victim can be made very clear. Milgram did this by using a condition in which the participants had to force the learner's hand onto the shockplate. This approximately halved the percentage of participants who were totally obedient compared to the standard condition.

Second, steps can be taken to reduce the perceived authority of the person who is issuing the orders. Milgram did this in various ways. One effective method was to reduce the status of the experimenter from a white-coated scientist to an ordinary member of the public. This reduced total obedience to only 10% of the participants. Even more effective at undermining the power of the experimenter was providing the participant with a confederate who refused to give electric shocks. Only 10% of the participants were fully obedient in this condition, which shows that people are much better able to resist authority when they feel they have someone else's support.

If we develop a good understanding of obedience, then we should be able to make people more capable of resisting obeying others when their orders are unreasonable. Based on our knowledge, it seems likely that the following methods would work:

- Educate people about the problems of "blind obedience".
- Remind people that they should take responsibility for their own actions.
- Provide role models who refuse to obey.
- Question the motives of authority when they issue unreasonable orders.

How can we reduce conformity behaviour or majority influence? Asch (1951, 1956) identified two important factors. First, he found that conformity dropped dramatically from 37% to 5% when one confederate gave the correct answer on all trials. As with obedience to authority, the presence of some support makes it much easier to resist social pressures. Second, it is easier to avoid conforming when the number of people ranged against you is relatively small than when it is large.

We conclude this section by considering an interesting study by Gamson, Fireman, and Rytina (1982). It shows how majority influence can play an important role in resisting obedience. More specifically, Gamson et al. found that rebellion in a group situation can create disobedience.

Gamson et al. set up a fictitious public relations firm called MHRC, and participants were employed to help the company collect opinions on moral standards. The participants met at a motel, and were asked to engage in a discussion that would be videotaped. The discussion was about Mr C, who had managed a service station for an oil company. However, his franchise had been revoked because, the company claimed, he had behaved immorally and this made him unfit to be their local representative (he was living with a young woman and they were not married). Mr C was suing the company for unfair dismissal. It also transpired that Mr C had spoken out on television against higher petrol prices. The participants were asked to discuss their attitudes towards Mr C's lifestyle, during which the coordinator switched the cameras on and off at various times while instructing the groups to argue as if they were offended by Mr C's behaviour. The groups soon realised they were being manipulated to produce evidence supporting the oil company's position. In some of the groups, the participants threatened to confiscate the videotapes of the discussion, and to expose the oil company to the media. In all groups there was some rebellion, and all but four of the groups refused to sign the affidavit giving MHRC permission to use the videotape in a trial.

This study provides a marked contrast with Milgram because in 29 out of the 33 groups there was successful resistance to unjust authority. Why did rebellion occur instead of obedience? In the MHRC groups, there were no confederates. One member in each group spontaneously rebelled and this minority opinion swayed most of the groups. It is possible that this change in behaviour reflects the fact that this study took place at a time when Americans had come to be more challenging of authority. It may also be that the MHRC coordinator had less authority than the experimenter in Milgram's study. Finally, it may be because the MHRC study involved groups, which behave differently from individuals because the possibility of collective action exists (i.e. everyone knows that they can group together to resist authority).

Individual differences

There are large individual differences between participants in their responses to situations, such as those devised by Asch and by Milgram. As we will see, various

? In the light of Gamson et al.'s (1982) study how can we re-interpret Asch's research (see page 229)?

? How would you explain the findings of Gamson et al.'s research?

attempts have been made to identify the personality and other characteristics of individuals whose behaviour is independent.

Crowne and Marlowe (1964) reported a number of studies in which conformity was assessed in high and low scorers on the Marlowe–Crowne Social Desirability Scale. This scale provides a measure of the need for social approval. As might be expected, those low in need for social approval were more likely to show independent behaviour by refusing to conform in the Asch situation. In other conformity studies (e.g. Stang, 1972) it has been found that individuals high in self-esteem are more likely to behave independently than those low in self-esteem.

When Milgram used female participants in his experiment he found that obedience rates were much the same. However, other studies have found some gender differences. Kilham and Mann (1974) used the Milgram baseline experiment and found that Australian women were less obedient than men (16% vs 40%), whereas Eagly and Carli (1981), as previously mentioned, claimed that women are more likely to be influenced than men, but this may be because women are more oriented towards interpersonal goals and therefore *appear* to be more influenced.

It is also likely that a tendency to prefer an autonomous state would be associated with greater desire for personal control, as Burger and Cooper (1979) found (see page 240).

Finally, we go back to Milgram's (1974) finding that individuals with an authoritarian personality were more likely than other people to be very obedient to authority. It follows of course that individuals who *don't* have an authoritarian personality are more likely than others to be independent and to resist pressures to obey authority figures.

Evaluation of individual differences

There are two main reasons why some individuals might show more independent behaviour than most other people. First, they may have a high opinion of themselves and of the correctness of their own judgements, explaining why those high in self-esteem, who believe themselves to be highly competent, who are intelligent, and who have leadership ability, show little conformity behaviour. Second, the "independent" types may be relatively unconcerned about the approval of others, and so have little motive for submitting to the judgements of other people. That explains why those low in need for social approval and high in assertiveness may behave in an independent way.

? Why is it that people high in self-esteem are more likely to resist orders to obey?

Do leaders share any common characteristics?

Two final points need to be made. First, the personality and other characteristics of those who show independent behaviour often differ surprisingly little from those who conform. Second, research into independent behaviour is important, because it serves to remind us that conformity behaviour or majority influence and obedience to authority depend on two factors: (1) the individual; and (2) the social situation. Majority influence and obedience to authority also depend on the behaviour that is being requested—conforming to traffic rules or obeying a traffic warden is one thing, whereas conforming to anti-social behaviour or obeying an unjust request is quite another.

In terms of dispositional/personality factors, there is a greater likelihood of resisting obedience if the person:

- wants to maintain control;
- is confident enough to be independent;
- has a high level of moral development;
- has a need to maintain their individuality.

The Surprising Nature of Milgram's Findings

Why is Milgram's research on obedience to authority so important? The main reasons are because of the light it sheds on human behaviour and the surprising findings he obtained. However, it seems to portray a very depressing view of human nature. According to Milgram (1974):

The capacity for man to abandon his humanity, indeed the inevitability that he does so, as he merges his unique personality into the larger institutional structures ... is the fatal flaw nature has designed into us, and which in the long run gives our species only a modest chance for survival.

Milgram (1974) seems to have been rather pessimistic in his conclusions. Most of the obedient participants experienced a strong conflict between the demands of the experimenter and the dictates of their consciences—being tense and nervous, perspiring, biting their lips, and repeatedly clenching their fists. Such behaviour does *not* suggest that they were simply in an agentic state.

Milgram and others have suggested that there are links between his findings and the horrors of Nazi Germany. However, there are various reasons why we shouldn't exaggerate the similarities. First, the values underlying Milgram's studies were the positive ones of understanding more about human learning and memory, whereas the values in Nazi Germany were morally vile. Second, most of the participants in Milgram's studies needed to be watched closely to ensure their obedience, whereas this was not necessary in Nazi Germany. Third, as we have seen, most of Milgram's participants were in a state of great conflict and agitation. In contrast, those who carried

CASE STUDY: STANLEY MILGRAM'S OTHER RESEARCH

Milgram's name is synonymous with obedience research, however he did conduct a number of other studies and was always seeking to test new ideas. Tavris (1974) called him "a man with a thousand ideas". He wrote songs, including a musical, and devised light-shows and machines.

In relation to conformity, he tried the following with a group of students (Tavris, 1974). He asked them to go up to someone on an underground train and say "Can I have your seat?" They all recoiled in horror at the idea. Why were they so frightened? Milgram tried the task himself, assuming that it would be easy, but when he tried to say the actual words to a stranger on the underground he froze. He found he was overwhelmed by paralysing inhibition, and suggested that this shows how social rules exert extremely strong pressure. ■

out the atrocities in Nazi Germany typically seemed unconcerned about moral issues.

Attribution

Why was the actual behaviour of the participants in Milgram's studies so different from what most people would have expected? Part of the answer is probably to be found in the **fundamental attribution error:** when we try to work out the factors determining someone else's behaviour, we tend to *underestimate* the role of situational factors in determining behaviour, and to *overestimate* the role of personality and other personal characteristics. When asked to decide how many people would show total obedience in Milgram's situation, we tend to think along the following lines: "Only a psychopath would give massive electric shocks to another person. There aren't many psychopaths about, and so only a tiny percentage of people would be totally obedient." This line of reasoning focuses exclusively on the individual participant's characteristics. In line with the fundamental attribution error, it ignores the relevant situational factors.

> ■ **Activity:** On the basis of the psychological evidence, what advice would you give to the management committee of a children's home for difficult children? They want to know how to increase obedience and reduce group conformity. List three things for obedience and three things for conformity, citing the relevant evidence to support your argument.

SECTION SUMMARY

❖ Obedience to authority is behaving as instructed, usually in response to an individual rather than a group.

❖ It can usually be considered a desirable social influence, unless it is unjust, and is generally a positive response to social instruction.

❖ Obedience and influence (majority and minority) differ in terms of the source of the social pressure and the extent to which private opinion is changed.

What is obedience to authority?

❖ Classic research studies into obedience include
  – Milgram
  – Hofling
  – Meeus and Raaijmakers

❖ Milgram's classic study on obedience showed that people were more obedient than we would imagine.

❖ The main criticisms of his research concern the lack of internal and external validity, and the contravention of ethical codes.

Research studies into obedience

❖ Obedience research has been criticised in terms of:
Internal validity:
  – This describes the extent to which a participant believes in the experimental manipulation and therefore the extent to which the participants' behaviour can tell us anything about real behaviour.
  – The roles of demand characteristics and social contracts are important considerations.
  – Milgram's research raised questions as to whether the participants believed the "victim" was receiving shocks and was in pain.
External validity:
  – This describes the extent to which the results of a study can be applied to other everyday life situations and other individuals.

Issues of validity associated with research into obedience

- Laboratory experiments are often seen as artificial and unreal (they lack mundane realism). However, if they have experimental realism this may give them external validity (if the participants regard the experimental situation as real).
- Further support for external validity comes from research with similar results in other cultures, showing that the findings can be applied to other situations and other people.
- Milgram's experiment raises questions as to whether any parallels to the Holocaust can be drawn from his research.

Ethical concerns associated with research into obedience

❖ Other criticisms of Milgram's research and other research into obedience focus on ethical concerns. These include:
  - Causing distress.
  - Deceiving participants.
  - A lack of informed consent.
  - Participants not being given the opportunity to withdraw from the study.
❖ Milgram responded to these criticisms by arguing that:
  - The distress was not anticipated and there was no long-term harm.
  - The deception was necessary and the means justified the ends.
  - Informed consent was replace by presumptive consent.
  - Debriefing took place.
❖ Both Milgram and Aronson argued that people made ethical objections because of the actual (distasteful) findings, not because of the methods used.

Explanations of why people obey

❖ There are situational and dispositional (personality) explanations for obedience, as there were for conformity.
❖ Situational explanations include:
  - Being in a socially obedient environment.
  - Agreeing to smaller demands first: graduated commitments.
  - The presence of buffers.
❖ Dispositional explanations include:
  - Authoritarian personality: individuals with authoritarian personalities have suppressed their hostility towards controlling parents and remain submissive to authority.
❖ According to Milgram, we often adopt the agentic state when given orders by an authority figure. This causes us to surrender our sense of responsibility and simply do what we have been told to do.

Independent behaviour, and why people may resist obedience

❖ As Milgram demonstrated, not everyone is obedient to authority. Independent behaviour may be influenced by the following factors:
  - Situational explanations: The presence of dissenters, the possibility of collective action, as in Gamson's study.
  - Dispositional explanations: The need for social approval, self-esteem, gender, and personal control.
❖ The unexpected nature of Milgram's findings should give us cause for thought. Our surprise may be explained in terms for the fundamental attribution error. It was the situational factors rather than personal factors that explained the participant's behaviour.

See pp.120–126 of the revision guide.

SECTION 19—CRITICAL ISSUE
ETHICAL ISSUES IN PSYCHOLOGICAL RESEARCH

The questions of ethics is critical to psychological research. Not least because a professional group of people is one that "polices" itself and therefore these ethical standards are a key feature of the professionalism of psychology. In this section, we will consider some important ethical issues in detail and relate these to the social influence research we have been examining. At the end we will consider how psychologists deal with these issues using ethical guidelines. Note that important ethical issues raised by obedience research are discussed on page 250.

Ethics in Psychology

Ethics are a set of moral principles used to guide human behaviour. There are no absolutes in ethics but any society or group of people develops ethics as a means of determining what is considered right and wrong for that group. The term "ethics" tends to be used when considering moral behaviour among professionals, such as doctors or lawyers. The term "morals" is used to refer to everyday standards of right and wrong, such as honesty and kindness. Ethics are determined by a balance between means and ends, or a **cost–benefit analysis**. Certain things may be less acceptable than others, but if the ultimate end is for the good of humankind, then we may feel that an undesirable behaviour is acceptable. For example, far more people accept that it is ethically justified to cause suffering to animals in order to find a cure for some serious human illness than it is merely to develop a new cosmetic.

Scientists often confront important ethical questions in the course of their work. Was it morally defensible for physicists to develop the atomic bomb during the 1940s? Can research on human embryos be justified? Should scientists participate in the development of chemical weapons that could kill millions of people? All these questions are hard to answer, because there are good arguments for and against each programme of research.

There are probably more major ethical issues associated with research in psychology than in any other scientific discipline. There are various reasons for this. First, all psychological experiments involve the study of living creatures (whether human or the members of some other species), and the rights of these participants to be treated in a caring and respectful way can easily be infringed by an unprincipled or careless experimenter.

Second, the findings of psychological research may reveal what seem to be unpleasant or unacceptable facts about human nature, or about certain groups within society. No matter how morally upright the experimenter may be, there is always the danger that extreme political organisations will use research findings to further their political aims. Such research is often described as "socially sensitive", and psychologists have a responsibility to consider very carefully the uses to which their findings may be put.

Third, these political aims may include social control. There is the danger that the techniques discovered in psychological research might be exploited by dictators or others seeking to exert unjustifiable influence on society or to inflame people's prejudices.

? Which do you think are more important, the interests of the individual or the interests of society as a whole?

EXAM HINT
If you are asked to outline the ethical issues in social influence research, make sure you focus on the *issues* and not the guidelines. You should be considering the use of deception, informed consent, and the protection of participants from harm, and using the research of Milgram, Zimbardo, and others to back up your answer.

The key ethical issues to consider are: the use of deception, informed consent, and the protection of participants from harm. These issues are especially relevant to research into social influence because of the potential for harm to participants and the potential uses of the findings.

The Use of Deception

Honesty is a key moral and ethical principle. It is a fundamental expectation to be given full information when you agree to take part in psychological research. However, deception is sometimes necessary. A well-known example of research involving deception is the work of Asch (1951, 1956, see page 229) on group pressure. If the participants had been told the experiment was designed to study conformity to group pressure, and that all the other participants were confederates of the experimenter, then this important study would have been pointless.

Deception is certainly widespread. Menges (1973) considered about 1000 experimental studies that had been carried out in the United States. Full information about what was going to happen was provided in only 3% of cases. However, the substantial increase in concern about ethical issues means that full informed consent is far more common nowadays than it was over 30 years ago.

One possible reaction is to argue that there should never be any deception in psychological experiments, even if that means that some lines of research have to stop. However, this ignores the fact that many forms of deception are entirely harmless. For example, some memory researchers are interested in incidental learning (see Chapter 2), which involves people's ability to remember information they were not asked to remember. This can only be done by deceiving the participants as to the true purpose of the experiment until the memory test is presented. Nearly everyone would agree that such deception is perfectly acceptable.

When is deception justified? There is no simple answer. Various relevant factors need to be taken into consideration. First, the less potentially damaging the consequences of the deception, the more likely it is to be acceptable. Second, it is easier to justify the use of deception in studies that are important in scientific terms than in those that are trivial. Third, deception is more justifiable when there are no alternative, deception-free ways of studying an issue.

Handling the deception issue

One way of avoiding the ethical problems associated with deception is the use of **role-playing experiments** (see discussion on page 251). The participants are asked to play the role of participants in a deception experiment. They are told beforehand about the experimental manipulations (e.g. there are no actual shocks in the Milgram situation), but have to try to behave as if they didn't know. This approach eliminates the ethical problems of deception studies, but it is not clear that it is a satisfactory way of studying behaviour. The obvious problem is that the behaviour displayed by role-playing participants may not correspond to the behaviour that would be displayed by participants who didn't know about the deception. The study by Meeus and Raaijmakers (1995, see page 249) also involved role playing. Deception was largely avoided but distress was again caused.

Debriefing

Debriefing is an important method of dealing with deception and other ethical issues. At the end of the research study, participants should be told the actual

KEY TERM

Deception: this is an ethical guideline, which states that deception of the participants during the research process should be avoided wherever possible. Deception refers to the withholding of information that might affect the participant's decision to take part in the research. It is an issue because this might lead to psychological harm. Deception is a particularly common issue because the withholding of the research hypothesis is often considered necessary in order to avoid demand characteristics.

nature and purpose of the research, and asked not to tell any future participants. In addition, debriefing typically involves providing information about the findings of the experiment and offering participatants the opportunity to have their results excluded from the study if they so wish.

Debriefing can also be used to reduce any distress that may have been caused by the experiment. However, the fact that participants are debriefed *doesn't* justify carrying out any unethical procedures. According to Aronson (1988) participants should leave the research situation in "a frame of mind that is at least as sound as it was when they entered". This might *not* be the case even after debriefing. You might consider Milgram's research in this context. For example, if you had been fully obedient in a Milgram-type experiment, you might feel somewhat guilty afterwards that you had allowed yourself to give what might been fatal electric shocks to someone with a heart condition.

Role-playing experiments can be used to avoid deceiving participants. How could a role-playing experiment be used in this teachers' meeting?

Informed Consent

It is considered the right of participants, wherever possible, to provide voluntary **informed consent**. This means several things: being informed about what will be required, being informed about the purpose of the research, being informed of your rights (e.g. the right to confidentiality, the right to leave the research at any time), and finally, giving your consent. There are many situations where this is not possible:

- When children or participants who have impairments that limit understanding and/or communication are involved. In this case, the informed consent of an adult is sought, although some critics might feel that this is not sufficient.
- When deception is a necessary part of the research design, as in Asch's or Milgram's experiment. We have seen that role-playing experiments can be used to provide informed consent, but such experiments have serious limitations.

KEY TERM

Informed consent: this is an ethical guideline, which states that participants' agreement to take part in research should be based on their full knowledge of the nature and purpose of the research. Thus, they should be made aware of any tasks required of them and their right to withdraw, and any other aspects of the research that might affect their willingness to participate.

CASE STUDY: SUBJECTS OR PARTICIPANTS?

Until recently members of the public who took part in psychology experiments were called "subjects". This reflected the view that they were only passively involved in the research process (they did what the researcher told them) and it emphasised the power of the researcher (as the person in authority). The subject in a psychological experiment was in a rather vulnerable and exploitable position. Kelman (1972, p.993) pointed out, "most ethical problems arising in social research can be traced to the subject's power deficiency." It follows that steps need to be taken to ensure that the participant is not placed in a powerless and vulnerable position. This is the task of an ethical code.

As a consequence of this insight it has become the practice to refer to such individuals as participants rather than subjects. Perhaps this process is analogous to the historical shift from having a political regime with "rulers and subjects" to the more modern conception of "leaders and followers". Both participants and followers have an active role to play and it would be foolish to think otherwise. The change in terminology allows for a more humane respect for individuals who participate in psychology experiments. ∎

? How does a field experiment differ from a laboratory experiment?

- In field experiments when participants are not even aware that they are taking part in a piece of psychological research. A classic study by Piliavin et al. (1969) involved a confederate pretending to collapse on an underground train with the aim of finding out how many people would offer help. None of the participants gave their consent. Bickman's (1974) study of obedience (see page 248) was also a field experiment.

- Retrospective case studies, where data in the public domain are used as psychological evidence (such as the case of Kitty Genovese on page 22).

- There is even the question as to whether truly informed consent is ever possible. How easy is it for a non-psychologist to understand the aims of psychological research and fully comprehend what is expected of him or her? Prior to participation, would the "teacher" in Milgram's experiment have anticipated how they would feel when giving shocks? The evidence of Milgram's pre-experiment surveys suggests that people would not have anticipated their own behaviour, let alone how they would *feel*.

Other ways to obtain consent

One possibility is to ascertain the acceptability of a given experiment by asking the opinions of members of the population from which the participants in the research are to be drawn. This is what Milgram did, and it is called seeking **presumptive consent**.

? Could the approach adopted by Gamson et al. be adapted to handle the deception issue in most kinds of research?

An alternative approach is to gain **prior general consent** (sometimes referred to as *partially informed consent*). This is what Gamson et al. (1982) did. In their study (described on page 256) they gained participants' consent using the following ruse: they advertised for participants and when interested individuals telephoned, the potential participants were asked whether they were willing to take part in any or all of the following kinds of research:

1. Research on brand recognition of commercial products.
2. Research on product safety.
3. Research in which you will be misled about the purpose until afterwards.
4. Research involving group standards.

■ **Activity:** You might try out Gamson et al.'s technique with various people. Pretend that you are about to conduct an experiment and ask the potential participants whether they are willing to take part in any of the following kinds of research. Show them the list from Gamson et al.'s study. Afterwards, debrief them by telling them the true purpose of your research and ask what they felt about the deception and the use of prior general consent.

Most people said "Yes" to all four and then were told that only the last kind of research was in progress. However, they had agreed to the third kind of research and thus consented to be deceived, probably without really being aware of it. So the experimenters felt ethically vindicated and they also had participants who were not primed to be suspicious about the purpose of the research.

The right to withhold data

Another means of offering informed consent is to do it retrospectively. After the research, during debriefing, the participant should be offered the opportunity to withhold their data. In essence, this gives them the same power as if they had refused to take part in the first place. If they withhold their data it is as if they had been informed at the start and not consented to take part. However, participants who exercise their right to withhold data may nevertheless have had experiences during the experiment that they would not have agreed to if they had realised beforehand what was going to happen to them.

Protection from Harm

"Harm" can mean a number of different things. It encompasses both physical and psychological damage. The key test of whether or not a participant has been harmed is to ask whether the risk of harm was greater than in ordinary life.

Physical harm

We might include excessive anxiety as physical harm because the results can be physically evident. For example, if you consider the description of some of Milgram's participants it is clear that they experienced physical as well as psychological harm—some of them had full-blown seizures, whereas many perspired and bit their lips. We also know from Chapter 5 that stress (a psychological state) has a physical basis.

Psychological harm

Psychological harm is much more difficult to measure, but there is no doubt that many studies infringe what might be called psychological "safety". It has been suggested that Milgram's participants would have felt disappointed with their own apparent willingness to obey unjust authority, which may have led to decreased self-esteem, a form of psychological harm

We can also consider the issues of **confidentiality** and the **right to privacy** as forms of protection of participants from psychological harm. Confidentiality means that no information (especially sensitive information) about any given participant should be revealed by the experimenter to anyone else. Right to privacy is a matter of concern when conducting observational research. It would not be appropriate, for example, to observe a person's behaviour in their bedroom without their permission. However, it would be acceptable to observe people in a public place, such as a park, where public scrutiny is expected.

Finally, you might consider the study by Berkun et al. (1962), which shows how enormously attitudes

When setting up observational research it is important to consider whether the participants would normally expect to be observed by strangers in the situation. For example, making observations of the people in this picture would be acceptable, but observing them in a changing room would not.

> ? If you recall, Watson and Rayner claimed that their experiment with Little Albert was ethical because the psychological harm inflicted was no greater than what he might experience in real life. Is this acceptable?

> **KEY TERM**
> **Protection of participants from psychological harm**: an ethical guideline, which states that participants should be protected from psychological harm, such as distress, ridicule, or loss of self-esteem. The risk of harm during the research study should be no greater than the participants would experience in their everyday life. Debriefing can be used to offer support if a study has resulted in psychological harm.

to psychological research have changed. This research didn't cause an outcry at the time, but would certainly be regarded as totally unacceptable nowadays. In one of Berkun et al.'s experiments to observe the effects of fear on behaviour, the participants were flying in a military plane when apparently one of the engines failed and they were misled to believe that the plane would ditch into the sea. There was another study in which soldiers were on their own out in the field, and could only communicate with base by using a radio transmitter. Some of the soldiers were exposed to explosions sounding like artillery shells, others were told that there had been an accident causing dangerous radioactive fallout in the area, and still others were enveloped in smoke so that they thought a forest fire had broken out. When they tried to contact base, they discovered that their radio transmitters would not work.

Some might argue that as these studies were carried out in an environment where individuals expect some loss of personal control this makes them ethically more acceptable. The BPS code (see page 269) does advise that risks should be similar to those that individuals experience in their everyday lives.

People used to be more accepting of the ways that experimental participants were treated, whereas this kind of physical and psychological harm is unacceptable now. Indeed, hard though it is to believe now, there was a time when many members of the public thought that much psychological research involved administering electric shocks to people!

CASE STUDY: ZIMBARDO'S DEFENCE

Zimbardo pointed out that all of his participants had signed a formal informed consent form, which indicated that there would be an invasion of privacy, loss of some civil rights, and harassment. He also noted that day-long debriefing sessions were held with the participants, so that they could understand the moral conflicts being studied. However, Zimbardo failed to protect his participants from physical and mental harm. It was entirely predictable that the mock guards would attack the mock prisoners, because that is exactly what had happened in a pilot study that Zimbardo carried out before the main study. ∎

EXAM HINT

If you are asked to identify two ethical issues, you should back this up with research:

- Deception works well for Milgram as there were so many forms of deception.
- Lack of protection works well for Zimbardo given the consequent distress for prisoners and guards in the study and the fact the study was ended early.

? **Why do you think that views about the kinds of research that are ethically acceptable have changed over the years?**

KEY TERM

Ethical guidelines: a written code of conduct designed to aid psychologists when designing and running their research. The guidelines set out standards of what is and is not acceptable. The code focuses on the need to treat participants with respect and to not cause them harm or distress. For example, the BPS code of conduct advises of "the need to preserve an overriding high regard for the well-being and dignity of research participants" (BPS, 1993).

Ethical Guidelines

The need for ethical control leads to the establishment of a set of rules or **ethical guidelines** that can be used to judge the acceptability of behaviour. During the Second World War, the Nazis conducted many horrific experiments with their concentration camp prisoners. At the end of the war, those responsible were tried in Nuremberg and one of the outcomes was that it became apparent that a code of ethics was needed as a reference point for what is acceptable in scientific research. The 10-point "Nuremberg code" was drawn up which introduced important concepts, such as that of informed consent.

This code has been adapted by professional bodies all over the world. Within psychology there are such organisations in every country, each with their own code of conduct, such as the British Psychological Society (BPS), the American Psychological Association (APA), and the German Psychology Association (Deutschen Gesellschaft für Psychologie, DGP).

Ethical committees

One way of trying to ensure that psychological research is ethically acceptable is by setting up **ethical committees**. Most institutions (e.g. universities; research units; hospitals) in which research is carried out now have their own ethical committee, which considers all research proposals from the perspective of the rights and dignity of the participants. The existence of such committees helps to

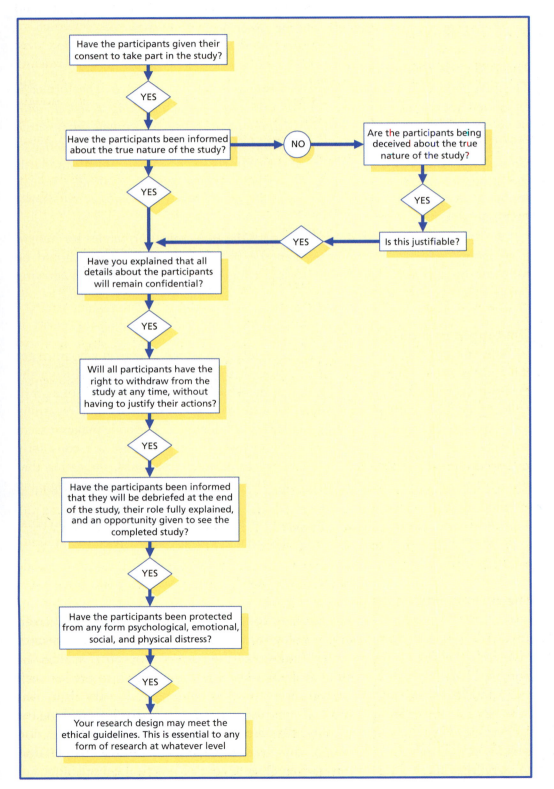

This flow chart shows ethical decisions to be taken by researchers designing a psychological study.

correct the power imbalance between experimenter and participant. However, if all the members of an ethical committee are researchers in psychology, they may be disinclined to turn down proposals from professional colleagues. For this and other reasons, it is desirable for every ethical committee to include some non-psychologists and at least one non-expert member of the public.

In the United States, every complaint against psychologists is investigated by the American Psychological Association's Committee on Scientific and Professional Ethics. If the complaint is found to be justified, then the psychologist concerned is either suspended or expelled from the Association.

The BPS code of conduct

The BPS code of conduct concerns (a) research and (b) practice. The former is enshrined in two documents: *Ethical principles for conducting research with human participants* (1993) and *Guidelines for the use of animals in research* (1965); the latter is represented in the *Guidelines for the professional practice of clinical psychology* (1983). As part of their efforts to encourage ethical standards the British Psychological Society has a system whereby suitably qualified Clinical, Occupational, Health Psychologists, and others are given the status of Chartered Psychologists.

We are only concerned in this book with the BPS ethical principles for human participants, which are summarised in the box on the right. They should be followed by all researchers in the United Kingdom, including students carrying out research as part of their course.

Limitations of ethical guidelines

In reality most professional guidelines have only some force. A person who infringes the code is not committing a crime, although they may well be barred from the professional organisation. There are other drawbacks. The establishment of a set of ethical guidelines enshrines its principles and may close off discussions regarding more appropriate solutions to a particular ethical dilemma. The code makes it seem as if there are ethical "truths". In fact, however, such guidelines are constantly reviewed, and they vary from one country to another (see later), indicating that there are no universal ethical truths (Gale, 1995). This is partly because of changing social attitudes.

Ethical codes may also take personal responsibility away from the individual researcher, and may invite individuals to find loopholes and "play the system" (Homan, 1991).

? **Without ethical guidelines, how difficult would it be to express misgivings about questionable research methods?**

The cost–benefit analysis

Diener and Crandall (1978) suggested the following drawbacks to the cost–benefit approach that underlies much psychological research. The cost–benefit approach involves weighing up the potential findings of the research (benefits) against the potential harm (costs). First of all it is difficult, if not impossible, to predict both costs and benefits prior to conducting a study. Second, even after the study it is hard to assess them accurately, partly because it can depend on who is making the judgements. A participant may judge the costs differently from the researcher, and benefits may be judged differently in years to come. Finally, cost–benefit analyses tend to ignore the important rights of individuals in favour of practical considerations of possible usefulness of the findings.

Ethical Guidelines for Research With Human Participants

(based on standards put forward by the British Psychological Society)

1. Introduction

Ethical guidelines are necessary to clarify the conditions under which psychological research is acceptable.

2. General

The essential principle is that the investigation should be considered from the standpoint of all participants; foreseeable threats to their psychological well-being, health, values, or dignity should be eliminated. It should be borne in mind that the best judge of whether an investigation will cause offence may be members of the population from which the participants in the research are to be drawn.

3. Consent

Participants should be informed of the objectives of the investigation and all other aspects of the research that might reasonably be expected to influence their willingness to participate—only such information allows informed consent to be given. Special care needs to be taken when research is conducted with children or with participants who have impairments that limit understanding and/or communication such that they are unable to give their real consent. This situation requires special safeguarding procedures.

4. Deception

Intentional deception of the participant over the purpose and general nature of the investigation should be avoided wherever possible. Participants should never be deliberately misled without extremely strong scientific or medical justification.

5. Debriefing

In the studies where the participants are aware that they have taken part in an investigation, when the data have been collected, the investigator should provide the participants with any necessary information to complete their understanding of the nature of the research in order to monitor any unforeseen negative effects or misconceptions.

6. Withdrawal from the investigation

At the onset of the investigation investigators should make plain to participants their right to withdraw from the research at any time, irrespective of whether or not payment or other inducement has been offered. In the light of experience of the investigation or as a result of debriefing, the participant has the right to withdraw retrospectively any consent given, and to require that their own data be destroyed.

7. Confidentiality

Subject to the requirements of legislation, information obtained about a participant during an investigation is confidential unless otherwise agreed in advance. Investigators who are put under pressure to disclose confidential information should draw this point to the attention of those exerting such pressure.

8. Protection of participants

Investigators have a primary responsibility to protect participants from physical and mental harm during the investigation. Normally the risk of harm must be no greater than in ordinary life, i.e. participants should not be exposed to risks greater than or additional to those encountered in their normal lifestyles. Where research may involve behaviour or experiences that participants may regard as personal and private, the participants must be protected from stress by all appropriate measures, including the assurance that answers to personal questions need not be given. In research involving children, great caution should be exercised when discussing the results with parents, teachers, or those in *loco parentis*, as evaluative statements may carry unintended weight.

9. Observational research

Studies based on observation must respect the privacy and psychological well-being of the individuals studied. Unless those being observed give their consent to being observed, observational research is only acceptable in situations where those observed would expect to be observed by strangers.

10. Giving advice

During research, an investigator may obtain evidence of psychological or physical problems of which a participant is apparently unaware. In such cases the investigator has a responsibility to inform the participant if the investigator believes that by not doing so the participant's future well-being may be endangered.

Baumrind (1975) has made the point that cost–benefit analyses inevitably lead to moral dilemmas, yet the function of ethical guidelines is precisely to avoid such dilemmas.

Cross-cultural comparisons

Kimmel (1996) compared the ethical codes produced by 11 different countries. An ethical code in psychology was first published in the United States in 1953. Several other countries (Australia, France, Germany, and the Netherlands) followed in the 1960s. The United Kingdom had its first ethical code in psychology in 1978, followed by Slovenia (1982), Canada (1986), and Scandinavia (1989). Finally, Spain and Switzerland produced ethical codes in the early 1990s.

There are important similarities among the ethical codes produced by the various countries. Most focus on three basic principles:

1. Protection of individuals from physical harm.
2. Protection of individuals from psychological harm.
3. Confidentiality of the data obtained from individual participants.

Confidentiality and anonymity

Anonymity is an important part of confidentiality. The discussion of case notes at a public lecture or in a published article or book must not involve identifying the client. A breach of this aspect of confidentiality could result in the client or client's relatives taking legal action against the therapist concerned. In situations like these, and of course with the permission of those involved, clients are usually identified by pseudonyms or initials only.

It is argued in nearly all of the ethical codes that informed consent and avoidance of deception are important in ensuring that the first two principles are achieved.

There are some differences in the ethical codes adopted by different countries. The French ethical code emphasises the fundamental rights of individuals, but has little to say about the ways in which research should be conducted, or on the importance of informed consent. The British ethical code differs from many others in that it is mainly concerned with research rather than the ethical issues posed by the professional activities of clinical psychologists. The ethical code in the Netherlands contains many very general statements, and so is hard to use in practice. One example is as follows: "The psychologist shall not employ methods that are in any way detrimental to the client's dignity or that penetrate into the client's private life deeper than is necessary for the objectives set." Another example is: "The psychologist shall do everything within his power to ensure that the client is entirely free to decide in a responsible manner whether to enter into the professional relationship."

There is a valuable feature of the American and Canadian ethical codes that is absent from the other nine. These two codes made use of an empirical approach, in which professional psychologists were asked to indicate how they *personally* resolved ethical issues. As a result, the American and Canadian codes contain case examples and applications of key research principles. These concrete examples make it easier for psychologists to follow ethical principles in the ways intended.

Justification of studies

As we have seen, it is essential ethically to focus on the interests of participants to ensure they are treated properly. However, we also need to take account of the potential importance of any research when deciding when it is acceptable. As the

American Psychological Association Committee on Ethical Standards in Psychological Research pointed out several years ago, "The general ethical question is whether there is a negative effect upon the dignity and welfare of the participants that the importance of the research does not warrant." In other words, deciding whether a given experiment should be carried out involves considering the potential benefits as well as the possible costs.

To what extent can we justify influence (majority and minority) and obedience research in terms of its importance? In both areas of research, the key findings have been extremely influential in developing our understanding of people as social beings. Most people are aware that their behaviour is influenced to some extent by other people, but Asch's research showed clearly that our behaviour is influenced considerably more by other people than we believe. The same is true of obedience research: people were aware that they often obey the instructions of authority figures. However, as Milgram (1974) discovered, they greatly underestimated the extent to which most people would obey very unreasonable (or even immoral) orders that might cause the death of another human being. Thus, the findings of Asch and of Milgram are important because they are surprising and unexpected.

Research on influence (majority and minority) and obedience is also important because it warns us of the dangers of being influenced too much by other people. It is desirable for us to be influenced to some extent by other group members and to obey authority much of the time. However, Asch and Milgram have shown us that too much conformity to others or too much obedience to authority can be very undesirable. The lessons learned from such research are of value to us in our everyday lives, and this practical relevance should be taken into account when deciding whether research on conformity and obedience should be permitted.

> **EXAM HINT**
> Prepare for two types of ethics essay questions:
>
> 1. "Were the studies justified given the ethical issues?"
> 2. "How successfully have psychologists resolved ethical issues?"
>
> The questions require two very different answers. See the essay plans in the AS Workbook for ideas.

SECTION SUMMARY

❖ The term "ethics" is used when considering moral behaviour among professionals. There are three key ethical issues:
1. Deception.
2. Informed consent.
3. Protection from harm.

❖ These issues apply especially to research in social psychology.

❖ Deception is not desirable but is sometimes necessary.   *Deception*
❖ It is not always harmful, such as in research involving incidental learning.
❖ Objections can be overcome by conducting role-playing experiments and carrying out adequate debriefing.

❖ Participants should always give informed consent when taking part in an   *Informed consent*
experiment, but this is not always possible as in the case of field experiments, retrospective case studies, and when the participants are children.
❖ Informed consent may be obtained by:
  – Presumptive consent.
  – General prior consent.
  – Withdrawal of data after retrospective consent.

Protecting participants from both psychological and physical harm

- ❖ Participants should be protected from both physical and psychological harm.
- ❖ Confidentiality and privacy are rights.
- ❖ Psychologists can assume that anything which occurs during "ordinary life" would not constitute "harm".
- ❖ An ethical code or set of guidelines is developed by separate professional bodies as a means of judging what behaviour is or is not acceptable to that professional group. In this country the British Psychological Society (BPS) regularly produces updated versions of ethical guidelines for psychologists.
- ❖ The problems with such guidelines include:
  - – They are difficult to enforce.
  - – It is hard to be objective and universal.
  - – There are variations in the ethical codes between different countries.
  - – The guidelines may remove personal responsibility from the researcher.
- ❖ In their attempt to justify research that breaks some of the codes, psychologists have suggested using a cost–benefit analysis, but this is difficult to quantify and there are cross-cultural difficulties.
- ❖ Case studies may be a useful way of demonstrating how to resolve ethical issues.

See pp.127–132 of the revision guide.

> You have reached the end of the chapter on social psychology. Social psychology is an approach or perspective in psychology. The material in this chapter has exemplified the way that social psychologists explain behaviour. They look at behaviour in terms of the ways in which other people affect our behaviour. Nowhere is this clearer than in social influence research. Ancient astrologers believed that people's actions were affected by an airy fluid that flowed down from the heavenly bodies. This fluid force-field was called *"influentia"*. The concept of influences comes from this—they are both invisible and very powerful, as we have seen.

FURTHER READING

Most of the topics discussed in this chapter are dealt with in various chapters in M. Hewstone and W. Stroebe (Eds.) (2001) *Introduction to social psychology (3rd Edn.)* Oxford, UK: Blackwell. Social influence and ethical issues are both considered in some detail in M.W. Eysenck (2000) *Psychology: A student's handbook* (Hove, UK: Psychology Press). Anyone who is considering carrying out any kind of study on human participants is strongly urged to consult the following before proceeding: British Psychological Society (2000) *Code of conduct*. Leicester, UK: British Psychological Society.

REVISION QUESTIONS

The examination questions aim to sample the material in this whole chapter. For advice on how to answer such questions refer to Chapter 1, Section 2.

Whenever you are asked to describe a study try to include some or all of the following details: research aim(s), participants, research method (e.g. experiment or observation), procedure, findings, and conclusion.

You will always have a choice of two questions in the AQA AS-level exam and 30 minutes in which to answer the question you choose:

Question 1 (AQA, 2004)

a. (i) Explain what is meant by social influence. (3 marks)
   (ii) Select *two* forms of social influence and explain the difference
       between them. (3 marks)
b. Outline the findings from **one** study of obedience to authority and give
   one criticism of this study. (3 marks + 3 marks)
c. "Most studies of majority influence have been carried out in laboratories
   and thus might not tell us much about the way people conform in the
   real world." Briefly outline findings from studies of majority influence
   (conformity) and consider the value of such studies. (18 marks)

Question 2

a. Explain what is meant by the terms "internal validity" and "external
   validity". (3 marks + 3 marks)
b. Describe the conclusions of *one* study of conformity and give *one* criticism
   of this study. (3 marks + 3 marks)
c. To what extent do studies of obedience infringe ethical guidelines? (18 marks)

The difference between "common sense" ideas about what causes behaviour and theories in psychology is that psychological theories are tested to see if they are true (or false!). In order to test theories systematically, psychologists conduct research.

SECTION 20
Quantitative and qualitative research methods p.275

Some research methods aim to quantify behaviour by counting frequencies (called quantitative research); others focus more on experience (called qualitative research). What are the relative advantages and limitations of both methods? How are they used? What ethical issues are raised?

Specification content: The nature and usage of the following research methods, their advantages and weaknesses, and how they relate to the scientific nature of psychology. The nature and usage of ethical guidelines in psychology. Experiments (including laboratory, field, and natural experiments), investigations using correlational analysis, naturalistic observations, questionnaires, and interviews.

SECTION 21
Research design and implementation p.296

In order to conduct meaningful research psychologists have developed standard procedures that aim to avoid bias.

Specification content: Aims and hypotheses (including the generation of appropriate aims, the formulation of different types of the experimental/alternative hypothesis [directional/non-directional]). Experimental design: independent groups, repeated measures, and matched participants. The design of naturalistic observations, questionnaires, and interviews. Factors associated with research design, including the operationalisation of the IV/DV, conducting pilot studies, control of extraneous variables, ways of assessing and improving reliability and internal and external validity. Ethical issues associated with research design and ways of dealing with them. The selection of participants including random, opportunity, and volunteer sampling. The relationship between researchers and participants (including demand characteristics and investigator effects).

SECTION 22
Data analysis p.314

A key aspect of the research process is the final interpretation of the results. What statistical methods enable us to interpret research findings and draw conclusions?

Specification content: The nature of qualitative data including strengths and weaknesses. Measures of central tendency and dispersion (including the appropriate use and interpretation of medians, means, modes, ranges, and standard deviations). The nature of positive and negative correlations and the interpretation of correlation coefficients. Graphs and charts, including the appropriate use and interpretation of histograms, bar charts, and scattergraphs.

RESEARCH METHODS

In a sense, we are all "armchair psychologists"—everyone has opinions about human behaviour. Psychologists don't just present theories about why people behave as they do, but they also seek to support or challenge these theories with research—systematic study of a problem—including experiments, interviews, and case studies. Throughout this book we have relied on such evidence as a means of analysing theories. In this chapter, we will consider the different methods used to conduct research, as well as other important features of the research process.

8

SECTION 20
QUANTITATIVE AND QUALITATIVE RESEARCH METHODS

The Scientific Approach

In common with other **sciences**, psychology is concerned with theories and with data. All sciences share one fundamental feature: they aim to discover facts about the world by using systematic and objective methods of investigation. The research process starts with casual observations about one feature of the world, for example, that people imitate the violence they see on television or that there are concerns about how the Nazis so easily made ordinary people obey them (see page 258). These observations collectively form a **theory** (a general explanation or account of certain findings or data). For example, someone might put forward a theory in which it is assumed that genetic factors play a role in all mental disorders.

Theories invariably produce a number of further expectations, which can be stated as a **research hypothesis**—a formal and unambiguous statement about what you believe to be true. Here is an example of a hypothesis: Anorexia nervosa is a condition that depends in part on genetic factors (see page 211). A hypothesis is stated with the purpose of attempting to prove or disprove it. And that is what scientists conduct research to do—prove or disprove their hypotheses. If it is disproved, then the theory has to be adjusted, and a new hypothesis produced, and tested, and so on. This process is shown in the diagram below.

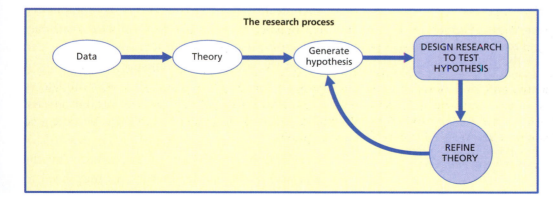

The research process

Data → Theory → Generate hypothesis → DESIGN RESEARCH TO TEST HYPOTHESIS → REFINE THEORY

KEY TERM

Research hypothesis: a statement put forward at the beginning of a study stating what you expect to happen, generated by a theory.

? What have you observed in your own life that could be the basis of real research? Can you think of a casual observation that leads you to think or believe something about behaviour?

Psychologists spend a lot of their time collecting data in order to test various hypotheses. In addition to **laboratory experiments**, they make use of many different methods of investigation, each of which can provide useful information about human behaviour.

The Experimental Method

The most-used method of investigation is the experimental method. Use of this method can involve experiments that are conducted in a laboratory or other contrived setting that is not the participants' natural environment. This method is not the *only* scientific method, but it is perhaps the *most* scientific because it is highly objective and systematic.

Dependent and independent variables

In order to understand what is involved in the experimental method, we will consider a concrete example. Put yourself in the position of the British psychologist Alan Baddeley (1966), who thought that acoustic coding was important in short-term memory, with people tending to confuse similar-sounding words when they tried to recall them in the right order. This led him to test the following hypothesis: More errors will be made in recalling acoustically similar word lists in the correct order than in recalling acoustically dissimilar word lists (see page 48).

In order to test this hypothesis, Baddeley compared the numbers of errors in short-term memory with lists of words that were acoustically similar and others that were acoustically dissimilar. This hypothesis refers to two **variables**—whether the list words were acoustically similar or dissimilar and the performance of the people learning the lists (errors made). The variable directly manipulated by the experimenter is called the **independent variable (IV)**, i.e. acoustic similarity vs dissimilarity. The other variable, the one affected by the IV, is called the **dependent variable (DV)**, i.e. how many errors are made on each type of list. (It is called *dependent* because it depends on something the experimenter controls.) The DV is some aspect of behaviour that is going to be measured or assessed, to decide whether or not the IV caused a change in behaviour.

A variable is something that varies! How long you sleep each night is a variable, whereas the number of days in a week is a fixed quantity.

The experimental process can be summarised thus:

- Experimenter acts on IV
- Changes in IV lead to changes in DV
- Changes in DV measured by experimenter

Apply this by referring to one of the experiments into short-term memory processing (e.g. Baddeley, 1966; Jacobs, 1887; Peterson & Peterson, 1959) and operationalise the IV and DV.

Experimental control

We come now to the most important principle of the experimental method: control. The IV is manipulated and the DV is free to vary. However, all other variables *must* be *controlled*, i.e. kept constant, so we can assume that the only variable causing any subsequent change in the DV *must* be the IV. In our example, we would control all aspects of the situation (**extraneous variables**) other than acoustic similarity by trying to make sure that both types of word lists had words of the same length, frequency of occurrence in the language, and so on. Other factors we may need to control when using the experimental method are

KEY TERM

Extraneous variables: variables that can affect the behaviour of participants in a research study, such as age, gender, intelligence, personality, type of task, noise, temperature etc. If extraneous variables are randomised across groups or held constant (e.g. all participants are the same age), then they should not bias results. However, if they vary systematically with the independent variable (e.g. if all the participants in the experimental group are male and all those in the control group are female) they become a *confounding* variable that may bias results.

always using the same room for the experiment, keeping the temperature the same, and having the same lighting.

Confounding variables

The variables that are *not* controlled may become confounding variables. Confounding variables are not of interest to the researcher, but may get in the way of the link between the independent and dependent variable. For example, suppose the words used in the acoustically similar lists were much longer words than those used in the acoustically dissimilar lists. We wouldn't know whether the higher number of errors with acoustically similar

The type of experimenter could act as a confounding variable. Some participants may feel more comfortable than others in the study situation...

lists than with acoustically dissimilar lists was due to the independent variable (acoustic similarity vs dissimilarity) or to the confounding variable of word length. The presence of any confounding variables is really serious, because it prevents us from being able to interpret our findings.

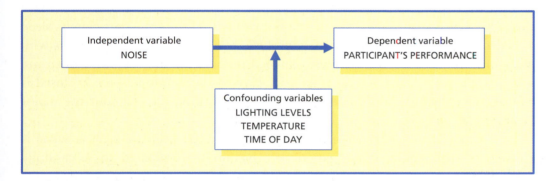

You might think that it would be easy to ensure that there were no confounding variables in an experiment. However, there are many well-known experiments containing confounding variables. Consider, for example, the study by Jenkins and Dallenbach (1924) described on page 65. They gave a learning task to a group of participants in the morning, and then tested their memory for the material later in the day. The same learning task was given to a second group of participants in the evening, and their memory was tested the following morning after a night's sleep.

What did Jenkins and Dallenbach find? Memory performance was much higher for the second group than for the first. They argued that this was due to there being less interference with memory when people are asleep than when they are awake. Can you see the flaw in this argument? The two groups learned the material at different times of day, and so time of day was a confounding variable. Hockey et al. (1972) discovered many years later that the time of day at which learning occurs is much more important than whether or not the participants sleep between learning and the memory test.

EXAM HINT
- There are so many different types of research methods question that it really is a good idea to prepare for the different types of question as you work your way through the topic.
- PRACTISE, PRACTISE, PRACTISE—it's more important than with any of the other topics to go through as many past exam papers as you can because unlike the other topics where you can know all the possible questions without looking at an exam paper, with this question you need to be familiar with the research summary that is part of the question.
- Contextualise—research methods questions often include the phrase ". . . in the context of this investigation", which means you must relate your answer to the study described in the question. For example, if you are asked to give a criticism don't generalise, but instead pick up on something specific from the summary in the question.

? **How else do you think students, as research participants, might differ from society in general?**

? **Can you think of another example of a situation in which a wrong causal inference could be made, i.e. *y* followed *x*, but *x* did not cause *y*?**

? **What are the main obstacles to replication in research using human participants?**

Participants in psychological experiment should be tested under constant controlled conditions (e.g. consistent lighting, temperature, and sound levels).

Participants and settings

Proper use of the experimental method requires careful consideration of the ways in which the participants are allocated to the various conditions. The main way of guarding against this possibility is by means of **randomisation**, in which participants are allocated at random.

Numerous studies are carried out using students as participants, raising the issue of whether students are representative of society as a whole. For example, students tend to be more intelligent and much younger than most members of society. However, they are representative in the sense that about half of all students are male and half are female.

Advantages of the experimental method

What is generally regarded as the greatest advantage of the experimental method is that it can allow us to establish causal (or cause and effect) relationships. In the terms we have been using, the independent variable in an experiment is often regarded as a cause, and the dependent variable is the effect. We assume that, if *y* (e.g. many errors in recall) follows *x* (e.g. acoustically similar word list), then it is reasonable to infer that *x* caused *y*.

But findings from studies based on the experimental method do *not* necessarily establish causality. For example, consider the following imaginary study. An experiment is carried out in a hot country. Half of the participants sleep in bedrooms with the windows open, and the other half sleep in bedrooms with the windows closed. Those sleeping in bedrooms with the windows open are found to be more likely to catch malaria. Having the window open or closed is *relevant* to catching the disease, but it tells us nothing direct about the major causal factor in malaria (infected mosquitoes).

The other major advantage of the experimental method concerns what is known as **replication**. If an experiment has been conducted in a carefully controlled way, other researchers should be able to repeat or replicate the findings. That would help to establish internal validity.

Replication is important in order to confirm an experimental result. If the result is "real", then it should be possible to obtain the same result when you repeat the experiment, but if it was a fluke, then it is not likely to be repeatable. Therefore, it is highly desirable in research to be able to replicate a study using precisely the same techniques and conditions. If the conditions aren't the same, that may explain why the results are not the same. This may allow us to make sense of the inconsistent findings from studies following up on Hofling et al.'s (1966) study on nurses obeying doctors when they shouldn't (see page 248).

Then there is the issue of objectivity. The experimental method is a more objective method than others. However, total objectivity is impossible since the experimenter's interests, values, and judgements will always have some influence, and the control of all confounding variables is impossible. Nevertheless, the experimental method offers the best chance of objectivity.

Disadvantages of the experimental method

It would appear that one disadvantage of most uses of the experimental method is that of artificiality. In fact, however, there are different views on this issue. Heather (1976) declared that the only thing learned from laboratory experiments is how people behave in laboratory experiments. But Coolican (1998) pointed out that, "In scientific investigation, it is often *necessary* to create artificial circumstances in order to *isolate* a hypothesised effect." If we are interested in studying basic cognitive processes, such as those involved in perception or attention, then the artificiality of the laboratory is unlikely to affect the results. On the other hand, if we are interested in studying social behaviour, then the issue of artificiality *does* matter.

Carlsmith et al. (1976) drew a distinction between **mundane realism** and **experimental realism** (see Chapter 7). Experimental realism (where participants are fooled that an artificial set-up is real) may be more important than mundane realism (where an artificial situation closely resembles a real-life situation) in producing findings that generalise to real-life situations.

An important reason why laboratory experiments are more artificial than other research methods is because the participants in laboratory experiments are aware that their behaviour is being observed. As Silverman (1977) pointed out, "Virtually the only condition in which a [participant] in a psychological study will not behave as a [participant] is if he does not know he is in one." One consequence of being observed is that the participants try to work out the experimenter's hypothesis, and then act accordingly. In this connection, Orne (1962) emphasised the importance of **demand characteristics**—the features of an experiment that "invite" participants to behave in certain predictable ways. Demand characteristics may help us to explain why Milgram (1963, 1974) found higher levels of obedience in his experiments at Yale University than in a run-down office building (65% vs 48%, respectively). Demand characteristics were also probably involved in Zimbardo's Stanford Prison Experiment, where the prison-like environment suggests that certain forms of behaviour were expected.

Another consequence of the participants in laboratory experiments knowing they are being observed is **evaluation apprehension**, a term used by Rosenberg (1965). The basic idea is that most people are anxious about being observed by the experimenter, and want him/her to evaluate them favourably. This may lead them to behave in ways they normally wouldn't.

Sigall, Aronson, and Van Hoose (1970) contrasted the effects of demand characteristics and evaluation apprehension on the task of copying telephone numbers. The experimenter told participants doing the task for the second time that he expected them to perform it at a rate *slower* than their previous performance. Adherence to demand characteristics would have led to slow performance, whereas evaluation apprehension and the need to be evaluated positively by the experimenter would have produced *fast* times. The participants actually performed more quickly than they had done before, indicating the greater importance of evaluation apprehension.

This conclusion was strengthened by the findings from a second condition, in which the experimenter not only said that he expected the participants to perform at a slower rate, but also told them that those who rush are probably obsessive-compulsive. The participants in this condition performed the task slowly, because they wanted to be evaluated positively.

Experiments and ethical issues

Ethical issues in psychological research are discussed in detail in Chapter 7, Section 19. Here are a few ethical issues of special relevance to laboratory experiments. In an experiment, there is a danger that the participants will be willing to behave in a laboratory in ways they would not behave elsewhere. Milgram (1974) found in

? If Milgram's experiment is an example of experimental realism, can you think of an example of mundane realism?

■ **Activity:** Experimental method
Asch's famous line-matching experiment had experimental realism (see p.229). Discuss with a partner or in a small group how you could adapt the experiment to increase its mundane realism, and produce a list of your recommendations.

Participants in psychological experiments usually try to perform the task set by the experimenter as well as they can, in order to gain his or her approval.

? Psychology students often use other psychology students as the participants in their research. What problems are likely to arise, for example, in terms of evaluation apprehension and demand characteristics?

his work on obedience to authority that 65% of his participants were prepared to give very intense electric shocks to someone else when the experiment took place in a laboratory at Yale University. In contrast, the figure was only 48% when the same study was carried out in a run-down office building.

Another ethical issue that applies especially to laboratory experiments concerns the participant's **right to withdraw** from the experiment at any time. It is general practice to inform participants of this right at the start of the experiment. However, participants may feel reluctant to exercise this right if they think it will cause serious disruption to the experimenter's research.

There can be ethical issues with experiments that initially seem totally acceptable. For example, consider the study by Bahrick et al. (1975; see page 51) on very long-term memory for the faces and names of fellow students. It is possible that this experiment may have caused unhappy or stressful memories to resurface for some of the participants.

Field Experiments

Field experiments are carried out in natural settings such as in the street, in a school, or at work. Some of the advantages of the experimental method are shared by both laboratory and field experiments. Field experiments, like laboratory experiments, involve direct control of the independent variable by the experimenter and also direct allocation of participants to conditions. This means that causal relationships can be determined (provided the experiment is carried out carefully and confounding variables are avoided!). Field experiments are also reasonably well controlled, which means that they can be replicated.

As an example of a field experiment, let us consider a study by Shotland and Straw (1976). They arranged for a man and a woman to stage an argument and a fight fairly close to a number of bystanders. In one condition, the woman screamed, "I don't know you!" In a second condition, she screamed, "I don't know why I ever married you!" When the bystanders thought the fight involved strangers, 65% of them intervened, against only 19% when they thought it involved a married couple. Thus, the experiment showed that people were less likely to lend a helping hand when it was a "lovers' quarrel" than when it was not. The bystanders were convinced that the fight was genuine, as was shown by the fact that 30% of the women were so alarmed that they shut the doors of their rooms, turned off the lights, and locked their doors.

Laboratory vs field experiments

The greatest advantage of laboratory experiments over field experiments is that it is generally easier to eliminate confounding variables in the laboratory than in the field. The experimenter is unlikely to be able to control every aspect of a natural situation. Another clear advantage of laboratory experiments over field experiments is that it is much easier to obtain large amounts of very detailed information from participants in the laboratory. Field experiments are limited in this way because (1) it is not generally possible to introduce bulky equipment into a natural setting, and (2) the participants in a field experiment are likely to realise they are taking part in an experiment if attempts are made to obtain a lot of information from them, and then the study loses its "naturalness".

One of the advantages of field experiments over laboratory experiments is that the behaviour of the participants is often more *typical* of their normal behaviour and therefore less artificial, i.e. field experiments tend to have greater external validity.

The respective strengths and weaknesses of laboratory experiments and field experiments can be summed up with reference to the two different kinds of validity:

- **Internal validity**—the validity of an experiment within the confines of the context in which it is carried out.
- **External validity**—the validity of an experiment outside the research situation itself.

Laboratory experiments tend to be high in internal validity but low in external validity. In contrast, field experiments are high in external validity but low in internal validity.

> **Field experiments**
>
> *Advantages*:
>
> - Establishes cause and effect relationships
> - Allows for replication
> - Behaviour of participants more typical than in a laboratory experiment, high external validity
>
> *Limitations*:
>
> - Ethical issues, such as a lack of voluntary informed consent
> - Low in internal validity, poor control
>
> To apply this, describe a field study and clearly identify its advantages and disadvantages (e.g. Bickman, 1974).

Field experiments and ethical issues

So far as field experiments are concerned, the main ethical issue relates to the principle of voluntary informed consent, which is regarded as central to ethical human research (see Chapter 7, Section 19). By their very nature, most field experiments don't lend themselves to obtaining informed consent from the participants. For example, the study by Shotland and Straw (1976) would have been rendered almost meaningless if the participants had been asked beforehand to give their consent to witnessing a staged quarrel! In addition, the participants in that study could reasonably have complained about being exposed to a violent quarrel.

Another ethical issue is that it is impossible to offer the right to withdraw or **debriefing**. Obviously participants who don't even know they are taking part in an experiment can't be given the right to withdraw from it!

> ■ **Activity:** Field experiments and ethics
> Find a partner, and toss a coin to see who is going to support doing field experiments and who is going to oppose them on ethical grounds. Then give yourselves 5 minutes to write an argument supporting your view of why these experiments are, or are not, ethically all right. Exchange your written comments, and discuss what each of you have said.

Quasi-experiments

"True" experiments based on the experimental method provide the best way of being able to draw causal inferences with confidence. However, there are often practical or ethical reasons why it is simply not possible to carry out a **true experiment**. So investigators often carry out what is known as a **quasi-experiment**—these "resemble experiments but

> **KEY TERMS**
>
> **Internal validity**: the validity of an experiment in terms of the context in which it is carried out. Concerns events within the experiment as distinct from external validity.
> **External validity**: the validity of an experiment outside of the research situation itself; the extent to which the findings of a research study are applicable to other situations, especially "everyday" situations.

are weak on some of the characteristics" (Raulin & Graziano, 1994). The two main differences between true and quasi-experiments are as follows:

1. The manipulation of the independent variable is often not under the control of the experimenter in quasi-experiments.
2. It is usually not possible to allocate the participants randomly to groups in quasi-experiments.

There are numerous hypotheses in psychology that can only be studied by means of quasi-experiments rather than true experiments. For example, if we are interested in studying the effects of divorce on young children we could do this by comparing children of divorced and married parents—but random allocation would not be possible! Studies in which pre-existing groups are compared often qualify as quasi-experiments, e.g. comparing the learning performance of males and females (gender is the IV).

A good example of a quasi-experiment is the famous study on personality and coronary heart disease (CHD) carried out by Friedman and Rosenman (1974; see page 163). They found that men with Type A personality (competitive; stressed; hostile) were much more likely to suffer from CHD than those with Type B personality (more relaxed and laid-back). This is a quasi-experiment because the researchers didn't allocate individuals at random to the Type A and Type B groups—these groups were pre-existing.

> **A true experiment involves manipulation of the IV by the experimenter. How is a quasi-experiment different?**

Quasi-experiments

Advantages

- Participants behave naturally
- Investigates the effects of independent variables that it would be unethical to manipulate

Limitations

- IV not directly manipulated
- Participants not allocated at random to conditions
- Difficult to identify what aspects of the independent variable have caused the effects on behaviour
- Requires ethical sensitivity

Natural experiments

In the studies just described, use is made of pre-existing groups of people. We might also make use of a naturally occurring event for research purposes. Such **natural experiments** are a kind of quasi-experiment. Such studies don't qualify as genuine experiments. Use of the experimental method requires that the independent variable is *manipulated* by the experimenter, but clearly the experimenter cannot decide whether a given person is going to be male or female for the purposes of the study!

An example of a natural experiment is a study reported by Charlton (1998) and Charlton et al. (2000). There has been much controversy as to whether watching television increases violence among young people, but it has proved hard to obtain convincing findings. The natural experiment was based on the introduction of television to the island of St. Helena, which is best known for the fact that Napoleon spent the last few years of his life there. Its inhabitants received television for the first time in 1995 (the naturally occurring event), but there was no evidence of any negative effects on the children. According to Charlton (1998):

> **What might be the practical uses of results such as those from the Mount St. Helena study?**

The argument that watching television turns youngsters to violence is not borne out, and this study on St. Helena is the clearest proof yet. The children have watched the same amounts of violence, and in many cases the same programmes as British children. But they have not gone out and copied what they have seen on TV.

Charlton et al. (2000) compared the children's playground behaviour 4 months before and 5 years after television broadcasting began. There was no increase at all in anti-social behaviour (e.g. fighting), and hardly any changes in helping and cooperative behaviour.

The issue of whether or not there is a correlation between violence on television and aggressive behaviour is frequently debated in the media.

Another example of a natural experiment is the study by Hodges and Tizard (1989; see page 121) on the long-term effects of privation in children who had been taken into care when very young. Some of the children were adopted whereas others returned to their natural home. The decision about whether each child should be adopted or should be restored to his/her home was the naturally occurring event outside the control of the researchers. Contrary to what might have been expected, the adopted children on average showed better emotional adjustment than the restored children.

Advantages of natural experiments

The main advantage is that the participants in natural experiments are often not aware they are taking part in an experiment, even though they are likely to know that their behaviour is being observed, so they behave more naturally. Also natural experiments allow us to study the effects on behaviour of independent variables that it would be unethical for the experimenter to manipulate. For example, consider the study by Hodges and Tizard (1989). No ethical committee would have allowed children to be taken into care and then either adopted or restored to their natural home to satisfy the requirements of the researchers. The obvious risks to the well-being of the children concerned mean that studies on the effects of adoption can only possibly be carried out as a natural experiment rather than as a true experiment.

Studies on flashbulb memories (vivid and long-lasting memories of dramatic events) provide another example (see study by Conway et al., 1994, page 72). It would be unethical for researchers deliberately to expose participants to tragic and stressful events. However, they have no responsibility for events such as 11 September 2001, or the death of Princess Diana, and so it is acceptable to study them.

Limitations of natural experiments

The greatest limitation occurs because the participants have not been assigned at random to conditions, so observed differences in behaviour between groups may be due to differences in the types of participants in the groups rather than to the effects of the independent variable. For example, in the study by Hodges and Tizard (1989), there was evidence that the children who were adopted were *initially* better adjusted than the children who were restored to their natural home. Thus, the finding that the adopted children subsequently showed better emotional adjustment than the restored children may be due to their personality or early experiences rather than to the fact that they were adopted.

It is usually possible to check whether the participants in the various conditions are comparable, with respect to variables such as age, sex, socioeconomic status, and so on. If the groups do differ significantly in some respects irrelevant to the independent variable, then this greatly complicates the task of interpreting the findings of a natural experiment.

The other major limitation of natural experiments involves the independent variable. In some natural experiments, it is hard to know exactly what aspects of the independent variable have caused any effects on behaviour. For example, it is usually assumed in studies on flashbulb memories that participants remember dramatic world events better than more ordinary events because of their emotional reaction when they first learn about the dramatic event. However, it is also possible that dramatic events are better remembered because they are talked about more with other people and are thought about more than is the case with ordinary events.

Natural experiments and ethical issues

It can be argued that there are fewer ethical issues with natural experiments than with many other kinds of research, as the experimenter is not responsible for the fact that the participants have been exposed to the independent variable. But various ethical issues include: (1) the question of voluntary informed consent, as the participants are typically not aware that they are taking part in an experiment, and (2) experimenters need to be sensitive to the situation in which the participants find themselves. For example, the researchers are not responsible for the dramatic world events causing flashbulb memories. However, they need to be aware of the sensitivities of some of the participants (e.g. some of them may have lost relatives in the 11 September attacks on New York).

■ **Activity:** In groups of three, design a summary table to illustrate the ethical issues involved in laboratory, field, and natural experiments, with each group member taking one type of experiment then reporting back to the group.

Studies Using Correlational Analysis

If we were interested in the hypothesis that watching violence on television leads to aggressive behaviour, we could test this hypothesis by obtaining information from a number of people about: (1) the amount of violent television they watched, and (2) the extent to which they behaved aggressively in various situations. If the hypothesis is correct, we would expect that those who have seen the most violence on television would tend to be the most aggressive, i.e. this study would be looking for a **correlation**, or association, between watching violent programmes and being aggressive. The closer the link between them, the greater would be the correlation or association.

One of the best-known uses of the correlational approach is in the study of life events and stress-related illnesses. For example, Rahe et al. (1970; see page 153) found that there was a significant positive correlation between the stress of recent life events (taking account of the number and severity of these events) and physical illness. These findings support those of many other researchers.

? **When would one have to use a correlational design?**

Limitations of correlational studies

Correlational designs are generally regarded as inferior to experimental designs, because it is hard (or impossible) to establish cause and effect. In our first example, the existence of an association between the amount of television violence watched and aggressive behaviour would certainly be consistent with the hypothesis that watching violent programmes can *cause* aggressive behaviour. However, it could equally be that aggressive individuals may choose to watch more violent programmes than those who are less aggressive, in other words the causality operates in the other direction. Or there is a third variable accounting for the association between watching violent programmes and aggressive behaviour, e.g. people in disadvantaged families may watch more television and their deprived circumstances may also cause them to behave aggressively. If that were the case, then the number of violent television programmes watched might have no direct effect at all on aggressive behaviour.

In our second example (Rahe et al., 1970), it is possible that stressful life events play a role in causing physical illness. However, it is also possible that illness increases the chance of experiencing life events. Alternatively, it may be that there is a third variable at work which accounts for the correlation between stressful life events and physical illness. Perhaps some people are naturally rather weak physically and psychologically, and this makes them tend to experience negative life events and to suffer from physical illness.

Correlation or causation?

Advantages of correlational studies

In spite of the interpretive problems posed by the findings of correlational studies, there are several reasons why psychologists continue to use this method. First, many hypotheses cannot be examined directly by means of experimental designs. For example, the hypothesis that life events cause various physical diseases cannot be tested by forcing some people to experience lots of negative events! All that can be done is to examine correlations or associations between the number and severity of negative life events and the probability of suffering from various diseases. Such a study might start with the hypothesis that "life events are related to ill health", and a correlational study would obtain data for each individual about, for example, the number and types of life events (negative and positive) they have experienced over a period of time and the types of physical illness from which they have suffered.

Second, it is often possible to obtain large amounts of data on a number of variables in a correlational study much more rapidly and efficiently than would be possible using experimental designs. Use of a questionnaire, for example, would permit a researcher to investigate the associations between aggressive behaviour and a wide range of activities (such as watching violent films in the cinema, reading violent books, being frustrated at work or at home).

Third, correlational research *can* produce reasonably definite information about causal relationships if there is *no* association between the two **co-variables**. For example, if it were found that there was no association at all between stressful life events and physical illness, this would provide fairly strong evidence that physical illnesses are *not* caused by stressful life events.

Correlational studies

Advantages

- Allows study of hypotheses that cannot be examined directly
- More data on more variables can be collected more quickly than in an experimental set-up
- Problems of interpretation are reduced when no association is found

Limitations

- Interpretation of results is difficult
- Cause and effect cannot be established
- Direction of causality is uncertain
- Variables other than the one of interest may be operating

To apply this, consider a correlational study that looks at the relationship between stress and the immune system, or stress and personality. With reference to this study identify the advantages and disadvantages as outlined above.

Finally, the greatest use of **correlational analysis** is in prediction, because if you find that two variables are correlated, you can predict one from another. It is also a useful method when manipulation of variables is impossible.

Correlational studies and ethical issues

There is the possibility that the public at large will misinterpret the findings from correlational studies. For example, the finding that there is a correlation between the amount of television violence watched by children and their level of aggression led many influential people to argue that television violence was having a damaging effect. In other words, they mistakenly supposed that correlational evidence can demonstrate a causal relation. Television companies may have suffered from such over-interpretation of findings. In similar fashion, the findings on Type A and coronary heart disease reported by Friedman and Rosenman (1974) may have unduly alarmed many people who feared that their Type A personality meant they were almost certain to have a heart attack.

Correlational analyses are often used in research that raises political and/or social issues. For example, consider the correlational evidence suggesting that individual differences in intelligence depend in part on genetic factors. Some people have argued, mistakenly, that this implies that *race* differences in intelligence also depend on genetic factors. The key ethical issue here (and in many other correlational studies) is for the researcher to be fully aware of the social sensitivity of the findings that he/she has obtained, and the lack of causal evidence.

Naturalistic observation, for example, observing children's behaviour in a playground, can provide more extensive information than a laboratory study. However, the participants' behaviour may alter if they are aware that they are being observed.

Naturalistic Observation

Naturalistic observation involves methods designed to examine behaviour *without* the experimenter interfering with it in any way. This approach was originally developed by the **ethologists** such as Lorenz (see Chapter 4) who studied non-human animals in their natural habitat and discovered much about the animals' behaviour. An example of the use of naturalistic observation in human research is the attachment study by Anderson (1972). He observed children in a London park and noticed that it was rare indeed to see a child under the age of 3 who wandered further than 200 feet from his/her mother before returning, perhaps just to touch her knee or come close.

Naturalistic observation was also used by Schaffer and Emerson (1964), who carried out a longitudinal observational study on children. They obtained clear evidence that children differ considerably from each other in their attachment behaviour. However, most children develop fairly strong attachments to one or more adults during early childhood. We can compare the approach to attachment behaviour taken by Schaffer and Emerson (1964) with that of Ainsworth and Bell (1970; see page 95). Ainsworth and Bell used structured observation, which has been criticised for being rather artificial.

? What advantages might be gained by observing children in a naturalistic environment rather than in a laboratory?

Intrusion

One of the key requirements of the method of naturalistic observation is to avoid *intrusion*. Dane (1994, p.1149) defined this as "anything that lessens the participants' perception of an event as natural". Intrusion can occur through the environment being one the participants regard as a research setting, or through the participants being aware that they are being observed, e.g. with the researcher in the same room—in this case, the researcher may try to become a familiar and predictable part of the situation before any observations are recorded.

Advantages of naturalistic observation

First, if the participants are unaware that they are being observed, this method provides a way of observing people behaving naturally, so there are no problems from demand characteristics and evaluation apprehension (seeking the approval of the researcher).

Second, observational data can be reliable or consistent provided that a few simple rules are followed. It is important for the researchers to spend some initial time observing the behaviour of participants in order to identify the relevant categories of behaviour. After that they need to develop precise categories. Finally, observers need to be trained in the use of the system of categories to produce high reliability. This can be assessed by correlating the observational records of two or more different observers, producing a measure of inter-observer reliability (sometimes known as *inter-rater* or *inter-judge reliability*). Naturalistic observation studies increasingly involve the use of video recordings, and this can be helpful in ensuring that all observers are categorising behaviour in the same way.

Third, many studies based on naturalistic observation provide richer and fuller information than typical laboratory experiments. For example, Schaffer and Emerson's (1964) naturalistic observations on attachment behaviour in children can be compared with Ainsworth and Bell's (1970) structural observation research. Schaffer and Emerson's approach allowed them to show very clearly that young children often form multiple important attachments, an important finding that was not considered by Ainsworth and Bell.

Fourth, it is sometimes possible to use naturalistic observation when other methods cannot be used, e.g. with unwilling participants, or where they cannot be disrupted at work. And finally, some participants don't cope well with other forms of research, such as children and non-human animals, so naturalistic observation is a more suitable method.

■ **Activity:** Observations
This could be done in small groups. People often assume that boys' play is more rough than girls' play. This is a casual observation, but you could devise a hypothesis from it, then operationalise this. How would you do your observations, and how would you ensure inter-observer reliability? What behavioural categories would you use? What might be problems in doing this naturalistic observation? One person should act as the recorder and make a list of what the group says, and this could then be shared with other groups.

As we have seen, naturalistic observations can provide reliable (consistent) and valid information provided that a few simple rules are followed. However, it is time-consuming to construct a good set of categories of behaviour and to have fully trained observers, and many researchers have not done these things. As a result, the data emerging from naturalistic observation studies are often unreliable.

Limitations of naturalistic observation

There are a number of limitations. First, the experimenter has essentially no control over the situation, making it very hard (or impossible) to decide what caused the participants to behave as they did. Second, the participants are often aware they are being observed, so their behaviour is not natural. Third, we have seen that there are ways of ensuring reliable observational data, but they are time-consuming. Many researchers have not taken the time to develop

Naturalistic observation

Advantages

- People tend to behave naturally
- Information that is gathered is rich and full
- Can be used where other methods are not possible

Limitations

- Experimenter has no control over the situation
- Participants can be aware of being watched and this can affect behaviour
- Problems of reliability due to bias or imprecise categorisation of behaviour
- Problems of validity due to observers' or coders' assumptions
- Replication is not usually possible

To apply this, consider a developmental study that has used observation as its research method. Using this study, identify its advantages and limitations.

precise categories of behaviour and to train their observers thoroughly, leading to unreliable data. Fourth, there can be problems of replication with studies of naturalistic observation. For example, consider naturalistic observation studies carried out in schools. As you will probably agree, there are enormous differences in character among schools, and this is likely to produce large differences in observational data from one school to the next.

Naturalistic observations and ethical issues

All research in psychology raises ethical issues, and this has led to the development of ethical guidelines for use by researchers (see page 269). Naturalistic observation poses ethical problems if the participants don't realise their behaviour is being observed (**undisclosed observation**), e.g. the use of one-way mirrors and participants being observed in public places, as voluntary informed consent cannot be given. There can also be problems about **confidentiality**—even if names are not mentioned in the published report, many people reading it will probably be able to

? Sometimes it is not possible to write field notes as events are happening. What does memory research tell us about the usefulness and accuracy of notes written after the event?

identify the place because they know that the researchers made detailed observations there.

Another issue was raised by Coolican (1994) in his discussion of the work of Whyte (1943). Whyte joined an Italian street gang in Chicago, and became a **participant observer**. The problem he encountered in interpreting his observations was that his presence in the gang influenced their behaviour. A member of the gang expressed this point as follows: "You've slowed me down plenty since you've been down here. Now, when I do something, I have to think what Bill Whyte would want me to know about it and how I can explain it." This is an important ethical concern related to observations. The observer has actually changed the participants, possibly without their prior consent.

Try to fit in as a member of the group and remain detached as an observer.

Interviews and Questionnaires

Interviews and questionnaires come in many different forms. Interviews vary in terms of the amount of structure and whether they are conducted face to face (interviews) or require written answers (**questionnaires**). Coolican (1994) identified the following interview types.

Non-directive interviews

These possess the least structure, with the person interviewed (the interviewee) being free to discuss almost anything he/she wants. The interviewer guides the discussion and encourages the interviewee to be more forthcoming. Such interviews are used in treatment of mental disorders, but have little relevance to research.

Informal interviews

These resemble non-directive interviews, in that the interviewer listens patiently and focuses mainly on encouraging the interviewee to discuss issues in more depth or detail. But there are certain general topics that the interviewer wishes to explore. One well-known example was a large-scale study of workers at the Hawthorne Western Electric plant (see page 309) that explored industrial relations via a series of interviews. What emerged was that the relatively minor issues initially raised by the workers generally reflected deeper and more serious worries (Roethlisberger & Dickson, 1939).

Semi-structured or guided interviews

These possess a little more structure than informal interviews. The interviewer identifies the issues to be addressed beforehand. During the interview, further decisions are made about how and when to raise these issues. All interviewees are asked precisely the same questions in the same order.

There are various types of interviews used for psychological experimentation, from non-directive interviews to fully structured designs that have a standard set of questions with restricted-choice answers.

Clinical interviews

These resemble the guided interview. All of the interviewees are asked the same questions, but the choice of follow-up questions depends on the answers given. The researcher can be given the flexibility to ask questions in various ways. Often used by clinical psychologists to assess patients with mental disorders. Clinical interviews give interviewers the flexibility to explore interesting or unexpected answers as they see fit.

Fully structured interviews

In this type of interview, a standard set of questions is asked in the same fixed order to all of the interviewees, and they are only allowed to choose their answers from a restricted set of possibilities (e.g. "Yes", "No", "Don't know"). As Coolican (1994, pp.121–122) points out, "this approach is hardly an interview worth the name at all. It is a face-to-face data-gathering technique, but could be conducted by telephone or by post."

Questionnaires

It is important to note at the outset that questionnaires are used for many purposes. For example, questionnaires are used to assess personality (e.g. Friedman & Rosenman, 1974, research on Type A personality and coronary heart disease). They are also used to assess the types of life events that someone has experienced over a period of time (e.g. the Social Readjustment Rating Scale developed by Holmes & Rahe, 1967). In addition, however, some written questionnaires are a special form of interview, where respondents are asked to record their own answers. The advantage of this method is that large amounts of data can be collected at relatively little cost. However the method is clearly only suitable for participants who are literate and willing to spend time filling in a questionnaire, so the sample is often biased. Designing questionnaires requires considerable skill, as discussed in the Case Study on the right.

Advantages of interviews

As might be expected, the precise advantages depend on the type of interview. Unstructured interviews can produce *qualitative* rather than quantitative data. The difference is that qualitative data typically involve using various categories (e.g. generally suitable; generally unsuitable), whereas quantitative data involve attaching numbers (e.g. 7 out of 10 for general suitability). The differences between quantitative and qualitative data are discussed more fully on page 293.

Structured interviews can compare the responses of different interviewees, all of whom have been asked the same questions. Another advantage is good reliability, in that two different interviewers are likely to obtain similar responses from an interviewee when they ask exactly the same questions in the same order. Also there is a reasonable probability of being able to replicate the findings in another study. Finally, it is usually fairly easy to analyse the data obtained from them because the data tend to be more *quantitative* rather than qualitative.

Limitations of interviews

Unstructured interviews have a problem with the unsystematic variation of information obtained from different interviewees, making the data hard to analyse. Also, what the interviewee says is determined in a complex way by the interaction between him/her and the interviewer, i.e. the personality and other characteristics of the interviewer typically influence the course of the interview, and make it hard to work out which of the interviewee's contributions are and are not affected by the interviewer—this is called **interviewer bias**. Finally, the fact that the information obtained from interviewees is influenced by the interviewer means the data obtained can be viewed as unreliable.

? **Have you ever been interviewed while out shopping? How would you classify this interview style?**

? **How would research results be affected by the possibility that people might decide to give the socially acceptable response to statements such as "Smacking children is an appropriate form of punishment"?**

CASE STUDY: QUESTIONNAIRE CONSTRUCTION

The first step is to generate as many ideas as possible that might be relevant to the questionnaire. Then discard those ideas that seem of little relevance, working on the basis (Dyer, 1995, p.114) that: "It is better to ask carefully designed and quite detailed questions about a few precisely defined issues than the same number on a very wide range of topics."

Closed and open questions

There is an important distinction between closed and open questions. Closed questions invite the respondent to select from various possible answers (e.g. yes or no; yes, unsure, or no; putting different answers in rank order), whereas open questions allow respondents to answer in whatever way they prefer. Most questionnaires use closed questions, because the answers are easy to score and to analyse. Open questions have the disadvantage of being much harder to analyse, but they can be more informative than closed questions.

Ambiguity and bias

Questions that are ambiguous or are likely to be interpreted in various ways should be avoided. Questions that are very long or complicated should also be avoided, because they are likely to be misunderstood. Emotive questions should be avoided because they make people defensive and result in answers that are not true. Finally, questions that are biased should be avoided. Here is an example of a biased question: "In view of the superiority of Britain, why should we consider further political integration with the rest of Europe?"

Attitude scale construction

One of the most common ways to construct an attitude scale is to use the Likert procedure. Initially various statements are collected together, and the participants' task is to indicate their level of agreement on a 5-point scale running from "strongly disagree" at one end to "strongly agree" at the other end. For positive statements (e.g. "Most Hollywood stars are outstanding actors"), strongly disagree is scored as 1 and strongly agree as 5, with intermediate points being scored 2, 3, or

4. For negative statements (e.g. "Most Hollywood stars are not outstanding actors"), the scoring is reversed so that strongly disagree is scored as 5 and strongly agree as 1.

■ **Activity:** Construct your own questionnaire

1. Select an area of study from the work you are doing in class.
2. Research the topic to gain ideas about the possible questions to ask.
3. Develop sub-topics to investigate. It may be best to generate questions with a group of people because more varied ideas are produced (brainstorming). Each group member should put forward ideas which are received uncritically by the group. Later, the group can select the best questions.
4. Write the questions. It may help to include some irrelevant "filler" questions to mislead the respondent as to the main purpose of the survey.
5. Decide on a sequence for the questions. It is best to start with easy ones.
6. Write standardised instructions, which must include guidance regarding respondents' ethical rights.
7. Conduct a pilot run and redraft your questionnaire in response to areas of confusion or difficulty.
8. After you have conducted your questionnaire, analyse the results using descriptive data (see next section, "Data Analysis").
9. Debrief participants and advise them of your findings. ■

Question styles: A survey on chocolate

Closed question: Do you like chocolate? (tick one)

YES   NO   NOT SURE

Open question: Why do you like or dislike chocolate?
Ambiguous question: Is chocolate likely to do you more harm than a diet that consists mainly of junk food?
Biased question: Plain chocolate is a more sophisticated taste than milk chocolate. Which type do you prefer?

In structured interviews, what the interviewee says may be somewhat constrained and artificial because of the high level of structure built into the interview. Interviewees may find this off-putting and it may lead them to give short, formal answers. Also, there is little or none of the flexibility associated with unstructured interviews.

Three limitations are common to all types of interview (with the first two also being common to most questionnaires). First, there is the issue of **social desirability bias**. Most people want to present a favourable impression of themselves to other people, so they may distort their answers to personal questions. For example, people are much more willing to admit that they are unhappy when filling in a questionnaire anonymously than when being interviewed (Eysenck, 1990). This

People adjust what they say to fit the circumstances.

can be overcome by using a **lie scale**, where some of the questions assess the extent to which the respondent is telling the truth or whether they are giving socially desirable answers. For example, a question about honesty might be included: "Do you always tell the truth?" An honest answer would be "No". If a respondent demonstrates a social desirability bias on a range of lie scale questions, then we might exclude their responses from our sample.

A second problem with interviews is that we can only extract information of which the interviewee is consciously aware. This is a significant limitation, because people are often unaware of the reasons why they behave in certain ways (Nisbett & Wilson, 1977). Third, many interviewers lack some of the skills necessary to conduct interviews successfully. Good interviewers can make an interview seem natural, are sensitive to non-verbal cues, and have well-developed listening skills (Coolican, 1994).

Interviews and ethical issues

Interviews (especially clinical interviews) are often concerned with personal issues about which the interviewee is sensitive, raising the issue of confidentiality. There are various ways in which confidentiality can be broken. For example, Coolican (1994) discussed a study by Vidich and Bensman (1958) in which direct quotations from interviewees in Springdale in the United States were published. Made-up names were used, but the people of Springdale were able to identify the actual individuals on the basis of what they said.

Confidentiality can also be broken if a detailed written account or video-recording of an interview falls into the wrong hands. Finally, of course, the interviewer himself/herself could disclose sensitive personal information about the interviewee to other people.

There is another ethical issue that is of particular importance with structured interviews. Interviewees may be aware that several other interviewees are being asked the same questions, and that their answers will be compared, so some interviewees may feel that they must answer embarrassing questions in order not to spoil the research study.

? Think back to what you learned about eyewitness testimony (see p. 79). How might Loftus' work relate to researching by asking questions? What would researchers have to be very careful about in forming questions for the interview?

Interviews and questionnaires

Advantages:

- Unstructured interviews can be more revealing
- Structured interviews permit comparison between interviewees and facilitate replication
- Questionnaires allow for collection of large amounts of data

Limitations:

- Interviewer bias
- Social desirability bias
- People don't always know what they think
- Good interviewing requires skill

To apply this, consider a study that has used the interview technique to obtain data (e.g. Friedman & Rosenman, 1959). Either obtain a copy of the original journal article to see what sort of questions were asked or try to design your own questions that might have been asked.

Quantitative and Qualitative Research Methods Compared

In this section, we have been considering various research methods. Most of them are **quantitative research methods**, meaning that the emphasis is on measuring behaviour by assigning numbers to it. Most studies involving experiments (whether laboratory experiments, field experiments, quasi-experiments, or natural experiments) tend to use quantitative research methods. In previous chapters we have discussed several Key Studies using quantitative research methods. Here are a few examples showing the main data of interest:

■ **Activity:** Divide the class into small groups and ask each group to prepare one kind of interview technique. They should present a short demonstration to the class. Which ones worked best? What problems arose? Which would be the best ways to collect data?

1. Peterson and Peterson (1959): Number of trials on which trigram was recalled.
2. Kiecolt-Glaser et al. (1995): Length of time for a wound to heal.
3. Milgram (1963): Maximum level of electric shock delivered by the participant to the learner.

There are also **qualitative research methods**, in which there is *no* emphasis on expressing participants' behaviour in numerical form. Instead, the focus is on participants' experience and/or assigning their behaviour to a given category. Most research involving interview techniques is qualitative in nature. Very often we are trying to obtain an overall impression of what someone else is like and this overall impression is expressed in qualitative terms. Other examples of qualitative research methods are discussed on page 314. Of the Key Studies we have discussed, a few are closer to a qualitative approach than a quantitative one in terms of the main data of interest:

1. Ainsworth and Bell (1970): Three categories of attachment style.
2. Holland et al. (1988): Twin of an individual with anorexia nervosa has or does not have anorexia nervosa. This study is in some ways quantitative, in that the focus is on percentages of twins showing concordance or agreement in diagnosis with their co-twin. However, since each individual is assigned to one of two categories (i.e. absence of anorexia vs presence of anorexia), the basic data are in the form of categories rather than numbers.

Here are some general points relating to the differences between quantitative and qualitative research methods:

- Many research methods produce quantitative *and* qualitative data. For example, we can measure obedience to authority in terms of willingness to administer shocks of various intensities, but we can also obtain qualitative measures by asking participants about the thoughts and feelings they had while deciding what to do. We can use interviews to produce a qualitative impression of the interviewee or we can give him/her numerical marks on various measures (e.g. honesty; clarity of thinking). In view of their differing strengths, it is very often a good idea to collect *both* qualitative and quantitative data when carrying out a study.
- Quantitative research methods tend to produce precise data that can be obtained in subsequent experiments.

? Can you describe the difference between quantitative and qualitative data?

- Quantitative research methods typically produce data that are limited in scope, focusing on only a few aspects of participants' behaviour.
  - Qualitative research methods often produce potentially rich data, as when interview techniques obtain information about the interviewee's past life.
  - Qualitative research methods tend to produce imprecise data that are hard to repeat in subsequent research.

> ■ **Activity:** List all the research methods covered in this section and, for each of them, say how they might produce qualitative and quantitative data.

SECTION SUMMARY

The scientific approach

❖ All research is scientific. The scientific method involves:
  - Making observations.
  - Formulating theories that generate hypotheses.
  - Testing the hypotheses by designing research, then collecting data, and finally revising the theory in line with the new data.

The experimental method

❖ The key principle of the experimental method is that an independent variable is manipulated (with all confounding variables controlled) in order to observe its effect on a dependent variable.
❖ Participants should be randomly allocated to conditions to further rule out confounding variables.
❖ Use of the experimental method often (but by no means always) allows us to infer causality, and it aims to be replicable.
❖ The experimental method is used in laboratory and field experiments.

Laboratory experiments

❖ Advantages of laboratory experiments:
  - Laboratory experiments permit greater removal of confounding variables.
  - They also allow more detailed data collection than field experiments.
❖ However, they tend to be artificial (lacking external validity and mundane realism).
❖ This artificiality can be compensated for by increased experimental realism (internal validity).
❖ Other concerns include:
  - The problems arising from knowing you are being observed (demand characteristics and evaluation apprehension).
  - Ethical issues such as being obedient to authority and the right to withdraw.

Field experiments

❖ Advantages of field experiments:
  - Field experiments are less artificial (higher external validity) than laboratory experiments.
  - They suffer less from factors such as demand characteristics and evaluation apprehension.

❖ Limitations of field experiments:
  – They are less controlled (lower internal validity).
  – They create ethical problems in terms of lack of informed consent.

❖ Quasi-experiments fall short of true experiments because: *Quasi-experiments*
  – The experimenter has not manipulated the independent variable.
  – The participants are not allocated at random to conditions.
❖ Natural experiments are quasi-experiments involving some naturally occurring independent variable.
❖ Advantages of natural experiments:
  – One advantage of natural experiments is that the participants are unaware they are taking part in an experiment, which prevents demand characteristics.
  – Natural experiments also permit the study of variables that couldn't ethically be manipulated by an experimenter.
❖ Limitations of natural experiments:
  – These include problems of interpreting the findings due to a lack of randomisation.
  – There is also an ethical concern about taking advantage of people at a time of possible high stress.

❖ Advantages of correlational analysis: *Investigations using*
  – Many issues can only be studied by assessing correlations or associations   *correlational analysis*
    between variables.
  – Correlational studies determine the extent that co-variables vary together, and offer the possibility of obtaining large amounts of data very rapidly.
❖ Limitations of correlational analysis:
  – Investigations using correlational analysis are less useful than experimental designs, because they don't permit inferences about causality.
  – In terms of ethical concerns, we should be wary of misinterpretations of correlational evidence.

❖ Naturalistic observation involves the use of methods designed to assess   *Naturalistic observations*
  behaviour without the experimenter interfering in any way.
❖ Advantages of naturalistic observations:
  – Naturalistic observation can provide rich and full information from people who are usually unaware they are being observed.
  – It is especially suitable for some situations (e.g. workplace studies) and some kinds of participants (e.g. children).
❖ Limitations of naturalistic observations:
  – The researcher has essentially no control over the situation.
  – The participants are sometimes aware they are being observed, and there can be problems with reliability and replication.
  – There are also ethical concerns such as lack of informed consent. Participant observation may raise ethical objections.

❖ There are several types of interview ranging from the unstructured to the   *Questionnaires and*
  totally structured.   *interviews*

❖ Unstructured interviews:
  – These are responsive to the personality, interests, and motivations of the interviewee, therefore tend to produce more qualitative data.
  – However, the data obtained tend to be unreliable.
❖ Structured interviews:
  – In contrast, structured interviews permit comparisons among interviewees, and they tend to be fairly reliable.
  – However, what the interviewee says can be constrained and artificial, and the data collected tend to be more quantitative.
❖ Questionnaires are written, highly structured interviews which permit large amounts of data to be collected but are not suitable for all participants.
❖ All types of interviews can produce problems due to social desirability bias, and interviewees can only provide information of which they are consciously aware.
❖ Ethically we might be concerned with the issue of confidentiality.

See pp.135–144 of the revision guide.

SECTION 21
RESEARCH DESIGN AND IMPLEMENTATION

In order to carry out a study successfully, care and attention must be devoted to each stage in its design and implementation. This section is concerned with these issues. We will focus on *experimental* designs, although many of the same issues also apply to non-experimental designs. As we will see, several decisions need to be made when designing an experimental study.

? In what way are research aims and hypotheses different?

Aims and Hypotheses

The first step when designing a study is to decide on the **aims** and **hypotheses** of the study. The aims are usually more general than the hypotheses, and they help to explain the reasons for the investigator deciding to test some specific hypothesis or hypotheses. In other words, the aims tell us *why* a given study is being carried out, whereas the hypotheses tell us *what* the study is designed to test.

As as example, suppose we decide to test the levels of processing theory put forward by Craik and Lockhart (1972, see Chapter 3), which states that information that has been processed for meaning will be remembered better than information that has not. We might present all of our participants with the same list of nouns and then ask them to provide free recall 30 minutes later. Half of them might be asked to think of adjectives to go with the nouns (processing of meaning or semantic processing), whereas the other half could be asked to think of rhyming words (non-

Common sense recommends a quiet rather than a noisy place for study—but to test the hypothesis that noise interferes with learning requires an experimental design.

semantic processing). So the main *aim* is to investigate levels of processing theory, or, more generally, to see whether long-term memory is influenced by the kind of processing that occurs at the time of learning. The *hypothesis* is more specific: "Free recall from long-term memory is higher when there is semantic processing at the time of learning than when there is non-semantic processing".

Hypotheses

The experimental/alternative hypothesis

Most experimental research using the experimental method starts with someone thinking of an **experimental hypothesis** so that they are clear about what they aim to prove or disprove. The experimental hypothesis is a prediction (or forecast) of what the researcher thinks will happen to the dependent variable when the independent variable changes. For example, "loud noise will have an effect on people's ability to learn the information in a chapter of an introductory psychology textbook".

We have just seen that we talk about an experimental hypothesis in the context of a proper experiment. However, there is a more general term (**alternative hypothesis**) that can be used to refer to *all* hypotheses that are not null hypotheses (see below). Thus, every experimental hypothesis is also an alternative hypothesis, but *not* every alternative hypothesis is also an experimental hypothesis. For example, we might carry out a correlational study, and form the hypothesis that Type A behaviour will be associated with coronary heart disease. That is an alternative hypothesis but *not* an experimental hypothesis.

There are two types of experimental or alternative hypothesis: directional and non-directional. A **directional**, or **one-tailed**, **hypothesis** predicts the *nature* of the effect of the independent variable on the dependent variable, e.g. "Loud noise will *reduce* people's ability to learn the information contained in this chapter of a textbook". In contrast, a non-directional, or two-tailed hypothesis predicts that the independent variable will have an effect on the dependent variable, but the *direction* of the effect is not specified, e.g. "Loud noise will have *an effect on* people's ability to learn the information contained in the chapter of a textbook". This latter hypothesis allows for the possibility that loud noise might actually improve learning, perhaps by making people more alert. So, a one-tailed hypothesis states that the independent variable will lead to either an increase or a decrease in the dependent variable, whereas a two-tailed hypothesis just predicts a change—but not its direction.

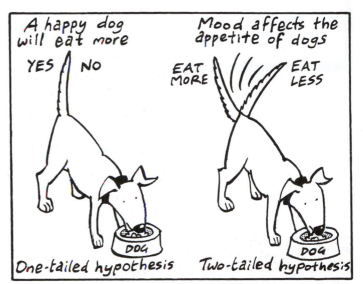

The null hypothesis

The **null hypothesis** can simply state that the independent variable will have no effect on the dependent variable. For example, "loud noise will have no effect on people's ability to learn the information contained in the chapter of the textbook". Sometimes it is easier to state the null hypothesis in relation to group differences. For example, "there will be no significant difference between groups a and b, and any observed differences will be due to chance factors". The purpose of most studies using the experimental method is to decide between the merits of the experimental hypothesis and those of the null hypothesis. Why do we need a null hypothesis when what we are interested in is the experimental hypothesis? The answer is *precision* and *proof*.

KEY TERM

Research/ experimental/ alternative hypothesis: a statement put forward at the beginning of a study stating what you expect to happen, generated by a theory.

Consider the null hypothesis that loud noise will have no effect on people's learning ability. This is *precise* because it leads to a prediction that the single most likely outcome is that performance will be equal in the loud noise and no noise conditions. Failing that, there will probably only be a small difference between the two conditions, with the difference being equally likely to go in either direction. In contrast, consider the experimental hypothesis that loud noise will reduce people's learning ability. This hypothesis is very *imprecise*, because it doesn't indicate how much learning will be impaired. This lack of precision makes it impossible to decide the exact extent to which the findings support (or fail to support) the experimental hypothesis.

If every time I toss a coin it comes down heads, we might form the hypothesis that there are heads on both sides of the coin. But we can't prove this. The more heads we see, the more likely it would appear that the hypothesis is correct. But, if on one occasion we see tails, we have disproved the hypothesis. It is possible to disprove something but not to prove it. Therefore, we propose a null hypothesis that can be disproved (or rejected) and this implies that we can accept the alternative hypothesis. The issues of precision and proof are aspects of the same thing: being able to reject the null hypothesis.

> ■ **Activity:** Devising hypotheses
> Devise suitable null and experimental hypotheses for the following:
>
> * An investigator considers the effect of noise on students' ability to concentrate and complete a word-grid. One group only is subjected to the noise in the form of a distractor, i.e. a television programme.
> * An investigator explores the view that there might be a link between the amount of television children watch and their behaviour at school.

Variables

Experimental hypotheses predict that some aspect of the situation (e.g. the presence of loud noise) will have an effect on the participants' behaviour (e.g. their learning of the information in the chapter). The experimental hypothesis refers to an **independent variable** (the aspect of the experimental situation manipulated by the experimenter), e.g. the presence versus absence of loud noise. The hypothesis also refers to a **dependent variable** (an aspect of the participants' behaviour that is measured or assessed by the experimenter), e.g. measuring learning.

> ■ **Activity:** In order to confirm that you do understand what independent (IV) and dependent (DV) variables are, try identifying them in the following examples. The answers are given on page 300 (don't peek!)
> Remember:
>
> * The DV depends on the IV.
> * The IV is manipulated by the experimenter or varies naturally.
> * The DV is the one we measure.
>
> 1. Long-term separation affects emotional development more than short-term separation. (The two variables are length of separation and emotional development.)
> 2. Participants conform more when the model is someone they respect. (The two variables are
>
> extent of conformity and degree of respect for the model.)
> 3. Participants remember more words before lunch than after lunch. (The two variables are number of words remembered and whether the test is before or after lunch.)
> 4. Boys are better than girls at throwing a ball. (The two variables are gender and ability to throw a ball.)
> 5. Physical attractiveness makes a person more likeable. (The two variables are the attractiveness of a person's photograph and whether they are rated as more or less likeable.)
>
> See page 300 for the answers.

In a nutshell, experimental hypotheses predict that a given independent variable will have some specified effect on a given dependent variable. However, some alternative hypotheses do *not* do this. For example, consider the longitudinal study by Friedman and Rosenman (1974) on Type A and coronary heart disease. Their null hypothesis could have been expressed as follows: "There is no relation between personality (Type A vs Type B) and coronary heart disease."

Operationalisation

Psychologists carry out studies to test hypotheses, such as "anxiety impairs performance" or "maternal deprivation leads to maladjustment", but there is little or no agreement on the best way to measure psychological concepts or variables such as "anxiety", "performance", "maternal deprivation", or "maladjustment". The most common approach to this problem is to make use of **operationalisation**—defining each variable of interest in terms of the operations taken to measure it. Such a definition is termed an operational definition. For example, memory might be defined as the number of words that can be recalled in 5 minutes; maternal deprivation as the number of months during which a child was separated from its main caregiver; and stress-related health problem as high blood pressure.

Operationalisation generally provides a clear and objective definition of even complex variables. However, there are various limitations associated with the use of operational definitions. First, operational definitions are entirely circular and arbitrary. For example, you can define memory as the number of words recalled in 5 minutes and I can define it as the number of words recalled in 10 minutes, but it is very hard to decide whose definition is preferable.

Second, an operational definition typically only covers part of the meaning of the variable or concept. For example, defining memory as word recall in 5 minutes ignores the fact that memory can be assessed by using a recognition test instead of recall or focusing on memory for sentences rather than words.

In spite of these important limitations with operational definitions, it is hard to carry out research without using them. As Stretch (1994) pointed out, the time to worry is when the findings using one operational definition of a variable are very different from the findings using a different operational definition of the same variable. That means that something is wrong, but it may be hard to discover exactly *what* is wrong.

Non-experimental research

In non-experimental research (e.g. correlations, interviews, and observations), it is still useful to have hypotheses, but these will not identify a potentially causal relationship. For example, the aim of an observational study might be "to study the feeding behaviour of geese". The researcher may have a number of hypotheses, such as "one goose always acts as the lookout" and "geese work systematically through the field", which will be important for designing research.

? It might be said that the operational definition of "intelligence" is "that which is measured by intelligence tests". What is the main weakness of this definition?

? What might be an operational definition of fatigue, or hunger?

■ Activity: Generating a hypothesis

1. Generate a hypothesis for each of these questions:
   - What are "football hooligans" really like?
   - Do children play differently at different ages?
   - What are the effects of caffeine on attention and concentration?
2. Identify the independent variable (IV) and dependent variable (DV) from each hypothesis.
3. Identify whether your hypotheses are one-tailed or two-tailed (remember, a one-tailed hypothesis predicts the direction of the effect of the IV on the DV, whereas a two-tailed hypothesis does not).
4. Write a null hypothesis for each of the experimental hypotheses.

Experimental Designs

The second step in the research process is to identify an appropriate design. We will consider experimental design, as well as some issues related to the design of qualitative research methods.

If we wish to compare two groups with respect to a given independent variable, they must not differ in any other important way. This general rule is important when it comes to selecting participants, e.g. if all the least able participants received the loud noise, and all the most able participants received no noise, we would not know whether it was the loud noise or the low ability level causing poor learning performance. How should we select our participants so as to avoid this problem? There are three main methods.

1. *Independent groups design.* Each participant is selected for only one group (e.g. no noise or loud noise), most commonly by randomisation. This could involve using a random process such as tossing a coin to allocate one of two conditions for all participants, or you could let all participants draw slips of paper, numbered 1 and 2, from a hat. This **random allocation** means that in most cases the participants in the two groups do end up equivalent in terms of ability, age, and so on. An example of a study using an independent groups design is the study by Loftus and Palmer (1974; see page 79) on eyewitness testimony. Each group was asked a different question concerning the speed of the cars involved in the accident.

2. *Matched participants design.* Each participant is selected for only one group, but the participants in the two groups are matched for some relevant factor or factors (e.g. ability, sex, age). In our example, using information about the participants' ability levels would ensure that the two groups were matched in terms of range of ability. For example, the study by Kiecolt-Glaser et al. (1995) on slowing of wound healing by psychological stress involved a matched participants design. The group of women caring for a relative with Alzheimer's disease were matched with the control women in terms of age and family income. This helped to ensure that differences between the groups in time for wound healing could be attributed to the stress of caregiving rather than some other factor.

3. *Repeated measures design.* Each participant appears in both groups, so that there are exactly the same participants in each group. In our example, that would mean that each participant learns the chapter in the loud noise condition, and also in the no noise condition. We don't need to worry about the participants in one group being cleverer than those in the other group, as the same participants appear in both groups! An example of a study using a repeated measures design is the one by Peterson and Peterson (1959; see page 46) on short-term forgetting at various retention intervals. In other words, all of the participants were tested at all of the retention intervals.

Counterbalancing

The main problem with using the repeated measures design is that there may be **order effects**. Participants may perform better when they appear in the second group because they have gained useful information about the experiment or about the task, or less well because of tiredness or boredom. It would be hard to use a

■ **Activity answers (from page 298)**

1. IV = length of separation, DV = emotional development.
2. IV = degree of respect for model, DV = degree of conformity.
3. IV = whether test is before or after lunch, DV = number of words recalled.
4. IV = gender, DV = ability to throw a ball.
5. IV = attractiveness, DV = rating for likeability.

repeated measures design in our earlier example: participants are almost certain to show better learning of the chapter the second time they read it, regardless of whether they are exposed to loud noise. However, there is a way around this, using **counterbalancing**—half the participants learn the chapter first in loud noise and then in no noise, while the other half learn the chapter first in no noise and then in loud noise. In that way, any order effects would be balanced out.

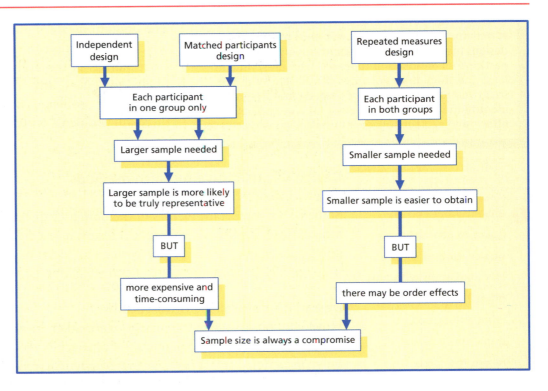

Experimental and control groups

In some experiments control is applied to establishing a baseline. In our example, one group receives the **experimental treatment** (noise) whereas the other receives nothing (no noise). This latter group serves as a **control group**. Their behaviour informs us about how people behave when they are not exposed to the experimental treatment so that we can make comparisons. The group who have the noise are called the **experimental group**.

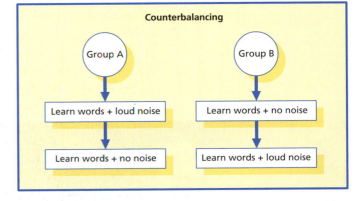

If a repeated measures design is used, then we have two different conditions: a control condition and an experimental condition.

Advantages and limitations of different research designs

Advantages of the **independent groups design** are that there are no order effects, no participants are lost between trials, and it can be used when a repeated measures design is inappropriate (e.g. when looking at gender differences). Limitations include the fact that there may be important individual differences between participants to start with (to minimise this there should be randomisation), and you need more participants than you do with a repeated measures design.

The **matched participants design** does control for some individual differences between participants and can be used when a repeated measures design is inappropriate. However, it is quite difficult to match participants in pairs and you need a large pool of participants from which to select (more than with a repeated measures design).

Advantages of the repeated measures design are that it controls for *all* individual differences, and it requires fewer participants than the other designs.

Activity: Research designs. For each of the three designs mentioned (independent design, matched participants design, and repeated measures), find at least one study that illustrates the design. With the study you have chosen for repeated measures design, identify the measures that were taken to prevent order effects and explain how counterbalancing was achieved.

The limitations are that it cannot be used in studies in which participation in one condition has large effects on responses in the other, or in which participants are likely to guess the purpose of the study, thus introducing problems with demand characteristics, and there are problems with order effects.

Design of qualitative research methods
Questionnaires and interviews

Some of the important factors in the design of questionnaires and interviews have already been discussed. In practical terms, a researcher needs guidance on writing good questions to avoid problems such as social desirability bias. The Case Study on page 291 provides guidance in constructing good questions.

? Imagine that you are going to conduct an observation of children in a playgroup with two other researchers. To what extent do you think that you will all record the same behaviours? How might you cope with any disagreements?

Designing naturalistic observations

How can observers avoid being overloaded in their attempts to record their observation of others' behaviour? Approaches include **event sampling**, focusing only on actions or events that are of particular interest to the researcher; **time sampling**, where observations are only made during specified time periods (e.g. the first 10 minutes of each hour); and **point sampling**, where one individual is observed in order to categorise their current behaviour, after which a second individual is observed, and so on.

In considering the data obtained from naturalistic observation, it is important to distinguish between recording and interpretation (coding), e.g. an observer may record that the participant has moved forwards, and interpret that movement as an aggressive action. In practice, however, observers typically only focus on interpretation. For example, Bales (1950) developed the interaction process analysis, which allows observers to watch groups of people talking together or interacting. The observers record inferred meanings for the forms of behaviour shown by members of a group (e.g. "offers suggestion" or "gives information").

There have been various attempts to develop ways of categorising people's behaviour in naturalistic observation without interpreting it. McGrew (1972) devised a detailed and comprehensive recording system to place the social interactions of children at nursery school into 110 categories.

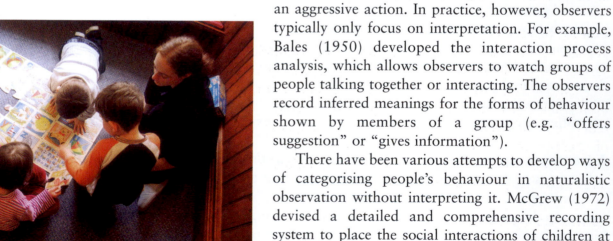

When conducting observational studies, psychologists need to categorise behaviour. When McGrew (1972) studied the interactions of nursery school children he used an observational rating system with 110 categories.

Factors Associated With Research Design

In order for a study to be designed and carried out successfully, the researcher needs to bear several considerations in mind, some of which apply to all kinds of research, whereas others are specific to experiments.

Standardised instructions and procedures

In order to carry out an experiment successfully, it is very important that every participant in a given condition is treated in the same way, so it is necessary to use standardised procedures. For example, the experimenter should write down a set of **standardised instructions**. He/she should then either read them to the participants, or ask the participants to read them to themselves. An example is given in the box on the right.

In similar fashion, **standardised procedures** should be used for the collection of data. This applies to all research, not just experiments. In our noise example, a standardised procedure would be to ask all of the participants the same set of, say, 20 questions relating to the chapter. Each participant then obtains a score between 0 and 20 as a measure of what he or she has learned.

It is not easy to make sure that standardised procedures are being used. Most experiments or other kinds of study can be thought of as social encounters between the researcher and the participant, and it is customary to behave in different ways towards different people. Rosenthal (1966) studied some of the ways in which researchers fall short of standardised procedures, e.g. male researchers were more pleasant, friendly, honest, encouraging, and relaxed when their participants were female, leading him to conclude: "Male and female [participants] may, psychologically, simply not be in the same experiment at all", i.e. the results would not be comparable.

Control of variables

We have previously discussed the control of **confounding variables**. These are variables that may mask the effect of the independent variable.

Confounding variables are a form of **constant error**, present when the effects of any unwanted variable on the dependent variable differ between conditions. There are numerous types of constant error: the participants in one condition may be more tired than those in another condition, more intelligent, or more motivated.

Controlled variables

How do we avoid having any confounding variables? One useful approach is to turn them into **controlled variables**, i.e. variables that are held constant or controlled. If we suspect that time of day may have an effect on learning, it could become a controlled variable by testing all of our participants at a given time of day, such as late morning or early evening. If we did this, we would know that time of day couldn't distort our findings.

Pilot studies

An important consideration in designing good studies is to try out your planned procedures in a small-scale trial run, called a **pilot study**. Such a preliminary study

---

A set of standardised instructions

Kelley (1950) conducted a field experiment to see whether class members would form different impressions of a lecturer if he was described as "warm" or as "cold". The standardised instructions for the experiment were:

"Your regular instructor is out of town today, and since we of Economics 70 are interested in the general problem of how various classes react to different instructors, we're going to have an instructor today you've never had before, Mr ____. Then, at the end of the period, I want you to fill out some forms about him. In order to give you some idea of what he's like, we've had a person who knows him write up a little biographical note about him. I'll pass this out now and you can read it before he arrives. Please read these to yourselves and don't talk about this among yourselves until the class is over so he won't get wind of what's going on."

The participants were then given the biographical note with the word "warm" or "cold" inserted. Kelley found that the "warm" lecturer was rated more positively.

To apply the concept of standardised instructions, use one of the studies that you have looked at in detail and write a set of standardised instructions that researchers might have used.

? If an experimenter used different wording in the instructions to different participants, how might this affect the results of the study?

■ **Activity:** Standardised instructions
Look back at Milgram's original obedience study (see p.244) and write out full standardised instructions as if you were going to run the experiment just as he did. Swap your standardised instructions with your neighbour and see if they have missed out any points, or if they have some extra points which you missed out. Though, of course, in today's world we could not do this experiment at all!

EXAM HINT
You may be asked to explain what a pilot study is and why it should be conducted Remember:

- A pilot study is carried out to trial-run the materials and procedure.
- It identifies any flaws or areas for improvement that can then be corrected before the main study such as clarity of instructions, ambiguity of questions, or timing.

makes it possible to check out standardised procedures and general design before investing time and money in the major study.

Improving and Measuring Reliability

One of the main goals of research is to design and carry out studies in such a way that replication or repetition of one's findings is possible. In order to achieve that goal, it is important that the measures we use should possess good **reliability**. Reliability can be considered in terms of internal reliability, which is how consistently a method measures within itself, and external reliability, which is how consistently a method measures over time, population, and location when repeated.

Determining the reliability of observations

Problems relating to reliability are likely to arise when a researcher is trying to code the complex behaviour of participants using a manageable number of categories. For example, a study might require a record to be made of the number of aggressive acts performed by an individual. If only one person observes the behaviour this would produce a rather subjective judgement, and so usually two (or more) judges are asked to provide ratings of a behaviour. The ratings can then be compared to provide a measure of **inter-judge**/inter-rater or **inter-observer reliability** (see discussion on naturalistic observation on page 286 of this chapter).

Internal and external reliability

Internal reliability = consistency within the method of measurement.
For instance, a ruler should be measuring the same distance between 0 and 5 centimetres as between 5 and 10 centimetres.
External reliability = consistency between uses of the method of measurement. For instance, the ruler should measure the same on a Monday as it does on a Friday.

- Reliability = consistent and stable.
- Validity = measuring what is intended.
- Standardisation = comparisons can be made between studies and samples.
- Reliability = consistent and stable. For example, Milgram's study (1963, 1974; see page 244) on obedience to authority produced findings that have been repeated numerous times in many countries, and are thus reliable.
- Validity = measuring what is intended. For example, Rahe et al.'s study (1970; see page 153) showed that scores on the Social Readjustment Rating Scale were associated with physical illness. The findings suggest (but don't prove) that the Social Readjustment Rating Scale is a valid measure of the stress created by life events.

Determining the reliability of psychological tests

Reliability is established on psychological tests by using the **test–retest** method where the same test is given to participants on two separate occasions to see if their scores remain relatively similar. The interval between testings must be long enough to prevent a **practice effect** occurring.

A second method of establishing reliability is called the **split-half technique**. Items from a test are randomly assigned to two sub-tests and then scores compared on both tests in the same way as on the test–retest method. The same person does both sub-tests during the same experimental session.

Improving and Measuring Validity

One of the key requirements of research is that any findings obtained are valid, in the sense that they are genuine and provide us with useful information about the phenomenon being studied (valid means "true"). Campbell and Stanley (1966) drew a distinction between internal validity, which refers to the issue of whether the effects observed are genuine and are caused by the independent variable, and external validity, which refers to the extent to which the findings of a study can be generalised to situations and samples other than those used in the study. This distinction is important: many experiments possess internal validity while lacking external validity (validity was discussed in Chapter 7, Section 18.)

The distinction between internal and external validity is especially relevant to experiments and quasi-experiments because of their potential artificiality, so we will focus on experimental research.

Internal validity

Coolican (1994) pointed out that there are many threats to the internal validity of an experiment, most of which were discussed earlier in this chapter. These include the existence of any confounding factors; the use of unreliable or inconsistent measures; lack of standardisation and randomisation; or **experimenter effects, demand characteristics**, and **participant reactivity** (all discussed later in this chapter).

In a nutshell, virtually all of the principles of experimental design are intended to enhance internal validity, and failure to apply these principles threatens internal validity. If internal validity is high, replication of the findings is likely; if it is low, it may be difficult or impossible.

External validity and generalisability

What about external validity? There are close links between external validity and **generalisability**, because both are concerned with the issue of whether the findings of an experiment or study are applicable to other situations. More specifically, Coolican (1994) argued that there are four main aspects to external validity or generalisability:

1. *Populations*: Do the findings obtained from a given sample of individuals generalise to a larger population from which the sample was selected?
2. *Locations*: Do the findings of the study generalise to other settings or situations? If they do, the study is said to possess external validity. Silverman (1977, p.108) was sceptical about the external validity of laboratory experiments: "The conclusions we draw from our laboratory studies pertain to the behaviour of organisms [living creatures] in conditions of their own confinement and control and are probably generalisable only to similar situations (institutions, perhaps, such as schools or prisons or hospitals)."
3. *Measures or constructs*: Do the findings of the experiment or study generalise to other measures of the variables used? For example, suppose we find using one method of assessing Type A that it is associated with an increased risk of coronary heart disease. Would we obtain the same findings if Type A were assessed by a different questionnaire?
4. *Times*: Do the findings generalise to the past and to the future? For example, it could be argued that sweeping changes in many cultures in recent decades have affected majority influence as studied by Asch, and obedience to authority as studied by Milgram (see Chapter 7).

Our culture today is different from the culture of the 1950s. This means that research conducted then, for example surveying women's attitudes towards domestic work, may not generalise to women's attitudes today.

Many laboratory-based experiments in psychology show low external validity—that is, their findings do not translate reliably to behaviour outside the laboratory

How can we maximise the external validity of an experiment? Unfortunately, there is no easy answer to that question. The external validity of an experiment usually only becomes clear when other researchers try to generalise the findings to other samples or populations, locations, measures, and times. It might be thought that the findings of field experiments are more likely than those of laboratory experiments to generalise to other real-life locations or settings, but that is not necessarily so.

Meta-analyses

One way of trying to determine whether certain findings generalise is to carry out what is known as a **meta-analysis**. In a meta-analysis, *all* the findings from many studies testing a given hypothesis are combined into a single analysis. If the meta-analysis indicates that some finding has been obtained consistently, this suggests that it generalises across populations, locations, measures, and times. For example, Smith and Bond (1993) carried out a meta-analysis on 133 Asch-type studies drawn from 17 countries. Their meta-analysis revealed that majority influence in the Asch situation is found in numerous countries, but there was a suggestion that it is greater in collectivistic societies (e.g. China) in which there is an emphasis on cooperating with others.

The greatest limitation of meta-analyses is that differences in the quality of individual studies are often ignored. This can lead to the situation in which a finding is accepted as genuine when it has been obtained in several poorly-designed studies but not in a smaller number of well-designed studies. Another problem is that it is often hard to know which studies to include and which to exclude. For example, the studies reviewed by Bond and Smith didn't use identical procedures and therefore they are not directly comparable. It is also quite possible that the task didn't have the same meaning for people in different cultures.

Ethics

We should finally consider the fact that good research design involves ethics. All research strives to satisfy the requirements of the psychologists' code of ethics. The details of this are discussed in Chapter 7, Section 19.

The Selection of Participants

Studies in psychology rarely involve more than about 100 participants. However, researchers generally want their findings to apply to a much larger group of people than those acting as participants. In technical terms, the participants selected for a study form a **sample** taken from some larger **population** (called the target or sample population), which consists of all the members of the group from which the sample has been drawn. For example, we might select a sample of 20 children aged 5 for a study. The target population would consist of all the

5-year-olds living in England or the population might be the 5-year-olds in a particular primary school, depending on where we selected our sample.

When we carry out a study, we want the findings obtained from our sample to be true of the population from which they were drawn. In order to achieve this, we must use a **representative sample**, i.e. participants who are representative or typical of the population in question. Only if we have a representative sample can we generalise from the behaviour of our sample to the target population in general. In other words, as in the example, we can only make statements about all 5-year-olds in the population studied, i.e. those in England or in the school, not those in the rest of the world. Many studies actually have non-representative samples. Such studies are said to have a **sampling bias**. Coolican (1994, p.36) was pessimistic about the chances of truly selecting a representative sample, calling it an "abstract ideal", and stressing the importance of removing "as much sampling bias as possible".

Random sampling

The best way of obtaining a representative sample from a population (e.g. students) would be to use **random sampling**. This could be done by picking students' names out of a hat, or by assigning a number to everyone in the population from which the sample is to be selected. After that, a computer or random number tables could be used to generate a series of random numbers to select the sample.

If we wanted to have a representative sample of the entire adult population, then we could apply one of the methods of random selection just described to the electoral roll. However, even that would be an imperfect procedure because several groups of people, including children and young people, the homeless, illegal immigrants, and prisoners, are not listed.

As Cardwell et al. (1996) pointed out, **systematic sampling** involves selecting the participants by a quasi-random procedure. This procedure is not as effective as random sampling because it cannot be claimed that every member of the population is equally likely to be selected.

Evaluation of random sampling

As it is actually very hard for an experimenter to obtain a random sample, this method typically fails to produce a truly representative sample, for various reasons:

1. It may not be possible to identify all of the members of the larger population from which the sample is to be selected.
2. It may not be possible to contact all those who have been selected randomly to appear in the sample—they may have moved house, or be away on holiday. You would end up with a sample that is definitely not random.
3. Some of those who are selected to be in the sample are likely to refuse to take part in the study. This might not matter if those who agreed to take part in research were very similar in every way to those who didn't. However, there is considerable evidence that a **volunteer sample** differs in various ways from

Activity: Target populations
Identify an appropriate target population for each project below. You would select your research sample from this population.

- To discover whether there are enough youth facilities in your community.
- To discover whether cats like dried or tinned cat food.
- To discover whether children aged between 5 and 11 watch too much violent television.
- To discover the causes of anxiety experienced by participants in research studies.

The questions in an examination aim to sample your knowledge. You will feel unhappy if that sample doesn't touch on what you know!

Systematic sampling is not as effective as random sampling but it does help to overcome the biases of the researcher. If we select every hundredth name on the list, we avoid missing names that we cannot pronounce, or do not like the look of, for whatever reason.

KEY TERM

Volunteer sample: refers to participants who volunteer to take part in a research study, for instance by replying to an advertisement. Some researchers believe that people who volunteer may be different from non-volunteers, for instance in personality, and so may not be a truly representative sample. This makes generalising the findings to the non-volunteering population questionable.

Ideally, psychological experiments should select a random sample of the population, although true randomness can be hard to achieve

a random sample. This is called a **volunteer bias**. Manstead and Semin (1996, p.93) discussed some of the evidence, and concluded, "there *are* systematic personality differences between volunteers and non-volunteers". Volunteers tend to be more sensitive to demand characteristics (cues used by participants to work out what a study is about), and they are also more likely to comply with those demand characteristics.

In sum, it is worth bearing in mind what Coolican (1998, p.720) had to say about random samples: "Many students write that their sample was 'randomly selected'. In fact, research samples are very rarely selected at random." Usually students and many psychologists actually use opportunity sampling.

Opportunity sampling

Random sampling is often expensive and time-consuming. As a result, many researchers use **opportunity sampling**. This involves selecting participants on the basis of their availability rather than by any other method. Opportunity sampling is often used by students carrying out experiments, and it is also very common in natural experiments.

> ■ **Activity:** Sampling. Find a study to illustrate volunteer sampling and another one to illustrate opportunity sampling. (Clue: most of the studies you have covered used a volunteer sample, whereas some of the studies have used opportunity samples.)

Evaluation of opportunity sampling

Opportunity sampling is the easiest method to use. However, it has the severe disadvantage that the participants may be nothing like a representative sample. For example, students who are friends of the student carrying out a study may be more likely to take part than students who are not. The twin study by Holland et al. (1988; see page 211) on anorexia nervosa successfully used an opportunity sample. However, it is very hard to know whether the use of such a sample distorted the results in some way.

Opportunity sampling gives the illusion of being drawn from a large population whereas it generally is from a very small sample, such as people who shop in the centre of town on a weekday. In other words, the sample really depends on who is available at the time. This type of group almost certainly constitutes a *biased sample*.

? Why do you think volunteers are more likely than non-volunteers to be sensitive to the demand characteristics of a study?

Sample size

One of the issues that anyone carrying out a piece of research has to consider is the total number of participants to be included. What is the ideal number of participants in each condition? That is a bit like asking how long is a piece of string (i.e. there is no definite answer), but here are some of the relevant factors:

- It is generally expensive and time consuming to make use of large samples running into hundreds of participants.

> **KEY TERM**
>
> **Opportunity sampling:** participants are selected because they are available, not because they are representative of a population.

- If we use very small samples (fewer than 10 participants in each condition), then this reduces the chances of obtaining a meaningful effect.
- In general terms, sampling bias is likely to be greater with small samples than with large ones.
- You should also remember that the size of the sample population matters. If a relatively small sample is drawn from a large and diverse population (e.g. entire population of the UK), it is very likely to be biased.

If there is a golden rule that applies to deciding on sample size, it is the following:

The smaller the likely effect being studied, the larger the sample size needed to demonstrate it.

For most purposes, however, having about 15 participants in each condition is a reasonable number.

Consider the total number of participants to be included...

The Relationship Between Researchers and Participants

In most experimental research (and some non-experimental research), the researcher and the participants *interact* with each other. This can produce various kinds of problems. How researchers behave and talk may influence the behaviour of the participants in ways having nothing to do with the independent variable or other variables being controlled. In addition, the participants may form mistaken ideas of what the study is about, and these mistaken ideas may affect their behaviour. Some of the main problems stemming from the relationship between the researcher and the participants are discussed next.

Participant reactivity

A weakness found in many studies is **participant reactivity**. This refers to a situation in which an independent variable has an effect on behaviour simply because the participants know they are being observed or studied. Any measure of the participants' behaviour that could suffer from this effect is called a reactive measure, and reactivity is the term used to refer to the changes in behaviour produced in this way.

In order to clarify the meaning of participant reactivity, we can consider a series of studies carried out at the Hawthorne Western Electric plant in Chicago (Roethlisberger & Dickson, 1939). In general, productivity increased when *any* changes were made to the working conditions, whether these

The way in which experimenters behave and talk may influence the behaviour of the participant.

changes were to wages, length of the working day, amount of lighting, or to rest. Productivity even improved when there was a return to the original working conditions. Presumably what happened was that the workers responded to the interest being shown in them, rather than to the specific changes in their working environment.

The term "**Hawthorne effect**" came to be used to refer to changes produced as a result of people knowing they are being studied, although the same phenomenon is now generally referred to as participant reactivity. It is a serious problem, because it can lead us to misinterpret our findings. To avoid this, we need to make sure that participant reactivity is the same in both conditions, by making it equally clear to both groups that they are being studied and that their behaviour is of interest. If the effect is still found, then it cannot have been due to participant reactivity.

Examples of participant reactivity include evaluation apprehension and demand characteristics. Evaluation apprehension (which involves participants doing their best to be regarded positively by the experimenter) is a real issue in many experiments, and is discussed fully on page 279.

? **When would you not expect to find evidence of participant reactivity?**

Demand characteristics

A common criticism of laboratory research is that the situation is so artificial that participants behave very differently from normal. Claxton (1980) discussed an amusing example of this. He considered a laboratory task, in which participants have to decide as rapidly as possible whether sentences such as "Can canaries fly?" are true or false. Under laboratory conditions, people perform this task uncomplainingly. However, as Claxton pointed out, "If someone asks me 'Can canaries fly?' in the pub I will suspect either that he is an idiot or that he is about to tell me a joke."

Why do people behave in unusual ways under laboratory conditions? We have already considered demand characteristics. Orne (1962) believed that most participants do their best to comply with what they perceive to be the demands of the experimental situation, so they try to guess what is expected using any available clues and these then become demand characteristics. Of course, their perceptions may often be inaccurate.

There is another problem with demand characteristics, which applies to participants who have previously taken part in an experiment in which they were deceived about the experimental purpose. Remember that psychological research often relies on psychology students as participants, and they take part in a number of studies. As a result of being deceived, some participants tend thereafter to respond in the opposite direction to the one suggested by an experiment's demand characteristics. Why should this be so? Silverman et al. (1970) explained this effect in the following way:

? **Is honesty the best policy? Would demand characteristics be reduced if both participants and experimenters knew the true aims of the experiment?**

Deceived [participants] may have become so alerted to possible further deceptions that they tend to respond counter to any cues regarding the experimenter's hypothesis. An element of gamesmanship may enter the experimental situation in that [participants] become wary of "tricks" underlying the obvious, and do not want to be caught in them.

Reducing demand characteristics

Information about the demand characteristics in any given experimental setting can be obtained by asking the participants afterwards to describe in detail what they felt the experiment was about. The experimenter can then take steps to make sure that the results of future experiments are not adversely affected by demand characteristics.

Some (but not all) of the problems of demand characteristics can be reduced by the **single blind** procedure, in which the participants are not informed of the condition in which they have been placed. Instead, they are usually given a false account of the purpose of the experiment so that they will not seek for cues about the nature of the research. The problem with this is that it raises ethical issues, because full informed consent cannot be obtained in such circumstances.

Investigator effects

The ideal experimenter is someone who behaves in exactly the same mildly positive way with every participant, and who doesn't allow his/her expectations and experimental hypotheses to influence the conduct of a study. In reality, the experimenter's expectations, personal characteristics, and so on often have an effect on the participants' behaviour. These are known as **investigator (experimenter) effects**.

Experimenter expectancy

One of the most important investigator effects is **experimenter expectancy**, in which the experimenter's expectations have a systematic effect on the performance of the participants. Perhaps the first systematic demonstration of experimenter expectancy involved a horse known as Clever Hans, studied by Pfungst (1911). The horse was apparently able to count, tapping its hoof the right number of times when asked a simple mathematical question (e.g. 8 + 6). Pfungst studied Clever Hans, and found it couldn't produce the correct answer when blindfolded. What happened normally was that the experimenter made slight movements when the horse had tapped out the correct number, and Clever Hans simply used those movements as the cue to stop tapping. Rosenthal (1966) experimentally demonstrated the power of unconscious cues in a study of flatworms, where participants recorded twice as many movements in the flatworms they had been told would be "highly active" than the ones that they had been told would be "inactive".

In another experiment, Rosenthal and Fode (1963) demonstrated an expectancy effect when students were working with rats, some of which they were told had been specially bred for high intelligence and could learn mazes very quickly. Other participants were told they had been bred for dullness. The rats were actually *randomly* assigned to the students, who trained them to learn mazes. The "maze-bright" rats actually performed the maze tasks significantly faster than the "maze-dull" rats.

Clever Hans, the "counting" horse who was in reality responding to unconscious cues from his trainer. In the same way, experimenters can unconsciously communicate cues to their participants.

? Greenspoon (1955) found that he could alter participants' responses by saying "mm-hmm" or "uh-huh" at strategic moments. In what way is this "Greenspoon effect" an example of experimenter expectancy?

EXAM HINT
You may be asked to describe one way that investigator effects might threaten the validity of your study. Consider one of the following:

- Researcher bias when setting the research question (formulation).
- In the carrying out of research (e.g. giving away the demand characteristics and the research expectancy effect.
- In the analysis of the results (manipulation of data).
- In the interpretation of results.

? Could the results of Rosenthal and Fode's experiment be explained in terms of deviation from the standardised procedure rather than the expectancy effect?

It would seem that the students had in some way communicated their expectations to their rats, an example of an experimenter effect or **experimenter bias**.

Coolican (1994) reported that at least 40 experiments specifically designed to test for the expectancy effect have found no evidence of it. There is evidence that the behaviour of human participants, especially those high in need for approval, can be influenced by the experimenter's behaviour. However, it seems less likely that flatworms and rats would respond to a smile or a frown from the experimenter!

Reducing investigator effects

What steps can be taken to minimise investigator effects? One approach is to use a **double blind** procedure, in which neither the investigator working with the participants nor the participants know the research hypothesis (or hypotheses) being tested. The double blind procedure reduces the possibility of investigator bias, but it is often too expensive and impractical to use. As more and more studies involve participants interacting with computers rather than with human investigators, the incidence of investigator effects is probably less than it used to be. In addition, data are increasingly stored directly in computers, making it harder to misrecord the information obtained from participants.

> **EXAM HINT**
>
> Questions on designing a further study and predicting results often make up the last two sub-parts of the research methods question. They test A03: design, implementation, and reporting of psychological research. To help you cover the design features, ask yourself:
>
> - Who—sample?
> - How—method/design/controls?
> - What—variables (IV and DV or V1 and V2) and materials?
> - When—timings and procedure.
>
> When asked to predict results, think about whether you are testing for a difference or correlation so that you predict correctly how the variables will change.

SECTION SUMMARY

Aims and hypotheses

- ❖ The first stage in designing a study is to decide on its aims and hypotheses.
- ❖ Aims tell us *why*, and hypotheses tell us *what*.
- ❖ The null hypothesis:
  - – The null hypothesis is a statement of no effect.
  - – It increases precision. One can prove (accept) the experimental/alternative hypothesis by rejecting the null hypothesis.
- ❖ The experimental/alternative hypothesis:
  - – This may be directional or one-tailed, or it may be non-directional and two-tailed.
- ❖ Non-experimental research may also have aims and hypotheses.

Experimental design

- ❖ There are three main types of experimental design:
  1. Independent groups design: where there may be an experimental and a control *group*.
  2. Repeated measures design: where there may be an experimental and a control *condition*.
  3. Matched participants design.
- ❖ With an independent groups design, random allocation is generally used to distribute participants to groups. The aim is to ensure that both groups are equivalent.

❖ Repeated measures compensate for any participant variation because the participants in both conditions are the same. However there is the problem of order effects, which may be overcome using counterbalancing.

❖ Matched participants design uses independent groups of participants who are similar. Control groups/conditions provide a baseline measure.

The design of naturalistic observations

❖ The design of qualitative research concerns how to construct questionnaires and interviews, and the choice of various observational methods.

❖ Methods of data collection include event sampling, time sampling, and point sampling.

❖ We should distinguish between data recording and interpretation.

Factors associated with research design

Factors in research design that are important to "good practice" include the following:

❖ The use of standardised instructions and procedures.

❖ It is important to avoid confounding variables and other forms of constant error by turning them into controlled variables.

❖ Operationalisation is useful, but operational definitions typically cover only part of the meaning of the variable in question.

❖ Pilot studies are important for testing the extent to which the design works in practice, before committing time and money to a full-scale study.

❖ Reliability and validity are also part of good research design:
  – The measures used in a study should possess good reliability or consistency. If they don't, then they are inadequate measures of the variables in question, and it will be hard to replicate or repeat any findings obtained.
  – Reliability can be determined by calculating inter-observer reliability, test–retest, and split-half measures.

❖ Internal and external validity are also part of good research design:
  – A study should also have internal validity. This means that the findings are genuine and caused by the independent variable.
  – External validity refers to the extent to which the findings of a study can be generalised. It is important to be able to make generalisations about populations, locations, measures, and historical times. Information about the generalisability of any particular findings can be obtained by means of a meta-analysis.

❖ Finally, ethics are a key consideration for good practice.

Selection of participants

❖ The participants selected for a study represent a sample from some target population. They should form a representative sample and be selected to avoid sampling bias.

❖ Random sampling: The best approach is random sampling, but this is difficult to achieve in practice because of problems in identifying whole populations, finding all participants, and obtaining responses from them.

❖ Opportunity sampling: This is the easiest (but least satisfactory) method. The ideal sample size depends on the likely size of the effect being studied. Fifteen participants in each experimental condition is generally a reasonable size.

The relationship between researchers and participants

❖ Most research involves interactions between the researcher and the participants.

❖ This can introduce various systematic biases, which can be divided into:
  – Participant reactivity (i.e. the Hawthorne effect and demand characteristics).
  – Investigator effects.

See pp.145–153 of the revision guide.

❖ Demand characteristics involve the participants responding on the basis of their beliefs about the research hypothesis or hypotheses. These can be minimised by using a single blind experimental design.

❖ Investigator effects include experimenter expectancy (e.g. Clever Hans). Double blind procedure is one way to overcome these effects.

SECTION 22
DATA ANALYSIS

The mean height of these children is 132cm. Stating the mean is one way of describing the data (in this case height).

The data obtained from a study may or may not be in numerical or quantitative form, i.e. in the form of numbers. Even if the data are not in quantitative form, we can still carry out *qualitative* analyses based on the experiences of the individual participants. If the data are in numerical form, then we typically start by working out some descriptive statistics to summarise the pattern of findings. These **descriptive statistics** include measures of central tendency within a sample (e.g. mean) and measures of the spread of scores within a sample (e.g. range). Another useful way of summarising the findings is through the use of graphs. Several such ways of summarising quantitative data are discussed later in this section. First, we will consider the qualitative analysis of data.

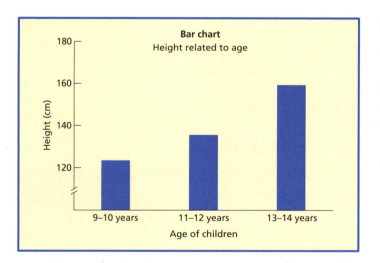

An investigator might study attitudes towards A-level psychology by carrying out interviews with several A-level students. One of the categories into which their statements are then placed might be "negative attitudes towards statistics". A consideration of the various statements in this category might reveal numerous reasons why A-level psychology students dislike statistics!

Qualitative Analysis of Data

- There is an important distinction between quantitative research and qualitative research.

- In **quantitative research**, the information obtained from the participants is expressed in numerical form (e.g. the number of items recalled; reaction times; the number of aggressive acts).

- In **qualitative research**, the information obtained from participants is *not* expressed in numerical form. The emphasis is on the stated experiences of the participants and on the stated meanings they attach to themselves, to other people, and to their environment.

- Content analysis is a very useful qualitative method for analysing messages in the media, including articles published in newspapers, speeches made by politicians on radio and television, and health records. For example, Cumberbatch (1990) found using content analysis that only about 25% of the women in advertisements on British television seemed to be over 30 years old, compared to about 75% of men. On the face of it, this appears to reflect sexist bias. Note that in this study (as in many qualitative studies), some numbers creep into the analysis!

- Discourse analysis is a form of qualitative analysis concerned with all kinds of speaking and writing. Its main emphasis is on meaning (i.e. what is the speaker or writer trying to say), and the key underlying assumption is that the ways we use language are greatly affected by the social context. For example, scientists are much more confident about the meaning of their findings when interviewed than they are in their writings (Gilbert & Mulkay, 1984).

- When researchers carry out a **case study**, they often include some raw data (e.g. direct quotations from the participant) as part of the qualitative analysis. For example, Griffiths (1993) chronicled one teenage boy's descent into pathological gambling and his subsequent recovery. Most of the data were collected in separate interviews with "David" and his mother. Here is part of what David had to say:

I always got the feeling of being 'high' or 'stoned' … Although winning money was the first thing that attracted me to playing fruit machines, this gradually converted to light, sounds and excitement … I was always very upset about losing all my money and I returned many times to try to win back my losses … The only time I found it possible to think about giving up was after leaving the arcade at closing time and [vowing] never to return … Whenever I felt depressed (which was practically all the time) or rejected, the urge to play machines became even bigger.

- Some observational studies make use of qualitative analysis whereas others focus mainly on quantitative analysis. An example of an observational study mostly relying on qualitative analysis is the one by Ainsworth and Bell (1970; see page 95). It was mainly qualitative because the emphasis was on assigning the young children into three attachment categories on the basis of observations of their behaviour in the Strange Situation.

- Strength: Qualitative research offers the prospect of understanding people as founded individuals in a social context, and is often broader in scope than quantitative research.

- Strength: Qualitative research often suggests interesting hypotheses that can be tested in subsequent research. For example, Griffiths' (1993) study on the teenage gambler David suggested that depression was responsible in part for his starting to gamble and then continuing to do so.

- Strength: Qualitative research such as the study by Ainsworth and Bell (1970) can successfully reduce very complex forms of behaviour to a manageable numbers of categories of theoretical importance.

Content analysis of advertising can tell us a great deal about society's attitudes to men and women.

? Many of the data in Griffiths' (1993) study were retrospective. How do you feel this may have affected the results?

■ **Activity:** Qualitative and quantitative analysis
Ask each of the class or another group of people to answer two questions:
a. Does having a tan make a person look more attractive? Yes/no
b. Is it healthy and safe to stay out in the sun for as long as possible in the summer? Yes/no

Then count your answers and make two bar charts. Is this qualitative or quantitative analysis?
Do the two bar charts match or not? Why? Is this now qualitative or quantitative analysis?

How would you interpret this behaviour? Is this person a dedicated supporter of an important cause, or a hooligan?

- Strength: Some qualitative research (e.g. discourse analysis) has been very successful in showing the ways in which what we say or write is strongly influenced by the immediate social context.
- Weakness: The greatest limitation of the qualitative approach is that the findings reported tend to be unreliable and hard to replicate. This is due in part to the fact that the qualitative approach is subjective and impressionistic.
- Weakness: The qualitative data collected in, for example, discourse analysis and case studies can be distorted by various factors. First, there is **social desirability bias,** the tendency for people to present themselves in the best possible light so they say things that are not strictly true. Second, there is the **self-fulfilling prophecy,** which is the tendency for someone's (e.g. the researcher's) expectations about another person (e.g. the participant in a case study) to lead to the fulfilment of those expectations. For example, if someone believed that depression leads to gambling, he/she might ask numerous questions about whether a gambler had ever felt very sad or depressed.
- Weakness: If the researcher accumulates a huge amount of material, as is the case with many case studies, he/she can easily show bias by emphasising only those bits of the material which fit his/her favoured hypothesis.
- Weakness: Qualitative analysis is not very useful in several areas of psychology (e.g. memory). For example, it would not have very useful for Peterson and Peterson (1959; see page 46) in their study of forgetting in short-term memory simply to describe their findings in qualitative terms!

■ **Activity:** Investigating conformity quantitatively and qualitatively

One way to investigate conformity is to stand near a traffic light and observe how many cars go through the red light, i.e. the drivers do not conform to our traffic regulations. The results of such a study would involve a frequency count of the number of people who did this. You could distinguish between male and female drivers, and people who are on their own or with passengers.

A qualitative approach would be to interview individuals about their driving habits and consider the reasons given as to why people do not always conform to traffic signals.

Which approach would provide "better" or more useful information?

Quantitative Analysis: Descriptive Statistics

Suppose we have carried out an experiment on the effects of noise on learning with three groups of nine participants each. One group was exposed to very loud noise, another to moderately loud noise, and the third was not exposed to any noise. What they had learned from a book chapter was assessed by giving them a set of questions, producing a score between 0 and 20.

What is to be done with the **raw scores**? There are two key types of measures that can be taken whenever we have a set of scores from participants in a given condition: **measures of central tendency,** and **measures of dispersion.**

Measures of central tendency

Measures of central tendency describe how the data cluster together around a central point. They provide some indication of the size of average or typical scores.

? **How can an experiment tell us more about "why" a behaviour has occurred than an observational study can?**

There are three main measures of central tendency: the mean, the median, and the mode.

Mean

The **mean** in each group or condition is calculated by adding up all the scores in a given condition, and then dividing by the number of participants in that condition. Suppose that the scores of the nine participants in the no-noise condition are as follows: 1, 2, 4, 5, 7, 9, 9, 9, 17. The mean is given by the total (63), divided by the number of participants (9) giving 7 (see the box on the right).

The mean takes all the scores into account, making it a **sensitive** measure of central tendency, especially if the scores resemble the **normal distribution**, which is a bell-shaped distribution in which most scores cluster fairly close to the mean.

However, the mean can be very misleading if the distribution differs markedly from normal and there are one or two extreme scores in one direction. Suppose that eight people complete one lap of a track in go-karts. For seven of them, the times taken (in seconds) are as follows: 25, 27, 28, 29, 34, 39, and 42. The eighth person's go-kart breaks down, and so the driver has to push it around the track, taking 288 seconds to complete the lap. The resulting overall mean of 64 seconds (see the box on the right) is clearly misleading, because no-one took even close to 64 seconds to complete one lap.

Median

Another way of describing the general level of performance in each condition is known as the **median**. If there is an odd number of scores, then the median is simply the middle score, having an equal number of scores higher and lower than it. In the example with nine scores in the no-noise condition, the median is 7 (see the box overleaf). Matters are slightly more complex if there is an even number of scores. In that case, we take the two central values and work out their mean. For example, suppose that we have the following scores in size order: 2, 5, 5, 7, 8, 9. The two central values are 5 and 7, and so the median is $(5 + 7)/2 = 6$.

The main advantage of the median is that it is unaffected by a few extreme scores, because it focuses only on scores in the middle of the

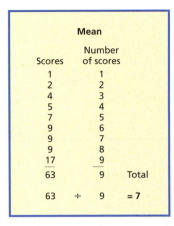

Mean		
Scores	Number of scores	
1	1	
2	2	
4	3	
5	4	
7	5	
9	6	
9	7	
9	8	
17	9	
63	9	Total
63	÷ 9	= 7

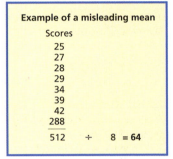

Example of a misleading mean

Scores
25
27
28
29
34
39
42
288
512 ÷ 8 = 64

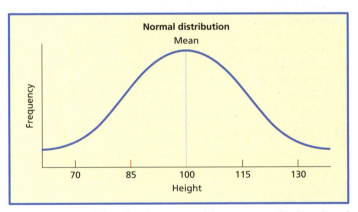

This is a normal distribution. It could represent the height of people in your class or the x-axis could be the "life-time" of a light bulb, given in weeks. Most of the scores will be clustered around the mean. The further away from the mean you get, the fewer cases there are.

LAP: 10 | TOTAL TIME: 20m 15 sec | FASTEST LAP: 1m 58 sec | THIS LAP: 2m 30 sec ↑ | MEAN LAP: 2m 15 sec ↑

An unexpected breakdown would cause the mean lap time to be very misleading.

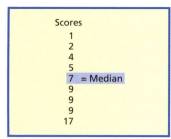

```
        Scores
          1
          2
          4
          5
          7   = Median
          9
          9
          9
          17
```

```
        Scores
          1
          2
          4
          5
          7
          9
          9   = Mode
          9
          17
```

distribution. In the case of our go-kart data the median would be 31.5, a more accurate "average" in this case than the mean. The median also has the advantage that it tends to be easier to work out than the mean.

The main limitation of the median is that it ignores most of the scores, and so it is often less sensitive than the mean. It is also not always representative of the scores obtained, especially if there are only a few scores.

Mode

The final measure of central tendency is the **mode**. This is simply the most frequently occurring score. In the no-noise condition example, this is 9 (see the box on the left).

The mode is unaffected by one or two extreme scores, and is the easiest measure of central tendency to work out. It can be worked out even when some of the extreme scores are not known.

However, its limitations generally outweigh these advantages. The greatest limitation is that the mode tends to be unreliable. For example, suppose we have the following scores: 4, 4, 6, 7, 8, 8, 12, 12, 12. The mode of these scores is 12. If just one score changed (a 12 becoming a 4), the mode would change to 4! Also, information about the exact values of the scores obtained is ignored in working out the mode. This makes it a less sensitive measure than the mean.

A final consideration is that it is possible for there to be more than one mode. In the case of the following scores 4, 4, 4, 4, 5, 6, 6, 8, 8, 8, 8 there are two modes (4 and 8) and the scores are therefore called **bimodal**. And some sets of data have no mode, as in our go-kart data.

> The mode is useful where other measures of central tendency are meaningless, for example when calculating the number of children in the average family. It would be unusual to have 0.4 or 0.6 of a child!

Summary

? The term "average" is rather vague. The mean, median, and mode are *all averages*.

The mean is the most generally useful measure of central tendency, whereas the mode is the least useful. However, there are circumstances in which the mean is less useful, such as when the distribution of scores is very unusual or there are a few extreme scores in the data.

Measures of dispersion

In addition to having an estimate of central tendency, it is also useful to work out what are known as measures of dispersion, such as the range and standard deviation. These measures indicate the extent to which the scores cluster around the average or are spread out.

The range

The simplest of these measures is the **range**, which can be defined as the difference between the highest and the lowest score in any condition. In the case of the following numbers: 4, 5, 5, 7, 9, 9, 9, 17, the range is calculated as follows: highest number − lowest number, or 17 − 4 = 13.

In fact, it is preferable to calculate the range in a slightly different way (Coolican, 1994). The revised formula (when we are dealing with whole numbers) is as follows: (highest score − lowest score) + 1, i.e. (17 − 4) + 1 = 14. This formula is preferable because it takes account of the fact that the scores were rounded to whole numbers. In our sample data, a score of 17 stands for all values between 16.5 and 17.5, and a score of 4 represents a value between 3.5 and 4.5. If we take the range as the interval between the highest possible value (17.5) and the lowest possible value (3.5), this gives us a range of 14, which is precisely the figure produced by the formula.

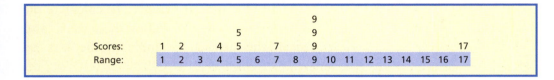

What has been said so far about the range applies only to whole numbers. Suppose that we measure the time taken to perform a task to the nearest tenth of a second, with the fastest time being 21.3 seconds and the slowest time being 36.8 seconds. The figure of 21.3 represents a value between 21.25 and 21.35, and 36.8 represents a value between 36.75 and 36.85. As a result, the range is $36.85 - 21.25$, which is 15.6 seconds, whereas $36.8 - 21.3 = 15.5$.

The range is easy to calculate and takes full account of extreme values. However, it can be greatly influenced by one score that is very different from all of the others. In the example above, the inclusion of the participant scoring 17 increases the range from 9 to 17. Also, it ignores all but two of the scores, and so is likely to provide an inadequate measure of the general spread or dispersion of the scores around the mean or median.

The interquartile range

The **interquartile range** is defined as the spread of the middle 50% of scores. For example, suppose we have the following scores: 4, 5, 6, 6, 7, 8, 8, 9, 11, 11, 14, 15, 17, 18, 18, 19. There are 16 scores, which can be divided into the bottom 25% (4), the middle 50% (8), and the top 25% (4). The middle 50% of scores starts with 7 and runs through to 15. The upper boundary of the interquartile range lies between 15 and 17, and is given by the mean of those two values, i.e. 16. The lower boundary of the interquartile range lies between 6 and 7, and is the mean, i.e. 6.5. The interquartile range is the difference between the upper and lower boundaries, i.e. $16 - 6.5 = 9.5$.

The interquartile range has the advantage over the range that it is not influenced by a single extreme score. Thus, it is more likely to provide an accurate reflection of the spread or dispersion of the scores. It has the disadvantage that it ignores information from the top and bottom 25% of scores.

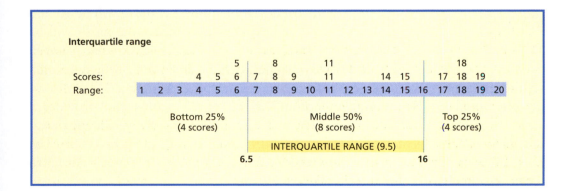

Standard deviation: A worked example

Participant	Score (x)	Mean ($\bar{x}$)	Deviation ($x - \bar{x}$)	Deviation² ($x - \bar{x}$)²
1	13	10	3	9
2	6	10	−4	16
3	10	10	0	0
4	15	10	5	25
5	10	10	0	0
6	15	10	5	25
7	5	10	−5	25
8	9	10	−1	1
9	10	10	0	0
10	13	10	3	9
11	6	10	−4	16
12	11	10	1	1
13	7	10	−3	9
13	130	10		$\Sigma(x - \bar{x})^2 = 136$

Total of scores (Σx) = 130

Number of participants (N) = 13

Mean ($\bar{x}$) = $\frac{\Sigma x}{N} = \frac{130}{13} = 10$

Σ means "the sum of"

$\bar{x}$ is the symbol for the mean

Variance (s^2) = $\frac{136}{13-1} = 11.33$

Standard deviation (SD) = $\sqrt{11.3} = 3.37$

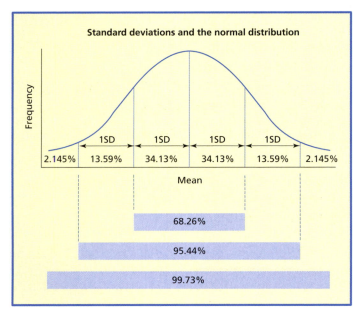

Standard deviations and the normal distribution

Frequency

1SD | 1SD | 1SD | 1SD

2.145% | 13.59% | 34.13% | 34.13% | 13.59% | 2.145%

Mean

68.26%

95.44%

99.73%

Two-thirds of a normally distributed population (or 68.26%) are located within one standard deviation of the mean, 95.44% fall within two standard deviations, and 99.73% fall within three standard deviations.

Standard deviation

The most generally useful measure of dispersion is the **standard deviation**. It is harder to calculate than the range, but generally provides a more accurate measure of the spread of scores. However, many calculators allow the standard deviation to be worked out rapidly and effortlessly. To calculate the standard deviation manually, follow these steps (also illustrated in the worked example in the box on the left):

1. Work out the mean of the sample. This is given by the total of all of the participants' scores $\Sigma x = 130$ (the symbol Σ means "the sum of") divided by the number of participants (N = 13). Thus, the mean ($\bar{x}$) is 10.
2. Subtract the mean in turn from each score ($x = \bar{x}$). The calculations are shown in the fourth column.
3. Square each of the scores in the fourth column $(x - \bar{x})^2$.
4. Work out the total of all the squared scores, $\Sigma(x - \bar{x})^2$. This comes to 136.
5. Divide by one less than the number of participants, N − 1 = 12. This gives us 136 divided by 12, which equals 11.33. This is known as the **variance** (s^2), which is in squared units.
6. Use a calculator to take the square root of the variance. This produces a figure of 3.37. This is the standard deviation (SD).

This method is used when we want to estimate the standard deviation of the population. If we want merely to describe the spread of scores in our sample, then the fifth step is to divide the result of the fourth step by N.

Where data are normally distributed, about two-thirds of the scores in a sample should lie within one standard deviation of the mean. This is shown in the graph on the left.

In our example, the mean of the sample is 10.0, one standard deviation above the mean will be 13.366 and one standard deviation below the mean will be 6.634. Eight out of the thirteen scores lie between these two values, which is 61.5%, which is only slightly below the expected percentage.

The standard deviation takes account of all of the scores and provides a sensitive measure of dispersion. As we have seen, it also has the advantage that it describes the spread of scores in a normal distribution with great precision. The most obvious disadvantage of the standard deviation is that it is much harder to work out than the other measures of dispersion.

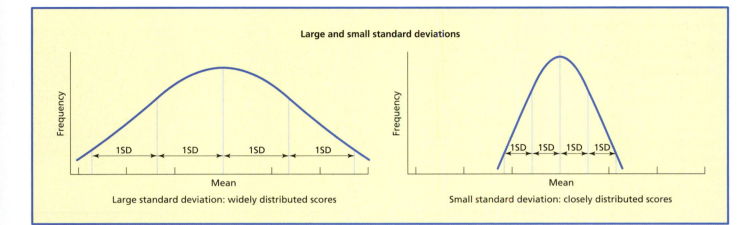

Large and small standard deviations

Large standard deviation: widely distributed scores

Small standard deviation: closely distributed scores

The Nature of Correlations

In Section 20, we considered studies using correlational analysis. Strictly speaking correlation is not a research method but a method of analysing data. Therefore it is appropriate to consider correlation further in this section on data analysis.

Positive and negative correlation

A **positive correlation** is when two variables increase together. You can also have a **negative correlation** when there is an inverse relationship between co-variables—as one increases, the other decreases (illustrations of positive and negative correlations are shown in the box on the right). The co-variables still vary together, though in opposite directions. This can be seen in exposure to loud noise and hearing. As your exposure increases, in general your hearing abilities decrease. The two variables are still correlated because there is a clear and predictable association; the co-variables vary systematically together.

Correlation coefficients

We assess the extent to which the co-variables are correlated using the **correlation coefficient**. A coefficient is a number that expresses the degree to which two things are related. If two variables are perfectly related then the coefficient is 1.0. Perfect positive correlation is +1.0 and perfect negative correlation is −1.0. Of course, perfect correlation is rare. A correlation coefficient of −0.75 would reflect a close inverse relationship between two variables. A correlation coefficient of −0.85 would suggest an even closer inverse relationship. A correlation coefficient of −0.25 or +0.25 would suggest a poor relationship between the two variables. A zero correlation coefficient (0.0) is a complete lack of relationship.

It is possible to calculate the correlation coefficient between co-variables using a statistical test, but this is not covered at AS level.

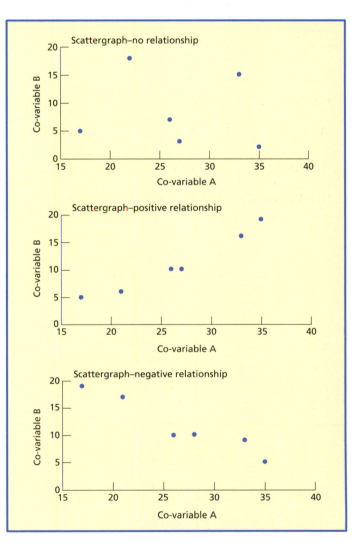

Graphs and Charts

Graphs and charts should be clearly labelled and presented so that the reader can rapidly make sense of the information contained in them. It is also helpful to use squared paper when recording numbers and drawing graphs.

Measures of central tendency and of range are ways of summarising data. Perhaps it is even more helpful to use visual displays to summarise information and get a feel for what it means. If information is presented in a graph or chart, this may make it easier for people to understand what has been found, compared to simply presenting information about the central tendency and dispersion.

Suppose that we ask 25 male athletes to run 400 metres as rapidly as possible, and record their times (in seconds). Having worked out a table of frequencies (see the boxed example below), there are several ways to present these data.

25 Athletes running 400 metres

Raw data

Athlete	1	2	3	4	5	6	7	8	9
Speed	71	77	84	49	63	62	56	67	52

Athlete	10	11	12	13	14	15	16	17	18
Speed	61	63	59	48	61	65	68	54	61

Athlete	19	20	21	22	23	24	25
Speed	58	66	55	57	58	56	53

Table of frequencies (number of athletes obtaining each speed)

Speed	48	49	52	53	54	55	56	57	58	59	61	62	63	65	66	67	68	71	77	84
Athlete no.	13	4	9	25	17	21	7 24	22	19 23	12	10 14 18	6	5 11	15	20	8	16	1	2	3
Number	1	1	1	1	1	1	2	1	2	1	3	1	2	1	1	1	1	1	1	1

Histogram

In a **histogram** (see below), the scores are indicated on the horizontal axis and the frequencies are shown on the vertical axis. The frequencies are indicated by rectangular columns all the same width but varying in height in accordance with the corresponding frequencies. It is important to make sure that the class intervals are not too broad or too narrow. All class intervals are represented, even if there are no scores in some of them. Class intervals are indicated by their mid-point at the centre of the columns. In the present example (see left), the histogram indicates that most of the athletes ran 400 metres fairly quickly. Only a few had extreme times that were below 55 seconds or greater than 70 seconds.

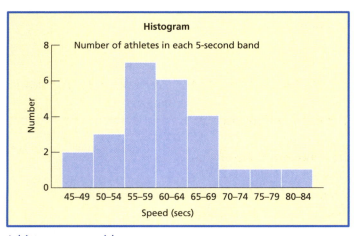

A histogram provides a means of summarising the data.

Bar charts

Bar charts are often used when the data are in categories. The categories are shown along the horizontal axis, and the frequencies are indicated on the vertical axis, as in a histogram (see box opposite). The categories in bar charts cannot be ordered numerically in a meaningful way, but in ascending (or descending) order of popularity. The rectangles in a **bar chart** don't usually touch each other.

The scale on the vertical axis of a bar chart normally starts at zero, although it is sometimes convenient for presentational purposes to have it start at some higher value. If so, it should be made clear in the bar chart that the lower part of the vertical scale is missing. The columns in a bar chart often represent frequencies, but they can also represent means or percentages for different groups (Coolican, 1994).

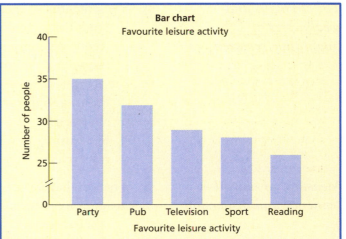

A bar chart makes it easy to compare the popularity of different leisure activities. We can see at a glance that going to a party was the most popular leisure activity, whereas reading a good book was the least popular. The data in this chart are in nominal categories.

Scattergraphs

In the case of correlational studies, the data, in the form of two measures of behaviour from each member of a single group of participants (called co-variables), can be presented in the form of a **scattergraph** (or **scattergram**), with a dot for each participant indicating where he or she falls on the two dimensions. If there is a positive relationship the dots should form a pattern going from the bottom left of the scattergraph to the top right (see examples on page 321). If there is no relationship between the two variables, then the dots should be distributed in a fairly random way within the scattergraph. If there is a negative relationship between the two variables, then the dots will form a pattern going from the top left to the bottom right. The scattergraph gives you a rough idea of the association between two variables. To be more precise you need to calculate an inferential statistic called a "correlation coefficient", but these statistics are not covered at AS level.

You have reached the end of the chapter on research methods in psychology. Research is fundamental to the status of psychology as a scientific subject. It enables us to be more than "armchair psychologists". We should be able to provide systematic, reliable, and valid evidence for our views.

SECTION SUMMARY

❖ Qualitative research is concerned with the experiences of the participants, and with the meanings they attach to themselves and their lives.

❖ A key principle of qualitative analysis is that theoretical understanding emerges from the data, and is not imposed by the researcher.

❖ Qualitative researchers typically categorise the data after taking account of all the data and the participants' own categories.

❖ There are various forms of qualitative research including:
  – content analysis,
  – discourse analysis,
  – case studies,
  – some observational studies.

The nature of qualitative research

The strengths and weaknesses of qualitative research

❖ The strengths of qualitative research include:
  – Studying people in a social context.
  – Reducing complex data into a manageable number of categories.
  – Producing findings that suggest new hypotheses.
❖ The weaknesses of qualitative research include:
  – Biases and distortions in the data collected and in the ways those data are analysed.
  – In addition, it is often hard to replicate the findings obtained in qualitative research.

Measures of central tendency and dispersion

❖ When we have obtained scores from a group of participants, we can summarise our data by working out:
  – A measure of central tendency (average).
  – A measure of dispersion or spread of scores around the central tendency.
❖ The mean is the most generally useful measure of central tendency because it takes all the scores into account.
❖ However, other measures include the median and mode.
❖ The median is less affected than the mean by extreme values.
❖ The standard deviation is the most useful and precise measure of dispersion, but the range is a much simpler figure to calculate, although it is affected by extreme scores.

Positive and negative correlations

❖ The correlations between two variables can be positive (variables increase together) or negative (variables change in an inverse fashion—as one increases, the other decreases).
❖ The extent to which the co-variables are related is expressed by a correlation coefficient.
❖ Perfect correlation is $+1.0$ or -1.0 for positive or negative correlation respectively.

Presentation of data

❖ Summary data from a study can be presented in the form of a figure or table of frequencies so that it is easy to observe general trends.
❖ Among the possible ways of presenting the data in a figure are the following:
  – Histogram: used when scores can be ordered from low to high.
  – Bar chart: used when the scores are in the form of categories.
  – Scattergraph: the data from correlational studies can be presented in a scattergraph where the scores on two co-variables are recorded from every participant as a dot.

See pp.154–158 of the revision guide.

FURTHER READING

A book that covers most research methods in an accessible way is H. Coolican (1994) *Research methods and statistics in psychology* (London: Hodder & Stoughton). A shorter version of the Coolican (1994) textbook is H. Coolican (1995) *Introduction to research methods and statistics in psychology* (London: Hodder & Stoughton). A good reasonably priced student book is by A. Searle (1999) *Introducing research and data in psychology* (London: Routledge). Another useful textbook is J.J. Foster and J. Parker (1995) *Carrying out investigations in psychology: Methods and statistics* (Leicester, UK: BPS Books). The various forms of non-experimental study are described in C. Dyer (1995) *Beginning research in psychology* (Oxford, UK: Blackwell).

EXAM HINT
Refer to the *Psychology for AS Level Workbook* for different types of exam questions that may come up in the research methods section.

REVISION QUESTIONS

The examination questions aim to *sample* the material in this whole chapter. For advice on how to answer such questions refer to Chapter 1, Section 2.

In this section of the examination there is only one question, worth 30 marks, and this is compulsory. You have approximately 30 minutes to do this question.

Question (AQA, 2004)

As part of their coursework, a small group of AS-level psychology students decided to examine the relationship between stress and physical illness. They designed a scale to measure stress using a list of 20 life events (e.g. exams, driving test, end of a relationship). After getting permission from their Head Teacher and the participants' parents to conduct the study, they obtained a random sample of 15 students from the 6th Form.

They asked the participants to tick any of the life events that they had experienced in the past two years. This was used to establish a stress score between 0 and 20. On this scale a high score indicates a lot of stress. After each participant had completed the stress scale, they were asked how many days they had taken off school through illness that year.

Previous research had led the psychology students to expect a positive correlation between stress and illness.

After statistical analysis, the results showed a correlation coefficient of −0.734.

a. How were the variables "stress" and "illness" operationalised by the
    students who designed the study?   (2 marks + 2 marks)
b. (i)   What is meant by investigator effects?   (1 mark)
    (ii) Give an example of *one* possible investigator effect in this study.   (2 marks)
    (iii) Describe how this investigator effect might be overcome in this study.   (2 marks)
c. (i)   What is meant by the term correlation coefficient?   (2 marks)
    (ii) Using the information from the correlation coefficient, describe the
          relationship between stress and illness that the researchers found in this study.   (2 marks)
    (iii) Give *one* advantage and *one* disadvantage of an investigation using a
          correlational analysis.   (2 marks + 2 marks)
d. (i)   Explain how students might have selected their random sample.   (2 marks)
    (ii) Give *one* limitation of random sampling.   (2 marks)
e. Although the students correctly obtained permission from their Head Teacher
    and the participants' parents,
    (i)   identify *one* ethical issue that they do not seem to have considered   (1 mark)
    (ii) explain how the researchers could have dealt with this ethical issue.   (2 marks)
f. Due to the unexpected nature of the findings, the students felt it would be useful
    to gather some qualitative data about the participants' experiences of stress and illness.
    (i)   Explain how they could obtain such qualitative data about participants'
          experiences.   (3 marks)
    (ii) Outline how they could analyse the data collected.   (3 marks)

GLOSSARY

The following list is a glossary of the key terms and concepts that are presented throughout the book in **bold**. It is important that you are able to define the key terms (listed in blue), as many questions will ask you for definitions. The key term definitions provided are worth 3 marks each, and this is usually the detail that is required to get full marks in the exam. The remainder of the terms (listed in black) are for your information only, and you will not be asked to define these in the exam.

Abnormal or **atypical psychology**: the study of individuals who differ from the norm, such as those with mental disorders.

Abnormality: behaviour that is considered to deviate from the norm (statistical or social), or ideal mental health. It is dysfunctional because it is harmful or causes distress to the individual or others and so is considered to be a failure to function adequately. Abnormality is characterised by the fact that it is an undesirable state that causes severe impairment in the personal and social functioning of the individual, and often causes the person great anguish depending on how much insight they have into their illness.

Acoustic coding: encoding words in terms of their sound using information stored in long-term memory.

Adaptive: the extent to which a behaviour increases the reproductive potential of an individual and survival of its genes.

Adrenal glands: the endocrine glands that are located adjacent to, and covering, the upper part of the kidneys.

Adrenaline: one of the hormones (along with noradrenaline) produced by the adrenal glands, which increases arousal by activating the sympathetic nervous system and reducing activity in the parasympathetic system.

Adrenocorticotrophic hormone (ACTH): a hormone produced by the anterior pituitary gland which stimulates the adrenal cortex.

Affectionless psychopathy: a condition where individuals appear to experience little guilt or emotion, lack normal affection, and are unable to form permanent relationships.

Agentic state: a state of feeling controlled by an authority figure, and therefore lacking a sense of personal responsibility.

Aims: the purpose of a research study.

Alternative hypothesis: another term for the experimental hypothesis. The experimental hypothesis is the alternative to the null hypothesis.

Amnesia: a partial loss of long-term memory, usually as a result of brain damage.

Anaclitic depression: a severe form of depression in infants who experience prolonged separations from their mothers. The term "anaclitic" means "arising from emotional dependency on another".

Animal behaviour: the study of non-human animals in their own right.

Anorexia nervosa: an eating disorder characterised by the individual being severely underweight; 85% or less than expected for size and height. There is also anxiety, as the anorexic has an intense fear of becoming fat and a distorted body image. The individual does not have an accurate perception of their body size, seeing themselves as "normal", when they are in fact significantly underweight, and they may minimise the dangers of being severely underweight.

ANS (autonomic nervous system): that part of the nervous system that controls vital body functions, which is self-regulating and needs no conscious control (automatic).

Attachment: this is a strong, reciprocal, emotional bond between an infant and his or her caregiver(s) that is characterised by a desire to maintain proximity. Attachments take different forms, such as secure or insecure. Infants display attachment through the degree of separation distress shown when separated from the caregiver, pleasure at reunion with the caregiver, and stranger anxiety.

Authoritarian personality: identified by Adorno et al. as someone who is more likely to be obedient. They tend to hold rigid beliefs, be hostile towards other groups, and submissive to authority.

Autokinetic effect: a visual illusion where a small spot of light in a darkened room appears to be moving when in fact it is stationary.

Autonomous state: being aware of the consequences of our actions and therefore taking voluntary control of our behaviour.

Avoidant attachment (type A): an insecure attachment of an infant to its mother. The child avoids contact on reunion.

Bar chart: like a histogram, a representation of frequency data but the categories do not have to be continuous; used for nominal data.

Behavioural model of abnormality: a model of abnormality that considers individuals who suffer from mental disorders possess maladaptive forms of behaviour, which have been learned.

Benzodiazepines: anti-anxiety drugs such as Valium and Librium. They work by reducing serotonin levels.

Bimodal: a distribution with two modes.

Biochemistry: the study of the chemical processes of living organisms.

Biofeedback: a technique that aims to control involuntary (autonomic) muscles through the use of feedback about current physiological functioning. Relaxation is an important aspect of its success when used in the context of stress.

Biological (medical) model: a model of abnormality that regards mental disorders as illnesses with a physical cause.

Black box: the term used by behaviourists to refer to the mind. Their focus was on what goes in (a stimulus) and what comes out (a response).

Bond disruption: when a child is deprived of their main attachment object, in the short or long term, and receives no substitute emotional care.

Bonding: the process of forming close ties with another.

Buffers: term used to refer to aspects of situations that protect people from having to confront the results of their actions.

Bulimia nervosa: an eating disorder in which excessive (binge) eating is followed by compensatory behaviour such as self-induced vomiting or misuse of laxatives. It is often experienced as an unbreakable cycle where the bulimic impulsively overeats and then has to purge to reduce anxiety and feelings of guilt about the amount of food consumed, which can be thousands of calories at a time. This disorder is not associated with excessive weight loss.

Burnout: physical and/or emotional exhaustion produced especially by stress.

Buspirone: a more recent anti-anxiety drug, which increases the production of serotonin and has fewer side effects than benzodiazepines.

Capacity: a measure of how much can be held in either short-term or long-term memory.

Cardiovascular disorders: these are disorders of the cardiovascular system, which includes the heart and its supporting systems. An example is atherosclerosis, which is the thickening of the arteries due to high levels of cholesterol in the bloodstream. Another disorder is hypertension or high blood pressure, which puts pressure on the heart as it has to work harder to beat at high pressure.

Caregiving sensitivity hypothesis: secure attachments are due to a caregiver's sensitivity and responsiveness, which creates independence in the infant.

Case study: detailed study of a single individual, event, or group.

Central executive: the key component of working memory. It is a modality-free system (i.e. not visual or auditory) of limited capacity and similar to "paying attention" to something.

Chunks: integrated units of information.

Chunking: the process of combining individual items (e.g. letters; numbers) into larger, meaningful units.

Classical conditioning: learning through association; a neutral stimulus becomes associated with a known stimulus–reflex response.

Client-centred therapy: a form of humanistic therapy introduced by Rogers and designed to increase the client's self-esteem and reduce incongruence between self and ideal self.

Clinician (or clinical psychologist): a person who works in clinical psychology, concerned with the diagnosis and treatment of abnormal behaviour.

CNS (central nervous system): part of the nervous system that consists of the brain and the spinal cord.

Cognitive development: the development of the child's mental processes such as thought, reasoning, and memory. IQ tests and the child's academic performance at school are used to assess cognitive development. Cognitive development is determined by an interaction of biological predisposition and the environment.

Cognitive interview: an interview technique that is based on our knowledge about the way human memory works, paying attention, for example, to the use of retrieval cues.

Cognitive model of abnormality: a model of abnormality which considers that individuals who suffer from mental disorders have distorted or irrational thinking.

Cognitive therapies: a form of treatment that involves attempts to change or restructure the client's thoughts and beliefs.

Cognitive triad: negative thoughts about the self, the world, and the future, found in depressed clients.

Collectivistic: a culture where individuals share tasks, belongings, and income. The people may live in large family groups and value interdependence.

Compliance: conforming to the majority view in order to be liked, avoid ridicule or social exclusion. Compliance occurs more readily with public behaviour than private behaviour, and is based on power.

Concordance rates: the extent to which two measures are in agreement, such as if one twin has a condition and so does the other.

Conditioning: when one response is made dependent on another.

Confederate: a colleague of the experimenter who acts a part during the experiment unknown to the real participant(s) who are unaware of the confederate's relationship with the experimenter.

Confidentiality: the requirement for ethical research that information provided by participants in research is not made available to other people.

Confounding variables: variables that are mistakenly manipulated or allowed to vary along with the independent variable and therefore affect the dependent variable.

Constant error: any unwanted variable that has a systematically different effect on the dependent variable in different conditions.

Control: this refers to the perception of being in command (control) of one's responses to stimuli, such as stressors. Self-perception is the crux of this, as according to the transactional model, a lack of control and consequently stress may be experienced when there is a mismatch between the perceived demands of the situation and the individual's perceived ability to cope. Perception of control gives the individual a sense of self-efficacy, that is, they perceive that they can cope with the stressor.

Control group: the group of participants who receive no treatment and act as a comparison to the experimental group to study any effects of the treatment.

Controlled variables: variables, not of interest to the experimenter, that are held constant or controlled.

Conversion: the influence of the minority on the majority. This is likely to effect private beliefs more than public behaviour.

Correlation: an association that is found between two variables.

Correlation coefficient: a number that expresses the extent to which two variables are related or vary together.

Correlational analysis: testing a hypothesis using an association that is found between two variables.

Cortisol: a hormone produced by the adrenal gland which elevates blood sugar and is important in digestion, especially at times of stress.

Cost–benefit analysis: a comparison between the costs of something and the related benefits, in order to decide on a course of action.

Counterbalancing: used with repeated measures design to overcome the problems of practice and order effects, and involves ensuring that each condition is equally likely to be used first and second by participants.

Co-variables: the variables involved in a correlational study that may vary together (co-vary).

Critical period: a biologically determined period of time during which an animal is exclusively receptive to certain changes.

Cross-cultural evidence: data collected from different cultures.

Cross-cultural variations in attachment: cross-cultural variations refer to the fact that behaviour, attitudes, norms, and values differ across cultures. This is because cultures socially construct different values and norms, etc. Thus, the relationships between infants and caregivers vary across cultures because of different childrearing styles and beliefs about which qualities should be nurtured. This is evident in the cross-cultural differences that research has suggested between individualistic and collectivist cultures.

Cue-dependent forgetting: forgetting that occurs when the sought-for information is in long-term memory because of the absence of a suitable retrieval cue.

Cued recall: after presenting the material to be learned, cues are provided to help recall.

Cultural relativism: the view that one cannot judge behaviour properly unless it is viewed in the context from which it originates. This is because different cultures have different constructions of behaviour and so interpretations of behaviour may differ across cultures. A lack of cultural relativism can lead to ethnocentrism, where only the perspective of one's own culture is taken.

Cultures: groups of people who are bound by the same rules, morals, and methods of interaction.

Day care: this refers to care that is provided by people other than the parent or relatives of the infant. It can take different forms, for example, nurseries, childminders, play groups, etc. It is distinct from institutionalised care, which provides permanent substitute care; day care is a temporary alternative to the caregiver.

Debriefing: attempts by the experimenter at the end of a study to provide detailed information for the participants about the study and to reduce any distress they might have felt.

Deception: this is an ethical guideline, which states that deception of the participants during the research process should be avoided wherever possible. Deception refers to the withholding of information that might affect the participant's decision to take part in the research. It is an issue because this might lead to psychological harm. Deception is a particularly common issue because the withholding of the research hypothesis is often considered necessary in order to avoid demand characteristics.

Declarative knowledge: knowledge related to "knowing that", including episodic and semantic memory.

Defence mechanisms: strategies used by the ego to defend itself against anxiety.

Deindividuation: losing one's sense of personal identity.

Demand characteristics: features of an experiment that help participants to work out what is expected of them, and lead them to behave in certain predictable ways.

Dependent variable (DV): an aspect of the participant's behaviour that is measured in the study.

Deprivation: to lose something, such as the care of an attachment figure for a period of time.

Deprivation dwarfism: physical underdevelopment found in children reared in isolation or in institutions. Thought to be an effect of the stress associated with emotional deprivation.

Depth of processing: the extent to which something is processed, not in terms of how much processing is done (as in repetition) but in terms of how much meaning is extracted.

Descriptive statistics: a diagram or numbers used to describe research data.

Deviation from ideal mental health: deviation from optimal psychological well-being (a state of contentment that we all strive to achieve). Deviation is characterised by a lack of positive self-attitudes, personal growth, autonomy, accurate view of reality, environmental mastery, and resistance to stress; all of which prevent the individual from accessing their potential, which is known as self-actualisation.

Deviation from social norms: behaviour that does not follow socially accepted patterns; violation of them is considered abnormal. These unwritten social rules are culturally relative and era-dependent. For example, homosexuality was once illegal and considered to be a mental disorder because it deviated from the social norm. Now there are campaigns for gay marriages to be recognised and afforded the same benefits as heterosexual marriages, and this shows the extent to which this definition of abnormality is subject to change.

Diathesis–stress model: the notion that psychological disorders occur when there is a genetically determined vulnerability (diathesis) and relevant stressful conditions.

Directional (one-tailed) hypothesis: a prediction that there will be a difference or correlation between two variables and a statement of the direction of this difference.

Disorganised attachment (type D): the infant shows no set pattern of behaviour at separation or reunion (thus "disorganised"). This kind of behaviour is associated with abused children or those whose mothers are chronically depressed.

Displacement: the pushing out of information from short-term memory by new information before it has been processed for long enough to pass on to long-term memory.

Dispositional explanation: deciding that other people's actions are caused by their internal characteristics or dispositions.

Dissociation: minority ideas absorbed into the majority viewpoint without anyone remembering where they came from.

Dizygotic (DZ) twins: non-identical twins formed from two eggs (ova). Genetically as similar as any pair of siblings.

Double blind: a procedure where neither the participant nor the experimenter knows the precise aims of the study. This reduces experimenter effects.

DSM-IV: the most recent version of *the Diagnostic and Statistical Manual of Mental Disorders* published by the American Psychiatric Association, provides a means of classifying and diagnosing mental disorders.

Duration: this refers to how long a memory lasts. The existence of two distinct memory stores is supported by differences in duration because this differs between short-term memory (STM) and long-term memory (LTM). STM has a very limited duration of 18–30 seconds. In contrast, LTM potentially lasts forever and so a memory may endure permanently.

DV (dependent variable): an aspect of the participant's behaviour that is measured in the study.

Eating disorder: a dysfunctional relationship with food. The dysfunction may be gross under-eating (anorexia), binge–purging (bulimia), over-eating (obesity), or healthy eating (orthorexia). These disorders may be characterised by faulty cognition and emotional responses to food, maladaptive conditioning, dysfunctional family relationships, early childhood conflicts, or a biological and genetic basis, but the nature and expression of eating disorders show great individual variation.

Ego: the conscious, rational part of the mind which is guided by the reality principle.

Ego defence: strategies used by the ego to defend itself against anxiety.

Elaboration of processing: a form of deep processing, achieved by engaging in complex processing.

Encoding: this involves the transfer of information into code, leading to the creation of a memory trace, which can be registered in the memory store. There is evidence that STM and LTM are dependent on different codes, as in STM encoding it is primarily acoustic (based on the sound of the word) and in LTM encoding it is primarily semantic (based on the meaning of the word).

Encoding specificity principle: the notion that memory is best when there is a large overlap between the information available at the time of retrieval and the information in the memory trace.

Endocrine system: a system of a number of ductless glands located throughout the body which produce the body's chemical messengers, called hormones.

Enmeshment: a situation in which all of the members of a family lack a clear sense of their own personal identity.

Episodic memory: long-term memory for autobiographical or personal events, usually including information about the time and place of an episode or event.

et al.: Latin, meaning "and others".

Ethical committees: committees of psychologists and lay individuals who consider all research proposals from the perspective of the rights and dignity of the participants.

Ethical guidelines: a written code of conduct designed to aid psychologists when designing and running their research. The guidelines set out standards of what is and is not acceptable. The code focuses on the need to treat participants with respect and to not cause them harm or distress. For example, the BPS code of conduct advises of "the need to preserve an overriding high regard for the well-being and dignity of research participants" (BPS, 1993).

Ethical issues: ethical issues arise in the implementing of research when there is conflict between how the research should be carried out (e.g. with no deception to the participants) and the methodological consequences of observing this (e.g. reduced validity of the findings). Another issue is that of participants versus society. Is it justifiable to infringe upon the rights of participants if the research will be of benefit to society? Such issues are an inevitable consequence of researching people and resolving the issues can be difficult.

Ethics: a set of moral principles used to guide human behaviour.

Ethologists: individuals who study animal behaviour in its natural environment, focusing on the importance of innate capacities and the functions of behaviours.

Evaluation apprehension: concern felt by research participants that their performance is being judged.

Event sampling: a technique for collecting data in an observational study. The observer focuses only on actions or events that are of particular interest to the study.

Experiment: a procedure undertaken to make a discovery about causal relationships. The experimenter manipulates one variable to see its effect on another variable.

Experimental group: the group receiving the experimental treatment.

Experimental hypothesis: the hypothesis written prior to conducting an experiment, it usually specifies the independent and dependent variables.

Experimental realism: the use of an artificial situation in which participants become so involved that they are fooled into thinking the set-up is real rather than artificial.

Experimental treatment: the alteration of the independent variable.

Experimenter bias: the effect that the experimenter's expectations have on the participants and therefore the results of the study.

Experimenter effects: see investigator effects.

Experimenter expectancy: the systematic effects that an experimenter's expectations have on the performance of the participants.

Expert witness: a person who offers testimony in a trial in relation to their professional knowledge, such as a medical expert or an expert on hypnosis.

External validity: the validity of an experiment outside the research situation itself; the extent to which the findings of a research study are applicable to other situations, especially "everyday" situations.

Extraneous variables: variables that can affect the behaviour of participants in a research study, such as age, gender, intelligence, personality, type of task, noise, temperature etc. If extraneous variables are randomised across groups or held constant (e.g. all participants are the same age), then they should not bias results. However, if they vary systematically with the independent variable (e.g. if all the participants in the experimental group are male and all those in the control group are female) they become a *confounding* variable that may bias results.

Eyewitness testimony: Evidence supplied by people who witness a specific event or crime, relying only on their memory. Statements often include descriptions of the criminal (facial appearance and other identifiable characteristics) and subsequent identification, and details of the crime scene (e.g. the sequence of events, time of day, and if others witnessed the event, etc.). There is good evidence that eyewitness testimony can be incorrect, because eyewitness memories of events tend to be fragile and easily distorted (e.g. by leading questions).

F (Fascism) Scale: a test of tendencies towards fascism. High scorers are prejudiced and racist.

Failure to function adequately: a model of abnormality based on an inability to cope with day-to-day life caused by psychological distress or discomfort.

False memory syndrome: a condition where an adult "recovers" apparently repressed memories. In fact the memories are for events that did not happen, thus "false memory".

Field experiment: a study in which the experimental method is used in a more naturalistic situation.

Fixation: in Freudian terms, spending a long time at a given stage of development because of over- or under-gratification.

Flashbulb memory: a long-lasting and vivid memory of a specific event and the context in which it occurred. The event is important and emotionally significant (e.g. a national or personal event). The term "flashbulb" refers to the fact that it is as if a photographic image of the event and setting has been encoded, as the memory is so detailed and accurate. Examples include the atrocities of September 11th 2001, and the deaths of Princess Diana and John F. Kennedy.

Forgetting: this is the inability to recall or recognise information. Forgetting may occur because the information no longer exists in memory and so is not available for retrieval. Alternatively, it can occur because it cannot be found and so is not accessible (cue-dependent forgetting). Forgetting is more likely with information that needs to be recalled, as recognition is generally easier than recall.

Fundamental attribution error: the tendency to explain the causes of another person's behaviour in terms of dispositional rather than situational factors.

GABA: a neurotransmitter that is produced at times of stress.

Gene: a unit of inheritance that forms part of a chromosome. Some characteristics are determined by one gene whereas for others many genes are involved.

Gene-mapping: determining the effect of a particular gene on physical or psychological characteristics.

General Adaptation Syndrome (GAS): the body's non-specific response to stress that consists of three stages: the alarm reaction, when the body responds with the heightened physiological reactivity of the "fight or flight" response to meet the demands of the stressor; resistance, when the body tries to cope with the stressor and outwardly appears to have returned to normal but inwardly is releasing high levels of stress hormones; and exhaustion, where resources are depleted and the body's defence against disease and illness is decreased.

Generalisability: the extent to which the findings of a study can be applied to other settings, populations, times, and measures.

Generalisation: the tendency to transfer a response from one stimulus to another that is quite similar.

Genetic: information from genes, the units of inheritance.

Genetic vulnerability: an inherited susceptibility to a particular condition or characteristic.

Glucose: a form of sugar that is one of the main sources of energy for the brain.

Hardiness: a cluster of traits possessed by those people best able to cope with stress.

Hawthorne effect: the changes that take place to participants' behaviour as a result of knowing that they are being observed.

Hindsight bias: the tendency to be wise after the event, using the benefit of hindsight.

Histogram: a graph in which the frequencies of scores in each category are represented by a vertical column; data on the y-axis must be continuous with a true zero.

Homeostasis: the process of maintaining a reasonably constant internal environment.

Hormones: chemical substances produced by the body.

Humanistic psychology: an approach to psychology that focuses on higher motivation, self-development, and on each individual as unique.

Hypermnesia: an enhanced ability to remember information, claimed to be found in hypnotised individuals.

Hypertension: a condition associated with very high blood pressure.

Hypothalamus: the part of the brain that integrates the activity of the autonomic nervous system. Involved with emotion, stress, motivation, and hunger.

Hypothesis: a statement of what you believe to be true.

Id: in Freudian theory, that part of the mind, motivated by the pleasure principle and sexual instincts.

Ideal mental health: a state of contentment that we all strive to achieve.

Identification: conforming to the demands of a given role because of a desire to be like a particular person in that role.

Immune system: a system of cells (white blood cells) within the body that is concerned with fighting disease. The white blood cells, called leucocytes, include T and B cells and natural killer cells. They help prevent illness by fighting invading antigens such as viruses and bacteria.

Imposed etic: the use of a technique developed in one culture to study another culture.

Imprinting: a kind of restricted form of learning that takes place rapidly and has both short-term effects (e.g. a following response) and long-lasting effects (e.g. choice of reproductive partner).

Independent behaviour: resisting the pressures to conform or to obey authority.

Independent groups design: a research design in which each participant is in one condition only. Each separate group of participants experiences different levels of the IV. Sometimes referred to as an unrelated or between subjects design.

Independent variable (IV): some aspect of the research situation that is manipulated by the researcher in order to observe whether a change occurs in another variable.

Individual differences: the characteristics that vary from one individual to another.

Individualistic: a culture that emphasises individuality, individual needs, and independence. People tend to live in small nuclear families.

Informational social influence: this occurs when someone conforms because others are thought to possess more knowledge.

Informed consent: this is an ethical guideline, which states that participants' agreement to take part in research should be based on their full knowledge of the nature and purpose of the research. Thus, they should be made aware of any tasks required of them and their right to withdraw, and any other aspects of the research that might affect their willingness to participate.

Innate: inborn, a product of genetic factors.

Insecure attachment: the attachment bond is weaker in insecure attachments and this may result in an anxious and insecure relationship between the infant and caregiver, such as avoidant and resistant attachments. Insecure attachments are assessed by the infant's separation distress, lack of stranger anxiety, and either avoidant or resistant reactions when reunited with the caregiver. The insecure attachment has a negative effect on development, as the infant has a negative working model of him/herself and others.

Interference: one set of information competes with another, causing it to be "overwritten" or physically destroyed.

Inter-judge reliability: the extent to which ratings from two judges are consistent.

Internalisation: conformity behaviour where the individual has completely accepted the views of the majority.

Internal validity: the validity of an experiment in terms of the context in which it is carried out. Concerns events within the experiment as distinct from external validity.

Internal working model: a mental model of the world that enables individuals to predict, control, and manipulate their environment. The infant has many of these, some of which will be related to relationships.

Inter-observer reliability: the extent to which the ratings from two observers are consistent, or in agreement.

Interquartile range: The spread of the middle 50% of an ordered or ranked set of scores.

Interview: a verbal research method in which the participant answers a series of questions.

Interviewer bias: the effects of an interviewer's expectations on the responses made by an interviewee.

Introspection: the process by which a person considers their inner thoughts as a means of understanding how the mind works.

Investigator effects: the effects of an investigator's expectations on the response of a participant. Sometimes referred to as experimenter expectancy effect.

IV (independent variable): some aspect of the research situation that is manipulated by the researcher in order to observe whether a change occurs in another variable.

Laboratory experiment: an experiment conducted in a laboratory setting or other contrived setting away from the participants' normal environments. The experimenter is able to manipulate the IV and accurately measure the DV, and considerable control can be exercised over confounding variables.

Leading questions: questions are relevant to eyewitness testimony. They are questions phrased in such a way as to lead witnesses to a particular answer, such as "Did you see THE broken glass?" instead of "Did you see ANY broken glass?". Another example would be Loftus and Palmer's

(1974) study showing that speed estimates varied with the word (contacted, bumped, smashed etc.) used in the question.

Learning: a relatively permanent change in behaviour, which is not due to maturation.

Learning theory: the explanation of behaviour using the principles of classical and operant conditioning; the view that all behaviour is learned.

Legitimate authority: the assumption that people in positions of power have earned the right to tell others what to do because they have superior expertise, knowledge, or ability.

Leucocytes: white blood cells that find and destroy antigens.

Levels of processing: the extent to which something (e.g. a list of words) is processed, not in terms of how much processing is done (as in repetition), but in terms of how much meaning is extracted. Shallow processing focuses on the superficial features of the information (e.g. whether a word is in upper or lower case). In contrast, deep processing focuses on the meaning of the information and generally (but not always) leads to better long-term memory.

Lie scale: a set of questions in an interview to determine the extent to which a respondent is telling the truth.

Life changes: life changes require some degree of social readjustment or alteration in the individual's current life patterns (life change), which is the response to a significant life event. For example, death, divorce, a change of job, marriage, vacation, or Christmas. Each life event is assigned a life change unit (LCU) based on how much readjustment the change would necessitate. The adaptation needed to cope with the life change absorbs energy, and so depletes the body's resources, and thus life changes are a source of stress.

Life events: events that are common to many people which involve change from a steady state.

Long-term memory: a relatively permanent store, which has unlimited capacity and duration. Different kinds of long-term memory have been identified, including episodic (memory for personal events), semantic (memory for facts and information), and procedural (memory for actions and skills).

Majority influence: this occurs when people adopt the behaviour, attitudes, or values of the majority (dominant or largest group) after being exposed to their values or behaviour. In this sense they publicly yield to group pressure (compliance), although in some cases they yield privately (internalisation). The majority is able to influence because of other people's desire to be accepted (normative) or their desire to be right (informational).

Maladaptive: the extent to which a behaviour is not adaptive.

Matched participants design: a research design that matches participants on a one-to-one basis rather than as a whole group.

Maternal deprivation hypothesis: the view, suggested by Bowlby, that separation from the primary caregiver (maternal deprivation) leads to bond disruption and possibly the breaking of the attachment bond. This has long-term effects on emotional development. Bowlby believed that once broken the attachment bond could not be fixed and so the damage would be permanent.

Mean: an average worked out by dividing the total of participants' scores by the number of participants.

Measures of central tendency: any means of representing the mid-point of a set of data, such as the mean, median, and mode.

Measures of dispersion: any means of expressing the spread of the data, such as range or standard deviation.

Median: the middle score out of all the participants' scores.

Memory: the mental processes used to encode, store, and retrieve information. Encoding takes many forms; visual, auditory, semantic, taste, and smell. Storage refers to the amount of information that can be held in memory. Retrieval refers to the processes by which information is "dug out" of memory, and includes recognition, recall, and reconstruction. It is useful to distinguish between two types of memory: short-term or immediate memory and long-term or more permanent memory.

Memory span: an assessment of how much can be stored in STM at any time.

Memory trace: the physical record or "trace" of the memory, presumably a chemical change in the brain cells.

Meta-analysis: a form of analysis in which the data from several related studies are combined to obtain an overall estimate.

Metabolism: all the chemical processes within the living organism.

Minority influence: a majority being influenced to accept the beliefs or behaviour of a minority. This usually involves a shift in private opinion, as the majority needs to accept the minority as "right" if they are to reject the dominant majority. This private change involves a process of conversion, which is more likely to occur when the minority is consistent and flexible, as this is more persuasive.

Mode: the most frequently occurring score among participants' scores in a given condition.

Modelling: a form of learning or therapy based on observing a model and imitating that behaviour.

Monotropy hypothesis: the notion that infants have an innate tendency to form strong bonds with one caregiver, usually their mother.

Monozygotic (MZ) twins: identical twins formed from the same egg (zygote).

Mood-state-dependent memory: memory is better when a person is in the same mood when trying to retrieve a memory as they were at the time of learning.

Multi-store model: the notion that memory is divided into three kinds of store (sensory memory; short-term memory; and long-term memory). It is often assumed that attention is used to select some information from sensory memory for processing in the short-term store, whereas verbal rehearsal is involved when information is transferred from the short-term memory store to the long-term memory store. It is increasingly doubted that there is a single long-term memory store.

Mundane realism: the use of an artifical situation that closely resembles a natural situation.

Mutations: a genetic change that can then be inherited by any offspring.

Natural experiment: a type of experiment where use is made of some naturally occurring variable(s).

Natural selection: the process by which individuals are selected because they are best adapted to their environment.

Naturalistic observation: an unobtrusive observational study conducted in a natural setting.

Negative correlation: as one co-variable increases the other decreases. They still vary in a constant relationship.

Neuroanatomy: the anatomy of the nervous system, i.e. the study of its structure and function.

Nonsense syllables: meaningless sets of letters.

Noradrenaline: one of the hormones (along with adrenaline) produced by the adrenal glands that increases arousal by activating the sympathetic nervous system and reducing activity in the parasympathetic system.

Normal distribution: a bell-shaped distribution in which most of the scores are close to the mean. This characteristic shape is produced when measuring many psychological and biological variables, such as IQ and height.

Normative social influence: this occurs when someone conforms in order to gain liking or respect from others.

Norms: cultural expectations, standards of behaviour.

Null hypothesis: a hypothesis that states that any findings are due to chance factors and do not reflect a true difference, effect, or relationship.

Obedience: behaving as instructed, usually in response to individual rather than group pressure. Unlikely to involve a change of private opinion.

Obedience to authority: behaving as instructed, usually in response to individual rather than group pressure. This usually takes place in a hierarchy where the person issuing the order is of higher status than the person obeying the order. Obedience occurs because the individual feels they have little choice; they cannot resist or refuse to obey. It is unlikely to involve a change in private opinion.

Observational learning: learning through imitating or copying the behaviour of others.

Oedipus complex: Freud's explanation of how a boy resolves his love for his mother and feelings of rivalry towards his father by identifying with his father.

Operant conditioning: learning through reinforcement; a behaviour becomes more likely because the outcome is reinforced. Learning that is contingent on the response.

Operationalisation: defining all variables in such a way that it is easy to measure them.

Opportunity sampling: participants are selected because they are available, not because they are representative of a population.

Order effects: participants' performance on two conditions may be affected by the order in which they are performed, e.g. because of being bored or having more practice.

Paired-associate learning: participants are given word pairs to learn and then tested by presenting them with one of the words and asking them to recall the other word.

Parasympathetic branch: the part of the autonomic nervous system that monitors the relaxed state, conserving resources, and promoting digestion and metabolism.

Participant observer: an observer who is also taking part in the activity being observed.

Participant reactivity: the situation in which an independent variable has an effect on participants merely because they know they are being observed.

Phonemic processing: processing material by attending to the sounds of the words (phonemes are sounds).

Phonological loop: a component of the working memory system concerned with speech perception and production.

Physiological: concerning the study of living organisms and their parts.

Physiological approaches to stress management: techniques that try to control the body's response to stress by reducing physiological reactivity. For example, anti-anxiety drugs decrease the "fight or flight" response such as high blood pressure, increased heart rate, etc. Biofeedback is another technique, which works by training the participants to recognise their heightened physiological reactivity and reduce it through relaxation exercises.

Pilot study: a smaller, preliminary study that makes it possible to check out standardised procedures and general design before investing time and money in the major study.

Pituitary gland: an endocrine gland located in the brain. Called the "master gland" because it directs much of the activity of the endocrine system.

Planning fallacy: the false belief that a plan will succeed even though past experience suggests it won't.

Pleasure principle: the drive to do things that produce pleasure or gratification.

PNS (peripheral nervous system): part of the nervous system that excludes the brain and spinal cord, but consists of all other nerve cells in the body. The PNS is divided into the somatic nervous system and the autonomic nervous system.

Point sampling: a technique used in an observational study. One individual is observed in order to categorise their current behaviour, after which a second individual is observed.

Population: the total number of cases about which a specific statement can be made. This in itself may be unrepresentative.

Positive correlation: when two co-variables increase at the same time.

Practice effect: an improvement in performance as a result of having done the task before.

Presumptive consent: a substitute for voluntary informed consent, it is presumed that if one set of people regard an experimental procedure as acceptable this applies to all people, including the experimental participants whose consent has not been obtained.

Prior general consent: obtaining apparent consent from research participants by arranging for them to agree in general to taking part in certain kinds of research before enlisting their involvement in an experiment.

Privation: the lack of any attachments, as distinct from the loss of attachments (deprivation). This is due to the lack of an appropriate attachment figure. Privation is more likely than deprivation to cause permanent emotional damage or "affectionless psychopathy"; the condition diagnosed by Bowlby as involving permanent emotional damage.

Proactive interference: current learning and memory being disrupted by previous learning.

Procedural knowledge: knowledge related to "knowing how", including motor skills.

Processing: changing the form or structure of something.

Projection: attributing one's undesirable characteristics to others, as a means of coping with emotionally threatening information and protecting the ego.

Protection of participants from psychological harm: an ethical guideline, which states that participants should be protected from psychological harm, such as distress, ridicule, or loss of self-esteem. The risk of harm during the research study should be no greater than the participants would experience in their everyday life. Debriefing can be used to offer support if a study has resulted in psychological harm.

Psychiatrist: a medically trained person who specialises in the diagnosis and treatment of mental disorders.

Psychoanalysis: the form of therapy derived from psychoanalytic theory.

Psychodynamic model: a model of abnormality that regards the origin of mental disorders as psychological rather than physical, and suggests that mental illness arises out of unresolved unconscious conflicts.

Psychological approaches to stress management: techniques that try to control the cognitive, social, and emotional responses to stress. They attempt to address the underlying causes of stress, such as faulty thinking and disproportionate emotional responses (overreactions and underreactions). Psychological techniques work by changing the person's perception of the stressor and/or increasing the individual's perception of control.

Psychoneuroimmunology (PNI): the study of the effects of both stress and other psychological factors on the immune system.

Psychosexual development: Freud's stages in personality development based on the child's changing focus on different parts of the body (e.g. the mouth and the anal region). "Sexual" is roughly equivalent to "physical pleasure".

Psychotherapy: any psychological form of treatment of a mental disorder or illness, as distinct from medical forms of treatment.

Qualitative research methods: concerned with how things are expressed, what it feels like, meanings or explanations; i.e. the quality. An example of qualitative data would be that obtained from a media interview.

Quantitative research methods: concerned with how much data are presented in numerical terms. An example of quantitative data would be a measurement of height or weight.

Quasi-experiment: research that is similar to an experiment but certain key features are lacking, such as the direct manipulation of the independent variable by the experimenter and random allocation of participants to conditions.

Questionnaire: a survey requiring written answers.

Random allocation: placing participants in different experimental conditions using random methods to ensure no differences between the groups.

Random sampling: selecting participants on some random basis (e.g. numbers out of a hat). Every member of the population has an equal chance of being selected.

Randomisation: the allocation of participants to conditions on a random basis, i.e. totally unbiased distribution.

Range: the difference between the highest and lowest score in any condition.

Raw scores: the data before they have been summarised in some way.

Reactance: reacting against attempts to control or restrict one's personal choices.

Reality principle: the drive to accommodate to the demands of the environment.

Recency effect: free recall of the last few items in a list, where higher performance is due to the information being in short-term store.

Reconstructive memory: it is often assumed that recall from long-term memory involves reconstruction. This is an active process in which information from the to-be-remembered material *and* information from our knowledge and experience of the world are combined. Information based on our knowledge and experience of the world is contained in schemas, which are packets of knowledge. What often happens is that what we recall is *not* an accurate reproduction of the original material, because our recall is distorted by schemas, which have been used to fill in the gaps in our memory.

Reductionist: an argument or theory that reduces complex factors to a set of simple principles.

Regression: in Freudian terms, returning to an earlier stage of development as a means of coping with anxiety.

Rehearsal: the verbal repetition of information (often words), which typically has the effect of increasing our long-term memory for the rehearsed information.

Reinforced: a behaviour is more likely to re-occur because the response was agreeable.

Reliability: the extent to which a method of measurement or test produces consistent findings.

Repeated measures design: a research design where the same participants are used for all conditions in the experiment.

Replication: the ability to repeat the methods used in a study and achieve the same findings.

Representative sample: the notion that the sample *is* representative of the whole population from which it is drawn.

Repression: this is one of the main defence mechanisms suggested by Freud. What happens is that memories causing great anxiety (e.g. traumatic memories) are kept out of conscious awareness in order to protect the individual. Thus, repression is a good example of motivated forgetting. Information that has been repressed still exists, and can often be recalled during psychoanalysis.

Research: the process of gaining knowledge and understanding via either theory or empirical data collection.

Research/experimental/alternative hypothesis: a statement put forward at the beginning of a study stating what you expect to happen, generated by a theory.

Resistant attachment (type C): an insecure attachment of an infant to its mother. The child resists contact on reunion.

Retrieval: this is a process of recovering information stored in long-term memory. If retrieval is successful, the individual remembers the information in question.

Retroactive interference: this is what happens when subsequent learning disrupts memory for previous learning. It is one of the ways in which forgetting occurs.

Right to privacy: the requirement for ethical research that no participants are observed in situations that would be considered as private.

Right to withdraw: the basic right of participants in a research study to stop their involvement at any point, and to withdraw their results if they wish to do so.

Role conflict: when the demands of various jobs or roles produce opposing requirements.

Role-playing experiments: studies in which participants are asked to imagine how they would behave in certain situations.

Sample: a part of a population selected such that it is considered to be representative of the population as a whole.

Sampling bias: some people have a greater or lesser chance of being selected than they should be, given their frequency in the population.

Scattergraph/scattergram: two-dimensional representation of all the participants' scores in a correlational study.

Schema: an "organised" packet of information about the world, events, or people that is stored in long-term memory. For example, most people have a schema containing information about the normal sequence of events when having a meal in a restaurant.

Schema theory: the view that memory is affected by schemas.

Science: a branch of knowledge conducted on objective principles. It is both an activity and an organised body of knowledge.

Secondary reinforcer: a reinforcer that has no natural properties of reinforcement but, through association with a primary reinforcer, becomes a reinforcer, i.e. it is learned.

Secure attachment (type B): a strong contented bond between the infant and caregiver. The secure infant shows distress at separation but is easily comforted by the caregiver when reunited. This characterises the majority of attachments and is related to healthy development as the infant has a positive working model of relationships.

Self-actualisation: fulfilling one's potential in the broadest sense.

Self-esteem: the feelings that an individual has about himself or herself.

Self-fulfilling prophecy: the tendency for someone's expectations about another person to lead to a fulfilment of those expectations.

Semantic coding: encoding or processing words in terms of their meaning based on information stored in long-term memory.

Semantic memory: organised knowledge about the world and about language, stored in long-term memory.

Semantic processing: processing material according to its meaning.

Sensitive: in the context of statistics, "sensitive" means more precise, able to reflect small differences or changes.

Sensitive period: a looser interpretation of the concept of a critical period—changes are more likely during the period of time rather than being exclusive to it.

Separation: this refers to the absence of the caregiver (e.g. due to work commitments, divorce, or hospitalisation), which usually causes great distress, but not necessarily permanent bond disruption. Separation has a number of effects, such as protest, despair, or detachment, and if prolonged it may result in deprivation.

Separation anxiety: the sense of concern felt by a child when separated from their attachment figure.

Separation protest: the infant's behaviour when separated—crying or holding out their arms. Some insecurely attached infants show no protest when left by their attachment figure, whereas securely attached children do.

Serotonin: a neurotransmitter that is associated with lower arousal, sleepiness, and reduced anxiety.

Shallow processing: a minimal amount of processing, such as in the physical analysis of information.

Short-term memory: a temporary place for storing information during which it receives limited processing (e.g. verbal rehearsal). Short-term memory has a very limited capacity and short duration, unless the information in it is maintained through rehearsal.

Single blind: a procedure in which the participants are not informed of the condition in which they have been placed.

Situational explanation: deciding that people's actions are caused by the situation in which they find themselves rather than by their personality.

Sociability: the tendency to seek and enjoy the company of others.

Social desirability bias: the tendency to provide socially desirable rather than honest answers on questionnaires or in interviews.

Social development: the development of the child's social competence includes social skills, ability to relate and empathise with others, and formation of close and meaningful relationships. Social development is determined by an interaction of biological predisposition and the environment.

Social impact theory: a way of explaining social influence in terms of cumulative factors, such as the number and status of people present, the consistency of the message, and closeness to the influencer.

Social influence: the influence of a group (majority influence) or individual (minority influence or obedience) to modify the thinking, attitudes, and/or behaviour of others. For example, fashion trends are a consequence of majority influence; political and religious leaders are an example of minority influence; and complying with the demands of an authority figure, such as an employer, is an example of obedience.

Social learning theory: the view that behaviour can be explained in terms of direct and indirect reinforcement, through imitation, identification, and modelling.

Social releasers: a social behaviour or characteristic that elicits a caregiving reaction. Bowlby suggested that these were innate and critical in the process of forming attachments.

Specific phobia: extreme fear and avoidance of specific kinds of stimuli (e.g. snakes, spiders).

Split-half technique: a technique used to establish reliability by assigning items from one test randomly to two sub-tests (split-halves). The same person does both sub-tests simultaneously and their scores are compared to see if they are similar, which would suggest that the test items are reliable.

SQ3R: five strategies for effective reading: Survey, Question, Read, Recite, Review.

S–R link: an abbreviation for stimulus–response link.

Standard deviation: a measure of the spread of the scores around the mean. It is the square root of the variance and takes account of every measurement.

Standardised instructions: instructions given to each participant which are kept identical to help to prevent experimenter bias.

Standardised procedures: the same procedures are used on every trial of an experiment to ensure that no confounding variables affect the dependent variable.

Statistical infrequency/deviation from statistical norms: behaviours that are statistically rare or deviate from the average/statistical norm as illustrated by the normal distribution curve, are classed as abnormal. Thus, any behaviour that is atypical of the majority would be statistically infrequent, and so abnormal (e.g. schizophrenia is suffered by 1 in 100 people and so is statistically rare).

Stereotype: a social perception of an individual in terms of some readily available feature, such as skin colour or gender, rather than their actual personal attributes.

Storage: storing a memory for a period of time so that it can be used later.

Strange Situation: an experimental procedure used to test the security of a child's attachment to a caregiver. The key features are what the child does when it is left by the caregiver and the child's behaviour at reunion, as well as responses to a stranger.

Stranger anxiety: the distress experienced by a child when approached by a stranger.

Stress: a state of psychological and physical tension produced, according to the transactional model, when there is a mismatch between the perceived demands of a situation (the stressor[s]) and the individual's perceived ability to cope. The consequent state of tension can be adaptive (eustress) or maladaptive (distress).

Stress inoculation training: a technique to reduce stress through the use of stress-management techniques and self-statements that aim to restructure the way the client thinks.

Stress management: stress management is the attempt to cope with stress through reduction of the stress response. This may be aimed at the physiological effects of stress (e.g. anti-anxiety drugs or biofeedback) and the psychological effects of stress (e.g. stress inoculation training or hardiness training). Stress management is often based on changing the person's perception of the stressor and/or increasing the individual's perception of control.

Stressor: an event that triggers the stress response because it throws the body out of balance and forces it to respond. For example, life changes (e.g. divorce, bereavement), daily hassles (e.g. traffic, lost keys), workplace stressors (e.g. role strain, lack of control), and environmental stressors (e.g. noise, temperature, overcrowding). Stressors are not objective in that they do not produce the same response in all people, as this depends on the individual's perception of the stressor. Thus, nothing is a stressor unless it is thought to be so!

Superego: the part of the mind that embodies one's conscience. It is formed through identification with the same-sex parent.

Sympathetic branch: the part of the autonomic nervous system that activates internal organs.

Systematic sampling: a modified version of random sampling in which the participants are selected in a quasi-random way (e.g. every 100th name from a population list).

Temperament: innate and characteristic modes of emotional response, such as sociability.

Temperament hypothesis: the view that a child's temperament is responsible for the quality of attachment between the child and its caregiver, as opposed to the view that experience is more important.

Test–retest: a technique used to establish reliability, by giving the same test to participants on two separate occasions to see if their scores remain relatively similar.

Theory: a general explanation of a set of findings. It is used to produce an experimental hypothesis.

Theory of evolution: an explanation for the diversity of living species. Darwin's theory was based on the principle of natural selection.

Time sampling: a technique used in observational studies. Observations are only made during specified time periods (e.g. the first 10 minutes of each hour).

Trace decay: the physical disappearance of a memory trace from the brain. Trace decay is one reason for forgetting. It should be distinguished from cue-dependent forgetting, in which the memory trace has *not* decayed but is hard to find.

Trait: a characteristic distinguishing a particular individual.

Transactional model: an explanation for behaviour which focuses on the interaction between various factors. The transactional model of stress explains stress in terms of the interaction between the demands of the environment and the individual's ability to cope.

True experiment: research where an independent variable is manipulated to observe its effects on a dependent variable and so determine a cause-and-effect relationship.

Type A personality: in biopsychology, a personality type who is typically impatient, competitive, time pressured, and hostile.

Undisclosed observation: an observational study where the participants have not been informed that it is taking place.

Validity: the soundness of the measurement tool, the extent to which it is measuring something that is real or valid.

Variables: things that vary or change.

Variance: the extent of variation of the scores around the mean.

Vicarious reinforcement: receiving reinforcement through another person.

Visuo-spatial sketch pad: a component within the working memory system designed for spatial and/or visual coding.

Volunteer bias: the systematic difference between volunteers and non-volunteers.

Volunteer sample: refers to participants who volunteer to take part in a research study, for instance by replying to an advertisement. Some researchers believe that people who volunteer may be different from non-volunteers, for instance in personality, and so may not be a truly representative sample. This makes generalising the findings to the non-volunteering population questionable.

Working memory model: a model of memory proposed by Baddeley and Hitch as an alternative to the multi-store model. The model consists of a central executive (an attentional system, which has a limited capacity and which is involved in decision-making), together with two slave systems (the articulatory-phonological loop, and visuo-spatial sketch pad). This model is concerned with both active processing and the brief storage of information.

Working memory system: the concept that short-term (or working) memory can be subdivided into other stores which handle different modalities (sound and visual data).

Workplace stressor: factors in the work environment or aspects of the job that cause stress. For example, overcrowding, noise, and temperature are factors in the environment. Lack of control, interpersonal relationships, role ambiguity, and work overload are all examples of work pressures that cause stress.

REFERENCES

Abernethy, E.M. (1940). The effect of changed environmental conditions upon the results of college examinations. *Journal of Psychology, 10*, 293–301.

Adorno, T.W., Frenkel-Brunswik, E., Levinson, D., & Sanford, R. (1950). *The authoritarian personality*. New York: Harper.

Ainsworth, M.D.S. (1982). Infant–mother attachment. *American Psychologist, 34*, 932–937.

Ainsworth, M.D.S., & Bell, S.M. (1970). Attachment, exploration and separation: Illustrated by the behaviour of one-year-olds in a strange situation. *Child Development, 41*, 49–67.

Ainsworth, M.D.S., Bell, S.M., & Stayton, D.J. (1971). Individual differences in strange situation behaviour of one-year-olds. In H.R. Schaffer (Ed.), *The origins of human social relations*. London: Academic Press.

Ainsworth, M.D.S., Bell, S.M., & Stayton, D.J. (1974). Infant/mother attachment and social development as a product of reciprocal responsiveness to signals. In M.P.M. Richards (Ed.), *The integration of the child into a social world*. Cambridge, UK: Cambridge University Press.

Ainsworth, M.D.S., Blehar, M.C., Waters, E., & Wall, S. (1978). *Patterns of attachment: A psychological study of the strange situation*. Hillsdale, NJ: Lawrence Erlbaum Associates Inc.

Allport, G.W., & Postman, L. (1947). *The psychology of rumour*. New York: Holt, Rinehart, & Winston.

Ancona, L., & Pareyson, R. (1968). Contribution to the study of aggression: The dynamics of destructive obedience. *Archivio di Psicologia, Neurologia, e Psichiatria, 29*, 340–372.

Anderson, J. (1972). Attachment out of doors. In N. Blurton-Jones (Ed.), *Ethological studies of child behaviour*. Cambridge, UK: Cambridge University Press.

Anderson, L.P. (1991). Acculturative stress: A theory of relevance to Black Americans. *Clinical Psychology Review, 11*, 685–702.

Anderson, N.B., Lane, J.D., Taguchi, F., Williams, R.B., & Houseworth, S.J. (1989). Race, parental history of hypertension and patterns of cardiovascular reactivity in women. *Psychophysiology, 26*, 39–47.

Andersson, B.-E. (1992). Effects of daycare on cognitive and socioemotional competence of thirteen-year-old Swedish schoolchildren. *Child Development, 63*, 20–36.

Andreasen, N.C., & Black, D.W. (2001). *Introductory textbook of psychiatry* (3rd Edn.). Washington, DC: American Psychiatric Association.

Arendt, H. (1963). *Eichmann in Jerusalem: A report on the banality of evil*. New York: Viking Press.

Aronson, E. (1988). *The social animal* (5th Edn.). New York: Freeman.

Asch, S.E. (1951). Effects of group pressure on the modification and distortion of judgements. In H. Guetzkow (Ed.), *Groups, leadership and men*. Pittsburgh, PA: Carnegie.

Asch, S.E. (1956). Studies of independence and conformity: A minority of one against a unanimous majority. *Psychological Monographs, 70*(Whole no. 416).

Ashton, H. (1997). Benzodiazepine dependency. In A. Baum, S. Newman, J. Weinman, R. West, & C. McManus (Eds.), *Cambridge handbook of psychology, health and medicine*. Cambridge, UK: Cambridge University Press.

Atkinson, R.C., & Shiffrin, R.M. (1968). Human memory: A proposed system and its control processes. In K.W. Spence & J.T. Spence (Eds.), *The psychology of learning and motivation, Vol. 2*. London: Academic Press.

Attanasio, V., Andrasik, F., Burke, E.J., Blake, D.D., Kabela, E., & McCarran, M.S. (1985). Clinical issues in utilizing biofeedback with children. *Clinical Biofeedback and Health, 8*, 134–141.

Bachen, E., Cohen, S., & Marsland, A.L. (1997). Psychoimmunology. In A. Baum, S. Newman, J. Weinman, R. West, & C. McManus (Eds.), *Cambridge handbook of psychology, health, and medicine*. Cambridge, UK: Cambridge University Press.

Baddeley, A.D. (1966). The influence of acoustic and semantic similarity on long-term memory for word sequences. *Quarterly Journal of Experimental Psychology, 18*, 302–309.

Baddeley, A.D., & Hitch, G.J. (1974). Working memory. In G.H. Bower (Ed.), *The psychology of learning and motivation, Vol. 8*. London: Academic Press.

Baddeley, A.D., & Lewis, V.J. (1981). Inner active processes in reading: The inner voice, the inner ear and the inner eye. In A.M. Lesgold & C.A. Perfetti (Eds.), *Interactive processes in reading*. Hillsdale, NJ: Lawrence Erlbaum Associates Inc.

Baddeley, A.D., Thomson, N., & Buchanan, M. (1975). Word length and the structure of short-term memory. *Journal of Verbal Learning and Verbal Behavior, 14*, 575–589.

Bahrick, H.P., Bahrick, P.O., & Wittinger, R.P. (1975). Fifty years of memory for names and faces: A cross-sectional approach. *Journal of Experimental Psychology: General, 104*, 54–75.

Bailey, F.J., & Dua, J. (1999). Individualism–collectivism, coping styles and stress in international and Anglo-Australian students: A comparative study. *Australian Psychologist, 34*, 177–183.

Bales, R.F. (1950). *Interaction process analysis: A method for the study of small groups*. Reading, MA: Addison-Wesley.

Bandura, A. (1965). Influences of models' reinforcement contingencies on the acquisition of initiative responses. *Journal of Personality and Social Psychology, 1*, 589–593.

Bandura, A. (1986). *Social foundations of thought and action: A social cognitive theory*. Englewood Cliffs, NJ: Prentice Hall.

Bandura, A., & Rosenthal, T.L. (1966). Vicarious classical conditioning as a function of arousal level. *Journal of Personality and Social Psychology, 3*, 54–62.

Bandura, A., Ross, D., & Ross, S.A. (1961). Transmission of aggression through imitation of aggressive models. *Journal of Abnormal and Social Psychology, 63*, 575–582.

Banyard, P., & Hayes, N. (1994). *Psychology: Theory and application*. London: Chapman & Hall.

Bar-Heim, Y., Sutton, B., Fox, N.A., & Marvin, R.S. (2000). Stability and change of attachment at 14, 24, and 58 months of age: Behaviour, representation, and life events. *Journal of Child Psychology and Psychiatry, 41*, 381–388.

Barlow, D.H., & Durand, V.M. (1995). *Abnormal psychology: An integrative approach*. New York: Brooks/Cole.

Barr, C.E., Mednick, S.A., & Munk-Jorgenson, P. (1990). Exposure to influenza epidemics during gestation and adult schizophrenia: A forty-year study. *Archives of General Psychiatry, 47*, 869–874.

Barrett, H. (1997). How young children cope with separation: Toward a new conceptualization. *British Journal of Medical Psychology, 70*, 339–358.

Bartlett, F.C. (1932). *Remembering: A study in experimental and social psychology*. Cambridge, UK: Cambridge University Press.

Baumrind, D. (1964). Some thoughts on ethics of research: After reading Milgram's behavioural study of obedience. *American Psychologist, 19*, 421–423.

Baumrind, D. (1975). Metaethical and normative considerations governing the treatment of human subjects in the behavioural sciences. In E.C. Kennedy (Ed.), *Human rights and psychological research: A debate on psychology and ethics*. New York: Thomas Y. Crowell.

Beck, A.T. (1976). *Cognitive therapy of the emotional disorders*. New York: New American Library.

Beck, A.T., & Clark, D.A. (1988). Anxiety and depression: An information processing perspective. *Anxiety Research, 1*, 23–36.

Behar, R., Delabarra, M., & Michelot, J. (2001). Gender identity and eating disorders. *Rev Med Chile, 129*, 1003–1011.

Belsky, J., & Rovine, M. (1987). Temperament and attachment security in the Strange Situation: A rapprochement. *Child Development, 58*, 787–795.

Belsky, J., & Rovine, M.J. (1988). Nonmaternal care in the first year of life and the security of parent–infant attachment. *Child Development, 59*, 157–167.

Berkun, M.M., Bialek, H.M., Kern, R.P., & Yagi, K. (1962). Experimental studies of psychological stress in man. *Psychological Monographs, 76*(Whole no. 15).

Berrettini, W.H. (2000). Susceptibility loci for bipolar disorder: Overlap with inherited vulnerability to schizophrenia. *Biological Psychiatry, 47*, 245–251.

Bickman, L. (1974). Clothes make the person. *Psychology Today, 8*(4), 48–51.

Blos, P. (1967). The second individuation process of adolescence. *Psychoanalytic Study of the Child, 22*, 162–186.

Bogdonoff, M.D., Klein, E.J., Shaw, D.M., & Back, K.W. (1961). The modifying effect of conforming behaviour upon lipid responses accompanying CNS arousal. *Clinical Research, 9*, 135.

Bower, G.H., Black, J.B., & Turner, T.J. (1979). Scripts in memory for text. *Cognitive Psychology, 11*, 177–220.

Bowlby, J. (1944). Forty-four juvenile thieves: Their characters and home life. *International Journal of Psycho-Analysis, 25*, 19–52 and 107–127.

Bowlby, J. (1951). *Maternal care and mental health*. Geneva, Switzerland: World Health Organisation.

Bowlby, J. (1953). *Child care and the growth of love*. Harmondsworth, UK: Penguin.

Bowlby, J. (1958). The nature of the child's tie to his mother. *International Journal of Psycho-Analysis, 39*, 350–373.

Bowlby, J. (1969). *Attachment and love, Vol. 1: Attachment*. London: Hogarth.

Bowlby, J. (1988). *A secure base: Clinical applications of attachment theory*. London: Routledge.

Bowlby, J., Ainsworth, M., Boston, M., & Rosenbluth, D. (1956). The effects of mother–child separation: A follow-up study. *British Journal of Medical Psychology, 29*, 211–247.

Brady, J.V. (1958). Ulcers in executive monkeys. *Scientific American, 199*, 95–100.

Bransford, J.D. (1979). *Human cognition: Learning understanding and remembering*. Belmont, CA: Wadsworth.

Brewin, C.R., Andrews, B., & Gotlib, I.H. (1993). Psychopathology and early experience: A reappraisal of retrospective reports. *Psychological Bulletin, 113*, 82–98.

British Psychological Society (1993). *Code of conduct, ethical principles and guidelines*. Leicester, UK: British Psychological Society.

Broberg, G., Wessels, H., Lamb, M.E., & Hwang, C.P. (1997). Effects of daycare on the development of cognitive abilities in 8-year-olds: A longitudinal study. *Developmental Psychology, 33*, 62–69.

Brown, G.W., & Harris, T. (1978). *Social origins of depression*. London: Tavistock.

Brown, R. (1986). *Social psychology: The second edition*. New York: The Free Press.

Brown, R., & Kulik, J. (1977). Flashbulb memories. *Cognition, 5*, 73–99.

Bruch, H. (1971). Family transactions in eating disorders. *Comprehensive Psychiatry, 12*, 238–248.

Bryant, B., Harris, M., & Newton, D. (1980). *Children and minders*. London: Grant McIntyre.

Buehler, R., Griffin, D., & Ross, M. (1994). Exploring the "planning fallacy": Why people underestimate their task completion times. *Journal of Personality and Social Psychology, 67*, 366–381.

Burchinal, M., Lee, M., & Ramey, C. (1989). Type of daycare and preschool intellectual development in disadvantaged children. *Child Development, 60*, 128–137.

Burger, J.M., & Cooper, H.M. (1979). The desirability of control. *Motivation and emotion, 3*, 381–393.

Bus, A.G., & van IJzendoorn, M.H. (1988). Attachment and early reading: A longitudinal study. *Journal of Genetic Psychology, 149*(2), 199–210.

Bushnell, I.W.R., Sai, F., & Mullin, J.T. (1989). Neonatal recognition of the mother's face. *British Journal of Developmental Psychology, 7*, 3–13.

Cahill, L., & McGaugh, J.L. (1998). Mechanisms of emotional arousal and lasting declarative memory. *Trends in Neuroscience, 21*, 294–299.

Campbell, D.T., & Stanley, J.C. (1966). *Experimental and quasi-experimental designs for research.* Chicago: Rand McNally.

Cardwell, M., Clark, L., & Meldrum, C. (1996). *Psychology for A level.* London: Collins Educational.

Carlsmith, H., Ellsworth, P., & Aronson, E. (1976). *Methods of research in social psychology.* Reading, MA: Addison-Wesley.

Carpenter, G. (1975). Mother's face and the newborn. In R. Lewin (Ed.), *Child alive.* London: Temple Smith.

Carrasco, J.L., Diaz-Marsa, M., Hollander, E., Cesar, J., & Saiz-Ruiz, J. (2000). Decreased platelet monoamine oxidase activity in female bulimia nervosa. *European Neuropsychopharmacology, 10*, 113–117.

Caspi, A., Mofitt, T.E., Newman, D.L., & Silva, P.A. (1996). Behavioral observations at age 3 years predict adult psychiatric disorders: Longitudinal evidence from a birth cohort. *Archives of General Psychiatry, 53*, 1033–1039.

Chadda, R.K., & Ahuja, N. (1990). Dhat syndrome. A sex neurosis of the Indian subcontinent. *British Journal of Psychiatry, 156*, 577–579.

Charlton, A. (1998). TV violence has little impact on children, study finds. *The Times*, 12 January, p.5.

Charlton, T., Panting, C., Davie, R., Coles, D., & Whitmarsh, L. (2000). Children's playground behaviour across five years of broadcast television: A naturalistic study in a remote community. *Emotional and Behavioural Difficulties, 5*, 4–12.

Clarke, A.M., & Clarke, A.D.B. (1976). *Early experience: Myth and evidence.* New York: Free Press.

Clarke, A.M., & Clarke, A.D.B. (1998). Early experience and the life path. *The Psychologist, 11*(9), 433–436.

Clarke-Stewart, K.A., Gruber, C.P., & Fitzgerald, L.M. (1994). *Children at home and in day care.* Hillsdale, NJ: Lawrence Erlbaum Associates Inc.

Claxton, G. (1980). Cognitive psychology: A suitable case for what sort of treatment? In G. Claxton (Ed.), *Cognitive psychology: New directions.* London: Routledge & Kegan Paul.

Cobb, S., & Rose, R.M. (1973). Hypertension, peptic ulcer, and diabetes in air traffic controllers. *Journal of the American Medical Association, 224*, 489–492.

Cockett, M., & Tripp, J. (1994). Children living in disordered families. *Social policy research findings: 45.* Joseph Rowntree Foundation.

Cohen, C.E. (1981). Person categories and social perception: Testing some boundaries of the processing effects of prior knowledge. *Journal of Personality and Social Psychology, 40*, 441–452.

Cohen, G. (1983). *The psychology of cognition* (2nd Edn.). London: Academic Press.

Cohen, N.J., & Squire, L.R. (1980). Preserved learning and retention of pattern-analysing skill in amnesia using perceptual learning. *Cortex, 17*, 273–278.

Cohen, S., Tyrrell, D.A.J., & Smith, A.P. (1991). Psychological stress and susceptibility to the common cold. *New England Journal of Medicine, 325*, 606–612.

Collins, B.E. (1970). *Social psychology.* Reading, MA: Addison-Wesley.

Comer, R.J. (2001). *Abnormal psychology* (4th Edn.). New York: Worth.

Conrad, R. (1964). Acoustic confusions in immediate memory. *British Journal of Psychology, 55*, 75–84.

Conway, M.A., Anderson, S.J., Larsen, S.F., Donnelly, C.M., McDaniel, M.A., McClelland, A.G.R., & Rawles, R.E. (1994). The formation of flashbulb memories. *Memory and Cognition, 22*, 326–343.

Coolican, H. (1990). *Research methods and statistics in psychology.* London: Hodder & Stoughton.

Coolican, H. (1994). *Research methods and statistics in psychology* (2nd Edn.). London: Hodder & Stoughton.

Coolican, H. (1996). *Introduction to research methods and statistics in psychology.* London: Hodder & Stoughton.

Coolican, H. (1998). Research methods. In M.W. Eysenck (Ed.), *Psychology: An integrated approach.* London: Addison-Wesley Longman.

Cooper, P.J. (1994). Eating disorders. In A.M. Coleman (Ed.), *Companion encyclopaedia of psychology, Vol. 2.* London: Routledge.

Cooper, P.J., & Taylor, M.J. (1988). Body image disturbance in bulimia nervosa. *British Journal of Psychiatry, 153*, 32–36.

Cooper, R.S., Rotimi, C.N., & Ward, R. (1999). The puzzle of hypertension in African-Americans. *Scientific American, 253*, 36–43.

Cox, T. (1978). *Stress.* London: Macmillan Press.

Craik, F.I.M., & Lockhart, R.S. (1972). Levels of processing: A framework for memory research. *Journal of Verbal Learning and Verbal Behavior, 11*, 671–684.

Craik, F.I.M., & Tulving, E. (1975). Depth of processing and the retention of words in episodic memory. *Journal of Experimental Psychology, 104*, 268–294.

Crowne, D.P., & Marlowe, D. (1964). *The approval motive: Studies in evaluative dependence.* New York: Wiley.

Cumberbatch, G. (1990). *Television advertising and sex role stereotyping: A content analysis* (Working paper IV for the Broadcasting Standards Council), Communications Research Group, Aston University, Birmingham, UK.

Curtis, A. (2000). *Psychology and health.* London: Routledge.

Curtiss, S. (1989). The independence and task-specificity of language. In M.H. Bornstein & J.S. Bruner (Eds.), *Interaction in human development.* Hillsdale, NJ: Lawrence Erlbaum Associates Inc.

Dane, F.C. (1994). Survey methods, naturalistic observations, and case-studies. In A.M. Colman (Ed.), *Companion encyclopaedia of psychology, Vol. 2.* London: Routledge.

Darley, J.M., & Latané, B. (1968). Bystander intervention in emergencies: Diffusion of responsibility. *Journal of Personality and Social Psychology, 8*, 377–383.

David, B., & Turner, J.C. (1996). Studies in self-categorization and minority conversion: Is being a member of an outgroup an advantage? *British Journal of*

Social Psychology (Special Issue on Minority Influences), 35, 179–199.

Davison, G.C., & Neale, J.M. (1996). *Abnormal psychology* (rev. 6th Edn.). New York: Wiley.

de Chateau, P., & Wiberg, B. (1977). Long-term effect on mother–infant behavior of extra contact during the first hour post-partum: I. First observation at 36 hours. *Acta Paediatrica Scandinavica, 66,* 137–144.

Delahanty, D.L., Dougall, A.L., Hawken, L., Trakowski, J.H., Schmitz, J.B., Jenkins, F.J., & Baum, A. (1996). Time course of natural killer cell activity and lymphocyte proliferation in healthy men. *Health Psychology, 15,* 48–55.

DeLongis, A., Coyne, J.C., Dakof, G., Folkman, S., & Lazarus, R.S. (1982). The impact of daily hassles, uplifts and major life events to health status. *Health Psychology, 1,* 119–136.

DeLongis, A., Folkman, S., & Lazarus, R.S. (1988). The impact of daily stress on health and mood: Psychological and social resources as mediators. *Journal of Personality and Social Psychology, 54,* 486–495.

Deutsch, M., & Gerard, H.B. (1955). A study of normative and informational influence upon individual judgement. *Journal of Abnormal and Social Psychology, 51,* 629–636.

Devlin, P. (1976). *Report to the Secretary of State for the Home Department of the Departmental Committee on evidence of identification in criminal cases.* London: Her Majesty's Stationary Office.

Diener, E., & Crandall, R. (1978). *Ethics in social and behavioural research.* Chicago: The University of Chicago Press.

DiNardo, P.A., Guzy, L.T., Jenkins, J.A., Bak, R.M., Tomasi, S.F., & Copland, M. (1988). Aetiology and maintenance of dog fears. *Behaviour Research and Therapy, 26,* 241–244.

Dollard, J., & Miller, N.E. (1950). *Personality and psychotherapy.* New York: McGraw-Hill.

Douglas, J.W.B. (1975). Early hospital admissions and later disturbances of behaviour and learning. *Developmental Medical Child Neurology, 17,* 456–480.

Durkin, K. (1995). *Developmental social psychology: From infancy to old age.* Oxford, UK: Blackwell.

Dworkin, B.R., & Dworkin, S. (1988). The treatment of scoliosis by continuous automated postural feedback. In R. Ader, R. Weiner, & A. Baum (Eds.), *Experimental foundations of behavioural medicine: Conditioning approaches.* Hillsdale, NJ: Lawrence Erlbaum Associates Inc.

Dyer, C. (1995). *Beginning research in psychology.* Oxford, UK: Blackwell.

Eagly, A.H. (1978). Sex differences in influenceability. *Psychological Bulletin, 85,* 86–116.

Eagly, A.H., & Carli, L. (1981). Sex of researchers and sex-typed communications as determinants of sex differences in influenceability: A meta-analysis of social influence studies. *Psychological Bulletin, 90,* 1–20.

Eakin, D.K., Schreiber, T.A., & Sergent-Marshall, S. (2003). Misinformation effects in eyewitness memory: The presence and absence of memory impairment as a function of warning and misinformation accessibility. *Journal of Experimental Psychology: Learning, Memory, and Cognition, 29,* 813–825.

Ebbinghaus, H. (1885/1913). *Uber das Gedachtnis.* Leipzig: Dunker. (Trans. H. Ruyer & C.E. Bussenius).

In *Memory.* New York: Teachers College, Columbia University. (Original work published 1885.)

Egeland, B., & Hiester, M. (1995). The long-term consequences of infant day-care and mother–infant attachment. *Child Development, 66,* 474–485.

Eibl-Eibesfeldt, I. (1995). The evolution of family and its consequences. *Futura, 10*(4), 253–264.

Endler, N.S., & Parker, J.D.A. (1990). Multidimensional assessment of coping: A critical evaluation. *Journal of Personality and Social Psychology, 58,* 844–854.

Erikson, M. (1968). The inhumanity of ordinary people. *International Journal of Psychiatry, 6,* 278–279.

Evans, P. (1998). Stress and coping. In M. Pitts & K. Phillips (Eds.), *The psychology of health* (2nd Edn.). London: Routledge.

Evans, P., Clow, A., & Hucklebridge, F. (1997). Stress and the immune system. *The Psychologist, 10*(7), 303–307.

Eysenck, M.W. (1990). *Happiness: Facts and myths.* Hove, UK: Psychology Press.

Eysenck, M.W. (1994). *Individual differences: Normal and abnormal.* Hove, UK: Psychology Press.

Eysenck, M.W., & Eysenck, M.C. (1980). Effects of processing depth, distinctiveness, and word frequency on retention. *British Journal of Psychology, 71,* 263–274.

Fallon, A.E., & Rozin, P. (1985). Sex differences in perceptions of desirable body shape. *Journal of Abnormal Psychology, 94,* 102–105.

Fava, M., Copeland, P.M., Schweiger, U., & Herzog, D.B. (1989). Neurochemical abnormalities of anorexia and bulimia nervosa. *American Journal of Psychiatry, 47,* 213–219.

Finlay-Jones, R.A., & Brown, G.W. (1981). Types of stressful life events and the onset of anxiety and depressive disorders. *Psychological Medicine, 11,* 803–815.

Fischhoff, B. (1977). Perceived informativeness of facts. *Journal of Experimental Psychology: Human Perception and Performance, 3,* 349–358.

Fischhoff, B., & Beyth, R. (1975). "I knew it would happen": Remembered probabilities of once-future things. *Organizational Behaviour and Human Performance, 13,* 1–16.

Fischman, J. (1987). Getting touch. *Psychology Today, 21,* 26–28.

Fisher, R.P., Geiselman, R.E., Raymond, D.S., Jurkevich, L.M., & Warhaftig, M.L. (1987). Enhancing enhanced eyewitness memory: Refining the cognitive interview. *Journal of Police Science and Administration, 15,* 291–297.

Forman, R.F., & McCauley, C. (1986). Validity of the positive control polygraph test using the field practice model. *Journal of Applied Psychology, 71,* 691–698.

Fox, N. (1977). Attachment of Kibbutz infants to mother and metapelet. *Child Development, 48,* 1228–1239.

Fraley, R.C., & Spieker, S.J. (2003). Are infant attachment patterns continuously or categorically distributed? A taxometric analysis of Strange Situation behaviour. *Developmental Psychology, 39,* 387–404.

Frankenhaeuser, M., Dunne, E., & Lundberg, U. (1976). Sex differences in sympathetic adrenal medullary reactions induced by different stressors. *Psychopharmacology, 47,* 1–5.

Franzoi, S.L. (1996). *Social psychology.* Madison, WI: Brown & Benchmark.

Freedman, J.L. (1969). Role playing: Psychology by consensus. *Journal of Personality and Social Psychology, 13*, 107–114.

Freud, A., & Dann, S. (1951). An experiment in group upbringing. *Psychoanalytic Study of the Child, 6*, 127–168.

Freud, S. (1915). Repression. In *Freud's collected papers, Vol. IV*. London: Hogarth.

Freud, S. (1924). *A general introduction to psychoanalysis*. New York: Washington Square Press.

Friedman, M., & Rosenman, R.H. (1959). Association of specific overt behaviour pattern with blood and cardiovascular findings. *Journal of the American Medical Association, 96*, 1286–1296.

Friedman, M., & Rosenman, R.H. (1974). *Type A behaviour and your heart*. New York: Knopf.

Friedman, M.I., Tordoff, M.G., & Ramirez, I. (1986). Integrated metabolic control of food intake. *Brain Research Bulletin, 17*, 855–859.

Funk, S.C. (1992). Hardiness: A review of theory and research. *Health Psychology, 11*, 335–345.

Gale, A. (1995). Ethical issues in psychological research. In A.M. Coleman (Ed.), *Psychological research methods and statistics*. London: Longman.

Gamson, W.B., Fireman, B., & Rytina, S. (1982). *Encounters with unjust authority*. Homewood, IL: Dorsey Press.

Ganellen, R.J., & Blaney, P.H. (1984). Hardiness and social support as moderators of the effects of life stress. *Journal of Personality and Social Psychology, 47*, 156–163.

Ganster, D.C., Schaubroeck, J., Sime, W.E., & Mayes, B.T. (1991). The nomological validity of the Type A personality among employed adults. *Journal of Applied Psychology, 76*, 143–168.

Gardner, G.A. (1978). The effects of human subject regulations on data obtained in environmental stressor research. *Journal of Personality and Social Psychology, 36*, 317–349.

Garfinkel, P.E., & Garner, D.M. (1982). *Anorexia nervosa: A multidimensional perspective*. New York: Basic Books.

Gatchel, R. (1997). Biofeedback. In A. Baum, S. Newman, J. Weinman, R. West, & C. McManus (Eds.), *Cambridge handbook of psychology, health, and medicine*. Cambridge, UK: Cambridge University Press.

Gathercole, S. & Baddeley, A.D. (1990). Phonological memory deficits in language-disordered children: Is there a causal connection? *Journal of Memory and Language, 29*, 336–360.

Geiselman, R.E., Fisher, R.P., MacKinnon, D.P., & Holland, H.L. (1985). Eyewitness memory enhancement in police interview: Cognitive retrieval mnemonics versus hypnosis. *Journal of Applied Psychology, 70*, 401–412.

Gentry, W.D., Chesney, A.P., Hall, R.P., & Harburg, E. (1981). Effect of habitual anger-coping pattern on blood pressure in black/white, high/low stress area respondents. *Psychosomatic Medicine, 43*, 88–93.

Gevirtz, R. (2000). Physiology of stress. In D. Kenney, J. Carlson, J. Sheppard & F.J. McGuigan (Eds.), *Stress and health: Research and clinical applications*. Sydney: Harwood Academic Publishers.

Gilbert, G.N., & Mulkay, M. (1984). *Opening Pandora's box: A sociological analysis of scientists' discourse*. Cambridge: Cambridge University Press.

Glanzer, M., & Cunitz, A.R. (1966). Two storage mechanisms in free recall. *Journal of Verbal Learning and Verbal Behavior, 5*, 351–360.

Glass, D.C., Singer, J.E., & Friedman, L.W. (1969). Psychic cost of adaptation to an environmental stressor. *Journal of Personality and Social Psychology, 12*, 200–210.

Gleitman, H. (1986). *Psychology* (2nd Edn.). London: Norton.

Goa, K.L., & Ward, A. (1986). Buspirone: A preliminary review of its pharmacological properties and therapeutic efficacy as an anxiolytic. *Drugs, 32*, 114–129.

Goldfarb, W. (1947). Variations in adolescent adjustment of institutionally reared children. *American Journal of Orthopsychiatry, 17*, 499–557.

Goleman, D. (1991, November 26). Doctors find comfort is a potent medicine. *The New York Times*.

Greenberg, D.L. (2004). President Bush's false "flashbulb" memory of 9/11/01. *Applied Cognitive Psychology, 18*, 363–370.

Greenspoon, J. (1955). The reinforcing of two spoken sounds on the frequency of responses. *American Journal of Psychology, 68*, 409–416.

Griffiths, M.D. (1993). Fruit machine addiction in adolescence: A case study. *Journal of Gambling Studies, 9*(4), 387–399.

Gross, R. (1999). *Key studies in psychology* (3rd Edn.). London: Hodder & Stoughton.

Grossman, K., Grossman, K.E., Spangler, S., Suess, G., & Uzner, L. (1985). Maternal sensitivity and newborn responses as related to quality of attachment in Northern Germany. In J. Bretherton & E. Waters (Eds.), Growing points of attachment theory. *Monographs of the Society for Research in Child Development, 50*, No. 209.

Grossmann, K.E., & Grossmann, K. (1991). Attachment quality as an organizer of emotional and behavioural responses in a longitudinal perspective. In C.M. Parkes, J. Stevenson-Hinde, & P. Marris (Eds.), *Attachment across the life cycle*. London: Tavistock/Routledge.

Guiton, P. (1966). Early experience and sexual object choice in the brown leghorn. *Animal Behaviour, 14*, 534–538.

Guyton, A.C., & Hall, J.E. (2000). *Textbook of medical physiology* (10th Edn.). New York: W.B. Saunders.

Hailman, J. (1992). The necessity of a "show-me" attitude in science. In J.W. Grier & T. Burk, *Biology of animal behaviour* (2nd Edn.). Dubuque, IO: W.C. Brown.

Hallstein, E.A. (1965). Adolescent anorexia nervosa treated by desensitization. *Behaviour Research and Therapy, 3*(2), 87–91.

Harlow, H.F. (1959). Love in infant monkeys. *Scientific American, 200*, 68–74.

Harlow, H.F., & Harlow, M.K. (1962). Social deprivation in monkeys. *Scientific American, 207*(5), 136–146.

Harris, J.R. (1998). *The nurture assumption*. London: Bloomsbury.

Harris, T.O. (1997). Adult attachment processes and psychotherapy: A commentary on Bartholomew and Birtschnell. *British Journal of Medical Psychology, 70*, 281–290.

Harrison, L.J., & Ungerer, J.A. (2002). Maternal employment and infant–mother attachment security at 12 months postpartum. *Developmental Psychology, 38*, 758–773.

Hastrup, J.L., Light, K.C., & Obrist, P.A. (1980). Relationship of cardiovascular stress response to parental history of hypertension and to sex differences. *Psychophysiology, 17,* 317–318.

Hay, D.F., & Vespo, J.E. (1988). Social learning perspectives on the development of the mother–child relationship. In B. Birns & D.F. Hay (Eds.), *The different faces of motherhood*. New York: Plenum Press.

Haynes, S.G., Feinleib, M., & Kannel, W.B. (1980). The relationship of psychosocial factors to coronary heart disease in the Framingham Study: III. Eight-year incidence of coronary heart disease. *American Journal of Epidemiology, 111,* 37–58.

Hazan, C., & Shaver, P.R. (1987). Romantic love conceptualised as an attachment process. *Journal of Personality and Social Psychology, 52,* 511–524.

Heath, W.P., & Erickson, J.R. (1998). Memory for central and peripheral actions and props after various post-event presentations. *Legal and Criminal Psychology, 3,* 321–346.

Heather, N. (1976). *Radical perspectives in psychology*. London: Methuen.

Hirschfeld, R.M. (1999). Efficacy of SSRIs and newer antidepressants in severe depression: Comparison with TCAs. *Journal of Clinical Psychiatry, 60,* 326–335.

Hitch, G., & Baddeley, A.D. (1976). Verbal reasoning and working memory. *Quarterly Journal of Experimental Psychology, 28,* 603–621.

Hockey, G.R.J., Davies, S., & Gray, M.M. (1972). Forgetting as a function of sleep at different times of day. *Quarterly Journal of Experimental Psychology, 24,* 386–393.

Hodges, J., & Tizard, B. (1989). Social and family relationships of ex-institutional adolescents. *Journal of Child Psychology and Psychiatry, 30,* 77–97.

Hofling, K.C., Brotzman, E., Dalrymple, S., Graves, N., & Pierce, C.M. (1966). An experimental study in the nurse–physician relationship. *Journal of Nervous and Mental Disorders, 143,* 171–180.

Holland, A.J., Sicotte, N., & Treasure, J. (1988). Anorexia nervosa: Evidence for a genetic basis. *Journal of Psychosomatic Research, 32,* 561–572.

Holmes, T.H., & Rahe, R.H. (1967). The social readjustment rating scale. *Journal of Psychosomatic Research, 11,* 213–218.

Holroyd, K.A., & French, D.J. (1994). Recent developments in the psychological assessment and management of recurrent headache disorders. In A.J. Greczyny (Ed.), *Handbook of health and rehabilitation psychology*. New York: Plenum Press.

Holroyd, K.A., Penzien, D., Hursey, K., Tobin, D., Rogen, L., Holm, J., Marcille, P., Hall, J., & Chila, A. (1984). Change mechanisms in EMG biofeedback training: Cognitive changes underlying improvements in tension headache. *Journal of Consulting and Clinical Psychology, 52,* 1039–1053.

Homan, R. (1991). *The ethics of social research*. London: Longman.

Howes, C., Galinsky, E., & Kontos, S. (1998). Caregiver sensitivity and attachment. *Social Development, 7*(1), 25–36.

Howes, C., Matheson, C.C., & Hamilton, C.E. (1994). Maternal, teacher, and child care correlates of children's relationships with peers. *Child Development, 65*(1), 264–273.

Hsu, L.K. (1990). *Eating disorders*. New York: Guilford Press.

Humphrey, L.L., Apple, R.F., & Kirschenbaum, D.S. (1986). Differentiating bulimic-anorexic from normal families

using interpersonal and behavioural observational systems. *Journal of Consulting and Clinical Psychology, 54,* 190–195.

Immelmann, K. (1972). Sexual and other long-term aspects of imprinting in birds and other species. In D.S. Lehrmann, R.A. Hinde, & E. Shaw (Eds.), *Advances in the study of behaviour, Vol. 4*. New York: Academic Press.

Isabella, R.A., Belsky, J., & Von Eye, A. (1989). Origins of infant–mother attachment: An examination of interactional synchrony during the infant's first year. *Developmental Psychology, 25,* 12–21.

Jacobs, J. (1887). Experiments on 'prehension'. *Mind, 12,* 75–79.

Jacobson, J.L., & Wille, D.E. (1986). The influence of attachment pattern on developmental changes in peer interaction from the toddler to the preschool period. *Child Development, 57,* 338–347.

Jacoby, L.L., Debner, J.A., & Hay, J.F. (2001). Proactive interference, accessibility bias, and process dissociations: Valid subjective reports of memory. *Journal of Experimental Psychology: Learning, Memory, & Cognition, 27,* 686–700.

Jaeger, B., Ruggiero, G.M., Gomez-Perretta, C., Lang, F., Mohammadkhani, P., Sahleen-Veasey, C., Schomer, H., & Lamprecht, F. (2002). Body dissatisfaction and its interrelations with other risk factors for bulimia in 12 countries. *Psychotherapy and Psychosomatics, 71,* 54–61.

Jahoda, M. (1958). *Current concepts of positive mental health*. New York: Basic Books.

James, O. (1997). Serotonin: A chemical feel-good factor. *Psychology Review, 4,* 34.

Janis, I. (1972). *Victims of groupthink: A psychological study of foreign-policy decisions and fiascos*. Boston: Houghton-Mifflin.

Jenkins, J.G., & Dallenbach, K.M. (1924). Obliviscence during sleep and waking. *American Journal of Psychology, 35,* 605–612.

Jenness, A. (1932). The role of discussion in changing opinion regarding matter of fact. *Journal of Abnormal and Social Psychology, 27,* 279–296.

Johansson, G., Aronson, G., & Lindstroem, B.O. (1978). Social psychological and neuroendocrine stress reactions in highly mechanised work. *Ergonomics, 21,* 583–599.

Johnson, R.D., & Downing, L.L. (1979). Deindividuation and valence of cues: Effects on prosocial and antisocial behaviour. *Journal of Personality and Social Psychology, 39,* 1532–1538.

Jones, D.N., Pickett, J., Oates, M.R., & Barbor, P. (1987). *Understanding child abuse* (2nd Edn.). London: Macmillan.

Kagan, J. (1984). *The nature of the child*. New York: Basic Books.

Kagan, J., Kearsley, R.B., & Zelazo, P.R. (1980). *Infancy: Its place in human development*. Cambridge, MA: Harvard University Press.

Kahneman, D., & Tversky, A. (1979). Intuitive prediction: Biases and corrective procedures. *TIMS Studies in Management Science, 12,* 313–327.

Kalucy, R.S., Crisp, A.H., & Harding, B. (1977). A study of 56 families with anorexia nervosa. *British Journal of Medical Psychology, 50,* 381–395.

Kelley, H.H. (1950). The warm–cold variable in first impressions of people. *Journal of Personality, 18,* 431–439.

Kelman, H.C. (1958). Compliance, identification and internalisation: Three processes of attitude change. *Journal of Conflict Resolution, 2,* 51–60.

Kelman, H.C. (1972). The rights of the subject in social research: An analysis in terms of relative power and legitimacy. *American Psychologist, 27,* 989–1016.

Kelman, H. & Lawrence, L. (1972). Assignment of responsibility in the case of Lt. Calley: Preliminary report on a national survey. *Journal of Social Issues, 28,* 177–212.

Kendler, K.S., Maclean, C., Neale, M., Kessler, R., Heath, A., & Eaves, L. (1991). The genetic epidemiology of bulimia nervosa. *American Journal of Psychiatry, 148,* 1627–1637.

Kendler, K.S., Masterson, C.C., & Davis, K.L. (1985). Psychiatric illness in first degree relatives of patients with paranoid psychosis, schizophrenia and medical controls. *British Journal of Psychiatry, 147,* 524–531.

Kendler, K.S., Neale, M.C., Prescott, C.A., Kessler, R.C., Heath, A.C., Corey, L.A., & Eaves, L.J. (1996). Childhood parental loss and alcoholism in women: A causal analysis using a twin-family design. *Psychological Medicine, 26,* 79–95.

Keppel, G., & Underwood, B.J. (1962). Proactive inhibition in short-term retention of single items. *Journal of Verbal Learning and Verbal Behavior, 1,* 153–161.

Kettlewell, H.B.D. (1955). Selection experiments on industrial melanism in the Lepidoptera. *Heredity, 9,* 323–342.

Khan, F., & Patel, P. (1996). A study of the impact of hassles versus life events on health outcome measures in students and the general population. *Proceedings of the British Psychological Society, 4(1),* 32.

Kiecolt-Glaser, J.K., Garner, W., Speicher, C.E., Penn, G.M., Holliday, J., & Glaser, R. (1984). Psychosocial modifiers of immunocompetence in medical students. *Psychosomatic Medicine, 46,* 7–14.

Kiecolt-Glaser, J.K., Marucha, P.T., Malarkey, W.B., Mercado, A.M., & Glaser, R. (1995). Slowing of wound healing by psychological stress. *Lancet, 346,* 1194–1196.

Kilham, W., & Mann, L. (1974). Level of destructive obedience as a function of transmitter and expectant roles in the Milgram obedience paradigm. *Journal of Personality and Social Psychology, 29,* 696–702.

Klaus, M.H., & Kennell, J.H. (1976). *Parent–infant bonding.* St Louis: Mosby.

Kobasa, S.C. (1979). Stressful events, personality, and health: An inquiry into hardiness. *Journal of Personality and Social Psychology, 37,* 1–11.

Kobasa, S.C. (1986). How much stress can you survive? In M.G. Walraven & H.E. Fitzgerald (Eds.), *Annual editions: Human development 86/87.* Guilford, CT: Dushkin.

Kobasa, S.C., Maddi, S.R., & Puccetti, M.C. (1982). Personality and exercise as buffers in the stress–illness relationship. *Journal of Behavioural Medicine, 5,* 391–404.

Kobasa, S.C., Maddi, S.R., Puccetti, M.C., & Zola, M.A. (1985). Effectiveness of hardiness, exercise and social support as resources against illness. *Journal of Psychosomatic Research, 29,* 525–533.

Kohnken, G., Milne, R., Memon, A., & Bull, R. (1999). The cognitive interview: A meta-analysis. *Psychology of Crime Law, 5,* 3–27.

Koluchová, J. (1976). The further development of twins after severe and prolonged deprivation: A second report. *Journal of Child Psychology and Psychiatry, 17,* 181–188.

Koluchová, J. (1991). Severely deprived twins after twenty-two years' observation. *Studia Psychologica, 33,* 23–28.

Langer, E.J., & Rodin, J. (1976). The effects of choice and enhanced personal responsibility for the aged. *Journal of Personality and Social Psychology, 34,* 191–198.

Latané, B., & Wolf, S. (1981). The social impact of majorities and minorities. *Psychological Review, 88,* 438–453.

Lau, J., Antman, E.M., Jimenez-Silva, J., Kuperlnik, B., Mostpeller, F., & Chalmers, T.C. (1992). Cumulative meta-analysis of therapeutic trials for myocardial infarction. *New England Journal of Medicine, 327,* 248–254.

Lazar, I., & Darlington, R. (1982). Lasting effects of early education: A report from the Consortium of Longitudinal Studies. *Monographs for the Society for Research in Child Development, 47(2–3; Serial No. 195).*

Lazarus, R.S., & Folkman, S. (1984). *Stress, appraisal and coping.* New York: Springer.

Lee, S., Hsu, L.K.G., & Wing, Y.K. (1992). Bulimia nervosa in Hong Kong Chinese patients. *British Journal of Psychiatry, 161,* 545–551.

Leitenberg, H., Agras, W.S., & Thomson, L.E. (1968). A sequential analysis of the effect of selective positive reinforcement in modifying anorexia nervosa. *Behaviour Research and Therapy, 6,* 211–218.

Leon, G.R. (1984). *Case histories of deviant behaviour* (3rd Edn.). Boston: Allyn & Bacon.

Lesar, T.S., Briceland, L., & Stein, D.S. (1997). Factors related to errors in medication prescribing. *Journal of the American Medical Association, 277,* 312–317.

Levinger, G., & Clark, J. (1961). Emotional factors and the forgetting of word associations. *Journal of Abnormal Social Psychology, 62,* 99–102.

Lewinsohn, P.M., Joiner, T.E., Jr., & Rohde, P. (2001). Evaluation of cognitive diathesis–stress models in predicting major depressive disorder in adolescents. *Journal of Abnormal Psychology, 110,* 203–215.

Lewis, M., Feiring, C., McGuffog, C., & Jaskir, J. (1984). Predicting psychopathy in six-year-olds from early social relations. *Child Development, 55,* 123–136.

Locke, E.A. (1968). Toward a theory of task motivation and incentives. *Organizational Behavior and Human Performance, 3,* 157–189.

Loftus, E. (1979). *Eyewitness testimony.* Cambridge, MA: Harvard University Press.

Loftus, E.F. (2004). Memories of things unseen. *Current Directions in Psychological Science, 13,* 145–147.

Loftus, E.F., & Palmer, J.C. (1974). Reconstruction of automobile destruction: An example of the interaction between language and memory. *Journal of Verbal Learning and Verbal Behavior, 13,* 585–589.

Loftus, E.F., & Zanni, G. (1975). Eyewitness testimony: The influence of the wording of a question. *Bulletin of the Psychonomic Society, 5,* 86–88.

Lozoff, B. (1983). Birth and "bonding" in non-industrial societies. *Developmental Medicine and Child Neurology, 25*, 595–600.

Lynch, M., & Roberts, J. (1982). *Consequences of child abuse*. London: Academic Press.

Maccoby, E.E. (1980). *Social development: Psychological growth and the parent–child relationship*. San Diego: Harcourt Brace Jovanovich.

Maher, B.A. (1966). *Principles of psychopathology: An experimental approach*. New York: McGraw-Hill.

Main, M., Kaplan, N., & Cassidy, J. (1985). Security in infancy: A move to a level of representation. In I. Bretherton & E. Waters (Eds.), Growing points of attachment theory and research. *Monographs of the Society for Research in Child Development, 50*(1–2; Serial no. 209).

Main, M., & Soloman, J. (1986). Discovery of a disorganised disoriented attachment pattern. In T.B. Brazelton & M.W. Yogman (Eds.), *Affective development in infancy*. Norwood, NJ: Ablex.

Main, M., & Weston, D.R. (1981). The quality of the toddler's relationship to mother and father: Related to conflict behaviour and the readiness to establish new relationships. *Child Development, 52*, 932–940.

Mandler, G. (1967). Organisation and memory. In K.W. Spence & J.T. Spence (Eds.), *The psychology of learning and motivation: Advances in research and theory, Vol. 1*. London: Academic Press.

Manstead, A.S.R., & Semin, G.R. (1996). Methodology in social psychology: Putting ideas to the test. In M. Hewstone, W. Stroebe, & G.M. Stephenson (Eds.), *Introduction to social psychology* (2nd Edn.). Oxford, UK: Blackwell.

Margolis, B., & Kroes, W. (1974). Work and the health of man. In J. O'Toole (Ed.), *Work and the quality of life*. Cambridge, MA: MIT Press.

Marmot, M.G., Bosma, H., Hemingway, H., Brunner, E., & Stansfeld, S. (1997). Contribution of job control and other risk factors to social variations in coronary heart disease incidence. *Lancet, 350*, 235–239.

Martin, R.A. (1989). Techniques for data acquisition and analysis in field investigations of stress. In R.W.J. Neufeld (Ed.), *Advances in the investigation of psychological stress*. New York: Wiley.

Maslach, C., & Jackson, S.E. (1982). Burnout in health professions: A social psychological analysis. In G.S. Sanders & J. Suls (Eds.), *Social psychology of health and illness*. Hillsdale, NJ: Lawrence Erlbaum Associates Inc.

Maslow, A.H. (1954). *Motivation and personality*. New York: Harper.

Mason, J.W. (1975). A historical view of the stress field. *Journal of Human Stress, 1*, 22–36.

Matthews, K.A., Glass, D.C., Rosenman, R.H., & Bortner, R.W. (1977). Competitive drive, Pattern A, and coronary heart disease: A further analysis of some data from the Western Collaborative Group. *Journal of Chronic Diseases, 30*, 489–498.

Maurer, D., & Maurer, C. (1989). *The world of the newborn*. London: Viking.

Mayall, B., & Petrie, P. (1983). *Childminding and day nurseries: What kind of care?* London: Heinemann Educational Books.

McGrew, W.C. (1972). *An ethological study of children's behaviour*. New York: Academic Press.

McKenzie, S.J., Willliamson, D.A., & Cubic, B.A. (1993). Stable and reactive body image disturbances in bulimia nervosa. *Behavior Therapy, 24*, 1958–2220.

Meeus, W.H.J., & Raaijmakers, Q.A.W. (1995). Obedience in modern society: The Utrecht studies. *Journal of Social Issues, 51*(3), 155–175.

Meichenbaum, D. (1977). *Cognitive-behaviour modification: An integrative approach*. New York: Plenum Press.

Meichenbaum, D. (1985). *Stress inoculation training*. New York: Pergamon.

Melhuish, E.C. (1993). Behaviour measures: A measure of love? An overview of the assessment of attachment. *ACPP Review and Newsletter, 15*(6), 269–275.

Menges, R.J. (1973). Openness and honesty versus coercion and deception in psychological research. *American Psychologist, 28*, 1030–1034.

Menzies, R.G., & Clarke, J.C. (1993). The aetiology of childhood water phobia. *Behaviour Research and Therapy, 31*, 499–501.

Milgram, S. (1963). Behavioural study of obedience. *Journal of Abnormal and Social Psychology, 67*, 371–378.

Milgram, S. (1974). *Obedience to authority: An experimental view*. New York: Harper & Row.

Milgram, S. (1992). *The individual in a social world* (2nd Edn.). New York: McGraw-Hill.

Miller, G.A. (1956). The magical number seven, plus or minus two: Some limits on our capacity for processing information. *Psychological Review, 63*, 81–97.

Miller, M.A., & Rahe, R.H. (1997). Life changes. Scaling for the 1990s. *Journal of Psychosomatic Research, 43*, 279–292.

Miller, N., & DiCara, L. (1967). Instrumental learning of heart rate changes in curarised rats: Shaping and specificity to discriminative stimulus. *Journal of Comparative and Physiological Psychology, 63*, 12–19.

Miller, T.Q., Turner, C.W., Tindale, R.S., Posavac, E.J., & Dugoni, B.L. (1991). Reasons for the trend toward null findings in research on Type A behaviour. *Psychological Bulletin, 110*, 469–485.

Mineka, S., Davidson, M., Cook, M., & Kuir, R. (1984). Observational conditioning of snake fear in rhesus monkeys. *Journal of Abnormal Psychology, 93*, 355–372.

Minuchin, S., Rosman, B.L., & Baker, L. (1978). *Psychosomatic families: Anorexia nervosa in context*. Cambridge, MA: Harvard University Press.

Morris, C.D., Bransford, J.D., & Franks, J.J. (1977). Levels of processing versus transfer appropriate processing. *Journal of Verbal Learning and Verbal Behavior, 16*, 519–533.

Morris, P.E. (1979). Strategies for learning and recall. In M.M. Gruneberg & P.E. Morris (Eds.), *Applied problems in memory*. London: Academic Press.

Morris, T., Greer, S., Pettingale, R.W., & Watson, M. (1981). Patterns of expression of anger and their psychological correlates in women with breast cancer. *Journal of Psychosomatic Research, 25*, 111–117.

Moscovici, S. (1976). *Social influence and social change*. London: Academic Press.

Moscovici, S. (1980). Toward a theory of conversion behaviour. In L. Berkowitz (Ed.), *Advances in experimental social psychology, Vol. 13*. New York: Academic Press.

Moscovici, S. (1985). Social influence and conformity. In G. Lindzey & E. Aronson (Eds.), *Handbook of social psychology* (3rd Edn.). New York: Random House.

Moscovici, S., Lage, E., & Naffrenchoux, M. (1969). Influence of a consistent minority on the responses of a majority in a colour perception task. *Sociometry, 32*, 365–380.

Moscovitz, S. (1983). *Love despite hate: Child survivors of the Holocaust and their adult lives*. New York: Schocken.

Mowrer, O.H. (1947). On the dual nature of learning: A reinterpretation of "conditioning" and "problem-solving". *Harvard Educational Review, 17*, 102–148.

Mugny, G. & Perez, J.A. (1991). *The social psychology of minority group influence*. New York: Cambridge University Press.

Nasser, M. (1986). Eating disorders: The cultural dimension. *Social Psychiatry and Psychiatric Epidemiology, 23*, 184–187.

Nemeth, C., Swedlund, M., & Kanki, G. (1974). Patterning of the minority's responses and their influence on the majority. *European Journal of Social Psychology, 4*, 53–64.

Newmark, C.S., Frerking, R.A., Cook, L., & Newmark, L. (1973). Endorsement of Ellis' irrational beliefs as a function of psychopathology. *Journal of Clinical Psychology, 29*, 300–302.

NICHD Early Child Care Research Network (1997). The effects of infant child care on infant–mother attachment security: Results of the NICHD study of early child care. *Child Development, 68*(5), 860–879.

Nisbett, R.E., & Wilson, T.D. (1977). Telling more than we can know: Verbal reports on mental processes. *Psychological Review, 84*, 231–259.

Nuckolls, K.B., Cassel, J., & Kaplan, B.H. (1972). Psychological assets, life crisis and the prognosis of pregnancy. *American Journal of Epidemiology, 95*, 431–441.

Ogden, J. (2000). *Health psychology* (2nd Edn.). Milton Keynes, UK: Open University Press.

Orne, M.T. (1962). On the social psychology of the psychological experiment: With particular reference to demand characteristics and their implications. *American Psychologist, 17*, 776–783.

Orne, M.T., & Holland, C.C. (1968). On the ecological validity of laboratory deceptions. *International Journal of Psychiatry, 6*(4), 282–293.

Oyserman, D., Coon, H.M., & Kemmelmeier, M. (2002). Rethinking individualism and collectivism: Evaluation of theoretical assumptions and meta-analyses. *Psychological Bulletin, 128*, 3–72.

Park, R.J., Lawrie, J.M., & Freeman, C.P. (1995). Post-viral onset of anorexia nervosa. *British Journal of Psychology, 166*, 386–389.

Parke, R.D. (1981). *Fathers*. Cambridge, MA: Harvard University Press.

Pennebaker, J.W., Hendler, C.S., Durrett, M.E., & Richards, P. (1981). Social factors influencing absenteeism due to illness in nursery school children. *Child Development, 52*, 692–700.

Perrin, S., & Spencer, C. (1980). The Asch effect: A child of its time. *Bulletin of the British Psychological Society, 33*, 405–406.

Peterson, C., Seligman, M.E., & Valliant, G.E. (1988). Pessimistic explanatory style is a risk factor for physical illness: A thirty-five year longitudinal study. *Journal of Personality and Social Psychology, 55*, 23–27.

Peterson, L.R., & Peterson, M.J. (1959). Short-term retention of individual verbal items. *Journal of Experimental Psychology, 58*, 193–198.

Pfungst, O. (1911). *Clever Hans, the horse of Mr. von Osten*. New York: Holt, Rinehart & Winston.

Piliavin, I.M., Rodin, J., & Piliavin, J.A. (1969). Good samaritanism: An underground phenomenon? *Journal of Personality and Social Psychology, 13*, 289–299.

Pinel, J.P.J. (1997). *Biopsychology* (3rd Edn.). Boston: Allyn & Bacon.

Posner, M.I. (1969). Abstraction and the process of recognition. In J.T. Spence & G.H. Bower (Eds.), *The psychology of learning and motivation: Advances in learning and motivation, Vol. 3*. New York: Academic Press.

Putnam, B. (1979). Hypnosis and distortions in eyewitness memory. *International Journal of Clinical and Experimental Hypnosis, 27*, 437–448.

Quinton, D., & Rutter, M. (1976). Early hospital admissions and later disturbance of behaviour: An attempted replication of Douglas's findings. *Developmental Medicine and Child Neurology, 18*, 447–459.

Quinton, D., Rutter, M., & Liddle, C. (1984). Institutional rearing, parenting difficulties, and marital support. *Psychological Medicine, 14*, 107–124.

Rahe, R.H., & Arthur, R.J. (1977). Life change patterns surrounding illness experience. In A. Monat & R.S. Lazarus (Eds.), *Stress and coping*. New York: Columbia University Press.

Rahe, R.H., Mahan, J., & Arthur, R. (1970). Prediction of near-future health-change from subjects' preceding life changes. *Journal of Psychosomatic Research, 14*, 401–406.

Rank, S.G., & Jacobsen, C.K. (1977). Hospital nurses' compliance with medication overdose orders: A failure to replicate. *Journal of Health and Social Behaviour, 18*, 188–193.

Raulin, M.L., & Graziano, A.M. (1994). Quasi-experiments and correlational studies. In A.M. Colman (Ed.), *Companion encyclopaedia of psychology, Vol. 2*. London: Routledge.

Riley, V. (1981). Psychoneuroendocrine influence on immuno-competence and neoplasia. *Science, 212*, 1100–1109.

Robertson, J., & Bowlby, J. (1952). Responses of young children to separation from their mothers. *Courier Centre International de l'Enfance, 2*, 131–142.

Robertson, J., & Robertson, J. (1971). Young children in brief separation. *Psychoanalytic Study of the Child, 26*, 264–315.

Roethlisberger, F.J., & Dickson, W.J. (1939). *Management and the worker*. Cambridge, MA: Harvard University Press.

Rogers, C.R. (1959). A theory of therapy, personality, and interpersonal relationships as developed in the client-centred framework. In S. Koch (Ed.), *Psychology: A study of a science*. New York: McGraw-Hill.

Roggman, L.A., Langlois, J.H., Hubbs-Tait, L., & Rieser-Danner, L.A. (1994). Infant daycare, attachment and the "file-drawer" problem. *Child Development, 65*, 1429–1443.

Rosen, J.C., & Leitenberg, H. (1985). Exposure plus response prevention treatment of bulimia. In D.M. Garner & P.E. Garfinkel (Eds.), *Handbook of psychotherapy for anorexia nervosa and bulimia*. New York: Guilford Press.

Rosenberg, M.J. (1965). When dissonance fails: On eliminating evaluation apprehension from attitude measurement. *Journal of Personality and Social Psychology, 1*, 28–42.

Rosenblum, L.A., & Harlow, H.F. (1963). Approach–avoidance conflict in the mother–surrogate situation. *Psychology Reports, 12*, 83–85.

Rosenhan, D. (1969). Some origins of concern for others. In P. Mussen, J. Langer, & M. Covington (Eds.), *Trends and issues in developmental psychology*. New York: Holt, Rinehart & Winston.

Rosenhan, D.L., & Seligman, M.E.P. (1989). *Abnormal psychology* (2nd Edn.). New York: Norton.

Rosenthal, A.M. (1964). *Thirty-eight witnesses*. New York: McGraw-Hill.

Rosenthal, R. (1966). *Experimenter effects in behavioural research*. New York: Appleton-Century-Crofts.

Rosenthal, R., & Fode, K.L. (1963). The effect of experimenter bias on the performance of the albino rat. *Behavioural Science, 8*(3), 183–189.

Roy, D.F. (1991). Improving recall by eyewitnesses through the cognitive interview: Practical applications and implications for the police service. *The Psychologist: Bulletin of the British Psychological Society, 4*, 398–400.

Russell, G.F. (1972). Premenstrual tension and "psychogenic" amenorrhoea: Psycho-physical interactions. *Journal of Psychosomatic Research, 16*(4), 279–287.

Rutter, M. (1972). *Maternal deprivation reassessed* (1st Edn.). Harmondsworth, UK: Penguin.

Rutter, M. (1981). *Maternal deprivation reassessed* (2nd Edn.). Harmondsworth, UK: Penguin.

Rutter, M., Graham, P., Chadwick, D.F.D., & Yule, W. (1976). Adolescent turmoil: Fact or fiction. *Journal of Child Psychology and Psychiatry, 17*, 35–56.

Rutter, M., & The ERA Study Team (1998). Developmental catch-up and deficit following adoption after severe early privation. *Journal of Child Psychology and Psychiatry, 39*, 465–476.

Ryle, G. (1949). *The concept of mind*. London: Hutchinson.

Rymer, R. (1993). *Genie: Escape from a silent childhood*. London: Michael Joseph.

Sagi, A., van IJzendoorn, M.H., & Koren-Karie, N. (1991). Primary appraisal of the Strange Situation: A cross-cultural analysis of the pre-separation episodes. *Developmental Psychology, 27*, 587–596.

Sarafino, E.P. (1990). *Health psychology: Biosocial interactions*. New York: John Wiley & Sons.

Savin, H.B. (1973). Professors and psychological researchers: Conflicting values in conflicting roles. *Cognition, 2*, 147–149.

Schaefer, C., Coyne, J.C., & Lazarus, R.S. (1981). The health-related functions of social support. *Journal of Behavioral Medicine, 4*, 381–406.

Schafer, W. (1992). *Stress management for wellness* (2nd Edn.). New York: Harcourt Brace Jovanovich.

Schaffer, H.R. (1998). *Making decisions about children*. Oxford, UK: Blackwell.

Schaffer, H.R., & Emerson, P.E. (1964). The development of social attachments in infancy. *Monographs of the Society for Research on Child Development* (Whole no. 29).

Schliefer, S.J., Keller, S.E., Camerino, M., Thornton, J.C., & Stein, M. (1983). Suppression of lymphocyte stimulation following bereavement. *Journal of the American Medical Association, 250*, 374–377.

Schmied, L.A., & Lawler, K.A. (1986). Hardiness, Type A behaviour, and stress–illness relation in working women. *Journal of Personality and Social Psychology, 51*, 1218–1223.

Schurz, G. (1985). Experimental examination of the relationship between personality characteristics and the readiness of destructive obedience to authorities. *Zeitschrift für experimentelle und angewandte psychologie, 32*, 160–177.

Selye, H. (1936). A syndrome produced by diverse nocuous agents. *Nature, 138*, 32.

Selye, H. (1950). *Stress*. Montreal, Canada: Acta.

Shaffer, D.R. (1993). *Developmental psychology*. Pacific Grove, CA: Brooks/Cole.

Shallice, T., & Warrington, E.K. (1970). Independent functioning of verbal memory stores: A neuropsychological study. *Quarterly Journal of Experimental Psychology, 22*, 261–273.

Shea, J.D.C. (1981). Changes in interpersonal distances and categories of play behaviour in the early weeks of preschool. *Developmental Psychology, 17*, 417–425.

Sherif, M. (1935). A study of some factors in perception. *Archives of Psychology, 27*, 187.

Shirom, A. (1989). Burnout in work organisations. In C.L. Cooper & I. Robertson (Eds.), *International review of industrial and organisational psychology*. Chichester, UK: Wiley.

Shotland, R.L., & Straw, M.K. (1976). Bystander response to an assault: When a man attacks a woman. *Journal of Personality and Social Psychology, 34*, 990–999.

Sigall, H., Aronson, E., & Van Hoose, T. (1970). The cooperative subject: Myth or reality? *Journal of Experimental Social Psychology, 6*, 1–10.

Silverman, I. (1977). *The human subject in the psychological laboratory*. Oxford, UK: Pergamon.

Silverman, I., Shulman, A.D., & Wiesenthal, D. (1970). Effects of deceiving and debriefing psychological subjects on performance in later experiments. *Journal of Personality and Social Psychology, 21*, 219–227.

Simon, H.A. (1974). How big is a chunk? *Science, 183*, 483–488.

Smith, E.R., & Mackie, D.M. (2000). *Social psychology* (2nd Edn.). New York, NY: Psychology Press.

Smith, P., & Bond, M.H. (1993). *Social psychology across cultures: Analysis and perspectives*. New York: Harvester Wheatsheaf.

Solso, R.L. (1991). *Cognitive psychology* (3rd Edn.). London: Allyn & Bacon.

Spangler, G. (1990). Mother, child, and situational correlates of toddlers' social competence. *Infant Behavior and Development, 13*, 405–419.

Spencer, C., & Perrin, S. (1998). Innovation and conformity. *Psychology Review, 5*(2), 23–26.

Spiers, H.J., Maguire, E.A., & Burgess, N. (2001). Hippocampal amnesia. *Neurocase, 7*, 357–382.

Spitz, R.A. (1945). Hospitalism: An inquiry into the genesis of psychiatric conditions in early childhood. *Psychoanalytic Study of the Child, 1*, 113–117.

Spitz, R.A., & Wolf, K.M. (1946). Anaclitic depression. *Psychoanalytic Study of the Child, 2,* 313–342.

Sroufe, L.A. (1990). An organizational perspective on the self. In D. Cicchetti & M. Beeghly (Eds.), *The self in transition: Infancy to childhood.* Chicago: University of Chicago Press.

Stams, G.-J.J.M., Juffer, F., & van IJzendoorn, M.H. (2002). Maternal sensitivity, infant attachment, and temperament in early childhood predict adjustment in middle childhood: The case of adopted children and their biologically unrelated parents. *Developmental Psychology, 38,* 806–821.

Standing, L.G., Conezio, J., & Haber, N. (1970). Perception and memory for pictures: Single-trial learning of 2500 visual stimuli. *Psychonomic Science, 19,* 73–74.

Stang, D.J. (1972). Conformity, ability, and self-esteem. *Representative Research in Social Psychology, 3,* 97–103.

Steblay, N.M. (1997). Social influence in eyewitness recall: A meta-analytic review of line-up instruction effects. *Law and Human Behavior, 21,* 283–298.

Steinhausen, H.C. (1994). Anorexia and bulimia nervosa. In M. Rutter, E. Taylor, & L. Hersov (Eds.), *Child and adolescent psychiatry.* Oxford: Blackwell.

Stirling, J.D., & Hellewell, J.S.E. (1999). *Psychopathology.* London: Routledge.

Stone, S.V., Dembroski, T.M., Costa, P.T., Jr., & McDougall, J.M. (1990). Gender differences in cardiovascular reactivity. *Journal of Behavioural Medicine, 13,* 137–157.

Stretch, D.D. (1994). Experimental design. In A.M. Colman (Ed.), *Companion encyclopedia of psychology, Vol. 2.* London: Routledge.

Strober, M., & Humphrey, L.L. (1987). Familial contributions to the aetiology and course of anorexia nervosa and bulimia. *Journal of Consulting and Clinical Psychology, 55,* 654–659.

Sue, D., Sue, D., & Sue, S. (1994). *Understanding abnormal behaviour.* Boston, MA: Houghton Mifflin.

Symington, T., Currie, A.R., Curran, R.S., & Davidson, J. (1955). The reaction of the adrenal cortex in conditions of stress. *Ciba Foundations Colloquia on Endocrinology, 20,* 156–164.

Szasz, T.S. (1960). *The myth of mental illness.* London: Paladin.

Tache, J., Selye, H., & Day, S. (1979). *Cancer, stress, and death.* New York: Plenum Press.

Talarico, J.M., & Rubin, D.C. (2003). Confidence, not consistency, characterises flashbulb memories. *Psychological Science, 14,* 455–461.

Tarvis, C. (1974). The frozen world of the familiar stranger. *Psychology Today, June,* 71–80.

Taylor, S. (1995). Anxiety sensitivity: Theoretical perspectives and recent findings. *Behaviour Research and Therapy, 33,* 243–258.

Taylor, S.E., Cousino-Klein, L., Lewis, B.P., Grunewald, T.L., & Updegraff, J.A. (2000). Behavioral response to stress in females: Tend and befriend, not fight-or-flight. *Psychological Review, 107,* 411–429.

Thomas, C.B., & Duszynski, K.R. (1974). Closeness to parents and the family constellation in a prospective study of five disease states: Suicide, mental illness, malignant tumour, hypertension and coronary heart disease. *Johns Hopkins Medical Journal, 134,* 251–270.

Thomas, L.K. (1998). *Multicultural aspects of attachment.* http://www.bereavement.demon.co.uk/lbn/attachment/ lennox.html. [See also Thomas, L.K. (1995). Psychotherapy in the context of race and culture. In S. Fernando (Ed.), *Mental health in a multi-ethnic society.* London: Routledge.]

Tizard, B. (1979). Language at home and at school. In C.B. Cazden & D. Harvey (Eds.), *Language in early childhood education.* Washington, DC: National Association for the Education of Young Children.

Tronick, E.Z., Morelli, G.A., & Ivey, P.K. (1992). The Efe forager infant and toddler's pattern of social relationships: Multiple and simultaneous. *Developmental Psychology, 28,* 568–577.

Tuckey, M.R., & Brewer, N. (2003a). How schemas affect eyewitness memory over repeated retrieval attempts. *Applied Cognitive Psychology, 7,* 785–800.

Tuckey, M.R., & Brewer, N. (2003b). The influence of schemas, stimulus ambiguity, and interview schedule on eyewitness memory over time. *Journal of Experimental Psychology: Applied, 9,* 101–118.

Tulving, E. (1972). Episodic and semantic memory. In E. Tulving & W. Donaldson (Eds.), *Organisation of memory.* Hillsdale, NJ: Lawrence Erlbaum Associates Inc.

Tulving, E. (1979). Relation between encoding specificity and levels of processing. In L.S. Cermak & F.I.M. Craik (Eds.), *Levels of processing in human memory.* Hillsdale, NJ: Lawrence Erlbaum Associates Inc.

Tulving, E., & Psotka, J. (1971). Retroactive inhibition in free recall: Inaccessibility of information available in the memory store. *Journal of Experimental Psychology, 87,* 1–8.

Turner, L.H., & Solomon, R.L. (1962). Human traumatic avoidance learning: Theory and experiments on the operant–respondent distinction and failures to learn. *Psychological Monographs, 76*(40; Whole no. 559).

Tyrell, J.B., & Baxter, J.D. (1981). Glucocorticoid therapy. In P. Felig, J.D. Baxter, A.E. Broadus, & L.A. Frohman (Eds.), *Endocrinology and metabolism.* New York: McGraw-Hill.

Ucros, C.G. (1989). Mood state-dependent memory: A meta-analysis. *Cognition and Emotion, 3,* 139–167.

Underwood, B.J., & Postman, L. (1960). Extra-experimental sources of interference in forgetting. *Psychological Review, 67,* 73–95.

Vandell, D.L., & Corasaniti, M.A. (1990). *Variations in early child care: Do they predict subsequent social, emotional, and cognitive differences?* Unpublished manuscript, University of Wisconsin, Madison. [Noted in Andersson, B.-E. (1992). Effects of daycare on cognitive and socioemotional competence of thirteen-year-old Swedish schoolchildren. *Child Development, 63,* 20–36.]

van IJzendoorn, M.H., & Kroonenberg, P.M. (1988). Cross-cultural patterns of attachment: A meta-analysis of the Strange Situation. *Child Development, 59,* 147–156.

Vargha-Khadem, F., Gadian, D.G., Watkins, K.E., Connelly, A., Van Paesschen, W. et al. (1997). Differential aspects of early hippocampal pathology on episodic and semantic memory. *Science, 277,* 376–380.

Venkatesan, M. (1966). Consumer behaviour: Conformity and independence. *Journal of Marketing Research, 3.*

Vidich, A.J., & Bensman, J. (1958). *Small town in mass society.* Princeton, NJ: Princeton University Press.

Wade, C., & Tavris, C. (1993). *Psychology.* New York: HarperCollins.

Warren, R., & Zgourides, G.D. (1991). *Anxiety disorders: A rational–emotive perspective*. New York: Pergamon Press.

Warrington, E.K., & Shallice, T. (1972). Neuropsychological evidence of visual storage in short-term memory tasks. *Quarterly Journal of Experimental Psychology, 24*, 30–40.

Watkins, M.J., Watkins, O.C., Craik, F.I.M., & Mazauryk, G. (1973). Effect of nonverbal distraction on short-term storage. *Journal of Experimental Psychology, 101*, 296–300.

Watson, J.B. (1928). *Psychological care of infant and child*. New York: Norton.

Watson, J.B., & Rayner, R. (1920). Conditioned emotional reactions. *Journal of Experimental Psychology, 3*, 1–14.

Waugh, N.C., & Norman, D.A. (1965). Primary memory. *Psychological Review, 72*, 89–104.

Weg, R.B. (1983). Changing physiology of ageing. In D.S. Woodruff & J.E. Birren (Eds.), *Ageing: Scientific perspectives and social issues* (2nd Edn.). Monterey: Brooks/Cole.

Weiner, H., Thaler, M., Reiser, M.F., & Mirsky, I.A. (1957). Etiology of duodenal ulcer: I. Relation to specific psychological characteristics to rate of gastric secretion (serum pepsinogen). *Psychosomatic Medicine, 19*, 1–10.

Wells, G.L., Liepe, M.R., & Ostrom, T.M. (1979). Guidelines for empirically assessing the fairness of a lineup. *Law and Human Behaviour, 3*, 285–293.

Westen, D. (1996). *Psychology: Mind, brain, and culture*. New York: Wiley.

Whyte, W.F. (1943). *Street corner society: The social structure of an Italian slum*. Chicago: University of Chicago Press.

Widdowson, E.M. (1951). Mental contentment and physical growth. *Lancet, 1*, 1316–1318.

Williams, L.M. (1994). Recall of childhood trauma: A prospective study of women's memories of childhood abuse. *Journal of Consulting and Clinical Psychology, 62*, 1167–1176.

Williams, T.P., & Sogon, S. (1984). Group composition and conforming behaviour in Japanese students. *Japanese Psychological Research, 26*, 231–234.

Winningham, R.G., Hyman, I.E., & Dinnel, D.L. (2000). Flashbulb memories? The effects of when the initial memory report was obtained. *Memory, 8*, 209–216.

Yerkes, R.M., & Morgulis, S. (1909). The method of Pavlov in animal psychology. *Psychological Bulletin, 6*, 257–273.

Yuille, J.C., & Cutshall, J.L. (1986). A case study of eyewitness memory of a crime. *Journal of Applied Psychology, 71*, 291–301.

Zimbardo, P. (1969). The human choice: Individuation, reason, and order versus deindividuation, impulse, and chaos. In W.J. Arnold & D. Levine (Eds.), *Nebraska Symposium on Motivation, 17*. Lincoln, NE: University of Nebraska Press.

Zimbardo, P.G. (1973). On the ethics of intervention in human psychological research: With special reference to the Stanford prison experiment. *Cognition, 2*, 243–256.

AUTHOR INDEX

SUBJECT INDEX

Page numbers in **bold** indicate glossary definitions.

ILLUSTRATION CREDITS